Post–Mining of Association Rules:
Techniques for Effective Knowledge Extraction

Yanchang Zhao
University of Technology, Sydney, Australia

Chengqi Zhang
University of Technology, Sydney, Australia

Longbing Cao
University of Technology, Sydney, Australia

INFORMATION SCIENCE REFERENCE

Hershey · New York

Director of Editorial Content:	Kristin Klinger
Senior Managing Editor:	Jamie Snavely
Managing Editor:	Jeff Ash
Assistant Managing Editor:	Carole Coulson
Typesetter:	Lindsay Bergman
Cover Design:	Lisa Tosheff
Printed at:	Yurchak Printing Inc.

Published in the United States of America by
Information Science Reference (an imprint of IGI Global)
701 E. Chocolate Avenue, Suite 200
Hershey PA 17033
Tel: 717-533-8845
Fax: 717-533-8661
E-mail: cust@igi-global.com
Web site: http://www.igi-global.com/reference

and in the United Kingdom by
Information Science Reference (an imprint of IGI Global)
3 Henrietta Street
Covent Garden
London WC2E 8LU
Tel: 44 20 7240 0856
Fax: 44 20 7379 0609
Web site: http://www.eurospanbookstore.com

Library of Congress Cataloging-in-Publication Data

Post-mining of association rules : techniques for effective knowledge extraction / Yanchang Zhao, Chengqi Zhang, and Longbing Cao, editors.
    p. cm.
  Includes bibliographical references and index. Summary: "This book provides a systematic collection on the post-mining, summarization and presentation of association rule, as well as new forms of association rules"--Provided by publisher. ISBN 978-1-60566-404-0 (hardcover) -- ISBN 978-1-60566-405-7 (ebook) 1. Paired-association learning. 2. Association of ideas. 3. Data mining. I. Zhao, Yanchang, 1977- II. Zhang, Chengqi, 1957- III. Cao, Longbing, 1969- BF319.5.P34P67 2009
  006.3'12--dc22
                        2008047731

British Cataloguing in Publication Data
A Cataloguing in Publication record for this book is available from the British Library.

All work contributed to this book is new, previously-unpublished material. The views expressed in this book are those of the authors, but not necessarily of the publisher.

Editorial Advisory Board

Table of Contents

Section I
Introduction

Chapter I

Paul D. McNicholas, University of Guelph, Ontario, Canada
Yanchang Zhao, University of Technology, Sydney, Australia

Section II
Identifying Interesting Rules

Chapter II

Mirko Boettcher, University of Magdeburg, Germany
Georg Ruß, University of Magdeburg, Germany
Detlef Nauck, BT Group plc, UK
Rudolf Kruse, University of Magdeburg, Germany

Chapter III

Solange Oliveira Rezende, University of São Paulo, Brazil
Edson Augusto Melanda, Federal University of São Carlos, Brazil
Magaly Lika Fujimoto, University of São Paulo, Brazil
Roberta Akemi Sinoara, University of São Paulo, Brazil
Veronica Oliveira de Carvalho, University of Oeste Paulista, Brazil

Section III
Post-Analysis and Post-Mining of Association Rules

Section IV
Rule Selection for Classification

Section V
Visualization and Representation of Association Rules

Section VI
Maintenance of Association Rules and New Forms of Association Rules

Detailed Table of Contents

Section I
Introduction

Chapter I

Paul D. McNicholas, University of Guelph, Ontario, Canada
Yanchang Zhao, University of Technology, Sydney, Australia

This chapter discusses the origin of association rules and the functions by which association rules are traditionally characterized. The formal definition of an association rule, and its support, confidence and lift are presented, and the techniques for rule generation are introduced. It also discusses negations and negative association rules, rule pruning, the measures of interestingness, and the post-mining stage of the association rule paradigm.

Section II
Identifying Interesting Rules

Chapter II

Mirko Boettcher, University of Magdeburg, Germany
Georg Ruß, University of Magdeburg, Germany
Detlef Nauck, BT Group plc, UK
Rudolf Kruse, University of Magdeburg, Germany

This chapter presents a unified view on assessing rule interestingness with the combination of rule change mining and relevance feedback. Rule change mining extends standard association rule mining by generating potentially interesting time-dependent features for an association rule during post-mining, and the existing textual description of a rule and those newly derived objective features are combined by using relevance feedback methods from information retrieval. The proposed technique yields a powerful, intuitive way for exploring the typically vast set of association rules.

Chapter III

Solange Oliveira Rezende, University of São Paulo, Brazil
Edson Augusto Melanda, Federal University of São Carlos, Brazil
Magaly Lika Fujimoto, University of São Paulo, Brazil
Roberta Akemi Sinoara, University of São Paulo, Brazil
Veronica Oliveira de Carvalho, University of Oeste Paulista, Brazil

This chapter presents a new methodology for combining data-driven and user-driven evaluation measures to identify interesting rules. Both data-driven (or objective measures) and user-driven (or subjective measures) are discussed and then analyzed for their pros and cons. With the proposed new methodology, data-driven measures can be used to select some potentially interesting rules for the user's evaluation, and the rules and the knowledge obtained during the evaluation can be employed to calculate user-driven measures for identifying interesting rules.

Chapter IV

Julien Blanchard, Polytechnic School of Nantes University, France
Fabrice Guillet, Polytechnic School of Nantes University, France
Pascale Kuntz, Polytechnic School of Nantes University, France

The authors present a semantics-based classification of rule interestingness measures in this chapter. They propose a novel and useful classification of interestingness measures according to three criteria: the subject, the scope, and the nature of the measure. These criteria are essential to grasp the meaning of the measures, and therefore to help the users to choose the ones he/she wants to apply. Moreover, the classification allows one to compare the rules to closely related concepts such as similarities, implications, and equivalences.

Section III
Post-Analysis and Post-Mining of Association Rules

Chapter V

Huawen Liu, Jilin University, P.R. China
Jigui Sun, Jilin University, P.R. China
Huijie Zhang, Northeast Normal University, P.R. China

This chapter's authors present a technique on post-processing for rule reduction using closed set. Superfluous rules are filtered out from knowledge base in a post-processing manner. With dependent relation discovered by closed set mining technique, redundant rules can be eliminated efficiently.

Chapter VI

A Conformity Measure Using Background Knowledge for Association Rules:

Hacène Cherfi, INRIA Sophia Antipolis, France
Amedeo Napoli, LORIA—INRIA, France
Yannick Toussaint, LORIA—INRIA, France

This chapter presents a new technique to combine data mining and semantic techniques for post-mining and selection of association rules. To focus on the result interpretation and discover new knowledge units, they introduce an original approach to classify association rules according to qualitative criteria using domain model as background knowledge. Its successful application on text mining in molecular biology shows the benefits of taking into account a knowledge domain model of the data.

Chapter VII

Hetal Thakkar, University of California, Los Angeles, USA
Barzan Mozafari, University of California, Los Angeles, USA
Carlo Zaniolo, University of California, Los Angeles, USA

In the case of stream data, the post-mining of association is more challenging. This chapter presents a technique for continuous post-mining of association rules in a data stream management system. The chapter describes the architecture and techniques used to achieve this advanced functionality in the Stream Mill Miner (SMM) prototype, an SQL-based DSMS designed to support continuous mining queries.

Chapter VIII

Ronaldo Cristiano Prati, UFABC Universidade Federal do ABC, Brazil

The Receiver Operating Characteristics (ROC) graph is a popular way of assessing the performance of classification rules, but they are inappropriate to evaluate the quality of association rules, as there is no class in association rule mining and the consequent part of two different association rules might not have any correlation at all. Chapter VIII presents a novel technique of QROC, a variation of ROC space to analyze itemset costs/benefits in association rules. It can be used to help analysts to evaluate the relative interestingness among different association rules in different cost scenarios.

Section IV
Rule Selection for Classification

Chapter IX

Maria-Luiza Antonie, University of Alberta, Canada
David Chodos, University of Alberta, Canada
Osmar Zaïane, University of Alberta, Canada

This chapter presents the rule generation, pruning and selection in associative classifier, which is a classification model based on association rules. Several variations on the associative classifier model are presented, which are mining data sets with re-occurring items, using negative association rules, and pruning rules using graph-based techniques. They also present a system, ARC-UI, that allows a user to analyze the results of classifying an item using an associative classifier.

Chapter X

Chiusano and Garza discuss the selection of high quality rules in associative classification. They present a comparative study of five well-known classification rule pruning methods and analyze the characteristics of both the selected and pruned rule sets in terms of information content. A large set of experiments has been run to empirically evaluate the effect of the pruning methods when applied individually as well as when combined.

Section V
Visualization and Representation of Association Rules

The authors present two meta-knowledge-based approaches for an interactive visualization of large amounts of association rules. Different from traditional methods of association rule visualization where association rule extraction and visualization are treated separately in a one-way process, the two proposed approaches that use meta-knowledge to guide the user during the mining process in an integrated framework covering both steps of the data mining process. The first one builds a roadmap of compact representation of association rules from which the user can explore generic bases of association rules and derive, if desired, redundant ones without information loss. The second approach clusters the set of association rules or its generic bases, and uses a fisheye view technique to help the user during the mining of association rules.

This chapter also discusses the visualization techniques to assist the generation and exploration of association rules. It presents an overview of the many approaches on using visual representations and information visualization techniques to assist association rule mining. A classification of the different approaches that rely on visual representations is introduced, based on the role played by the visualization technique in the exploration of rule sets. A methodology that supports visually assisted selective generation of association rules based on identifying clusters of similar itemsets is also presented. Then, a case study and some trends/issues for further developments are presented.

Chapter XIII

Pasquier presents frequent closed itemset based condensed representations for association rules. Many applications of association rules to data from different domains have shown that techniques for filtering irrelevant and useless association rules are required to simplify their interpretation by the end-user. This chapter focuses on condensed representations that are characterized in the frequent closed itemsets framework to expose their advantages and drawbacks.

Section VI
Maintenance of Association Rules and New Forms of Association Rules

This chapter presents a survey of the techniques for the maintenance of frequent patterns. The frequent pattern maintenance problem is summarized with a study on how the space of frequent patterns evolves in response to data updates. Focusing on incremental and decremental maintenance, four major types of maintenance algorithms are introduced, and the advantages and limitations of these algorithms are studied from both the theoretical and experimental perspectives. Possible solutions to certain limitations and potential research opportunities and emerging trends in frequent pattern maintenance are also discussed.

Conditional contrast patterns are designed by the authors of this chapter. It is related to contrast mining, where one considers the mining of patterns/models that contrast two or more datasets, classes, conditions, time periods, etc. Roughly speaking, conditional contrasts capture situations where a small change in patterns is associated with a big change in the matching data of the patterns. It offers insights on "discriminating" patterns for a given condition. It can also be viewed as a new direction for the analysis and mining of frequent patterns. The chapter formalizes the concepts of conditional contrast and provides theoretical results on conditional contrast mining. An efficient algorithm is proposed based on the results and experiment results are reported.

Chapter XVI

This chapter presents a technique for multidimensional model-based decision rules mining, which can output generalized rules with different degree of generalization. A method of decision rules mining from different abstract levels is provided in the chapter, which aims to improve the efficiency of decision rules mining by combining the hierarchical structure of multidimensional model and the techniques of rough set theory.

Foreword

Since its introduction for market basket analysis in the early 1990s, association rule mining has had a lot of research attention, and it is now widely used in many fields, for example in retail, telecom, insurance, and bioinformatics applications.

One familiar problem encountered in association mining exercises is that they frequently produce large numbers of rules, and this makes it difficult for users to identify those that are of interest. To tackle this problem and facilitate the extraction of useful knowledge from learned rules, Zhao, Zhang, and Cao edited this book to present a systemic collection of the up-to-date techniques for reducing the numbers of association rules, after mining. Such *post-mining* touches on many and varied practical issues, such as the interestingness, redundancy, summarization, generalisation, presentation, visualisation, and maintenance of the rules, and it also involves the understanding of processes and outcomes, as well as new trends and challenges for the analysis of association rules.

This book should be of use to academic researchers in the field of data mining and to industrial data miners. However, it involves clustering, classification and many other techniques of data mining, as well as statistics and artificial intelligence, and it is therefore of wider interest.

This book is composed of six sections, each containing its own chapters. Section I presents an introduction to association rule mining, which covers the association of attributes, and post-mining issues to do with pruning methods, interestingness measures and negative associations. Section II focuses on identifying interesting rules using objective measures, subjective measures, user feedback and combinations of these. A semantics-based classification of interestingness measures is also presented. Section III presents four techniques for the post-analysis of association rules. They are post-processing with a closed set mining technique to eliminate insignificant rules, combining data mining and semantic techniques for classifying the extracted rules, continuous post-mining of association rules, and using a variation of ROC for association rule evaluation. Section IV addresses the needs of associative classifiers and considers how to select high-quality rules for associative classification. Section V presents three new techniques for easy-to-use condensed representation, visualisation, and interactive exploration of association rules. Finally, Section VI presents a survey of methods for the maintenance of association rules, and deals with "conditional contrast pattern mining" and an interesting extension of association mining for multidimensional data models.

This is a stimulating series of chapters, and we believe that they will promote interest and progress in this important aspect of data mining.

David Bell
Queen's University Belfast, UK

David Bell has been a full professor at Queen's University of Belfast since 2002 and before that he was a full professor at University of Ulster since 1986. He holds a DSc and a PhD degree from the University of Ulster. His research addresses the issues of functionality and performance in data and knowledge management systems, and linking these to reasoning under uncertainty, machine learning, and other artificial intelligence techniques – exploiting the close relationship between evidence and data. For many years he has been a programme committee member of the IEEE Conference on Data Engineering, and several other International Conferences. He has been programme committee chairman of several international conferences, including Very Large Database (VLDB) Conference in 1993. He was a panel member (1994-98) of the UK Cabinet Office's Technology Foresight programme and continues to be an associate member. He is an associate editor of the Pergamon Press journal "Information Systems" and was previously editor-in-chief of another Pergamon Press Journal "Database Technology" and the Computer Journal. He has refereed for many journals. His publication list contains well over 300 papers and books.

Preface

SUMMARY

This book examines the post-analysis and post-mining of association rules to find useful knowledge from a large number of discovered rules and presents a systematic view of the above topic. It introduces up-to-date research on extracting useful knowledge from a large number of discovered association rules, and covers interestingness, post-mining, rule selection, summarization, representation and visualization of association rules, as well as new forms of association rules and new trends of association rule mining.

BACKGROUND

As one of the key techniques for data mining, association rule mining was first proposed in 1993, and is today widely used in many applications. An association rule is designed in the form of A→B, where A and B are items or itemsets, for example, beer→diaper. There are often a huge number of association rules discovered from a dataset, and it is sometimes very difficult for a user to identify interesting and useful ones. Therefore, it is important to remove insignificant rules, prune redundancy, summarize, post-mine, and visualize the discovered rules. Moreover, the discovered association rules are in the simple form of A→B, from which the information we can get is very limited. Some recent research has focused on new forms of association rules, such as combined association rules, class association rules, quantitative association rules, contrast patterns and multi-dimensional association rules.

Although there have already been a quite few publications on the post-analysis and post-mining of association rules, there are no books specifically on the above topic. Therefore, we have edited this book to provide a collection of work on the post-mining of association rules and present a whole picture of the post-mining stage of association rule mining.

OBJECTIVES AND SIGNIFICANCE

The objectives of this book are to emphasize the importance of post-mining of association rules, to show a whole picture on the post-mining of association rules, and to present the up-to-date progress of the research on how to extract useful knowledge from a large number of discovered association rules.

The unique characteristic of this book is the comprehensive collection of the current research on post-mining and summarization of association rules and new trends of association rules. It aims to answer the question "we have discovered many association rules, and so what?" It presents readers what we can do or shall do to extract useful and actionable knowledge after discovering a large number of association rules, instead of algorithms or models for mining association rules themselves. It presents academia with a whole picture of the current research progress on post-mining and summarization of association rules. It may help industry to learn from the ideas and apply them to find useful and actionable knowledge in real-world applications. This book also aims to expand the research on association rules to new areas, such as new forms of association rules. The ideas of post-analysis may also be used in the step of association rule mining and help to make new efficient algorithms for mining more useful association rules.

TARGET AUDIENCES

This book is aimed at researchers, postgraduate students, and practitioners in the field of data mining. For researchers whose interests include data mining, this book presents them with a survey of techniques for post-mining of association rules, the up-to-date research progress and the emerging trends/directions in this area. It may spark new ideas on applying other techniques in data mining, machine learning, statistics, and so forth, to the post-mining phase of association rules, or using the post-mining techniques for association rules to tackle the problems in other fields.

For postgraduate students who are interested in data mining, this book presents an overview of association rule techniques and introduces the origin, interestingness, redundancy, visualization, and maintenance of association rules, as well as associative classification and new forms of association rules. It presents not only the post-mining stage of association rules, but also many techniques that are actually used in association rule mining procedure.

For data miners from the industry, this book provides techniques and methodologies for extracting useful and interesting knowledge from a huge number of association rules learned in a data mining practice. It presents a whole picture of what to do after association rule mining and advanced techniques to post-mine the learned rules. Moreover, it also presents a number of real-life case studies and applications, which may help data miners to design and develop their own data mining projects.

However, the audiences are not limited to those interested in association rules, because the post-mining of association rules involves visualization, clustering, classification and many other techniques of data mining, statistics and machine learning, which are actually beyond association rule mining itself.

ORGANIZATION

This book is composed of six sections. **Section I** gives an introduction to association rules and the current research in the related topics, including the preliminary of association rules and the classic algorithms for association rule mining. **Section II** presents three techniques on using interestingness measures to select useful association rules. **Section III** presents four techniques for the post-processing of associations. **Section IV** presents two techniques for selecting high-quality rules for associative classification. **Section V** discusses three techniques for visualization and representation of association rules. **Section VI** presents the maintenance of association rules and new forms of rules.

Section I presents an introduction to association rule techniques. In **Chapter I**, Paul D. McNicholas and Yanchang Zhao discuss the origin of association rules and the functions by which association rules are traditionally characterised. The formal definition of an association rule, and its support, confidence and lift are presented, and the techniques for rule generation are introduced. It also discusses negations and negative association rules, rule pruning, the measures of interestingness, and the post-mining stage of the association rule paradigm.

Section II studies how to identify interesting rules. In **Chapter II**, Mirko Boettcher, Georg Ruß, Detlef Nauch, and Rudolf Kruse presented a unified view on assessing rule interestingness with the combination of rule change mining and relevance feedback. Rule change mining extends standard association rule mining by generating potentially interesting time-dependent features for an association rule during post-mining, and the existing textual description of a rule and those newly derived objective features are combined by using relevance feedback methods from information retrieval. The proposed technique yields a powerful, intuitive way for exploring the typically vast set of association rules.

Chapter III by Solange Oliveira Rezende et al., presents a new methodology for combining data-driven and user-driven evaluation measures to identify interesting rules. Both data-driven (or objective measures) and user-driven (or subjective measures) are discussed and then analysed for their pros and cons. With the proposed new methodology, data-driven measures can be used to select some potentially interesting rules for the user's evaluation and the rules and the knowledge obtained during the evaluation can be employed to calculate user-driven measures for identifying interesting rules.

Julien Blanchard, Fabrice Guillet, and Pascale Juntz present a semantics-based classification of rule interestingness measures in **Chapter IV**. They propose a novel and useful classification of interestingness measures according to three criteria: the subject, the scope, and the nature of the measure. These criteria are essential to grasp the meaning of the measures, and therefore to help the users to choose the ones he/she wants to apply. Moreover, the classification allows one to compare the rules to closely related concepts such as similarities, implications, and equivalences.

Section III presents four techniques on post-analysis and post-mining of association rules. **Chapter V** by Huawen Liu, Jigui Sun, and Huijie Zhang presents a technique on post-processing for rule reduction using closed set. Superfluous rules are filtered out from knowledge base in a post-processing manner. With dependent relation discovered by closed set mining technique, redundant rules can be eliminated efficiently.

In **Chapter VI**, Hacène Cherfi, Amedeo Napoli, and Yannick Toussaint present a new technique to combine data mining and semantic techniques for post-mining and selection of association rules. To focus on the result interpretation and discover new knowledge units, they introduce an original approach to classify association rules according to qualitative criteria using domain model as background knowledge. Its successful application on text mining in molecular biology shows the benefits of taking into account a knowledge domain model of the data.

In the case of stream data, the post-mining of association is more challenging. **Chapter VII** by Hetal Thakkar, Barzan Mozafari, and Carlo Zaniolo present a technique for continuous post-mining of association rules in a data stream management system. The chapter describes the architecture and techniques used to achieve this advanced functionality in the Stream Mill Miner (SMM) prototype, an SQL-based DSMS designed to support continuous mining queries.

The Receiver Operating Characteristics (ROC) graph is a popular way of assessing the performance of classification rules, but they are inappropriate to evaluate the quality of association rules, as there is no class in association rule mining and the consequent part of two different association rules might not have any correlation at all. Ronaldo Cristinano Prati presents in **Chapter VIII** a novel technique of QROC, a variation of ROC space to analyse itemset costs/benefits in association rules. It can be used to help analysts to evaluate the relative interestingness among different association rules in different cost scenarios.

Section IV presents rule selection techniques for classification. **Chapter IX** by Maria-Luiza Antonie, David Chodos, and Osmar Zaïane presents the rule generation, pruning, and selection in associative classifier, which is a classification model based on association rules. Several variations on the associative classifier model are presented, which are mining data sets with re-occurring items, using negative association rules, and pruning rules using graph-based techniques. They also present a system, ARC-UI, which allows a user to analyze the results of classifying an item using an associative classifier.

In **Chapter X**, Silvia Chiusano and Paolo Garza discuss the selection of high-quality rules in associative classification. They present a comparative study of five well-known classification rule pruning methods and analyze the characteristics of both the selected and pruned rule sets in terms of information content. A large set of experiments has been run to empirically evaluate the effect of the pruning methods when applied individually as well as when combined.

Section V presents the visualization and representation techniques for the presentation and exploration of association rules. In **Chapter XI**, Sadok Ben Yahia, Olivier Couturier, Tarek Hamrouni, and Engelbert Mephu Nguifo, present two meta-knowledge based approaches for an interactive visualization of large amounts of association rules. Different from traditional methods of association rule visualization where association rule extraction and visualization are treated separately in a one-way process, the two proposed approaches that use meta-knowledge to guide the user during the mining process in an integrated framework covering both steps of the data mining process. The first one builds a roadmap of compact representation of association rules from which the user can explore generic bases of association rules and derive, if desired, redundant ones without information loss. The second approach clusters the set of association rules or its generic bases, and uses a fisheye view technique to help the user during the mining of association rules.

Chapter XII by Claudio Haruo Yamamoto, Maria Cristina Ferreira de Oliveira, and Solange Oliveira Rezende also discusses the visualization techniques to assist the generation and exploration of association rules. It presents an overview of the many approaches on using visual representations and information visualization techniques to assist association rule mining. A classification of the different approaches that rely on visual representations is introduced, based on the role played by the visualization technique in the exploration of rule sets. A methodology that supports visually assisted selective generation of association rules based on identifying clusters of similar itemsets is also presented. Then, a case study and some trends/issues for further developments are presented.

Nicolas Pasquier presents in **Chapter XIII** frequent closed itemset based condensed representations for association rules. Many applications of association rules to data from different domains have shown that techniques for filtering irrelevant and useless association rules are required to simplify their interpretation by the end-user. This chapter focuses on condensed representations that are characterized in the frequent closed itemsets framework to expose their advantages and drawbacks.

Section VI present techniques on the maintenance of association rules and new forms of association rules. **Chapter XIV** by Mengling Feng, Jinyan Li, Guozhu Dong, and Limsoon Wong presents a survey of the techniques for the maintenance of frequent patterns. The frequent pattern maintenance problem is summarized with a study on how the space of frequent patterns evolves in response to data updates. Focusing on incremental and decremental maintenance, four major types of maintenance algorithms are introduced, and the advantages and limitations of these algorithms are studied from both the theoretical and experimental perspectives. Possible solutions to certain limitations and potential research opportunities and emerging trends in frequent pattern maintenance are also discussed.

Conditional contrast patterns are designed by Guozhu Dong, Jinyan Li, Guimei Liu, and Limsoon Wong in **Chapter XV**. It is related to contrast mining, where one considers the mining of patterns/ models that contrast two or more datasets, classes, conditions, time periods, etc. Roughly speaking, conditional contrasts capture situations where a small change in patterns is associated with a big change in the matching data of the patterns. It offers insights on "discriminating" patterns for a given condition. It can also be viewed as a new direction for the analysis and mining of frequent patterns. The chapter formalizes the concepts of conditional contrast and provides theoretical results on conditional contrast mining. An efficient algorithm is proposed based on the results and experiment results are reported.

In **Chapter XVI**, Qinrong Feng, Duoqian Miao, and Ruizhi Wang present a technique for multidimensional model-based decision rules mining, which can output generalized rules with different degree of generalization. A method of decision rules mining from different abstract levels is provided in the chapter, which aims to improve the efficiency of decision rules mining by combining the hierarchical structure of multidimensional model and the techniques of rough set theory.

IMPACTS AND CONTRIBUTIONS

By collecting the research on the post-mining, summarization and presentation of association rule, as well as new forms and trends of association rules, this book shows the advanced techniques for the post-processing stage of association rules and presents readers what can be done to extract useful and actionable knowledge after discovering a large number of association rules. It will foster the research in the above topic and will benefit the use of association rule mining in real world applications. The readers can develop a clear picture on what can be done after discovering many association rules to extract useful knowledge and actionable patterns. Readers from industry can benefit by discovering how to deal with the large number of rules discovered and how to summarize or visualize the discovered rules to make them applicable in business applications. As editors, we hope this book will encourage more research into this area, stimulate new ideas on the related topics, and lead to implementations of the presented techniques in real-world applications.

Acknowledgment

This book dates back all the way to August 2007, when our book prospectus was submitted to IGI Global as a response to the Data Mining Techniques Call 2007. After its approval, this project began from October 2007 and ended in October 2008. During the process, more than one thousand e-mails have been sent and received, interacting with authors, reviewers, advisory board members, and the IGI Global team. We also received a lot of support from colleagues, researchers, and the development team from IGI Global. We would like to take this opportunity to thank them for their unreserved help and support.

Firstly, we would like to thank the authors for their excellent work and formatting by following the guidelines closely. Some authors also took the painful procedure to convert their manuscripts from LaTex to WORD format as required. We are grateful for their patience and quick response to our many requests.

We also greatly appreciate the efforts of the reviewers, for responding on time, their constructive comments and helpful suggestions in the detailed review reports. Their work helped the authors to improve their manuscripts and also helped us to select high-quality papers as the book chapters.

Our thanks go to the members of the Editorial Advisory Board, Prof. Jean-Francois Boulicaut, Prof. Ramamohanarao Kotagiri, Prof. Jian Pei, Prof. Jaideep Srivastava and Prof. Philip S. Yu. Their insightful comments and suggestions helped to make the book coherent and consistent.

We would like to thank the IGI Global team for their supports throughout the one-year book development. We thank Ms. Julia Mosemann for her comments, suggestions and supports, which ensured the completion of this book within the planned timeframe. We also thank Ms. Kristin M. Klinger and Ms. Jan Travers for their help on our book proposal and project contract.

We would also like to express our gratitude to our colleagues for their support and comments on this book and for their encouragement during the book editing procedure.

Last but not least, we would like to thank Australian Research Council (ARC) for the grant on a Linkage Project (LP0775041), and University of Technology, Sydney (UTS), Australia for the Early Career Researcher Grant, which supported our research in the past two years.

Yanchang Zhao
University of Technology, Sydney, Australia

Chengqi Zhang
University of Technology, Sydney, Australia

Longbing Cao
University of Technology, Sydney, Australia

Section I
Introduction

Chapter I
Association Rules:
An Overview

Paul D. McNicholas
University of Guelph, Guelph, Ontario, Canada

Yanchang Zhao
University of Technology, Sydney, Australia

ABSTRACT

Association rules present one of the most versatile techniques for the analysis of binary data, with applications in areas as diverse as retail, bioinformatics, and sociology. In this chapter, the origin of association rules is discussed along with the functions by which association rules are traditionally characterised. Following the formal definition of an association rule, these functions – support, confidence and lift – are defined and various methods of rule generation are presented, spanning 15 years of development. There is some discussion about negations and negative association rules and an analogy between association rules and 2×2 tables is outlined. Pruning methods are discussed, followed by an overview of measures of interestingness. Finally, the post-mining stage of the association rule paradigm is put in the context of the preceding stages of the mining process.

INTRODUCTION

In general, association rules present an efficient method of analysing very large binary, or discretized, data sets. One common application is to discover relationships between binary variables in transaction databases, and this type of analysis is called a 'market basket analysis'. While association rules have been used to analyse non-binary data, such analyses typically involve the data being coded as binary before proceeding. Association rules present one of the most versatile methods of analysing large binary datasets; recent applications have ranged from detection of bio-terrorist attacks (Fienberg and Shmeeli, 2005) and the analysis of gene expression data (Carmona-Saez *et al.*, 2006), to the analysis of Irish third level education applications (McNicholas, 2007).

There are two or three steps involved in a typical association rule analysis (as shown in Box 1).

This book focuses on the third step, post-mining, and the purpose of this chapter is to set the scene for this focus. This chapter begins with a look back towards the foundations of thought on the association of attributes: the idea of an association rule is then introduced, followed by discussion about rule generation. Finally, there is a broad review of pruning and interestingness.

BACKGROUND

Although formally introduced towards the end of the twentieth century (Agrawal *et al.* 1993), many of the ideas behind association rules can be seen in the literature over a century earlier. Yule (1903) wrote about associations between attributes and, in doing so, he built upon the earlier writings of De Mogran (1847), Boole (1847, 1854) and Jevons (1890). Yule (1903) raised many of the issues that are now central to association rule analysis. In fact, Yule (1903) built the idea of not possessing an attribute into his paradigm, from the outset, as an important concept. Yet, it was several years after the introduction of association rules before

such issues were seriously considered and it is still the case that the absence of items from transactions is often ignored in analyses. We will revisit this issue later in this chapter, when discussing negative association rules and negations.

ASSOCIATION RULES

Definitions

Given a non-empty set I, an association rule is a statement of the form $A \Rightarrow B$, where $A, B \subset I$ such that $A \neq \emptyset, B \neq \emptyset$, and $A \cap B = \emptyset$. The set A is called the antecedent of the rule, the set B is called the consequent of the rule, and we shall call I the master itemset. Association rules are generated over a large set of transactions, denoted by T. An association rule can be deemed interesting if the items involved occur together often and there are suggestions that one of the sets might in some sense lead to the presence of the other set. Association rules are traditionally characterised as interesting, or not, based on mathematical notions called 'support', 'confidence' and 'lift'. Although there are now a multitude of measures of interestingness available to the analyst, many of them are still based on these three functions.

The notation $P(A)$ is used to represent the proportion of times that the set A appears in the transaction set T. Similarly, $P(A, B)$ represents the proportion of times that the sets A and B coincide in transactions in T. It is also necessary to define

Box 1. Steps involved in a typical association rule analysis

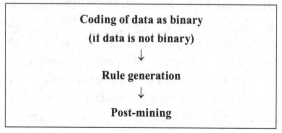

Table 1. Traditional functions of association rules

Function	Definition
Support	$s(A \Rightarrow B) = P(A, B)$
Confidence	$c(A \Rightarrow B) = P(B \mid A)$
Lift	$L(A \Rightarrow B) = c(A \Rightarrow B)/P(B)$

$$P(B \mid A) = \frac{P(A,B)}{P(A)},$$

which is the proportion of times that the set B appears in all of the transactions involving the presence of the set A. Table 1 contains the definitions for the functions by which association rules are traditionally characterised.

The lift, or as it is sometimes called, the 'interest', of an association rule can be viewed as some measure of the distance between $P(B \mid A)$ and $P(B)$ or, equivalently, as a function giving the extent to which A and B are dependent on one another. The support of the antecedent part of the rule, $P(A)$, is sometimes called the 'coverage' of the rule and that of the consequent part, $P(B)$, is referred to as the 'expected confidence' because it is the value that the confidence would take if the antecedent and consequent were independent.

Negations and Negative Association Rules

In many applications, it is not only the presence of items in the antecedent and the consequent parts of an association rule that may be of interest. Consideration, in many cases, should be given to the relationship between the absence of items from the antecedent part and the presence or absence of items from the consequent part. Further, the presence of items in the antecedent part can be related to the absence of items from the consequent part; for example, a rule such as {margarine} $\Rightarrow$ {not butter}, which might be referred to as a 'replacement rule'.

Table 2. A cross-tabulation of A versus B.

		A	
		1	0
B	1	a	b
	0	c	d

One way to incorporate the absence of items into the association rule mining paradigm is to consider rules of the form $A \nRightarrow B$ (Savasere *et al.*, 1998). Another is to think in terms of negations. Suppose $A \subset I$, then write $\neg A$ to denote the absence or negation of the item, or items, in A from a transaction. Considering A as a binary $\{0, 1\}$ variable, the presence of the items in A is equivalent to $A = 1$, while the negation $\neg A$ is equivalent to $A = 0$. The concept of considering association rules involving negations, or "negative implications", is due to Silverstein *et al.* (1998).

The Relationship to 2×2 Tables

Table 2, which is a cross-tabulation of A versus B, can be regarded as a representation of the supports of all of the rules that can be formed with antecedent A ($A = 1$) or $\neg A$ ($A = 0$) and consequent B ($B = 1$) or $\neg B$ ($B = 0$).

The odds ratio associated with Table 2 is given by ad/bc. This odds ratio can be used to provide a partition of the eight possibly interesting association rules that can be formed from A, B and their respective negations: if odds ratio > 1, then only rules involving A and B or $\neg A$ and $\neg B$ may be of interest, while if odds ratio < 1, then only rules involving exactly one of $\neg A$ and $\neg B$ may be of interest.

RULE GENERATION

Introduction

Since their formal introduction in the year 1993 (Agrawal *et al.* 1993), most of the published work on association rules has focused on effective and fast techniques for rule generation. In the original formulation of the association rule mining problem, mining was performed by generating rules with support and confidence above predefined thresholds.

In general, the generation of association rules can be broken into two steps: frequent itemset counting and rule generation. A frequent itemset is an itemset with support no less than some pre-specified threshold. The first step counts the frequency of itemsets and finds frequent ones, and the second step generates high confidence rules from frequent itemsets. The first step is of exponential complexity in that, given m items, there are 2^m possible candidate itemsets. The lattice of itemsets is shown in Figure 1, where the dashed line shows the boundary between frequent itemsets and infrequent ones. The itemsets above the line are frequent, while those below it are infrequent. Due to the huge search space of itemsets, many researchers work on frequent itemset counting, and more than two dozen publications and implementations on the topic can be found at the FIMI (Frequent Itemset Mining Implementations) Repository (http://fimi.cs.helsinki.fi/).

The Apriori Algorithm

Due to the explosion in the number of candidate itemsets as the number of items increases, much research work has focused on efficient searching strategies for looking for frequent itemsets. The apriori algorithm was introduced by Agrawal and Srikant (1994). To improve the efficiency of searching, the algorithm exploits the downward-closure property of support (also called the anti-monotonicity property); that is, if an itemset is infrequent, then all of its supersets are also infrequent. To put it in another way, if an itemset is frequent, then all of its subsets are frequent. The above property is often employed to efficiently traverse the search space. For example, in the item lattice shown in Figure 1, if {ABC} is a frequent itemset, then {AB}, {AC}, {BC}, {A}, {B} and {C} are all frequent itemsets. If {AD} is infrequent, then {ABD}, {ACD} and {ABCD} are infrequent.

Alternative Algorithms

To reduce the number of candidate itemsets, the ideas of discovering only closed itemsets or maximal frequent itemsets were proposed. A closed itemset is an itemset without any immediate supersets having the same support (Pasquier *et al.*, 1999; Zaki and Hsiao, 2005), and an itemset is a maximum frequent itemset if none of its im-

Figure 1. An example of an item lattice

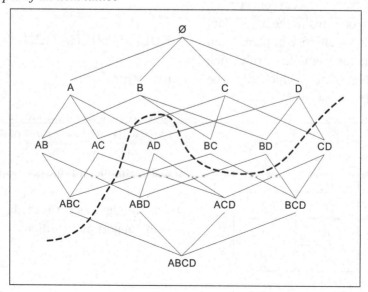

mediate supersets are frequent (Gouda and Zaki, 2001, Xiao *et al.*, 2003). For example, {ABC} and {BD} are two maximum frequent itemsets in the itemset lattice in Figure 1.

Alternatives to the apriori algorithm have been proposed, that count items in different ways, such as 'dynamic itemset counting' (Brin *et al.*, 1997). However, recent improvements in the implementation of the apriori algorithm by Borgelt and Kruse (2002) and Borgelt (2003) have made it very efficient. Zaki *et al.* (1997) introduced the ECLAT algorithm, which was later implemented efficiently by Bolgelt (2003). The ECLAT algorithm is a viable alternative to the apriori algorithm that is based on equivalence class clustering using some predefined support threshold.

For searching in the item lattice shown in Figure 1, there are two different approaches: breadth-first search and depth-first search. A typical example of a breadth-first search is the apriori algorithm. Depth-first traversal of itemset lattice was proposed by Burdick *et al.* (2001). Han *et al.* (2004) designed a frequent-pattern tree (FP-tree) structure as a compressed representation of the database, and proposed the FP-growth algorithm for mining the complete set of frequent patterns by pattern fragment growth.

Throughout the literature, there have been alternatives to support-based rule generation. The idea of discovering association rules based on conditional independencies was introduced by Castelo *et al.* (2001) in the form of the MAMBO algorithm. Pasquier *et al.* (1999) showed that it is

not necessary to use support pruning in order to find all interesting association rules and that it is sufficient to mine the closed frequent itemsets. Pei *et al.* (2000) and Zaki and Hsiao (2005) propose efficient algorithms for this purpose, called CLOSET and CHARM respectively.

The problem of finding efficient parallel routines for association rule generation has gone through several iterations. Aggarwal and Yu (1998) present an excellent review of work carried out up to that time, encompassing the contributions of Mueller (1995), Park *et al.* (1995) and Agrawal and Shafer (1996), amongst others. More recent work on parallel techniques for association rule generation, includes that of Zäiane *et al.* (2001) and Holt and Chung (2007).

A detailed introduction to a variety of association rule mining algorithms is given by Ceglar and Roddick (2006).

PRUNING

Pruning and Visualisation

Hofmann and Wilhelm (2001) discusss methods of visualising association rules, amongst which are doubledecker plots and two-key plots. Doubledecker plots are mosaic plots (Hartigan and Kleiner, 1981) that can be used to visualise the support and confidence of different combinations of presence and absence of the consequent part and the items in the antecedent part of a rule. Doubledecker plots can be used to implicitly find interesting rules involving negations but are of limited use for this purpose when the consequent is not singleton. A two-key plot is a scatter plot of confidence versus support, where each point lies on a line through the origin and each such line represents rules with a common antecedent. Two-key plots can be used to perform visual pruning since all rules with support of at least s and confidence of at least c will lie in a rectangle with corners $(s, 1)$, $(1, 1)$, $(1, c)$ and (s, c).

Figure 2. The apriori algorithm

```
k ← 1;
L₁ ← frequent items;
Repeat until Lₖ is empty
        Generate candidate (k+1)-itemsets Cₖ₊₁ from Lₖ;
        Lₖ₊₁ ← {X | X ∈ Cₖ₊₁ and supp(X) ≥ minsupp};
        k ← k + 1;
End loop;
```

The Three-Step Approach

There have been some statistically-based pruning methods mentioned in the association rules literature. One such method was given by Bruzzese and Davino (2001), who presented three tests. Initially, association rules are mined with certain support and confidence thresholds, then three statistical tests are employed; an association rule is only retained if it 'passes' all three tests. These tests can be carried out using the software PISSARRO (Keller and Schlögl, 2002). By comparing the confidence of a rule to its expected confidence, the first test prunes rules that have high confidence due to the presence of frequent items in the consequent part of the rule. The second test involves performing a chi-squared test on each set of rules with the same antecedent part. The third test evaluates the strength of the association between the antecedent and the consequent of a rule by comparing the support of the rule with the support of its antecedent part. This pruning approach will, in many cases, be excessive. This third test in particular can cause the pruning of rules that one may wish to keep. Furthermore, this procedure can greatly slow down the post-mining stage of the process.

Pruning Methods Based on the Chi-Squared Test

Although the relationship that we have outlined between association rules and 2×2 tables might make pruning methods based on the chi-squared test seem attractive, they will suffer from the usual sample size-related problems attached to chi-squared tests. An excellent critique of pruning methods based on the chi-squared test is given by Wilhelm (2002).

INTERESTINGNESS

Background

Apart from the staples of support, confidence and lift, a whole host of other functions have been introduced to measure the interestingness of an association rule. Interestingness is viewed by some as an alternative to pruning: rules can be ranked by interestingness and the pruning stage can then be omitted. However, interestingness can also be used before pruning or to break ties during pruning.

Measures of rule interestingness can be considered as falling into one of two categories: subjective and objective (Silberschatz and Tuzhilin, 1996; Freitas, 1998). Subjective measures of interestingness focus on finding interesting patterns by matching against a given set of user beliefs, while objective ones measure the interestingness in terms of their probabilities.

In this section, a selection of objective measures of interestingness is given and briefly discussed. More extensive reviews of measures of interestingness are given elsewhere in this book.

Selected Measures of Interestingness

The lift of an association rule, which was defined in Table 1, is often used as a measure of interestingness. One notable feature of lift is that it is symmetric, in that the lift of the rule $A \Rightarrow B$ is the same as the lift of the rule $B \Rightarrow A$. A rule with a lift value of 1 means that the antecedent and consequent parts of the rule are independent. However, lift is not symmetric about 1 and it is not clear how far lift needs to be from 1 before a rule can be considered interesting. In an attempt to solve this latter problem, McNicholas *et al.* (2008) introduced the standardised lift of an association rule. Their standardised lift gives a measure of the interestingness of an association rule by standardising the value of the lift to give a number in the interval [0,1]. This standardisation takes into account the support of the antecedent, the support of the consequent, the support of the rule and any support or confidence thresholds that may have been used in the mining process.

The 'conviction' (Brin *et al.*, 1997) of an association rule $A \Rightarrow B$, which is given by

$$\text{Con}(A \Rightarrow B) = \frac{P(A)P(\neg B)}{P(A, \neg B)},$$

presents an alternative to some of the more traditional measures of interestingness such as confidence and lift. Conviction takes the value 1 when A and B have no items in common and it is undefined when the rule $A \Rightarrow B$ always holds.

Gray and Orlowska (1998) define the interestingness of an association rule $A \Rightarrow B$ as

$$\text{Int}(A \Rightarrow B; K, M) = \left[\left(\frac{P(A,B)}{P(A)P(B)} \right)^K - 1 \right] (P(A)P(B))^M$$

This is the distance of the Kth power of lift from 1 multiplied by the respective magnitudes of $P(A)$ and $P(B)$ raised to the Mth power. Since lift is symmetric, so is Gray and Orlowska's interestingness

Other Measures of Interestingness

A whole host of other measures of interestingness exist. More than twenty measures of interestingness are reviewed by Tan *et al.* (2002): these include the Φ-coefficient, kappa, mutual information, the J-measure and the Gini index. The unexpected confidence interestingness and isolated interestingness of an association rule were introduced by Dong and Li (1998) by considering the unexpectedness of the rule in terms of other association rules in its neighbourhood. In addition, any-confidence, all-confidence and bond were given by Omiecinski (2003) and utility was

used by Chan *et al.* (2003). More recently, Weiß (2008) introduced the notions of α-precision and σ-precision.

POST-MINING

Pruning and interestingness, as discussed previously in this chapter, are employed in the post-mining stage of the association rule mining paradigm. However, there are a host of other techniques used in the post-mining stage that do not naturally fall under either of these headings. Some such techniques are in the area of redundancy-removal.

There are often a huge number of association rules to contend with in the post-mining stage and it can be very difficult for the user to identify which ones are interesting. Therefore, it is important to remove insignificant rules, prune redundancy and do further post-mining on the discovered rules (Liu and Hsu, 1996; Liu *et al.*, 1999). Liu *et al.* (1999) proposed a technique for pruning and summarising discovered association rules by first removing those insignificant associations and then forming direction-setting rules, which provide a sort of summary of the discovered association rules. Lent *et al.* (1997) proposed clustering the discovered association rules. A host of techniques on post mining of association rules will be introduced in the following chapters of this book.

SUMMARY

Whilst there has been much work on improving the algorithmic efficiency of association rule generation, relatively little has been done to investigate the in-depth implications of association rule analyses. With this chapter presenting some background and an overview of some of the developments in the area, the remainder of this book will focus on the post-mining stage of association rule mining.

REFERENCES

Aggarwal, C. C., & Yu, P. S. (1998). Mining Large Itemsets for Association Rules. *In Bulletin of the Technical Committee, IEEE Computer Society, 21(1)* 23-31.

Agrawal, R., Imielinski, T., & Swami, A. (1993). Mining association rules between sets of items in very large databases. *In Proceedings of the ACM SIGMOD Conference on Management of data,* Washington, USA (pp. 207-216).

Agrawal, R., & Srikant R. (1994). Fast Algorithms for Mining Association Rules in Large Databases. *In Proceedings of the 20th International Conference on Very Large Data Bases,* Santiago, Chile (pp. 478-499).

Agrawal, R., & Shafer, J. (1996). Parallel Mining of Association Rules: Design, Implementation, and Experience. *Technical Report RJ10004, IBM Almaden Research Center,* San Jose, California, USA.

Boole, G. (1847). *The Mathematical Analysis of Logic.* Cambridge: Macmillan, Barclay and Macmillan.

Boole, G. (1854). *An Investigation of the Laws of Thought.* Cambridge: Macmillan and Co.

Borgelt, C. (2003). Efficient implementations of apriori and éclat. *In Workshop on Frequent Itemset Mining Implementations.* Melbourne, FL.

Borgelt, C., & Kruse, R. (2002). Induction of association rules: Apriori implementation. *In 15th COMPSTAT Conference,* Berlin, Germany.

Brin, S., Motwani, R., Ullman, J. D., & Tsur, S. (1997). Dynamic itemset counting and implication rules for market basket data. *In SIGMOD '97: Proceedings of the 1997 ACM SIGMOD international conference on Management of data,* Tucson, Arizona, USA (pp 255-264).

Bruzzese, D., & Davino, C. (2001). Statistical pruning of discovered association rules. *Computational Statistics, 16(3),* 387-398.

Burdick, D., Calimlim, M., & Calimlim, M. (2001). MAFIA: A Maximal Frequent Itemset Algorithm for Transactional Databases. *Proceedings of the 17th International Conference on Data Engineering,* IEEE Computer Society (pp. 443-452).

Carmona-Saez, P., Chagoyen, M., Rodriguez, A., Trelles, O., Carazo, J. M., & Pascual-Montano, A. (2006). Integrated analysis of gene expression by association rules discovery. *BMC Bioinformatics, 7(54).*

Castelo, R., Feelders, A., & Siebes, A. (2001). MAMBO: Discovering association rules based on conditional independencies. *In Proceedings of 4th International Symposium on Intelligent Data Analysis,* Cascais, Portugal.

Ceglar, A., & Roddick, J. F. (2006). Association mining. *ACM Computing Surveys, 38*(2), 5.

Chan, R., Yang, Q., & Shen, Y.-D. (2003). Mining high utility itemsets Data Mining, *In ICDM 2003: Third IEEE International Conference on Data Mining,* Melbourne, Florida, USA (pp. 19-26).

De Morgan, A. (1847). *Formal Logic or, The Calculus of Inference, Necessary and Probable.* London: Taylor and Walton.

Dong, G., & Li, J. (1998), Interestingness of discovered association rules in terms of neighborhood-based unexpectedness. *In Pacific-Asia Conference on Knowledge Discovery and Data Mining.* Melbourne, Australia (pp. 72-86).

Fienberg, S. E., & Shmueli, G. (2005). Statistical issues and challenges associated with rapid detection of bio-terrorist attacks. *Statistics in Medicine, 24(4),* 513-529.

Freitas, A. A. (1998). On Objective Measures of Rule Surprisingness. *PKDD '98: Proceedings of the Second European Symposium on Principles of*

Data Mining and Knowledge Discovery, Springer-Verlag, Nantes, France (pp. 1-9).

Gouda, K., & Zaki, M. J. (2001). Efficiently Mining Maximal Frequent Itemsets. *ICDM '01: Proceedings of the 2001 IEEE International Conference on Data Mining*, San Jose, California, USA (pp. 163-170).

Gray, B., & Orlowska, M. (1998). CCAIIA: Clustering categorical attributes into interesting association rules. *In Pacific-Asia Conference on Knowledge Discovery and Data Mining*, Melbourne, Australia (pp. 132-143).

Han, J., Pei, J., Yin, Y., & Mao, R. (2004). Mining frequent patterns without candidate generation. *Data Mining and Knowledge Discovery, 8*, 53-87.

Hartigan, J. A., & Kleiner, B. (1981). Mosaics for contingency tables. In W. F. Eddy (Ed.), *13th Symposium on the Interface Between Computer Science and Statistics*, New York: Springer-Verlag.

Hofmann, H., & Wilhelm, A. (2001). Visual comparison of association rules. *Computational Statistics, 16(3)*, 399-415.

Holt, J. D., & Chung, S. M. (2007). Parallel mining of association rules from text databases. *The Journal of Supercomputing, 39(3)*, 273-299.

Jevons, W. S. (1890). *Pure Logic and Other Minor Works*. London: Macmillan.

Keller, R., & Schlögl, A. (2002). *PISSARRO: Picturing interactively statistically sensible association rules reporting overviews*. Department of Computer Oriented Statistics and Data Analysis, Augsburg University, Germany.

Lent, B., Swami, A. N., & Widom, J. (1997). Clustering Association Rules. *Proceedings of the Thirteenth International Conference on Data Engineering*. Birmingham U.K., IEEE Computer Society (pp. 220-231).

Liu, B., & Hsu, W. (1996). Post-Analysis of Learned Rules. *AAAI/IAAI, 1*(1996), 828-834.

Liu, B., Hsu, W., & Ma, Y. (1999). Pruning and summarizing the discovered associations. *Proceedings of the fifth ACM SIGKDD international conference on Knowledge discovery and data mining (KDD-99)*, ACM Press (pp. 125-134).

McNicholas, P. D. (2007). Association rule analysis of CAO data (with discussion). *Journal of the Statistical and Social Inquiry Society of Ireland, 36*, 44-83.

McNicholas, P. D., Murphy, T. B., & O'Regan, M. (2008). Standardising the Lift of an Association Rule, *Computational Statistics and Data Analysis, 52(10)*, 4712-4721.

Mueller A. (1995). Fast sequential and parallel methods for association rule mining: A comparison. *Technical Report CS-TR-3515, Department of Computer Science, University of Maryland*, College Park, MD.

Omiecinski, E. R. (2003). Alternative Interest Measures for Mining Associations in Databases. *IEEE Transactions on Knowledge and Data Engineering, 15*, 57-69.

Park, J. S., Chen, M. S., & Yu, P. S. (1995). Efficient Parallel Data Mining of Association Rules. *In Fourth International Conference on Information and Knowledge Management*, Baltimore, Maryland. (pp. 31-36).

Pasquier, N., Bastide, Y., Taouil, R., & Lakhal, L. (1999). Discovering Frequent Closed Itemsets for Association Rules. *Proceeding of the 7th International Conference on Database Theory*, Lecture Notes in Computer Science (LNCS 1540), Springer, 1999, 398-416.

Pei, J., Han, J., & Mao, R. (2000). CLOSET: An efficient algorithm for mining frequent closed itemsets. *Proceedings of ACM SIGMOD Workshop on Research Issues in Data Mining and Knowledge Discovery*, 2000.

Savasere, A., Omiecinski, E., & Navathe, S. B. (1998). Mining for strong negative associations in a large database of customer transactions. *Proceedings of the 14th International Conference on Data Engineering*, Washington DC, USA, 1998, (pp. 494–502).

Silberschatz, A., & Tuzhilin, A. (1996). What Makes Patterns Interesting in Knowledge Discovery Systems. *IEEE Transactions on Knowledge and Data Engineering, IEEE Educational Activities Department, 8*, 970-974.

Silverstien, C., Brin, S., & Motwani, R. (1998). Beyond Market Baskets: Generalizing Association Rules to Dependence Rules. *Data Mining and Knowledge Discovery, 2(1)*, 39-68.

Tan, P., Kumar, V., & Srivastava, J. (2002). Selecting the right interestingness measure for association patterns. *KDD '02: Proceedings of the eighth ACM SIGKDD international conference on Knowledge discovery and data mining*, ACM Press, 2002, (pp. 32-41).

Weiß, C. H. (2008). Statistical mining of interesting association rules. *Statistics and Computing, 18*(2), 185-194.

Wilhelm, A. (2002). Statistical tests for pruning association rules. *In Computational Statistics: 15th Symposium*, Berlin, Germany.

Xiao, Y., Yao, J., Li, Z., & Dunham, M. H. (2003). Efficient Data Mining for Maximal Frequent Subtrees. *ICDM '03: Proceedings of the Third IEEE International Conference on Data Mining*, IEEE Computer Society, *379*.

Yule, G. U. (1903). Notes on the theory of association of attributes in statistics. *Biometrika, 2*(2), 121–134.

Zaki, M. J., Parthasarathy, S., Ogihara, M., & Li, W. (1997). New algorithms for fast discovery of association rules. *Technical Report 651, Computer Science Department, University of Rochester*, Rochester, NY 14627.

Zaki, M. J., & Hsiao, C. (2005). Efficient Algorithms for Mining Closed Itemsets and Their Lattice Structure. *IEEE Transactions on Knowledge and Data Engineering, 17*, 462-478.

Zäiane, O. R., El-Hajj, M., & Lu, P. (2001). Fast Parallel Association Rule Mining without Candidacy Generation. *In First IEEE International Conference on Data Mining* (pp. 665-668).

Section II
Identifying Interesting Rules

Chapter II
From Change Mining to Relevance Feedback:
A Unified View on Assessing Rule Interestingness

Mirko Boettcher
University of Magdeburg, Germany

Georg Ruß
University of Magdeburg, Germany

Detlef Nauck
BT Group plc, UK

Rudolf Kruse
University of Magdeburg, Germany

ABSTRACT

Association rule mining typically produces large numbers of rules, thereby creating a second-order data mining problem: which of the generated rules are the most interesting? And: should interestingness be measured objectively or subjectively? To tackle the amount of rules that are created during the mining step, the authors propose the combination of two novel ideas: first, there is rule change mining, which is a novel extension to standard association rule mining which generates potentially interesting time-dependent features for an association rule. It does not require changes in the existing rule mining algorithms and can therefore be applied during post-mining of association rules. Second, the authors make use of the existing textual description of a rule and those newly derived objective features and combine them with a novel approach towards subjective interestingness by using relevance feedback methods from information retrieval. The combination of these two new approaches yields a powerful, intuitive way of exploring the typically vast set of association rules. It is able to combine objective and subjective measures of interestingness and will incorporate user feedback. Hence, it increases the probability of finding the most interesting rules given a large set of association rules.

INTRODUCTION

Nowadays, the discovery of association rules is a relatively mature and well-researched topic. Many algorithms have been proposed to ever faster discover and maintain association rules. However, one of the biggest problems of association rules still remains unresolved. Usually, the number of discovered associations will be immense, easily in the thousands or even tens of thousands. Clearly, the large numbers make rules difficult to examine by a user. Moreover, many of the discovered rules will be obvious, already known, or not relevant.

For this reason a considerable amount of methods have been proposed to assist a user in detecting the most interesting or relevant ones. Studies about interestingness measures can roughly be divided into two classes: objective and subjective measures. Objective (data-driven) measures are usually derived from statistics, information theory or machine learning and assess numerical or structural properties of a rule and the data to produce a ranking. In contrast to objective measures, subjective (user-driven) measures incorporate a user's background knowledge and mostly rank rules based on some notion of actionability and unexpectedness.

In spite of a multitude of available publications the problem of interestingness assessment still is regarded as one of the unsolved problems in data mining and still experiencing slow progress (Piatetsky-Shapiro, 2000). The search for a general solution is one of the big challenges of today's data mining research (Fayyad et al., 2003). Existing approaches for interestingness assessment have several shortcomings which render them inadequate for many real-world applications.

Nonetheless, objective and subjective measures both have their justification to be used within the process of interestingness assessment. Objective measures help a user to get a first impression at what has been discovered and to obtain a starting point for further exploration of the rule set.

This exploration step can then be accomplished by methods for subjective interestingness assessment. Ideally, the interestingness assessment of association rules should therefore be seen as a two step process. It is clear that for this process to be optimal it is necessary that both, the calculus used for the objective and the subjective rating, are based on the same notion of interestingness. Nevertheless, most approaches for objective and subjective ratings have been developed independently from each other with no interaction in mind such that the information utilized for the objective is neglected for the subjective rating. In fact, approaches rarely do fit together.

In this article we discuss a framework which combines objective and subjective interestingness measures to a powerful tool for interestingness assessment and addresses the problems mentioned above. Our framework incorporates several concepts which only recently have been introduced to the area of interestingness assessment: rule change mining and user dynamics. In particular, we show how to analyse association rules for *changes* and how information about change can be used to derive meaningful and interpretable objective interestingness measures. Based on the notion of change, we discuss a novel *relevance feedback* approach for association rules. We relate the problem of subjective interestingness to the field of Information Retrieval where relevance estimation is a rather mature and well-researched field. By using a vector-based representation of rules and by utilizing concepts from information retrieval we provide the necessary tool set to incorporate the knowledge about change into the relevance feedback process.

BACKGROUND

Significant research has been conducted into methods which assess the relevance, or interestingness, of a rule. Studies concerning interestingness assessment can roughly be divided into two classes. The first class are objective measures. These are usually derived from statistics, information theory or machine learning and assess numerical or structural properties of a rule and the data to produce a ranking (Tan et al., 2004). Objective measures do not take any background information into account and are therefore suitable if an unbiased ranking is required, e.g. in off-the-shelf data mining tools. Examples of such measures are lift, conviction, odds ratio and information gain. Overviews can be found in (Tan and Kumar, 2000), (McGarry, 2005), and (Geng and Hamilton, 2006). In (Tan et al., 2004) it is empirically shown that some measures produce similar rankings while others almost reverse the order. This poses the problem of choosing the right measure for a given scenario. One solution is to discover all rules that are interesting to any measure out of a predefined set (Bayardo, Jr. and Agrawal, 1999). A different approach is presented by (Tan et al., 2004). They developed two preprocessing methods which–integrated into a mining algorithm–render many measures consistent with each other. The same publication also presents an algorithm which finds a measure that best fits the requirements of a domain expert. This is accomplished by an interactive interestingness rating of a small set of patterns.

The second class are subjective measures which incorporate a user's background knowledge. In this class a rule is considered interesting if it is either *actionable* or *unexpected*. Actionability of a rule means that the user "can act upon it to his advantage" (Silberschatz and Tuzhilin, 1996). Their focal point is on rules that are advantageous for the user's goals. The actionability approach needs detailed knowledge about the current goals and also about the cost and risks of possible actions. Systems that utilise it are hence very domain specific, like the *KEFIR* system described in (Piatetsky-Shapiro and Matheus, 1994).

A rule is unexpected if it contradicts the user's knowledge about the domain. Systems that build upon this approach require the user to express his

domain knowledge–a sometimes difficult, long and tedious task. The methods are usually based on pairwise comparison of a discovered rule with rules representing the user knowledge. This comparison can be logic-based, as in (Padmanabhan and Tuzhilin, 1999), (Padmanabhan and Tuzhilin, 2000) or (Padmanabhan and Tuzhilin, 2002) or syntax-based (Liu et al., 1997). In logic-based systems a contradiction is determined by means of a logical calculus, whereas in syntax-based systems a rule contradicts if it has a similar antecedent but a dissimilar consequent.

In (Padmanabhan and Tuzhilin, 1999), (Padmanabhan and Tuzhilin, 2000) and (Padmanabhan and Tuzhilin, 2002) the authors connect belief models with association rules. In particular, they assume that a belief system has been provided by the user whereby beliefs are defined as association rules. Based on this definition they provide a set of conditions to verify whether a rule is *unexpected* with respect to the belief on the rule database *D*. They propose an algorithm *ZoomUR* which discovers the set of unexpected rules regarding a specified set of beliefs. The algorithm itself consists of two different discovery strategies: *ZoominUR* discovers all unexpected rules that are refinements (or specialisations). On the other hand, *ZoomoutUR* discovers all unexpected rules that are more general.

In (Liu et al., 1997) the authors address the insufficiency of objective interestingness measures by focusing on the unexpectedness of generalised association rules. They assume that taxonomies exist among association rules' attributes. In subsequent work (Liu et al., 2000), human knowledge is recognised to have different degrees of certainty or preciseness. Their system allows for three degrees, notably *general impressions, reasonably precise concepts* and *precise knowledge*. The approach they propose accounts for these degrees and uses the gathered knowledge to find rules which are unexpected in regard to the expressed knowledge. The approach works iteratively: first, the user specifies his knowledge or modifies previously specified knowledge, supported by the specification language; second, the system analyses the association rules according to conformity and unexpectedness; and third, the user inspects the analysis results (aided by visualisation), saves interesting rules and discards uninteresting rules.

How to incorporate user dynamics into the relevance assessment has been studied in (Wang et al., 2003). They propose an approach based on two models which a user has to specify prior to any analysis: a model of his existing knowledge and a model of how he likes to apply this knowledge. The degree of unexpectedness of each discovered rule is calculated with respect to these two models. Their approach is based on what they call the See-and-Know assumption. Once a user has seen a rule, the rule itself and similar rules are not of interest anymore. Our approach, in contrast, uses two classes of seen rules, relevant and non-relevant ones. The ranking is calculated by aggregating the (dis-)similarity of a rule with respect to rules in both classes. Our approach also does not require a user to specify any kind of prior model of his knowledge.

In the area of rule change mining the discovery of interesting changes in histories for association rules has been studied by several authors. In (Agrawal and Psaila, 1995) a query language for history shapes is introduced. In (Dong and Li, 1999) and (Zhang et al., 2000) efficient algorithms which detect emerging itemsets are proposed. A fuzzy approach to reveal the regularities in how measures for rules change and to predict future changes was presented by (Au and Chan, 2005). In (Chakrabarti et al., 1998) an algorithm that ranks itemsets based on a change measure derived from the minimum description length principle is presented. (Liu et al., 2001b) proposes a statistical approach to distinguish trend, semi-stable and stable rules with respect to their histories of confidence and support. In (Liu et al., 2001a) a method to detect so-called fundamental rule changes is presented.

PROBLEMS

Data mining aims at discovering patterns in data which are novel, potentially useful and understandable (Fayyad et al., 1996). While being understandable is an inherent property of association rules which largely contributes to their popularity, it is the task of interestingness assessment to decide which of the many rules discovered are novel and useful. In practise, nevertheless, existing methods often perform poorly in reaching this goal.

Objective measures rely on a user's ability to choose the right measure for a given scenario out of a huge set of available ones. In (Tan et al., 2004) it is empirically shown that some measures produce similar rankings while others almost reverse the order. This poses the problem of choosing the right measure for a given scenario. Moreover, due to their rather mathematical foundations most measures lack interpretability and meaningfulness because the rule properties they measure rarely reflect the practical considerations of a user. For a user it is often unclear which measure to choose and how to link its results to his application scenario. Consequently many rules deemed interesting will not be very useful. Because objective measures do not memorize the past they are unable to identify patterns which have already been discovered multiple times in the past, which are diminishing or emerging. This ability, in turn, is crucial for distinguishing novel patterns from prevalent ones which often represent domain knowledge and thus are of less interest.

Subjective measures, on the other hand, require a user to be aware what he knows, to have a rough idea what he is looking for, and to be able to specify this knowledge in advance. A lot of effort is necessary to collect, organise and finally incorporate domain knowledge into a knowledge base against which association rules will be compared. Moreover, domain experts often forget certain key aspects or may not remember others which come into play under rarer circumstances. This problem can be termed 'expert dilemma' and has already been observed by designers of expert systems in the 1980s (Fogel, 1997). Building a knowledge base can also become a task never to be finished. During the knowledge acquisition process domain knowledge may become outdated, invalid, or loose its relevance. On the other hand, new knowledge may evolve. Users almost always have only partial, if any, awareness about this knowledge ageing process. Because of these knowledge dynamics it is often difficult to obtain a complete knowledge base. In contrast, subjective approaches treat domain knowledge as something static that never changes. Hence, they do not account for the ageing of knowledge nor do they support the user in maintaining it. Consequently, there is a risk that patterns are regarded as interesting based on outdated knowledge while a user is being left uninformed about the outdatedness itself.

ON THE INTERESTINGNESS OF CHANGE

While it is very challenging to design an algorithmic method to assess the interestingness of a rule, it is astonishingly simple for us humans to decide what is relevant to us and what is not. One of the clues to how humans judge the interestingness of an object is that they take its past and how it changes into account. When investing in stocks or buying expensive consumer goods one does not only look at the current price but also how it developed other the last couple of months. When we like to place a bet we do not only look at how a team scored last weekend but during the whole season. When we drive a car we could see many objects in our field of vision but we focus only on those which change, for example visually, like warning signs, or spatially, like pedestrians and cars.

For a business change can mean a risk (like a shrinking subgroup of target customers) or opportunity (like an evolving market niche). In either case, the business has to detect the change in order to survive or to win. In some business domains the value of information about change as a key enabler for anticipating events and conditions that may arise has been known for a long time. For example, stock traders aim to optimize buy and sell decisions by analyzing stock price behaviour over time. Moreover, many data collected are already time-stamped. In fact, the time dimension is the one dimension which is present in every data warehouse (Kimball, 1996). Due to its temporal nature business data reflect external influences like management decisions, economic and market trends and thus capture the changes a business is interested in.

Change, therefore, has some inherent interestingness for a user, and is likewise a concept that is easy to understand and can directly lead to business actions. For this reason it provides a basis for assessing a rule's interestingness and has already proven to be successful in a variety of applications, e.g. retail marketing (Chen et al., 2005), exception detection (Baron et al., 2003) and customer segmentation (Boettcher et al., 2007). Rules which change hint at unknown or surprising changes in the underlying data-generating process which may require intervening action (Chakrabarti et al., 1998). A downward trend in a rule's confidence indicates that it may disappear from the discovered rule set in the future, while an upward trend may hint at a rule which has emerged recently. On the other hand, rules which are stable over time often represent invariant properties of the data-generating process and thus are either already known, or, if discovered once, should not be displayed to the user a second time. Nonetheless, information about stability can be useful if a domain is only poorly understood. In the context of change, the information whether a rule has a high confidence is of less interest than the information that the confidence has a trend or other regular, or surprising characteristics.

HISTORIES OF ASSOCIATION RULE MEASURES

The underlying idea of our framework is to detect interesting association rules by analysing their support and confidence along the time axis. The starting point of such a *rule change mining* approach is as follows: a timestamped data set is partitioned into intervals along the time axis. Association rule discovery is then applied to each of these subsets. This yields sequences—or *histories*—of support and confidence for each rule, which can be analysed further. Of particular interest are regularities in the histories which we call *change patterns*. They allow us to make statements about the future development of a rule and thus provide a basis for proactive decision making.

In the following we will denote an association rule r as $X \rightarrow Y$ where X and Y are itemsets, $|Y| > 0$ and $X \cap Y = \varnothing$. If for two rules $r : X \rightarrow y$ and $r' : X' \rightarrow y$, $X \subset X'$ holds, then it is said that r is a *generalisation* of r'. This is denoted by $r' \prec r$. As usual, the reliability of a rule $r : X \rightarrow y$ is measured by its *confidence* conf(r) and the statistical significance measured by its *support* supp(r). We also use the support of an itemset X denoted by supp(X).

Further, let D be a time-stamped data set and $[t_0, t_n]$ the minimum time span that covers all its tuples. The interval $[t_0, t_n]$ is divided into $n > 1$ non-overlapping periods $T_i := [t_{i-1}, t_i]$, such that the corresponding subsets $D(T_i) \subset D$ each have a size $|D(T_i)| \gg 1$. Let $\hat{T} := \{T_1, \dots, T_n\}$ be the set of all periods, then for each $T_i \in \hat{T}$ association rule mining is applied to the transaction set $D(T_i)$ to derive rule sets $R(D(T_i))$.

Because the measures, like confidence and support, of every rule $r : X \rightarrow y$ are now related to a specific transaction set $D(T_i)$ and thus to a certain time period T_i we need to extend their notation. This is done straightforwardly and yields supp(r,T_i) and conf(r,T_i).

Each rule

$$r \in \hat{R}(D) := \bigcap_{i=1}^{n} R(D(T_i))$$

is therefore described by n values for each measure. Imposed by the order of time the values form sequences called *confidence history*

$$H_{conf}(r) := (conf(r, T_1), \dots conf(r, T_n))$$

and *support history*

$$H_{supp}(r) := (supp(r, T_1), \dots supp(r, T_n))$$

of the rule r. These histories are the input to most rule change mining approaches, which then detect interesting change patterns.

FRAMEWORK FOR RULE INTERESTINGNESS ASSESSMENT

In order to analyse rules for change *rule histories* need to be derived which in turn serve as the basis for both objective and subjective interestingness assessment. To derive a history, data sets collected during many consecutive periods have to be analysed for association rules. After each analysis session the discovered rules have to be compared to those discovered in previous periods and their histories have to be extended. On the other hand, history values may be discarded if their age exceeds an application-dependent threshold. Therefore, rules and histories have to be stored on a long-term basis. Taking all of the aforesaid into account the first task of our framework is:

1. Association rules have to be *discovered* and their histories efficiently stored, managed and maintained.

If histories with a sufficient length are available, the next task is straightforward and constitutes the core component of rule change mining:

2. Histories that exhibit specific change patterns have to be reliably *detected*.

Association rule discovery is generally connected with two problems. In the first place, a vast number of rules will be detected, which is also referred to as the *rule quantity problem*. Secondly, rules may be obvious, already known or not relevant, which is also referred to as the *rule quality problem* (Tan and Kumar, 2000).

Since a history is derived for each rule, the rule quantity problem also affects rule change mining: it has to deal with a vast number of histories and thus it is likely that many change patterns will be detected. Moreover, as we will briefly discuss in the following section methods that were developed to deal with this problem for association rules cannot be used in rule change mining. Furthermore, there is also a quality problem: not all of the detected change patterns are equally interesting to a user and the most interesting are hidden among many irrelevant ones. Overall, the third task is:

3. Histories with a change pattern have to be analysed for redundancies and *evaluated* according to their interestingness.

Such an initial interestingness ranking for association rules proves to be helpful in providing a user with a first overview over the discovered rules and their changes. Still, it is also clear that the user starts to build his own notion of interestingness as soon as he starts browsing the rules and histories. Our framework should support this dynamics of interestingness and therefore the fourth task is:

4. A user's feedback about the rules and histories seen thus far should be collected, analysed and used to obtain a new interestingness ranking.

Because the aforementioned tasks build upon each other, they can be seen as layers of a processing framework termed *Rule Discovery*, *Change Analysis*, *Objective Interestingness*, and *Subjective Interestingness*. The framework itself has first been described in (Boettcher et al, 2006) and evaluated in a real-life scenario in (Boettcher et al, 2007). Figure 1 illustrates and summarises the workflow.

RULE DISCOVERY

Given a timestamped data set collected during a certain period, the task of the Rule Discovery layer is to discover and store the association rules hidden in it. Therefore, the first component of this layer is an association rule mining system, its second component is a database that stores and manages rules and their histories. Both components, but also the choice of the time periods, will be explained in the following.

Figure 1. Detailed design of each layer

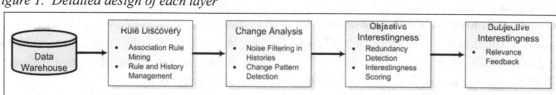

In order to obtain the data set, the period length has to be chosen. Two aspects have to be considered. Long periods lead to many transactions in the individual data sets for the different periods and thus can enhance the reliability of the metrics used. However, due to this coarse-grainedness interesting short-duration patterns may be missed. Short periods allow for measuring a rule's statistics more frequently. The reduced robustness in the model estimation makes it then more difficult to distinguish true change patterns from incidental worthless patterns. The choice of period length should therefore depend on the application. Data often is collected in regular intervals, for instance survey may be conducted weekly or bulk updates to a database may be carried out daily. In practise, these application-specific intervals can then be used to guide the choice of the time period.

After the data set is available, association rule mining is applied to it. A typical system for association rule mining may not only consist of the rule miner itself, but also of methods for pruning, constrained mining and interestingness assessment. Such methods have been developed to cope with the problem of a vast amount of discovered rules in each period. A huge number of histories has to be processed and consequently far too many change patterns will be reported. In order to cope with this problem, pruning methods are used to constrain the set of generated rules. From the perspective of rule change mining such pruning methods treat rule sets independently from each other. However, in rule change mining we have many, temporally ordered rule sets. Thus the rule property utilized for pruning—in general a measure based on rule statistics—may vary for some rules over time, but still match the pruning criterion in each rule set. Although these variations may render rules interesting, they are discarded by approaches for association rule pruning. Consequently, conventional pruning approaches should not directly be used in conjunction with rule change mining.

CHANGE ANALYSIS

The task of change analysis is to discover change patterns in rule histories. In this article, however, we only discuss how histories are detected that are stable or exhibit a trend. The Change Analysis layer fulfils its task by a two-step approach. In the first step a filter is applied to the histories to reduce the noise contained in them. In a second step statistical tests for trend and stability are conducted.

Rule histories inherently may contain random *noise*. Random noise may influence subsequent analysis steps in such a way that wrong and misleading results are produced. To reduce this effect we use *double exponential smoothing* (Chatfield, 2003) in order to reveal more clearly any trend or stability. It is a simple and fast, yet effective method, which can easily be automated. Nevertheless, it has to be considered that after smoothing association rule measures may be inconsistent with each other. For example, the confidence of a rule can in general not be obtained anymore by dividing the rule's support by the support of its antecedent itemset.

Detection of Trends

A trend is present if a sequence exhibits steady upward growth or a downward decline over its whole length. This definition is rather loose, but in fact there exists no fully satisfactory definition for trend (Chatfield, 2003). From a data mining perspective a trend describes the pattern that each value is likely to be larger or smaller than all its predecessors within a sequence, depending on whether the trend is upward or downward. Hence it is a qualitative statement about the current and likely future development of a sequence. However, taking aspects of interpretability and usefulness into account, such a statement is sufficient in the case of rule change mining. When faced with a vast number of rules and their histories, a user often has a basic expectation whether they should exhibit a trend and of what kind. By comparing his expectations with reality he will mostly be able to roughly assess the implications for its business. On the other hand, a user will rarely know in advance how trends should look like quantitatively, e.g., their shape or target values. Thus he may be unable to exploit the advantages of more sophisticated trend descriptions, like regression models.

To choose a method for trend detection, it has to be taken into account that the number of sequences to examine is huge. Whenever a trend is reported the user is basically forced to rely on the correctness of this statement, because it is infeasible for him to verify each trend manually. In addition to the requirement of reliable detection, the method should incorporate no assumptions about any underlying model, because it is very unlikely that it will hold for all or at least most sequences. Therefore non-parametric statistical tests are the appropriate choice for trend detection.

Within our framework we provide two statistical tests for trend, the *Mann-Kendall test* (Mann, 1945) and the *Cox-Stuart test* (Cox and Stuart, 1955). The Cox-Stuart test exploits fewer features of the sequence, leading to a computational effort that increases linearly with the sequence length. Although this may render the Cox-Stuart test susceptible to noise, because the influence of artefacts on the test result is stronger, it is considerably faster for long sequences. In contrast to this, the Mann-Kendall test is much more robust, but its computational effort increases quadratically with the sequence length. Therefore it has to be determined which of the two issues—speed or robustness—is more important depending on the actual application scenario.

Detection of Stability

Roughly speaking, a history is considered stable if its mean level and variance are constant over time and the variance is reasonably small. Similar to trends, a clear definition of stability is difficult.

For example, a sequence may exhibit a cyclical variation, but may nevertheless be stable on a long term scale. Depending on the problem domain, either the one or the other may have to be emphasised. From a data mining perspective, stability describes the pattern that each value is likely to be close to a constant value, estimated by the mean of its predecessors. Thus it is, like a trend, a qualitative statement about the future development of a sequence. However, in contrast to a trend, it can easily be modelled in an interpretable and useful way, e.g., by the sequence's sample mean and variance. Generally, stable rules are more reliable and can be trusted—an eminently useful and desirable property for long-term business planning (Liu et al., 2001b).

To test for stability we use a method based on the well-known chi-square test which was proposed in (Liu et al., 2001b). However, since the test does not take the inherent order of a history's values into account, the single use of this method may infrequently also classify histories as stable which actually exhibit a trend. Therefore, we chose to perform the stability test as the last one in our sequence of tests for change patterns.

OBJECTIVE INTERESTINGNESS

Since usually a vast number of change patterns will be detected, it is essential to provide methods which reduce their number and identify potentially interesting ones. This is the task of objective interestingness assessment. To reduce the number of change patterns to assess we use a redundancy detection approach, based on so-called derivable histories.

Non-Derivable Rules Filter

Generally, most changes captured in a history and consequently also change patterns are simply the snowball effect of the changes of other rules (Liu et al., 2001a). Suppose we are looking at churn prevention and our framework would discover that the support of the rule

$$r_1 : \text{Age} > 50 \rightarrow \text{Complain} = \text{Yes}$$

shows an upward trend. That is, the fraction of customers over 50 who complain increased. However, if the fraction of males among all over 50 year old complaining customers is stable over time, the history of

$$r_2 : \text{Age} > 50, \text{Gender} = \text{Male} \rightarrow \text{Complain} = \text{Yes}$$

shows qualitatively the same trend. In fact, the history of rule r_2 can be *derived* from the one of r_1 by multiplying it with a gender-related constant factor. For this reason, the rule r_2 is *temporally redundant* with respect to its history of support.

It is reasonable to assume that a user will generally be interested in rules with non-derivable and thus non-redundant histories, because they are likely key drivers for changes. Moreover, derivable rules may lead to wrong business decisions. In the above example a decision based on the change in rule would account for the gender as one significant factor for the observed trend. In fact, the gender is completely irrelevant. Therefore, the aim is to find rules that are non-redundant in the sense that their history is not a derivative of related rules' histories. In a way, the approach is to search for and discard rules that are not the root cause of a change pattern which, in turn, can be seen as a form of pruning. In order to find derivable rules we have to answer the following questions. First, what is meant by *related* rules, and second, what makes a history a *derivative* of other histories. Regarding the first question, a natural relation between association rules is *generalisation*. We therefore define that a rule r' is *related to a rule* r iff r' is more general than r, i.e. $r \prec r'$.

The following definition for derivable measure histories includes those of itemsets as a generalisation from rules. Thereby, the superset relation is used to define *related itemsets*: an itemset Y is related to an itemset X iff $X \prec Y := X \supset Y$. As before, XY is written for $X \cup Y$.

Definition 1: Let s, $s_1, s_2 \ldots s_p$ be rules or itemsets with $s \prec s_i$ for all i and p>0. In case of rules, let the antecedent itemsets of the s_i be pairwise disjoint, in case of itemsets let the s_i be pairwise disjoint. Let m be a measure like support or confidence, $m(T) := m(s, T)$ and $m_i(T) := m(s_i, T)$ its functions over time and $\mathcal{M} := \{g : \mathbb{R} \rightarrow \mathbb{R}\}$ be the set of real-valued functions over time. The history $H_m(s)$ regarding the measure m is called derivable iff a function $f : \mathcal{M}^p \rightarrow \mathcal{M}$ exists such that for all $T \in \hat{T}$

$$m(T) = f(m_1, m_2, \ldots, m_p)(T) \tag{1}$$

For simplicity, we call a rule or itemset *derivable with respect to a measure* m iff its history of m is derivable. The temporal redundancy of a rule therefore depends on the measure under consideration, e.g. a rule can be redundant (derivable) with respect to its support history, but not redundant (not derivable) with respect to its confidence history. This in turn is consistent with existing rule change mining approaches, because they typically process histories of different measures independently from another.

The main idea behind the above definition is that the history of a rule (itemset) is derivable, if it can be constructed as a mapping of the histories of more general rules (itemsets). To compute the value m(s,T) the values $m(s_i,T)$ are thereby considered. The definition above does not allow for a pointwise definition of f on just the $T \in \hat{T}$ but instead states a general relationship between the measures of the rules independent from the point in time. It can therefore be used to predict the value of, for example, supp(s) given future values of the supp(s_i). A simple example we will see below is $m = f(m_1) = cm_1$, i.e. the history of a rule can be obtained by multiplying the history of a more general rule with a constant c.

In the following we introduce three criteria for detecting derivable histories which can be used in combination or independently from another. The first two criteria deal with itemsets and can therefore be directly applied to the support of rules as well. The last criterion is related to histories of rule confidences. The functions f are quite simple and we make sure that they are intuitive.

The first criterion checks if the support of an itemset can be explained with the support of exactly one less specific itemset.

Criterion 1: The term supp(XY,T)/supp(Y,T) is constant over $T \in \hat{T}$ given disjoint itemsets X and Y.

When being rewritten as

$$c = supp(XY,T) / supp(Y,T) = $$
$$P(XY|T) / P(Y|T) = P(X|YT)$$

with a constant c the meaning of the criterion becomes clear. The probability of X is required to be constant over time given Y, so the fraction of transactions containing X additionally to Y constantly grows in the same proportion as Y. Due to

$$supp(XY,T) = c \cdot supp(Y,T) \qquad (2)$$

with c=supp(XY,T)/supp(Y,T) for any $T \in \hat{T}$, XY is obviously a derivative of Y with respect to support history as defined in Definition 1.

Figure 2 and Figure 3 show an example of a derivable support history of a rule. The histories have been generated from a customer survey dataset which is described in (Boettcher et al, 2006). Figure 2 shows the support histories of the less specific rule at the top and the more specific rule underneath over 20 time periods. The shape of the two curves is obviously very similar and it turns out that the history of the more specific rule can be approximately reconstructed using the less specific one based on (2). As shown in Figure 3 the reconstruction is not exact due to noise.

Opposed to the criterion above, the following is based on the idea of explaining the support of an itemset with the support values of two subsets.

Criterion 2: The term

$$\frac{supp(XY,T)}{supp(X,T)supp(Y,T)}$$

is constant over $T \in \hat{T}$ given disjoint itemsets X and Y.

supp(XY,T) measures the probability of the itemset XY in period T which is P(XY|T). The term

$$\frac{supp(XY,T)}{supp(X,T),supp(Y,T)} = \frac{P(XY|T)}{P(X|T)P(Y|T)}$$

Figure 2. Histories of the rule $X \rightarrow z$ and its derivable rule $Xy \rightarrow z$

Figure 3. Reconstructed history of $Xy \rightarrow z$ using the history of $X \rightarrow z$

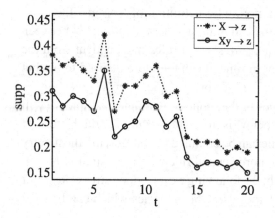

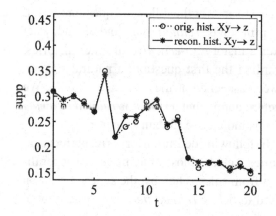

is quite extensively used in data mining to measure the degree of dependence of X and Y at time T. Particularly in association rule mining this measure is also known as *lift* (Webb, 2000). The criterion therefore expresses that the degree of dependence between both itemsets is constant over time. The support history of XY can then be constructed using

$$supp(XY, T) = c \cdot supp(X, T) supp(Y, T) \qquad (3)$$

with $c = supp(XY,T)/(supp(X,T)supp(Y,T))$ for any $T \in \hat{T}$, that is, the individual support values of the less specific itemsets are used corrected with the constant degree of dependence on another. According to Definition 1 the support history of XY is therefore derivable.

Overall, an itemset is considered derivable with respect to support if more general itemsets can be found, such that at least one of the Criteria 1 or 2 holds.

Finally, the last criterion deals with derivable confidence histories of rules.

Criterion 3: The term

$$\frac{conf(r, T)}{conf(r', T)}$$

is constant over $T \in \hat{T}$ given two rules r and r' with $r \prec r'$.

Assuming the rules $r : XY \rightarrow z$ and $r' : Y \rightarrow z$ with disjoint itemsets X and Y, the criterion translates to

$$\frac{P(z|XYT)}{P(z|YT)}$$

being constant over time. This basically means that the contribution of X in addition to Y to predict z relative to the predictive power of Y remains stable over time and can therefore be neglected. The confidence history of r is derivable because of the following. Be $c = conf(r, T) / conf(r', T)$ for any $T \in \hat{T}$, then for all $T \in \hat{T}$

$$conf(r, T) = c \cdot conf(r', T) \qquad (4)$$

Suitable statistical tests for these criterions have been proposed in (Boettcher et al, 2005).

Objective Interestingness Measures

To assess the interestingness of detected trends and stabilities it has to be considered that each history is linked to a rule, which, prior to rule change mining, has a certain relevance to a user. However, the detection of a specific change pattern may significantly influence this prior relevance. In this sense a rule can have different degrees of interestingness, each related to another history. However, there is no broadly accepted and reliable way of measuring a rule's interestingness up to now (Tan et al., 2004). Therefore we consider any statement about the interestingness of a history also as a statement about the interestingness of its related rule.

To assess stable histories two things should be considered. Firstly, association rule discovery typically assumes that the domain under consideration is stable over time. Secondly, measures like support and confidence are interestingness measures for rules themselves. It is summarised by the mean of its values, which in turn can then be treated as an objective interestingness measure. Here the variance of the history can be neglected, since it is constrained by the stability detection method.

Developing objective interestingness measures for trends is more complex due to their richness of features. For identifying salient features of a given trend, it is essential to provide reference points for comparison. As such we chose the assumptions a user naively makes in the absence of any knowledge about the changes in rule histories. From a psychological perspective they can be seen as the anchors relative to which histories with a trend are assessed: a trend becomes more interesting with increasing inconsistency between its features and the user's naive assumptions. We identified three such assumptions and defined heuristic measures for the discrepancy between a history and an assumption:

- **Stability:** Unless other information is provided, a user assumes that histories are stable over time. This assumption does not mean that he expects no trends at all, but expresses his naive expectations in the absence of precise knowledge about a trend. It should be noted that this is consistent with conventional association rule mining, which implicitly assumes that the associations hidden in the data are stable over time. The confidence histories of the rule XY → z in Figure 4 would violate the stability assumption because its trend is very clear.

- **Non-rapid change:** Since a user shapes his business, he will be aware that the domain under consideration changes over time. However, he will assume that any change is continuous in its direction and moderate in its value. For example, if a business starts a new campaign, it will probably assume that the desired effect evolves moderately, because, for instance, not all people will see a commercial immediately. On the other hand, a rapid change in this context attracts more attention, because it may hint at an overwhelming success or an undesired side effect. For example, the history of the rule Y → z in Figure 4 would be very interesting according to the non-rapid change assumption because the depicted trend is very pronounced and steep.

- **Homogeneous change:** If the support of a rule (itemset) changes over time, it is assumed that the rate and direction of changes in the support of all its specialisations are the same. This basically means that the observed change in the rule (itemset) does not depend on further items. For example, a user may know that the fraction of satisfied customers increases. The homogeneous change assumption states that the observed change in satisfaction affects all customers and not only selected subpopulations, e.g. females over 40. If, on the other hand, the confidence of a rule changes over time, it is assumed that the confidence of all more specialised rules changes at the same rate. For example, the history of the rule XY → z in Figure 4 would be very interesting because its shape is completely different from those of its more general rules.

SUBJECTIVE INTERESTINGNESS

Conservative approaches that employ mostly objective measures of interestingness only insufficiently reflect the way a user searches for relevant rules because a user's perception of relevance is not a static but rather a dynamic process due to several reasons: firstly, when a user starts to explore a set of discovered association rules he only has a very vague notion about which rules might be relevant to him. Secondly, while seeing more rules his knowledge about the domain of interest changes, some aspects might gain while others might lose importance. His notion of relevance depends on these changes and thus changes too, almost always becoming clearer. The more rules

Figure 4. Examples of interesting histories which exhibit a trend

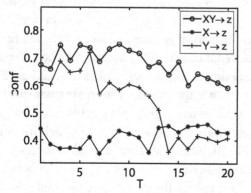

a user examines, the more knowledge he gathers about the domain of interest. This knowledge then helps him to decide for newly encountered rules whether they are (non-)relevant for him, for example, because they are kind-of similar to previously seen (non-)relevant ones.

The importance of user dynamics and incremental knowledge gathering in assessing the relevance of data mining results only recently gained attention in the research community (Wang et al., 2003). However, it is a rather well-researched topic in the field of information retrieval where it has been known for a long time that a user cannot express his information need from scratch. For example, when using an internet search engine to search documents about a non-trivial topic most users start with a rather simple query. By analyzing the search results they gain more knowledge about what they actually look for and thus are able to further refine their initial query, i.e. to express their notion of relevance more clearly. To support a user in this process techniques like relevance feedback based on document similarities have been developed.

In fact, the way a user builds up his internal notion of relevance when searching for the most relevant association rules described above is very similar to the models of user behaviour used in information retrieval (cf. (Baeza-Yates and Ribeiro-Neto, 1999)). Based on these similarities we present a new approach to the problem of finding the most relevant rules out of a large set of association rules which is inspired by ideas from information retrieval. Our approach, as described in, e.g., (Ruß, 2007),or (Ruß, 2008) , uses relevance feedback to acquire users' preferences and to build a knowledge base of what he considers to be relevant and non-relevant, respectively. By calculating the (dis-)similarity of each unexamined rule with the rules in the knowledge base and aggregating the scores we obtain a relevance score which—with each feedback provided—better reflects the user's notion of relevance.

Using Concepts from Information Retrieval

Existing approaches to assess the relevance of association rules strongly require a user to explicitly specify his existing knowledge in advance. This leads to two major drawbacks. In the first place, when specifying their existing knowledge, domain experts often forget certain key aspects or may not remember others which come into play under rarer circumstances. This problem can be termed 'expert dilemma' and has already been observed by designers of expert systems in the 1980s (Fogel, 1997). Secondly, at the beginning of an analysis session a user can only very vaguely specify what he considers to be relevant. His notion of relevance only becomes clearer the more rules he examines. This problem, that a user is incapable of specifying his information need from scratch, is very well-known in the field of information retrieval (Baeza-Yates and Ribeiro-Neto, 1999) where it lead to the development of relevance feedback methods.

Relevance feedback is an intuitive technique that has been introduced to information retrieval in the mid-1960s (Salton, 1971). In information retrieval it is a controlled, semi-automatic, iterative process for query reformulation that can greatly improve the usability of an information retrieval system (Jaakkola and Siegelmann, 2001). Relevance feedback allows a user to express what he considers to be relevant by marking rules as relevant and non-relevant, respectively. Whenever a rule has been marked as relevant, it is added to the set of relevant rules R_r. Whenever a rule is marked as non-relevant, it is added to the set of non-relevant rules R_n. For simplicity, we will assume that in each feedback cycle exactly one rule is marked.

After each feedback cycle the remaining rules are compared to the set of annotated rules and a new relevance score is calculated. The set of annotated rules, in turn, can be seen as a representation of the user's notion of relevance. Hence it also provides a solution to the first of the above-mentioned drawbacks by supporting an iterative, easy way for a user to specify his knowledge about a domain. For example, he may annotate rules that are already known as non-relevant and some novel rules as relevant.

In order to develop a feedback system for association rules the following questions need to be answered:

- How do we represent association rules for the purpose of relevance feedback?
- How do we score the likely relevance of a rule in relation to a rule already marked as (non-)relevant?
- How do we aggregate those scores to an overall relevance score?

We will provide answers to these questions in the subsequent sections. In particular we are aiming at adapting established methods from information retrieval.

Rule Representation

To be the core building block of a relevance feedback approach it is necessary to transform the rules into an equivalent representation. In particular, such a representation should have a couple of properties. Firstly, rather than relying on generalisation and specialisation relationships among rules as a key to rule similarity it should support a less crisp and thus more flexible definition. For example, rules that have the same consequent and share items in their antecedent should be regarded as similar to a certain degree. Secondly, items have a different importance to a user. For example, an item that is contained in almost every rule does not contribute much towards a user's understanding of the domain, whereas an item that is only contained in a few rules can contribute considerably. This importance should be reflected in the rule representation. Thirdly, it should be easy to extend the rule representation

by further numeric properties of a rule. As we pointed out in the first part of this article, there has been increasing interest into the change of a rule's support and confidence values (cf. (Liu et al., 2001b; Boettcher et al., 2006)) as a key to rule interestingness. In this scenario the rule representation should account for the change of rules and allow for change information, which can be histories of support or confidence, or higher order features derived thereupon, to be incorporated in order to enable similarity calculations based on rule change. To illustrate the usage of further information about rules for relevance feedback we will use the example of rule change throughout this article.

As a representation that fulfils all of the above requirements we define a *feature vector of an association rule* r whose elements are numerical values and which consists of three components: a representation of the rule's antecedent, a representation of the rule's consequent and a rule's time series. The latter component can easily be replaced by other numeric features of a rule or completely omitted. The different components can be seen as a projection of $\vec{r}$ and will be referred to as follows:

$$\vec{r}_{body} = (r_1, \ldots, r_b) \tag{5}$$

$$\vec{r}_{head} = (r_{b+1}, \ldots, r_{b+h}) \tag{6}$$

$$\vec{r}_{sym} = (r_1, \ldots, r_{b+h}) \tag{7}$$

$$\vec{r}_{time} = (r_{b+h+1}, \ldots, r_{b+h+t}) \tag{8}$$

To calculate the *item weights* r_i we adapted the well-known TF-IDF approach (Salton and Buckley, 1987) from information retrieval. The TF-IDF approach weights terms according to their appearance in a document and in the overall document collection. A high term weight, which is correlated with a high importance of that particular term, is achieved if the term appears frequently in the document (term frequency, TF) but much less frequently in the document collection (inverse document frequency, IDF). This approach filters out commonly used terms and tries to capture the perceived relevance of certain terms.

This method, carried over to association rules, means that items that appear in the vast majority of rules will get a very low weight whereas items that are rather infrequent will get a rather high weight. Since item appearance in rules is linked to item appearance in a data set this also means that infrequent attribute values in the data set will receive a high weight.

The term frequency tf of an item x in an association rule r is calculated as follows:

$$tf(x,r) = \begin{cases} 1 & x \in r \\ 0 & \text{otherwise} \end{cases} \qquad (9)$$

The inverse document frequency idf of an item x in an association rule r and in regard to a rule set R is calculated as follows:

$$idf(x,R) = 1 - \frac{\ln|r : r \in R \wedge x \in r|}{\ln|R|} \qquad (10)$$

To generate $\vec{r}_{body}$ and $\vec{r}_{head}$ a series of steps has to be performed. For antecedent and consequent separately, a set of items is generated: $I_{body} = \{x_1,...,x_b\}$ and $I_{head} = \{x_1,...,x_h\}$ where the x_i are the items that occur in antecedent or consequent of the association rules in R, respectively. Each item of these sets is assigned exactly one vector dimension in $\vec{r}_{body}$ or $\vec{r}_{head}$, respectively. Hence, the values for *b* and *h* in - are the cardinalities of the respective itemsets: $b = |I_{body}|$ and $h = |I_{head}|$

The part of the feature vector of an association rule r which covers antecedent and consequent consists of TF-IDF values. Let x_i the *i*-th item of the alphabetically ordered set I_{body} and let r_i be the *i*-th component of $\vec{r}_{body}$. Then, $\vec{r}_{body}$ is defined as follows:

$$r_i = tf(x_i,r) \cdot idf(x_i,R), \quad i = 1,...,b \qquad (11)$$

$\vec{r}_{head}$ is treated in the same way, except that x_j is the j-th item of the alphabetically ordered set $\vec{r}_{head}$

$$r_{b+j} = tf(x_j,r) \cdot idf(x_j,R), \quad j = 1,...,h \qquad (12)$$

Pairwise Similarity

A relevance feedback system must have the ability to compare unrated rules, or features of those, with rules previously rated as (non-)relevant. Instead of utilizing the generalisation and specialisation relationships among rules we choose a more flexible approach based on a notion of similarity among rules. As a similarity measure we have chosen the cosine similarity. It calculates the cosine of the angle between two n-dimensional vectors r and s as follows:

$$sim(\vec{r}, \vec{s}) = \frac{\sum_{i=1}^{n} r_i s_i}{\sqrt{r_i^2} \sqrt{s_i^2}} \qquad (13)$$

Since the cosine measure yields values in [0,1], the corresponding dissimilarity measure is:

$$dissim(\vec{r}, \vec{s}) = 1 - sim(\vec{r}, \vec{s}) \qquad (14)$$

The cosine similarity compared to other similarity measures, like ones based on the Euclidean distance, has the advantage that it does not take missing items in a rule into account. For example, when measuring the similarity between a rule $Xy \to z$ and its more general rule $X \to z$ only the item weights contained in both rules (i.e. X and z) contribute towards the similarity measure. This property of the cosine measure is also the reason why it is frequently used in information retrieval systems. When comparing, for example, a query with a document it is desirable only to take the actual words contained in the query into account and not each of the many words the user did not specify.

The similarity between rules' antecedents or rules' consequents can be calculated straight-forwardly using the cosine measure, yielding $\text{sim}(\vec{r}_{\text{head}}, \vec{s}_{\text{head}})$ and $\text{sim}(\vec{r}_{\text{body}}, \vec{s}_{\text{body}})$, respectively. We aim to emphasize antecedent and consequent equally, so by averaging both we obtain the similarity of a rule $\vec{r}_{\text{sym}}$ with regard to a rule $\vec{s}_{\text{sym}}$:

$$\text{sim}(\vec{r}_{\text{sym}}, \vec{s}_{\text{sym}}) = \\ 0.5\text{sim}(\vec{r}_{\text{body}}, \vec{s}_{\text{body}}) + 0.5\text{sim}(\vec{r}_{\text{head}}, \vec{s}_{\text{head}}) \quad (15)$$

The cosine measure is also suitable as a measure of similarity $\text{sim}(\vec{r}_{\text{time}}, \vec{s}_{\text{time}})$ of a time series which we use in this article as an example of further information about rules embedded into the rule vector. For time series the cosine measure has the advantage only to reflect the magnitude of the angle between two vectors but—compared with other distance measures (e.g. Euclidean distance)—to ignore the magnitude difference between the two vectors. This means, it is robust w.r.t. different variation ranges of the time series. It is, however, not robust w.r.t. shifts of the time series' mean value. Nevertheless, robustness can be achieved by subtracting from both time series their respective mean value prior to similarity calculation.

Similarity Aggregation

So far, we have discussed how to calculate pair-wise similarities between vectors which represent certain features of a rule like its consequent, antecedent or a time series of rule measures. For the purpose of relevance feedback it is necessary to measure the similarity of a feature of an un-rated rule r relative to the features contained in the elements of a rule set R which may represent relevant and non-relevant rules. Generally, we define the similarity of a vector $\vec{r}$ relative to a set $R = \{\vec{s}_1, \ldots, \vec{s}_m\}$ as

$$\text{sim}_{\text{rs}}(\vec{r}, R) = \Omega(\{\text{sim}(\vec{r}, \vec{s}_1), \ldots, \text{sim}(\vec{r}, \vec{s}_m)\}) \quad (16)$$

whereby Ω denotes a suitable aggregation operator which we will describe in the next section. As in the previous section the dissimilarity of a vector relative to a set is defined as

$$\text{dissim}_{\text{rs}}(\vec{r}, R) = 1 - \text{sim}_{\text{rs}}(\vec{r}, R) \quad (17)$$

The OWA Operator

Our choice of the aggregation operator Ω is guided by two requirements: firstly, the user should be able to influence the aggregation operator, either implicitly or explicitly. Secondly, to obtain comparable results, the aggregation operator should be able to represent also simple aggregation operators like min, max or median. These two requirements are met by the family of OWA operators, which originate in the Fuzzy Domain and have been introduced by (Yager, 1988). An OWA operator Ω is a mapping $\Omega: S \to R$, where S is a set of numerical values with $S \neq \emptyset$ and $|S| = n$. The OWA operator Ω has an associated weighting vector $W = (w_1, w_2, \ldots, w_n)^T$ with $w_j \in [0,1]$ and

$$\sum_{j=1}^{n} w_j = 1.$$

It is defined as:

$$\Omega(\{s_1, s_2, \ldots, s_n\}) = \sum_{j=1}^{n} w_j b_j \quad (18)$$

with b_j being the j-th largest of the s_i.

The most important feature of this operator is the ordering of the arguments by value. The OWA operator is in a way very general in that it allows different conventional aggregation operators. This is achieved by appropriately setting the weights in W–different arguments can be emphasised based upon their position in the ordering.

Min, max, mean, and *median* are special cases for the OWA operator and were described by (Yager, 1997). They illustrate the generality and flexibility of the OWA operator. By setting the weights accordingly, the user can influence the relevance score to suit the needs of his particular application scenario. For example, $(1/n,1/n,...1/n)^T$ yields the mean, whereas $(1,0,...,0)^T$ yields the maximum operator.

Furthermore, the OWA operator is strongly related to the concept of linguistic quantifiers, such as *many, a few, most*. In (Yager, 1988) the connection to linguistic quantifiers is presented by explaining how the weights of the OWA expression can be obtained by using the membership function of any linguistic quantifier.

Relative Importance of Recent Relevance Choices

The retrieval of relevant association rules is a consecutive, iterative process. The user's knowledge, his beliefs and assumptions change during the relevance feedback cycle as he sees more rules. Therefore, the user's latest choices should be considered as having a higher priority over the first, relatively uninformed ones. This concept can be captured as the *decay of a relevant or non-relevant* rule's importance over time. The similarity aggregation should account for this and thus should weight recently selected rules higher than older ones.

Let $t(r)$ be the *age* of a relevant or non-relevant association rule r. This means, $t(r)$ is the number of feedback cycles that have been performed since the rule r was marked as being (non-)relevant, thereby a newly selected rule receives $t=0$. Two possibilities to model such relevance decay are:

$$\tau_{exp}(r) = (1-\delta)^{t(r)} \tag{19}$$

$$\tau_{lin}(r) = \max(1-t(r)\cdot\delta,0) \tag{20}$$

with (19) for an exponential type of decay and (20) for a linear decay down to a minimum of zero, whereby $\delta \in [0,1]$ is a decay constant that controls the speed of decay.

This concept can also be described as a kind of *memory* of the relevance feedback engine. The higher the decay factor δ, the faster the system

forgets what has been chosen in an earlier step. If we set $\delta=1$ then our approach would only consider the user's latest relevance decision in its relevance score calculation. The value of $\delta=0$ would deactivate the decay completely. Values of δ in between those bounds activate a gradual decay. Using the time-weighted importance we refine our definition of the similarity of a vector to a set R and yield

$$sim_{rs}(\vec{r},R) = \Omega(\{\tau(\vec{s}_1)sim(\vec{r},\vec{s}_1),$$
$$...,\tau(\vec{s}_m)sim(\vec{r},\vec{s}_m)\}) \tag{21}$$

Relevance Scoring

Based on the similarity measure we defined in the last section we can develop a notion of a rule's pairwise score, i.e. its relevance score with respect to a certain rule that was marked as relevant. While in information retrieval it is mostly assumed that those documents which are similar to (non-)relevant ones are (non-)relevant too, we use a slightly different approach.

For rules marked as relevant we assume that once a user has seen such a rule rather than being interested in similar ones his attention is attracted by those which are similar in certain features but dissimilar in others. This means, a user aims for rules which have an element of surprise. For example, a rule could have a very similar antecedent, but a rather dissimilar consequent when compared to a relevant one. It would therefore be surprising to a user because it is an exception to his previous knowledge. This approach also captures the case of rule contradiction employed by other authors (Liu et al., 1997; Padmanabhan and Tuzhilin, 2002), albeit in a fuzzy, less crisp way.

Table 1 shows three of such interesting combinations of rule features. The case discussed above is named C_1 in this table. Another example is C_2. It assigns a high score to those rules that are very different in their symbolic representation, but exhibit a similar time series. Such a combina-

Table 1. Interestingness matrix

		dissimilar		
		consequent	time series	symbolic
similar	antecedent	C_1	-	-
	time series	-	-	C_2
	symbolic	-	C_3	-

tion can hint at an unknown hidden cause for the observed changes, which in turn are of interest to a user who typically will assume that only similar rules change similarly. The remaining entry C_3 is basically the inversion of the last one. A rule is considered interesting if it is similar to a relevant one, but has a very dissimilar time series.

For rules marked as non-relevant we use an approach similar to the one used in information retrieval, i.e. rules that are similar to non-relevant ones are also considered non-relevant.

Based on these considerations our calculation of the overall relevance score is split into two parts: one each for the relevant and non-relevant rules, respectively.

Our definition of the relevance of a rule with regard to the set of relevant rules is rather straightforward and shown in , and for the three cases mentioned above. To pick up on our examples from the previous section, using C_1 a rule receives a high relevance score if its antecedent is similar to the rule antecedents in R_r and its consequent dissimilar to the rule consequents in R_r Likewise, the score for C_2 is calculated by multiplying the similarity of the rule/rule set combination for the time series with the dissimilarity of the rule/rule set combination for the symbolic representation.

$$C_1 \; : \; \Phi(\vec{r}, R_r) = \text{sim}_{rs}(\vec{r}_{body}, R_r) \text{dissim}_{rs}(\vec{r}_{head}, R_r)$$
(22)

$$C_2 \; : \; \Phi(\vec{r}, R_r) = \text{sim}_{rs}(\vec{r}_{time}, R_r) \text{dissim}_{rs}(\vec{r}_{sym}, R_r)$$
(23)

$$C_3 \; : \; \Phi(\vec{r}, R_r) = \text{sim}_{rs}(\vec{r}_{sym}, R_r) \text{dissim}_{rs}(\vec{r}_{time}, R_r)$$
(24)

For the non-relevant rules we assume that rules in R_n specify a subspace of the rule space where more non-relevant rules are located. To direct the user away from this subspace, rules that are far away from it will receive a higher score, whereas those in the vicinity will receive a low score. An unrated rule r should therefore receive a high interestingness score the more dissimilar it is from the set of non-relevant rules, i.e.

$$\Psi(\vec{r}, R_n) = \text{dissim}(\vec{r}, R_n)$$
(25)

Our final relevance score of an unrated rule r under consideration of the set of relevant and (non-)relevant rules consists of two parts, $\Phi(\vec{r}, R_r)$ and $\Psi(\vec{r}, R_n)$, which are both weighted to give the user more influence on the scoring.

$$F(\vec{r}, R_r, R_n) = w_{rel}\Phi(\vec{r}, R_r) + w_{nrel}\Psi(\vec{r}, R_n)$$
(26)

After every feedback cycle, i.e. after every update of R_r or R_n, each unrated rule r is being re-evaluated whereby a new score $F(\vec{r}, R_r, R_n)$ is assigned. Rules which previously have been ranked as rather non-relevant can now receive a higher score whereas others may lose their relevance.

EVALUATION

To evaluate the proposed framework we applied it to a data set from the customer relationship management domain in the context of a telecommunication company (Boettcher et al 2006; Boettcher et al, 2007). In particular we were looking into using association rule mining for detecting interesting changes of customer segments in data. Customer segmentation is the process of dividing customers into homogeneous groups on the basis of common attributes. Here, we define a customer segment as a set of customers who have certain features or attributes in common. Given a data set which describes customers any attribute value combination of each subset of its attributes therefore qualifies as a candidate customer segment. Thus, an association rule's antecedent can be seen as a customer segment whereas its consequent can be seen as one of its properties. Picking up our earlier example suppose that the following association rule has been discovered:

$$r : Age > 50, Gender = Male \rightarrow Complain = Yes$$

The antecedent of this rule describes the segment of customers which are over 50 years old and male. The support of this rule is the relative frequency of customers, who fall within this segment, i.e., it describes the relative size of a customer group. The confidence of this rule, in contrast, can be interpreted as the relative frequency of customers within the group of over 50 year old, male customers who did complain about something, i.e., it describes the frequency a certain property has within a group.

To evaluate our framework we extracted a representative dataset from the company's data warehouse. The dataset contains answers of customers to a survey collected over a period of 40 weeks. Each tuple is described by 33 nominal attributes with a domain size between 2 and 39. We transformed the dataset into a transaction set by recoding every (attribute, attribute value) combination as an item. Then we split the transaction set into 20 subsets, each corresponding to a period of two weeks. The subsets contain between 1480 and 2936 transactions. To each subset we applied the well-known apriori algorithm (Agrawal et al, 1993). From the obtained 20 rule sets we created a compound rule set by intersecting them. Its size is 77401 for the parameters $supp_{min} = 0.05$ and $conf_{min} = 0.2$, respectively. Subsequently we applied the proposed framework. Thereby we will first focus on two objectives within our evaluation. First, the number of trends and stabilities contained in histories has to be determined. Second, the number of derivable rule histories has to be determined.

The results for trend are shown in Table 2 whereby we only show the results for the Mann-Kendall test. Furthermore, the results for stability detection are included, since they depend on the outcome of a prior test for trend. Roughly 50% of support histories exhibit a trend, whereas the number of confidence histories with a trend is considerably smaller. On the other hand, around 30% of confidence histories are stable, compared to fewer than 3% for support. The significant difference can be explained with the density of the data. Since some items are highly correlated, it is very likely that many rules have a stable history of high confidence values. The support history of such rules, nonetheless, may exhibit a trend.

Only histories which exhibit change patterns were tested if they are a derivative of another history. The first row of Table 3 shows the obtained results for trends separately for support and confidence histories. As it can be seen between 40.7% (for confidence) and 66.3% (for support) of the histories are derivable. The second row shows that these numbers are considerably smaller for stable histories; ranging from 26.7% (for confidence) to 39.6% (for support).

Table 2. Fraction of histories with trend and stability

	Trend(%)			Stabil-ity(%)
	Down	Up	All	
conf	21.2	18	39.3	28.1
supp	37.5	17.1	54.7	2.6

Table 3. Fraction of derivable histories among all histories which have a trend or are stable

Pattern	Support		Confidence	
	#Histories	Derivable(%)	#Histories	Derivable(%)
Trend	42307	66.3	30387	40.7
Stable	2019	39.6	21753	26.7

Proving the utility of methods for interestingness assessment is rather difficult due to a lack of suitable public benchmark dataset's which in our case must contain time-stamped data. Moreover, interestingness is a highly subjective matter influenced by the role, experience and task of the person who does the actual evaluation which renders it problematic to use a precision-recall-based approach on the basis of predetermined interesting patterns. For these reasons we decided to trial our methods for interestingness assessment within a real business scenario of a telecommunication company with experienced users as the test persons in order to measure their acceptance and receive feedback.

We developed a user interface to display the ranked rules to a user, to allow for rule browsing, and to gather relevance feedback. The user interface is shown in Figure 5. Due to reasons of data protection those parts which reveal discovered rules are obfuscated. Its main part consists of a list of rules which are sorted by interestingness. The user can choose whether the rules are being ranked by a change-based objective measure or by the relevance feedback received so far. Here, the underlying assumption is that the user starts with an objective interestingness rating to get a first overview about the discovered associations

and to have a starting point for building up his notion of what is relevant and what is not. The user can filter the list by change pattern and rule measure. For instance, he could choose to display only rules which exhibit an upward trend in their confidence history, or rule which are stable in their support history. At any time he can select a rule as relevant or non-relevant using a context menu. The user can access the rules rated so far through another window which is not shown in Figure 5. He can also use this view to revise earlier rating decisions. Double-clicking on a rule opens a chart in the lower left part of the user interface which displays support and confidence histories. On the right hand side of the user interface there are several filters which allows for restricting the displayed rules based on the items contained in them.

The users with whom we trialed our interestingness framework are experienced analysts. Part of their role is to analyze the customer survey data we also used for our experiments on a regular basis by off-the-shelf business intelligence and statistics tools. Therefore the acceptance criterion for our framework and the prototype was whether they would discover anything completely novel or unexpected patterns, and the ease of relating the obtained knowledge to current business opera-

Figure 5. User Interface used for the Trial. For reasons of data protection rules are obfuscated

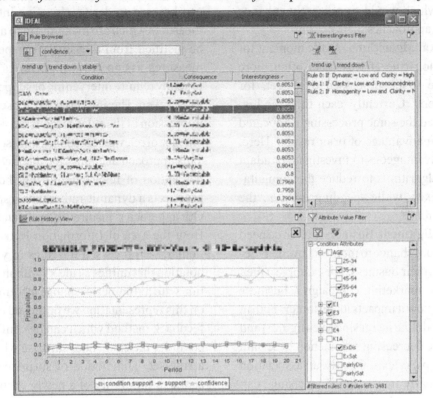

tions. The trial is still going on but we will the some feedback we received so far is very promising: The users reported that they did discover novel patterns and they also pointed out that they could easily reproduce why certain rules had been judged as interesting by the system. Most of them discovered interesting and unexpected rules within a few feedback cycles. There was very positive feedback that the change information is readily available and that the objective interestingness measures rank the most dramatic changes rather high. With other tools they first had to identify certain patterns and then manually trace their change over time. Since this approach is purely hypothesis driven it is clear that interesting trends might be missed if the analyst does not expect that these trends occur. For example, several rules could be identified whose change was rather unexpected. Further investigation showed that the trend in those rules was linked to a campaign (the trend started with the beginning of the campaign) and represented a positive, yet unexpected side-effect.

FUTURE TRENDS

The idea of assessing the interestingness of an association rule by analyzing histories of support and confidence can be traced back to the early days of association rule mining itself (Agrawal and Psaila, 1995; Chakrabarti et al., 1998). Still, it only recently received increasing attention in research publications (Liu et al., 2001b; Baron et al, 2003; Boettcher et al., 2006) and large scale business applications (Boettcher et al., 2007). Because it is an evolving field there are many challenges which still need to be addressed and solved. We have identified two areas that we believe merit future work which would significantly enhance the discussed approaches.

Incremental algorithms. At the moment for each association rule at least one, often more histories have to be processed to detect, for example, a trend. Currently, each time the history is extended the same processing is repeated without taking advantage of prior results. Here, it would be advantageous to investigate or adapt incremental algorithms to reduce the computational complexity while speeding up, e.g., the discovery of trends.

Business alignment. Businesses often do need knowledge about change to monitor how their decisions impact their business. For example, when starting a new marketing campaign a business wants to know how it impacts its customers both in terms of desired (like increasing sales figures) and undesired (like decreasing satisfaction in certain customer groups) effects. Clearly, an association rule is particularly interesting if its change can be related to recent business decisions. Such a *business-aligned* interestingness assessment would be objective in the sense that the required data about decisions and campaigns has not to be collected by a user but is often electronically available in corporate databases and document management systems. Still, change mining for association rules is only a first step in this direction; it also involves fields as diverse as data mining across heterogeneous sources, time series analysis, and maybe semantic technologies.

CONCLUSION

This article dealt with the cornerstones of a comprehensive interestingness assessment framework for association rules which provides a unified handling of objective and subjective interestingness measures based on a notion of rule change. In the first part we introduced our idea of change

mining of association rules and showed how it can be used to derive objective interestingness measures which are meaningful to a user and can be justified from a business perspective. These measures assign rules high ranks which most urgently require intervening or supporting actions to be taken. Having provided a user with a first impression of the rules discovered we introduced our idea of relevance feedback on association rules. This approach accounts for the fact that a user's perception of relevance during the exploration process is a dynamic rather than a static process. Our approach is inspired by well-known methods from the area of Information Retrieval. In particular, we processed the rules to yield a vector notation that unifies a rule's symbolic representation with its (numeric) change information. Based on this representation we proposed our relevance feedback method which can be configured to account for the element of surprise when exploring a rule set. This notion of surprise was defined as the dissimilarity of a newly encountered rule with the set of previously seen ones. Overall, our unified approach to interestingness assessment can greatly improve on the usability and the practicability of any association rule mining process by post-processing the rules accordingly and incorporating user feedback.

REFERENCES

Agrawal, R., Imieliński, T., & Swami, A. (1993). Mining association rules between sets of items in large databases. ACM *SIGMOD Record* 22(2),207-216

Agrawal, R., & Psaila, G. (1995). Active data mining. In U. M. Fayyad, & R. Uthurusamy, (Eds.), *Proceedings of the 1st ACM SIGKDD International Conference on Knowledge Discovery and Data Mining*, (pp. 3–8), Montreal, Quebec, Canada. AAAI Press, Menlo Park, CA, USA.

Au, W.-H., & Chan, K. (2005). Mining changes in association rules: A fuzzy approach. *Fuzzy Sets and Systems, 149*(1), 87–104.

Baeza-Yates, R. A., & Ribeiro-Neto, B. A. (1999). *Modern Information Retrieval.* ACM Press / Addison-Wesley.

Baron, S., Spiliopoulou, M., & Günther, O. (2003). Efficient monitoring of patterns in data mining environments. In *Proc. of 7th East-European Conf. on Advances in Databases and Inf. Sys. (ADBIS'03)*, LNCS, (pp. 253–265). Springer.

Bayardo, Jr., R. J., & Agrawal, R. (1999). Mining the most interesting rules. *In Proceedings of the 5th ACM SIGKDD International Conference on Knowledge Discovery and Data Mining*, (pp. 145–154).

Boettcher, M., Nauck, D., Ruta, D., & Spott, M. (2006). Towards a framework for change detection in datasets. In *Proceedings of the 26th SGAI International Conference on Innovative Techniques and Applications of Artificial Intelligence*, (pp. 115–128). Springer.

Boettcher, M., Nauck, D., & Spott, M. (2005). Detecting Temporally Redundant Association Rules. In *Proceedings of the 4th International Conference on Machine Learning and Applications*, (pp. 397-403). IEEE Computer Science Press.

Boettcher, M., Spott, M., & Nauck, D. (2007). A framework for discovering and analyzing changing customer segments. In *Proceedings of the 7th Industrial Conference on Data Mining (ICDM'2007)*, LNAI 4597, (pp. 255–268). Springer.

Chakrabarti, S., Sarawagi, S., & Dom, B. (1998). Mining surprising patterns using temporal description length. In *Proceedings of the 24th International Conference on Very Large Databases*, (pp. 606–617). Morgan Kaufmann Publishers Inc.

Chatfield, C. (2003). *The Analysis of Time Series: An Introduction, Sixth Edition (Texts in Statistical Science).* Chapman & Hall/CRC.

Chen, M.-C., Chiu, A.-L., & Chang, H.-H. (2005). Mining changes in customer behavior in retail marketing. *Expert Systems with Applications, 28*(4), 773–781.

Cox, D., & Stuart, A. (1955). Some quick sign tests for trend in location and dispersion. *Biometrika, 42*, 80–95.

Dong, G., & Li, J. (1999). Efficient mining of emerging patterns: Discovering trends and differences. *In Proceedings of the 5th ACM SIGKDD International Conference on Knowledge Discovery and Data Mining*, (pp. 43–52).

Fayyad, U. M., Piatetsky-Shapiro, G., Smyth, P., & Uthurusamy, R. (1996). *Advances in Knowledge Discovery and Data Mining.* AAAI Press and MIT Press, Menlo Park and Cambridge, MA, USA.

Fayyad, U. M., Piatetsky-Shapiro, G., & Uthurusamy, R. (2003). Summary from the KDD-03 panel: Data mining–the next 10 years. *SIGKDD Explorations Newsletter, 5*(2), 191–196.

Fogel, D. B. (1997). The advantages of evolutionary computation. In D. Lundh, B. Olsson, & A. Narayanan, (Eds.), *Bio-Computing and Emergent Computation.* World Scientific Press, Singapore.

Geng, L., & Hamilton, H. J. (2006). Interestingness measures for data mining: A survey. *ACM Computing Surveys, 38*(3), 9.

Jaakkola, T., & Siegelmann, H. (2001). Active information retrieval. In *Advances in Neural Information Processing Systems, 14*, 777–784. MIT Press.

Kimball, R. (1996). *Data Warehouse Toolkit: Practical Techniques for Building High Dimensional Data Warehouses.* John Wiley & Sons.

Liu, B., Hsu, W., & Chen, S. (1997). Using general impressions to analyze discovered classification rules. In *Proceedings of the 3rd ACM SIGKDD International Conference on Knowledge Discovery and Data Mining*, (pp. 31–36).

Liu, B., Hsu, W., Chen, S., & Ma, Y. (2000). Analyzing the subjective interestingness of association rules. *IEEE Intelligent Systems, 15*(5), 47–55.

Liu, B., Hsu, W., & Ma, Y. (2001a). Discovering the set of fundamental rule changes. In *Proceedings of the 7th ACM SIGKDD International Conference on Knowledge Discovery and Data Mining*, (pp. 335–340).

Liu, B., Ma, Y., & Lee, R. (2001b). Analyzing the interestingness of association rules from the temporal dimension. In *Proceedings of the IEEE International Conference on Data Mining*, (pp. 377–384). IEEE Computer Society.

Mann, H. (1945). Nonparametric tests against trend. *Econometrica, 13*, 245–259.

McGarry, K. (2005). A survey of interestingness measures for knowledge discovery. *The Knowledge Engineering Review, 20*(1), 39-61. Cambridge University Press.

Padmanabhan, B. & Tuzhilin, A. (1999). Unexpectedness as a measure of interestingness in knowledge discovery. *Decision Support Systems, 27*.

Padmanabhan, B., & Tuzhilin, A. (2000). Small is beautiful: discovering the minimal set of unexpected patterns. In *Proceedings of the 6th ACM SIGKDD International Conference on Knowledge Discovery and Data Mining*, (pp. 54–63).

Padmanabhan, B., & Tuzhilin, A. (2002). Knowledge refinement based on the discovery of unexpected patterns in data mining. *Decision Support Systems, 33*(3), 309–321.

Piatetsky-Shapiro, G. (2000). Knowledge discovery in databases: 10 years after. *SIGKDD Explorations Newsletter, 1*(2), 59–61.

Piatetsky-Shapiro, G., & Matheus, C. J. (1994). The interestingness of deviations. In *Proceedings of the AAAI Workshop on Knowledge Discovery in Databases*, (pp. 25–36).

Ruß, G., Boettcher, M., & Kruse, R. (2007). Relevance feedback for association rules using fuzzy score aggregation. In *Proc. Conf. North American Fuzzy Information Processing Society (NAFIPS 2007)*, (pp. 54–59).

Ruß, G., Kruse, R., Nauck, D., & Boettcher, M. (2008). Relevance feedback for association rules by leveraging concepts from information retrieval. In M. Bramer, (Ed,), *Research and Development in Intelligent Systems, 24* of *Proceedings of AI-2007*, (pp. 253–266). BCS SGAI, Springer.

Salton, G. (1971). *The SMART Information Retrieval System*. Englewood Cliffs, NJ: Prentice Hall.

Salton, G., & Buckley, C. (1987). Term weighting approaches in automatic text retrieval. *Information Processing and Management, 5*(24), 513–523.

Silberschatz, A., & Tuzhilin, A. (1996). What makes patterns interesting in knowledge discovery systems. *IEEE Transactions on Knowledge and Data Engineering, 8*(6), 970–974.

Tan, P., & Kumar, V. (2000). *Interestingness measures for association patterns: A perspective*. Technical Report 00-036, Department of Computer Science, University of Minnesota.

Tan, P.-N., Kumar, V., & Srivastava, J. (2004). Selecting the right objective measure for association analysis. *Information Systems, 29*(4), 293–313.

Wang, K., Jiang, Y., & Lakshmanan, L. V. S. (2003). Mining unexpected rules by pushing user dynamics. In *Proceedings of the 9th ACM*

SIGKDD International Conference on Knowledge Discovery and Data Mining, (pp. 246–255).

Webb, G. I. (2000). Efficient search for association rules. In *Proceedings of the 6th ACM SIGKDD International Conference on Knowledge Discovery and Data Mining*, (pp. 99–107).

Yager, R. R. (1988). On ordered weighted averaging aggregation operators in multicriteria decisionmaking. *IEEE Trans. Syst. Man Cybern., 18*(1), 183–190.

Yager, R. R. (1997). On the inclusion of importances in owa aggregations. In *The ordered weighted averaging operators: theory and applications*, (pp. 41–59), Norwell, MA, USA. Kluwer Academic Publishers.

Zhang, X., Dong, G., & Kotagiri, R. (2000). Exploring constraints to efficiently mine emerging patterns from large high-dimensional datasets. In *Proceedings of the 6th ACM SIGKDD International Conference on Knowledge Discovery and Data Mining*, (pp. 310–314).

Chapter III
Combining Data–Driven and User–Driven Evaluation Measures to Identify Interesting Rules

Solange Oliveira Rezende
University of São Paulo, Brazil

Edson Augusto Melanda
Federal University of São Carlos, Brazil

Magaly Lika Fujimoto
University of São Paulo, Brazil

Roberta Akemi Sinoara
University of São Paulo, Brazil

Veronica Oliveira de Carvalho
University of Oeste Paulista, Brazil

ABSTRACT

Association rule mining is a data mining task that is applied in several real problems. However, due to the huge number of association rules that can be generated, the knowledge post-processing phase becomes very complex and challenging. There are several evaluation measures that can be used in this phase to assist users in finding interesting rules. These measures, which can be divided into data-driven (or objective measures) and user-driven (or subjective measures), are first discussed and then analyzed for their pros and cons. A new methodology that combines them, aiming to use the advantages of each kind of measure and to make user's participation easier, is presented. In this way, data-driven measures can be used to select some potentially interesting rules for the user's evaluation. These rules and the knowledge obtained during the evaluation can be used to calculate user-driven measures, which are used to aid the user in identifying interesting rules. In order to identify interesting rules that use our methodology, an approach is described, as well as an exploratory environment and a case study to show that the proposed methodology is feasible. Interesting results were obtained. In the end of the chapter tendencies related to the subject are discussed.

INTRODUCTION

It can be said that the objective of the data mining process is to find knowledge from a group of data to be used in a decision making process. Therefore, it is important that the discovered knowledge is comprehensible and interesting to the final users. However, from the user's point of view, one of the main problems is the difficulty of understanding the extracted models. These models can be very complex or difficult to understand by the domain experts. In the case of association rules, the fundamental issue in the analysis and interpretation of the extracted knowledge is the great number of patterns that makes the manual interpretation infeasible. Besides, few of these patterns are really interesting to the user.

One of the most used techniques in the evaluation of rules and search for interesting ones is the application of knowledge evaluation measures (Natarajan & Shekar, 2005). These measures are usually classified as data-driven or user-driven. The data-driven measures (or objective measures) depend exclusively on the pattern structure and the data used in the process of knowledge extraction, while the user-driven measures (or subjective measures) depend fundamentally on the final user's interest and/or needs. Therefore, the data-driven measures are more general and independent of the domain in which the data mining process is carried out. These measures can be insufficient to identify the interesting rules, because the objectives and the specialists' knowledge are not considered. Although the user-driven measures consider these factors, there

can be some limitations in their use. A specialist can have difficulty in expressing himself/herself when supplying a system with his/her knowledge and interests that uses the user-driven measures. A good alternative to aid in the identification of interesting rules can be the combined use of data-driven and user-driven measures, exploiting the advantages of each type. This combination can facilitate the domain's (or the final user's) participation in the knowledge post-processing phase and allow a more efficient identification of interesting association rules than with the use of just one measure type.

In this context, the objective of this chapter is to discuss the evaluation of rules using data-driven and user-driven measures by presenting the advantages, difficulties and limitations in their use. Then, a methodology to identify interesting association rules is presented. This methodology combines the use of data-driven and user-driven measures, focusing strongly on the interaction with the expert user. Using this methodology it is possible to overcome some of the difficulties and limitations found in the post-processing of association rules.

Considering the established objective, a literature review is initially presented in the background section to discuss the challenges of using data mining and the association technique in real databases. Then the evaluation of rules is covered by evaluating the interestingness of these rules, considering the objective and subjective aspects. Some of the main techniques used in the identification of interesting rules are introduced, among them the application of knowledge evaluation measures. Then, we propose a methodology that takes advantage of data-driven and user-driven measures for the identification of interesting knowledge.

The chapter also presents the RulEE environment, a Web based environment that supports the user in identifying interesting rules according to the methodology developed by us. Special focus is given to its modules. These modules are developed to aid in the evaluation of the association rules. In sequence a case study is presented which mentions the interesting results and demonstrates the feasibility of the proposed methodology. Finally, our conclusions are presented along with a discussion on the tendencies about the identification of interesting rules supported by data-driven and user-driven measures.

BACKGROUND

This section presents some challenges related to the use of association rules, the objective and subjective aspects of the interestingness, objective and subjective measures for the evaluation of association rules and some environments that support the identification of interesting association rules.

Challenges of the Application of Association Rules

Since the proposition of the technique for extracting association rules by Agrawal et al. (1993), most of the efforts in previous works on the subject has been aimed at improving the algorithm performance on extracting the rules, especially with aim at proposing more efficient solutions for the problem of identifying and counting the itemsets. At the same time, several algorithms and applications were developed incorporating the progress of these previous works. Some algorithms for obtaining frequent itemsets are described in Ceglar & Roddick (2006).

Despite these efforts, there is an association rule issue related to the support. If the defined support is low, the number of generated rules is very high and in most of the times even exceeds the dimension of the mined database, inhibiting a better human interpretation of those rules. In contrast, if the support is high and the number of generated rules is smaller, the probability to find trivial rules and to lose important rules is high. Therefore, the great challenge is to find a balance point, because the domain expert or the final user is interested in a small fraction of the rules, those rules that present some useful, interesting or innovative knowledge. These rules can be small disjuncts, which are discussed in the next section.

Considering the need to find that balance point, we are developing a post-processing environment called RulEE, described ahead in this chapter. This environment allows that the huge number of association rules generated with low support are loaded and explored interactively with the aid of different types of measures and graphs for visualization.

Interestingness of Rules: Objective and Subjective Aspects

The interestingness refers to the degree of the user's interest regarding a discovered rule. It is related to factors such as innovation, usefulness, relevance and statistical significance. Liu et al. (1999) define that the problem of the interestingness consists of determining the group of interesting patterns and ranking these patterns in accordance with the degree of the user's interest in a certain moment. Therefore, it is necessary to consider some factors that can be used to classify a rule as not interesting for the user, such as redundancy. Redundant rules correspond to a previous knowledge or are related to non-interesting attributes for this user.

Several previous works have been carried out in order to solve the problem of the interestingness.

Some of these works were aimed at the development of general rule selection and ranking techniques in accordance with their interestingness, considering objective aspects for this evaluation. In contrast, other works also consider subjective aspects, related to the user and the application domain. The objective and subjective aspects of the interestingness are presented ahead.

Regarding the objective aspects, which only consider the data and structure of the patterns, the interestingness can be estimated by using statistical measures. It is important to highlight that only the statistical significance doesn't guarantee that a rule is interesting. Piatetsky-Shapiro (1991) proposes intuitive principles that a measure should fulfill in order to evaluate the degree of interest of a rule. According to the author, this type of measures should associate high values to strong rules and low values to weak rules. A "strong rule" can be defined as a description of regularity with high confidence for a great number of examples, and a "weak rule" represents regularity with high confidence for a reduced number of examples.

Freitas (1999) proposed other principles that should be considered in the evaluation of the interestingness such as the disjunct size and the cost of attributes. Considering the size of the disjunct, a group of rules can be seen as a separation of rules, so that each rule can be seen as a disjunct. The size of the disjunct represents the number of examples of the data group in which the conditional part of the rule is true, that is, the number of examples covered by the rule. Thus, small disjuncts are rules in which the number of covered examples is small, in accordance with a pre-defined criterion. During the execution of the pattern extraction algorithms the small disjuncts are usually eliminated from the models, because they can represent an irregularity in the data. However, the small disjuncts can also represent an exception that really happens in the data. Therefore, the small disjuncts should be treated more carefully, therefore avoiding the elimination of potentially interesting knowledge. In relation

to the cost of attributes, in many domains the attributes can have different cost to be collected. In medical diagnostic, for example, some attributes can represent a simple medical exam while others can only be determined by sophisticated exams. In those cases, a cost can be associated to each attribute and used during the evaluation of rules. Then, it can be considered that the less the cost, the more interesting (or less interesting) the rule.

Many other previous works have been carried out focusing on the development of methods to support the users in identifying interesting knowledge using objective measures (Carvalho et al., 2005; Hébert & Crémilleux, 2007; Hilderman & Hamilton, 2001; Natarajan & Shekar, 2005; Omiecinski, 2003; Sheikh et al., 2004; Tamir & Singer, 2006; Tan et al., 2004).

In relation to the subjective aspects of the interestingness, the interest in a rule is associated to the user's belief, knowledge and needs. Therefore, the interestingness implies in establishing a commitment among the three factors as mentioned before, in which the balance among the factors depends on the domain and the established objectives. From the user's point of view, a group of factors can determine if a rule is interesting or not. These factors are confidence, actionability, usefulness, originality and surprise (Hussain et al., 2000). Some of the factors are orthogonal among themselves, others present some overlap.

Several methods were proposed to try to capture the interestingness of rules subjectively. The main idea is to obtain and to use the knowledge, the experiences and the users' interests in the search for interesting rules. This knowledge has been used both in the pattern extraction stage (Wang et al., 2003) and in the post-processing (Liu et al., 2000). The capture of knowledge or interest of the domain expert can take place in different ways such as: specification of a taxonomy on the domain (Shekar & Natarajan, 2004), specification of rules in different syntaxes (Liu et al., 2000; Zheng & Zhao, 2003) and evaluation of some rules carried out by the domain expert (Sahar, 1999).

Data-Driven and User-Driven Evaluation of Association Rules

The objective measures are more general than the subjective ones, depending only on the pattern structure and the data used in the knowledge extraction process. In contrast, the subjective measures consider the rule structure, the data used in the discovery process, the knowledge the user possesses and his/her interest at the moment of the pattern analysis. It is important to highlight that, despite considering the user's subjectivity, the values of the subjective measures are usually obtained objectively, through mathematical formulas. Some objective measures shown in Table 1 and used to evaluate the performance or interestingness of rules can be found in Tan

et al., 2004; Geng & Hamilton, 2006; Ohsaki et al., 2004; Lavrač et al., 1999. In Table 1, LHS denotes the antecedent of the rule and $\overline{LHS}$ its complement; RHS denotes the consequent of the rule and $\overline{RHS}$ its complement;

$$f(X) = \frac{n(X)}{N},$$

where $n(X)$ denotes the number of transactions that X is true and N the total number of transactions.

Considering the subjective aspects in the rule interestingness evaluation, in other words, considering the user's interest at the moment of the evaluation, Silberschatz & Tuzhilin (1996) proposed a classification for the subjective measures. This classification identifies the two main reasons

Table 1. Example of some objective measures used to evaluate rules

Measure	Definition
Support	$f(LHS\ RHS)$
Confidence	$f(RHS \mid LHS)$
Interest Factor / Lift	$\dfrac{f(RHS \mid LHS)}{f(RHS)}$ or $\dfrac{f(LHS\ RHS)}{f(LHS) * f(RHS)}$
Conviction	$\dfrac{f(LHS) * f(\overline{RHS})}{f(LHS\ \overline{RHS})}$
Specificity	$f(\overline{RHS} \mid \overline{LHS})$
Added Value	$f(RHS \mid LHS) - f(RHS)$
Piatetsky-Shapiro / Rule Interest / Novelty / Leverage	$f(LHS\ RHS) - f(LHS) * f(RHS)$
Certainty Factor	$\dfrac{f(RHS \mid LHS) - f(RHS)}{1 - f(RHS)}$

that make the knowledge interesting, which are Unexpectedness and Actionability. Unexpectedness states that the knowledge is interesting if it surprises the user, which means that it is new for the user or it contradicts his/her previous knowledge or his/her expectation. Actionability means that the knowledge is interesting if the user can use it to make a decision and obtain some advantage. These two concepts do not exclude each other. Therefore, interesting rules can be presented in a combined way, being: unexpected and useful, unexpected and useless or expected and useful. Although the unexpectedness and the actionability are important, the actionability is the main characteristic in most of the applications, because useful rules allow the user to do his/her work better (Liu et al., 2000; Silberschatz & Tuzhilin, 1996). However, the usefulness of the rules is more difficult to be evaluated, because it involves classifying rules and obtaining actions that should be taken for each user. Furthermore, these actions can vary along the time. Thus, the works carried out in this area focus more on the evaluation of the unexpectedness and hope to reach the usefulness, believing that most of the useful rules are also unexpected and vice-versa.

Liu et al. (2000) propose four measures to identify expected and unexpected association rules considering the user's previous knowledge of the domain. Such measures are conforming, unexpected antecedent, unexpected consequent, and both-side unexpected. These measures are defined in relation to the degree to which the antecedent and/or the consequent of the discovered rule match with the knowledge provided by the user. The values of these factors range from 0 (for no conformity) to 1 (for complete conformity).

Environments for Identifying Interesting Rules

Different tools have been developed to support the evaluation of association rules. Some of these tools are presented ahead.

In Jorge et al. (2002) the environment PEAR (Post-processing Environment for Association Rules) is presented. This is a Web environment used to explore large sets of association rules based on the approach of Web browsing. Each page presents a group of rules and in order to change the page, restrictions and operators are implemented. The restrictions can be limitations regarding the support and confidence. In contrast, the operators can transform a single rule (or a group of rules) into another group of rules. The module also permits the visualization of the support and confidence measures through dispersion and bar graphs.

In Liu et al. (2000) the AIAS application (Association Interestingness Analysis System) is introduced, which uses subjective measures to evaluate association rules. Through the AIAS the identification of interesting rules, especially unexpected rules, starts from a set of association rules and the user provides his/her domain knowledge. Then, the domain knowledge is applied to rank the rules according to the types of unexpectedness. In this environment the user can use the results of the analyses to visualize the rules, to save those that are interesting and to remove those he/she doesn't want. The knowledge that the user has on the domain is supplied to the system through a predefined language.

The system VisAR uses a visualization technique based on matrices and graphs described in Techapichetvanich & Datta (2005) to explore association rules. In order to apply such a technique it is necessary that the user specifies the items of interest in the antecedent. So the system can filter the rules according to those items. Moreover, the user should specify if the rules should be ranked according to the values of support or confidence.

The module of visualization of association rules developed by Chakravarthy & Zhang (2003) consists of visualizing the association rules in table format and in the 3D space. The visualization of association rules in table format consists of presenting the antecedent, consequent and values of support and confidence. In the table, the rules can be filtered through SQL queries and by ranking them according to the values of the support and confidence measures. In contrast, the 3D visualization allows the representation of these measures in the matrix format.

In Blanchard et al. (2007) a module called ARVis is described. It uses a form of visual representation different from the others by representing subsets of association rules in a three-dimensional landscape. The landscape is a metaphor, in which each rule is represented by a sphere over a cone. The sphere represents the support and the cone the confidence. Furthermore, the position of the rule represents the intensity implication, which is a measure that evaluates how much a rule is surprising, and the coloration provides a general idea of the quality of the rule.

In Yamamoto et al. (2007) and Yamamoto et al. (2008), the authors proposed a new methodology to carry out association rule mining tasks in a flexible and interactive way aiming at the insertion of the user into the discovery process. Firstly, the methodology allows users to redefine the parameters for the algorithm during the process. Secondly, the process itself is developed interactively (according to the steps of Apriori), so that the users can visually take part in the itemset exploration, which increases his/her awareness of the process. Furthermore, employing a selection policy along with a filtering policy, the user can obtain compact sets of association rules, which reduces his/her tiredness during rule exploration. Finally, rule exploration is enormously facilitated by the use of visual pairwise comparisons to reduce cognitive load during the selection of interesting rules. The authors presented the I2E System, which implements the methodology proposed, and consists of the I2E module and the RulEx module. With I2E module, miners can take part of the itemset exploration to generate compact sets of rules, which can be explored with RulEx.

APPROACH FOR IDENTIFYING INTERESTING RULES USING DATA-DRIVEN AND USER-DRIVEN MEASURES

The main advantage of the objective measures is that they can be used to evaluate rules of any domain without the need of depending on an expert. However, despite its efficiency in many cases, the objective measures cannot help on the identification of really interesting rules for the user in some cases. This happens because the degree of interest, that a certain rule possesses, can vary depending on the user's objective and needs. There is also the factor that the expert's knowledge can change along the time due to studies and new experiences. Therefore, a rule considered interesting in a certain evaluation cannot be interesting in another moment, given that the expert's previous knowledge or his objectives might have changed.

The subjectivity use can be very useful to capture the variation of interest the user can have, therefore the subjective measures are calculated based on the user's knowledge and needs at the moment of evaluation. However, the subjective approach presents some limitations, as the uncertainty in expressing the personal criteria and difficulty with the language used to express the knowledge. These limitations can raise the user's difficulties to express his/her knowledge when supplying it to the system that supports him/her in the process of identifying interesting rules.

The combination of these two types of measures is an alternative to minimize the presented unfavorable aspects. The objective measures can be used to filter the ruleset, which is frequently formed by a huge number of rules, whereas the subjective measures can be used in the end of the process, supporting the user in the analysis of the rules according to his/her previous knowledge. The support of a computational environment can improve the evaluation of the rules, and certainly overcome many of the existing limitations.

Considering the arguments above presented, in the methodology proposed by us, the objective measures are first used, aiming to filter the rule set, which usually has a large number of rules. Afterwards, the subjective measures are used at the end of the process, to assist the user in analyzing the rules according to his/her knowledge and goals. Figure 1 shows the four phases of the methodology: objective analysis, user's knowledge and interest extraction, evaluation processing, and subjective analysis.

Objective Analysis

The aim of the objective analysis phase is to use objective measures in the selection of a subset of the rules generated by an extraction algorithm. Then that subset can be evaluated by the user. There are many objective measures that can be used in this phase. The analysis stream proposed by Melanda & Rezende (2004) presents an approach for choosing the best measures according to the

ruleset. Therefore, this stream is suitable for the objective analysis phase, supporting the selection of a rule subset by using rule set querying and objective evaluation measures.

The rule set querying is defined by the user if there is the wish to analyze rules that contain certain items. If the user is not interested in specific items, the focus rule set is formed by the whole rule set. After defining the focus rule set the analysis using objective measures can start. For each measure a graphical analysis can be carried out through its value distribution in the focus rule set using scatter charts, bar charts, and Pareto's analysis graphs. After the distribution analysis of objective measure values a cut point is set to select a subset of the rules. The cut point filters the focus rule set for each measure. The union or the intersection of the subsets defined by each measure forms the subset of potentially interesting rules (PIR). After presenting this subset to the user, the next phase of the methodology starts with the user's knowledge and interest extraction.

Figure 1. Methodology to interesting association rules identification

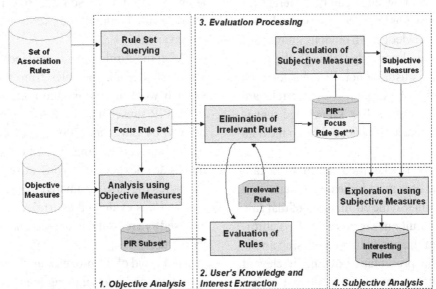

* Subset of Potentially Interesting Rules
** Subset of Evaluated Potentially Interesting Rules without Irrelevant Rules
*** Focus Rule Set without Irrelevant Rules

User's Knowledge and Interest Extraction

The user's knowledge and interest extraction can be seen as an interview with the user to evaluate the rules from the PIR subset. In order to optimize the evaluation, the rules are ordered according to the itemset length. Rules with smaller itemset are presented first because they are simpler, which facilitates its comprehension. For each rule from the PIR subset, the user has to indicate one or more evaluation options. Each evaluation option classifies the knowledge represented by the rule. The options are: unexpected knowledge, useful knowledge, obvious knowledge, previous knowledge, and irrelevant knowledge considering the analysis goals.

A rule evaluated as an unexpected knowledge represents a novelty, something that the user has never thought of or something that contradicts his/her previous knowledge. The useful knowledge option indicates that the rule represents a knowledge which can be used to assist the user in some decision-making. A rule evaluated as a previous knowledge represents a user's knowledge which was formed by his/her past experiences. So, the previous knowledge can be different for each user. The obvious knowledge option indicates solid domain knowledge. An obvious knowledge is also a previous knowledge, though the obvious knowledge is usually not different for each user. A rule might be evaluated as an irrelevant knowledge if it represents a knowledge that is not important or necessary according to the data mining goals.

When a rule is classified as an irrelevant knowledge, the user must indicate the items that make it irrelevant. So the elimination of that rule and other irrelevant ones is possible. This elimination is part of the evaluation processing and is done to avoid the presentation of other irrelevant rules, whose items have been evaluated before as irrelevant by the user. After the evaluation of every rule in the PIR subset, the subjective measures are calculated as part of the evaluation processing phase.

Evaluation Processing

After the user's evaluation for each rule from PIR subset, the evaluation processing starts in the focus rule set defined in the objective analysis. This processing consists of eliminating irrelevant rules and calculating subjective measures.

Every time a rule is classified as irrelevant knowledge by the user means that the user is not interested in the relation among the items that he/she indicates, therefore all similar rules from the focus rule set, those with the items indicated by the user, are eliminated. These rules represent irrelevant knowledge according to the items indicated by the user. First, the rules that contain the items in the same rule side (antecedent or consequent) are eliminated. For example, if the user classifies the rule $a, b \Rightarrow c, d$ as irrelevant and indicates the items a in the antecedent and d in the consequent, then every rule that has a in the antecedent and d in the consequent are eliminated from the focus ruleset. After that, it is checked whether there are rules in the focus rule set which contain these items in different sides. When a rule is found, the user is asked about its irrelevance.

After the elimination, the subjective measures are calculated for the rules from the focus rule set that were not eliminated and do not belong to the PIR subset. These subjective measures are defined by Liu et al. (2000) (conforming, unexpected antecedent, unexpected consequent, and both-side unexpected). In order to calculate these measures the rules evaluated by the user, except for the rules evaluated as irrelevant knowledge, are used as a reasonably precise concept provided by the user.

At the end of the processing, the user can analyze the focus rule set using the subjective measures, in the next phase of the methodology.

Subjective Analysis

The user can explore the resultant focus rule set using the subjective measures defined by Liu et al. (2000) as a guide. The user accesses the rules according to each measure and considers each evaluated rule. This exploration should be carried out according to the goals of the user during the analysis. For example, if the user wishes to confirm his/her previous knowledge, he/she can use the conforming measure and list the rules that conform to the rules that had been evaluated as obvious or previous knowledge; but if his/her aim is to find new knowledge, he/she can use the unexpected antecedent, unexpected consequent, and both-side unexpected measures, and list the rules that are contrary to an evaluated rule.

By browsing the focus rule set, the user identifies his/her rules of interest. Thus, at the end of the analysis, the user will have a set of the rules which were considered interesting.

Data-Driven and User-Driven Combined Evaluation: An Overview

Considering the pros and cons of the objective and subjective analysis, we proposed a methodology that combines the application of objective and subjective measures. The combined use of these measures can be useful for identifying interesting association rules, considering that the objective measures can filter the rule set and decrease the number of rules to be presented and evaluated by the user. Through the evaluation of these rules, it is possible to obtain the user's knowledge and interest needed to calculate the subjective measures. The subjective measures can be used to rank the rules according to the user's interest facilitating the identification of interesting rules.

As the methodology uses the analysis stream proposed by Melanda & Rezende (2004), combined with the subjective measures defined by Liu et al. (2000), it reaches two aspects that make an association rule interesting: the presence of interesting items and the presence of interesting association among the items. The rules that contain items, which are in the interest of the users, can be selected through the rule set querying during the objective analysis. The rules that contain interesting associations can be identified using the subjective measures.

An aspect of our methodology that must be considered a relevant contribution is the way the user's subjectivity is obtained. The user's knowledge and interest are obtained through the evaluation of some rules. Thus, some frequent limitations of subjective analysis, such as the language that the user has to use to express its knowledge to a system, are suppressed. As the user does not have to provide his/her knowledge explicitly to calculate the subjective measures, he/she does not need to use a specific language and to quantify his/her imprecise concepts.

Another relevant contribution of our methodology for the user's knowledge and interest extraction is the identification of the knowledge that is irrelevant to the user. This identification is very important, because when a rule is evaluated as irrelevant knowledge other rules are also eliminated from the focus rule set. The elimination of irrelevant rules assists in identifying interesting rules during the subjective analysis, regarding that the number of rules to be analyzed decreases. However, if all the rules from the PIR subset are classified as irrelevant, it will not be possible to calculate the subjective measures and another objective analysis must be carried out to define a new PIR subset for the user's evaluation.

EXPLORATORY ENVIRONMENT TO AID THE IDENTIFICATION PROCESS OF INTERESTING RULES

The computational environment for exploration of rules denominated RulEE (Rule Exploration Environment) was developed to support the post-processing phase and make knowledge available in the data mining process. This environment was designed with the aim to integrate different techniques and measures to evaluate the rules in a single system, where several types of analyses could be made in association, classification and regression rules. The environment RulEE has been improved at the Laboratory of Computational Intelligence (LABIC (http://labic.icmc.usp.br/)), with continuous increment of its functionalities for knowledge evaluation.

An important feature of the RulEE is facilitating the access to discovered knowledge. This is done through an interface based on the Web that makes the knowledge available. Consequently, some important features of Web are incorporated into the environment, such as the platform independence and the ease of use by users regardless of their physical location and the tool used for knowledge extraction.

Besides the combined evaluation of objective and subjective measures, the following features for association rules are also available in this environment: analysis with objective measures; generalization of association rules; interactive exploration of generalized rules and semi-automatic construction of taxonomies. These features are described ahead in accordance with the type of possible analysis.

Objective Analysis

The functionalities for the objective analysis in the RulEE are made available by the module ARInE (Association Rules Interactive Exploration). ARInE was designed and implemented to provide an interactive process of post-processing for the association rules. The module aims at supporting the evaluation of association rules with objective measures as defined by the approach proposed by Melanda & Rezende (2004). The goal of this methodology is to identify a small subset of potentially interesting rules (PIR) according to one or more objective measures.

The objective analysis, which is the first stage of the methodology proposed in this chapter, is carried out in ARInE. The analysis of the rules starts with the definition of a focus rule set. The user defines his/her focus rule set by conducting queries on the rule set resulting from the pattern extraction phase. In these queries the items of interest may be specified and it may be defined if these items should occur in the antecedent, consequent or any part of the rule. Afterwards, graphical analyses are carried out for each considered measure in order to identify ranges of values that may indicate potentially interesting rules. Additionally, it is possible to combine two or more measures and thereby obtain an even more restricted PIR set, formed by rules defined as potentially interesting for more than one measure.

Subjective Analysis

The functionalities for subjective analysis of association rules, in the RulEE environment, are made available by the module RulEE-SEAR (Subjective Exploration of Association Rules), which was developed for interactive and iterative exploration with subjective measures. In the module the process of subjective analysis follows the approach proposed in this chapter by initially capturing the knowledge and interests of the domain expert. The domain expert evaluates each rule of the focus rule set. Along with this evaluation the irrelevant knowledge is eliminated as part of the evaluation process. When the expert classifies a rule as irrelevant knowledge, this rule and similar rules are removed from the focus set.

After completing the evaluation, the second phase of processing starts. The second phase consists of calculating the subjective measures. These measures are calculated for the rules from the focus set which were not eliminated based on the evaluation of the rules. After calculating the values of the subjective measures, the analysis with these measures can begin. This is the last stage of the methodology proposed in this chapter. During this analysis the expert uses subjective measures to guide him/her in the exploration of the resulting rules in the focus set and in identifying the interesting rules.

Generalized Association Rules Functionalities

The association rule mining technique generates all possible rules considering only the items contained in the data set, which leads to specialized knowledge. Aiming to obtain a more general knowledge, the generalized association rules (GAR), which are rules composed by items contained in any level of a given taxonomy, were introduced by Srikant & Agrawal (1995). Taxonomies reflect arbitrary individual or collective views according to which the set of items is hierarchically organized (Adamo, 2001).

The RulEE environment has three modules related to generalized association rules. The RulEE-SACT (Semi-automatic Construction of Taxonomies) module implements a methodology to semi-automatically construct taxonomies to be used in obtaining generalized rules (Martins & Rezende, 2006). This methodology includes automatic and interactive procedures in order to construct the taxonomies, using the expert's knowledge and also assisting in identifying groups of items. With the use of this module, the knowledge and effort needed to carry out this task are reduced, providing greater speed and quality in the construction of taxonomies.

Taxonomies can be used in the different phases of the data mining process. The focus in the RulEE environment is to apply taxonomies in the post-processing phase. The RulEE-RAG module, which is an improvement of the methodology implemented by the RulEE-GAR module (Domingues & Rezende, 2005), allows that a set of traditional association rules (called specific rules) is generalized automatically, based on the taxonomies specified by the user (Carvalho et al.,

2007a). Additional parameters make it possible for the generalization to take place in various levels of abstraction, on any side of the rule, or on both sides, and that the relation between generalization and loss of knowledge is also considered.

For further analysis of the generalized rules obtained by the available modules the module RulEE-GARVis is being implemented, which provides various types of visualization and exploration for this type of rule.

CASE STUDY

This section describes an experiment carried out with a real database in order to exemplify the application of our methodology, implemented in the RulEE environment. The entire data mining process was conducted. A domain expert participated in the pre-processing of the dataset and especially in the post-processing of the rules, which included the user's knowledge and interest extraction (the second phase of our methodology). The goal of this data mining process was to find associations among the features of certain urban sectors which influence the residents' quality of life. The database used in this experiment is about urban life quality (ULQ) and is composed of 120 examples, each one representing an urban sector of the city of São Carlos, SP, Brazil. All of its 19 attributes are continuous and do not have missing values. In order to generate the association rules, the database attributes were discretized under the domain expert's supervision. The domain expert presented a good number of intervals for each attribute and the method equal-width binning of the Weka (Witten & Frank, 2000) tool was used to discretize each attribute.

The association rules were generated by the Apriori implementation carried out by Chistian Borgelt (http://fuzzy.cs.uni-magdeburg. de/~borgelt/software.html), with minimum support and minimum confidence equal to 20% and 50%, respectively. Another parameter of the

Apriori implementation used is the maximum number of items per rule. That parameter was set at 3, aiming to improve the rules' comprehension. 4122 rules were obtained. In the post-processing of these rules, our methodology was applied using the ARInE and RulEE-SEAR tools available in the RulEE environment. The description of the activities are divided into: ULQ rules' objective analysis, related to the first phase of the methodology and ULQ rules' subjective exploration, related to the user's knowledge and interest extraction, evaluation processing, and subjective analysis.

ULQ Rules' Objective Analysis

The focus rule set was formed by all the 4122 extracted rules considering that the user does not have interest in a specific item. In order to verify the similarity among the 31 objective measures used by the ARInE tool (Melanda, 2004), the factor analysis was applied. The result of this analysis was used to divide the measures into four groups, according to the behavior of each measure in the rule set.

The groups that had the measures support (Tan et al., 2004) and confidence (Tan et al., 2004) were discarded, because those measures had already been used to generate the rules, consequently they were not suitable to filter the same rules. So, one measure of the other two groups was selected to filter the focus rule set so that the PIR subset could be formed. The selected measures were: lift (Tan et al., 2004), and relative specificity (Lavrač et al., 1999). These measures were selected because they belong to only one group, what means that they have a clear behavior in the rule set, and because their meaning has an easy interpretation.

To verify the value distribution of the measure lift and relative specificity in the focus rule set, scatter charts were generated in the ARInE tool. Figure 2 presents these charts. In each chart, for each rule from the focus rule set, identified by its number in the rule set (x axis) there is a number (y axis) referring to the measure value.

The measure lift indicates the dependency level between the antecedent and the consequent of the rule. For rules with a lift value greater than 1, the antecedent positively influences the consequent. These rules can be considered interesting. It can be observed (Figure 2 (a)) that few rules have high values for the measure lift. So the rules from the focus rule set with lift value greater than 2 were selected.

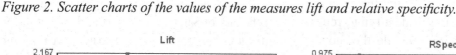

Figure 2. Scatter charts of the values of the measures lift and relative specificity.

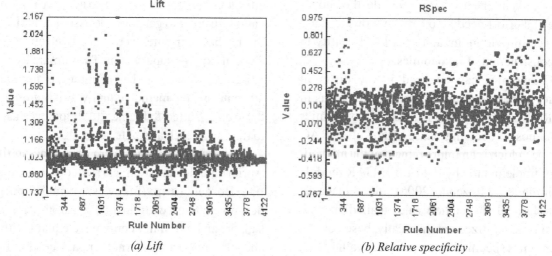

(a) Lift *(b) Relative specificity*

The measure relative specificity indicates the rule specificity gains when the consequent is added. Thus, interesting rules might have high values of this measure. Figure 2 (b) shows the distribution of the relative specificity values in the focus rule set. As observed that few rules have higher values (values close to 1), the rules having relative specificity value greater than 0.9 were selected.

After completing the objective analysis, only 20 rules were selected from the focus rule set (set composed by 4122 rules). Each of these rules has support > 0.2, confidence > 0.5, lift > 2 and relative specificity > 0.9. Thus, all of them were considered potentially interesting and were used to form the PIR subset.

ULQ Rules' Subjective Exploration

First, the user evaluated seven rules from the PIR subset. One rule was evaluated as unexpected knowledge, two as useful knowledge, one as obvious knowledge, and three as previous knowledge. The three rules classified as unexpected or useful knowledge were also considered interesting by the user. The four classified as obvious or previous knowledge were also classified as irrelevant knowledge. Most of the rules from PIR subset were not evaluated because they contained items considered as irrelevant during the evaluation. So these rules were eliminated during the evaluation without being presented to the user.

In the evaluation processing the irrelevant rules were eliminated during the evaluation, and the subjective measures were calculated. For each rule evaluated as irrelevant knowledge, the rules from the focus rule set that contained the irrelevant items were eliminated. From the four rules classified as irrelevant, 272 other rules were eliminated, including 13 rules from PIR subset that were not presented to the user during the evaluation. After that, the four subjective measures defined by Liu et al. (2000) were calculated for each rule from the focus rule set that was not eliminated and does

not belong to the PIR subset. This calculation is based on the three rules that were evaluated and were not eliminated.

Using the subjective measures, the user analyzed the focus rule set. In this subjective analysis, other five interesting rules, that did not belong to the PIR subset, were identified.

Considerations about the Example

This experiment shows that the application of the methodology is feasible, since the use of the objective measures reduced the number of rules to be evaluated by the user and the analysis using the subjective measures allowed the identification of interesting rules, which were not found in the objective analysis.

During the evaluation, the user noticed that some database attributes were correlated. The rules which contained these attributes were classified as irrelevant. The identification of four irrelevant rules led to the elimination of 276 rules from the focus rule set. In order to verify the validity of the elimination, the rules from PIR subset that had been automatically eliminated were presented to the user. Analyzing the 20 rules from PIR subset, the user concluded that those rules represented only six different kinds of knowledge. All of them were evaluated during the user's knowledge and interest extraction. So, the elimination of irrelevant rules did not miss any kind of knowledge.

It can be noticed that the three rules considered interesting in the evaluation are the same three rules that were selected using the measure lift in the objective analysis. Moreover, all of the rules, that were selected using the measure relative specificity, were classified as irrelevant. In addition, the values of relative specificity for the interesting rules, which were identified in the subjective analysis phase, are relatively low, in contrast, the values of lift are closer to the cut point set in the objective analysis. Therefore, in this experiment the measure lift represented better the user's interest as it did not point out rules with correlated attributes.

CONCLUSION AND FUTURE TRENDS

This chapter presented a methodology proposed to identify interesting association rules through the combination of objective and subjective measures. The main goal of the combination is to make the user's participation easier. As the objective measures are more general, they are used as filters to select a subset of potentially interesting rules. These rules are presented to the user, who evaluates them according to his/her knowledge and interest. Through this evaluation the user's subjectivity is obtained. This process may not be difficult for the user, considering that the user does not need to provide explicitly his/her knowledge. He/she just needs to evaluate the rules by choosing one or more options that indicate the kind of knowledge the rule represents. Based on the evaluated rules, subjective measures values of conforming, unexpected antecedent, unexpected consequent, and both-side unexpected can be calculated. So, these measures are used in the last phase of our methodology to guide the user in the analysis of the rules.

In order to exemplify the application of our methodology, an experiment was carried out with the participation of a specialist in urban life quality. This experiment shows that with the application of our methodology it is possible to identify interesting association rules by using the advantages of both objective and subjective measures.

Some future trends related with this work which can be developed are: to establish which approach should be used in a certain context considering the objectives of the application, the type of application, the data used in the extraction of rules (structured, semi-structured, non-struc-

tured), etc; and to study the behavior of existing post-processing approaches in non-traditional association rules, as the work of (Carvalho et al., 2007b).

In our future work, other experiments using our methodology with different real databases and specialists in other domains will be carried out.

ACKNOWLEDGMENT

The authors acknowledge the financial support of FAPESP and CNPq.

REFERENCES

Adamo, J.-M. (2001). *Data Mining for Association Rules and Sequential Patterns*. Springer-Verlag.

Agrawal, R., Imieliński, T., & Swami, A. (1993). Mining association rules between sets of items in large databases. In P. Buneman, S. Jajodia (Eds.), *Proceedings of the 1993 ACM SIGMOD International Conference on Management of Data* (pp. 207-216). ACM Press.

Blanchard, J., Guillet, F., & Briand, H. (2007). Interactive visual exploration of association rules with rule-focusing methodology. *Knowledge and Information Systems, 13*(1), 43-75.

Carvalho, D. R., Freitas, A. A., & Ebecken, N. (2005). Evaluating the correlation between objective rule interestingness measures and real human interest. *Knowledge Discovery in Databases. Lecture Notes in Artificial Intelligence 3731* (pp. 453–461). Springer-Verlag Press.

Carvalho, V. O., Rezende, S. O., & Castro, M. (2007a). Obtaining and evaluating generalized association rules. In *Proceedings of the 9th International Conference on Enterprise Information Systems (ICEIS)*, Volume 2 - Artificial Intelligence and Decision Support Systems, (pp. 310–315).

Carvalho, V. O., Rezende, S. O., & Castro, M. (2007b). An analytical evaluation of objective measures behavior for generalized association rules. In *Proceedings of the IEEE Symposium on Computational Intelligence and Data Mining (CIDM-2007)*, (pp. 43–50).

Ceglar, A., & Roddick, J. F. (2006). Association mining. *ACM Computing Survey, 38*(2).

Chakravarthy, S., & Zhang, H. (2003). Visualization of association rules over relational dbmss. In *Proceedings of the 2003 ACM Symposium on Applied Computing* (pp. 922–926). ACM Press.

Domingues, M. A., & Rezende, S. O. (2005). Using taxonomies to facilitate the analysis of the association rules. In *Proceedings of ECML/ PKDD'05 – The Second International Workshop on Knowledge Discovery and Ontologies (KDO-2005)*, (pp. 59–66).

Freitas, A. A. (1999). On rule interestingness measures. *Knowledge-Based Systems, 12*(5), 309-315.

Geng, L., & Hamilton, H. J. (2006). Interestingness measures for data mining: A survey. In *ACM Computing Surveys, 38*. ACM Press.

Hébert, C., & Crémilleux, B. (2007). A unified view of objective interestingness measures. In Petra Perner (Eds.), *Machine Learning and Data Mining in Pattern Recognition* (pp. 533-547). Springer-Verlag Press.

Hilderman, R. J., & Hamilton, H. J. (2001). Evaluation of interestingness measures for ranking discovered knowledge. In D. W. Cheung, G. J. Williams, Q. Li (Eds.), *Proceedings of the 5th Pacific-Asia Conference on Knowledge Discovery and Data Mining* (pp. 247–259). Springer-Verlag Press.

Hussain, F., Liu, H., & Lu, H. (2000). Relative measure for mining interesting rules. In *4th European Conference on Principles and Practice of*

Knowledge Discovery in Databases - Workshop in Knowledge Management: Theory and Applications (pp. 117-132). Springer-Verlag Press.

Jorge, A., Poças, J., & Azevedo, P. (2002). A post-processing environment for browsing large sets of association rules. In *Proceedings of Second International Workshop on Integration and Collaboration Aspects of Data Mining, Decision Support and Meta-Learning* (pp. 53-64). Springer-Verlag Press.

Lavrač, N., Flach, P., & Zupan, R. (1999). Rule evaluation measures: A unifying view. In S. Dzeroski, P. Flach (Eds.), *Proceedings of the 9th International Workshop on Inductive Logic Programming*, ILP 1999, Volume 1634 of Lecture Notes in Artificial Intelligence, (pp. 174–185). Springer-Verlag.

Liu, B., Hsu, W., Chen, S., & Ma, Y. (2000). Analyzing the subjective interestingness of association rules. *Intelligent Systems and Their Applications, IEEE 15*(5), 47–55.

Liu, B., Hsu, W., Mun, L., & Lee, H. (1999). Finding interesting patterns using user expectations. *IEEE Transactions on Knowledge and Data Engineering, 11*(6), 817-832.

Martins, C. D., & Rezende, S. O. (2006) Construção semi-automática de taxonomias para generalização de regras de associação. In *Proceedings of International Joint Conference IBERAMIA/SBIA/SBRN 2006 – 3rd Workshop on MSc dissertations and PhD thesis in Artificial Intelligence (WTDIA)*. São Carlos: ICMC/USP. v. 1. 10 p. (In Portuguese).

Melanda, E. A. (2004) *Post-processing of Association Rules*. PhD thesis, Instituto de Ciências Matemáticas e de Computação – USP – São Carlos. (In Portuguese).

Melanda, E. A., & Rezende, S. O. (2004). Combining quality measures to identify interesting association rules. In C. Lemaître, C. A. Reyes, J.

A. González (Eds.), *Advances in Artificial Intelligence* (pp. 441-453). Springer-Verlag Press.

Natarajan, R., & Shekar, B. (2005). A relatedness-based data-driven approach to determination of interestingness of association rules. In H. Haddad, L. M. Liebrock, A. Omicini, R. L. Wainwright (Eds.), *Proceedings of the 2005 ACM Symposium on Applied Computing* (pp. 551–552). ACM Press.

Ohsaki, M., Kitaguchi, S., Okamoto, K., Yokoi, H., & Yamaguchi, T. (2004). Evaluation of rule interestingness measures with a clinical dataset on hepatitis. In J.-F. Boulicaut, F. Esposito, F. Giannotti, D. Pedreschi (Eds.), *Proceedings of the 8th European Conference on Principles and Practice of Knowledge Discovery in Databases*, PKDD 2004, Volume 3202 of Lecture Notes in Artificial Intelligence, (pp. 362–373). Springer-Verlag New York, Inc.

Omiecinski, E. (2003). Alternative interest measures for mining associations in databases. *Knowledge and Data Engineering, IEEE 15*(1), 57–69.

Piatetsky-Shapiro, G. (1991). Discovery, analysis, and presentation of strong rules. In G. Piatetsky-Shapiro, W. Frawley (Eds.), *Knowledge Discovery in Databases* (pp. 229-248). AAAI/MIT Press.

Sahar, S. (1999). Interestingness via what is not interesting. In *Proceedings of the Fifth International Conference on Knowledge Discovery and Data Mining* (pp. 332-336). ACM Press.

Sheikh, L., Tanveer, B., & Hamdani, M. (2004). Interesting measures for mining association rules. In *Proceedings of International Multi Topic Conference* (pp. 641–644). IEEE Press.

Shekar, B., & Natarajan, R. (2004). A framework for evaluating knowledge-based interestingness of association rules. *Fuzzy Optimization and Decision Making, 3*(2), 157-185.

Silberschatz, A., & Tuzhilin, A. (1996). What makes patterns interesting in knowledge discovery systems. *IEEE Transactions on Knowledge and Data Engineering, 8*(6), 970-974.

Srikant, R., & Agrawal, R. (1995). Mining generalized association rules. In *Proceedings of the 21th International Conference on Very Large Databases* VLDB'95, (pp. 407–419).

Tamir, R., & Singer, Y. (2006). On a confidence gain measure for association rule discovery and scoring. *The VLDB Journal The International Journal on Very Large Databases, 15*(1), 40–52.

Tan, P. N., Kumar, V., & Srivastava, J. (2004). Selecting the right objective measure for association analysis. In *Knowledge Discovery and Data Mining, 29*(4), 293–313.

Techapichetvanich, K., & Datta, A. (2005). VisAR: A new technique for visualizing mined association rules. In *Advanced Data Mining and Applications* (pp. 88–95). Springer-Verlag Press.

Yamamoto, C. H., Oliveira, M. C. F., Fujimoto, M. L., & Rezende, S. O. (2007). An itemset-driven cluster-oriented approach to extract compact and meaningful sets of association rules. In *M. A. Wani (Eds.), The Sixth International Conference on Machine Learning and Applications* (pp. 87-92). Los Alamitos: IEEE Computer Society's Conference Publishing Services.

Yamamoto, C. H., Oliveira, M. C. F., Rezende, S. O., & Nomelini, J. (2008). Including the user in the knowledge discovery loop: Interactive itemset-driven rule. In *ACM Symposium on Applied Computing: Vol II*. Multimedia and Visualization (pp. 1212-1217). ACM Press.

Wang, K., Jiang, Y., & Lakshmanan, L. V. S. (2003). Mining unexpected rules by pushing user dynamics. In L. Getoor, T. E. Senator, P. Domingos, C. Faloutsos (Eds.), *Proceedings of the Ninth International Conference on Knowl-*

edge Discovery and Data Mining (pp. 246-255). ACM Press.

Witten, I. H., & Frank, E. (2000). *Data Mining: practical machine learning tools and techniques with Java implementations*. Morgan Kaufmann.

Zheng, C., & Zhao, Y. (2003). A distance-based approach to find interesting patterns. In Y. Kambayashi, K. Mohania, W. Wöß (Eds.), *Data Warehousing and Knowledge Discovery* (pp. 299-308). Springer-Verlag Press.

Chapter IV
Semantics–Based Classification of Rule Interestingness Measures

Julien Blanchard
Polytechnic School of Nantes University, France

Fabrice Guillet
Polytechnic School of Nantes University, France

Pascale Kuntz
Polytechnic School of Nantes University, France

ABSTRACT

Assessing rules with interestingness measures is the cornerstone of successful applications of association rule discovery. However, as numerous measures may be found in the literature, choosing the measures to be applied for a given application is a difficult task. In this chapter, the authors present a novel and useful classification of interestingness measures according to three criteria: the subject, the scope, and the nature of the measure. These criteria seem essential to grasp the meaning of the measures, and therefore to help the user to choose the ones (s)he wants to apply. Moreover, the classification allows one to compare the rules to closely related concepts such as similarities, implications, and equivalences. Finally, the classification shows that some interesting combinations of the criteria are not satisfied by any index.

INTRODUCTION

Most of association rule mining algorithms are unsupervised algorithms, i.e. they do not need any endogenous variable but search all the valid associations existing in the data. This makes the main interest of association rules, since the algorithms can discover relevant rules that the user didn't even think of beforehand. However, the unsupervised nature of association rules causes their principal drawback too: the number of rules generated increases exponentially with the number of variables. Then a very high number of rules can be extracted even from small datasets.

To help the user to find relevant knowledge in this mass of information, many Rule Interestingness Measures (RIM) have been proposed in the literature. RIMs allow one to assess, sort, and filter the rules according to various points of view. They are often classified into two categories: the subjective (user-oriented) ones and the objective (data-oriented) ones. Subjective RIMs take into account the user's goals and user's beliefs of the data domain (Silberschatz & Tuzhilin, 1996; Padmanabhan & Tuzhilin, 1999; Liu et al., 2000). On the other hand, the objective RIMs do not depend on the user but only on objective criteria such as data cardinalities or rule complexity. In this chapter, we are interested in the objective RIMs. This category is very heterogeneous: one can find both elementary measures based on frequency and sophisticated measures based on probabilistic models, as well as information-theoretic measures or statistical similarity measures. In practice, the use of RIMs is problematic since:

- The RIMs are too numerous, and sometimes redundant (Bayardo & Agrawal, 1999; Tan et al., 2004; Blanchard et al., 2005a; Huynh et al., 2006; Lenca et al., 2007).
- The meanings of the RIMs are often unclear, so that it is hard to know precisely what is measured.
- Finally, choosing the RIMs to apply for a given study remains a difficult task for the user.

The main contribution of this chapter is to present a novel and useful classification of RIMs according to three criteria: the subject, the scope, and the nature of the measure. These criteria seem to us essential to grasp the meaning of the RIMs,

and therefore to help the user to choose the ones (s)he wants to apply. Moreover, the classification allows one to compare the rules to closely related concepts such as similarities, implications, and equivalences. Finally, the classification shows that some interesting combinations of the criteria are not satisfied by any index.

The remainder of the chapter is organized as follows. In the next section, after introducing the notations, we formalize the concepts of *rule* and *interestingness measure*, and then take inventory of numerous measures traditionally used to assess rules. Section 3 defines the three classification criteria, presents our classification of rule interestingness measures, and describes two original measures that we specifically developed to complement the classification. Section 4 discusses the related works. Finally, we give our conclusion in section 5.

RULES AND INTERESTINGNESS MEASURES

Notations

We consider a set O of n objects described by boolean variables. In the association rule terminology, the objects are transactions stored in a database, the variables are called items, and the conjunctions of variables are called itemsets.

Let a be a boolean variable which is either an itemset, or the negation of an itemset[1]. The variable a^* is the negation of a. We note A the set of objects that verify a, and n_a the cardinality of A. The complementary set of A in O is the set A^* with cardinality n_{a^*}. The probability of the event "a is true" is noted $P(a)$. It is estimated by the empirical frequency: $P(a)=n_a/n$.

In the following, we study two boolean variables a and b. The repartition of the n objects in O with regard to a and b is given by the contingency Table 1, where the value n_{ab} is the number of objects that verify both a and b.

Table 1. Contingency table for two boolean variables a and b. 0 and 1 refer to true and false

a \ b	1	0	
1	n_{ab}	n_{ab^*}	n_a
0	n_{a^*b}	$n_{a^*b^*}$	n_{a^*}
	n_b	n_{b^*}	n

Rules

In this chapter, we study the rule interestingness measures as mathematical functions. To do so, we need a general mathematical definition of the concept of *rule* that does not rely on any data mining algorithm.[2]

Definition 1. A **rule** is a couple of boolean variables (a, b) noted $a \rightarrow b$. The examples of the rule are the objects which verify the antecedent a and the consequent b, while the counter-examples are the objects which verify a but not b (Figure 1). A rule is better when it has many examples and few counter-examples.

With this definition, an association rule is a special kind of rule. This is simply a rule where a and b are two itemsets which have no items in common.

Rule Connections

From two variables a and b, one can build eight different rules:

- $a \rightarrow b$,
- $b \rightarrow a$,
- $a \rightarrow b^*$,
- $b \rightarrow a^*$,
- $a^* \rightarrow b$,
- $b^* \rightarrow a$,
- $a^* \rightarrow b^*$,
- $b^* \rightarrow a^*$.

For a rule $a \rightarrow b$, $a \rightarrow b^*$ is the opposite rule, $b \rightarrow a$ is the converse rule, and $b^* \rightarrow a^*$ is the contrapositive rule.

Rule Modeling

In the same way that the contingency table of two boolean variables is determined by four independent cardinalities, a rule can be modeled with four parameters. Commonly, in the literature, the parameters are n_a, n_b, n and one cardinality of the joint distribution of the two variables such as n_{ab} or n_{ab^*}[3]. Like Piatetsky-Shapiro (1991), we choose as fourth parameter the number of examples n_{ab}. So each rule $a \rightarrow b$ is modeled by (n_{ab}, n_a, n_b, n). In the following, we do not differentiate between a rule and its model: $(a \rightarrow b) = (n_{ab}, n_a, n_b, n)$. The set **R** of all the possible rules is the following subset of $\aleph^4$:

Figure 1. Venn diagram for the rule a → b

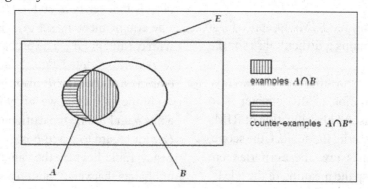

$$\mathbf{R} = \{ (n_{ab}, n_a, n_b, n) \mid n_a \leq n, n_b \leq n,$$
$$max(0, n_a + n_b - n) \leq n_{ab} \leq min(n_a, n_b) \}$$

The choice of the modeling parameters is important since it determines the way of studying rules by inducing a particular point of view for their variations. For example, let us assume that we are interested in the behavior of a rule when n_{ab} varies. If n_{ab} and n_a are among the chosen modeling parameters, then one will tend to fix n_a and therefore to consider that $n_{ab*} = n_a - n_{ab}$ decreases when n_{ab} increases. On the other hand, if n_{ab} and n_{ab*} are among the chosen modeling parameters, then one will tend to fix n_{ab*} and therefore to consider that $n_a = n_{ab} + n_{ab*}$ increases with n_{ab}, which is a totally different scenario. Unfortunately, the choice of the modeling parameters is generally not specified in the literature about rule interestingness (this is an implicit assumption). Few authors have alluded to this problem (see for example (Freitas, 1999)).

Rule Interestingness

A huge number of indexes can be found in the literature to assess associations between categorical variables. Before giving a definition of the rule interestingness measures, we explain why some of these indexes are not appropriate to assess rules.

Associations Measures Between Categorical Variables

We differentiate two kinds of association measures between two nominal categorical variables (see Table 2):

- The association measures between (possibly) multivalued variables, in which all the values of the variables are treated in the same way.
- The association measures between (necessarily) binary variables, in which the two values are not treated in the same way.

An association measure between two multivalued variables is not altered by a permutation among the values of a variable. On the other hand, an association measure between binary variables is altered. For such a measure M and two binary variables v_1 and v_2, let us denote v_1^* and v_2^* the variables coming from v_1 and v_2 by permutation of the values (v_1^* and v_2^* are the negations of v_1 and v_2 in the boolean case). Then we have:

$$M(v_1, v_2) \neq M(v_1, v_2^*) \quad \text{and}$$
$$M(v_1, v_2) \neq M(v_1^*, v_2)$$

As a rule concerns boolean variables, measures between multivalued variables are few appropriate to rule assessment. Indeed, by treating identically

Table 2. Examples of association measures between two nominal categorical variables

	symmetrical	directed
measures between multivalued variables	χ^2, Cramer's V, Tschuprow's T, mutual information	Goodman and Kruskal's λ and τ, Theil uncertainty coefficient, J-measure, Gini index
measures between binary variables	Jaccard index, Dice index, Kulczynski index, Yule index	confidence, Loevinger index, implication intensity, conviction

all the values, these measures do not differentiate *true* and *false*, and in particular examples and counter-examples. They systematically give the same score to $a \rightarrow b$, $a \rightarrow b*$, and $a* \rightarrow b$. However, if $a \rightarrow b$ is a strong rule, then intuitively $a \rightarrow b*$ and $a* \rightarrow b$ should be weak ($a \rightarrow b$ and $a \rightarrow b*$ have opposite meanings). As pointed out by Jaroszewicz and Simovici (2001), a rule should not be assessed on the full joint distribution of the antecedent and consequent.

Interestingness Measures

The two basic rule interestingness measures are support and confidence (Agrawal et al., 1993). Support evaluates the generality of the rule; it is the proportion of objects which satisfy the rule in the dataset:

$$\text{support}(a \rightarrow b) = n_{ab}/n$$

Confidence evaluates the validity of the rule (success rate); it is the proportion of objects which satisfy the consequent among those which satisfy the antecedent:

$$\text{confidence}(a \rightarrow b) = n_{ab}/n_a$$

Support and confidence are simple measures, but they are very commonly used. This popularity can be explained by two major reasons: they are highly intelligible, and they are at the root of the association rule mining algorithms.

Nevertheless, it is now well-known that the support-confidence framework is rather poor to evaluate rule interestingness (Brin et al., 1997a; Bayardo & Agrawal, 1999; Tan et al., 2004). Numerous rule interestingness measures have been proposed to complement this framework (lists can be found for example in (Tan et al., 2004; Geng & Hamilton, 2007)). To unify all the approaches, we propose below a definition of the concept of *rule interestingness measure*.

Definition 2. A **rule interestingness measure (RIM)** is a function $M(n_{ab}, n_a, n_b, n)$ from **R** to $\Re$ which increases with n_{ab} and decreases with n_a when the other parameters are fixed. The variations are not strict.

In this chapter, we have taken inventory of numerous measures which are traditionally used as RIM. They are listed in the Table 3. The Definition 2 is general enough to include all the measures of the Table 3. The definition is also specific enough to discard all the association measures between multivalued variables (these measures cannot satisfy the variations in the definition because of their symmetries). Information-theoretic measures are not studied in this chapter because they are generally association measures between multivalued variables. The reader can refer to (Blanchard et al., 2005b) for a specific survey on this kind of measures.

The variations of a RIM with regard to n_{ab} and n_a were originally mentioned by Piatetsky-Shapiro (1991) as desirable features of a measure. Here we consider them as the foundations of the concept of RIM. Piatetsky-Shapiro considers that a good measure has to decrease with n_b too, but this requirement is too restricting to appear in a general definition of RIM. More precisely, with regard to n_b or n, RIMs have no particular behavior: some increase, others decrease, and others do not depend on these parameters.

Comparison to Similarity Measures

Similarity measures are indexes used in data analysis to study objects described by binary variables. They allow one to assess the likeness between two objects or two variables. Lerman gives the following definition for similarity measures (Lerman, 1981).

Definition 3. We note **S** the following subset of $\mathbb{N}^4$: $\mathbf{S} = \{ (n_{ab}, n_{ab*}, n_{a*b}, n) \mid n_{ab} + n_{ab*} + n_{a*b} \leq n \}$. A **similarity measure** is a function $S(n_{ab}, n_{ab*}, n_{a*b}, n)$

Table 3. The main RIMs

Measure M	$M(a \rightarrow b) =$	References
confidence	$\frac{n_{ab}}{n_a}$	[Agrawal et al., 1993]
Laplace	$\frac{n_{ab}+1}{n_a+2}$	[Bayardo and Agrawal, 1999] [Clark and Boswell, 1991]
Sebag and Schoenauer index	$\frac{n_{ab}}{n_{ab^*}}$	[Sebag and Schoenauer, 1988]
example and counter-example ratio	$\frac{n_{ab}-n_{ab^*}}{n_{ab}}$	[Huynh et al., 2006]
Ganascia index	$\frac{n_{ab}-n_{ab^*}}{n_a}$	[Ganascia, 1991]
least-contradiction	$\frac{n_{ab}-n_{ab^*}}{n_b}$	[Aze and Kodratoff, 2002]
inclusion index	$\sqrt[4]{I^2_{b/a=1} I^2_{a^*/b=0}}$	[Blanchard et al., 2003]
Loevinger index	$1 - \frac{n n_{ab^*}}{n_a n_{b^*}}$	[Loevinger, 1947]
correlation coefficient	$\frac{n n_{ab}-n_a n_b}{\sqrt{n_a n_b n_{a^*} n_{b^*}}}$	[Pearson, 1896]
rule-interest	$n_{ab} - \frac{n_a n_b}{n}$	[Piatetsky-Shapiro, 1991]
novelty (leverage)	$\frac{n_{ab}}{n} - \frac{n_a n_b}{n^2}$	[Lavrac et al., 1999]
lift (interest)	$\frac{n n_{ab}}{n_a n_b}$	[Brin et al., 1997a]
conviction	$\frac{n_a n_{b^*}}{n n_{ab^*}}$	[Brin et al., 1997b]
collective strength	$\frac{n_{ab}+n_{a^*b^*}}{n_a n_b+n_{a^*} n_{b^*}} \frac{n^2-n_a n_b-n_{a^*} n_{b^*}}{n-n_{ab}-n_{a^*b^*}}$	[Aggarwal and Yu, 2001]
Yule index	$\frac{n_{ab} n_{a^*b^*} - n_{ab^*} n_{a^*b}}{n_{ab} n_{a^*b^*} + n_{ab^*} n_{a^*b}}$	[Yule, 1900]
odds ratio	$\frac{n_{ab} n_{a^*b^*}}{n_{ab^*} n_{a^*b}}$	[Mosteller, 1968]
Bayes factor	$\frac{n_{ab} n_{b^*}}{n_{ab^*} n_b}$	[Jeffreys, 1935]
κ	$\frac{n n_{ab}+n n_{a^*b^*}-n_a n_b-n_{a^*} n_{b^*}}{n^2-n_a n_b-n_{a^*} n_{b^*}}$	[Cohen, 1960]
implication intensity	$\mathrm{P}(Poisson(\frac{n_a n_{b^*}}{n}) > n_{ab^*})$	[Gras and Kuntz, 2008]
likelihood linkage index	$\mathrm{P}(Poisson(\frac{n_a n_b}{n}) < n_{ab})$	[Lerman, 1993]
implication index	$-\frac{n_{ab^*} - \frac{n_a n_{b^*}}{n}}{\sqrt{\frac{n_a n_{b^*}}{n}}}$	[Gras and Kuntz, 2008]
directed contribution to χ^2	$\frac{n_{ab} - \frac{n_a n_b}{n}}{\sqrt{\frac{n_a n_b}{n}}}$	[Lerman, 1993]
support (Russel-Rao index)	$\frac{n_{ab}}{n}$	[Agrawal et al., 1993] [Russel and Rao, 1940]
causal support (Sokal-Michener index)	$\frac{n_{ab}+n_{a^*b^*}}{n}$	[Kodratoff, 2001] [Sokal and Michener, 1958]
Rogers-Tanimoto index	$\frac{n-n_{ab^*}-n_{a^*b}}{n+n_{ab^*}+n_{a^*b}}$	[Rogers and Tanimoto, 1960]
Jaccard index	$\frac{n_{ab}}{n-n_{a^*b^*}}$	[Jaccard, 1901]
Dice index	$\frac{n_{ab}}{n_{ab}+\frac{1}{2}(n_{ab^*}+n_{a^*b})}$	[Dice, 1945]
Ochiai index (cosine)	$\frac{n_{ab}}{\sqrt{n_a n_b}}$	[Ochiai, 1957]
Kulczynski index	$\frac{1}{2}\left(\frac{n_{ab}}{n_a} + \frac{n_{ab}}{n_b}\right)$	[Kulczynski, 1927]

from **S** to $\Re$ which is positive, symmetrical with n_{ab*} and n_{a*b}, increases with n_{ab} and decreases with n_{ab*} when the other parameters are fixed. The variations are strict.

Within the Table 3, the similarity measures are the indexes of Russel and Rao (support), Sokal and Michener (causal support), Rogers and Tanimoto, Jaccard, Dice, Ochiai, and Kulczynski. Below we prove that a similarity measure is a RIM.

Proof 1. Let S be a similarity measure. Given $(n_{ab}, n_a, n_b, n) \in$ **R**, we have $(n_{ab}, n_a-n_{ab}, n_b-n_{ab}, n) \in$ **S**. Thus we can define the following function I from **R** to $\Re$:

$$\forall\ (n_{ab}, n_a, n_b, n) \in \mathbf{R}, I(n_{ab}, n_a, n_b, n)$$
$$=S(n_{ab}, n_a-n_{ab}, n_b-n_{ab}, n)$$

The function I is a RIM if it increases with n_{ab} and decreases with n_a when the other parameters are fixed. Let us make n_{ab} increase while n_a, n_b, and n are fixed. n_a-n_{ab} and n_b-n_{ab} decrease. As S increases with its first parameter and decreases with its second and third parameters, we conclude that I increases. Let us make n_a increase while n_{ab}, n_b, and n are fixed. S decreases with its second parameter, so I decreases. $\square$

On the other hand, a RIM is not systematically a similarity measure, even if it is positive and symmetrical with a and b. For example, the lift can decrease when n_{ab} increases while n_{ab*}, n_{a*b}, and n are fixed.

CLASSIFICATION OF INTERESTINGNESS MEASURES

In this section, we present an original classification of RIMs according to three criteria: the subject, the scope, and the nature of the measure. In brief, the subject is the notion measured by the index, the scope is the entity concerned by the result of the measure, and the nature is the descriptive or statistical feature of the index. These criteria

seem to us essential to grasp the meaning of the measures, and therefore to help the user to choose the ones (s)he wants to apply.

Subject of a RIM

An rule is better when it has many examples and few counter-examples (Definition 1). Thus, given the cardinalities n_a, n_b, and n, the interestingness of $a \rightarrow b$ is maximal when $n_{ab}=min(n_a,\ n_b)$ and minimal when $n_{ab}=max(0, n_a+n_b-n)$. Between these extreme situations, there exist two significant configurations in which the rules appear non-directed relations and therefore can be considered as neutral or non-existing: the independence and the equilibrium. If a rule is in this configuration, then it must be discarded.

Independence

The binary variables a and b are independent iff $P(a \cap b)=P(a) \times P(b)$, i.e. $\boldsymbol{n.n_{ab}=n_a n_b}$. In this case, each variable gives no information about the other, since knowing the value taken by one of the variables does not alter the probability distribution of the other variable: $P(b \mid a)=P(b \mid a*)=P(b)$ and $P(b* \mid a)=P(b* \mid a*)=P(b*)$ (same for the probabilities of a and $a*$ given b or $b*$). In other words, knowing the value taken by a variable lets our uncertainty about the other variable intact.

Table 4. Cardinalities at independence between a and b.

a \ b	1	0	
1	$\frac{n_a \times n_b}{n}$	$\frac{n_a \times n_{b*}}{n}$	n_a
0	$\frac{n_{a*} \times n_b}{n}$	$\frac{n_{a*} \times n_{b*}}{n}$	n_{a*}
	n_b	n_{b*}	n

Given two variables a and b, there exists only one independence situation, common to the eight rules $a \rightarrow b$, $a \rightarrow b^*$, $a^* \rightarrow b$, $a^* \rightarrow b^*$, $b \rightarrow a$, $b \rightarrow a^*$, $b^* \rightarrow a$, and $b^* \rightarrow a^*$. The contingency table of two independent variables is given in Table 4. There are two ways of deviating from the independence:

- Either the variables a and b are positively correlated ($P(a \cap b) > P(a) \times P(b)$), and the four rules $a \rightarrow b$, $a^* \rightarrow b^*$, $b \rightarrow a$, and $b^* \rightarrow a^*$ appear in data (Table 5).
- Or they are negatively correlated ($P(a \cap b) < P(a) \times P(b)$), and the opposite four rules appear in data: $a \rightarrow b^*$, $a^* \rightarrow b$, $b \rightarrow a^*$, and $b^* \rightarrow a$ (Table 6).

This dichotomy between the rules and their opposites is due to the fact that two opposite rules are contravariant, since the examples of the one are the counter-examples of the other and vice versa.

Equilibrium

We define the equilibrium of a rule $a \rightarrow b$ as the situation where examples and counter-examples are equal in numbers: $\boldsymbol{n_{ab} = n_{ab^*} = n_a/2}$ (Blanchard et al., 2005a). This corresponds to the maximum uncertainty of b given that a is true. In this situation, the event $a=1$ is as concomitant with $b=1$ as with $b=0$ in the data. So a rule $a \rightarrow b$ at equilibrium is as directed towards b as towards b^*.

The equilibrium $n_{ab} = n_{ab^*}$ is not defined for the two variables a and b but for the variable b with regard to the literal $a=1$. Thus, with two variables, there exist four different equilibriums, each being common to two opposite rules. Table 7 gives the cardinalities for the equilibrium of b with regard to $a=1$ under the form of a contingency half-table. There are two ways of deviating from the equilibrium:

- Either $a=1$ is more concomitant with $b=1$ than with $b=0$, and the rule $a \rightarrow b$ appears in data (Table 8).

Table 5. Positive correlation between a and b with a degree of freedom $\Delta > 0$.

a \ b	1	0	
1	$\frac{n_a \times n_b}{n} + \Delta$	$\frac{n_a \times n_{b^*}}{n} - \Delta$	n_a
0	$\frac{n_{a^*} \times n_b}{n} - \Delta$	$\frac{n_{a^*} \times n_{b^*}}{n} + \Delta$	n_{a^*}
	n_b	n_{b^*}	n

Table 6. Negative correlation between a and b with a degree of freedom $\Delta > 0$.

a \ b	1	0	
1	$\frac{n_a \times n_b}{n} - \Delta$	$\frac{n_a \times n_{b^*}}{n} + \Delta$	n_a
0	$\frac{n_{a^*} \times n_b}{n} + \Delta$	$\frac{n_{a^*} \times n_{b^*}}{n} - \Delta$	n_{a^*}
	n_b	n_{b^*}	n

Table 7. Cardinalities at the equilibrium of b with regard to $a=1$.

a \ b	1	0	
1	$\frac{n_a}{2}$	$\frac{n_a}{2}$	n_a
	n_{ab}	n_{ab^*}	n_a

Table 8. Imbalance of b in favor of $b=1$ with regard to $a=1$ (degree of freedom $\Delta > 0$).

a \ b	1	0	
1	$\frac{n_a}{2} + \Delta$	$\frac{n_a}{2} - \Delta$	n_a
	n_{ab}	n_{ab^*}	n_a

Table 9. Imbalance of b in favor of b=0 with regard to a=1 (degree of freedom Δ>0).

a \ b	1	0	
1	$\frac{n_a}{2} - \Delta$	$\frac{n_a}{2} + \Delta$	n_a
	n_{ab}	n_{ab^*}	n_a

- Or *a=1* is more concomitant with *b=0* than with *b=1*, and the opposite rule $a \rightarrow b^*$ appears in data (Table 9).

Deviations from Independence and Equilibrium

The fact that there exist two different notions of neutrality for the rules proves that rule interestingness must be assessed from (at least) two complementary points of view: the deviation from independence and the deviation from equilibrium (Blanchard, 2005). These deviations are directed in favor of examples and in disfavor of counter-examples.

Definition 4. The subject of a RIM *M* is the **deviation from independence** iff the measure has a fixed value at independence:

$M(n_a n_b/n, n_a, n_b, n) = $ constant

Definition 5. The subject of a RIM *M* is the **deviation from equilibrium** iff the measure has a fixed value at equilibrium:

$M(n_a/2, n_a, n_b, n) = $ constant

Any rule such as $M(a \rightarrow b) \leq constant$ has to be discarded. Also the constant values can be used as reference for setting thresholds to filter the rules. Relevant thresholds are above the constant value.

Regarding the deviation from independence, a rule $a \rightarrow b$ with a good deviation means:

"When *a* is true, then *b* is more often true." (more than usual, i.e. more than without any information about *a*)

On the other hand, regarding the deviation from equilibrium, a rule $a \rightarrow b$ with a good deviation means:

"When *a* is true, then *b* is very often true."

Deviation from independence is a comparison relatively to an expected situation (characterized by n_b), whereas deviation from equilibrium is an absolute statement. From a general point of view, the measures of deviation from independence are useful to discover relations between *a* and *b* (do the truth of *a* influence the truth of *b*?), while the measures of deviation from equilibrium are useful to take decisions or make predictions about *b* (knowing or assuming that *a* is true, is *b* true or false?).

Example. Let us consider a rule *smoking → cancer* assessed by means of confidence and lift. Its deviation from equilibrium is measured by a 30% confidence, which means that 30% of smokers have cancer; its deviation from independence is measured by a lift of 10, which means that smoking increases the risk of cancer by a factor of 10. A smoker that wants to know whether (s)he could have cancer is more interested in deviation from equilibrium. On the contrary, somebody that does not smoke but hesitates to start is more interested in deviation from independence. □

Independence is defined by means of the four parameters n_{ab}, n_a, n_b and n, whereas equilibrium is defined only by means of the two parameters n_{ab} and n_a. Thus, all the measures of deviation from independence depend on the four parameters, whereas there is no reason for any measure of deviation from equilibrium to depend on n_b or n. To the best of our knowledge, the only exceptions to this principle are the inclusion index (Blanchard et al., 2003) and least-contradiction (Aze & Kodratoff, 2002):

- The inclusion index depends on n_b and n because it combines two measures. One is for the direct rule (function of n_{ab} and n_a), and the other is for the contrapositive rule (function of n_{a*b*} and n_{b*}, i.e. $n-n_a-n_b+n_{ab}$ and $n-n_b$). This is the contribution of the contrapositive which introduces a dependency regarding n_b and n.
- The least-contradiction depends on n_b. This is an hybrid measure which has a fixed value at equilibrium thanks to its numerator –as the measures of deviation from equilibrium– but decreases with n_b thanks to its denominator –as the measures of deviation from independence.

Some RIMs evaluate neither the deviation from equilibrium, nor the deviation from independence. These measures are the similarity indexes of Russel and Rao (support), Sokal and Michener (causal support), Rogers and Tanimoto, Jaccard, Dice, Ochiai, and Kulczynski. They generally have a fixed value only for the rules with no counter-examples ($n_{ab*}=0$) or for the rules with no examples ($n_{ab}=0$). In our classification, we have to create a third class for the similarity measures. They can have various meanings:

- Support evaluates the generality/specificity of the rule.
- Causal support can also be considered as a measure of generality/specificity, but for a rule and its contrapositive;
- Ochiai index is the geometric mean of the confidences of $a \to b$ and $b \to a$
- Kulczynski index is the arithmetic mean of the confidences of $a \to b$ and $b \to a$

The signification of the other similarity measures cannot be easily expressed in terms of rules.

Preorder Comparison

Let M_{idp} and M_{eql} be two RIMs which measure the deviations from independence and equilibrium respectively. The fixed values at independence and equilibrium are noted v_{idp} and v_{eql}:

$$M_{idp}(n_a n_b/n, n_a, n_b, n) = v_{idp} \qquad (1)$$

$$M_{eql}(n_a/2, n_a, n_b, n) = v_{eql} \qquad (2)$$

Here we want to exhibit two rules r_1 and r_2 which are differently ordered by M_{idp} and M_{eql}, i.e. $M_{idp}(r_1) \le M_{idp}(r_2)$ and $M_{eql}(r_1) \ge M_{eql}(r_2)$. To do so, we present below two categories of rules which are always ordered differently.

Let us consider a rule (n_{ab}, n_a, n_b, n). By varying n_{ab} with fixed n_a, n_b, and n, one can distinguish two different cases (see Figure 2):

Figure 2. Two possible cases for equilibrium and independence

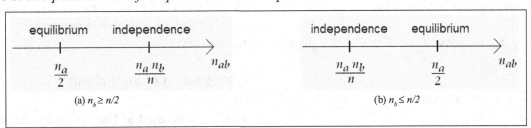

- If $n_b \geq n/2$ (case 1), then $n_a n_b/n \geq n_a/2$, so the rule goes through the equilibrium before going through the independence when n_{ab} increases.

- If $n_b \leq n/2$ (case 2), then $n_a n_b/n \leq n_a/2$, so the rule goes through the independence before going through the equilibrium when n_{ab} increases.

Let us assume that n_{ab} is between $n_a/2$ and $n_a n_b/n$. The rule is between equilibrium and independence. More precisely:

- In case 1, we have $n_a/2 \leq n_{ab} \leq n_a n_b/n$. Since a RIM increases with n_{ab} when the other parameters are fixed, from (1) and (2) we get that

$$M_{idp}(n_{ab}, n_a, n_b, n) \leq v_{idp}$$
$$\text{and } M_{eql}(n_{ab}, n_a, n_b, n) \geq v_{eql} \qquad (3)$$

The rule is to be discarded according to its deviation from independence, but it is acceptable according to its deviation from equilibrium.

- In case 2, we have $n_a n_b/n \leq n_{ab} \leq n_a/2$. In the same way, from (1) and (2) we get that
$$M_{idp}(n_{ab}, n_a, n_b, n) \geq v_{idp}$$
$$\text{and } M_{eql}(n_{ab}, n_a, n_b, n) \leq v_{eql} \qquad (4)$$

The rule is to be discarded according to its deviation from equilibrium, but it is acceptable according to its deviation from independence.

Thus, to exhibit two rules r_1 and r_2 which are ordered differently by M_{idp} and M_{eql}, one only needs to choose r_1 between equilibrium and independence in case 1 and r_2 between equilibrium and independence in case 2, i.e.:

$r_1 = (n_{ab1}, n_{a1}, n_{b1}, n_1)$ with $n_{a1}/2 \leq n_{ab1} \leq n_{a1}n_{b1}/n_1$ and $n_{b1} \geq n_1/2$

$r_2 = (n_{ab2}, n_{a2}, n_{b2}, n_2)$ with $n_{a2}n_{b2}/n_2 \leq n_{ab2} \leq n_{a2}/2$ and $n_{b2} \leq n_2/2$

($n_1 = n_2$ if one wants to choose two rules coming from the same dataset)

The inequalities (3) and (4) applied to r_1 and r_2 respectively lead to:

$$M_{idp}(r_1) \leq v_{idp} \leq M_{idp}(r_2)$$
$$\text{and } M_{eql}(r_2) \leq v_{eql} \leq M_{eql}(r_1)$$

Example. Let us consider the rules $r_1 = (800, 1000, 4500, 5000)$ and $r_2 = (400, 1000, 1000, 5000)$ assessed by means of confidence (measure of deviation from equilibrium) and lift (measure of deviation from independence). Confidence is worth 0.5 at equilibrium and lift is worth 1 at independence. We obtain

confidence(r_1)=0.8 and *lift(r_1)=0.9*
confidence(r_2)=0.4 and *lift(r_2)=2.*

The rule r_1 is good according to confidence but bad according to lift, whereas the rule r_2 is good according to lift but bad according to confidence. We do have that *confidence(r_1)* $\geq$ *confidence(r_2)* and *lift(r_1)* $\leq$ *lift(r_2)*. $\square$

A measure of deviation from independence and a measure of deviation from equilibrium do not create the same preorder on **R**. This demonstrates that a RIM (unless being constant) cannot measure both the deviations from independence and equilibrium. This also confirms that the two deviations are two different aspects of rule interestingness. A rule can have a good deviation from equilibrium with a bad deviation from independence, and vice versa. Surprisingly, even if this idea underlies various works about association rules, it seems that it has never been claimed clearly that rule objective interestingness lies in the two deviations.

Comparison of the Filtering Capacities

RIMs can be used to filter rules by discarding those that do not satisfy a minimal threshold.

We now compare the filtering capacities of a measure of deviation from equilibrium M_{eql} and of a measure of deviation from independence M_{idp}. For the comparison to be fair, we assume that the two measures have similar behaviors: same value for zero counter-examples, same value for equilibrium/independence, same decrease speed with regard to the counter-examples. For example, M_{eql} and M_{idp} can be the Ganascia and Loevinger indexes (cf. the definitions in Table 3).

Let us consider the cases 1 and 2 introduced in the previous section. As shown in Figure 3, M_{idp} is more filtering than M_{eql} in case 1, whereas M_{eql} is more filtering than M_{idp} in case 2. In other words, in case 1, it is M_{idp} which contributes to rejecting the bad rules, while in case 2 it is M_{eql}. This shows that the measures of deviations from equilibrium and from independence have to be regarded as complementary, the second ones not being systematically "better" than the first ones[4]. In particular, the measures of deviation from equilibrium must not be neglected when the realizations of the studied variables are rare. Indeed, in this situation, should the user not take an interest in the rules having non-realizations (which is confirmed in practice), case 2 is more frequent than case 1.

Scope of a RIM

Quasi-Implication

At first sight, one can think that a rule is an approximation of the logical implication (also called material implication) which accepts counter-examples. However, rules and implications are actually not so similar. This can be seen by comparing the Tables 10.(a) and (b), which are the contingency table of the rule $a \rightarrow b$ and the truth table of the logical implication $a \supset b$.

The cases with the same role for the rule and the implication are the cases ($a=1$ and $b=1$) and ($a=1$ and $b=0$): the first ones satisfy the rule and the implication, while the second ones contradict them. On the other hand, the cases ($a=0$ and $b=1$) and ($a=0$ and $b=0$) do not play the same role for $a \rightarrow b$ and $a \supset b$: they satisfy the implication but are not examples of the rule. Actually, a rule only conveys the tendency of the consequent to be true when the antecedent is true. The fact that cases ($a=0$ and $b=1$) and ($a=0$ and $b=0$) satisfy the implication is often considered as a paradox of logical implication (a false antecedent can imply any consequent). Paradoxes like this one have motivated the development of nonclassical logics

Figure 3. Comparison of Ganascia and Loevinger indexes. (E: equilibrium, I: independence)

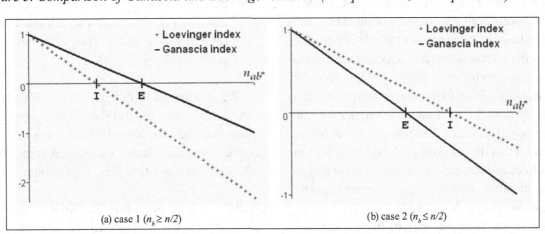

(a) case 1 ($n_b \geq n/2$)   (b) case 2 ($n_b \leq n/2$)

Table 10. Comparison of a rule to the logical implication

b / a	1	0	
1	examples n_{ab}	counter-examples n_{ab^*}	n_a
0	n_{a^*b}	$n_{a^*b^*}$	n_{a^*}
	n_b	n_{b^*}	n

(a) Contingency table of the rule $a \rightarrow b$.

b / a	1	0
1	1	0
0	1	1

(b) Truth table of the logical implication $a \supset b$.

aiming at representing the common sense "logic" more faithfully. In these logics, the implication does not give rise (or gives less rise) to counter-intuitive statements. These are the modal logics, the conditional logics, and the relevant logics (Dunn, 1986).

A logical implication $a \supset b$ is equivalent to its contrapositive $b^* \supset a^*$. Thus, the following deductions are possible:

- Either by affirming the antecedent a (*Modus ponens*) –the direct form of the implication is used
- Or by denying the consequent b (*Modus tollens*) –the contrapositive of the implication is used.

On the other hand, in the general case, a rule $a \rightarrow b$ is not equivalent to its contrapositive $b^* \rightarrow a^*$: the tendency of the consequent to be true when the antecedent is true is not systematically identical to the tendency of the antecedent to be false when the consequent is false. In particular, some RIMs can measure very different interestingness for a rule and its contrapositive[5]. The user can nevertheless interpret that the meaning of the rule lies both in the direct and contrapositive forms, as for a logical implication. In this case, one can legitimately assess the relation discovered in data not as a rule stricto sensu. More precisely, behind the notation

$a \rightarrow b$, Kodratoff (Kodratoff, 2000) distinguishes two types of relations with implicative meaning that can be discovered in data:

- Some associations noted $a \rightarrow b$ express a rule for the user, such as "crows are black" (*crows* $\rightarrow$ *black*). They must be invalidated each time that (a=1 and b=0) is observed, and validated each time that (a=1 and b=1) is observed. In accordance with Hempel's paradox[6], the cases (a=0 and b=0) which validate the contrapositive are not taken into account.
- Some associations noted $a \rightarrow b$ express a quasi-implication for the user, such as "smoking causes cancer" (*smoking* $\rightarrow$ *cancer*). Their meaning is more causal. They must be invalidated each time that (a=1 and b=0) is observed, and validated each time that (a=1 and b=1) or (a=0 and b=0) is observed.

We note the quasi-implications $a \Rightarrow b$. By considering the cases (a=0 and b=0) as examples, a quasi-implication is not a rule stricto sensu since it conveys both the rule $a \rightarrow b$ and the contrapositive $b^* \rightarrow a^*$ (similarly to logical implication).

Definition 6. A quasi-implication is a couple of boolean variables (a, b) noted $a \Rightarrow b$. The examples

Table 11. Contingency table of the quasi-implication $a \Rightarrow b$

a \ b	**1**	**0**	
1	examples n_{ab}	counter-examples n_{ab^*}	n_a
0	n_{a^*b}	examples $n_{a^*b^*}$	n_{a^*}
	n_b	n_{b^*}	n

of the quasi-implication are the objects in $A \cap B$ and $A^* \cap B^*$, while the counter-examples are the objects in $A \cap B^*$ (see Table 11). So $a \Rightarrow b$ is equivalent to its contrapositive $b^* \Rightarrow a^*$. A quasi-implication is better when it has many examples and few counter-examples.

Since quasi-implications rather express a causality for the user, it must be possible to use them to do "quasi-deductions" in the direct way or in the contrapositive way. So the measures M used to assess quasi-implications must render the interestingness of the two rules: $M(a \Rightarrow b) = M(a \rightarrow b) = M(b^* \rightarrow a^*)$.

Definition 7. The scope of a RIM M is **quasi-implication** iff $M(a \rightarrow b) = M(b^* \rightarrow a^*)$, i.e. $M(n_{ab}, n_a, n_b, n) = M(n - n_a - n_b + n_{ab}, n - n_b, n - n_a, n)$.

In practice, if the user is sure that contrapositive rules are not relevant for the current application, then (s)he should not apply RIMs whose scope is quasi-implication since the resulting scores are interfered by the interestingness of the contrapositive.

Quasi-Conjunction

Following the quasi-implication which approximates the logical implication, we define the quasi-conjunction which approximates the logical conjunction[7].

Definition 8. A **quasi-conjunction** is a couple of boolean variables (a, b) noted $a \leftrightarrow b$. The examples of the quasi-conjunction are the objects in $A \cap B$, while the counter-examples are the objects in $A \cap B^*$ and $A^* \cap B$. So $a \leftrightarrow b$ is equivalent to its converse $b \leftrightarrow a$. A quasi-conjunction is better when it has many examples and few counter-examples.

The contingency table of the quasi-conjunction $a \leftrightarrow b$ and the truth table of the logical conjunction $a \wedge b$ are given in Tables 12.(a) and (b). As for quasi-implication and its logical counterpart, 75% of the cases play the same role:

- The cases ($a=1$ and $b=1$) satisfy the quasi-conjunction and the conjunction,

Table 12. Comparison of a quasi-conjunction to the logical conjunction

a \ b	**1**	**0**	
1	examples n_{ab}	counter-examples n_{ab^*}	n_a
0	counter-examples n_{a^*b}	$n_{a^*b^*}$	n_{a^*}
	n_b	n_{b^*}	n

(a) Contingency table of the quasi-conjunction $a \leftrightarrow b$.

a \ b	**1**	**0**
1	1	0
0	0	0

(b) Truth table of the logical conjunction $a \wedge b$.

- The cases ($a=1$ and $b=0$) and ($a=0$ and $b=1$) contradict the quasi-conjunction and the conjunction.
- Only cases ($a=0$ and $b=0$) are considered differently: they contradict the conjunction but have no precise role for the quasi-conjunction.

A quasi-conjunction $a \leftrightarrow b$ conveys both the rule $a \to b$ and its converse $b \to a$. Similarly to quasi-implication, we propose to assess quasi-conjunctions with RIMs that render the interestingness of both $a \to b$ and $b \to a$.

Definition 9. The scope of a RIM M is **quasi-conjunction** iff $M(a \to b)=M(b \to a)$, i.e. $M(n_{ab}, n_a, n_b, n)=M(n_{ab}, n_b, n_a, n)$.

If the user intuitively gives sense to the rule $b \to a$ when (s)he reads a rule $a \to b$, then RIMs whose scope is quasi-conjunction should be applied.

The scope of a similarity measure is quasi-conjunction, since a similarity measure is a RIM (see Proof 1) and is symmetrical with a and b. On the other hand, a RIM whose scope is quasi-conjunction (even a positive RIM such as lift) is not a similarity measure according to the Definition 3.

Quasi-Equivalence

Definition 10. A **quasi-equivalence** is a couple of boolean variables (a, b) noted $a \Leftrightarrow b$. The ex-

amples of the quasi-equivalence are the objects in $A \cap B$ and $A^* \cap B^*$, while the counter-examples are the objects in $A \cap B^*$ and $A^* \cap B$. So $a \Leftrightarrow b$ is equivalent to its contrapositive $b^* \Leftrightarrow a^*$ and to its converse $b \Leftrightarrow a$. A quasi-equivalence is better when it has many examples and few counter-examples.

The contingency table of the quasi-equivalence $a \Leftrightarrow b$ and the truth table of the logical equivalence $a \equiv b$ are given in Tables 13.(a) and (b) (see also (Zembowicz & Zytkow, 1996)). The analogy is strong since all the cases play the same role:

- The cases ($a=1$ and $b=1$) and ($a=0$ and $b=0$) satisfy the quasi-equivalence and the equivalence.
- The cases ($a=1$ and $b=0$) and ($a=0$ and $b=1$) contradict the quasi-equivalence and the equivalence.

A quasi-equivalence lies on the four rules $a \to b$, $b \to a$, $b^* \to a^*$, and $a^* \to b^*$. We propose to assess quasi-equivalence with RIMs that render the interestingness of the four rules.

Definition 11. The scope of a RIM M is **quasi-equivalence** iff $M(a \to b)=M(b \to a)=M(b^* \to a^*)=M(a^* \to b^*)$, i.e. $M(n_{ab}, n_a, n_b, n)=M(n_{ab}, n_b, n_a, n)=M(n-n_a-n_b+n_{ab}, n-n_b, n-n_a, n)$
$=M(n-n_a-n_b+n_{ab}, n-n_a, n-n_b, n)$

Table 13. Comparison of a quasi-equivalence to the logical equivalence

a \ b	1	0	
1	examples n_{ab}	counter-examples n_{ab^*}	n_a
0	counter-examples n_{a^*b}	examples $n_{a^*b^*}$	n_{a^*}
	n_b	n_{b^*}	n

(a) Contingency table of the quasi-equivalence $a \Leftrightarrow b$.

a \ b	1	0
1	1	0
0	0	1

(b) Truth table of the logical equivalence $a \equiv b$.

If the scope of a RIM is quasi-equivalence, then it evaluates both a quasi-implication and a quasi-conjunction. The scope of a similarity measure is not necessarily quasi-equivalence. Among the measures of Table 3, only the Sokal-Michener and Rogers-Tanimoto indexes evaluate quasi-equivalence.

Nature of a RIM

Our last classification criterion is the descriptive or statistical nature of RIMs.

Descriptive Measures

Definition 12. The nature of a RIM *M* is **descriptive** (or frequency-based) iff the measure does not vary with cardinality expansion (when all the data cardinalities are increased or decreased in equal proportion), i.e.

$$\forall \; \alpha > 0, \; M(n_{ab}, n_a, n_b, n) = M(\alpha.n_{ab}, \alpha.n_a, \alpha.n_b, \alpha.n)$$

Descriptive measures take the data contingencies into account only in a relative way (by means of the probabilities $P(a)$, $P(b)$, $P(a \cap b)$) an not in an absolute way (by means of the cardinalities n_a, n_b, n_{ab}).

Statistical Measures

Definition 13. The nature of a RIM *M* is **statistical** iff the measure varies with cardinality expansion.

Statistical measures take into account the size of the phenomena studied. Indeed, a rule is statistically all the more reliable since it is assessed on a large amount of data.

Among the statistical measures, there are some measures based on a probabilistic model. They compare the observed data distribution to an expected distribution. Two probabilistic measures

come from the LLA method (likelihood linkage analysis), a method developed by Lerman in 1981 for the hierarchical clustering of variables (Lerman, 1981):

- The likelihood linkage index of Lerman $P(N_{ab} < n_{ab})$ (Lerman, 1993).
- The implication intensity of Gras $P(N_{ab*} > n_{ab*})$ (Gras, 1996; Gras & Kuntz, 2008),

where N_{ab} and N_{ab*} are the random variables for the numbers of examples and counter-examples under the hypothesis H_0 of independence between *a* and *b*. These measures respectively quantify the unlikelihood of the greatness of the number of examples n_{ab} and the unlikelihood of the smallness of the number of counter-examples n_{ab*}, with respect to the hypothesis H_0. Although they can be seen as the complement to 1 of the p-value of a hypothesis test, the aim is not testing the hypothesis H_0 but actually using it as a reference to evaluate and sort the rules.

Lerman (1981) proposed three possible random models for H_0. According to the model chosen, the random variables N_{ab} and N_{ab*} can be hypergeometric, binomial, or poissonian. To analyze rules, the most appropriate model is the poissonian one which is the most asymmetric. Then the likelihood linkage index *LLI* and implication intensity *II* are:

$$\text{LLI}(a \rightarrow b) = P(\text{Poisson}(n_a n_b / n) < n_{ab})$$
$$\text{II}(a \rightarrow b) = P(\text{Poisson}(n_a n_{b*} / n) > n_{ab*})$$

With the poissonian model, *LLI* evaluates the quasi-conjunction $a \leftrightarrow b$ while *II* evaluates the quasi-implication $a \Rightarrow b$. Of course they both measure deviation from independence. As the two measures are probabilities, they have the advantage of referring to an intelligible scale of values (scale of probabilities). This is not the case for many RIMs. Also, *LLI* and *II* facilitate the choice of a threshold for filtering the rules, since the complement to 1 of the threshold has the meaning of the significance level of a hypothesis test (generally in a test, one chooses $\alpha \in \{0.1\%, 1\%, 5\%\}$).

As they are statistical, the probabilistic measures take into account the size of the phenomena studied. However, this is also their main limit: the probabilistic measures have a low discriminating power when the size of the phenomena is large (beyond around 10^4) (Elder & Pregibon, 1996). Indeed, with regard to large cardinalities, even minor deviations can be statistically significant.

Classification

The classification of RIMs according to subject, scope, and nature is given in Table 14 (Blanchard, 2005). Some cells are empty. First, as a similarity index is symmetrical with a and b, it can evaluate neither a single rule, nor a quasi-implication. Then, there exists no measure of quasi-conjunction or quasi-equivalence for deviation from equilibrium. Such RIMs could be developed, but they would require to combine rules whose equilibriums are not the same. Contrary to independence, the equilibrium of a rule $a \rightarrow b$ is indeed neither the equilibrium of $b \rightarrow a$, nor the one of $b^* \rightarrow a^*$, nor the one of $a^* \rightarrow b^*$. The only RIM which combines different equilibriums (rule and contrapositive) is the inclusion index.

Whereas one generally considers that RIMs are very numerous, or even too numerous, the classification shows that there are actually few measures whose scope is a single rule. In particular, the only measure of deviation from independence whose scope is a rule stricto sensu is Bayes factor (Jeffreys, 1935). Also the classification shows that there is no statistical RIM measuring the deviation from equilibrium.

Two Original RIMs

Using the previous classification, we were able to identify gaps and propose two novel RIMs with unique features in (Blanchard et al., 2005a) and (Blanchard et al., 2005b).

Probabilistic Measure of Deviation from Equilibrium *IPEE* (Blanchard et al., 2005a)

IPEE evaluates the deviation from equilibrium while having a statistical nature, which is a unique feature for a RIM according to our classification. More precisely, *IPEE* is based on a probabilistic model and measures the statistical significance of the deviation from equilibrium (whereas implication intensity or likelihood linkage index, for example, measure the statistical significance of the deviation from independence). The measure has the advantage of taking into account the size of the phenomena studied, contrary to the other measures of deviation from equilibrium. Experimental studies show that *IPEE* is efficient even to assess rules with no counter-examples, and well adapted to the search for specific rules ("nuggets").

Directed Information Ratio *DIR* (Blanchard et al., 2005b)

Information-theoretic measures are particularly useful to assess rules since they can be interpreted in terms of information. More precisely, as pointed out by Smyth and Goodman (1992), there is an interesting parallel to draw between the use of information theory in communication systems and the use of information theory to evaluate rules. In communication systems, a channel has a high capacity if it can carry a great deal of information from the source to the receiver. As for a rule, the relation is interesting when the antecedent provides a great deal of information about the consequent. The main drawback of information-theoretic measures is that they do not respect the value-based semantics of association rules, i.e. they systematically give the same value to $a \rightarrow b$ and to its opposite $a \rightarrow b^*$. However, if

Table 14. Classification of RIMs

Subject \ Scope	Rule	Quasi-implication	Quasi-conjunction	Quasi-equivalence
Deviation from equilibrium	– confidence, – Sebag and Schoenauer index, – example and counter-example ratio, – Laplace[8], – Ganascia index, – least-contradiction	– inclusion index		– correlation coefficient, – novelty; – collective strength, – κ, – Yule index, – odds ratio
Deviation from independence	– Bayes factor	– Loevinger index, – conviction – **implication intensity,** – **implication index**	– lift – **likelihood linkage index,** – **directed contribution to χ^2**	– **rule-interest**
Similarity			– support (Russel and Rao), – Jaccard index, – Dice index, – Ochiai index, – Kulczynski index	– causal support (Sokal and Michener), – Rogers and – Tanimoto index

The nature of RIMs is given by the font: the measures in **bold** are statistical, while the others are descriptive.

$a \rightarrow b$ is strong, then intuitively $a \rightarrow b*$ should be weak.

In (Blanchard et al., 2005b), we presented a new RIM based on information theory which respects the value-based semantics of association rules. This new measure named *DIR* is the only RIM which rejects both independence and equilibrium. In other words, with only one fixed threshold *DIR* discards both the rules whose antecedent and consequent are negatively correlated, and the rules which have more counter-examples than examples[8]. Formal and empirical experiments show that *DIR* is a very filtering measure, which is useful for association rule post-processing.

COMPARISON WITH RELATED WORKS

In 1991, Piatetsky-Shapiro has proposed three principles for an objectively "good" RIM M (Piatetsky-Shapiro, 1991):

- P1. $M(a \rightarrow b)=0$ if a and b are statistically independent.
- P2. M monotically increases with n_{ab} when all other parameters remain the same.
- P3. M monotically increases with n_a or n_b when all other parameters remain the same[10].

We think that the principles P1 and P3 (concerning n_b) are too restricting. They lead to discard a wide range of RIMs whereas practical experiment can show that these measures are useful for certain applications. For example, it is well-known that confidence is an appropriate RIM to analyze market basket data, and more generally sparse data. Nevertheless, these principles have been used in many later works (Brin et al., 1997a; Freitas, 1999; Yao & Zhong, 1999; Tan & Kumar, 2000; McGarry, 2005).

More recently, more general works have been conducted to study RIM properties with formal or empirical experiments. Bayardo (1999) showed that several RIMs are redundant when n_b is fixed. In this case, using support and confidence is enough to discover the best rules. Tan et al. (2004) compared 20 symmetrical or symmetrized[11] RIMs according to different formal criteria and on synthetic rule sets. The measures show to be sometimes redundant, sometimes conflicting, and none is significantly better than all the others. Closer to our work is the paper of Lenca et al. (2007) who study 20 RIMs according to the eight following formal criteria:

- C1. symmetry with regard to a and b;
- C2. decrease with n_b;
- C3. value at independence;
- C4. value for rules with no counter-example;
- C5. linearity with n_{ab*} around 0^+;
- C6. sensitivity to n;
- C7. easiness to fix a threshold;
- C8. intelligibility.

The criteria C1 and C3 can be retrieved from our classification. In our opinion, the other criteria, although interesting, do not seem closely related to the meaning of the measures, i.e. they do not help to understand what is measured. With these criteria, Lenca et al. partition the 20 RIM in two ways: first they build a formal partition from the matrix measures×criteria, then they build an experimental partition by comparing the measure behaviors on real rule sets. It is interesting to notice that the resulting clusters tend to greatly confirm our classification, especially regarding subject and scope:

- Measures with different subjects belong to different clusters
- Measures of quasi-implication and measures of quasi-conjunction/quasi-equivalence belong to different clusters.

Another approach close to our work is the experimental study of Huynh et al. (2006) performed on 36 RIMs. From two datasets, they mine the association rules and then partition the RIMs using their correlations. If the datasets are considered singly, the resulting clusters differ from our classification. On the other hand, if the partitions are merged by intersecting clusters, then the clusters tend to confirm our classification, again especially regarding subject and scope. The comparison of our semantics-based classification to data-based partitions needs to be explored further with numerous datasets. Indeed, the results of data-based approaches depend on the data and on the biases induced by the parameters of the association rule mining algorithms (support threshold, confidence threshold, maximum number of items, considering of item negations). Actually, a formal classification like ours can be seen as a data-based analysis performed on a rule set that would be the unbiased theoretical set **R**.

CONCLUSION

By defining the notions of *rule* and *rule interestingness measure*, this chapter provides a formal framework to study rules. Within this framework, we are able to compare the rules to closely related concepts such as similarities, implications, and equivalences. Also we make a novel and useful classification of interestingness measures according to three criteria: the subject, the scope, and the nature of the measure.

- The subject is the notion measured by the index. It can be either the deviation from equilibrium, or the deviation from independence, or a similarity. Deviations from equilibrium and from independence are two different but complementary aspects of rule interestingness.
- The scope is the entity concerned by the result of the measure. It can be either a single rule, or a rule and its contrapositive (quasi-implication), or a rule and its converse (quasi-conjunction), or a rule and its contrapositive and converse (quasi-equivalence).
- The nature is the descriptive or statistical feature of the index.

Finally, the classification shows that some interesting combinations of the criteria are not satisfied by any index. Hence we provide two innovative measures specifically developed to complement the classification: the probabilistic measure of deviation from equilibrium *IPEE*, and the directed information ratio *DIR* which rejects both equilibrium and independence.

The subject, scope, and nature seem to us essential to grasp the meaning of rule interestingness measures. Thus, the classification can help the user to choose the measures (s)he wants to apply for a given application. For example, the classification leads to wonder whether the user is interested only in single rules, or whether the contrapositive and converse can make sense. Also it is relevant to question whether the user wants to measure deviations from equilibrium or deviations from independence, or both. Without information from the user, we think that a judicious solution is using together a descriptive measure of deviation from equilibrium, a statistical measure of deviation from equilibrium, a descriptive measure of deviation from independence, and a statistical measure of deviation from independence. According to us, such a quadruplet of indexes allows one to measure four strongly "orthogonal" aspects of rule interestingness.

REFERENCES

Aggarwal, C. C., & Yu, P. S. (2001). Mining associations with the collective strength approach. *IEEE Transactions on Knowledge and Data Engineering, 13*(6), 863–873.

Agrawal, R., Imielienski, T., & Swami, A. (1993). Mining association rules between sets of items in large databases. In *Proceedings of the 1993 SIGMOD international conference on management of data*, (pp. 207–216). ACM Press.

Aze, J., & Kodratoff, Y. (2002). A study of the effect of noisy data in rule extraction systems. In Rappl, R. (Ed.), *Proceedings of the Sixteenth European Meeting on Cybernetics and Systems Research (EMCSR'02)*, 2, 781–786.

Bayardo, R. J., & Agrawal, R. (1999). Mining the most interesting rules. In *Proceedings of ACM KDD'1999*, (pp. 145–154). ACM Press.

Blanchard, J. (2005). *Un système de visualisation pour l'extraction, l'évaluation, et l'exploration interactives des règles d'association*. PhD thesis, University of Nantes.

Blanchard, J., Guillet, F., Briand, H., & Gras, R. (2005a). Assessing rule interestingness with a probabilistic measure of deviation from equilibrium. In *Proceedings of the 11th international symposium onApplied Stochastic Models and Data Analysis ASMDA-2005*, (pp. 191–200).

Blanchard, J., Guillet, F., Gras, R., & Briand, H. (2005b). Using information-theoretic measures to assess association rule interestingness. In *Proceedings of the fifth IEEE international conference on data mining ICDM'05*, (pp. 66–73). IEEE Computer Society.

Blanchard, J., Kuntz, P., Guillet, F., & Gras, R. (2003). Implication intensity: from the basic statistical definition to the entropic version. In *Statistical Data Mining and Knowledge Discovery*, (pp. 473–485). Chapman & Hall.

Brin, S., Motwani, R., & Silverstein, C. (1997a). Beyond market baskets: Generalizing association rules to correlations. *SIGMOD Record*, *26*(2), 265–276.

Brin, S., Motwani, R., Ullman, J. D., & Tsur, S. (1997b). Dynamic itemset counting and implica-

tion rules for market basket data. *SIGMOD Record*, *26*(2), 255–264.

Clark, P., & Boswell, R. (1991). Rule induction with CN2: Some recent improvements. In *EWSL'91: Proceedings of the European Working Session on Machine Learning*, (pp. 151–163). Springer.

Cohen, J. (1960). A coefficient of agreement for nominal scales. *Educational and Psychological Measurement*, (20), 37–46.

Dice, L. (1945). Measures of the amount of ecologic association between species. *Ecology*, (26), 297–302.

Dunn, J. M. (1986). Relevance logic and entailment. In D. Gabbay, & F. Guenthner (Ed.), *Handbook of Philosophical Logic*, *3*, 117–224. Kluwer Academic Publishers.

Elder, J. F., & Pregibon, D. (1996). A statistical perspective on knowledge discovery in databases. In U. M. Fayyad, G. Piatetsky-Shapiro, P. Smyth, & R. Uthurusamy, (Eds.), *Advances in knowledge discovery and data mining*, (pp. 83–113). AAAI/MIT Press.

Freitas, A. (1999). On rule interestingness measures. *Knowledge-Based Systems Journal*, *12*(5-6), 309–315.

Ganascia, J. G. (1991). Deriving the learning bias from rule properties. In *Machine intelligence 12: towards an automated logic of human thought*, (pp. 151–167). Clarendon Press.

Geng, L., & Hamilton, H. J. (2007). Choosing the right lens: Finding what is interesting in data mining. In F. Guillet & H. J. Hamilton (Ed.), *Quality Measures in Data Mining*, volume 43 of *Studies in Computational Intelligence*, (pp. 3–24). Springer.

Gras, R. (1996). *L'implication statistique : nouvelle méthode exploratoire de données*. La Pensée Sauvage Editions.

Gras, R., & Kuntz, P. (2008). An overview of the statistical implicative analysis development. In Gras, R., Suzuki, E., Guillet, F., & Spagnolo, F. (Ed.), *Statistical Implicative Analysis: Theory and Applications*, volume 127 of *Studies in Computational Intelligence*, (pp. 21–52). Springer.

Huynh, X.-H., Guillet, F., & Briand, H. (2006). Evaluating interestingness measures with linear correlation graph. In *Proceedings of the 19th International Conference on Industrial, Engineering and Other Applications of Applied Intelligent Systems (IEA/AIE)*, volume 4031 of *Lecture Notes in Computer Science*, (pp. 312–321). Springer.

Jaccard, P. (1901). Etude comparative de la distribution florale dans une portion des Alpes et du Jura. *Bulletin de la Société Vaudoise des Sciences Naturelles*, (37), 547–579.

Jaroszewicz, S., & Simovici, D. A. (2001). A general measure of rule interestingness. In *Proceedings of PKDD'2001*, (pp. 253–265). Springer.

Jeffreys, H. (1935). Some tests of significance treated by the theory of probability. In *Proceedings of the Cambridge Philosophical Society*, (pp. 203–222).

Kodratoff, Y. (2000). Extraction de connaissances à partir des données et des textes. In *Actes des journées sur la fouille dans les données par la méthode d'analyse statistique implicative*, (pp. 151–165). Presses de l'Université de Rennes 1.

Kodratoff, Y. (2001). Comparing machine learning and knowledge discovery in databases: an application to knowledge discovery in texts. In Paliouras, G., Karkaletsis, V., and Spyropoulos, C. (Ed.), *Machine Learning and Its Applications*, volume 2049 of *Lecture Notes in Artificial Intelligence*, (pp. 1–21). Springer.

Kulczynski, S. (1927). Die pflanzenassoziationen der pieninen. *Bulletin International de l'Académie Polonaise des Sciences et des Lettres. Classe des Sciences Mathématiques et Naturelles*, (suppl. II), 57–203. série B.

Lavrac, N., Flach, P. A., & Zupan, B. (1999). Rule evaluation measures: a unifying view. In *ILP'99: Proceedings of the ninth International Workshop on Inductive Logic Programming*, (pp. 174–185). Springer-Verlag.

Lenca, P., Vaillant, B., Meyer, P., & Lallich, S. (2007). Association rule interestingness measures: Experimental and theoretical studies. In Guillet, F. and Hamilton, H. J. (Ed.), *Quality Measures in Data Mining*, volume 43 of *Studies in Computational Intelligence*, (pp. 51–76). Springer.

Lerman, I. C. (1981). *Classification et analyse ordinale des données*. Dunod.

Lerman, I. C. (1993). Likelihood linkage analysis (LLA) classification method: An example treated by hand. *Biochimie*, *75*(5), 379–397.

Liu, B., Hsu, W., Chen, S., & Ma, Y. (2000). Analyzing the subjective interestingness of association rules. *IEEE Intelligent Systems*, *15*(5), 47–55.

Loevinger, J. (1947). A systematic approach to the construction and evaluation of tests of ability. *Psychological Monographs*, *61*(4).

McGarry, K. (2005). A survey of interestingness measures for knowledge discovery. *The Knowledge Engineering Review*, *20*(1), 39–61.

Mosteller, F. (1968). Association and estimation in contingency tables. *Journal of the American Statistical Association*, *63*(321), 1–28.

Ochiai, A. (1957). Zoogeographic studies on the soleoid fishes found in japan and its neighbouring regions. *Bulletin of the Japanese Society of Scientific Fisheries*, (22), 526–530.

Padmanabhan, B., & Tuzhilin, A. (1999). Unexpectedness as a measure of interestingness in knowledge discovery. *Decision Support Systems*, *27*(3), 303–318.

Pearson, K. (1896). Mathematical contributions to the theory of evolution: regression, heredity and panmixia. *Philosophical Transactions of the Royal Society Of London*, series A(187), 253–318.

Piatetsky-Shapiro, G. (1991). Discovery, analysis, and presentation of strong rules. In *Knowledge Discovery in Databases*, (pp. 229–248). AAAI/ MIT Press.

Quinlan, J. (1993). *C4.5: Programs for Machine Learning*. Morgan Kaufmann.

Rogers, D., & Tanimoto, T. (1960). A computer program for classifying plants. *Science*, (132), 1115–1118.

Russel, P., & Rao, T. (1940). On habitat and association of species of anopheline larvae in southeastern madras. *Journal of the Malaria Institute of India*, (3):153–178.

Sebag, M., & Schoenauer, M. (1988). Generation of rules with certainty and confidence factors from incomplete and incoherent learning bases. In *Proceedings of EKAW88*, (pp. 28.1–28.20).

Silberschatz, A., & Tuzhilin, A. (1996). User-assisted knowledge discovery: how much should the user be involved. In *Proceedings of the 1996 SIGMOD workshop on research issues on data mining and knowledge discovery (DMKD)*.

Smyth, P., & Goodman, R. M. (1992). An information theoretic approach to rule induction from databases. *IEEE Transactions on Knowledge and Data Engineering*, *4*(4), 301–316.

Sokal, R., & Michener, C. (1958). A statistical method for evaluating systematic relationships. *University of Kansas Science Bulletin*, (38), 1409–1438.

Tan, P.-N., & Kumar, V. (2000). Interestingness measures for association patterns: a perspective. In *Proceedings of the KDD-2000 workshop on postprocessing in machine learning and data mining*.

Tan, P.-N., Kumar, V., & Srivastava, J. (2004). Selecting the right objective measure for association analysis. *Information Systems*, 29(4), 293–313.

Yao, Y. Y., & Zhong, N. (1999). An analysis of quantitative measures associated with rules. In *PAKDD'99: Proceedings of the Third Pacific-Asia Conference on Methodologies for Knowledge Discovery and Data Mining*, pages 479–488. Springer.

Yule, G. (1900). On the association of attributes in statistics. *Philosophical Transactions of the Royal Society of London*, series A(194), 257–319.

Zembowicz, R., & Zytkow, J. M. (1996). From contingency tables to various forms of knowledge in databases. In *Advances in knowledge discovery and data mining*, (pp. 328–349). American Association for Artificial Intelligence.

ENDNOTES

[1] In general, association rule mining algorithms do not handle negations of items or itemsets. In this chapter, in order to study the meaning of the interestingness measures, we have to consider negations too.

[2] The concept of *rule* defined here can refer to association rules as well as classification rules. Classification rules are generated for example by induction algorithms such as CN2 (Clark & Boswell, 1991) or decision tree algorithms such as C4.5 (Quinlan, 1993).

[3] Certain authors assume that n is constant, therefore they use only three parameters. However, this prevents from comparing rules coming from different datasets.

[4] Numerous authors consider that a good interestingness measure must vanish at independence (principle P1 originally proposed in (Piatetsky-Shapiro, 1991), see the "Related Works" section). This principle to-

tally denies the deviation from equilibrium. It amounts to say that measures of deviation from independence are better.

5   For example with $(n_{ab}, n_a, n_b, n) = (750; 800; 900; 1000)$, one have a *confidence(a→ b)=93%* and *confidence(b*→ a*)=50%*.

6   Hempel's paradox lies in the fact that a statement such as "All the crows are black" (logically equivalent to "Something not black is not a crow") is validated by the observation of anything which is not black: a white shoe, a traffic jam...

7   One can think that the counterpart of the implication is not the conjunction but the equivalence. However, it must be recalled that the implication $a \Rightarrow b$ is the disjunction $a* \vee b$.

8   Laplace varies only slightly with cardinality expansion. This is the reason why we classify it among the descriptive measures.

9   According to the classification presented in this chapter, *DIR* is a mesure of deviation from independence (it vanishes at independence). Nevertheless, as *DIR* is always negative or zero at equilibrium, any strictly positive threshold is enough to reject both independence and equilibrium.

10   This statement is not precise enough since the modeling parameters are not given. For example, we could use (n_{ab}, n_a, n_b, n) as well as $(n_{ab}, n_a, n_b, n_{a*b*})$ or even $(n_{ab}, n_a, n_b, n_{b*})$, which alters the principles. As explained in the section "Rule Modeling", the choice of the modeling parameters is generally an implicit assumption in the literature about rule interestingness.

11   The measures do not assess a rule stricto sensu since they estimate a rule and its converse identically: *M(a → b) = M(b → a)*.

Section III
Post-Analysis and Post-Mining of Association Rules

Chapter V
Post–Processing for Rule Reduction Using Closed Set

Huawen Liu
Jilin University, P.R. China

Jigui Sun
Jilin University, P.R. China

Huijie Zhang
Northeast Normal University, P.R. China

ABSTRACT

In data mining, rule management is getting more and more important. Usually, a large number of rules will be induced from large databases in many fields, especially when they are dense. This, however, directly leads to the gained knowledge hard to be understood and interpreted. To eliminate redundant rules from rule base, many efforts have been made and various efficient and outstanding algorithms have been proposed. However, end-users are often unable to complete a mining task because there are still insignificant rules. Thus, it becomes apparent that an efficient technique is needed to discard useless rules as more as possible, without information lossless. To achieve this goal, in this paper we propose an efficient method to filter superfluous rules from knowledge base in a post-processing manner. The main character of our method lies in that it eliminates redundancy of rules by dependent relation, which can be discovered by closed set mining technique. Their performance evaluations show that the compression degree achieved by our proposed method is better and its efficiency is also higher than those of other techniques.

INTRODUCTION

Knowledge discovery in databases (KDD) refers to the overall process of mapping low-level data in large databases into high-level forms that might be more compact, more abstract, or more useful (Fayyad et al., 1996). KDD can be viewed as a multidisciplinary activity because it exploits several research disciplines of artificial intelligence such as machine learning, pattern recognition, expert systems, knowledge acquisition, as well as mathematical disciplines (Bruha, 2000). Its objective is to extract previously unknown and potentially useful information hidden behind data from usually very large databases. As one of core components of KDD, data mining refers to the process of extracting interesting patterns from data by specific algorithms. Due to intuitional meaning and easy understandability, rule has now become one of major representation forms of extracted knowledge or patterns. Under this context, the result produced by data mining techniques is a set of rules, i.e., rule base.

Currently, the major challenge of data mining is not at its efficiency, but at the interpretability of discovered results. During mining stage, a considerable number of rules may be discovered when the real-world database is large. Particularly, if data is highly correlated, the situation will turn worse and quickly out of control. The huge quantity of rules makes themselves difficult to be explored, thus hampers global analysis of discovered knowledge. Furthermore, monitoring and managing of these rules are turned out to be extremely costly and difficult. The straight misfortune to users is that they can not effectively interpret or understand those overwhelming number of rules. Consequently, users may be buried within the masses of gained knowledge again, and nobody will directly benefit from the results of such data mining techniques (Berzal & Cubero, 2007). Hence, it is an urgent requisite for intelligent techniques to handle useless rules and help

users to understand the results from the rapidly growing volumes of digital data.

Post-processing, whose purpose is to enhance the quality of the mined knowledge, plays a vital role in circumventing the aforementioned dilemma. The main advantage of post-processing is that it can effectively assist end-users to understand and interpret the meaning knowledge nuggets (Baesens et al., 2000). The post-processing procedure usually consists of four main steps, i.e., quality processing, summarizing, grouping and visualization. At the core of these routines, rule quality processing (e.g., pruning and filtering) is considered to be the most important one (Bruha, 2000), because this procedure can eliminate lots of noisy, redundant or insignificant rules and provide users with compact and precise knowledge derived from databases by data mining methods. From the view of end-users, a concise or condensed rule base is more preferable, because on the ground of it, decision-makers can make a quick and precise response to unseen data without being distracted by noise information.

In data mining community, many attentions have now been paid on dealing with noise knowledge through measuring similarity or redundancy. For example, distance metrics, e.g., Euclidean distance (Waitman et al., 2006), are often used to measure the similarity between rules, and those rules with high similarity will be discarded. In addition, Chi-square tests (Liu et al., 1999) and entropy (Jaroszewicz and Simovici, 2002) are addressed to analyze the distance between rules in the post-processing phase. Besides, some classifiers explore efficient data structures, such as bitmap technique (Jacquene et al., 2006) and prefix tree (Li et al., 2001), to store and retrieve rules. Moreover, various interestingness measurements, both objective and subjective, are also considered in studying the issue of rules importance (Geng and Hamilton, 2006). As a representative example, Brin et al. (1997) outlined a conviction measurement to express rule interestingness.

Other endeavors have been attempted to prune the generated rule base directly. The typical case is rule cover technique addressed by Toivonen et al. (1995), where a rule is redundant if it is covered by others. Brijs et al. (2000) further improved its performance by virtue of integer-programming technique. However, Klemettinen et al. (1994) extracted interesting rules from the whole rule base through rule templates (or constraints). Whereas Srikant et al. (1995) organized a rule base as a hierarchical structure, and the rules lie in higher level are more general than those in low level. Additionally, Liu et al. (1999) divided a rule base into two parts (DS rules and Non-DS rules) by means of direction setting (DS). Under this scheme, the rules within the DS part have key information of the rule base, whilst those non-DS ones embody relevant detailed knowledge. Recently, Ashrafi et al. (2007) proposed fixed antecedent and consequent methods to remove redundant rules from the resultant rule set. In this method, a rule is redundant when a set of rules that also convey the same knowledge is found.

Note that most of methods mentioned above are only based on the analysis of rule structure or interestingness measurements, and little work has been done on analyzing relations between rules with respect to objects. This, however, may result in a problem, that is, redundant or insignificant rules still inhabit the pruned subset or rules. In this chapter, a fast rule reduction algorithm using closed set will be introduced. As we know, in data mining, a rule is supported or satisfied by many transactions, and each transaction supports several rules at the same time. As a matter of fact, this supported relation satisfies closed property and forms a Galois connection between transactions and rules. Fortunately, this closed dependency between rules can also be explored by the existing association rule techniques. Thus, we can utilize this closed dependency to eliminate insignificant rules. More specifically, our method is implemented in two steps. The first step is performing data mining algorithms on database, and then a closed mining method is carried out on the mined rule base to obtain closed rule-subsets. Reversely, these closed sets representing high-order relation between original rules are exploited to remove insignificant or useless rules from the rule base.

Compared with other pruning useless rule methods, the proposed one has several advantages. For example, our approach is conducted on the dependent relation among rules, rather than their internal structures. As a result, it is competent for eliminating more redundant rules, including those having little or even no common ingredients in structure. In addition, information will not be lost via our method, because the dependent relation is closed one. Moreover, the proposed method is capable of finding a good trade-off between classification capability and size for a classifier. These will be demonstrated by later evaluation experiments on benchmark datasets.

The rest of this chapter is arranged as follows. Section 2 briefly provides related work on pruning redundant rules. In Section 3, several notations about association rule mining are briefly reviewed. Section 4 firstly introduces the theoretical foundation of our method, i.e., formal representation of the dependent relation between rules and transactions. After that, a fast redundant rule elimination method using closed rule-sets is proposed. Experimental results conducted to evaluate the usefulness and effectiveness of our approach are presented in Section 5, and Section 6 closes this chapter with conclusions.

RELATED WORK

During past years, a modest number of proposals that address the redundancy elimination problem of rules have been witnessed. Roughly speaking, most of them can be classified into two categories: pre-pruning and post-pruning.

The task of the former is to prevent useless or redundant rules from being generated at mining stage. That is to say, the pruning operation occurs at the phase of rule generation, and the generated rules are all significant. As we know, association rule mining generally consists of two phases (Agrawal et al., 1993), namely, identifying frequent itemsets and then generating rules from these mined itemsets. For the first step, it is more computationally intensive. Thus, many pruning methods focus on the former step and seek condensed representations of frequent itemsets (Calders et al., 2006). For example, Pasquier et al. (2005) and Zaki (2004) substituted frequent itemset with its closed one and then induced minimal antecedent and maximal consequent rules from them. Calders and Goethals (2007) explored association rules from another lossless representation, called non-derivable itemset. Besides, other generalized concepts, such as maximal frequent itemset (Bayardo, 1998), disjunction-free set (Kryszkiewicz, 2005), free set (Boulicaut et al., 2003), heavy itemset (Palshikar et al., 2007) and δ-tolerance frequent itemset (Cheng et al., 2008), are also investigated. A comprehensive survey about association rule mining can be consulted the literature by Ceglar and Roddick (2006).

Contrastively, post-pruning technique mainly concerns that the pruning operation occurs after rules have been generated. Since it occurs at post-processing phase and is independent of specified mining algorithms, this method has attracted so many attentions that many outstanding pruning methods have been developed. Among them, rule cover is a representative case. It extracts a small subset from the original rule set without reducing database coverage. As an illustrative instance, Toivonen et al. (1995) replaced the generated rule base with a structural rule subset, which has the same database transaction rows with the original one. In this method, rules outside the subset are regarded as redundant ones and will be removed undoubtedly. Baralis and Chiusano (2004) presented another approach to yield a minimal rule subset, called essential rule set, from the whole one. A rule is essential if no other rules, which make the rule redundant, exist in the same rule set. In an analogical vein, Li (2006) provided a notion termed as family of optimal rule sets, which generalizes the *k*-optimal rule set (Webb and Zhang, 2005), to get useful rules. Additionally, Kryszkiewicz (1998) highlighted representative association rules to take place of the original rule base, where other insignificant rules can be derived from them.

To extract interesting rules, apriori knowledge has also been taken into account in literatures. For example, Domingues and Rezende (2005) applied knowledge taxonomies to reduce the quantity of rules, which are summarized from low-level to high-level. In addition, Baralis and Psaila (1997) stated that template-based constraint is also a good choice to draw interesting rules. A template denotes which attributes should occur in antecedent or consequent of rule. After rule templates have been pre-specified by users, system retrieves matching rules from the whole knowledge base. However, this method only summarizes rules and does not eliminate redundancy in the final model.

Besides, several special data structures are adopted to remove specific rules. The typical case is CMAR (Li et al., 2001), where a prefix tree structure, called CR-Tree, is employed to identify common components shared by rules. Jacquenet et al. (2006) grouped rules by virtue of bitmap technique, where each rule is encoded into a bitmap array with respect to items (or attributes). Thus, redundancy produced by duplicate or specific rules can be easily avoided by logic AND operation. Moreover, Brijs et al. (2000) resorted to integer programming model to select the most promising subset of characteristic rules. Whereas Chawla et al. (2004) investigated the mapping relation between certain classes of association rules with single consequent under the framework of directed hyper-graph and then addressed a local pruning method.

Apart from support and confidence, seeking other interesting measurements, such as Chi-squared test, Pearson's correlation, lift, information entropy and conviction (Brin et al., 1998, Geng and Hamilton, 2006), is another direction to determine whether a rule is significant or not. This is motivated by the fact that it is difficult to come up with single metric to quantify the interestingness or goodness of rule in some situations. As a typical example, Liu et al. (1999) argued that a rule is not interesting if its confidence is not distinguished from its specific ones by Chi-squared tests, and will be discarded if the confidence difference with any sub-rule is less than pre-specified threshold. In practice, however, many non-interesting rules will not be pruned, for they are not sensitive to low-threshold when the data is sparse. To alleviate this problem, Jaroszewicz and Simovici (2002) took maximum entropy means, which combines influence of specific rules to their general ones, to evaluate the interestingness of rules. While Bathoorn et al. (2006) removed redundant rules on the ground of the minimum description length principle.

Association rule mining technique is also mentioned in literatures to discard useless rules. For instance, Fernádez et al. (2001) employed the Apriori algorithm to reduce the decision rules obtained through rough sets. Recently, Berrado and Runger (2007) organized and grouped association rules using one-way rules (i.e., meta-rules), which also can be obtained by the Apriori algorithm. However, the main disadvantage of these approaches is that the computational cost is very high, especially when the number of association rules is huge. Our method works in a similar way. The difference lies in that we exploit approximate function dependency between rules to eliminate superfluous rules. Moreover, rather than extracting all association second-order rules, we only generate closed rule-sets, which is far less than association rules, to discard redundancy between discovered rules.

ASSOCIATION AND CLASSIFICATION RULES

Let I be a set of m distinct literals termed *items*, i.e., $I = \{i_1, \dots i_m\}$. A subset X of I is called an *itemset*, or a k-itemset if it contains k items, namely, $X = \{i_1, \dots i_k\}$. A *transaction t* over I is a couple $t = (tid, X)$ where tid and $X \subseteq I$ refer to transaction identifier and its corresponding itemset respectively. Formally, a *data mining context* is a triple $D = (T, I, R)$, where T and I are finite sets of *transactions* over I and *items* respectively, and $R \subseteq T \times I$ is a binary relation such that pair $(t, i) \in R$ denotes item i is related to the t-th transaction. Typically, the mining context D is organized as relation database form, where each row is a transaction representing as a set of items.

Given an itemset $X \subseteq I$ in $D = (T, I, R)$, its *cover* consists of the set of transactions in D that support X, i.e., $cover(X) = \{t \mid (t, Y) \in T, X \subseteq Y\}$. Additionally, the *support* of X, denoted as $\sigma(X)$, is the number of transactions in which it occurs as a subset, that is, $\sigma(X) = |cover(X)|$, where $|Y|$ is the cardinality of Y. An itemset X is called a *frequent* one if its support is larger than or equal to a user-specified minimum support threshold *minsup*, i.e., $\sigma(X) \geq minsup$.

An *association rule* is an implication expression of the form $X \rightarrow Y$, where $X \subseteq I$ and $Y \subseteq I$ are two itemsets, and $X \cap Y = \varnothing$. This rule form illustrates a kind of association relation, that is, if a transaction contains all items in X, then it also contains all items in Y at the same time. Given an association rule $X \rightarrow Y$, X and Y are called *antecedent* and *consequent* of the rule, respectively. Moreover, the *support* of rule $X \rightarrow Y$ refers to the number of transactions supporting X and Y simultaneously, i.e., $support(X \rightarrow Y) = \sigma(X \cup Y)$. Similarly, its *confidence* is the conditional probability of having Y contained in a transaction, given that X is also contained in the same transaction, that is, $confidence(X \rightarrow Y) = \sigma(X \cup Y) / \sigma(X)$. A rule is *interesting* or *valid* if its support and confidence are no less than user-specified minimum support and confidence thresholds respectively.

As aforesaid discussion, association rule mining generally comprises two phases (Agrawal et al., 1993). The first one is to identify all frequent itemsets from a given data mining context D. After that, association rules will be induced from these discovered itemsets at the second phase. However, it is a quite challenge problem to identify all frequent itemsets, for the computational cost is very high. Assume that the number of items within D is m, then the search space for enumerating all frequent itemsets is 2^m, which will exponentially increase with m. The worse thing is that the context D is usually full with massive transactions in real-world. Hence, the number of frequent itemsets may be extremely large, especially, when D is dense or inner highly correlated (Liu et al., 1999). This problem, however, can be circumvented by adopting other alternatives, e.g., non-derivable itemset (Calders and Goethals, 2007) and maximal frequent itemset (Bayardo, 1998). The most used and typical one is closed frequent itemset (Zaki, 2004).

Assume that $X \subseteq I$ is an itemset, X is *closed* if there has no other itemset $X' \supseteq X$ such that $cover(X') = cover(X)$. Further, X is a *closed*

frequent itemset if it is both closed and frequent itemset. The advantage brought by closed itemset is that it is a lossless representation and the number of closed frequent itemsets is often much smaller than those of corresponding frequent ones in a given context D (Zaki, 2004).

Classification rule is a special case of association rule, if the consequent of association rule is only constrained by class label attributes (Liu et al, 1998). However, classification rule has more readable form in practice. Apart from transaction database, it can also be derived from relation database or decision table. Theoretically, transaction database and relation database are two different representations of data and one can be transformed into another by one-one mapping. Just owing to this, the technique for mining association rule can also be utilized to uncover classification rule. The remarkable predominance is that only minor modification is needed as it faces with classification tasks.

Example 3.1. Let $D = (T, I, R)$ be a data mining context, as described in Table 1, where $I = \{i_0, \ldots, i_{13}\}$ and $T = \{t_0, \ldots, t_{10}\}$. For transaction $t_0, (t_0, i_0) \in R$ and $(t_0, i_1) \notin R$ hold, because item i_0 occurs in the itemset of t_0, while i_1 does not.

Table 1. A data mining context $D = (T, I, R)$

Tids	Itemset	Tids	Itemset	Tids	Itemset
t_0	i_0,i_2,i_6,i_8,i_{12}	t_4	i_0,i_4,i_5,i_8,i_{11}	t_8	i_1,i_4,i_6,i_8,i_{12}
t_1	i_0,i_3,i_5,i_8,i_{11}	t_5	i_0,i_4,i_6,i_8,i_{12}	t_9	$i_1,i_4,i_7,i_{10},i_{13}$
t_2	i_0,i_3,i_6,i_8,i_{12}	t_6	i_1,i_2,i_6,i_8,i_{12}	t_{10}	$i_1,i_3,i_7,i_{10},i_{13}$
t_3	i_0,i_3,i_6,i_9,i_{13}	t_7	i_1,i_3,i_6,i_8,i_{12}		

Table 2. Classification rules RS derived from the context $D = (T, I, R)$

id	rule	support	id	rule	support	id	rule	support
r_0	$i_6 i_8 \rightarrow i_{12}$	6	r_3	$i_2 \rightarrow i_{12}$	2	r_6	$i_7 \rightarrow i_{13}$	2
r_1	$i_1 i_6 \rightarrow i_{12}$	3	r_4	$i_5 \rightarrow i_{11}$	2	r_7	$i_{10} \rightarrow i_{13}$	2
r_2	$i_1 i_8 \rightarrow i_{12}$	3	r_5	$i_4 i_6 \rightarrow i_{12}$	2	r_8	$i_9 \rightarrow i_{13}$	1

Let itemset $X=\{i_0, i_6\}$, then its cover and support are $\{t_0,t_2,t_3,t_5\}$ and 4 respectively. For the sake of simplicity, hereafter we denote $\{i_0, i_6\}$ as i_0i_6 and $\{t_0,t_2,t_3,t_5\}$ as $t_0t_2t_3t_5$, as no confusion occurs. Itemset i_0i_6 is frequent, if the user-specified minimum support threshold *minsup* is zero. For itemset i_1i_7, it is not closed one because $cover(i_1i_7)=cover(i_1i_7i_{10}i_{13})$. In this case, $i_1i_7i_{10}i_{13}$ is closed itemset. Assume that the minimal confidence is one and the class labels are constrained within $i_{11}i_{12}i_{13}$, then nine interesting classification rules (Table 2) can be obtained from this context D by association rule mining, where *supp* is the support of classification rule.

REDUNDANT RULE ELIMINATION

The production of association mining is a rule base with hundreds to millions of rules. However, the number of interesting ones is less. In order to highlight those important ones in the rule base, in this section, a new method will be presented to filter insignificant rules. Before eliciting the details of our pruning algorithm, we firstly focus our attention on the dependent relation between transactions and rules. For convenience, we hereafter take the Example 3.1 as a running example.

Second-Order Rule

Given a data mining context $D = (T, I, R)$, any association rule r induced from D may be supported or satisfied by a set of transactions. Meanwhile, each transaction t in D may support or fire a set of rules. Unless otherwise specified, $D = (T, I, R)$ denotes a given data mining context and *RS* refers to the original *rule-set* (a set of rules) induced from D. Formally, this supported relation can be defined as follows.

Definition 4.1. *Let $D=(T, I, R)$ be a context and RS be the rule-set from it, a supported relation between rules and transactions is $S \subseteq RS \times T$*

where $(r,t) \in S$ denotes transaction t satisfies or supports rule r in D, and r is not satisfied by t otherwise.

From this definition, one may note that the supported relation S is tightly related with the notion of *cover*. As a matter of fact, for single rule $r : X \to Y$, if a transaction t is contained in the cover of itemset $X \cup Y$, i.e., $t \in cover(X \cup Y)$, then $(r,t) \in S$ holds on, and vice versa. This means that if the cover of itemset is known, the corresponding supported relation can be derived. For example, $t_6 \in cover(i_1i_8i_{12})$, then t_6 supports rule r_2 and $(r_2,t_6) \in S$. Similarly, $(r_2,t_7) \in S$ and $(r_2,t_8) \in S$ In addition, an important concept, named as transaction-rule context, can be derived from the supported relation S.

Definition 4.2. *Let D be a context and RS be the rule-set from it, a transaction-rule context is a triple $K=(T, RS, S)$, where $S \subseteq RS \times T$ is the supported relation between rules and transactions.*

Like data mining context D, the transaction-rule context $K=(T, RS, S)$ can also be arranged as the form of transaction database, where each row is a transaction $t=(tids, Rs)$ denoted as an unique identifier *tids* and a rule-set $Rs \subseteq RS$. For any $t=(tids, Rs)$ in K, if rule r in the rule-set RS subjects to $(r,t) \in S$, then $r \in Rs$. On the ground of this definition, the transaction-rule context K can be induced from D and RS in a straightforward way and its construction algorithm is shown in Box 1.

In this algorithm, *Rs* denotes the *rule-set* related with the transaction t. Assume that the number of transactions in D and association rules in RS are n and m respectively, the complexity of the construction algorithm is $O(nm)$. Under the framework of this context, the relation between transactions and rule-sets can be easily explored. As an illustration, given the context D in Table 1 and rule-set RS in Table 2, a transaction-rule

Box 1. Algorithm 1

Algorithm 1. Generating a transaction-rule context K from D and RS.
Input : a data mining context $D = (T, I, R)$, and a rule-set RS induced from D.
Output: the transaction-rule context $K = (T, RS, S)$.
1). Initialize the context $K = \varnothing$;
2). **For** each transaction $t \in T$ in D
3).   Initialize the rule-set Rs supported by t as an empty set, namely, $Rs = \varnothing$;
3).   **For** each association rule $r : X \to Y \in RS$
4).   **If** t supports or satisfies r, i.e., $(r,t) \in S$, or $t \in cover(X \cup Y)$ **then**
5). $Rs = Rs \cup \{r\}$;
6).   Insert the rule-set Rs into the context K as a transaction, i.e., $K = K \cup \{Rs\}$;

Table 3. A transaction-rule context $K=(T, RS, S)$

Tids	Rule-set	Tids	Rule-set	Tids	Rule-set
t_0	$r_0 r_3$	t_4	r_4	t_8	$r_0 r_1 r_2 r_5$
t_1	r_4	t_5	$r_0 r_5$	t_9	$r_6 r_7$
t_2	r_0	t_6	$r_0 r_1 r_2 r_3$	t_{10}	$r_6 r_7$
t_3	r_8	t_7	$r_0 r_1 r_2$		

context $K=(T, RS, S)$ can be induced from them by this algorithm and shown as Table 3.

Definition 4.3. *In the context $K=(T, RS, S)$, mapping $f : \rho(T) \to \rho(RS)$ is called a* satisfying *function, if $f(X) = \{r \in RS \mid \forall x \in X, (r,x) \in S\}$ for $X \subseteq T$, where $\rho(T)$ and $\rho(RS)$ are power sets of T and RS, respectively. Dually, mapping $h : \rho(RS) \to \rho(T)$ is a satisfied function, if $h(X) = \{t \in T \mid \forall x \in X, (x,t) \in S\}$ for rule-set $X \subseteq RS$.*

Similar with the relation between transaction and itemset in association mining, the mapping $f(X)$ is the rule-set satisfied by all transactions in X, while $h(X)$ contains transactions supporting all rules in X. For single rule $r : X \to Y \in RS$, one may notice that $h(r)=cover(X \cup Y)$ and its support is $\sigma(r)=|h(r)|$. Assume that $f(\varnothing) = RS$ and $h(\varnothing) = T$, we have $f(X_1 \cup X_2) = f(X_1) \cap f(X_2)$ and $h(Y_1 \cup Y_2) = h(Y_1) \cap h(Y_2)$. This implies mappings f and h meet order-reversing property, that is, $f(X_1) \subseteq f(X_2)$ and $h(Y_1) \subseteq h(Y_2)$ hold on for $X_2 \subseteq X_1$ and $Y_2 \subseteq Y_1$. For instance, $f(t_7) = r_0 r_1 r_2$, $h(r_1) = t_6 t_7 t_8$ and $f(t_5 t_8) = r_0 r_5$. Based on the satisfied function h, several concepts about rule cover can be achieved.

Definition 4.4. *In the context $K=(T, RS, S)$, rule $r \in RS$ is equivalent to rule $r' \in RS$, if $h(r) = h(r')$; r is a* cover-rule *of r' if $h(r') \subset h(r)$; otherwise, r is called a* covered-rule *of r'.*

As mentioned above, for single rule $r : X \to Y \in RS$, it is supported by transactions in $h(r)$ which is equal to its *cover*, i.e., $h(r) = cover(X \cup Y)$. Thus, rule r is a cover-rule of r', if any transaction supporting r' also supports r, no matter whether common ingredients (i.e., items) are shared by both rules or not. This indicates that specific rule or sub-rule in literatures is a special case of cover-rule. For instance, r_0 is a cover-rule of r_5, because $h(r_5) \subset h(r_0)$. However, the antecedent of r_0 is not contained in r_5, namely,

r_5 is not a specific one of r_0. In addition, the equivalent property denotes that if a transaction supports one of them, then it necessarily supports its equivalent rules at the same time. As a typical case, r_1 in Example 3.1 is equivalent to r_2 and both of them are covered-rules of r_0, because $h(r_1)=h(r_2)=t_6t_7t_8 \subset t_0t_2t_5t_6t_7t_8 = h(r_0)$.

For rule $r \in RS$, we use $Eq(r)$ to denote its equivalent class, where $Eq(r) =\{r' \in RS \mid h(r) = h(r')\}$. According to equivalence relation, we have the following property.

Property 4.1. *In $K=(T, RS, S)$, if rule $r \in RS$ is equivalent to rule $r' \in RS$, then $Eq(r)=Eq(r')$ and $h(Eq(r)) = h(r)$.*

This property tells us that equivalent rules in the same equivalent class have the same database cover or support power in the context K. Therefore, given an equivalent class $Eq(r)$, any rule r can be picked out from $Eq(r)$ to stand for other equivalent rules and the rest may be removed safely with reference to the context K. In selecting a rule from its equivalence, many interesting measurements are available. The common strategy is to choose the rule with highest confidence.

From the prediction perspective, covered-rules and some equivalent ones are useless, because they are supported by less transaction than their corresponding cover-rules or equivalent ones. That is to say, their capacities are covered by their corresponding rules. However, their existing may hinder users from exploration and analysis. Thus, it is necessary to prevent them from being generated during mining phase or discard them in post-processing. For two rules $r, r' \in RS$ in K, they may be supported by same transactions. At this point, r is related with r' with respect to T. Specifically, a dependent relation between two rule-sets is defined as follows.

Definition 4.5. *Let $R_1, R_2 \subseteq RS$ be two rule-sets in $K=(T, RS, S)$, if there are transactions supporting rule-set R_1 also support rule-set R_2 at the same time,*

that is, $t \in h(R_1)$ implies $t \in h(R_2)$, then R_2 is called depended on R_1 with degree k and represented as form $R_1 \Rightarrow_k R_2$, where $k = \mid h(R_1 \cup R_2) \mid / \mid h(R_1) \mid$ is its dependent degree.

Clearly, $0 \leq k \leq 1$. Rule-set R_2 *partially depends* on R_1 if $k < 1$; Otherwise R_2 *totally depends* on R_1, denoted as $R_1 \Rightarrow R_2$, if $k=1$. For those rule-sets with single rule, if r in one rule-set R_1 is a covered-rule of r' in another rule-set R_2, then R_2 depends totally on R_1 (i.e., $r \Rightarrow r'$) because of $h(r) \subseteq h(r')$. In addition, both $r \Rightarrow r'$ and $r \Rightarrow r'$ hold, if r equivalent to r'. These imply a very interesting thing that both covered-rules and equivalent rules can also be represented as this kind of function dependence. Therefore, we can take this dependence property of rules as evaluation criterion to determine whether a rule is insignificant or not. For instance, rules r_1 and r_2 in the running example are all totally dependent on r_0, i.e., $r_1 \Rightarrow r_0$ and $r_2 \Rightarrow r_0$.

In order to locate this kind of dependent relation among rules, traditional data mining techniques or methods can be accessed. The distinctness between traditional mining and dependency discover lies in their input and output. The input of traditional mining is the data mining context D, while the input is the transaction-rule context K in this chapter. For the mined results, although they have the same form, the result of traditional mining is an association rule-set. However, the output of dependency discovery is the dependent relations among rules and they are called *second-order rules*, namely, rules of rules (e.g., $r_1 \Rightarrow r_0$). After these second-order rules are indentified by mining technique, they can be utilized to filter useless or insignificant rules out of the rule-set RS in K.

In a given context K, rule-set R_1 is a reduction representation of R_2, if $h(R_1) = h(R_2)$ and $R_1 \subseteq R_2$. For the whole rule-set RS in K, the aim of pruning redundant rules is to obtain minimal reduction of RS. Therefore, we need to single out a rule for each set of equivalent rules or remove all covered-rules for each cover-rule in RS. As a consequence, the size of RS is getting smaller and the last reduced rule-set RS is the desired minimal reduction. Fortunately, this aim can be achieved easily by virtue of second-order rule.

Redundant Rule Elimination

As discussed in subsection 4.1, insignificant rules usually refer to those covered-rules or equivalent ones, which are represented as the form of totally dependent relation among them (i.e., second-order rules). These second-order rules can be obtained by traditional mining methods, e.g., the Apriori algorithm. However, the computational cost is very high, because a huge number of second-order rules would be discovered when the context K is large. As we know, all interesting association rules can be derived from corresponding closed itemsets. Thus, we can also attain our reduction purpose by resorting to closed rule-set. Indeed, aggregating operations between the satisfying function f and the satisfied function h are closure ones over T and RS.

Property 4.2. *Let $X \in \rho(T)$ and $Y \in \rho(RS)$ in $K=(T, RS, S)$, mappings $c_{hf} : \rho(T) \to \rho(T)$ and $c_{fh} : \rho(RS) \to \rho(RS)$ are closure operators on power sets $\rho(T)$ and $\rho(RS)$ respectively, where $c_{hf}(X) = h \circ f(X) = h(f(X))$ and $c_{fh}(Y) = f \circ h(Y) = f(h(Y))$.*

Proof. Let $X_1 \subseteq X_2 \subseteq T$ and $Y_1 \subseteq Y_2 \subseteq RS$, in the following we will prove c_{hf} and c_{fh} are closure operations at three aspects.

Extension. For any rule $r \in Y_1$, we have $h(Y_1) \subseteq h(r)$ on the ground of the monotonic property of the satisfied function h. Similarly, $f \circ h(r) \subseteq f \circ h(Y_1)$ holds because f is an order-reversing function. Moreover, for any rule r, $r \in f \circ h(r)$ is always true. Thus, $r \in f \circ h(Y_1)$. This implies that $Y_1 \subseteq f \circ h(Y_1)$ holds.

Monotonicity. For any two rule-set $Y_1 \subseteq Y_2 \subseteq RS$, $Y_1 \subseteq Y_2$ implies $h(Y_2) \subseteq h(Y_1)$ in the light of the reverse monotonicity about h. Furthermore, we

have $f \circ h(Y_1) \subseteq f \circ h(Y_2)$, that is, the function c_{fh} is monotonic.

Idempotency. In terms of the extension property, one may note that $c_{fh}(Y_1) \subseteq c_{fh} \circ c_{fh}(Y_1)$, if $Y_1 \subseteq c_{fh}(Y_1)$. Additionally, $h(Y_1) \subseteq c_{hf} \circ h(Y_1)$ holds, because c_{hf} is monotonic. Further, $f \circ c_{hf} \circ h(Y_1) \subseteq f \circ h(Y_1)$, that is, $c_{fh} \circ c_{fh}(Y_1) \subseteq c_{fh}(Y_1)$. Consequently, $c_{fh} \circ c_{fh}(Y_1) = c_{fh}(Y_1)$.

On all accounts, $c_{fh} : \rho(RS) \to \rho(RS)$ is a closure operator on the power set $\rho(RS)$. In a similar vein, we also can prove the function $c_{hf} : \rho(T) \to \rho(T)$ is another closure operator on the power set $\rho(T)$.

On the basis of the closure operator $c_{fh} : \rho(RS) \to \rho(RS)$, a notion of closed rule-set, which is the foundation of our pruning approach, can be derived.

Definition 4.6. *In the context $K=(T, RS, S)$, for any rule-set $Rs \subseteq RS$, its closure is $c_{fh}(Rs)$. Additionally, Rs is called a closed rule-set if and only if its closure is itself, i.e., $Rs = c_{fh}(Rs)$.*

According to this definition, a rule-set Rs is a closed rule-set if there is no rule-set Rs' such that $Rs \subseteq Rs'$ and $h(Rs) = h(Rs')$. This gives us a good indication that a rule-set has the same property (e.g., *cover* and *support*) with its closure. As an illustration of this case, for rule-set $Rs=r_1 r_2$, its closure is $r_0 r_1 r_2$. Thus, it is not a closed rule-set. However, rule-set $r_6 r_7$ is closed for $c_{fh}(r_6 r_7) = r_6 r_7$.

As we know, all rule-sets can be induced from their corresponding closed rule-sets, and all association rules which are extracted from frequent rule-sets can also be explored from closed rule-sets (Pasquier et al., 2005). In addition, the number of closed rule-sets is typical smaller than that of rule-sets, and far less than second-order rules induced from them. Thus, in order to reduce redundancy, the only thing we need to do is to find those closed rule-sets in a given context K, instead of generating all second-order rules. Once the context K has been generated from D and its whole rule-set RS, closed rule-sets can be easily derived from K by adopting mature closed set mining algorithm, e.g., LCM (Uno et al., 2003) and CHARM (Zaki, 2004).

Proposition 4.1. *Let $K=(T, RS, S)$ be the context and CR be the set of closed rule-sets induced from K, For any rule $r \in RS$, r and its equivalent rules, together with its cover-rules, co-exist in the same closed rule-set $cr \in CR$, and $h(r) = h(cr)$.*

Proof. According to Definition 4.4 and Property 4.1, for any rule r, equation $h(r)=h(r')=h(Eq(r))$ holds, where r' is one of its equivalent ones. Since both r and its equivalent one r' are supported by the same transactions, they always co-occur in the same rule-set. This means that there is a closed rule-set cr in CR such that $Eq(r) \subseteq cr$. Assume that cr is the minimal closed rule-set with $Eq(r) \subseteq cr$, then we have $h(r) = h(cr)$. Otherwise if $h(r) \neq h(cr)$, there must exist another closed rule-set cr' such that $Eq(r) \subseteq cr' \subseteq cr$ according to the closed property. However, it is impossible because cr is the minimal one.

Now we will show the set Rs of cover-rules of r is also included within cr. For any cover-rule $r' \in Rs$, $h(r) \subseteq h(r')$ holds on the ground of definition. This implies a fact that any closed rule-sets cr containing r also includes its cover-rule r' at

the same time. That is to say, if $r \in cr$, then for any its cover-rule r', $r' \in cr$. Hence, $Rs \subseteq cr$ is satisfied.

As a consequence, this proposition holds on.

For example, rule r_6 is equivalent to r_7 and they co-exist in the closed rule-set $r_6 r_7$. Analogously, rules r_0, r_1 and r_2 are bound within the closed rule-set $r_0 r_1 r_2$, where r_0 is a cover-rule of r_1 and r_2. This proposition serves as a guide for us to discard useless rules in a manner of post-processing. Assume CR is the set of closed rule-sets induced from the context K, for each closed rule-set $cr \in CR$, if there have two elements r and r' in cr such that $h(r) = h(cr)$ and $h(cr) \subseteq h(r')$, then r is a covered-rule and r' is one of its cover-rule. At this case, r can be safely removed and the result will not be affected, because r' is preserved and $h(r) \subseteq h(r')$. However, if all elements r in the closed rule-set cr have the same support transactions, i.e., $h(r)=h(cr)$, rules in cr are equivalent to each other. Thus, only one rule with the most interesting is needed to be chosen, while others can be eliminated safely. If the cover of each rule r in cr is larger than $h(cr)$, then we will do nothing at this moment, except to omit it.

Since noise data may exist in data mining context, the dependent degree k between rules should be taken into consideration in filtering rules. The smaller the value of k is, the more rules will be removed and the less creditable the result

Box 2. Algorithm 2

Algorithm 2. Redundant rules elimination using closed rule-sets.
Input: A transaction-rule context $K=(T, RS, S)$, its set of closed rule-sets CR, and a pre-specified threshold k.
Output: A reduction representation of RS.
1). **For** each closed rule-set $cr \in CR$ **do**
2).   Sort cr according to the respective support of rule $r \in cr$ in an ascending order;
3).   **For** any rule r in the closed rule-set cr **do**
4).   **If** $h(cr)/h(r) \geq k$ **then**
5). $RS = RS \setminus \{r\}$;
6).   **End**;
7). **End**.

is. In practice, we should assign the dependent degree k with an appropriate value in the light of the specific problem on hand. After every closed rule-set has been processed, a minimal reduction representation of RS is achieved. Based on this principle, the pseudo-code of redundant rules elimination algorithm is presented as Algorithm 2 (Box 2).

This pruning algorithm works in a straightforward way. It begins with the first closed rule-set cr. For each closed set cr, all elements in it will be sorted according to their *supports* (i.e., the number of transactions supporting the corresponding rule) in an ascending order. After that, every rule r in cr, except the last one, will be processed one by one as follows (the If statement): the rule r is insignificant and would be removed from the whole rule-set RS if the ratio of the support of cr to that of r is larger than the pre-specified threshold k.

Asides from the sort criterion of support in line 2, other interesting measurements, such as confidence and length of rule, can also be used. One may notice that the last rule in each closed rule-set will not be processed (line 3). The reason behind it is that the current closed rule-set may only embody equivalent rules. If so, the last one is the most interesting and should be kept down. Otherwise, the support of the last rule is larger than that of the closed rule-set. At this point, the last one should not be discarded.

Assumed the number of closed rule-sets in CR is m, and there are n association rules in RS. Since the maximal number of rules in each closed rule-set is n, the time complexity of sort is $O(n \cdot \log n)$. Thus, the computational cost of the whole pruning algorithm is $O(mn \cdot \log n)$.

EXPERIMENTAL EVALUATION

In this section, the effectiveness of our method as a concise representation of rules is verified. Besides, its efficiency in eliminating redundancy is also compared with other classical methods, e.g., CHARM (Zaki, 2004), CBA (Liu et al., 1998) and the Apriori-like method (Berrado and Runger, 2007). All experiments described below were performed on a 2.8 GHz Pentium PC with 1GB of memory. The proposed algorithms were coded in VC++.

Table 4. Descriptions about real and synthetic datasets

Dataset	Number of items /attributes	Average size of trans- actions	Number of transactions/ objects
Chess	76	37	3,196
Mushroom	120	23	8,124
Pumsb	7,117	74	49,046
Pumsb*	7,117	50	49,046
T10I4D100K	1,000	10	100,000
T40I10D100K	1,000	40	100,000
Australian	15	15 (2)	690
Segment	20	20 (7)	2310
Vehicle	19	19 (4)	846
Lymph	19	19 (4)	148
Credit-a	16	16 (2)	690

Datasets

To roundly evaluate the proposed method, two group experiments were carried out. The first one is to prune insignificant association rules, while another group mainly removes useless association classification rules. To serve for this purpose, we have chosen eleven real and synthetic datasets for performance study. These datasets are widely used to evaluate performance of mining algorithms in literatures. The brief characteristics of these datasets, such as the total number of items, average size of transactions and the total number of transactions, are shown as Table 4. Except T10I4D100K and T40I10D100K, they are real ones and taken from the UCI Machine Learning Repository (Blake and Merz, 1998). T10I4D100K and T40I10D100K datasets are synthetic ones and generated with different parameters through using the data generator developed by the IBM Almaden Quest research group, which can be downloaded from the FIMI website (FIMI, 2003).

Among these eleven datasets in the table, the first six ones are used to validate effectiveness on association rules, while the rests are used to demonstrate that our method is capable of removing more insignificant classification rules and information will not be lost too much. In association rule mining, the four real datasets are very dense (i.e., a large number of items occurred very frequently in the transactions), and many long frequent itemsets would be induced from them when the support threshold is high. The rest two synthetic datasets (i.e., T10I4D100K and T40I10D100K) are relatively sparse. Note that the number within brackets in the last five datasets refers to the number of classes. More details about these datasets can be consulted the UCI Machine Learning website.

Experimental Settings

In experiments of the first group, our method is made a comparison with CHARM proposed by Zaki (2004), which is a traditional non-redundant rules mining algorithm using closed sets, on eliminating association rules. Additionally, CBA (Liu et al., 1998) is taken into consideration to prune classification rules in another group. CBA is a typical classifier using association rule mining technique. It removes non-predictive and over-fitting rules by virtue of information gain metric. Since both CHARM and CBA prune rules during the phase of rule generation, we only evaluate them with our method on compression ratio. In order to illustrate the proposed algorithm surpasses others in efficient aspect, the Apriori-like pruning algorithm is also adopted as the baseline, for this kind of method explores the dependent relation between rules and is similar to our method (Berrado and Runger, 2007).

Since our pruning method works in a manner of post-processing, some external tools or algorithms must be taken to produce rules from datasets. In experiments, the Apriori software developed by Borgelt (2000) and CBA are used to generate association and classification rules respectively. Specifically, our experimental procedure consists of three main steps. At first, each dataset D will be taken as input to be fed into the Apriori software (or CBA), and the result is the whole association (or classification) rule-set RS which will be pruned later. During the second step, a transaction-rule context K will be induced by Algorithm 1, whose inputs are the dataset D and its corresponding rule-set RS. Finally, the proposed elimination algorithm is performed on the rule-set RS by regulating dependent degree k. Thus, the final result is a desirable reduction of the original rule-set RS.

For evaluation criterion on association rule, two measurements are adopted to estimate the performance of pruning algorithms. The first metric is the number of rules, which is the most common one and widely used to weigh the effectiveness of a pruning algorithm. The less the number of rules is, the more effective the pruning algorithm is. In some literatures, the number of rules is represented as compression ratio, which is the proportion of the number of pruned rules to the total one (Baralis and Chiusano, 2004). Another criterion is computational time consumed in experiments. This parameter mainly measures the efficiency of pruning algorithms during the pruning stage. Moreover, classification capabilities, such as coverage and accuracy, are also taken into account in classification issue.

Experimental Results and Discussion

Association Rule Elimination

Table 5 presents the experimental results comparing our method with CHARM (Zaki, 2004) and Apriori-like method (i.e., meta-rule) (Berrado and Runger, 2007) on pruning useless association rules. In this table, the fourth column (i.e., Number of rules) denotes the number of association rules generated by traditional rule mining algorithm. From the results in Table 5, one can observe that the proposed method is competent for discarding most redundant rules and achieve a very low compression ratio. For example, the quantity of rules reduced by the proposed method is less than that of CHARM. This situation is more distinct when the dependent degree *k* gets a low value. It is worthy to mention that the quantity of rules obtained by the Apriori-like method is the same

with our method, as *k* was assigned to one. This is really true, because all meta-rules (i.e., one-way rules) can be derived from its corresponding closed sets.

Additionally, in experiments, we also find that the dependent degree *k* plays a vital role in eliminating useless rules. For instance, when *k* was set to 0.95, lots of rules, which would not be removed as *k*=1, were still deleted. However, this is not means that the smaller the dependent degree *k* is, the better the results are. The reason is some interesting information would be missing if *k* is too low.

Consumed time is another important criterion in evaluating the efficiency of pruning method. Since CHARM prevents insignificant rules from being generating during the mining phase, it does not work in a manner of post-pruning. Thus, we only compared our method with the Apriori-like one on the consumed time aspect. Table 6 lists the elapsed time of these two methods during the whole pruning procedure. According to the results, the proposed method took less time than the Apriori-like one on pruning rules. Consequently, it is more preferable in practice and has higher efficiency. As a matter of fact, it is not curious, for the Apriori-like algorithm not only need to identify all frequent rule-sets from the transaction-rule context, but also need to induce meta-rules from these mined frequent rule-sets. However, the only thing identified in our algorithm is closed rule-

Table 5. Number of association rules (Conf.=min. confidence, Sup.=min. support)

Dataset	Conf. (%)	Sup. (%)	Number of rules	CHARM	Meta-rule	Our proposed method			
						k=1.0	*k*=0.99	*k*=0.95	*k*=0.90
Chess	80	90	7,286	1,822	1,185	1,815	1,745	1,480	1,173
Mushroom	80	40	7,020	267	259	259	259	250	246
Pumsb	80	95	1,170	356	347	347	325	197	74
Pumsb*	80	60	2,358	192	152	152	138	115	70
T10I4D100K	80	0.5	749	524	519	519	515	480	458
T40I10D100K	80	1.5	9,049	6,258	6,251	6,251	6,251	6,085	4,369

Table 6. Comparison of elapsed time (s) on pruning association rules

Dataset	Meta-rule	Our proposed method
Chess	30.40	13.26
Mushroom	8.44	1.72
pumsb	39.01	2.53
pumsb	10.06	0.08
T10I4D100K	0.91	0.31
T40I10D100K	140.90	35.72

Table 7. Comparison of classification performance (%)

Dataset	Coverage				Accuracy			
	Total	CBA	Our method	CBA*	Total	CBA	Our method	CBA*
Australian	100	94.2	100	94.2	81.2	81.8	81.2	81.8
Segment	100	98.7	100	98.7	75.3	96.9	76.5	96.9
Vehicle	100	96.5	100	96.5	32.5	31.7	35.9	31.7
Lymph	100	96.5	100	96.5	73.3	73.3	73.3	73.3
Credit-a	100	92.8	100	92.8	89.9	85.9	86.1	85.9

Table 8. Comparison of number of classification rules and elapsed time

Dataset	Number of classification rules				Elapsed time (s)	
	Total	CBA	Our method	CBA*	Our method	Meta-rule
Australian	1,648	134	29	129	0.45	9.99
Segment	17,446	169	100	154	0.34	49.64
Vehicle	11,658	276	47	257	0.17	175.04
Lymph	4,062	36	14	36	0.26	571.92
Credit-a	4,226	167	67	167	1.83	-

sets, whose amount and computational cost are far less than those of frequent rule-sets, needless to say the generation of meta-rules.

Classification Rule Elimination

To validate the effectiveness of our method in classification issue, we further carried out experiments in comparison with CBA (Liu et al., 1998) and the Apriori-like method. CBA is a typical association classifier. Its pruning strategy is the distance measurement based on information gain. The experimental results on classification performance (coverage and accuracy) are provided in Table 7, where CBA* refers to the CBA classifier being performed our method again, after it eliminated insignificant rules using its strategy. In our experiments, the dependent degree k was set to one, i.e., $k=1.0$.

In terms of the experimental results, we can notice an important fact that information will not be lost at the coverage aspect, after the proposed method has been conducted. This mainly owes to the totally dependent property inhabiting among rules inherently. Although the accurate ratio induced by our method is lower than CBA at two cases, it is normal because the estimation strategy is standard voting. Similarly, the experimental results also tell us that the performance (i.e., coverage and accuracy) induced by our method and the Apriori-like one are the same with each other when $k=1$. Due to space limitations, the results have not been listed in here.

As illustrated in Table 8, the proposed method is also superior to CBA from the view of compression ratio. The number of rules induced by our method is less than those of CBA. Additionally, in comparison with CBA and CBA*, one may note that redundant rules still exist in the CBA classifier after using its own pruning strategy. This means that our method can remove more superfluous rules.

Despite that our method has the same effectiveness with the Apriori-like method, it has higher efficient. For our method, the pruning operation will be finished within several seconds in experiments. However, the time cost of the Apriori-like method is soaring up with the number of meta-rules generated during the pruning phase. Especially, in the case of the *Credit-a* dataset, a considerable number of meta-rules had been yielded and the pruning operation had lasted for longer than an hour without being ended.

CONCLUSION

In this chapter, we proposed an efficient post-processing method to remove superfluous rules from rule base. The primary idea behind our method is that it exploits the dependent relation inherently residing among rules to eliminate redundancy. This dependent relation is a closed one, and can be represented as second-order rule form. This means that in our method knowledge is used to manage knowledge itself.

Specifically, our pruning procedure consists of three stages. At first, a transaction-rule context will be derived from a given database and its rule-sets according to the supported relation between them. Based on this context, closed rule-sets can be obtained by using traditional closed set mining tools. After that, the pruning operation of rules will be conducted on the original rule set by virtue of these closed rule-sets. To validate the effectiveness of our method, experiments on several real and synthetic datasets have been carried out. The experimental results show that our method not only discards a large number of useless rules, but also has higher efficiency in comparing with the Apriori-like one.

Although the computational cost of our method is lower than the Apriori-like one, it is still relatively higher. Particularly, when the size of database and the number of mined rules are large, it will take much more time to generate transaction-rule context. Thus, our future work will be put on exploiting sampling technique or special data structure to further improve the efficiency of our method.

ACKNOWLEDGMENT

The authors would like to thank anonymous reviewers for their valuable comments which greatly improve the clarity of this paper. This work is supported by the Science Foundation for Young Teachers of Northeast Normal University (20081003).

REFERENCES

Agrawal, R., Imielinski, T., & Swami, T. (1993). Mining association rules between sets of items in large databases. *In Proceedings of the ACM Int. Conf. on Management of Data*, Washington, D.C., May 1993 (pp. 207-216).

Ashrafi, M. Z., Taniar, D., & Smith, K. (2007). Redundant association rules reduction techniques.

International Journal of Business Intelligence and Data Mining, 2(1), 29-63.

Baesens, B., Viaene, S., & Vanthienen, J. (2000). Post-processing of association rules. *In Proceedings of the Sixth ACM SIGKDD International Conference on Knowledge Discovery and Data Mining (KDD'2000),* Boston, Massachusetts, 20-23 Aug 2000 (pp. 2-8).

Baralis, E., & Chiusano, S. (2004). Essential Classification Rule Sets. *ACM Transactions on Database Systems, 29*(4), 635-674.

Baralis, E., & Psaila, G. (1997). Designing templates for mining association rules, *Journal of Intelligent Information Systems, 9*(1), 7-32.

Bathoorn, R., Koopman, A., & Siebes, A. (2006). *Frequent Patterns that Compress.* Institute of Information and Computing Sciences, Technical reports, UU-CS-2006-048, Utrecht University.

Bayardo, R. J. (1998). Efficiently Mining Long Patterns from Databases. *In Proceedings of the ACM SIGMOD International Conference on Management of Data* (pp. 85-93).

Berrado, A., & Runger, G.C. (2007). Using meta-rules to organize and group discovered association rules. *Data Mining and Knowledge Discovery, 14*(3), 409-431.

Berzal, F., & Cubero, J.C. (2007). Guest editors' introduction, *Data & Knowledge Engineering, Special section on Intelligent Data Mining, 60,* 1-4.

Blake, L. C., & Merz, J. C. (1998). *UCI Repository of Machine Learning Databases.* Department of Information and Computer Science, University of California, Irvine, http://www.ics.uci.edu/~mlearn/MLRepository.html.

Borgelt, C. (2000). *Apriori software.* Available from http://www.borgelt.net/software.html.

Boulicaut, J. F., Bykowski, A., & Rigotti, C. (2003). Free-sets: a condensed representation of boolean data for the approximation of frequency queries. *Data Mining and Knowledge Discovery, 7*(1), 5-22.

Brijs, T., Vanhoof, K., & Wets, G. (2000). Reducing Redundancy in Characteristic Rule Discovery By Using Integer Programming Techniques. *Intelligent Data Analysis Journal, 4*(3), 229-240.

Brin, S., Motwani, R., & Silverstein, C. (1998). Beyond market baskets: Generalizing association rules to dependence rules. *Data Mining and Knowledge Discovery, 2*(1), 39-68.

Brin, S., Motwani, R., Ullman, J. D., & Tsur, S. (1997). Dynamic itemset counting and implication rules for market basket data. *In Proceedings of the ACM SIGMOD Conference on Management of Data,* May 13-15, Tucson, Arizona, USA, 1997 (pp. 255-264).

Bruha, I. (2000). From machine learning to knowledge discovery: Survey of preprocessing and postprocessing. *Intelligent Data Analysis, 4*(3-4), 363-374.

Calders, T., & Goethals, B. (2007). Non-derivable itemset mining. *Data Mining and Knowledge Discovery, 14,* 171-206.

Calders, T., Rigotti, C., & Boulicaut, J. F. (2006). A Survey on Condensed Representations for Frequent Sets, In: J.F. Boulicaut, L.D. Raedt, & H. Mannila (Ed.), *Constraint-based mining and Inductive Databases* (pp. 64-80), Springer.

Ceglar, A., & Roddick, J.F. (2006). Association mining. *ACM Computing Survey, 38*(2), No.5.

Chawla, S., Davis, J., & Pandey G. (2004). On local pruning of association rules using directed hypergraphs. In Proceedings of the 20th International Conference on Data Engineering (pp. 832-841).

Cheng, J., Ke, Y., & Ng, W. (2008). Effective elimination of redundant association rules, *Data Mining and Knowledge Discovery, 16,* 221-249.

Domingues, M. A., & Rezende, S. O. (2005). Post-processing of Association Rules using Taxonomies. *In Proceedings of Portuguese Conference on Artificial Intelligence* (pp. 192-197).

Fayyad, U., Piatetsky-Shapiro, G., & Smyth, P. (1996). From data mining to knowledge discovery in databases. *AI Magazine, 17*, 37-54.

Fernádez, M. Z., Menasalvas, E., Marbán, O., Peña, J. M., & Millán S. (2001). Minimal Decision Rules Based on the Apriori Algorithm, *Internal Journal of Applied Mathematics and Computer Science, 11*(3), 691-704.

FIMI Dataset Repository. (2003). Available from http://fimi.cs.helsinki.fi/data/.

Geng, L., & Hamilton, H. J. (2006). Interestingness Measures for Data Mining: A Survey. *ACM Computing Surveys, 38*(3), No.9.

Jacquenet, F., Largeron, C., & Udrea, C. (2006). Efficient Management of Non Redundant Rules in Large Pattern Bases: A Bitmap Approach. *In Proceedings of the International Conference on Enterprise Information Systems*, 2006 (pp. 208-215).

Jaroszewicz, S., & Simovici, D.A. (2002). Pruning Redundant Association Rules Using Maximum Entropy Principle. *In Proceedings of the 6th Pacific-Asia Conference on Knowledge Discovery and Data Mining*, 2002 (pp. 135-147).

Klemettinen, M., Mannila, H., Ronkainen, P., Toivonen, H., & Verkamo, A.I. (1994). Finding interesting rules from large sets of discovered association rules. *In Proceedings of the Third International Conference on Information and Knowledge Management (CIKM'94)*, Gaithersburg, Maryland, USA (pp. 401-408).

Kryszkiewicz, M. (1998). Representative Association Rules and Minimum Condition Maximum Consequence Association Rules. *In Proceedings of the Principles of Data Mining and Knowledge Discovery Conference* (pp. 361-369).

Kryszkiewicz, M. (2005). Generalized disjunction-free representation of frequent patterns with negation. *Journal of Experimental and Theoretical Artificial Intelligence, 17*(1-2), 63-82.

Li, J. (2006). On Optimal Rule Discovery. *IEEE Transactions on Knowledge and Data Engineer, 18*(4), 460-471.

Li, W., Han, J., & Pei, J. (2001). CMAR: Accurate and Efficient Classification Based on Multiple Class-Association Rules, *In Proceedings of the 2001 IEEE International Conference on Data Mining*, 2001 (pp. 369-376).

Liu, B., Hsu, W., & Ma, Y. (1998). Integrating Classification and Association Rule Mining. In Proceedings of the 4th International Conference on Knowledge Discovery and Data Mining (pp. 27-31).

Liu, B., Hsu, W., & Ma, Y. (1999). Pruning and summarizing the discovered association. *In Proceedings of the 5th ACM SIGKDD International Conference on Knowledge Discovery and Data Mining*, 1999, Philadelphia, Penn (pp. 125-134).

Palshikar, G. K., Kale, M. S., & Apte, M. M. (2007). Association rules mining using heavy itemsets. *Data & Knowledge Engineering, 61*(1), 93-113.

Pasquier, N., Taouil, R., Bastide, Y., Stumme, G., & Lakhal, L. (2005). Generating a Condensed Representation for Association Rules. *Journal of Intelligent Information Systems, 24*(1), 29-60.

Srikant, R., & Agrawal, R. (1995). Mining Generalized Association Rules. *In Proceedings of the 1995 Int. Conf. Very Large Data Bases, Zurich, Switzerland*, 1995 (pp. 407--419).

Toivonen, H., Klemettinen, M., Ronkainen, P., Hätönen, K., & Mannila, H. (1995). Pruning and Grouping of Discovered Association Rules. *In Proceedings of ECML-95 Workshop on Statistics, Machine Learning, and Discovery in Databases*, Heraklion, Crete, Greece, 1995 (pp. 47-52).

Uno, T., Asai, T., Arimura, H. & Uchida, Y. (2003). LCM: An Efficient Algorithm for Enumerating Frequent Closed Item Sets. *In Proceedings of ICDM'03 Workshop on Frequent Itemset Mining Implementations* (pp. 1-10).

Waitman, L. R., Fisher, D. H., & King P. H. (2006). Bootstrapping rule induction to achieve rule stability and reduction. *Journal of Intelligent Information System, 27,* 49–77.

Webb, G. I., & Zhang, S. (2005). *K*-Optimal Rule Discovery. *Data Mining and Knowledge Discovery, 10*(1), 39-79.

Zaki, M. J. (2004). Mining Non-Redundant Association Rules. *Data Mining and Knowledge Discovery, 9,* 223-248.

Chapter VI
A Conformity Measure Using Background Knowledge for Association Rules:
Application to Text Mining

Hacène Cherfi
INRIA Sophia Antipolis, France

Amedeo Napoli
LORIA—INRIA, France

Yannick Toussaint
LORIA—INRIA, France

ABSTRACT

A text mining process using association rules generates a very large number of rules. According to experts of the domain, most of these rules basically convey a common knowledge, that is, rules which associate terms that experts may likely relate to each other. In order to focus on the result interpretation and discover new knowledge units, it is necessary to define criteria for classifying the extracted rules. Most of the rule classification methods are based on numerical quality measures. In this chapter, the authors introduce two classification methods: the first one is based on a classical numerical approach, that is, using quality measures, and the other one is based on domain knowledge. They propose the second original approach in order to classify association rules according to qualitative criteria using domain model as background knowledge. Hence, they extend the classical numerical approach in an effort to combine data mining and semantic techniques for post mining and selection of association rules. The authors mined a corpus of texts in molecular biology and present the results of both approaches, compare them, and give a discussion on the benefits of taking into account a knowledge domain model of the data.

INTRODUCTION

From the data mining point of view, texts are complex data giving raise to interesting challenges. First, texts may be considered as weakly structured, compared with databases that rely on a predefined schema. Moreover, texts are written in natural language, carrying out implicit knowledge, and ambiguities. Hence, the representation of the content of a text is often only partial and possibly noisy. One solution for handling a text or a collection of texts in a satisfying way is to take advantage of a knowledge model of the domain of the texts, for guiding the extraction of knowledge units from the texts.

In this chapter, we introduce a knowledge-based text mining process (KBTM) relying on the knowledge discovery process (KDD) defined in [Fayyad *et al.*, 1996]. The KBTM process relies on an interactive loop, where the analyst – an expert of the text domain – controls and guides the mining process. The objective of the mining process is to enrich the knowledge model of the text domain, and, in turn, to improve the capability of the knowledge-based text mining process itself.

Following a natural language processing of the texts described in [Cherfi *et al.*, 2006], the text mining process (also denoted by TM in the following) is applied to a binary table Texts × Keyterms, and produces a set of association rules (AR in the following). The set "Keyterms" includes a set of keyterms giving a kind of summary of the content of each text. The extraction of association rules is carried out thanks to a *frequent itemset* algorithm (namely the Close algorithm [Pasquier *et al.*, 1999]). Association rules show some advantages, among which the facts that AR are easily understandable and that they highlight regularities existing within the set of texts.

Two text mining approaches based on association rules are studied hereafter. The first approach is based on the use of statistical quality measures for classifying the extracted rules [Cherfi et al.,

2006]. A set of five quality measures is introduced, each of them expressing some particular aspects of the texts: e.g. rare keyterms, functional dependencies, or probabilistic correlations between keyterms. One limitation of this approach is due to the numerical characteristics of the classification process, which takes into account the distribution of the keyterms, and ignores the semantics carried by the keyterms. By contrast, a second approach is based on a domain knowledge model of the texts which is used to classify the extracted association rules. The knowledge model is a pair $(K, \sqsubseteq)$ where K is a finite set of keyterms and $\sqsubseteq$ is a specialisation relation (*i.e.*, a partial ordering). Hence, the quality of a rule depends on the conformity of the rule with respect to the knowledge model: a rule is interesting if it includes semantic relations that are not already known in the knowledge model. Thus, the knowledge model is used to guide the interpretation and the classification of the extracted association rules. This KBTM approach is original and relies on a qualitative approach rather than on a more classical approach based on statistical quality measures. Two experiments show that the KBTM approach gives substantial and good quality results, opening new perspectives in the difficult field of text mining. The objective of these experiments is to show how far our proposed Conformity measure is consistent with the text mining task in a specific domain (here molecular biology).

This chapter is organised as follows. Firstly, we introduce the context of association rule extraction for text mining, and we present and discuss an example, based on statistical quality measures. Then, we introduce the principles of the KBTM process. We analyse thanks to an example –the same as in the first part of the chapter– the KBTM process for the so-called simple and complex extracted AR. The following section sets up an experiment and a qualitative analysis based on real-world collection of texts with the help of an analyst. The AR are classified according to the conformity measure, in contrast with five statistical measure classifications. We continue the chapter with a discussion on the benefits of the KBTM approach, and we mention some related work. The chapter ends with a conclusion and draws future work.

EXTRACTION OF ASSOCIATION RULES FOR TEXT MINING

Text Processing for Data Mining Preparation

In our experiments, we dealt with a collection of texts (hereafter called corpus) in molecular biology. Basically, we start with a set of bibliographical records characterised by contextual metadata, *e.g.*, title, author(s), date, status (whether published or not), keywords, etc. Hereafter, we explain how we get the keyterms associated with each text.

Extracting textual fields in the sources: A first processing of this collection of records consists in extracting two textual fields, the title and the abstract.

Part-of-speech (POS) tagging: It is a natural language processing (NLP) technique which associates with each word of the texts a linguistic tag corresponding to its grammatical category (noun, adjective, verb, etc.). A POS-tagger needs a learning phase with a manually tagged vocabulary. A POS-tagger basically uses a statistical model to learn how to predict the category of a word with respect to the preceding word categorisation. Several taggers exist for English and show high performance of correctness [Paroubek, 2007]. For example, sentence (1) extracted from one of our texts gives the tagged sentence (2):

1. Two resistant strains were isolated after four rounds of selection.

2. Two/CD resistant/JJ strains/NNS:pl were/ VBD isolated/VBN after/IN four/CD rounds/NNS:pl of/IN selection/NN.

Terminological indexing: In our experiments, the texts have been processed and represented by a set of keyterms. A keyterm is a noun phrase (*i.e.*, one to many words) of our vocabulary which can be associated with a domain concept of our knowledge model, thus, it ensures the transition from the linguistic to the knowledge level.

Keyterm identification and variants: We have used the FASTR [Jacquemin, 1994] terminological extraction system for identifying the keyterms of our vocabulary in the text. It allows us to recognise a keyterm in several variant forms. For example, the expression "transfer of capsular biosynthesis genes" is considered as a variant form of the keyterm "gene transfer" which belongs to the vocabulary. However, all the variants are not acceptable; NLP meta-rules are used to keep the variants preserving the initial sense of the keyterm. The keyterm variants are identified using the meta-rules. A meta-rule is a transformation rule operating on the grammatical description of a keyterm and the linguistically authorised variation of this description. For example, the expression "transfer of genes" is recognised as a variation of the keyterm "gene transfer" (which belongs to the vocabulary) by a *permutation* meta-rule of "gene" and "transfer". The expression "transfer of capsular biosynthesis genes" is recognised as well by applying an *insertion* meta-rule (of "capsular biosynthesis"). In this way, the NLP keyterm identification contributes to reduce the word dispersion in the description of a text by unifying variants to a single keyterm.

Association Rules and Statistical Quality Measures

Let $T = \{t_1, t_2, ..., t_m\}$ be a set of m texts and $K = \{k_1, k_2, ..., k_n\}$ a set of n keyterms associated with these texts. An association rule is a weighted implication such as $A \rightarrow B$ where $A = \{k_1, k_2, ..., k_p\}$ (the *body*) and $B = \{k_{p+1}, k_{p+2}, ..., k_q\}$ (the *head*). The rule $A \rightarrow B$ means that if a text contains $\{k_1, k_2, ..., k_p\}$ then it tends to contain also $\{k_{p+1}, k_{p+2}, ..., k_q\}$ with a probability given by the confidence of the rule. Several algorithms aim at extracting association rules: Apriori [Agrawal *et al.*, 1996] or Close [Pasquier et *al.*, 1999] that will be used hereafter. The support and the confidence are two quality measures related to association rules that are used to reduce the number of the extracted units, hence reducing the complexity of the extraction process. The support of a rule $A \rightarrow B$ measures the number of texts containing both keyterms of A and B. The union of the keyterm sets A and B is denoted by $A \sqcap B$. The support may be normalised by the total number of texts. The confidence of a rule is defined by the ratio between the number of texts containing the keyterms in $A \sqcap B$, and the number of texts containing the keyterms in A. The confidence is seen as the conditional probability $P(B/A)$. The confidence of a rule measures the proportion of examples and counterexamples of the rule. A counterexample states that there exist texts having all the keyterms of A, but not necessarily all the keyterms of B. When the confidence of a rule is 1, the rule is *exact*, otherwise it is *approximate*. Two thresholds are defined, σ_s for the minimum support, and σ_c for the minimum confidence. A rule is valid whenever its support is greater than σ_s and its confidence is greater than σ_c.

Considering a rule such as $A \rightarrow B$, if A and B are frequent keyterm sets (*i.e.*, their support is above the σ_s threshold), then they are shared by a large proportion of texts, and the probabilities $P(A), P(B)$, and $P(A \sqcap B)$ are high (here probability stands for the number of texts containing a given keyterm set out of the total number of the texts). The importance of such frequent keyterm sets is rather small, from the KDD point of view. By contrast, when A and B are rare, i.e. they have a low probability, then these keyterm sets are shared by a low number of texts, i.e. the keyterms in A and B may be related in the context of the mined text set. However, the support and the confidence are not always sufficient for classifying extracted

association rules in a meaningful way. This reason leads to introduce a number of other statistical quality measures attached to the rules enlightening some particular aspects on the rules [Lavrac *et al.,*1999]. Five of these quality measures are presented hereafter, and have been used in our two experiments.

1. The *interest* measures the degree of independence of the keyterm sets A and B, and is defined by interest$(A \rightarrow B) = P(A \sqcap B)/P(A) \times P(B)$. The interest is symmetrical (interest$(A \rightarrow B)$ = interest$(A \rightarrow B)$) and has its range in the interval $[0, +\infty[$. It is equal to 1 whenever the "events" A and B are statistically independent. The more A and B are incompatible, the more $P(A \sqcap B)$, and hence the interest, tend to 0;

2. The *conviction* allows us to select among the rules $A \rightarrow B$ and $A \rightarrow B$ the one having the less counterexamples. The conviction is defined by conviction$(A \rightarrow B) = P(A) \times P(\neg B)/P(A \sqcap \neg B)$. The conviction is not symmetrical, and has its range in $[0, +\infty[$. It denotes a dependency between A and B whenever it is greater than 1, independence whenever it is equal to 1, and no dependency at all whenever it is lower than 1. The conviction is not computable for exact rules because $P(A \sqcap \neg B)$ is equal to 0 (there is no counterexample for exact rules);

3. The *dependency* measures the distance between the confidence of the rule and the independence case: dependency$(A \rightarrow B) = |P(B/A) - P(B)|$. This measure has its range in $[0, 1[$, where a dependency close to 0 (respectively to 1) means that A and B are independent (respectively dependent);

4. The *novelty* is defined by novelty$(A \rightarrow B) = P(A \sqcap B) - P(A) \times P(B)$, and has its range within $]-1, 1[$, with a negative value whenever $P(A \sqcap B) < P(A) \times P(B)$. The novelty tends to -1 for rules with a low support, i.e. $P(A \sqcap B) \simeq 0$. The novelty is symmetrical

although the rule A → B may have more counterexamples than the rule B → A. It leads to the definition of the following measure;

5. The *satisfaction* measure is defined by satisfaction(A → B) = P(¬B) − P(¬B|A)/P(¬B). The satisfaction has its range in [−∞, 1], and is equal to 0 whenever A and B are independent. The satisfaction cannot be used for classifying exact rules because, in this case, its value is equal to 1.

Using Quality Measures on a Small Example

An example borrowed from [Pasquier *et al.*, 1999] will be used to illustrate the behaviour of the statistical quality measures introduced above. Let us consider six texts $\{t_1, t_2, t_3, t_4, t_5, t_6\}$ described by a set of five keyterms, namely {a, b, c, d, e}. So the text t_1 is described by the keyterm set {b, c, e} (see Table 1), and hereafter more simply denoted by the bce. The extraction of the association rules has been performed with the Close algorithm [Pasquier *et al.*, 1999]. Twenty association rules, numbered $r_1, \ldots, r_{20}$, have their support greater than the threshold $\sigma_s = 1/6$ (where 6 is the total number of texts), and their confidence is greater than $\sigma_c = 0.1$ (or 10%). The set of extracted association rules is given in Table 2. The rules have been extracted from closed frequent keyterm sets. The Close algorithm is based on levelwise search

of *closed frequent* keyterm sets in the binary table Texts × Keyterms, starting from the smallest closed keyterm sets {ac, be} to the largest closed keyterm set abce. A closed frequent keyterm set corresponds to a maximal set of keyterms shared by a given subset of texts, with a support greater than the σ_s threshold. Once the closed frequent keyterm sets have been extracted, the association rules of the form $P_2 \rightarrow P_1 \setminus P_2$ may be derived, where for example b → ce stands for "b → bce \ b". The extracted association rules A → B have a minimal *body*, i.e. A corresponds to a generator, and a maximal head, i.e. B corresponds to a closed set for the Galois connection associated with the relation Texts × Keyterms (see for example [Bastide *et al.*, 2000]). For example, the association rules b → e and b → c ∧ e are extracted, because the corresponding keyterm sets be and bce are closed sets in the Galois connection.

The classification of the rules according to the different quality measures is given in Table 3. In each column of the table, the rules are classified according to the value of the measure in a decreasing order. Such a rule classification may be presented to an analyst, either for the whole set of measures or only one particular measure. An algorithm for classifying extracted association rules according to these quality measures (and their roles) is proposed in [Cherfi *et al.*, 2006].

Table 1.The textual database

Texts	Keyterms
t_1	acd
t_2	boo
t_3	abce
t_4	be
t_5	abce
t_6	bce

Table 2.The set of 20 valid AR

id	Rule	id	Rule
r_1	b → e	r_{11}	a → c
r_2	b → c ∧ e	r_{12}	b ∧ c → a ∧ e
r_3	a ∧ b → c ∧ e	r_{13}	d → a ∧ c
r_4	a → b ∧ c ∧ e	r_{14}	c → b ∧ e
r_5	b ∧ c → e	r_{15}	c → a ∧ d
r_6	b → a ∧ c ∧ e	r_{16}	c → a ∧ b ∧ e
r_7	e → b ∧ c	r_{17}	c ∧ e → b
r_8	a ∧ e → b ∧ c	r_{18}	c ∧ e → a ∧ b
r_9	a → c ∧ d	r_{19}	e → b
r_{10}	e → a ∧ b ∧ c	r_{20}	c → a

Table3.Statistical measures for the 20 valid AR in a decreasing order

id	support	id	confidence	id	interest	id	conviction	id	dependence	id	novelty	id	satisfaction
r_1	5	r_1	1.000	r_9	2.000	r_7	1.667	r_{13}	0.500	r_1	0.139	r_1	1.000
r_2	5	r_3	1.000	r_{13}	2.000	r_2	1.667	r_3	0.333	r_{19}	0.139	r_3	1.000
r_6	5	r_5	1.000	r_3	1.500	r_{12}	1.333	r_8	0.333	r_2	0.111	r_5	1.000
r_7	5	r_8	1.000	r_8	1.500	r_{18}	1.333	r_1	0.167	r_3	0.111	r_8	1.000
r_{10}	5	r_{11}	1.000	r_{12}	1.500	r_9	1.250	r_5	0.167	r_5	0.111	r_{11}	1.000
r_{14}	5	r_{13}	1.000	r_{18}	1.500	r_{20}	1.250	r_9	0.167	r_7	0.111	r_{13}	1.000
r_{15}	5	r_{17}	1.000	r_1	1.200	r_6	1.111	r_{11}	0.167	r_8	0.111	r_{17}	1.000
r_{16}	5	r_{19}	1.000	r_2	1.200	r_{10}	1.111	r_{12}	0.167	r_9	0.111	r_{19}	1.000
r_{19}	5	r_2	0.800	r_5	1.200	r_{16}	1.111	r_{17}	0.167	r_{11}	0.111	r_2	0.400
r_{20}	5	r_7	0.800	r_6	1.200	r_{15}	1.042	r_{18}	0.167	r_{12}	0.111	r_7	0.400
r_5	4	r_{14}	0.800	r_7	1.200	r_4	1.000	r_{19}	0.167	r_{13}	0.111	r_{12}	0.250
r_{12}	4	r_4	0.667	r_{10}	1.200	r_{14}	0.833	r_2	0.133	r_{17}	0.111	r_{18}	0.250
r_{17}	4	r_{20}	0.600	r_{11}	1.200	r_1	0.000	r_7	0.133	r_{18}	0.111	r_9	0.200
r_{18}	4	r_{12}	0.500	r_{15}	1.200	r_3	0.000	r_{20}	0.100	r_{20}	0.111	r_{20}	0.200
r_4	3	r_{18}	0.500	r_{16}	1.200	r_5	0.000	r_6	0.067	r_6	0.056	r_6	0.100
r_9	3	r_6	0.400	r_{17}	1.200	r_8	0.000	r_{10}	0.067	r_{10}	0.056	r_{10}	0.100
r_{11}	3	r_{10}	0.400	r_{19}	1.200	r_{11}	0.000	r_{16}	0.067	r_{16}	0.056	r_{16}	0.100
r_3	2	r_{16}	0.400	r_{20}	1.200	r_{13}	0.000	r_{14}	0.033	r_{15}	0.028	r_{15}	0.040
r_8	2	r_9	0.333	r_4	1.000	r_{17}	0.000	r_{15}	0.033	r_4	0.000	r_4	0.000
r_{13}	1	r_{15}	0.200	r_{14}	0.960	r_{19}	0.000	r_4	0.000	r_{14}	-0.028	r_{14}	-0.200

CONFORMITY OF AN ASSOCIATION RULE WITH RESPECT TO A KNOWLEDGE MODEL

Conformity for a Simple Rule

Definition 1. (Knowledge Model)

A knowledge model, denoted by (K, ⊑), is a finite, directed graph with K standing for the set of vertices (the keyterms), and the relation ⊑ defining the edges of the graph and the partial ordering over the keyterms in K. For each x, y ∈ K, x ⊑ y means that each instance of the keyterm concept x is also an instance of the keyterm concept y.

The principle of classifying AR according to their conformity with a knowledge model is stated as follows: we assign a high value of conformity to any association rule A → B that is "represented" in (K, ⊑) with a relation A ⊑ B existing between the keyterms a_i ∈ A and b_j ∈ B, i, j ≥ 1. We suppose in the following of this section that the rules are simple in the sense that their *body* and *head* are restricted to a single keyterm, for example b → e. The so-called complex rules where the *body* and/or the *head* are composed of more than one keyterm are considered in section 3.4.

Definition 2. (Conformity for a Simple AR with the Knowledge Model)

Let k_1, k_2 be in K, and let k_1 → k_2 be a valid AR. The conformity measure of k_1 → k_2 with (K, ⊑) is defined by the probability of finding out a path from k_1 to k_2 – called hereafter the probability *transition from k_1 to k_2 – in the directed graph of $(K, \sqsubseteq)$. This path can be composed of one to several edges.*

If we consider that updating the knowledge model consists in introducing new keyterms and new relations between keyterms in K, then an association rule x→y is conform to $(K, \sqsubseteq)$ (i.e., it has a high value of conformity) if the relation $x \sqsubseteq y$ exists in $(K, \sqsubseteq)$. Otherwise, the rule is not conform to the knowledge model (i.e., its conformity value is low). Indeed, we have to notice that a rule x→y extracted within the text mining process is not added to $(K, \sqsubseteq)$ without the control of the analyst in charge of updating a knowledge model of his domain. Any knowledge unit update is supervised by the analyst. The computation of the conformity is based on the principles of the spreading activation theory [Collins & Loftus,1975] stating that the propagation of an information marker through the graph of the knowledge model from a given vertex, say k_1, to another vertex, say k_2, relies on the strength associated to the marker. The value of the strength depends on: (i) the length of the path, and (ii) on the number of reachable keyterms starting from k_1 in $(K, \sqsubseteq)$. The strength of the marker monotonically decreases with respect to these two factors.

Definition 3. (Calculation of the Conformity Measure for Simple Rules)

The conformity of a simple rule k_1→k_2 is defined as the transition probability from the keyterm k_1 to the keyterm k_2, and is dependent on the minimal path length between k_1 and k_2, and the centrality of k_1 in $(K, \sqsubseteq)$ which depends on how many keyterms are related to k_1 in $(K \setminus k_1)$.

Transition Probability

Given the domain knowledge model $(K, \sqsubseteq)$, a probability transition table is set and used as a basis of the conformity calculation. The prob-

ability transition of k_i and k_j depends on the minimal distance $d(k_i, k_j)$ between a keyterm k_i and a keyterm k_j in $(K, \sqsubseteq)$. We distinguish two particular cases:

1. For each k_i, $d(k_i,k_i) = 1$ in order to take into account the reflexivity of the relation $\sqsubseteq$, and to avoid abnormally high probabilities in a case where there is no outgoing edge from k_i (as illustrated by the vertex c in Figure 1);

2. If it does not exist a path from a keyterm k_i to a keyterm k_j, then we set a "minimal" (non zero) transition probability by using $d(k_i,k_j) = 2N+1$, where N is the cardinal of the set of keyterms in K.

The transition probability from k_i to k_j, denoted by $Cty(k_i,k_j)$, defines the Conformity measure of the rule k_i→k_j, and relies on the product of two elements: (i) the distance from k_i to k_j, and (ii) a normalisation factor, denoted by $\delta(k_i)$. Moreover, two additional principles are used:

1. The higher the distance between two keyterms k_i and k_j is, the lower the conformity for k_i→k_j is;

2. The normalisation factor of a keyterm k_i depends on all the keyterms in K, either they are reachable from k_i or not. Putting things altogether, the formula for calculating the conformity for a simple rule is stated as follows: $Cty(k_i,k_j) = [d(k_i,k_j) \times \delta(k_i)]^{-1}$ where the normalisation factor of k_i is: $\delta(k_i) = \Sigma_{x \in K} 1/d(k_i,x)$.

Hence, $\delta(k_i)$ depends on the number of outgoing edges from k_i in K: the higher the number of outgoing edges from k_i is, the lower $\delta(k_i)$ is. In accordance, when there is no outgoing edge from a keyterm k_i; this keyterm k_i becomes "predominant" because the highest transition probability for k_i is the reflexive transition as $d(k_i,k_i) = 1$. The

Figure 1. The knowledge model **K**.

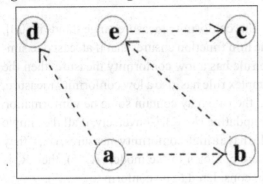

normalisation factor $\delta(k_i)$ is computed only once for each keyterm k_i of the knowledge model, and the following equation holds: $\Sigma_{x \in K} Cty(k_i, x) = 1$.

A Small Example for Simple AR

Let Figure 1 be an example of a knowledge model, where an edge between k_i and k_j vertices is interpreted as the specialisation relation $k_i \sqsubseteq k_j$. Based on this model, we may compute the conformity related to each transition as shown in Table 4. Next, we provide details for the computation of the conformity measure for two examples: firstly between a and c where there exists a path in the model, and secondly between c and d, where a path is missing in $(K, \sqsubseteq)$.

$$Cty(a, c) = [d(a,c) \times \Sigma_{x \in \{a,b,c,d,e\}} 1/d(a,x)]^{-1}$$
$$= [d(a,c) \times (1/d(a,a) + 1/d(a,b) + 1/d(a,c) + 1/d(a,d) + 1/d(a,e))]^{-1}$$
$$= [3 \times (1 + 1 + 1/3 + 1 + 1/2)]^{-1} = 2/23 = 0.09$$

$$Cty(c, d) = [d(c,d) \times \Sigma_{x \in \{a,b,c,d,e\}} 1/d(c,x)]^{-1}$$
$$= [d(c,d) \times (1/d(c,a) + 1/d(c,b) + 1/d(c,c) + 1/d(c,d) + 1/d(c,e))]^{-1}$$
$$= [11 \times (1/11 + 1/11 + 1 + 1/11 + 1/11)]^{-1} = 1/15$$
$$= 0.07$$

Once the computation of the Table 4 is completed, the conformity for each simple rule $k_i \rightarrow k_j$ is given by looking up to the corresponding row i and column j of this table. From the previous example given in Table 2: r_1, r_{19} and r_{11}, r_{20} are two pairs of symmetrical simple rules. Hence, the Table 4 gives their conformity as shown in Box 1.

According to the conformity measure – the classification of the rules is presented in the increasing order – the interesting rules have the lowest values in conformity with $(K, \sqsubseteq)$. For the four previous simple rules, the classification is established as follows: $\{r_{19}, r_{20}, r_{11}, r_1\}$.

The rule r_{11} (in 3rd position in the classification), is already known in $(K, \sqsubseteq)$: its conformity is low because the distance between the two vertices (a and c) is the longest one in $(K, \sqsubseteq)$. The first two rules r_{19} and r_{20} possibly could enrich the model under the supervision of the analyst. It should be noticed that these four rules are classified at very

Table 4. The conformity scores with the model (K, $\sqsubseteq$) of Figure 1

$\rightarrow$	a	b	c	d	e	Σ
a	0.26	0.26	0.09	0.26	0.13	1
b	0.03	0.37	0.19	0.03	0.37	1
c	0.07	0.07	0.73	0.07	0.07	1
d	0.07	0.07	0.07	0.73	0.07	1
e	0.04	0.04	0.44	0.04	0.44	1

Box 1. The conformity scores of four simple rules

(r19) : e→b with Cty(r19) = 0.04	(r20) : c→a with Cty(r20) = 0.07
(r1) : b→e with Cty(r1) = 0.37	(r11) : a→c with Cty(r11) = 0.09

different ranks depending on the statistical measures. Likely because we use an extra knowledge source (K, ⊑), along with the textual database used for the classification in Table 3.

If an analyst studies the rules sequentially, following any statistical measure, he may be overwhelmed by rules which reflect knowledge already known in (K, ⊑). Moreover, a major knowledge loss occurs when a number of extracted rules containing new pieces of interesting knowledge are classified at the bottom following the statistical classification lists. On the contrary, the classification given by the conformity measure may draw the attention of the analyst on the possible enrichment of the current domain model (K, ⊑) with interesting extensions and modifications.

Conformity for Complex Rules

The complex rules have their left and/or right parts composed of more than one keyterm. Three different kinds of rules may be distinguished. The first is called a 1—m rule: $k_1 \rightarrow k_2 \wedge ... \wedge k_{m+1}$ with $m \geq 2$, and it is composed of one keyterm on the left part and its right part has at least two keyterms. The second is called a n—1 rule: $k_1 \wedge ... \wedge k_n \rightarrow k_{n+1}$ with $n \geq 2$ that has its left part composed of at least two keyterms and a right part with a single keyterm. Finally, an n—m rule: $k_1 \wedge ... \wedge k_n \rightarrow k_{n+1} \wedge ... \wedge k_{n+m}$ where both $(n, m) \geq 2$. We generalize the conformity measure for complex rules by examining its definition for the three kinds (respectively, 1—m, n—1, and n—m) AR.

1—m rules. Let us consider the example of a 1—2 rule: $R_1 : x \rightarrow y \wedge z$. Following predicate logic, R1 can be rewritten in: $\neg x \vee (y \wedge z) = (\neg x \vee y) \wedge (\neg x \vee z)$. This rule can be normalised in a clausal form and decomposed into a conjunction of simple rules: $R_1 = (x \rightarrow y) \wedge (x \rightarrow z)$. Accordingly, the rule R1 is in conformity with (K, ⊑) if each simple rule of the decomposition is in conformity with (K, ⊑). The conformity for R1 is then defined by:

$$Cty(R_1 : x \rightarrow y \wedge z) = min(Cty(x \rightarrow y), Cty(x \rightarrow z))$$

The conformity measure range stands in [0,1[. The min function ensures that if at least one simple rule has a low conformity measure, then the complex rule has also a low conformity measure, i.e., the rule may contain some new information for updating (K, ⊑). Conversely, if all the simple rules have a high conformity measures, i.e., if they all are conform to the model (K, ⊑), then R_1 is also considered to be conform to (K, ⊑).

n—1 rules. Let us consider the example of the 2—1 rule $R_2: x \wedge y \rightarrow z$. Following predicate logic, R_2 can be rewritten in: $\neg(x \wedge y) \vee z = (\neg x \vee \neg y) \vee z = (\neg x \vee y) \vee (\neg y \vee z)$. This rule can be decomposed into a disjunction of two simple rules: $R_2 = (x \rightarrow z) \vee (y \rightarrow z)$. Thus, the rule R_2 is in conformity with (K, ⊑) if one of the simple rules of the decomposition is in conformity with (K, ⊑). The conformity for R_2 is then defined by: $Cty(R_2 : x \wedge y \rightarrow z) = max(Cty(x \rightarrow z), Cty(y \rightarrow z))$. The max function ensures that if at least one simple rule has a high conformity measure, then the complex rule has also a high conformity measure, i.e., (K, ⊑) already contains the information carried out by R_2. Conversely, if all the simple rules have a low conformity measure, i.e., if there is no simple rule that is conform to the model (K, ⊑), then R_2 is also considered as being not conform to (K, ⊑).

n—m rules. Following the same two ideas, a n—m rule is considered as a conjunction of disjunction of simple rules. The 3—2 rule $R_3 : x \wedge y \wedge z \rightarrow v \wedge w$ can be decomposed into $[(x \rightarrow v) \vee (y \rightarrow v) \vee (z \rightarrow v)] \wedge [(x \rightarrow w) \vee (y \rightarrow w) \vee (z \rightarrow w)]$. Hence, the conformity for R_3 is defined by: $min(max(Cty(x \rightarrow v), Cty(y \rightarrow v), Cty(z \rightarrow v)), max(Cty(x \rightarrow w), Cty(y \rightarrow w), Cty(z \rightarrow w)))$ and can be generalized for all simple and complex rules R into:

$$Cty(R : x_1 \wedge ... \wedge x_n \rightarrow y_1 \wedge ... \wedge y_m)$$
$$= min_{j=1}^{m}(max_{i=1}^{n}(Cty(x_i, x_j)))$$

In doing so, we have to mention that the combination of min and max in the conformity measure for complex rules may lead to loose the fact that some keyterms for R, among all others, are related in (K, ⊑). Since other relations are absent in (K, ⊑), R should be presented to the analyst. This case is illustrated by the following rule r_{12}:

$$Cty(b \wedge c \rightarrow a \wedge e)$$
$$= min(max(Cty(b, a), Cty(c, a)), max(Cty(b, e), Cty(c, e)))$$
$$= min((max(0.03, 0.07), max(\mathbf{0.37}, 0.07)))$$
$$= min(0.07, \mathbf{0.37}) = 0.07$$

A Small Example for Complex AR

Given (K, ⊑) in Figure 1, the Table 5 shows the classification of the 20 valid AR extracted – 16 complex and 4 simple – in an increasing order according to their conformity with (K, ⊑). We notice that the conformity classification for complex rules is, as we expected, different from the classification with the statistical measures given in Table 3. The difference is due to the use of an extra knowledge source (K, ⊑) for the former classification, rather than the text collection only as for the latter classification. The next section

Table 5. Conformity of the 20 AR in Table 2 with the model (K, ⊑) depicted in Figure 1

id	Rule Conformity		id	Rule Conformity	
r_6	$b \rightarrow a \wedge c \wedge e$	0.03	r_{18}	$c \wedge e \rightarrow a \wedge b$	0.07
r_7	$e \rightarrow b \wedge c$	0.04	r_{20}	$c \rightarrow a$	0.07
r_{10}	$e \rightarrow a \wedge b \wedge c$	0.04	r_9	$a \rightarrow c \wedge d$	0.09
r_{19}	$e \rightarrow b$	0.04	r_4	$a \rightarrow b \wedge c \wedge e$	0.09
r_{13}	$d \rightarrow a \wedge c$	0.07	r_{11}	$a \rightarrow c$	0.09
r_{14}	$c \rightarrow b \wedge e$	0.07	r_2	$b \rightarrow c \wedge e$	0.19
r_{15}	$c \rightarrow a \wedge d$	0.07	r_3	$a \wedge b \rightarrow c \wedge e$	0.19
r_{16}	$c \rightarrow a \wedge b \wedge e$	0.07	r_8	$a \wedge e \rightarrow b \wedge c$	0.26
r_{17}	$c \wedge e \rightarrow b$	0.07	r_5	$b \wedge c \rightarrow e$	0.37
$\mathbf{r_{12}}$	$b \wedge c \rightarrow a \wedge e$	0.07	r_1	$b \rightarrow e$	0.37

gives the main results of a qualitative analysis on real-word corpus. We follow the same principle as used for the simple example: by comparing conformity *versus* statistical measure classifications[1], and by considering the analyst's perspective on the appropriate knowledge units carried by the rules.

APPLICATION ON MOLECULAR BIOLOGY CORPUS

Description of the Experiment

On the one hand, there is a corpus of 1361 scientific paper abstracts holding on molecular biology[2] of about 240,000 words (1.6 M-Bytes). The theme of the texts is the phenomenon of gene mutation causing a bacterial resistance to antibiotics. The interpretation results from this specific domain needs a high degree of human expertise. On the other hand, there is a domain ontology – a set of semantically related concepts – used as a knowledge model (K, ⊑). The concepts of the ontology are the keyterms of the domain and constitute the pieces of information we mine in the texts. Moreover, we assume that cooccurrence of the keyterms in a text reflects a semantic link between keyterms [Anick & Pustejovsky, 1990]. We used UMLS [UMLS, 2000] restricted to the keyterms of the domain and all their parent keyterms represented by the specialisation relation (IsA). A keyterm is a noun phrase in the domain ontology which can be associated to a concept, and thus, it ensures the transition from the linguistic to the knowledge level. In this way, the corpus has been indexed with 14,374 keyterms, including 632 different keyterms. The minimal support σ_s for the AR extraction is set to 0.7% – occurring, at least in 10 texts – and the minimal confidence σ_c is set to 80%. We obtain 347 valid AR, including 128 exact rules. From the set of 347 rules, we kept 333 AR which do not deal with ambiguities in the keyterm meaning – two or more concept identi-

Table 6. Results on the model (K, ⊑) and the rule set extracted from our corpus

333 AR set	# concepts	# different concepts		
	364	94		
(K, ⊑) model	# concepts	# concepts (Is-A augmented)		
	510	1640		
Transition probability	# values	# non-zero values		
	831	108 (13%)		
AR class	1—1	1—n	n—1	n—m
	45	5	250	33

fiers (CUI) in the UMLS for the same keyterm. Thus, we discarded 14 AR, and there are 510 different concepts remaining (from 632 original ones). When the 510 concepts are augmented with their IsA-parents, K is composed of 1,640 vertices (concepts) and 4178 edges (⊑ relations). Among them, concepts appear 364 times in the 333 AR. There are 53 concepts in common with K (i.e., 56%), whereas 41 concepts are absent in K (i.e., 44%) out of the 94 different concepts from the AR set. There is a total number of 2,689,600 transitions probabilities computed from the 510 keyterms in K. The number of transition probabilities stored for the calculation in the 333 AR is: 419,906. The conformity computation operates 739 comparisons (min or max) for the probability transitions, yielding a total number of 831 values – with $108 \neq 0$ (i.e., 13%) and 21 different transitions, including Cty = 0. Finally, the conformity value range is [0, 0.231] with 18 different measure values and 75 out of 333 rules have their Cty > 0. We have to notice that the conformity measure is set to 0 for keyterms that does not appear in the (K, ⊑) rather than a minimal probability as stated in section 3.2, because the automatic computation of the probability transitions for (K, ⊑) is done once and regardless of the corpus. Finally, there are four classes of AR in the 333 set: 45 (1—1) simple rules (i.e., 13.51%), 5 (1—n) complex rules (i.e., 1.5%), 250 (n—1) complex rules (i.e., 75.08%), and 33 (n—m) complex rules (i.e., 9.9%). Table 6 summarizes these results.

Quality Analysis of AR rankings in the KBTM Process

The analysis is conducted as follows: For each rule in the four AR classes (1—n, 1—n, etc.), we compare its conformity measure, its statistical measures and whether or not it belongs to three groups based on the analyst's expertise: (i) interesting rules, (ii) relating known meronyms (especially hypernyms) and synonyms, and (iii) useless rules. Thanks to the conformity measure, we focus on a subset of 258 rules (*i.e.*, 77.5%) over the 333 rule set that are not conform to (K, ⊑) – as they relate keyterms that either are absent in K or isolated concepts following the relation ⊑. This gives a significant improving rate of 22.5% of extracted AR that are candidate to be discarded from the rule set. The discarded rules may be examined by their own in a further analysis (see summary in Table 7).

Table 7. Results of the subset presented to the domain expert for qualitative analysis

AR category	# AR	Percentage (%)
interesting (Cty=0)	258	77.5
useless (Cty>0)	75	22.5
Total	333	

In the following, and without exhaustiveness, we report the outcome through some examples: Firstly, we focus on two close n–1 rules interesting according to the analyst: one is conform and the other is not conform with regards to (K, ⊑). Next, we show and comment one simple AR belonging to the analyst's class: relating known keyterms. We end with an example of a useless AR according to the analyst. Some rules are identified as interesting by the analyst. For example, the mutation of the parC gene is interesting to comment in the following two (2—1) rules:

Rule Number: 221
"gyra gene" ∧ "substitution" → "quinolone"
Interest: "13.610" Conviction: "4.706"
Dependency: "0.741" Novelty: "0.008"
Satisfaction:"0.788" Conformity: "0"

Rule Number: 218
"gyra gene" ∧ "sparfloxacin" →
"ciprofloxacin"
Interest: "1.073" Conviction: "6.003"
Dependency: "0.770" Novelty: "0.007"
Satisfaction: "0.833" Conformity: "0.000215"

The rule #218, with Cty > 0, draws the resistance mechanism for two antibiotics sparfloxacin and ciprofloxacin that are subsumed (⊑) by the concept of quinolone (a family of antibiotics) in K. Moreover, the rule #221 is more precise by pointing out the specific resistance mechanism (namely substitution). We notice that the major good statistical measures for these rules are: conviction and satisfaction. Nevertheless, both measures give the reverse classification compared to the conformity and the analyst comments below. Some simple AR relate synonyms or hypernyms keyterms. They belong to the group: relating known keyterms according to the analyst. This group of rules shows that authors of the texts describe the same concept with different keyterms, and the text mining process reveals such usage.

Rule Number: 183:
"epidemic strain" ─→ "outbreak"
Interest: "17.449" Conviction: "undefined"
Dependency: "0.943" Novelty: "0.011"
Satisfaction: "1.000" Conformity: "0"

The statistical measure that gives a good quality for rule #183 is the dependency (which is used as the 3rd quality measure to check following the algorithm given in [Cherfi *et al.*, 2006]). The interest measure classes this rule in the middle of the corresponding list. Conversely, the conformity is 0, which gives it a chance to be analysed and update (K, ⊑) with two missing relations epidemic strain ⊑ outbreak and outbreak ⊑ epidemic strain.

Finally, the rules #268 and #269 are examples which are considered as wrong, hence useless for the analysis. It is due to the fact that keyterms: mycobacterium and tuberculosis are not significant in the molecular biology domain; however, these keyterms are extracted as keyterm index and are present as concepts in the general UMLS. The correct concept, in this context, would be the keyterm mycobacterium tuberculosis (see in [Cherfi *et al.*, 2006]).

Rule Number: 268
"mutation" ∧ "mycobacterium tuberculosis" → "tuberculosis"
Interest: "14.956" Conviction: "undefined" Dependency: "0.933" Novelty: "0.006"
Satisfaction: "1.000" Conformity: "0.000178"

Rule Number: 269
"mutation" ∧ "mycobacterium" → "tuberculosis"
Interest: "12.463" Conviction: "5.599" Dependency: "0.766" Novelty: "0.010"
Satisfaction: "0.821" Conformity: "0.00017809"

The rules #268 and #269 have the same non zero conformity, and have also good statistical quality measures. Hence, they will be presented to the analyst. Using the KBTM process, and without knowledge loss, we can discard the rules #268 and #269 from the rule set presented to the analyst because they are useless by introducing the artefacts mycobacterium and tuberculosis which are irrelevant in the context of molecular biology.

DISCUSSION

Among studies that intend to handle the large set of AR extracted with statistical quality measures, [Kuntz *et al.*, 2000] is similar to the work presented in section 2.2. This methodology is of great interest to highlight rule properties such as resistance to noise in the data set, or to establish whether a rule is extracted randomly or not (i.e., by chance). However, the limits of these measures come from the fact that they do not consider any knowledge model.

The background knowledge is used during the data mining process in [Jaroszewicz & Simovici, 2004] with a Bayesian Network [Pearl, 1988] to filter interesting frequent itemsets. A Bayesian network is similar to the knowledge model $(K, \sqsubseteq)$ described in this chapter; except that each vertex (*i.e.*, relation) is associated with a weight defined by the relation conditional probability (*e.g.*, for the specialisation $\sqsubseteq$) *wrt.* to the concept parent(s) in the Bayesian network. The distribution probabilities over the relations are set up, *a priori*, by expert's judgments. The authors propose an algorithm to compute the marginal distributions of the itemset (*e.g.*, corresponding to the keyterm sets when dealing with text applications) over the Bayesian network. Hence, the itemset marginal distributions are inferred from the Bayesian network structure. An itemset is interesting if its support in the corpus (*i.e.*, real support of appearing in the texts) deviates, with a given threshold, from the support inferred from the Bayesian network

(*i.e.*, its conditional probability to occur in the knowledge domain). A sampling-based approach algorithm for fast discovery of the interesting itemsets (called unexpected patterns) is given in [Jaroszewicz & Scheffer, 2005].

This methodology is extended in [Faure *et al.*, 2006] to drive both the AR extraction and the Bayesian network's weight updates. Hence, iteratively, the interesting AR identified in this way are candidates to update the Bayesian network. The similarities with the approach presented in this chapter are high. However, when [Faure *et al.*, 2006] deal with probabilistic reasoning and analyst's judgments on the structure of the Bayesian Network, we rather stick to more formal knowledge conveyed by an ontological (i.e., consensual) domain knowledge model. However, the approach in [Faure *et al.*, 2006] could be complementary to the KBTM approach presented in this chapter. Further studies can be conducted to study the AR rankings given by both approaches for a given domain corpus *wrt.* to, respectively, a knowledge model, and a Bayesian network.

Another interesting work for the post-mining of association rules involving user interaction as backgroung knowledge is [Sahar, 1999; Liu *et al.,* 2003]. Here, the user is asked to interact with the system in order to evaluate the quality of the rules. [Sahar, 1999] assumes the following hypothesis: if a simple rule $k_1 \rightarrow k_2$ is of low interest for the user, then all related complex rules – related rules are defined as rules containing k_1 in their body and k_2 in their head– are also considered as of low interest. The user does not have to study them and the number of rules to study is substantially reduced. The user is asked to classify simple rules in one of the four categories: (1) true but uninteresting, (2) false and interesting, (3) false and uninteresting, (4) true and interesting. If a simple rule is classified in class (1) or (3), then the rule itself and its complex related rules may be deleted from the set of rules. This work has some other interesting characteristics: (i) An appropriate algorithm has been developed to select the simple rules to be given first to the user. The selected rules are the ones connected to a large number of complex rules. In this way, the number of rules to study decreases more rapidly than a random choice. (ii) The approach takes into account the direction of the rule: the deletion by the user of the rule $k_1 \rightarrow k_2$ has no effect on the rule $k_2 \rightarrow k_1$. (iii) [Sahar, 1999] does not use a knowledge model but the subjective judgement of the user which may be seen as an informal knowledge model. (iv) Finally, the major difference between our approach and [Sahar, 1999] concerns the interpretation of complex rules. The assumption adopted in [Sahar, 1999] is that any complex rule, according to our interpretation, could be turned to a conjunction of simple rules. However, we have shown that such decomposition, in clausal form, is misleading: 1 — m rules can be rewritten into a conjunction of simple rules; whereas n — 1 rules are rewritten into a disjunction of simple rules.

[Basu *et al.*, 2001] proposes another approach and uses WORDNET lexical network to evaluate the quality of the rule where keyterms are, actually, words. The quality score of a simple rule $word_1 \rightarrow word_2$ is given by the semantic distance between $word_1$ and $word_2$ in the lexical network. The network is a weighted graph, and each semantic relation (syno/antonymy, hyper/hyponymy) has its own weight. The distance between two words is the lower weight path in the graph. For any complex rule, the quality score is the mean of the distance for each pair ($word_i$, $word_j$) where $word_i$ is in the body of the rule and $word_j$ is in its head. Here, as in [Sahar, 1999], the definition of the score for complex rules is logically false. The advantage in [Basu *et al.*, 2001] is the ability to deal with several semantic relations. However, the different properties of these relations cannot be formally expressed using a weighted graph and some assumptions are made such as: weight(synonymy) > weight(hypernymy), etc. This method, based on a network of lexical entities, could be adapted to a formal knowledge

model. However, it cannot be used to update a knowledge model: the weighting system and the mean calculation of the score for complex rules make impossible the association of a rule with a knowledge model as we did in Table 5.

CONCLUSION AND FUTURE WORK

In this chapter, we have proposed two methods for classifying association rules extracted within a KBTM process: the first one is based on statistical measures, and the second one is based on conformity with a knowledge model. Our present research study sets a knowledge-based text mining (KBTM) process driven by a knowledge model of the domain. Association rules that do not correspond to known relations of specialisation in the knowledge model are identified thanks to the conformity measure. The behaviour of the conformity measure is in agreement with the KBTM process. The conformity measure allows us both the enrichment of the knowledge model, and the TM process efficiency enhancement. An experiment on real-world textual corpus gives a significant improving rate and shows the benefits of the proposed approach to an analyst of the domain.

Furthermore, the conformity measure proposed in this first study can be extended to a number of promising directions in order to assess its effectiveness in different knowledge domains and contexts. Firstly, it could be interesting to take into account in the knowledge model of molecular biology domain other relations such as: causality (by considering rules involving instances of antibiotics → bacteria), temporal (the study of gene parC) mutation is anterior to gyrA study, how this relation has an impact on the resistance mechanism to antibiotics). In doing so, we will be able to have a deeper understanding of the texts and suggest an accurate modification of the knowledge model itself within the KBTM process.

REFERENCES

Agrawal, R., Mannila, H., Srikant, R., Toivonen, H., & Verkamo, A. I. (1996). Fast Discovery of Association Rules. In U. Fayyad, G. Piatetsky-Shapiro, P. Smyth, & R. Uthurusamy (Ed.), *Advances in Knowledge Discovery and Data Mining* (pp. 307–328). Menlo Park, CA: AAAI Press / MIT Press.

Anick, P., & Pustejovsky, J. (1990). An Application of lexical Semantics to Knowledge Acquisition from Corpora. *30ᵗʰ International Conf. on Computational Linguistics (COLING'90), 3*, 7–12. Helsinki, Finland.

Bastide, Y., Taouil, R., Pasquier, N., Stumme, G., & Lakhal, L. (2000). Mining frequent patterns with counting inference. *ACM SIGKDD Exploration Journal, 2*(2), 66–75.

Basu, S., Mooney, R. J., Pasupuleti, K. V., & Ghosh J. (2001). Evaluating the Novelty of Text-Mined Rules using Lexical Knowledge. *7th ACM SIGKDD International Conference on Knowledge Discovery in Databases* (pp. 233–238). San Francisco, CA: ACM Press.

Cherfi, H., Napoli, A., & Toussaint, Y. (2006). Towards a text mining methodology using frequent itemsets and association rules. *Soft Computing Journal - A Fusion of Foundations, Methodologies and Applications, 10*(5), 431–441. Special Issue on Recent Advances in Knowledge and Discovery. Springer-Verlag.

Collins A., & Loftus E. (1975). A spreading-activation of semantic processing. *Psychological Review, 82*(6), 407–428.

Faure, C., Delprat, D., Boulicaut, J. F., & Mille, A. (2006). Iterative Bayesian Network Implementation by using Annotated Association Rules. *15ᵗʰ Int'l Conf. on Knowledge Engineering and Knowledge Management – Managing Knowledge in a World of Networks, Vol. 4248 of Lecture Notes in Artificial Intelligence – LNAI* (pp. 326–333). Prague, Czech Republic: Springer-Verlag.

Fayyad, U., Piatetsky-Shapiro, G., Smyth, P., & Uthurusamy, R. (1996). *Advances in Knowledge Discovery and Data Mining.* Menlo Park, CA: AAAI Press / MIT Press.

Jacquemin, C. (1994). FASTR: A unification-based front-end to automatic indexing. *Information multimedia, information retrieval systems and management* (pp. 34–47). New-York, NY: Rockfeller University.

Jaroszewicz, S., & Scheffer, T. (2005). Fast Discovery of Unexpected Patterns in Data, Relative to a Bayesian Network. *ACM SIGKDD Conference on Knowledge Discovery in Databases* (pp. 118–127). Chicago, IL: ACM Press.

Jaroszewicz, S., & Simovici, D. A. (2004) Interestingness of Frequent Itemsets using Bayesian networks as Background Knowledge. *ACM SIGKDD Conference on Knowledge Discovery in Databases* (pp. 178–186). Seattle, WA: ACM Press.

Kuntz, P., Guillet, F., Lehn, R., & Briand, H. (2000). A User-Driven Process for Mining Association Rules. In D. Zighed, H. Komorowski, & J. Zytkow (Eds.), *4th Eur. Conf. on Principles of Data Mining and Knowledge Discovery (PKDD'00), Vol. 1910 of Lecture Notes in Computer Science – LNCS* (pp. 483–489), Lyon, France: Springer-Verlag.

Lavrac, N., Flach, P., & Zupan, B. (1999). Rule Evaluation Measures: A Unifying View. *9th Int'l Workshop on Inductive Logic Programming (ILP'99). Co-located with ICML'9., Vol. 1634 of Lecture Notes in Artificial Intelligence – LNAI* (pp. 174 185). Bled, Slovenia: Springer-Verlag, Heidelberg.

Liu, B., Ma, Y., Wong, C., & Yu, P. (2003). Scoring the Data Using Association Rules. *Applied Intelligence, 18*(2), 119–135.

Pasquier, N., Bastide, Y., Taouil, R., & Lakhal, L. (1999). Pruning closed itemset lattices for association rules. *International Journal of Information Systems, 24*(1), 25–46.

Paroubek, P. (2007). Evaluating Part-Of-Speech Tagging and Parsing – On the Evaluation of Automatic Parsing of Natural Language (Chapter 4). In L. Dybkaer, H. Hemsen, & W. Minker (Eds.), *Chapter 4 of Evaluation of Text and Speech Systems* (pp. 99–124). Springer.

Pearl, J. (1988). *Probabilistic Reasoning in Intelligent Systems: Networks of Plausible Inference.* San Fransisco, CA: Morgan Kaufmann.

Sahar, S. (1999). Interestingness via What is Not Interesting. In S. Chaudhuri, & D. Madigan, (Eds.), *5th ACM SIGKDD International Conference on Knowledge Discovery and Data Mining*

(KDD'99). (pp. 332–336). San Diego, CA: ACM Press.

UMLS (2000). *The Unified Medical Language System.* (11th edition). National Library of Medicine.

ENDNOTES

[1] The statistical measure classification is detailed in [Cherfi *et al.*, 2006], where an algorithm is proposed and an evaluation is carried out by an analyst – expert in molecular biology.

[2] The corpus is collected from the Pascal-BioMed documentary database of the French institute for scientific and technical information (INIST).

Chapter VII
Continuous Post–Mining of Association Rules in a Data Stream Management System

Hetal Thakkar
University of California, Los Angeles, USA

Barzan Mozafari
University of California, Los Angeles, USA

Carlo Zaniolo
University of California, Los Angeles, USA

ABSTRACT

The real-time (or just-on-time) requirement associated with online association rule mining implies the need to expedite the analysis and validation of the many candidate rules, which are typically created from the discovered frequent patterns. Moreover, the mining process, from data cleaning to post-mining, can no longer be structured as a sequence of steps performed by the analyst, but must be streamlined into a workflow supported by an efficient system providing quality of service guarantees that are expected from modern Data Stream Management Systems (DSMSs). This chapter describes the architecture and techniques used to achieve this advanced functionality in the Stream Mill Miner (SMM) prototype, an SQL-based DSMS designed to support continuous mining queries.

INTRODUCTION

Driven by the need to support a variety of applications, such as click stream analysis, intrusion detection, and web-purchase recommendation systems, much of recent research work has focused on the difficult problem of mining data streams for association rules. The paramount concern in previous works was how to devise frequent itemset algorithms that are fast and light enough for mining massive data streams continuously with real-time or quasi real-time response (Jiang, 2006). The problem of post-mining the association rules, so derived from the data streams, has so far received much less attention, although it is rich in practical importance and research challenges. Indeed, the challenge of validating the large number of generated rules is even harder in the time-constrained environment of on-line data mining, than it is in the traditional off-line environment. On the other hand, data stream mining is by nature a continuous and incremental process, which makes it possible to apply application-specific knowledge and meta-knowledge acquired in the past, to accelerate the search for new rules. Therefore, previous post-mining results can be used to prune and expedite both (i) the current search for new frequent patterns and (ii) the post processing of the candidate rules thus derived. These considerations have motivated the introduction of efficient and tightly-coupled primitives for mining and post-mining association rules in Stream Mill Miner (SMM), a DSMS designed for mining applications (Thakkar, 2008). SMM is the first of its kind and thus must address a full gamut of interrelated challenges pertaining to (i) functionality, (ii) performance, and (iii) usability. Toward that goal, SMM supports

- A rich library of mining methods and operators that are fast and light enough to be used for online mining of massive and often bursty data streams,
- The management of the complete DM process as a workflow, which (i) begins with the preprocessing of data (e.g., cleaning and normalization), (ii) continues with the core mining task (e.g., frequent pattern extraction), and (iii) completes with post-mining tasks for rule extraction, validation, and historical preservation.
- Usability based on high-level, user-friendly interfaces, but also customizability and extensibility to meet the specific demands of different classes of users.

Performing these tasks efficiently on data streams has proven difficult for all mining methods, but particularly so, for association rule min-

Figure 1. Post-mining flow

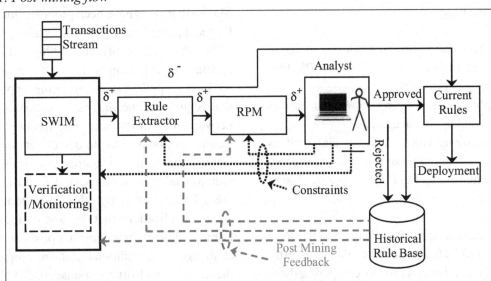

ing. Indeed, in many applications, such as click stream analysis and intrusion detection, time is of the essence, and new rules must be promptly deployed, while current ones must be revised in a timely manner to adapt to concept shifts and drifts. However, many of the generated rules are either trivial or nonsensical, and thus validation by the analyst is required, before they can be applied in the field. While this human validation step cannot be completely skipped, it can be greatly expedited by the approach taken in SMM where the bulk of the candidate rules are filtered out by the system, so that only a few highly prioritized rules are sent to analyst for validation. Figure 1 shows the architecture used in SMM to support the rule mining and post-mining process.

As shown in Figure 1, the first step consists in mining the data streams for frequent itemsets using an algorithm called SWIM (Mozafari, 2008) that incrementally mines the data stream partitioned into slides. As shown in Figure 1, SWIM can be directed by the analyst to (i) accept/reject interesting and uninteresting items, and (ii) monitor particular patterns of interest while avoiding the generation of others. Once SWIM generates these frequent patterns, a *Rule Extractor* module derives interesting association rules based on these patterns. Furthermore, SMM supports the following customization options to expedite the process:

1. Filtering and prioritizing rules by semantic criteria such as *correlation* and *PS* (Piatetsky-Shapiro, 1991),
2. Applying and passing down constraints specified by the analyst, and
3. Memorizing rules that were classified as good or bad in the past and then, using this information to filter out newly generated rules.

These candidate rules are passed to the *Rule Post-Miner (RPM)* module that evaluates them by various semantic criteria and by comparing them against a historical database of rules previously characterized by the analyst. Thus, the effect of the *RPM* is to (i) validate rules that match others approved by the analyst in the past, (ii) filter out rules that the analyst had rejected in the past, and (iii) prioritize the remaining rules and pass them to the analyst for a prompt review. As a result of this process the currently deployed rules are revised, and the historical rule repository is also updated. The analyst continuously monitors the system and by querying and revising the historical rule repository, he/she provides critical feedback to control and optimize the post-mining process.

The rest of the chapter is organized as follows. We present the related work in the next section, followed by the discussion of the SWIM algorithm and its ability to support (i) incremental pattern mining and (ii) feedback from later stages of the post-mining process. Then, we describe the techniques used to derive and to post-mine rules using semantic information provided by the analyst and the historical database. Then, we describe how such end-to-end processes are specified and supported in SMM. This is followed by discussion of the future work and conclusion.

RELATED WORK

Many algorithms have been proposed for mining frequent patterns over static databases (Agrawal, 1994; Han, 2000; Srikant, 1996; Zaki, 2002; Bastide, 2000). However, these methods are no longer applicable in emerging applications that require online mining. For instance, in a network monitoring scenario, frequent pattern mining can be utilized to detect network intrusions in real time. Click-stream analysis, online recommendation systems, and fraud detection are a few out of many other important stream mining applications that demand online pattern mining. Online stream mining poses significant challenges over traditional static mining, such as the need for real-time response, high volume of data and bursty arrival rate. Existing static mining methods (Agrawal, 1994; Han, 2000; Srikant, 1996; 40; Bastide, 2000) have limited use when facing such challenges. In fact, the main reason that most of the above algorithms are not suitable for data streams is because they require several passes through the data, or they are computationally too expensive. Thus, new algorithms have been proposed for mining of frequent patterns in the context of data streams (Cheung, 2003; Kumar, 2006; Leung, 2005; Pei, 2004; Chi, 2004; Mozafari, 2008). Due to space limitations, here we will only discuss those that are most relevant to this chapter.

In an attempt to cope with the overwhelming number of patterns, there has been work on representing frequent patterns in a more condensed form. For instance, Pei et al. (2000) and Zaki et al. (2002) present efficient algorithms, Closet and Charm respectively, to mine closed frequent itemsets; an itemset is called closed if none of its proper supersets has the same *support* as it has (Pasquier, 1999). Han et al. (2000), introduced an efficient data structure, called *fp-tree*, for compactly storing transactions for a given minimum *support* threshold. They also proposed an efficient algorithm (called FP-growth) for mining an *fp-tree* (Han, 2000). This efficient algorithm, however, leaves much to be desired for mining data streams; in fact, it requires two passes over each window (one for finding the frequent items and another for finding the frequent itemsets), and becomes prohibitively expensive for large windows. Our proposed verifiers (Mozafari, 2008) borrow this *fp-tree* structure and the conditionalization idea from (Han, 2000).

In a different line of research, delta-maintenance techniques (i.e., windows over data streams) have attracted a considerable amount of interest in online maintenance of frequent itemsets over data streams (Cheung, 2003; Leung, 2005; Chi, 2004; Jiang, 2006; Mao, 2007). Thus, Yu et al. (2006), propose a false negative based approach for mining of frequent itemsets over data streams.

Lee et al. (2005) propose generating k-candidate sets from (k-1)-candidate sets without verifying their frequency. Jiang et al. (2006) propose an algorithm for incrementally maintaining closed frequent itemsets over data streams. This avoids extra passes over the data and, according to the authors, does not result in too many additional candidate sets. Chi et al. (2004) propose the Moment algorithm for maintaining closed frequent itemsets over sliding windows. However, Moment does not scale well with larger slide sizes. Cats Tree (Cheung, 2003) and CanTree (Leung, 2005) support the incremental mining of frequent itemsets. These and also our incremental mining algorithm (SWIM) all utilize the *fp-tree* structure. The SWIM algorithm, supported in SMM (discussed in the next Section), significantly out-performs these algorithms (Mozafari, 2008).

There has also been a significant amount of work on counting candidate itemsets more efficiently. Hash-based counting methods, originally proposed in Park et al. (1995), are in fact used by many of the aforementioned frequent itemsets algorithms (Agrawal, 1994; Zaki, 2002; Park, 1995), whereas Brin et al. (1997), proposed a dynamic algorithm, called DIC, for efficiently counting itemset frequencies. The fast verifiers described in this chapter, utilize the *fp-tree* data structure and the conditionalization idea (which have been used for mining in (Han, 2000)) to achieve much faster counting of patterns and much faster delta-maintenance of frequent patterns on large windows. Thus, our approach improves upon the performance of state-of-the-art incremental frequent pattern mining algorithms.

Another relevant body of work is called association rule generation and summarization. Won et al. (2007) proposed a method for ontology driven hierarchical rule generation. The method concentrates on controlling the level of items, and rule categorization using hierarchical association rule clustering that groups the generated rules from the item space into hierarchical space. Similarly, Kumar et al. (2006) proposed a single pass algorithm based on hierarchy-aware counting and transaction pruning for mining association rules, once a hierarchical structure among items is given. Therefore, such generalization methods can be applied over the history of association rules to find generalized associations. Liu et al. (2001) proposed a technique to intuitively organize and summarize the discovered association rules. Specifically, this technique generalizes the rules and keeps track of the exceptions to the generalization. Other research projects in this category have focused on rule ordering based on interestingness measures (Li, 2001; Tan, 2002). For instance, Li et al. (2001) proposed rule ranking based on *confidence*, *support*, and number of items in the left hand side, to prune discovered rules. Our proposed approach allows integration of such ideas in end-to-end association rule mining, including post-mining.

FINDING FREQUENT PATTERNS IN DATA STREAMS

In this section, we briefly describe the SWIM algorithm (Mozafari, 2008), for mining and monitoring frequent patterns in large sliding windows on data streams; the algorithm is used in our SMM system, since it ensures excellent performance and flexibility in supporting a goal-driven mining process. Here we summarize the main ideas of the algorithm, whereas (Mozafari, 2008) can be consulted for more technical details.

Sliding Window Incremental Mining (SWIM)

Figure 2 illustrates the SWIM algorithm, which divides the data stream into segments, called windows. Each window is further divided into $n > 1$ slides, a.k.a. panes. For example in Figure 2, window W_4 consists of slides S_4, S_5 and S_6 (thus $n = 3$). The current slide completes after a given time interval has passed (logical window), or after a given number of tuples, each representing a transaction, has arrived (physical window). Upon completion of a new slide (of either kind) the whole window is moved forward by one slide. Therefore, in Figure 2, once S_7 completes, we have a new window W_7 which consists of slides S_5, S_6, and S_7.

SWIM keeps track of the counts of all the patterns that are frequent in any of the slides in the current window using a data structure

Figure 2. Visual Demonstration of the SWIM algorithm

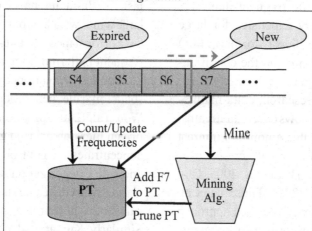

called *Pattern Tree* (*PT* in Figure 2), which is very similar to the *fp-tree* data structure. Thus, the patterns in *PT* form a superset of the actual frequent patterns over the current window. Upon completion of a new slide (e.g., S_7 in Figure 2), and the concomitant expiration of the old one (S_4 in Figure 2), we update the true count of every pattern in *PT*, by subtracting the count of this pattern in the expired slide, and by adding the count of the pattern in the new slide. Moreover, to assure that *PT* contains all patterns that are frequent in at least one of the slides of the current window, we must mine the new slide and add its frequent patterns to *PT* (in Figure 2, *F7* denotes the new frequent patterns found in S_7). The difficulty is that when a new pattern is added to *PT* for the first time, its true frequency in the whole window is not yet known, since this pattern was not counted in the previous $n - 1$ slides. Thus, we can either proceed eagerly and perform a count on those previous slides at once, or we cam operate lazily as described next. Under the laziest policy, SWIM waits to perform this computation until each of the successive $n - 1$ slides have expired and returned their counts for the pattern; at this point, if the sum of its frequencies in the individual n slides is above the threshold, the pattern is returned.

Thus, in the laziest policy, no additional pass through the window is required, but the pattern is reported after a delay of $n - 1$ slides. Intermediate policies, which trade-off delayed reporting with additional slide checking, are easily supported in this framework.

The pseudo-code for the SWIM algorithm is given in Figure 3, and the following mini-example shows how SWIM works. Note, *aux_arrays* in the pseudo code and the example below refers to an auxiliary data structure for storing the newly found patterns and their frequency.

Example 1: Assume that our input stream is partitioned into slides (S_1, S_2 ...) and we have 3 slides in each window.

Consider a pattern p which shows up as frequent in S_4 for the first time. Letting $p.f_i$ denote the frequency of p in the ith slide and $p.freq$ denote p's cumulative frequency in the current window, SWIM works as follows:

- $W_4 = \{S_2, S_3, S_4\}$: SWIM allocates an auxiliary array for p; $p.freq = p.f_4$ and $p.aux\_array = <>$

- $W_5 = \{S_3, S_4, S_5\}$: S_2 expires thus the algorithm computes $p.f_2$ storing it in the *aux_array*, also adds $p.f_5$ to the cumulative count of p; $p.freq = p.f_4 + p.f_5$ and $p.aux\_array = <p.f_2>$

Figure 3. SWIM pseudo code

```
For Each New Slide S
1: For each pattern p ∈ PT update p.freq over S
2: Mine S to compute σα(S)
3: For each existing pattern p ∈ σα(S) ∩ PT
     remember S as the last slide in which p is frequent
4: For each new pattern p ∈ σα(S) - PT
          PT ← PT U {p}
          remember S as the first slide in which p is frequent
          create auxiliary array for p and start monitoring it
For Each Expiring Slide S
5: For each pattern p ∈ PT
          update p.freq, if S has been counted in
          update p.aux_array, if applicable
          report p as delayed, if frequent but not reported at query time
          delete p.aux_array, if p has existed since arrival of S
delete p, if p no longer frequent in any of the current slides
```

- $W_6 = \{S_4, S_5, S_6\}$: S_3 expires thus the algorithm computes $p.f_3$ storing it in the *aux_array*, also adds $p.f_6$ to the cumulative count of p; $p.freq = p.f_4 + p.f_5 + p.f_6$ and $p.aux\_array = \langle p.f_2, p.f_3 \rangle$

- $W_7 = \{S_5, S_6, S_7\}$: S_4 expires thus the algorithm computes $p.f_4$; Then SWIM refers to the *aux_array* to see whether $p.f_2 + p.f_3 + p.f_4$ is greater than the *support* threshold; if so, p is reported as delayed. At this point, $p.f_2$ can be replaced with $p.f_4$ in the *aux_array*. SWIM also adds $p.f_7$ to the cumulative count of p and subtracts $p.f_4$; $p.freq = p.f_5 + p.f_6 + p.f_7$ and $p.aux\_array = \langle p.f_4, p.f_3 \rangle$

- $W_8 = \{S_6, S_7, S_8\}$: S_5 expires, thus the algorithm computes $p.f_5$; Then SWIM refers to the *aux_array* to see whether $p.f_3 + p.f_4 + p.f_5$ is greater than the *support* threshold; if so, p is reported as delayed. After this point SWIM discards the *aux_array* for p because its frequency is counted in all slides after S_4 and the count in slides before S_4 is no longer required. Therefore SWIM releases the *aux_array*; $p.freq = p.f_6 + p.f_7 + p.f_8$.

In next slides SWIM simply updates cumulative count of p until none of the 3 slides in the current window have p as frequent and then p is pruned from the Pattern Tree (*PT*).

Next, we briefly illustrate the concept of verification, which is the driving power of SWIM. In fact, counting represents the crux of the efficiency of SWIM (Step 1 in Figure 3), and verification addresses this problem via fast verifier algorithms.

VERIFICATION

Verification was first introduced in Mozafari et al. (2008).

Definition 1. *Let D be a transactional database, P be a given set of arbitrary patterns and min_freq a given minimum frequency, then function f is called a verifier, if it takes D, P and min_freq as input and for each $p \in P$ returns one of the following: (i) p's true frequency in D if it has occurred at least min_freq times or otherwise (ii) reports that it has occurred less than min_freq times (exact frequency not required in this case).*

It is important to notice the subtle difference between verification and simple counting. In the special case of *min_freq = 0*, a verifier simply counts the frequency of all $p \in P$, but in general if *min_freq > 0*, the verifier can skip any pattern whose frequency will be less than *min_freq*. This early pruning can be done by the Apriori property or by visiting more than $|D|$ - *min_freq* transactions. Also, note that verification is different from (and weaker than) mining. In mining the goal is to find all those patterns whose frequency is at least *min_freq*, but verification only verifies counts for a given set of patterns, i.e., verification does not discover additional patterns. Therefore, we can consider verification as a concept more general than counting, and different from (weaker than) mining. The challenge is to find a verification algorithm, which is faster than both mining and counting algorithms, since algorithms like SWIM benefit greatly from this efficiency. Therefore, we proposed such verification algorithms in (Mozafari, 2008), which result in significant performance improvements.

MANAGING ASSOCIATION RULES

The previous section discussed the mining of frequent patterns from windows over stream of transactions. Once, we find these frequent patterns the next task is to derive the set of association rules that satisfy the user-specified thresholds, such as *confidence*. While this task is simple compared to finding frequent patterns, it still requires considerable attention. The most naive algorithm to find association rules is as follows. For each frequent pattern P, consider all its subsets, S. For each subset S, create a 'counter subset' C, where a counter subset contains all items in pattern P that are not in subset S. Then, we compute the *confidence* of rule $S \rightarrow C$. If this *confidence* is above the user specified threshold then this rule qualifies as a frequent association rule. While this algorithm finds all qualifying association rules, it is rather inefficient, since it must construct all subsets of frequent patterns (exponential in the length of the patterns). Therefore, we must use faster algorithms to derive rules from frequent patterns.

For instance, Aggarwal et al. (1998), propose techniques to prune the subset space based on frequent pattern ordering. Aggarwal et al. (1998) also consider efficient generation of rules with only one item in the consequent, namely *single consequent rules* to further reduce the search space. Thus, an online mining system must include such advanced techniques to expedite rule generation. However, we note that association rule mining is an exhaustive mining method, thus it produces too many rules. Furthermore, many of the generated rules are either trivial or non-actionable, and thus validation is required by the analyst. While this human validation step cannot be skipped completely, the system must reduce the number of rules that require validation by the analyst. *Support* and *confidence* represent the most commonly used criteria to filter these rules. Here, *support* for an item or itemset is defined as the number of transactions in which it (item or itemset) occurs divided by the total number of transactions, and *confidence* is defined as the ratio between the *support* of the left hand side of the rule, and the *support* of the union of both left and right hand sides. While these measures filter some rules, they may not always produce the rules that the user is interested in. Thus, many other measures have been introduced to find rules that are more interesting to the user, as we discuss next.

OTHER MEASURES

Support and *confidence* represent the most commonly used constraints for association rule mining. However, these two constraints are not always sufficient for different mining cases. For instance, a rule that is frequently discovered when mining the data for a large department store is that people that buy maintenance contracts are likely to buy large appliances. Based on the *support* and *confidence* constraints, this represents a valid association; however we know that purchasing a maintenance contract represents the consequence, not the cause of purchasing a large appliance. Therefore, we may use different measures to discard such trivial rules and thus reduce the burden on the analyst. For instance, Piatetsky-Shapiro et al. (1991) proposed *leverage* as an alternate measure. *Leverage* for a given rule is defined as follows:

$$leverage(X \rightarrow Y) = Sup(X \cap Y) - Sup(X)*Sup(Y)$$

This essentially measures the difference of X and Y appearing together in the real-world data set and what would be expected, if X and Y where statistically independent. However, *leverage* tends to suffer from the rare item problem, whereby items that only appear a few times but have a clear association, will not be discovered. *Correlation* is another such measure that has gained some popularity among the research community. *Correlation* was first proposed in Brin et al. (1997) and it statistically shows whether and how strongly two itemsets are related. Thus, *correlation* between two itemsets X and Y is defined as follows:

$$corr(X \rightarrow Y) = Sup(X \cap Y) / Sup(X)*Sup(Y)$$

Unlike *confidence*, *correlation* is a symmetric measure, i.e., $corr(X \rightarrow Y) = corr(Y \rightarrow X)$. The *confidence* measure does not work well for items that are part of large percentage of the transactions. For example, let's consider the transaction database of Table 1.

Given that a customer buys bread, the percentage of customers that buy milk is 66%, which translates to a *confidence* of 0.66. However, the probability that any customer, regardless of whether he buys bread or not, buys milk is 80%. Thus, a customer who is known to buy bread is roughly 13% less likely to buy milk, however the *confidence* in this rule is pretty high. Thus, *confidence* is not a good indicator for the importance of the rule. On the other hand, the *correlation* for this rule,

$$corr(bread \rightarrow milk) = Sup(bread \cap milk) / Sup(bread)*Sup(milk)$$
$$= 0.2/(0.3*0.8) = 0.83$$

Thus, we see that the *correlation* between bread and milk is in fact negative. Other, thresholds such as *odds ratio*, a.k.a. cross-product ratio, have also been proposed (Lehmann, 1959).

Sheikh et al. (2004) provide an overview of other measures that are useful for pruning association rules. Similarly, Guillet et al. (2007) provide both theoretical and practical study of interesting measures for association rule mining. In general, we use a conjunction of these thresholds to prune the rules reported to the analyst. This serves the dual purposes of providing (i) more accurate and

(ii) less number of rules. Currently, the SMM system uses the *support* and the *confidence* measures.

VALIDATION WITH HISTORICAL RULE BASE

In a streaming environment we are presented with an additional opportunity for filtering based on rules that have been reported to the analyst in the past, i.e., we maintain the history of the rules and the pertaining statistics, which is utilized for further filtering. In fact, we also store the analyst's preferences, i.e., if the analyst accepted or rejected a rule in the past an utilizes it for filtering. Next, we discuss how these rules and their history is stored in SMM. Furthermore, this rule history can be used for further analysis and temporal mining as we discuss in Sections *Generalization and Summarization* and *Temporal Mining*.

Calders et al. (2006), proposed an approach to incorporate association rule mining in relational databases through virtual mining views. According to their proposal, the mining system should provide the following relational views for association rule mining and when the user queries these views, the system should invoke the corresponding mining methods.

Sets(sid int, item int);
Supports(sid int, supp real);
Rules(rid int, sida int, sidc int, sid int, conf int);

The table *Sets* stores the frequent patterns by its id (sid) and items. The table *Supports* stores the *support* of the frequent patterns (supp) by their id (sid). Finally, the table *Rules* stores the *confidence* of each rule (conf) by rule id (rid), rule antecedent id (sida), rule consequent id (sidc), and parent set id (sid, a set containing the union of antecedent and consequent). This idea is easily extended to work with data streams, by converting the *Supports* and the *Rules* tables into streams. Thus, we provide these mining views in SMM via User

Table 1. Simple transactions example

1	bread, ketchup, milk
2	cereal, milk
3	juice
4	bread, cereal, milk
5	bread, juice
6	milk
7	cereal, milk
8	cereal, milk
9	coco, milk
10	cereal, milk

Defined Aggregates (UDAs) and mining model types, as discussed in Section *Workflow and DSMS Integration*. Here, we discuss the organization of the history of these association rules.

We maintain a table called *HistoricalSets* that stores any sets that may have been frequent in at least one of the windows. Similarly, *Historical-Rules* table has an entry for each rule that may have satisfied user specified constraints, such as *support, confidence, correlation*, etc., in at least one window. Furthermore, it stores whether the user rejected the rule or not (*rejected* column). The schema for these tables and other supporting tables are provided below. Furthermore, we have a *HistoricalRuleStats* table that maintains the statistical history for each rule by the rid. For example this table stores the historical *confidence, correlation*, etc., for each time interval, denoted by startTime and endTime. Similarly, *Historical-SetStats* table stores historical statistics for the sets, by sid. See Box 1.

Such historical representation of association rules allows temporal analysis of rules. For instance, slice queries that ask for validity of a rule at a given time, or queries that ask for a set of rules that were valid at a given time, etc. Thus, any rules that are found to be valid in the current window are matched with the historical database to validate based on user preferences and rule history. Furthermore, the set of discovered rules can be generalized and summarized to restrict the number of rules that are reported to the analyst, as we discuss next.

GENERALIZATION AND SUMMARIZATION

Many research efforts have focused on generalization and summarization of association rules, as discussed in related work (Section *Related Work*). Instead, we focus on a particular technique for temporal analysis of association rules, proposed by Liu et al. (2001), which is particularly effective and is easily supported in SMM. The technique attempts to determine true and stable relationships in the domain. Given the history of the association rules and their attributes, including *support, confidence*, etc., (Liu, 2001)) divides the rules into the following three groups: *semi-stable rules, stable rules*, and *rules that exhibit trends*. *Semi-stable rules* are defined as rules whose *confidence* (or *support*) is statistically above the given thresholds; this allows these statistics to drop marginally below the specified threshold due to chance. Whereas *stable rules* are defined as semi-stable rules, whose *confidence* (or *support*) do not vary much over time, thus they are more reliable. We note that such analysis on the historical values of statistics is easily performed with a sequence query language, such as SQL-TS (Sadri, 2001). In fact, SQL-TS is fully supported in SMM precisely for such sequence queries, which are very difficult to express in standard SQL. SQL-TS queries are state-based operations on a set of tuples, which can be easily captured with the UDA framework supported in SMM. Therefore, we create an SQL-TS compiler that analyzes SQL-TS queries and automatically generates user defined aggregates.

Box 1.

```
HistoricalRules(rid int, sida int, sidc int, sid int, rejected int);
HistoricalSets(sid int, item int);
HistoricalRuleStats(rid int, confidence real, correlation real, startTime timestamp,
                    endTime timestamp);
HistoricalSetStats(sid int, support int, startTime timestamp, endTime timestamp);
```

Thus, post-analysis of temporal association rules, with the proposed method (Liu, 2001), is naturally supported in SMM.

Other methods of post-analysis of association rules may include rule correlation and periodicity analysis. For instance, in a market basket example, associations involving Christmas related goods only hold during holiday season and may not have the required *support* otherwise. Detecting such periodicity can provide increased insight to store managers. Next, we discuss temporal mining of association rules.

TEMPORAL MINING

The history of temporal association rules brings many opportunities for post-mining. For instance, association rule correlation provides further insight into correlated itemset behavior. More specifically, we look for association rules on top of the discovered association rules. Therefore, we view different time intervals as transactions and the discovered association rules as items in the transactions. Thus, we determine which association rules co-occur with each other. Furthermore, we can determine causalities, i.e., occurrence of a set of rules that implies another set of rules. Therefore, the analyst can further mine this history to gain more intelligence.

Similarly, we can perform collaborative filtering over this historical database. In this case, different time intervals are viewed as different users and the *support* and *confidence* of the rules is considered as user's ranking for the given rule. Then, we perform collaborative filtering over these rules. Therefore, we can predict the *support* and *confidence* of a given rule in a time interval, given similar time intervals. Here, similar time interval is defined as intervals with similar association rules, where similarity between a set of association rules is defined as an inverse of the cosine distance. This analysis is useful to determine anomalies in association rules. For

instance, if rules A, B, C, and D are important in time intervals T1, T2, and T3 and rule E is only reported as important in time intervals T1 and T3, it is very likely that E is also important in T2. These kinds of situations are very important from the view point of the analyst. Thus, temporal collection of association rule provides many opportunities for further mining.

WORKFLOW AND DSMS INTEGRATION

Integration of online mining algorithms with DSMSs represents an important research problem (Thakkar, 2008). Static data mining methods could be implemented outside the DBMS, since DBMS essentials such as atomicity, concurrency, etc. are not essential for the mining process. However, DSMS essentials such as load shedding, query scheduling, buffering, windowing, synopses, etc. play a critical role in online mining process. Furthermore, the real-time response requirements and the massive size of the stream data prohibit the traditional store-now-process-later approach. Thus, online mining algorithms should be integrated inside a DSMS to leverage DSMS essentials. This is specially true for association rule mining, which requires new fast and light, single pass mining algorithms that can take full advantage of the DSMS essentials discussed above. Thus, we discuss the integration of the SWIM algorithm, rule generation, and the post-mining of the generated rules in a DSMS, namely SMM.

SMM supports the Expressive Stream Language (ESL), which extends SQL with User Defined Aggregates (UDAs) (Bai, 2006) (UDAs can either be defined natively in SQL or in an external programming language such as C/C++). Furthermore, SMM supports different kinds of windows and slides over arbitrary UDAs. UDAs make SQL Turing-complete with regards to static data and non-blocking complete with respect to data streams (Wang, 2003). While this is proven theoretically (Wang, 2003), practically, this powerful framework extended with UDAs, can express many advanced applications, including sequence queries, integration of XML streams, data mining, etc. (Bai, 2006). Finally, SMM allows definition of new mining models, which are composed of one more tasks, each implemented as a UDA. For example, an association rule mining model is composed of frequent itemsets task, rule finding task, prioritization and summarization task. Furthermore, SMM allows modification of existing mining algorithms and definition of new mining algorithms (Thakkar, 2008).

There have also been previous research efforts to integrate association rule mining in relational DBMSs. For instance, OLE DB for DM supports association rule mining much in the same way as classification. However, the queries to invoke these algorithms get increasingly complex, due to the required structure of the data (Tang, 2005). Instead, Calders et al. (2006), propose an approach to incorporate association rule mining in relational databases through virtual mining views. Furthermore, this approach achieves much closer integration and allows the mining system to push down the constraints related to frequent itemsets mining for optimized execution. In addition to *support* and *confidence* thresholds, these also include specification of high (low) importance items that should always (never) be reported. Therefore Calders et al. (2006) proposes a 3-table view of the discovered association rules as discussed in Section *Validation with Historical Rule Base*. Furthermore, this framework is easily extended to work with data streams, by converting the Supports and Rules tables into streams.

Thus in SMM, we define a mining model that provides relational views similar to (Calders, 2006) over patterns and rules discovered from data streams. Furthermore, this mining model integrates post processing of the data in terms of matching with previously found rules and/ or rule ranking methods. A sample definition

of an association rule mining model is given in Example 2. Of course, the users can modify and/or extend this mining model to derive new mining models.

Example 2: Defining A ModelType for Association Rule Mining

In Example 2 (Box 2), association rule mining is decomposed to four sub-tasks, namely *FrequentItemsets*, *AssociationRule*, *PruneSummarizeRules*, and *MatchWithPastRules*. These are implemented as UDAs, as discussed previously (Bai, 2006). For instance, we use the SWIM algorithm to continually find the *FrequentItemsets* from a set of transactions. An instance of *AssociationRuleMiner* is created at the end of the examples. Thus, the analyst can invoke the tasks of the mining model, one after the other, in a step-by-step procedure, to create a flow of the data. Of course the analyst can pick, which tasks should be invoked and in which order. Furthermore, at each step the analyst can specify the thresholds associated with the task at hand. For instance, Example 3 shows a possible step-by-step invocation of this mining model.

Example 3: Invoking Association Rule Mining Model

Example 3 is shown in Box 3. In step 1, we invoke the frequent patterns mining algorithm, e.g. SWIM, over the *Transactions* input stream. We specify the size of the window and slide to instruct the algorithm to report frequent patterns every 100K (slide) transactions for the last 1 million (window) tuples. Furthermore, we specify the *support* threshold for the patterns. Also note that the user may specify a list of uninteresting items as a post-constraint, to allow additional filtering. In fact for greater efficiency, this post-constraint can be pushed down, before the mining step. Similarly, the user may also specify the list of patterns that should be always rejected (or accepted) regardless of their frequency. A continuous algorithm such

Box 2. Example 2: Defining a ModelType for association rule mining

```
CREATE MODELTYPE AssociationRuleMiner {
SHAREDTABLES (Sets, RulesHistory),
FrequentItemsets (UDA FindFrequentItemsets,
        WINDOW TRUE,
        PARTABLES(FreqParams),
        PARAMETERS(sup Int, uninterestingItems List, rejectedPats List, acceptedPats
...)
    ),
AssociationRules (UDA FindAssociationRules,
        WINDOW TRUE,
        PARTABLES(AssocParams),
        PARAMETERS(confidence Real, correlation Real)
    ),
PruneSummarizeRules (UDA PruneSummarizeRules,
        WINDOW TRUE,
        PARTABLES(PruneParams),
        PARAMETERS(chiSigniThresh Real)
    ),
MatchWithPastRules (UDA MatchPastRules,
        WINDOW TRUE,
        PARTABLES(AssocParams),
        PARAMETERS()
    ),
};
CREATE MODEL INSTANCE AssocRuleMinerInstance OF AssociationRuleMiner;
```

as SWIM can utilize this knowledge to efficiently prune (or keep) nodes (or include nodes) that may not be of interest (or are of interest regardless of frequency). Indeed, the framework presented above provides the parameters specified in the USING clause to the underlying algorithm for best utilization. Additionally, these parameters are inserted into the PARTABLES specified during mining model definition, which allows the user flexibility and the option to change the parameters, while the algorithm is being executed continuously. Of course, the algorithm must check for updates in parameter values periodically. Furthermore, the algorithm must also update the Sets

table based on the frequent itemsets. The results of this frequent patterns algorithm are inserted into the *FrequentPatterns* stream, denoted by the CREATE STREAM construct. The *FrequenPatterns* stream is in fact the same as the supports stream as proposed in Calders et al. (2006).

Step 2 finds the association rules based on the results of step 1, i.e., it takes *FrequentPatterns* stream as its input. The algorithm is implemented as a UDA, which is a combination of native ESL and C/C++. Any off-the-shelf algorithm that generates rules based on frequent patterns can be used for this step. This algorithm takes *confidence* and *correlation* thresholds to prune the resulting

Box 3. Example 3: Invoking association rule mining model

```
1: CREATE STREAM FrequentPatterns AS
   RUN AssocRuleMinerInstance.FrequentItemsets
   WITH Transactions USING sup > 10, window = 1M, slide = 100K;
2: CREATE STREAM AssocRules AS
   RUN AssocRuleMinerInstance.AssociationRules
   WITH FrequentPatterns USING confidence > 0.60 AND correlation > 1;
3: CREATE STREAM PrunedRules AS
   RUN AssocRuleMinerInstance.PruneSummarizeRules
   WITH AssocRules USING chiSigniThresh > 0.50;
4: CREATE STREAM NewRules AS
   RUN AssocRuleMinerInstance.MatchPastRules
   WITH PrunedRules;
```

association rules. This algorithm utilizes the Sets table to determine the association rules. Similarly, other tasks down stream may also utilize the Sets table, thus it is denoted as SHAREDTABLE in model type definition. Finally, the results of this mining task are inserted into the *AssocRules* stream.

Step 3 prunes and summarizes the resulting association rules, which is an optional step. Association rule mining finds all associations in the data that satisfy the specified *support* and *confidence* measures. Thus, it often produces a huge number of associations, which make difficult, if not impossible, for the analyst to manage and take action. Therefore many research efforts have focused on pruning and summarizing the results of association rule mining. For instance, Liu et al. (1999) present techniques for both pruning and summarizing. The approach finds rules that are insignificant or that over-fit the data. A rule is considered insignificant if it gives little extra information compared to other rules. For example, given

R1: Job = Yes → Loan_Approved = true
R2: Job = Yes, Credit = Good → Loan_Approved = true

R2 is insignificant, since R1 is more generic; this is of course assuming that the *support* and *confidence* values are close. The work (Liu, 1999) proposes to use chi-square test to determine the significance of the rules. Once the rules are pruned, the technique then finds a subset of un-pruned rules, called direction setting rules, to summarize the found associations. Therefore, while pruning and summarizing represent an optional step, it has significant practical value for the analyst. These pruning and summarization are implemented in SMM as a UDA (again natively or in an external programming language).

In a data stream setting we have a list of rules that have already been presented to the analyst. The DSMS maintains these patterns and their attributes, such as *support, confidence*, etc., in a table, namely *RulesHistory* (defined as shared in model type definition). Thus, new rules are matched with these old rules in step 4 (*MatchPastRules*), which allows the system to report only the changes in association rules, as opposed to providing a huge list of patterns again and again. Thus, the *NewRules* stream only has the new rules and the rules that just expired. In addition to simple matching with old rules, we may also record the statistics for each rule, to enable historical queries at a later point.

Therefore, SMM allows definition of new mining models, which the analyst can uniformly instantiate and invoke (The analyst also uses the same uniform syntax to instantiate and invoke built-in mining models.). This approach works particularly well for association rule mining, since it involves many steps. The analyst can pick the steps and the order in which he/she wants to invoke them. Finally, we note that the system also allows specification of data flow. Thus a naive user may simply invoke the flow, as opposed to determining, the order of the tasks to be invoked. In fact, multiple data flows can be defined as part of the same data mining model. For example, for the data mining model of Example 2, we define two separate data flows as follows:

F1: *FrequentItemsets → AssociationRules → PruneSummarizeRules → MatchPastRules*
F2: *FrequentItemsets → AssociationRules → MatchPastRules.*

Therefore, the analyst simply picks the flow he/she wants to execute. Thus, SMM provides an open system for data stream mining, which has been adapted to support end-to-end association rule mining. Furthermore, user can implement new techniques to achieve customization. Additionally, SMM imposes a negligible overhead (Thakkar, 2008). For instance, the overhead of integrating the SWIM algorithm in SMM is about 10-15% as compared to a stand-alone implementation. In return for this small cost, SMM brings many advantages, such as DSMS essentials (I/O buffering, synopses, load shedding, etc.), declarative implementation, and extensibility. This extensibility and declarativity has lead to the implementation of many mining algorithms in SMM, including Naïve Bayesian classifiers, decision tree classifiers, ensemble based methods for classification (Wang, 2003), IncDBScan (Ester, 1998), SWIM (Mozafari, 2008), and SQL-TS (Sadri, 2001).

FUTURE WORK

Currently the SMM does not provide much assistance in terms of visualizing the results of association rule mining. Thus, we are currently focusing on finding an appropriate interface for reporting rules and receiving feedback from the user for each rule. We are also looking to integrate more mining algorithms in the system, such as the Moment algorithm (Chi, 2004) or the CFI-stream algorithm (Jiang, 2006) for finding frequent patterns from a stream. We are testing our system on new application areas where the proposed solutions naturally apply. For instance, given a market basket data for a particular store (or a set of stores), we would like to extract frequent patterns and rules from the data and apply the post-mining techniques such as summarization, prioritization, temporal mining, etc. Thus, we are constantly looking for real-world datasets to determine the usefulness of the proposed approach. Finally, we are considering of running SMM in a distributed environment where multiple server parallely process data streams.

CONCLUSION

Although there have been many DSMS projects (Bai, 2006) and commercial startups, such as Coral8, StreamBase, etc., Stream Mill Miner is the first system that claims to have sufficient power and functionality to support the whole data stream mining process. In this paper, we have focused on the problem of post-mining association rules generated from the frequent patterns detected in the data streams. This has been accomplished by (i) the SWIM algorithm, which easily incorporates preferences and constraints to improve the search, (ii) a historical database of archived rules that supports summarization, clustering, and trend analysis, over these rules, (iii) a high level mining language to specify the mining process, and (iv) a powerful DSMS that can support the mining models and process specified in this language as continuous queries expressed in an extended SQL language with quality of service guarantees.

REFERENCES

Aggarwal, C. C., & Yu, P. S. (1998). Online generation of association rules. In *ICDE* (pp. 402-411).

Agrawal, R., & Srikant, R. (1994). Fast algorithms for mining association rules in large databases. In *VLDB* (pp. 487-499).

Bai, Y., Thakkar, H., Wang, H., Luo, C., & Zaniolo, C. (2000). A data stream language and system designed for power and extensibility. In *CIKM* (pp.337-346).

Bastide, Y., Pasquier, N., Taouil, R., Stumme, G., & Lakhal, L. (2000). Mining minimal non-redundant association rules using frequent closed itemsets. In *First International Conference on Computational Logic* (pp. 972-986).

Brin, S., Motwani, R., & Silverstein, C. (1997). Beyond market baskets: Generalizing association rules to correlations. In *SIGMOD* (pp. 265-276).

Brin, S., Motwani, S., Ullman, J. D., & Tsur, S. (1997). Dynamic itemset counting and implication rules for market basket data. In *SIGMOD* (pp. 255-264).

Calders, T., Goethals, B., & Prado, A. (2006) Integrating pattern mining in relational databases. In *PKDD*, volume 4213 of *Lecture Notes in Computer Science* (pp. 454-461). Springer.

Cheung, W., & Zaiane, O. R. (2003). Incremental mining of frequent patterns without candidate generation or support. In *7th Database Engineering and Applications Symposium International Proceedings*, (pp.111-116).

Chi, Y., Wang, H., Yu, P. S., & Muntz, R. R. (2004). Moment: Maintaining closed frequent itemsets over a stream sliding window. In *ICDM* (pp 59-66).

Ester, M., Kriegel, H.-P., Sander, J., Wimmer, M., & Xu, X. (1998). Incremental clustering for mining in a data warehousing environment. In *VLDB* (pp. 323-333).

Guillet, E., & Hamilton, H. J. (Ed.). (2007). *Quality Measures in Data Mining*. Studies in Computational Intelligence. Springer.

Han, J., Pei, J., & Yin, Y. (2000). Mining frequent patterns without candidate generation. In *SIGMOD* (pp. 1-12).

Jiang, N., & Gruenwald, D. L. (2006). Cfi-stream: mining closed frequent itemsets in data streams. In *SIGKDD* (pp. 592-597).

Jiang, N., & Gruenwald, L. (2006). Research issues in data stream association rule mining. *SIGMOD Record* (pp. 14-19).

Kumar, K. B., & Jotwani, N. (2006). Efficient algorithm for hierarchical online mining of association rules. In *COMAD*.

Lee, C., Lin, C., & Chen, M. (2005). Sliding window filtering: an efficient method for incremental mining on a time-variant database. *Information Systems* (pp. 227-244).

Lehmann, E. (1959). *Testing Statistical Hypotheses*. Wiley, New York.

Leung, C.-S., Khan, Q., & Hoque, T. (2005). Cantree: A tree structure for efficient incremental mining of frequent patterns. In *ICDM* (pp. 274-281).

Li, W., Han, J., & Pei, J. (2001). CMAR: Accurate and efficient classification based on multiple class-association rules. In *ICDM* (pp. 369-376).

Liu, B., Hsu, W., & Ma, Y. (1999). Pruning and summarizing the discovered associations. In *KDD* (pp. 125-134).

Liu, B., Hu, M., & Hsu, W. (2000). Multi-level organization and summarization of the discovered rules. In *Knowledge Discovery and Data Mining* (pp. 208-217).

Liu, B., Ma, Y., & Lee, R. (2001). Analyzing the interestingness of association rules from the temporal dimension. In *ICDM* (pp. 377-384).

Mao, G., Wu, X., Zhu, X., Chen, G., & Liu, C. (2007). Mining maximal frequent itemsets from data streams. *Information Science* (pp. 251-262).

Mozafari, B., Thakkar, H., & Zaniolo, C. (2008). Verifying and mining frequent patterns from large windows over data streams. *ICDE* (pp. 179-188).

Park, J. S., Chen, M.-S., & Yu, P. S. (1995). An effective hash-based algorithm for mining association rules. In *SIGMOD* (pp. 175-186).

Pasquier, N., Bastide, Y., Taouil, R., & Lakhal, L. (1999). Efficient mining of association rules using closed itemset lattices. *Information Systems* (pp. 25-46).

Pei, J., Han, J., & Mao, R. (2000). CLOSET: An efficient algorithm for mining frequent closed itemsets. In *SIGMOD* (pp. 21-30).

Pei, J., Han, J., Mortazavi-Asl, B., Wang, J., Pinto, H., Chen, Q., Dayal, U., & Hsu, M. (2004). Mining sequential patterns by pattern-growth: The PrefixSpan approach. *IEEE TKDE*, 16(11), 1424-1440.

Piatetsky-Shapiro, G. (1991). Discovery, analysis, and presentation of strong rules. In *KDD*.

Sadri, R., Zaniolo, C., Zarkesh, A., & Adibi, J. (2001). Optimization of sequence queries in database systems. In *PODS* (pp. 71-81).

Sheikh, L., Tanveer, B., & Hamdani, M. (2004). Interesting measures for mining association rules.

Multitopic Conference INMIC, 8th International (pp. 641-644).

Srikant, R., & Agrawal, R. (1996). Mining sequential patterns: Generalizations and performance improvements. In *EDBT* (pp. 3-17).

Tan, P., Kumar, V., & Srivastava, J. (2002). Selecting the right interestingness measure for association patterns. In *Knowledge Discovery and Data Mining* (pp. 32-41).

Tang, Z., Maclennan, J., & Kim, P. (2005). Building data mining solutions with OLE DB for DM and XML analysis. *SIGMOD Record*, *34*(2), 80-85.

Thakkar, H., Mozafari, B., & Zaniolo, C. (2008). Designing an inductive data stream management system: the stream mill experience. In *SSPS* (pp. 79-88).

Wang, H., Fan, W., Yu, P. S., & Han, J. (2003). Mining concept-drifting data streams using ensemble classifiers. *In SIGKDD (pp. 226-235)*.

Wang, H., & Zaniolo, C. (2003). Atlas: a native extension of sql for data minining. In *Proceedings of Third SIAM Int. Conference on Data Mining* (pp.130-141).

Won, D., & McLeod, D. (2007). Ontology-driven rule generalization and categorization for market data. *Data Engineering Workshop, 2007 IEEE 23rd International Conference on* (pp. 917-923).

Yu, J., Chong, Z., Lu, H., Zhang, Z., & Zhou, A.. A false negative approach to mining frequent itemsets from high speed transactional data streams. *Inf. Sci.* 176(14).

Zaki, M. J., & Hsiao, C. (2002). CHARM: An efficient algorithm for closed itemset mining. In *SIAM*.

Chapter VIII
QROC:
A Variation of ROC Space to Analyze Item Set Costs/Benefits in Association Rules

Ronaldo Cristiano Prati

UFABC Universidade Federal do ABC, Brazil

ABSTRACT

Receiver Operating Characteristics (ROC) graph is a popular way of assessing the performance of classification rules. However, as such graphs are based on class conditional probabilities, they are inappropriate to evaluate the quality of association rules. This follows from the fact that there is no class in association rule mining, and the consequent part of two different association rules might not have any correlation at all. This chapter presents an extension of ROC graphs, named QROC (for Quality ROC), which can be used in association rule context. Furthermore, QROC can be used to help analysts to evaluate the relative interestingness among different association rules in different cost scenarios.

INTRODUCTION

In numerous data mining applications, a key issue to discover useful and actionable knowledge from association rules is to properly select the (probably) most profitable rules out of a large set of generated rules. To this end, it would be desirable to properly take into account expected costs/benefits of different item sets of different rules.

Receiver Operating Characteristic (ROC) analysis was developed in the context of signal-detection theory in engineering applications to examine the association between the presence and absence of a signal and the ability of a detector to sense the difference between them (Egan, 1975). These methods have been widely adopted for use in machine learning and data mining research thanks to its ability in visualizing and organizing classification performance without regard to class distributions or misclassification costs, therefore providing a direct and natural way to incorporate cost/benefit analysis for different classification thresholds (Provost, Fawcett, & Kohavi, 1998). Furthermore, the ROC convex hull (ROCCH) provides a straightforward tool to select possibly optimal models and to discard sub-optimal ones, independently from (and prior to specifying) the cost context or the class distribution (Provost & Fawcett, 2001).

Nevertheless, the use of ROC analysis in machine learning and data mining concentrates mostly in classification tasks, where the area under the ROC curve (AUC) is used as a performance measure (Bradley, 1997). Although it is possible to plot association rules in the ROC space, the properties that make ROC analysis suitable for cost/benefit analysis in classification context do not hold in the association rule context. These properties came from the assumption that, even though cost context or class distribution are free to vary, in classification context they vary in the same way for all rules. This is because in classification, all classification rules have the same attribute in the consequent (the "target class" attribute). However, in the association rule context, the consequent is an item set that may contain any item (attribute) that does not appear in the rule antecedent. Therefore, ROC analysis cannot be used in the same direct and natural way to incorporate costs/benefits in association rule context.

This chapter proposes the use of a variation of ROC graphs, named QROC, for association rule evaluation. The benefit of using a ROC-like graph for analyzing association rules is twofold: first, this framework can be used to prune uninteresting rules from a large set of association rules. Second, it can help the expert in analyzing the performance of the association rules in different cost scenarios.

This chapter is organized as follows: Section "ROC space" presents some concepts of ROC analysis in the classification rule evaluation context,

as well as it describes some pitfalls of using ROC analysis to association rules evaluation. Section "Quality ROC – QROC" presents an extension to ROC analysis, named QROC, which can be used in the association rule context. This section also presents a geometric interpretation of the ROC re-scaling process from which the QROC space is derived, as well as how cost information can be used to derive cost-sensitive metrics for rule evaluation and geometric interpretations of some well-known rule measures used for association rules evaluation. Section "An illustrative example" presents example on how QROC can be used to analyze a set of association rules generated for basket analysis. Section "New trends and Related Work" present related research. Finally, Section "Concluding remarks" concludes.

BACKGROUND

Rule learning has been mainly addressed from two different perspectives: predictive and descriptive tasks. Rule learning in predictive tasks is mainly concerned in generating classification rules that form a classifier. On the other hand, rule generation in descriptive tasks focus in finding all rules over a certain confidence that summarizes the data. However, in a broader sense, rules (either predictive or descriptive) can be considered as an association of two binary variables: the rule antecedent and the rule consequent. Rules of the form:

antecedent → consequent,

where both antecedent and consequent are conjunctions of features (for classification rules, the consequent always refers to a single feature), whereas they do not have features in common. The antecedent is also called left-hand side, premise, condition, tail or body and the consequent is called right-hand side, conclusion or head. Throughout this chapter, we will also use the general notation

Table 1. A 2x2 contingency table

XY	y	ẏ	
x	n(xy)	n(xẏ)	Q
ẋ	n(ẋy)	n(xẏ)	Q̇
	P	Ṗ	N

$X \rightarrow Y$ (X corresponding to the antecedent and Y to the consequent, respectively) to denote a rule.

Assume we have a set of cases and a certain procedure by which for a given case and for every possible X and Y we can determine whether these variables are true or false. Therefore, the fundamental problem is to measure the strength of agreement between two random variables X and Y in a population, where X and Y have each two possible responses, and X is used as a criterion against Y is judged (*i.e.*, we are mainly concerned in evaluating the strength of $X \rightarrow Y$ agreement rather than the agreement between $Y \rightarrow X$).

To assess the agreement between X and Y, a 2×2 contingency table is a convenient way to tabulate statistics for evaluating the quality of an arbitrary rule. An example of a contingency table is shown in Table 1. In this table, x and $\dot{x}$ represents the events X=true and X=false and y and $\dot{y}$ represents the events Y=true and Y=false, respectively, meaning that the antecedent/consequent part of the rule is true/false. In this table, $n(xy)$, $n(\dot{x} y)$, $n(x\dot{y})$ and $n(\dot{x}\dot{y})$ represent antecedent/consequent true/false case counts, respectively. P, $\dot{P}$, Q and $\dot{Q}$ represent the marginal counts whether X/Y are true/false. N is the data set size.

ROC SPACE

Numerous rule evaluation measures can be derived from a contingency table. These measures are often aimed to evaluate the strength of the association between X and Y of a rule in a particular way. Among them, two measures are of special interest in ROC analysis, namely specificity (SP) and sensitivity (SE).

Sensitivity is defined as the conditional probability that X is true given that Y is true. In terms of the contingency table, it can be calculated as:

$$SE = p(x \mid y) = \frac{n(xy)}{n(xy) + n(x\dot{y})}$$

Specificity is defined as the conditional probability that X is false given that Y is false. It can be calculated as:

$$SP = p(\dot{x} \mid \dot{y}) = \frac{n(\dot{x}\dot{y})}{n(\dot{x}\dot{y}) + n(x\dot{y})}$$

The ROC space is a unite-square graph, where sensitivity is represented in the y-axis and the x-axis corresponds to 1 - specificity. Several points in the ROC space are worth noticing (Fawcett, 2006). The lower left corner (0, 0) represents the strategy of always implicating $\dot{y}$, *i.e.*, Y is always false. The upper right corner (1, 1) represents the opposite strategy, *i.e.*, always implicating y. The upper left corner (0, 1) represents perfect agreement between X and Y, while the lower right corner (1, 0) represents perfect disagreement between X and Y. Random associations between X and Y lies in the ascending diagonal.

ROC Analysis and Classification Rules

The fundamental proposal of the ROC method is that the performance of a binary classification model can be described geometrically by the location of (1 - SP, SE) in the ROC space. This proposal assumes that SP and SE do not depend on the Y distribution, so that performance of multiple models can be simultaneously compared by comparing their location in the ROC space. This assumption is necessary because a 2×2 contingency table has three degrees of freedom, meaning that if know three values in this table, and as long as these three values are not in the same line or column, the remaining values can be determined. Therefore, to fully characterize the performance, we need a three-dimensional space (Flach, 2003).

However, as specificity and sensitivity are conditional to *Y*, in a classification problem generally we can ignore the *y* and *ẏ* distributions and carry out performance analysis based only in SP and SE. This is true even if the proportion of examples over *y* and *ẏ* changes. The main requirement is that the *Y* conditional distributions do not change (Fawcett & Flach, 2005).

The ROC space is appropriate for measuring the quality of classification rules. Points close to the main diagonal usually have a poor correlation between *X* and *Y*. This is because they are only slightly better than chance. Furthermore, rules having a better trade-offs of SP and SE are close to the upper left corner in the ROC space. When comparing two classification models in the ROC space (including classification rules), if a model A has both a greater sensitivity and a greater specificity than a model B, A is the better of these two models. In this case we say A dominates B. A model is the best of a set of models if it dominates all other models. If an overall best model does not exist, models that might be optimal under varying SP and SE trade-offs form a convex hull (a Pareto front) in the ROC space. This projection works as follows:

The overall expected loss function is assumed to be:

$$L = p(\dot{x} \mid y)p(y)c(\dot{x}, y) + p(x, \dot{y})p(\dot{y})c(x, \dot{y})$$

where $c(\dot{x}, y)$ and $c(x, \dot{y})$ represents the costs related to the two possible disagreements between *X* and *Y* (either *X* is false and *Y* is true or vice-versa). *p(y)* and *p(ẏ)* are the corresponding *Y* = true and *Y* = false marginal probabilities.

Some algebraic manipulation can show that the location of all points with the same expected loss is a line segment with slope:

$$\frac{p(y)c(\dot{x}, y)}{p(\dot{y})c(x, \dot{y})}$$

We call this line an iso-performance line. Furthermore, lines "more northwest" (having a larger SE intercept) are better because they correspond to models with lower expected cost. Each possible combination of costs and class proportions defines a family of iso-performance lines, and for a given family, the optimal methods are those that lie on the "most-northwest" iso-performance line. Thus, a model is optimal for some conditions if and only if it lies on the upper convex hull of the set of points in the ROC space.

Figure 1 shows a ROC graph containing 5 classification rules (A, B, C, D and E). Three points compose the ROC convex hull: A, B and C. A dominates D. E is not dominated by any other point, but it lies inside the ROC convex hull. Furthermore, E is close to the main diagonal and thus its performance is only slightly better than random.

Any point in the convex hull can be obtained by alternating the prediction of the models associated to the points in the extremity of the line segment in consideration using a different weight for selecting each model. For classification, the ROC convex hull has the property that

Figure 1. A ROC graph and its corresponding convex hull

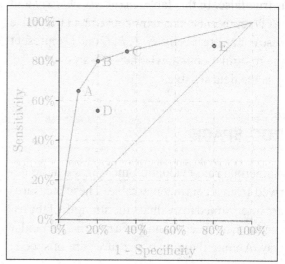

only the rules on the convex hull are potentially optimal under different trade-offs of SE and SP, rules that are outside the ROC convex hull can be discarded.

Pitfalls of Using ROC Analysis for Evaluating Association Rules

Although it is possible to calculate SP and SE for an association rule and plot it into the ROC space, this approach has some drawbacks. The reason is that the distribution of Y over the rules where the consequent is not constrained to a unique attribute is some unknown bi-varied distribution that may change from rule to rule. In other words, when dealing with association rules, the assumption often made in classification contexts that the conditional Y distributions are the same for all points in the ROC space does not hold.

When comparing two points in the ROC space corresponding to two association rules with different consequents, the general procedure of determining whether point A or point B is the dominant point is no longer valid. The same happens to the points lying in the ROC convex hull. As the consequent part of the rules lying in the convex hull might be different, the convex hull does not contain points having the best trade-offs between SP and SE.

However, differently from classification in which although the costs and class proportions are free to vary they are the same for all points in the ROC space, for association rules they can be very different, depending on the consequent part of the rule.

Let us analyze an example to understand the differences. Suppose we have two association rules with the following contingency tables: let rule 1 (R1) have the contingency table shown in Table 2 and let rule 2 (R2) have the contingency table shown in Table 3.

Figure 2 depicts the ROC graph of these two rules. As can be easily verified, if we apply the concept of dominance that is valid in the classification rule context, R1 dominates R2. However, if we assume equal cost for the two possible disagreements between *X* and *Y*, both rules have the same expected cost!

This can be verified by tracing the so-called iso-performance lines (the dotted lines in the graph) that passes through the points corresponding to the rules. The expected cost is proportional to the distance between the y-axis and the intercept of the iso-performance line (the dark dashed line

Table 2. Rule 1

XY	y	ẏ	
x	30	10	40
ẋ	20	90	110
	50	100	150

Table 3. Rule 2

XY	y	ẏ	
x	20	25	45
ẋ	80	25	105
	100	50	150

Figure 2. Two different association rules and their expected cost projections in the ROC space.

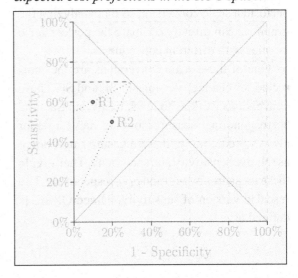

in the graph) in the descending diagonal (Drummond & Holte, 2006). As can be observed, both iso-performance lines intercept the descending diagonal at the same point and thus have the same expected cost.

This is because the SE and SP points plotted in the ROC graph for these two rules are in different "scales". In an association rule context, if the consequent parts of the rules are related to different features, each point corresponds to a different slice of a three-dimensional space. This is not the case of classification, where all points are assumed to be in the same slice of the three dimensional space.

QUALITY ROC: QROC

As mentioned in the previous section, rules with different consequents when plotted in the ROC space are in "different scales", and therefore not directly comparable. The procedure for analyzing measures in different scales is well known in physical sciences. For instance, when we have a temperature expressed in Fahrenheit and are used to temperatures reported in Celsius, or vice-versa, we can make a scale conversion so that temperatures expressed in one scale can be converted to another. Therefore, to be able to extend ROC analysis to association rules, we should previously perform a scale conversion so that analyzing the graph we can directly compare the performance of rules with different consequents.

One of these scale conversions are the "corrected for chance" versions of SE and SP. These conversions work as follows: firstly, subtract the corresponding measures by the naïve rule of always predicting y; these measures are known as relative sensitivity and specificity. Then divide these measures by $p(y)$ and $p(\dot{y})$, respectively. The rescaled version of sensitivity, named QRSE, is defined as:

$$QRSE = \frac{p(x \mid y) - p(y)}{p(\dot{y})}$$

and the rescaled version of specificity, named QRSP, is defined as:

$$QRSP = \frac{p(\dot{x} \mid \dot{y}) - p(\dot{y})}{p(y)}$$

These measures are also called Cohen's kappas: $\kappa(0)$ for QRSP and $\kappa(1)$ for QRSE. Because $\kappa(0)$ and $\kappa(1)$ reflect where both sensitivity and specificity lie between their random value and perfect agreement, they are often referred as sensitivity and specificity "corrected for chance" or "quality" sensitivity and specificity.

In medical domains, (Kraemer, 1992, 1988) propose to use these rescaled versions as the axis of the QROC space. The Quality Receiver Operating Characteristic space, the QROC space, is formed by $\kappa(0)$ on the x-axis and by $\kappa(1)$ on the y-axis.

QROC space has numerous interesting properties. Random performance, which lies in the ascending diagonal in the ROC space, corresponds to the point $(0, 0)$ in the ROC space. Therefore, instead of a line as in the ROC space, random performance is always represented by a single point in the ROC space regardless the consequent proportions or costs. The ideal point (perfect agreement between X and Y) is the upper right corner $(1, 1)$.

The ascending diagonal in QROC space is the place where $p(x) = p(y)$. The optimally specific rule (maximum $\kappa(0)$) is the point furthest to the right in the QROC space. The optimally sensitive rule (maximum $\kappa(1)$) is the highest point in the QROC space. All points in the QROC space are constrained to the maximum $\kappa(0)$ and $\kappa(1)$.

The location of all rules having the best trade-offs between $\kappa(0)$ and $\kappa(1)$ forms a leaf shaped convex line. This convex line is similar in spirit to the ROC convex hull in the case of classification. However, the interpretation is slightly different: instead of manipulating costs or class proportions to select classification rules to maximize expected cost under different conditions we are concerned in choosing rules which trades specificity and sensitivity. For instance, in market basket analysis, we may choose to market very specific products (maximum $\kappa(0)$) to a limited audience or quite general products (maximum $\kappa(1)$) for a broad audience, or decide for intermediary approaches which lie in this leaf shaped convex line.

Although the set of best trade-offs between $\kappa(0)$ and $\kappa(1)$ form this leaf-shaped convex line, the set of "most valuable" rules lies in the line segment between the optimal specific and optimal sensitive rules. This is because we would like to remove from consideration rules that have high sensitivity only because the consequent is high prevalent in the data set ($p(y)$ near 1) and rules that have high specificity only because the consequent is low prevalent in the data set ($p(y)$ near 0).

Figure 3 shows an example of a QROC graph containing 7 points (A, B, C, D, E, F and G). The leaf-shaped convex region is formed by the origin and other 5 points (A to E). Point B is the one with highest $\kappa(0)$. Point D is the one

with highest $\kappa(1)$. Points D to E are those with the most valuable trade off of $\kappa(0)$ and $\kappa(1)$, not taking into account those points which are in the convex region due to extreme (high or low) values of the prevalence of the consequent part of the rule (the shaded areas).

Geometric Derivation of the QROC Space

To gain more insight in the interpretation of QROC graphs, this section provides a geometric interpretation of the process of deriving a QROC from a ROC graph. To this end, we will use the concept of isometrics in the ROC space (Flach, 2003).

Prevalence is defined as the fraction of cases for which the consequent Y of a rule is true, *i.e.*, *Prev* = *p(y)*. The location of all points for which *Prev* = *p(x)* lies on a line connecting the ROC ideal point (0, 1) to the point (*p(x)*, *p(x)*) in the main diagonal. This line is often called diagnosis line in medical decision-making. Coverage isometrics with value equal to *p(y)* are parallel

Figure 3. The QROC space

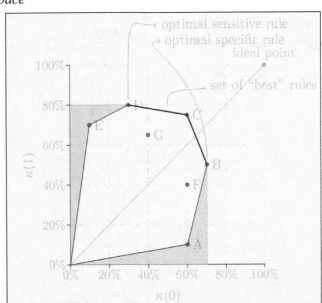

to the diagnosis line, although they intercept the main diagonal at the point $(p(y),p(y))$ As we move from a ROC plane with one value of $p(y)$ to others with different values of $p(y)$, the slope of this diagnosis line changes along the slope of every prevalence isometric.

Figure 4 shows isometric lines for two different values of $p(y)$. For the solid lines $p(y) = 0.5$, while for the dashed lines $p(y) = 0.25$. Note that as $p(y)$ changes, not only the slope changes but also the distance between the isometric lines. For $p(y) = 0.5$ all isometric lines are equally spaced, while for $p(y) = 0.25$ the bottom line is closer to the middle line than the top line. Because of this, the points in the corners of the ROC space are those where $p(y)$ is much greater (upper corner) or much less (lower corner) than $p(x)$. They are particularly problematic if $p(x)$ itself is near 0 or 1, generating a diagnosis line that is either very steep ($p(y)$ near zero) or flat ($p(y)$ near 1).

Clearly, for extreme values of $p(y)$ relative to $p(x)$, the points in the corners of the ROC space have very little room to move in the ROC space, as they are constrained to move along lines parallel to the diagnosis line along a coverage line of limited length. It is very difficult to see or to interpret what is going on in those corners.

The QROC plane is a re-scaling of the ROC space to give a chance to points at different levels of $p(y)$ to become more visible. The geometric re-scaling from the ROC to the QROC space can be interpreted as follows: consider the ROC graph shown in Figure 5. This graph has a diagnosis line crossing the main diagonal at the point (0.25, 0.25), and thus p(y) = 0.25. The prevalence isometric which pass through point A cross the main diagonal at the point (0.55, 0.55) and thus $p(y) = 0.55$.

In the graph represented in Figure 5, relative sensitivity is the line segment corresponding to the sensitivity minus the line segment corresponding to $p(y)$. If we trace a line parallel to the y-axis passing through the point $(p(y), p(y))$ in the main diagonal (the point corresponding to the rule of naively predicting y) relative accuracy is the portion of the line that is above the main diagonal. In other words, we are removing the portion of sensitivity "due to chance". This relative sensitivity is then weighed by a factor which is the line segment above the main diagonal crossing the chance rule. This factor aims to re-scale the relative sensitivity to the 0-1 range.

*Figure 4. Prevalence isometrics. Solid lines indicates isometrics for **p(y)**=0.5; dashed lines for* **p(y)** *= 0.25.*

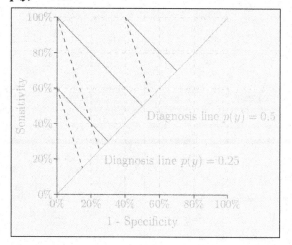

Figure 5. Scaling factors in ROC space for deriving QRSE

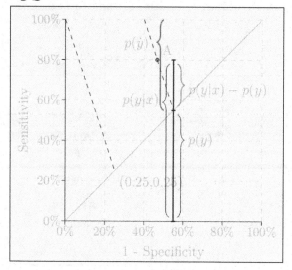

A similar procedure can be applied to specificity to derivate the QRSP.

Therefore, $\kappa(0)$ and $\kappa(1)$ are the ratio of two widths. If these ratios are equal to 1, the rule lies at the ideal point. If they are equal to zero, the point lies on the random line in the ROC space. The larger the ratio, the higher the "corrected by chance" version of SE and SP. Note that the scaling of SE and SP might be higher or lower, depending where the chance rule cross the main diagonal.

In the QROC space, the diagnosis line is always the main diagonal. Rules having $p(y) > p(x)$ are above the main diagonal. Rules having $p(y) < p(x)$ are below the main diagonal. Points that might be compressed in the corners of the ROC space are now spread out along the full length of the two main axis of the QROC space. Furthermore, all points have a great deal of space to move, regardless of the values of costs and consequent proportions.

Taking Costs into Account

An interesting property of the ROC graph is to analyze the behavior of classifiers under different misclassification costs scenarios. However, as described earlier, costs are uniform for all classification rules. This section describes how disagreement costs can be analyzed in the QROC space so that the expert can analyze the rules under different cost scenarios, and with rules having different non uniform costs. This approach can help the (often ad hoc) process of analyzing the rules under the expert's preferences.

The transformation of the ROC space to the QROC space is effective in alleviating the problem of different values of $p(y)$ in two different rules having two different consequents. Unfortunately, it does not take into account that the disagreement costs associated with two rules might be different. However, it is still possible to incorporate this information in the QROC space.

Suppose that for some rule, the relative cost of a negative antecedent and a positive consequent $c(\dot{x},y)$ is proportional to some value r ($0 \le r \le 1$), and the relative cost of $c(x,\dot{y})$ is some value $r' = 1-r$. The agreement between X and Y is assumed having zero cost. Then, the expected loss would be (Kraemer, 1992):

$$L = p(\dot{x}\,|\,y)p(y)r + p(x\,|\,\dot{y})p(\dot{y})r'$$

If the rule is random (there is no agreement between X and Y),

$$L = p(x)p(y)r + p(x)p(y)r'$$

and the gain given by the rule when compared to the random rule is obtained by subtraction:

$$G = L - L' = p(x)p(\dot{y})r\kappa(1) + p(\dot{x})p(y)r'\kappa(0)$$

The maximum possible gain would be when both $\kappa(0)$ and $\kappa(1)$ are both 1 (they have their maximal possible values):

$$\max G = p(x)p(\dot{y})r + p(\dot{x})p(y)r'$$

The relative gain of a given rule can then be defined as:

$$\kappa r = \frac{p(x)p(\dot{y})r\kappa(1) + p(\dot{x})p(y)r'\kappa(0)}{p(x)p(\dot{y})r + p(\dot{x})p(y)r'}$$

Note that $\kappa(r)$ is a weighted average of $\kappa(0)$ and $\kappa(1)$. It is also known as weighed kappa coefficient, where the weight reflects the context specific costs of the two possible disagreements between X and Y. Thus, $\kappa(r)$ can be used to select rules according to the relative cost r. Clearly, if $r = 1$, we are aiming to maximize $\kappa(1)$. If $r = 0$, then we are maximizing $\kappa(0)$. If $r = 0.5$ we are given equal cost to the two possible disagreement between X and Y, and are maximizing rule accuracy. Other values of r trade sensitivity and specificity in different ways.

It is very easy to obtain $\kappa(r)$ from a QROC graph. By tracing a line of slope

$$\frac{p(x)p(\dot{y})r}{p(\dot{x})p(y)r'}$$

passing through the point in the QROC space corresponding to a given rule, $\kappa(r)$ can be read by the intercept of this line in the main diagonal. This construction is shown in Figure 6 for an arbitrary point in the QROC space for three possible values of r (0, 0.5 and 1).

Geometric Interpretation of Rule Quality Measures in the QROC Space

This section presents geometric interpretation of some rule quality measures often used for evaluating association rules in the QROC space.

Coverage

Coverage isometrics in the ROC space were discussed in the section Geometric derivation of the QROC space. They are parallel lines in which the slope depends on *p(y)*. However, in QROC space coverage is well-behaved. Coverage can be written as:

$$Cov$$
$$= p(x)(p(x\,|\,y) - p(y)) + p(\dot{x})(p(\dot{x}\,|\,\dot{y}) - p(\dot{y}))$$
$$= p(x)p(\dot{y})\kappa(1) + p(\dot{x})p(y)\kappa(0)$$

Therefore, in terms of the QROC space:

$$\frac{\kappa(1)}{\kappa(0)} = \frac{p(\dot{x})p(y)}{p(x)p(\dot{y})}$$

As in QROC space, the main diagonal is the line where *p(y) = p(x)*, coverage isometrics in the QROC space are rotations of this line towards the origin. Lines above the main diagonal have *Cov > p(x)*, while lines below the main diagonal have *Cov < p(x)*. Figure 7 shows coverage isometrics in QROC space.

Chi-Square

The χ^2 index is the difference between observed and expected values for each inner cell in the contingency table, and is used as a measure of in-

Figure 6. Obtaining $\kappa(r)$ in QROC space

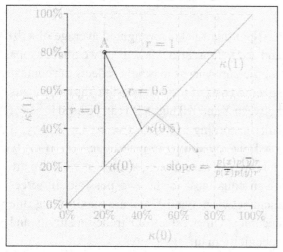

Figure 7. Coverage isometrics in QROC space

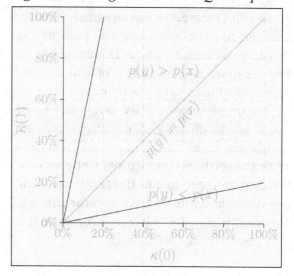

Figure 8. Geometric interpretation of χ^2

Figure 8. Geometric interpretation of χ^2

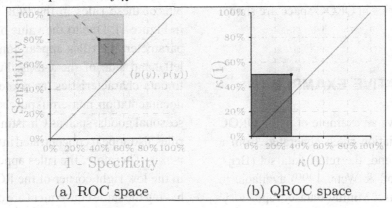

(a) ROC space   (b) QROC space

dependence between two variables. The expected value is obtained by multiplying the marginals. Its formulae is given by:

$$\chi^2 = \sum_{X \in \{x, \dot{x}\}, Y \in \{y, \dot{y}\}} \frac{(n(X,Y) - n(X)n(Y))^2}{n(X)n(Y)}$$

The relationship between χ^2 and ROC graphs was studied in (Bradley, 1996). The χ^2 isometrics are curves in the ROC space that depend on the proportion of cases between $p(y)$ and $p(\dot{x})$. Figure 8 shows the geometric interpretation of χ^2 in the ROC space. Observe that χ^2 is proportional to the area ratio between the two nested boxes (The value of χ^2 is this ratio multiplied by N). This geometric interpretation helps us to understand why χ^2 isometrics depends on $p(y)$. The shape of the boxes changes as $p(y)$ changes (due to change in the coverage isometrics).

χ^2 has a much simpler visualization in the QROC space. χ^2 can be re-written as (Kraemer, 1992):

$$\chi^2 = N\kappa(0)\kappa(1)$$

As shown in Figure 8, χ^2 is proportional to the area of the rectangular box formed by the point (0, 0) and $(\kappa(0), \kappa(1))$, regardless of $p(y)$. χ^2

isometrics in the QROC space are lines parallel to the descending diagonal.

Accuracy

Accuracy (the proportion of examples correctly classified) in the ROC space has the same behavior of the loss function, assuming equal unit costs for both possible disagreements between X and Y. Its isometrics in ROC space are similar in shape to coverage isometrics in the QROC space. In

Figure 9. Accuracy isometrics in QROC space

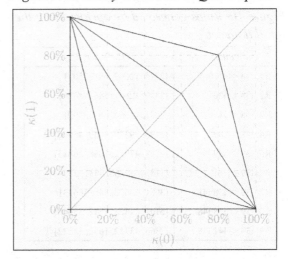

QROC space, accuracy is equivalent to $\kappa(0.5)$. Accuracy isometrics in QROC space are shown in Figure 9.

AN ILLUSTRATIVE EXAMPLE

This section shows an example of using QROC to analyze association rules generated from a data set. To this end, the retail data set (Brijs, Swinnen, Vanhoof, & Wets, 1999) available in the Frequent Itemset Mining dataset repository[1] is used. This data set contains retail market basket data provided by an anonymous Belgian retail supermarket store. The data are collected over three non-consecutive periods totalizing approximately 5 months of data, between the half of December 1999 to the end of November 2000. The total amount of receipts collected is 88,163. The average number of distinct items (*i.e.* different products) purchased per shopping visit is around 11, and most customers buy between 7 and 13 items per shopping visit.

We ran the implementation of Apriori from (Borgelt & Kruse, 2002)[2], and minimum support was set to 3% and minimum confidence was set to 70%. With these parameters, Apriori found 9 rules, shown in Figure 10, alongside their re-

spective true/false positive/negative counts. The plot of these rules in the ROC space is shown in Figure 11. Due to the value of the confidence parameter, the rules appear concentrated in the left hand side of the *x*-axis. Furthermore, due to data characteristics (as related in the dataset documentation, numerous purchases may contain seasonal goods, such as Christmas products), the rules also appear concentrated in the bottom of the *y*-axis. Therefore, the rules appear concentrated in the low right corner of the ROC graph. Rules having the same consequent are depicted with the same symbol: the item i38 in the consequent is represented by a triangle, the item i48 by a circle and the item i39 by an x. As argued in section Pitfalls of using ROC analysis for evaluating association rules, it is very difficult to draw a general conclusion by analyzing the ROC graph, as only the rules with the same consequent are directly comparable. Furthermore, several rules seem to have similar quality, as they appear closer to each other in the ROC space.

Figure 12 depicts the same set of rules in the QROC space. Unlike in ROC space, the points can be now directly comparable. Assuming an uniform cost (or profit) for all items, in our proposed framework it is more evident that rules having

Figure 10. Rules generated by apriori using the retail data set

Rule	[TP, FN, FP, TN]
R1: i38 <- i110	[2725, 12867, 69, 72501]
R2: i38 <- i36	[2790, 12801, 146, 72425]
R3: i38 <- i170	[3031, 12564, 68, 72499]
R4: i48 <- i89	[2798, 39319, 1039, 45006]
R5: i39 <- i89	[2719, 47912, 1088, 36413]
R6: i39 <- i41	[11414, 39268, 3531, 33949]
R7: i39 <- i38 i41	[3051, 47632, 846, 36633]
R8: i39 <- i38 i48	[6102, 44578, 1842, 35640]
R9: i39 <- i41 i48	[7366, 43322, 1652, 35822]

Figure 11. Association rules in the ROC space

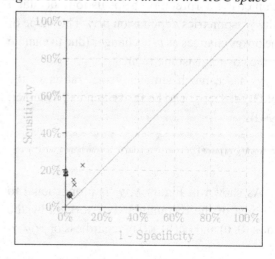

Figure 12. Association rules in the QROC space

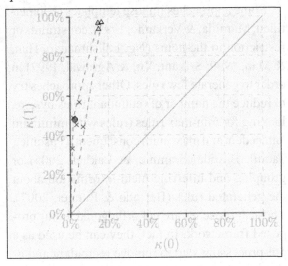

Figure 13. Using different costs per item to analyze rules

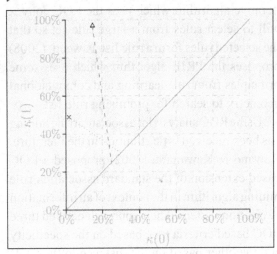

the item i39 in the consequent might be better than the others, as they appear in the upper left part of the QROC graph isolated from the others - remember that in the QROC space, the closer a point is to the upper right corner (1, 1) the better. This fact is masked in the ROC space because the prevalence of items i39 and i48 is larger than the prevalence of item i38. In other words, is easier to have a good sensitivity for rules having items i39 and i48 in the consequent because these items are very frequent in the transactions. On the other hand, although the sensitivity of the rules having the item i38 in the consequent is similar to some rules having the item i39 in the consequent, it is much harder to achieve such sensitivity because this item is less prevalent (the prevalence of item i38 is about one quarter of prevalence of item i39 and a third of the prevalence of item i48). This does not occur in the "corrected by chance" version of sensitivity $\kappa(0)$. We can also draw the leaf shaped closed area corresponding to the best trade-offs between $\kappa(0)$ and $\kappa(1)$. Note that although it is possible to draw the convex hull in the ROC graph, as discussed in section Pitfalls of using ROC analysis for evaluating association rules, this convex hull is meaningless.

As discussed in the section Taking costs into account, we can not only consider uniform trade-offs between $\kappa(0)$ and $\kappa(1)$ (as we have done in drawing the leaf-shaped closed area) but also different ones. For the sake of illustration, let us assume that item i38 is quite cheap, thus leading to a small profit, and item i39 has a good pay off so that the profit is greater, leading to a $\kappa(r)$ (see Section Taking costs into account,) as shown in Figure 13 (for the sake of visualization only the two first points which appears in the leaf shaped closed area are reproduced; the dashed line corresponds to the projection of a rule with the item i38 in the consequent, and the dotted corresponds to the rule with item i39). In this scenario, although the rule with consequent i38 has a greater "corrected by chance sensitivity", the rule with consequent 39 has a better pay off, having a greater $\kappa(r)$ than the first rule.

NEW TRENDS AND RELATED WORK

In classification rule learning, the ROC convex hull can be used to keep track of the best rule set which forms a classifier. This idea has been used by Prati & Flach, (2005), who proposed an iterative algorithm which uses the ROC convex hull to select rules from a large rule set so that the selected rules form a rule list. Fawcett, (2008) proposes the PRIE algorithm which uses some principles from rule learning and computational geometry to search for promising rule list.

Using ROC analysis for association rule mining has been received little attention in the literature. Kawano & Kawahara, (2002) proposed a ROC based extension of the standard association rule mining algorithm in the context of an information navigation system. Their approach derived three ROC based criteria (one based on the specificity and the other based on the distance to the (0, 1) point in the ROC space) for pruning association rules out of the association rule set. However, their approach to decide whether a case is a true/false positive one is strongly dependent to the domain they are working on: in their domain, items are keywords which indexes some bibliography; for a given association rule, a case is considered as a true positive if the keywords appearing in the rule are related to a subset of the bibliography a user is interested in or a false positive otherwise. Obviously, this cannot be generalized to the general association rule problem, as it is not possible to define an arbitrary criterion to decide beforehand whether a case covered by a rule is a true/false positive one.

Much work has been done in terms of rule interestingness measures (Guillet & Hamilton, 2007) aiming to select the most interesting rules out of a large set of discovered rules. In (Piatetsky-Shapiro et al., 2005), the authors present three principles of rule interestingness. In (Liu, Hsu, & Ma, 1999), the authors proposed the use of the χ^2 statistical test as a way of pruning uninteresting rules. The relationship of our proposed framework is presented in Section Chi-Squares. Kappa coefficients, which are used as the axis of the QROC graph in our framework, were also used for selecting rules (Tan, Kumar, & Srivastava,

2002). However, to the best of our knowledge, it has not been used for visualization.

Some approaches impose templates (Klemettinen, Mannila, & Verkamo, 1999), constraints or restriction to the items (Ng, Lakshmanan, Han, & Mah, 1999; Srikant, Vu, & Agrawal, 1997) in order to generate few rules. Other approaches try to reduce the number of redundant rules by, *e.g.*, looking for min-max rules (rules with minimum antecedent and maximum consequent) (Pasquier, Taouil, Bastide, Stumme, & Lakhal, 2005) or grouping and inferring meta-information about the generated rules (Berrado & Runger, 2007). Those approaches are not orthogonal to our proposed framework. In fact, they can be used as a pre-processing step to remove redundant and/or undesirable rules. The remaining rules can be plotted in the QROC space for analysis, where the domain expert can analyze the rules under different cost scenarios.

CONCLUDING REMARKS

In this paper we present an extension to ROC analysis, named QROC, which can be applied to association rules. This extension is necessary because in order to ROC analysis be applied in classification context, we often make the (sometimes implicit) assumption that class conditional likelihoods are constant. This assumption does not hold in association rule context because the consequent part of two different association rules might be very different from each other.

In a QROC graph, the axes are re-scaled so that points in QROC space can be directly compared regardless of the consequent. QROC is especially suitable when there is a strong skew ratio between the marginal probabilities in a 2 x 2 contingency table. In such situations, most points are constrained to the corner in the ROC space. On the other hand, in the QROC space, points in such situations have a great deal of space in which to move, regardless of $p(x)$ or $p(y)$.

The proposed extension is based on "corrected for chance" or quality versions of sensitivity and specificity. These measures are also known as Cohen's kappa coefficients. We also present the weighed kappa coefficient, which can be used to take different disagreement costs into account in the analysis. Furthermore, we present a geometric interpretation to the transformation of ROC space into the QROC space, as well as geometric interpretations of some rule quality measures often used for evaluation association rules.

REFERENCES

Berrado, A., & Runger, G. C. (2007). Using meta-rules to organize and group discovered association rules. *Data Mining and Knowledge Discovery, 14*(3), 409-431.

Borgelt, C., & Kruse, R. (2002). Induction of association rules: Apriori implementation. *Proceedings of the 15th Conference on Computational Statistics*, (pp. 395–400). *Berlin, Germany.*

Bradley, A. P. (1996). ROC curves and the x^2 test. *Pattern Recognition Letters, 17*(3), 287-294.

Bradley, A. P. (1997). The use of the area under the ROC curve in the evaluation of machine learning algorithms. *Pattern Recognition, 30*(7), 1145-1159.

Brijs, T., Swinnen, G., Vanhoof, K., & Wets, G. (1999). Using association rules for product assortment decisions: a case study. *Proceedings of the fifth ACM SIGKDD international conference on Knowledge discovery and data mining*, (pp. 254-260).

Drummond, C., & Holte, R. (2006). Cost curves: An improved method for visualizing classification performance. *Machine Learning, 65*(1), 95-130.

Egan, J. P. (1975). *Signal detection theory and ROC analysis.* New York: Academic Press.

Fawcett, T. (2006). An introduction to ROC analysis. *Pattern Recognition Letters, 27*(8), 861-874.

Fawcett, T. (2008). PRIE: A system to generate rulelists to maximize ROC performance. *Data Mining and Knowledge Discovery Journal, 17*(2), 207-224.

Fawcett, T., & Flach, P. A. (2005). A Response to Webb and Ting's On the Application of ROC Analysis to Predict Classification Performance Under Varying Class Distributions. *Machine Learning, 58*(1), 33-38.

Flach, P. A. (2003). The geometry of ROC space: Understanding machine learning metrics through ROC isometrics. *Proceedings of the Twentieth International Conference on Machine Learning,* (pp. 194–201).

Guillet, P. F., & Hamilton, H. J. (2007). *Quality Measures in Data Mining.* Springer.

Kawano, H., & Kawahara, M. (2002). Extended Association Algorithm Based on ROC Analysis for Visual Information Navigator. *Lecture Notes In Computer Science, 2281*, 640-649.

Klemettinen, M., Mannila, H., & Verkamo, A. I. (1999). Association rule selection in a data mining environment. *Principles of Data Mining and Knowledge Discovery (Proc. 4th European Conf.-PKDD-99), LNAI, 1704*, 372-377.

Kraemer, H. (1988). Assessment of 2×2 associations: generalization of signal-detection methodology. *The American statistician, 42*(1), 37-49.

Kraemer, H. (1992). *Evaluating medical tests.* Newbury Park, CA: Sage Publications.

Liu, B., Hsu, W., & Ma, Y. (1999). Pruning and summarizing the discovered associations. *Proceedings of the fifth ACM SIGKDD international conference on Knowledge discovery and data mining*, (pp. 125-134).

Ng, R., Lakshmanan, L. V. S., Han, J., & Mah, T. (1999). Exploratory mining via constrained frequent set queries. *Proceedings of the 1999 ACM SIGMOD international conference on Management of data*, (pp. 556-558).

Pasquier, N., Taouil, R., Bastide, Y., Stumme, G., & Lakhal, L. (2005). Generating a Condensed Representation for Association Rules. *Journal of Intelligent Information Systems*, *24*(1), 29-60.

Piatetsky-Shapiro, G., Piatetsky-Shapiro, G., Frawley, W. J., Brin, S., Motwani, R., Ullman, J. D., et al. (2005). Discovery, Analysis, and Presentation of Strong Rules. *Proceedings of the 11th international symposium on Applied Stochastic Models and Data Analysis ASMDA*, *16*, 191-200.

Prati, R., & Flach, P. (2005). ROCCER: an algorithm for rule learning based on ROC analysis. *Proceeding of the 19th International Joint Conference on Artificial Intelligence. Edinburgh, Scotland.*

Provost, F., & Fawcett, T. (2001). Robust Classification for Imprecise Environments. *Machine Learning*, *42*(3), 203-231.

Provost, F., Fawcett, T., & Kohavi, R. (1998). The case against accuracy estimation for comparing induction algorithms. Proceedings of the Fifteenth International Conference on Machine Learning, (pp. 445–453).

Srikant, R., Vu, Q., & Agrawal, R. (1997). Mining association rules with item constraints. KDD, 97, 67–73.

Tan, P. N., Kumar, V., & Srivastava, J. (2002). Selecting the right interestingness measure for association patterns. Proceedings of the eighth ACM SIGKDD international conference on Knowledge discovery and data mining, (pp. 32-41).

ENDNOTES

[1]   http://fimi.cs.helsinki.fi/data/

[2]   http://www.borgelt.net/apriori.html

Section IV
Rule Selection for Classification

Chapter IX
Variations on Associative Classifiers and Classification Results Analyses

Maria-Luiza Antonie
University of Alberta, Canada

David Chodos
University of Alberta, Canada

Osmar Zaïane
University of Alberta, Canada

ABSTRACT

*The chapter introduces the **associative classifier**, a classification model based on **association rules**, and describes the three phases of the model building process: **rule generation**, pruning, and selection. In the first part of the chapter, these phases are described in detail, and several variations on the **associative classifier** model are presented within the context of the relevant phase. These variations are: mining data sets with **re-occurring items**, using **negative association rules**, and pruning rules using **graph-based techniques**. Each of these departs from the standard model in a crucial way, and thus expands the classification potential. The second part of the chapter describes a system, ARC-UI that allows a user to analyze the results of classifying an item using an **associative classifier**. This system uses an intuitive, Web-based interface and, with this system, the user is able to see the rules that were used to classify an item, modify either the item being classified or the rule set that was used, view the relationship between attributes, rules and classes in the rule set, and analyze the training data set with respect to the item being classified.*

INTRODUCTION

The process of creating an **associative classifier** from a training data set has three main phases: (1) mining the training data for **association rules** and keeping only those that can classify instances, (2) pruning the mined rules to weed out irrelevant or noisy rules, and (3) selecting and combining the rules to classify unknown items. Within each of these steps, there is a great deal of potential for variation and improvement. The first three sections describe each of the three phases of the associative classification process in detail. In addition, three variations on this process are described, each within the context of the relevant classification phase. Each of these variations are outlined briefly in the following paragraphs and described using a running example of a department store sales dataset. To put the preceding paragraph into this context, we can imagine a store with data from previous months on the sales of various items in the store, and an assessment from a manager of whether the items were worth stocking. An **associative classifier** for this context would create a set of rules relating items' sales figures to their overall profitability, and allow the manager to assess the current month's stock based on data accumulated from previous months.

The first variation considers data sets with **re-occurring items**. **Associative classifiers** are typically concerned only with the presence of an attribute, which ignores potentially valuable information about the number of occurrences of that attribute. For example, in a text classification context, the number of occurrences of a word in a document and in a collection are crucial indicators of its importance. Or, to use the department store example, knowing *how many* shirts were sold might be more important than knowing whether or not any shirts were sold. A classification model by Rak et al (Rak, 2005) considers the number of occurrences of an attribute both in generating rules and in classifying items according to those rules. In the **rule generation** phase, the model increments a rule's support by an amount proportional to the number of attribute occurrences. In the item classification phase, the model uses the Cosine Measure to measure the similarity between an item and rules which have re-occurring attributes.

The second variation presents a classifier which works with both positive and negative rules. Negative rules either use attribute/negated value pairs, or imply a negative classification, and can capture patterns and relationships that would be missed by positive only rule-based **associative classifiers**. In the department store context, knowing that a store did not sell any shirts of a certain brand could help a manager decide not to stock more shirts of that brand. Generating a complete set of **negative association rules** from a set of positive rules is a very difficult task, and can result in an exponential growth in the number of **association rules**. A method developed by Antonie and Zaïane (Antonie, 2004c) deals with this issue in two ways. First, the negative rules generated are restricted to those where either the entire antecedent or consequent is negated. Thus, a rule that identifies one brand of shirt that *did not* sell and another that did would not be generated using this method. Second, the correlation coefficient between a pattern and a frequent itemset is used to guide the generation of **negative association rules**. This method also incorporates both negative and positive rules into the item classification process.

The third variation deals with the issue of pruning rules generated through frequent itemset mining. Since frequent itemset mining can generate hundreds or even thousands of rules, pruning this initial rule set is crucial for maintaining classification accuracy and comprehension. However, it is important not just to reduce the number of rules, but to do so in such a way that the accuracy of the classifier does not suffer. That is, one must reduce the number of rules while preserving the rules which do a good job of classification. To this end, a technique was developed that evaluates each rule by using the rule set to re-classify the training data set and measuring each rule's number of correct and incorrect classifications (Zaïane, 2005). These measurements are then plotted on a graph, and the rules are then categorized (e.g., frequently used and often inaccurate) and prioritized for pruning.

An important part of associative classification process that is often overlooked is the analysis of classification results by the user. Often, a user will be interested not only in the classification of an item, but in the reasons behind that classification, and how the classification might change with slightly different input. Returning to the department store example, a manager might want to know *why* a brand of shirt was classified as a "very profitable item"; is it because of customer demand, a supplier discount, or a beneficial profit margin? The second section of the chapter presents an analysis system for **association rule** classifiers, ARC-UI, which offers the user a variety of classification analysis and speculation tools.

The analysis tools offered by ARC-UI are based on research on analyzing the results of linear classifiers by Poulin *et al* (Poulin, 2006). However, these tools have been modified for use with **associative classifiers**, and deal with rule sets as opposed to weighted attributes. The decision speculation component offers robust speculation capabilities which allow the user to modify both the item being classified and the rules used to perform the classification. The decision evidence component shows the impact of all relevant rules on an item's classification, while the ranks of evidence component offers a concise graphical representation of the relationship between attributes, rules, and classes. Finally, the source of evidence component allows the user to analyze the relationship between the item being classified and the training data set used to generate the **associative classifier**.

ASSOCIATIVE CLASSIFIERS

The first reference to using **association rules** as classification rules is credited to Bayardo (Bayardo, 1997), while the first classifier using these **association rules** was CBA, introduced by Liu (Liu, 1998) and later improved in CMAR (Li, 2001), and ARC-AC and ARC-BC (Antonie, 2002a). Other **associative classifiers** that have been presented in the literature include CPAR (Yin, 2003), Harmony (J. Wang, 2005), and 2SARC (Antonie, 2006).

The idea behind these classifiers is relatively simple. Given a training set modeled with transactions, where each transaction contains all features of an object in addition to the class label of the object, we can constrain the mining process to generate **association rules** that always have a class label as their consequent. In other words, the problem consists of finding the subset of strong **association rules** of the form $X \rightarrow C$ where C is a class label and X is a conjunction of features.

The main steps in building an **associative classifier** when a training set is given are the following:

1. *Generating the set of **association rules** from the training set:* In this phase, **association rules** of the form *set_of_features → class_label* are discovered using a mining algorithm. This phase can be completed in two ways:
   - Using an **association rule** mining algorithm, generate all the strong **association rules**. Once these are generated, filter them so that only the rules of interest are kept (those that have a class label as the consequent and the antecedent composed of features other than class labels).
   - Modifying an **association rule** mining algorithm by imposing a constraint. The constraint is that the **association rules** must have a class label as the con-

sequent. This improves the algorithm's efficiency since less candidate items are generated. All of the candidate itemsets that are generated contain a class label on the right-hand side.

2. *Pruning the set of discovered rules:* The previous phase may generate a large set of **association rules**, especially when a low support is given. Thus, pruning techniques are used in order to discover the best set of rules that can cover the training set. In this phase, rules that may introduce errors or cause overfitting in the classification stage are weeded out.

3. *Classification phase:* At this level a system that can classify a new item is built. The challenge here is using the set of rules from the previous phase to classify new items effectively. In order to classify a new item effectively using these rules, we need a good way of selecting one or more rules to participate in the classification process. In addition, another challenge is dealing with conflicting rules – when multiple rules with the same antecedent point to different classes.

RULE GENERATION: FROM ASSOCIATION RULES TO CLASSIFICATION RULES

The first step in creating an **associative classifier** is to generate a complete set of **association rules** for the training data set. The key difference between **associative classifiers** and other rule-based classifiers is that **associative classifiers** seek to use a *complete* set of rules, rather than using heuristics to identify a small set of hopefully relevant rules. To start this process, the frequent itemsets are found using an established technique such as Apriori (Agrawal, 1993) or FP-Growth (Han, 2000). This set of frequent itemsets is converted into **association rules**, and these are pruned so

that only those rules with the class label in the consequent are kept. Finally, from this list, all of the **association rules** which do not meet a certain minimum confidence level are discarded. Thus, the resulting rule set contains *all* the rules which a) have a sufficient level of support in the training data set and b) may be used to classify an unknown item.

While this approach works in many situations, it makes some assumptions which may not always work best. For one, the rules that are generated are assumed to be positive rules – that is, they associate the presence of an attribute with a particular class label. They do not, however, explicitly consider the *absence* of an attribute, nor do they consider rules where a class label is ruled out, rather than implied. Second, the rules are binary, in the sense that they are concerned only with the presence of an attribute. However, there are situations where the cardinality (number of occurrences) of an attribute is as important as its presence (e.g. image classification, text classification). Two variations on this approach are described in the sections that follow which address each of these concerns.

Data Sets with Recurrent Items

Associative rule classifiers typically use rules which are based on the presence of an attribute. For example, market-basket analysis focuses on questions such as "has the customer purchased both cereal and milk". However, this ignores potentially important information about the number of times an attribute occurs in a transaction. For instance, returning to market-basket analysis, one might want to know how many cans of pop a customer has purchased. Or, in a text classification context, the number of occurrences of a word in a document and in a collection are crucial indicators of its importance. This section presents a **rule generation** algorithm and classification scheme by Rak *et al* which makes use of attribute frequency (Rak, 2005).

The task in this case is to combine associative classification with the problem of recurrent items. Stated more formally, the original approach is modified such that transactions of the form $<\{o_1 i_1, o_2 i_2, \ldots o_n i_n\}, c>$ are used, where o_k is the number of the occurrences of the item i_k in the transaction and c is a class label.

Association rules have been recognized as a useful tool for finding interesting hidden patterns in transactional databases. However, less research has been done considering transactions with recurrent items. In (W. Wang, 2004), the authors assign weights to items in transactions and introduce the WAR algorithm to mine the rules. This method has two phases: first, frequent itemsets are generated without considering weights, and then weighted association rules (WARs) are derived from each of these itemsets. The MaxOccur algorithm (Zaïane, 2000) is an efficient Apriori-based method for discovering **association rules** with recurrent items. It reduces the search space by making effective use of joining and pruning techniques. The FP'-tree approach presented in (Lim, 2001) extends the FP-tree design (Han, 2000) by combining it with concepts from the MaxOccur algorithm. For every distinct number of occurrences of a given item, a separate node is created. In the case where a new transaction is inserted into the tree, it might increase support count for the different path(s) of the tree as well. This is based on the intersection between these two itemsets. Given the complete tree, the enumeration process to find frequent patterns is similar to that of the FP-tree approach.

Description of Rule Generation Process

The rule generator differs from traditional, Apriori-based algorithms in two important respects. First, the **rule generation** process is designed for finding all frequent rules in the form of $<\{o_1 i_1, o_2 i_2, \ldots o_n i_n\}, c>$ from a given set of transactions

and is based on ARC-BC (Antonie, 2002a): transactions are divided by class, rules are generated from each subset and then the rule sets for each class are merged to create a rule set for the entire data set. Second, attribute frequency is taken into account when calculating the support for a particular pattern. A transaction may only add support to a pattern if its attributes occur at least as many times as in the pattern. Similarly, the amount of support a transaction adds to a pattern is proportional to the cardinality of its attributes, as compared to that of the pattern.

The rule generator for each class C_x takes into account recurrent items in a single transaction à la MaxOccur (Zaïane, 2000). To accomplish this, the support count is redefined. Typically, a support count is the number of transactions that contain an item. In our approach, the main difference is that a single transaction may increase the support of a given itemset by more than one. The formal definition of this approach is as follows: a transaction $T=<\{o_1 i_1, o_2 i_2, \ldots o_n i_n\}, c>$ supports itemset $I=\{l_1 i_1, l_2 i_2, \ldots l_n i_n\}$ if and only if $\forall\ i=1..n;\ l_1 \leq o_1 \wedge l_2 \leq o_2 \wedge \ldots \wedge l_n \leq o_n$. The number t by which T supports I is calculated according to the formula: $t=\min[o_i / l_i]\ \forall\ i=1..n,\ l_i \neq 0 \wedge o_i \neq 0$.

Description of Classifier

Because of the added complexity of attribute recurrence, the probability of obtaining an exact match between an item to be classified and an **association rule** in the rule set is quite low. Thus, the classifier must use some notion of similarity between an item and a non-matching rule. Several definitions were considered by Rak *et al* (Rak, 2005) and tested extensively. The measure which proved most effective was the Cosine Measure (CM), which measures the angle between the vector representations of an item and an **association rule**. A small angle between the vector representations indicates that the item and the rule are similar.

Negative Association Rules

Most **associative classifiers** are based on rules which are made up of attribute/value pairs and an implied classification. However, one may also consider negative rules – that is, rules which either use attribute/negated value pairs, or which imply a negative consequent. This section presents a classifier developed by Antonie and Zaïane (Antonie, 2004c) that is based on this type of rule.

Utility of Negative Association Rules

Negative association rules, in general, rely on or imply the absence of a particular attribute value or class, respectively. In other words, negated predicates can exist in the antecedent or consequent of the rule. Negative attribute value rules identify situations where the absence of an attribute value is an important indicator of an item's class.

Example 1. Let us consider an example from the context of market basket analysis. In this example we want to study the purchase of organic versus non-organic vegetables in a grocery store. Table 1 gives us the data collected from 100 baskets in the store. In Table 1 "organic" means the basket contains organic vegetables and "¬organic" means the basket does not contain organic vegetables. The same applies for the term "non-organic".

Using this data, let us find the positive **association rules** in the "support-confidence" framework. The **association rule** "non-organic → organic" has 20% support and 25% confidence (supp(non-organic ∧ organic)/supp(non-organic)).

The **association rule** "organic → non-organic" has 20% support and 50% confidence (supp(non-organic ∧ organic)/supp(organic)). The support is considered fairly high for both rules. Although we may reject the first rule on the basis of confidence, the second rule appears to be valid and may be analyzed more closely. Now, let us compute the statistical correlation between the *non-organic* and *organic* items. For more details on the correlation measure, see (Antonie, 2004b). The correlation coefficient between these two items is -0.61. This means that the two items are negatively correlated. This measure sheds new light on the data analysis for these items. The rule "organic → non-organic" is misleading. The correlation, therefore, provides new information that can help in devising better marketing strategies.

The example above illustrates some weaknesses in the "support-confidence" framework and shows the need for the discovery of more interesting rules. The "interestingness" of an **association rule** can be defined in terms of the measure associated with it and in terms of the form of the association.

Brin *et al* (Brin, 1997) were the first in the literature to mention the idea of negative relationships. Their model is chi-square based. Specifically, they use the chi-square statistical test to verify the independence between two variables. To determine the nature (positive or negative) of the relationship, a correlation metric is used. In (Savasere, 1998) the authors present a new idea to mine strong negative rules. They combine positive frequent itemsets with domain knowledge, in the form of a taxonomy, to mine negative associations. However, their algorithm is hard to generalize since it is domain dependant and

Table 1. Example 1 data

	organic	¬organic	Σ_{row}
non-organic	20	60	80
¬non-organic	20	0	20
Σ_{col}	40	60	100

requires a predefined taxonomy. Wu *et al* (Wu, 2002) derived another algorithm for generating both positive and **negative association rules**. They add a measure called *mininterest* to the support-confidence framework in order to better prune the frequent itemsets that are generated. In (Teng, 2002) the authors use only negative associations of the type $X \rightarrow \neg Y$ to substitute items in market basket analysis.

In (Antonie, 2004b) the authors define a *generalized **negative association rule*** as a rule that contains a negation of an item – that is, a rule whose antecedent or consequent can be formed by a conjunction of presence or absence of terms. An example of such an **association rule** is: $A \wedge \neg B \wedge \neg C \wedge D \rightarrow E \wedge \neg F$. To the best of our knowledge, there is no algorithm that can determine this type of **association rule**. Deriving such an algorithm would be quite difficult, since it involves expanding the itemset generation phase, which is already a very expensive part of the association rule mining process. Such an algorithm would need not only to consider all items in a transaction, but also all possible items absent from the transaction. There could be a considerable exponential growth in the candidate generation phase. This is especially true in datasets with highly correlated attributes. Thus, it is not feasible to extend the attribute space by adding the negated attributes and continuing to use existing **association rule** algorithms. In (Antonie, 2004b), the authors generate and use a subset of the generalized **negative association rules**, referred to as *confined **negative association rules***, in the classification process. A confined **negative association rule** is defined as follows: $\neg X \rightarrow Y$ or $X \rightarrow \neg Y$, where the entire antecedent or consequent must be a conjunction of negated attributes or a conjunction of non-negated attributes.

Finding Positive and Negative Rules for Classification

Generating a complete set of **negative association rules** is a very difficult task, as it involves

the identification of all possible patterns that do not exist in a data set. For a frequent pattern in a data set, there is an exponentially larger number of possible frequent negative patterns, since any attribute that is not in the frequent pattern may either be negated or be absent in the negative pattern. Antonie and Zaïane deal with this issue by restricting the rules that are generated to those that fit the definition of confined **negative association rules** (Antonie, 2004b), which was described previously. This reduces the problem to adding at most two negative rules for each positive rule, which means that the overall number of rules increases by a small constant factor.

When processing the training data set, the algorithm uses the correlation coefficient between an itemset in the data set and each class to efficiently generate both positive and negative rules. Specifically, for each itemset I in the data set, the correlation coefficient is calculated for each class c. If corr(I, c) is above a positive threshold, then a positive rule $(I \rightarrow c)$ is generated and, provided the rule's confidence is high enough, that rule is added to the positive rule set. However, if corr(I, c) is below a negative threshold, then negative rules $(\neg I \rightarrow c$ and $I \rightarrow \neg c)$ are generated and, if their confidence levels are high enough, added to the negative rule set. Finally, the positive and negative rule sets are combined to create the classifier's rule set.

Classification Using Positive and Negative Rules

In (Antonie, 2004a), the classification of an item using positive and negative rules occurs as in a positive rule-based classifier for the most part. The item is compared against each rule in the rule set, and a set of matching rules is generated. These matching rules are then divided by class, the average confidence for each class is calculated, and the item is assigned the class with the highest average confidence. Note that an item matches a rule with negative attributes if the item does not contain any of the attributes in the rule. The main variation comes when considering rules which imply a negative classification. When calculating the average confidence for a class, these rules subtract from the total confidence for the class, rather than adding to it.

The set of rules that are generated, as discussed in the previous section, make up the classifier's model. This model is used to assign classification labels to new objects. Given a new object, the classification process searches in this set of rules for those classes that are relevant to the object presented for classification. The set of positive and negative rules are ordered by confidence and support. This sorted set of rules forms the basis for ARC-PAN (**Association Rule** Classification with Positive And Negative) (Antonie, 2004a) **associative classifier**, which uses an average confidence per class as a score.

Association rules of the type $X \rightarrow C$ and $\neg X \rightarrow C$ can be treated in the same way. Both of them have an associated confidence value and class label. These types of rules can be considered together and their confidence can be added to the C class total. However, the rules of the type $X \rightarrow \neg C$ have to be treated differently. Their confidences are subtracted from the total confidence of their corresponding class since they strongly indicate that the object should not be assigned to this class.

RULE PRUNING: KEEPING THE ESSENTIAL

The completeness of the initial rule set is, in theory, an advantage of associative classification over other rule-based algorithms, in that it guarantees that the classifier will not miss any potentially relevant rules. That is, all the rules meeting our definition of "relevant" (i.e., above a certain confidence threshold) are generated and included in the initial rule set. Thus, by using the initial rule set, the classifier will be able to draw on the information from *all* the relevant rules. However, in practice, the size of the generated rule set is often prohibitively large, containing thousands of rules. Thus, **associative classifiers** use **rule pruning** techniques to maintain the comprehensiveness of the rule set, while reducing the rule set to a more manageable size.

There are several heuristics that are commonly used to prune rule sets, such as removing low-ranking specialized rules, removing conflicting rules, and using database coverage. Each of these will be discussed in the following paragraphs.

Specialized rules occur when two rules have different characteristics, but the same classification. Let us consider two rules, r_1 and r_2, where $r_1 = a_1 ... a_n \rightarrow c$ and $r_2 = b_1 ... b_m \rightarrow c$ ($a_1 ... a_n \subset b_1 ... b_m$). If $n < m$, then r_2 is considered a *specialized* version of r_1 – that is, they both provide the same classification, but r_2 requires a larger number of characteristics, and is arguably less useful than the more generally-applicable r_1. Moreover, if r_2 also has a lower confidence, then it can be safely pruned, since it requires more information than r_1 to make a classification decision, and is less confident about that decision in those cases when it is actually applicable.

Conflicting rules, meanwhile, occur when two rules have the same characteristics, but different classifications. Let us again consider two rules, r_1 and r_2, where $r_1 = a_1 ... a_n \rightarrow c_1$ and $r_1 = a_1 ... a_n \rightarrow c_2$. Thus, if we are attempting to classify an item that matches attributes $a_1 ... a_n$, r_1 implies that the item should be given the class label c_1, while r_2 implies that the label should be c_2. In this case, the obvious solution to the problem is simply to prune the rule with a lower confidence value, as it provides a less certain answer.

Database coverage consists of going over all the rules and evaluating them against the training instances. Whenever a rule applies correctly on some instances, the rule is marked and the instances eliminated until all training instances are covered. Finally, the unmarked rules are simply pruned.

An alternative approach to pruning described below, uses **graph-based techniques** to categorize rules according to their utility and accuracy, and then prune those rules accordingly (Zaïane, 2005).

Pruning Using Graph-Based Techniques

Rule Categorization

One crucial difficulty in pruning rules is that it is important not just to reduce the number of rules, but to do so in such a way that the accuracy of the classifier does not suffer. That is, one must reduce the number of rules while preserving the rules which do a good job of classification. To this end, Zaïane and Antonie (Zaïane, 2005) evaluate each rule in the rule set by using it to re-classify the training data. In doing so, they keep track of the number of correct and incorrect classifications made by each rule, and then graph each rule as a point on a plane, as shown in Figure 1. The graph may then be divided using various thresholds, for instance shown in Figure 1 with thick lines. Rules above the horizontal line have a large number of false positives. Rules above the diagonal line classify more items incorrectly than

they do correctly. Finally, rules to the right of the vertical line classify many items correctly.

Rule Pruning Strategies

Using the thresholds concept described previously, one may divide the graph into four quadrants or regions. Given the rule evaluation related to these quadrants, the authors propose a variety of **rule pruning** schemes based around eliminating rules from particular quadrants (illustrated in Figure 2):

1. **Eliminate the high offender rules:** By tracing a horizontal line at a given threshold, we can eliminate all the rules above the line. This is illustrated in the chart on the left in Figure 2. The authors suggest a line at 50% by default but a sliding line can also be possible aiming at a certain percentage of rules to eliminate.

2. **Eliminate the rules that misclassify more than they classify correctly:** By tracing a diagonal line such rules can be identified. This is illustrated in the chart in the middle of Figure 2. Notice that when the axes of the plot are normalized, the diagonal indicates the rules that correctly classify as many

Figure 1. Quadrants for pruning rules

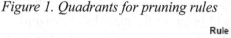

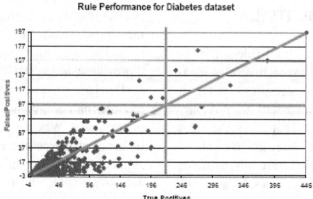

Figure 2. Filtering by quadrant and diagonal slicing

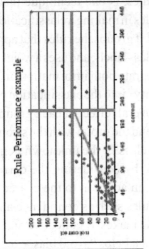

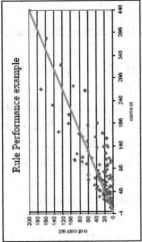

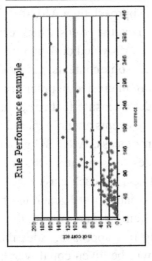

times as they misclassify. When the axes are not normalized, the diagonal indicates a relative ratio, which the authors advocate.

3. **Elimination by quadrant slicing:** The plot could be divided into four regions, as shown in the chart on the right of Figure 2. The top left (*Region A*) contains rules that are incorrect more than they are correct. The top right (*Region B*) contains rules that are frequently used but equally misclassify and correctly classify. The bottom left (*Region C*) has rules that are infrequently used but equally misclassify and correctly classify. Finally, the bottom right (*Region D*) contains the good rules which frequently classify correctly but seldom misclassify. The idea is to successively remove the rules that are in *Region A*, then *Region B*, then *Region C*.

4. **A combination of the above methods:** After removing regions *A* and *B*, eliminating the rules in *Region C* (bottom left) can be costly because many rules may be seldom used but have no replacements. Once removed, other rules are "forced" to play their role and can in consequence misclassify. The idea is to use a diagonal line to identify within *Region C* the rules that misclassify more than they are correct. This strategy strikes a good balance between removing a sufficient number of rules and retaining enough accurate rules to maintain effective classification.

Pruning classification rules is a delicate enterprise, because even if a rule misclassifies some objects, it has a role in correctly classifying other objects. When removed, there is no guarantee that the object the rule used to correctly classify will be correctly classified by the remaining rules. This is why we advocate progressive strategies depending upon the datasets at hand.

RULE SELECTION

Once the rule set has been pruned, all that remains is to classify unknown items using this optimized rule set. If for an unknown item only one relevant rule exists, then classifying the item would be quite straightforward: find the relevant rule for that item, and assign the class label implied by the relevant rule. However, even after pruning, rule sets for an **associative classifier** can contain a large number of rules. Thus, when classifying an item, it is very unlikely that only one rule will apply. Rather, there may be dozens or even hundreds of rules that apply for a particular item, meaning the potential application of a wide variety of class labels. How, then, does the classifier determine which class label to apply? Researchers have suggested a variety of answers to this problem. The following paragraphs will discuss four such techniques: CBA (Liu, 1998), CMAR (Li, 2001), ARC-AC and ARC-BC (Antonie, 2002a), and 2SARC (Antonie, 2006).

CBA may be viewed as the most straightforward of these techniques. It seeks to find a single "best" rule to classify the unknown item (Liu, 1998). Typically, the best rule is determined using Confidence, Support, size of Antecedent (CSA) ordering – that is, the rule with the highest confidence is used, unless there is a tie. In this case, the rule with the higher support is used. In the (highly unlikely) event that there is more than one rule with the same confidence and support, the size of the antecedent is used to break a tie. CBA has the advantage of being quite intuitive, and fairly straightforward to implement. However, relying on a single rule to classify an item can lead to incorrect classifications if that rule is not the best match for the item. For instance, a general rule with high confidence will invariably take precedence over a more specific rule with a slightly lower confidence. A way to solve this particular problem is to use ACS (antecedent, confidence, support) ordering, thus giving priority to more specific rules (Coenen, 2004). However,

the reliance on a single rule remains a drawback to the CBA technique, in general.

CMAR, Classification based on Multiple Association Rules, is one technique that considers groups of rules in making a classification decision. Specifically, it groups the rules that apply according to their class labels, and uses a weighted χ^2 measure to "integrate both information of correlation and popularity" into the classification process (Li, 2001). The overall effect of each group of rules is calculated, and the group with the strongest effect is chosen to classify the unknown item (Coenen, 2004). Thus, by considering the correlation between rules, in addition to the characteristics of individual rules such as confidence and support, the technique makes a "collective and all-round" decision which helps "avoid bias, exceptions and over-fitting" (Li, 2001).

The ARC-AC (Antonie, 2002a) technique takes a different approach to multiple rule-based classification. Like CMAR, ARC-AC groups rules according to their classification label. Instead of the weighted χ^2 value, however, ARC-AC calculates the average confidence for each class, and uses the class with the highest average confidence to classify the unknown item or the top scores based on dominance factor analysis if the application requires multi-label classification.

ARC-BC (Antonie, 2002a), Association Rule based Classification By Category, takes a slightly more refined approach than ARC-AC. This technique recognizes that rules which classify rare events may be "drowned out" by more common occurrences. In some contexts, such as classifying tumors, we are interested in precisely those rare cases. In order to ensure that rules that are able to classify rare events are not ignored during the classification process, ARC-BC generates classification rules by separating the training data into disjoint sets for each class label. Thus, the rules for class label c_i are generated from those items in the training data set with the class label c_i. By taking this approach, rules that classify rare events will be given equal weight as those that classify common events, thus ensuring that all rules are equally relevant in classifying an unknown item. The **rule selection** is also based on confidence average.

The above strategies assign classes to new objects based on the best rule applied or on some predefined scoring of multiple rules. Moreover, CMAR and ARC trade part of their comprehensibility inherited from the **association rules** for improved performance. This trade-off is the result of using a weighting score on the rules.

In (Antonie, 2006) a weighted voting scheme is proposed to combine the class predictions of the selected rules to produce a final classification. Instead of pre-defining the way in which weights are computed, 2SARC (Antonie, 2006) uses a second learning algorithm to automatically determine the weights for the application at hand. Therefore, with 2SARC, the learning takes place in two stages.

First, an **associative classifier** is learned using standard methods as described in the above sections. Second, predefined features computed on the outputs of the rules in the learned associative classifier are used as the inputs to another learning system, which is trained (using a separate training set) to weigh the features appropriately to produce highly accurate classifications. The advantage is that the **rule selection** can adapt to the data at hand rather than being static as CBA, CMAR and ARC.

CHALLENGES AND OPEN PROBLEMS

In each stage of the associative classification process, various techniques and heuristics are used to find the best balance between various factors. When generating rules, the **rule generation** algorithm must be carefully selected and tuned so as to return a set of rules that accurately reflects the connections between item attributes and classification labels. After this rule set has been

generated, it must be pruned to a manageable size, while maintaining the comprehensive quality that is one of the main advantages of associative classification over other rule-based classifiers. Once the rule set has been pruned appropriately, one must determine how to weigh the influence of numerous relevant rules in arriving at a single classification for an unknown item. At each of these stages, there is room for improvement in accuracy, flexibility and comprehensiveness. Figure 3 shows a chart of this process, with open problems clearly indicated.

In each of these open problem areas, researchers have been working to develop new solutions and techniques. In the area of **rule generation**, Wang, Do and Liu have recently developed a text classification scheme that uses a graph-based model in order to capture the relationships between terms (W. Wang, 2005). Thus, rules generated using this technique capture not only the frequency of items, but the connections between those items. This represents an important departure from conventional frequency-based rule sets, and thus requires novel approaches when determining large itemsets, significant rules, and so forth.

In the area of rule ranking, Arunaslam and Chawla have developed a new measure, the Complement Class Support (CCS) (Arunaslam, 2006). The CCS measure rules according to their strength in the class complement (that is, all classes except for the one matching the rule's class label), which results in stronger rules being assigned smaller CCS values. Using CCS results in rules which are guaranteed to be positively correlated, a desirable property when working with row enumeration algorithms, such as those used in analyzing microarray data. CCS is very well-suited for situations where there is an imbalanced distribution of classes, since it does not rely on class frequencies in the same manner as algorithms such as CBA and CMAR. Finally, CCS is relevant to **rule pruning** and threshold parameters, as it "allows the pruning of rules without the setting of any threshold parameter" (Arunaslam, 2006).

Figure 3. Open problems in associative classification

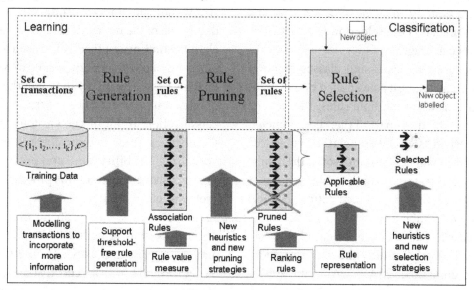

Coenen *et al* have done a great deal of work in automatically determining threshold values, thus contributing to the area of threshold-free algorithms (Coenen, 2007). In their work, they propose a hill-climbing method to determine the best threshold values when pruning rules, rather than using database coverage, a pruning technique discussed in the first part of Section 2.

Finally, in the area of rule representation, but not specifically for associative classifiers, Leung *et al* have developed a method of representing frequent itemsets based on wiring diagrams (Leung, 2007). This visualization technique follows established design principles such as minimizing edge crossings and using orthogonal coordinates in order to maximize readability and user comprehension. As well, the authors use a principle of overview and zoom in order to both manage the potentially large number of frequent itemsets and provide the user with meaningful analysis capabilities.

ANALYZING AND INTERPRETING ASSOCIATIVE CLASSIFIER RESULTS

The previous sections described the key concepts in the associative classification process, and presented several variations on this theme. Thus, the transition from raw data to classified information through the use of an **associative classifier** has been thoroughly described. However, this is not the whole story. Even the most rigorously trained and finely calibrated **associative classifier** is useless if the results are not properly interpreted by the person using it. Thus, a thorough discussion of the associative classification process is incomplete without exploring the analysis and interpretation of the classification results by the user. The following section presents the ARC-UI system, developed by Chodos and Zaïane which addresses this very issue.

Overview

The classification of items based on previously classified training data is an important area within data mining, and has many real-world applications. However, one drawback to many classification techniques, such as those based on neural networks or support vector machines (SVM), is that it is difficult for the user to understand the reasoning behind a classification result, or interpret the learned classification model. This is particularly important in a context where an expert user could make use of domain knowledge to either confirm or correct a dubious classification result.

Rule-based classifiers address this shortcoming by using a collection of simple rules to perform classification. Each rule is made up of one or more attribute/value pairs and a class, and is thus quite easy to understand. Most rule-based classifiers perform a heuristic search to discover classification rules, often missing important ones. **Associative classifiers**, on the other hand, use **association rule** mining to perform an exhaustive search to find classification rules. However, the set of rules generated by an associative classifier may contain hundreds of thousands of rules, and thus it is difficult for the user to ascertain which rules are relevant to the classification of an item, and to what extent the relevant rules influence a classification decision. The process of analyzing a set of generated **association rules**, referred to as post-mining, is a broad field and includes topics such as finding smaller, equally expressive, sets of rules and performing visual analysis on the set of rules. However, as the focus of this section is on the classification process, the discussion of post-mining will be focused on association rules used for classification.

This section presents ARC-UI, a tool that allows the user to understand the reasoning behind an associative classification result via a graphical, interactive interface. Furthermore, the user is able to modify the rules that are used and immediately see the results of this modification, thus allowing

the user to improve the accuracy of the classifier through the application of domain expertise. This capability has the added benefit of increasing the user's confidence in the classifier.

The screenshots that follow were taken from the system's use in the context of classifying mushrooms. The well-known "mushroom" data set, downloaded from the UCI data repository, contains over 8,000 mushrooms that have been classified as either poisionous or edible (Asuncion, 2007). Each item in the data set contains twenty-two characteristics, such as gills-attached, colour and odor, that help determine the item's classification. The Weka data analysis tool (Witten, 2005) was used to generate classification rules (1,275 in total), which were then imported into the system. Thus, the screenshots show the system analyzing the classification of an unknown mushroom using these rules.

Classification Analysis Component

The classification component shows the result of classifying the item, as well as all other possible classifications, as shown in Figure 4. This allows the user to compare the result with other possibilities, and thus assess the likelihood of an alternative result. The classification possibilities are listed in decreasing order of likelihood, to facilitate comparison between the various possibilities.

Decision Evidence Analysis Component

The decision evidence component shows the rules that were used to classify an item. This gives the user an initial understanding of the reasoning used by the classifier. If the relevant rule set is small enough, these rules are shown in a bar graph, as in Figure 5.

However, if the rule set is too large for this to be feasible, the bar graph is compressed in order to present the rule set characteristics in a meaningful, visual manner, as shown in Figure 6. By moving the mouse over the bars, details of individual rule is displayed. In either case, compressed or non compressed, the bar graph is colour-coded according to the class labels, to facilitate comparison among the rules shown. As well, the component presents a summary of the rules influencing each classification possibility. This summary includes the rules' confidence values and the overall confidence for each class, which is calculated by combining rules using different methods, as specified by the user.

Decision Speculation Component

The decision speculation component allows the user to modify the item being classified, the method used to calculate the confidence for each class, and the rules used in classification. After performing the desired modifications, the user is immediately shown the results of this modification. The decision speculation interface is shown in Figure 7. This allows the user to experiment with the classification engine, thus offering insight into the process behind item classification. In selecting the confidence calculation method, the user may choose between the best rule (Liu,

Figure 4. Classification component

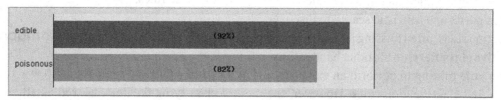

Figure 5. Decision evidence component

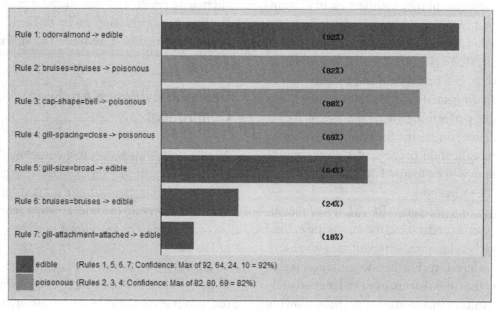

1998) and average rule methods (Antonie, 2002b). When editing the rules used in classification, the user can:

- Edit the classification or confidence for a rule
- Add, modify or delete clauses within a rule
- Remove a rule entirely (causing it to be ignored)
- Create a new rule

This editing capability is provided via a simple interface, as shown in Figure 8. Thus, the user can draw on expert knowledge to edit the computationally-generated rule set. Moreover, the user is shown immediately whether this modification improved the accuracy of the classifier. It should be noted that the speculative changes made by the user are not immediately made permanent. However, the user has the option of making the speculative changes permanent in the classification model, once the results of these changes have been presented, and accepted by the user. Thus, the tool offers the ability to interactively analyze and improve the classifier.

Figure 6. Decision evidence in compressed format

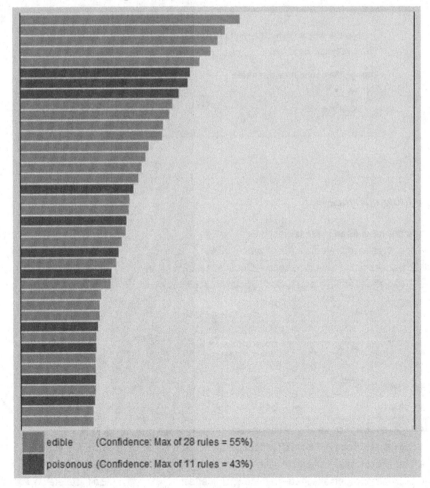

Figure 7. Decision speculation component

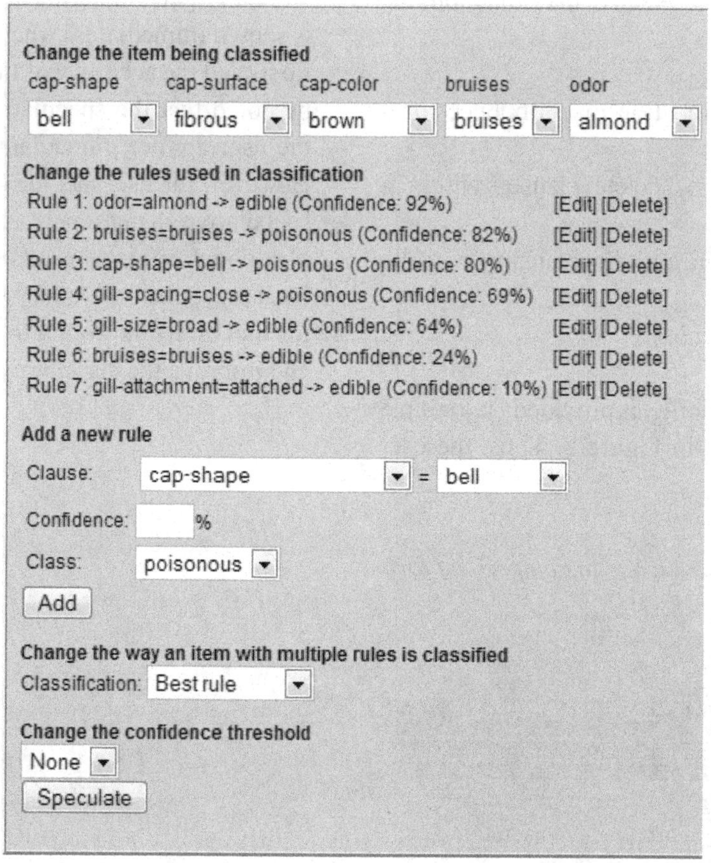

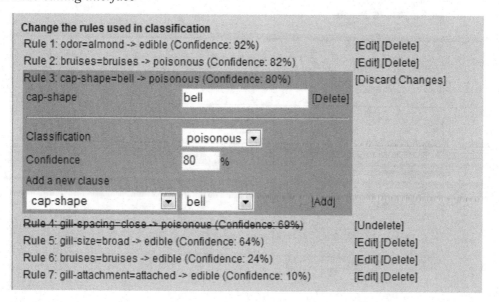

Figure 8. Rule editing interface

Ranks of Evidence Analysis Component

The ranks of evidence component shows the relationships between characteristics, **association rules** and classifications. This provides the user with further information about the way the classifier works, independent of any particular item or rule set. The system uses a colour-coded bar chart-based visualization scheme, as shown in Figure 9. The length of each bar indicates the total number of times a characteristic appears in the rule set. The colour-coded segments show the number of rules containing a given characteristic that result in a particular classification. By moving the mouse over each segment, the use is shown a more detailed summary of the rules that contain a given characteristic and result in

the selected classification. This approach is both visually appealing and scalable, which is quite beneficial when dealing with very large rule sets. In Figure 10, we see that the "gill-spacing" characteristic appears in three rules, two of which have the class "poisonous", and one with the class "edible" (represented by green and red segments, respectively). By placing the mouse over the "poisonous" segment of the bar for the "gill-spacing" characteristic, we are shown more information about the rules containing the "gill-spacing" characteristic where the class is "poisonous", as shown in Figure 9.

Source of Evidence Analysis Component

Finally, the source of evidence component allows the user to make connections between the item

Figure 9. Ranks of evidence component – attribute/value pair information

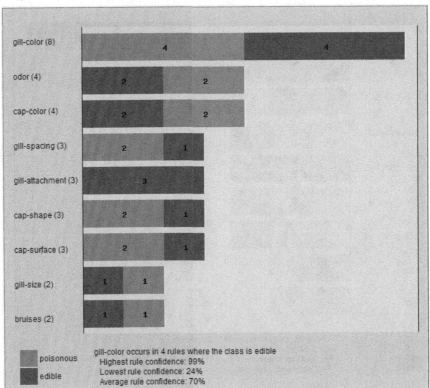

being classified and the entries in the data set that were used to generate the associative classification rules. This may be useful when investigating a dubious classification result — the user can check the data used in training the classifier to see if there were any anomalies in that original data. Specifically, the component shows the entries in the training set in a colour-coded list using shades of red and green, as shown in Figure 11. A green entry indicates that the entry has the same class as the item being analyzed, while a red entry indicates that they have different classes. The intensity of the colour indicates the proximity of the entry to the current item, in terms of matching attribute-value pairs. Finally, the user is able to specify a variety of further analysis options to restrict the list of entries to those matching certain classification or characteristic criteria. In particular, when filtering by attribute, the user is shown a chart of the distribution of that attribute among the possible classifications, divided by the possible attribute values. Figure 12 shows the class break-down for the possible values of the "cap-shape" attribute. For example, in 89% of the 402 items containing the "cap-shape=bell" attribute-value pair, the class was "edible". The table also shows that there were only two items which contained "cap-shape=conical" both of which poisonous, and thus this attribute-value pair had very little impact on the classification model.

CONCLUSION

Association rules, originally introduced in the context of market basket analysis, have many more

Figure 10. Ranks of evidence component – overall attribute information

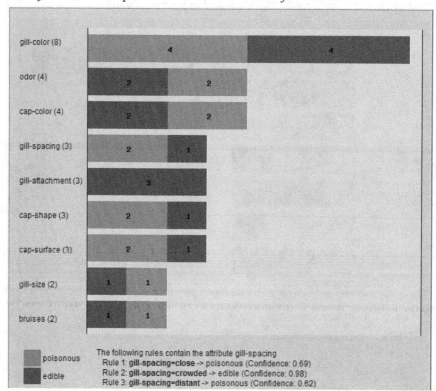

Figure 11. Source of evidence component

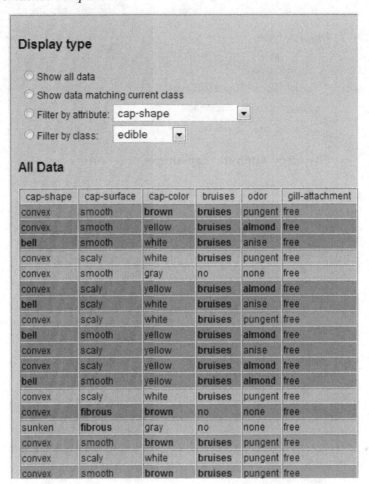

applications. We discussed here the use of **association rules** in building a classification model. Classifiers that use **association rule** mining to learn a classification model from a training set are called **associative classifiers**. In the first part of this chapter, the process of associative classification is explained briefly, and the three phases of the process – **rule generation**, **rule pruning**, and **rule selection** – are explored in detail. For each phase, the principal ideas of the phase are explained, and the phase is placed within the overall context of the associative classification process. As well, variations on each phase are

described; these variations expand and improve the classification possibilities in various ways. Finally, open problems in the field are identified, and work in these areas is briefly described.

In the second part, the issue of understanding associative classification results is addressed via ARC-UI, an analysis and speculation tool. Using the analysis tools, one can find out which rules were involved in the classification, the effect of different attribute values, and the connection between the item being classified and the entries in the training data set. Moreover, using the speculation tool, one can temporarily modify

Figure 12. Source of evidence chart

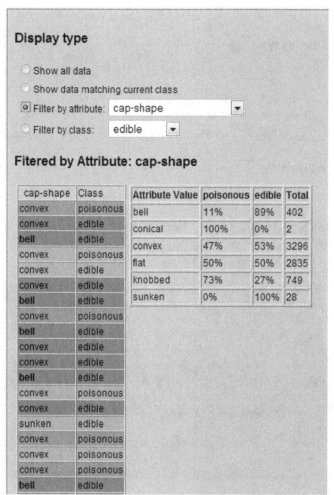

either the item being analyzed or the rules used in analysis, and see the classification that results from this modification. Thus, the user is given the ability to interactively test and improve the classifier, which increases both the classifier's accuracy and the user's trust in the system.

REFERENCES

Agrawal, R., Imieliński, T., & Swami, A. (1993). Mining association rules between sets of items in large databases. In *Proceedings of SIGMOD*, 22(2), 207–216.

Antonie, M.-L., & Zaïane, O. R. (2002a). Text document categorization by term association. In *Proceedings of ICDM*, (pp. 19–26).

Antonie, M.-L., & Zaïane, O. R. (2004a). An associative classifier based on positive and negative rules. In *9th ACM SIGMOD Workshop on Research Issues in Data Mining and Knowledge Discovery (DMKD-04)*, (pp. 64–69), Paris, France.

Antonie, M.-L., & Zaïane, O. R. (2004b). Mining positive and negative association rules: An approach for confined rules. In *8th European Conference on Principles and Practice of Knowl-*

edge Discovery in Databases (PKDD 04), (pp. 27–38), Pisa, Italy.

Antonie, M.-L., Zaïane, O. R., & Holte, R. (2006). Learning to use a learned model: A two-stage approach to classification. *In Proceedings of ICDM*, (pp. 33–42).

Antonie, M.-L., & Zaïane, O.R. (2002b). Text document categorization by term association. In *IEEE Data Mining (ICDM)*, (pp. 19–26).

Antonie, M.-L., & Zaïane, O.R. (2004c). An associative classifier based on positive and negative rules. In *DMKD '04: Proceedings of the ACM SIGMOD workshop on Research issues in data mining and knowledge discovery*, (pp. 64–69), New York, NY, USA.

Arunaslam, B., & Chawla, S. (2006). *CCCS: A top-down associative classifier for imbalanced class distribution* (Technical report). University of Sydney, School of IT.

Asuncion, A., & Newman, D.J. (2007). UCI machine learning repository.

Bayardo, R. (1997). Brute-force mining of high-confidence classification rules. In *SIGKDD 1997*, (pp. 123–126).

Brin, S., Motwani, R., & Silverstein, C. (1997). Beyond market basket: Generalizing association rules to correlations. *In Proceedings of the 1997 ACM-SIGMOD International Conference on the Management of Data*, (pp. 265–276), Tucson, Arizona.

Coenen, F., & Leng, P. (2007). The effect of threshold values on association rule based classification accuracy. In *Journal of Data and Knowledge Engineering*, *60*(2), 345–360.

Coenen, F., & Leng, P. (2004). An evaluation of approaches to classification rule selection. In *ICDM 2004*, (pp. 359–362).

Han, J., Pei, J., & Yin, Y. (2000). Mining frequent patterns without candidate generation. In *Proceedings of SIGMOD*, (pp. 1–12).

Leung, C. K., & Carmichael, C. (2007). *Frequent itemset visualization* (Technical report). University of Manitoba.

Li, W., Han, J., & Pei, J. (2001). CMAR: Accurate and efficient classifcation based on multiple class-association rules. In *ICDM 2001*, (pp. 369–376).

Liu, B., Hsu, W., & Ma, Y. (1998). Integrating classification and association rule mining. *Proceedings of SIGKDD*, (pp. 80–86).

Lim, W.-K., Ong E.-P., & Ng, K.-L (2001). Multi-level rules with recurrent items using fp'-tree. In *Proceedings of ICICS*.

Poulin, B., Eisner, R., Szafron, D., Lu, P., Greiner, R., Wishart, D.S., Fyshe, A., Pearcy, B., Mac-Donnell, C., & Anvik, J.. Visual explanation of evidence in additive classifiers. *In Proceedings of the Conference on Innovative Applications of Artificial Intelligence*, (pp. 1–8).

Rak, R., Stach, W., Zaïane, O.R., & Antonie, M. (2005). Considering re-occurring features in associative classifiers. In *PAKDD'05: Pacific-Asia Conf. on Knowledge Discovery and Data Mining*, (pp. 240–248).

Savasere, A., Omiecinski, E., & Navathe, S. (1998). Mining for strong negative associations in a large database of customer transactions. In *Proceedings of ICDE*, (pp. 494–502).

Teng, W. G., Hsieh, M. J., & Chen, M. S. (2002). On the mining of substitution rules for statistically dependent items. In *Proceedings of ICDM*, (pp. 442–449).

Wang, J., & Karypis, G. (2005). Harmony: Efficiently mining the best rules for classification. In *Proceedings of SIAM*.

Wang, W., Bich Do, D., & Lin, X. (2005). Term graph model for text classification. In *Advanced Data Mining and Applications*, pages 19–30.

Wang, W., Yang, J., & Yu, P. (2004). War: Weighted association rules for item intensities. *Knowledge and Information Systems*, *6*, 203–229.

Witten, I. H., & Frank, E. (2005). Data Mining: Practical machine learning tools and techniques. Morgan Kaufman, 2nd edition.

Wu, X., Zhang, C., & Zhang, S. (2002). Mining both positive and negative association rules. In *Proceedings of ICML*, (pp. 658–665).

Yin, X., & Han, J. (2003). CPAR: Classification based on predictive association rules. In *Proceedings of SDM*.

Zaïane, O. R., Han, J., & Zhu, H. (2000). Mining recurrent items in multimedia with progressive resolution refinement. In *Proceedings of ICDE*, (pp. 461–470).

Zaïane, O. R., & Antonie, M.-L. (2005) On pruning and tuning rules for associative classifiers. In *KES'05: Knowledge-Based Intelligence Information & Engineering Systems*, (pp. 966–973).

Chapter X
Selection of High Quality Rules in Associative Classification

Silvia Chiusano
Politecnico di Torino, Italy

Paolo Garza
Politecnico di Torino, Italy

ABSTRACT

In this chapter the authors make a comparative study of five well-known classification rule pruning methods with the aim of understanding their theoretical foundations and their impact on classification accuracy, percentage of pruned rules, model size, and number of wrongly and not classified data. Moreover, they analyze the characteristics of both the selected and pruned rule sets in terms of information content. A large set of experiments has been run in order to empirically evaluate the effect of the pruning methods when applied individually as well as when combined.

INTRODUCTION

Given a set of labeled data objects, denoted as training data set, classification rule mining aims at discovering a small set of rules to form a model, the classifier, which is then used to classify new data with unknown class label (Quinlan, 1993). The classification accuracy is evaluated on a different data set, the test data set.

Recently, associative classification methods have been proposed, which exploit association rule mining techniques to generate classification models for structured data (Arunasalam & Chawla, 2006; Baralis & Paolo, 2002; Baralis, Chiusano, & Garza, 2008; Dong, Zhang, Wong, & Li, 1999; Li, Han, & Pei, 2001; Liu, Hsu, & Ma, 1998; Liu, Ma, & Wong, 2000; Thabtah, Cowling, & Peng, 2004; Wang & Karypis, 2005; Wang, Zhou, & He,

2000; Yin & Han, 2003). Associative classification generates highly accurate classifiers, since, differently from decision trees (Quinlan, 1993), it considers the simultaneous correspondence of values of different attributes.

The generation of an associative classifier usually consists of two steps. First, a large set of classification rules is extracted from the training data to allow a wide selection of rules and the generation of accurate classifiers. Then, pruning techniques are applied to select a small subset of high quality rules and build an accurate model of the training data.

Similarly to decision tree based approaches, associative classification exploits pruning techniques (a) to deal with the problem of combinatorial explosion of the solution set and (b) to improve the accuracy in classification. While a pruning technique in case (a) aims at reducing the size of the rule set without affecting its accuracy, in case (b) pruning aims at removing those rules that can decrease classification accuracy, because introducing noise and overfitting.

So far, associative classification mainly exploited ad hoc versions of pruning methods previously proposed in decision tree based classification (Esposito, Malerba, & Semeraro, 1997) or high quality measures proposed for association rule selection (Tan, Kumar, & Srivastava, 2002). Significant improvements in classification accuracy have been obtained by slight modifications of the same pruning methods, and different combinations of them (Arunasalam & Chawla, 2006; Baralis & Paolo, 2002; Baralis, Chiusano, & Garza, 2008; Dong, Zhang, Wong, & Li, 1999; Li, Han, & Pei, 2001; Liu, Hsu, & Ma, 1998; Liu, Ma, & Wong, 2000; Thabtah, Cowling, & Peng, 2004; Wang & Karypis, 2005; Wang, Zhou, & He, 2000; Yin & Han, 2003). However, to the best of our knowledge, the specific contribution of the different techniques has never been investigated. Thabtah (2007) surveys the existing associative classification methods and the pruning techniques used by them. Differently from (Thabtah, 2007), this

chapter focuses on the pruning methods used in associative classification, and deeply investigates their theoretical properties and experimentally evaluates their effects. Because of the increasing relevance of associative classification, we believe that a systematic and experimental analysis of the effects of rule pruning in this context can be beneficial. A similar analysis concerning the effects of pruning in decision tree based classification was presented in (Esposito, Malerba, & Semeraro, 1997).

In the proposed chapter we present a comparative study of five well-known classification rule pruning methods with the aim of understanding their properties by a mathematical point of view, and their impact on classification accuracy, percentage of pruned rules, characteristics of the selected and pruned rules and their information content by means of a large set of experiments. We considered the following five classification rule pruning methods: database coverage (Baralis, Chiusano, & Garza, 2008; Li, Han, & Pei, 2001; Liu, Hsu, & Ma, 1998; Liu, Ma, & Wong, 2000; Thabtah, Cowling, & Peng, 2004), redundancy removal (Liu, Hsu, & Ma, 1998; Liu, Ma, & Wong, 2000; Wang, Zhou, & He, 2000), chi-square test (Baralis, Chiusano, & Garza, 2008; Li, Han, & Pei, 2001), pessimistic error rate (Liu, Hsu, & Ma, 1998; Liu, Ma, & Wong, 2000), and pruning based on minimum confidence threshold (Baralis, Chiusano, & Garza, 2008; Li, Han, & Pei, 2001; Liu, Hsu, & Ma, 1998; Liu, Ma, & Wong, 2000). We investigate first the effects of the pruning methods when applied individually, and next explore the effects of combining different techniques.

We perform our experiments by using a CBA-like framework. The CBA associative classifier (Liu, Hsu, & Ma, 1998) is one of the top 18 algorithms according to the ICDM'06 panel on "Top 10 Algorithms in Data Mining", and various associative classifiers are based on a CBA-like framework. Rules are sorted based on confidence, support, and length, and data are classified by using the first most confident matching rule approach.

Other rule sorting and classification approaches have been proposed (e.g., (Baralis, Chiusano, & Garza, 2008; Li, Han, & Pei, 2001)), and their effect on the considered pruning methods is an interesting topic. However, for sake of clarity, we do not consider them in this chapter.

The chapter is organized as follows. Firstly, we describe the associative classification. We also formally define the analyzed mathematical properties of the pruning techniques and the characteristics of the pruned and unpruned rules. Then, five commonly used classification rule pruning techniques are described and their properties are analyzed. Finally, a set of experimental results is reported for the five techniques and conclusions are drawn.

ASSOCIATIVE CLASSIFICATION

Traditional framework in associative classification represents the data set as a relational table D, which consists of N data cases described by k distinct attributes and a class attribute C. Attributes may be either categorical or continuous. To treat them uniformly, values in the domain of a categorical attribute are mapped to consecutive positive integers, and the value of a continuous attribute is discretized into intervals, that are then mapped into consecutive positive integers (Fayyad & Irani, 1993). In this way, each tuple in D can be described as a collection of pairs (attribute, integer value), plus a class label (a value belonging to the domain of class attribute C). Each pair (attribute, integer value) will be denoted as item in the paper. A training case is a tuple in relation D, where the class label is known, while a test case is a tuple in D where the class label is unknown.

Association rules are rules in the form $X \rightarrow Y$. In the context of associative classification, X is a set of items, while Y is a class label. A case d is matched by a set of items X when $X \subseteq d$. The quality of an association rule is measured by two parameters, its support, given by the number of cases matched by $X \cup Y$ over the number of cases in the data set, and its confidence given by the number of cases matched by $X \cup Y$ over the number of cases matched by X. Classification rules are usually characterized also by their length. The length of a classification rule $r: X \rightarrow c$ is the number of items in X and is denoted $len(r)$.

The generation of an associative classification model is usually performed in two main steps: (i) classification rule mining and (ii) rule selection. In the first step all the classification rules satisfying a minimum support threshold are extracted, while in the second step a small set of high quality rules is selected by applying rule pruning techniques and included in the associative classification model. In this chapter, we focus on the second step by analyzing five well-known rule pruning techniques.

To build the classifier, the data in D are bipartite into training and test data sets. The training data are used to extract the rules to form the classifier, while the test data to assess the accuracy of the classifier. A classification rule $X \rightarrow c$ is said to classify or match (or cover) a data d when $X \subseteq d$. A rule matching a data d is said to correctly or properly classify d when the class label of d and the class label of the rule are equal. The quality of the generated classification model is usually evaluated by using the accuracy measure.

Definition 1. (Classification accuracy). The accuracy of a classifier is expressed as the fraction of test data correctly classified over the whole test data set.

Since potentially more rules match a test data, the accuracy achieved by a rule set depends on which rules are actually used for classification. Usually, rules are sorted according to an order relation (Baralis, Chiusano, & Garza, 2008; Li, Han, & Pei, 2001; Liu, Hsu, & Ma, 1998; Liu, Ma, & Wong, 2000; Wang, Zhou, & He, 2000) and the rule with higher priority and matching the data is used for classification (Baralis, Chiusano, &

Garza, 2008; Liu, Hsu, & Ma, 1998; Liu, Ma, & Wong, 2000; Wang, Zhou, & He, 2000).

Definition 2. (Rule sorting). Let r_i and r_j be two rules, and let > be a total order relation. r_i is said to rank higher than r_j if it precedes r_j according to the relation >, and it is denoted as $r_i > r_j$.

Definition 3. (Most-confident-first principle (MCF)). Let consider a set of rules R, and the rules in R being sorted according to the total order relation >. The most-confident-first principle classifies a given data using the rule in R with higher priority according to > and matching the data.

The MCF principle was introduced in (Liu, Hsu, & Ma, 1998) and is based on the idea that rules with higher priority are the most predictive ones and therefore have to be preferred. The order relation commonly used lists the rules based on confidence, support, and length (Liu, Hsu, & Ma, 1998; Liu, Ma, & Wong, 2000; Wang, Zhou, & He, 2000).

Definition 4. (Rule sorting based on confidence, support, and length). Let r_i and r_j be two rules. r_i precedes r_j denoted as $r_i \gg r_j$, if (i) $conf(r_i) > conf(r_j)$, or (ii) $conf(r_i) = conf(r_j)$ and $sup(r_i) > sup(r_j)$, or (iii) $conf(r_i) = conf(r_j)$ and $sup(r_i) = sup(r_j)$ and $len(r_i) < len(r_j)$, or (iv) if $conf(r_i) = conf(r_j)$ and $sup(r_i) = sup(r_j)$ and $len(r_i) = len(r_j)$ and r_i precedes r_j based on the lexicographical order of items.

Li, Han, and Pei (2001) proposed an alternative to the MCF principle. Rules are sorted based on $\gg$, and for a given test data the first δ rules matching it are used to classify the test data by applying a majority classification approach.

In this chapter, we use a framework based on the MCF principle and the rule sorting based on confidence and support ($\gg$).

PROPERTIES OF PRUNING TECHNIQUES AND CLASSIFICATION RULES

This section formally defines the properties of pruning techniques that are useful to understand by a theoretical point of view the obtained results. They support in understanding the effects when different pruning techniques are joined together, as the characteristics of the selected rules. First, we define the idempotency, transparency, and commutative property for a pruning technique. Then, we define the concepts of specialization and general rule, and redundant and essential rule, which are used to characterize pruned and unpruned classification rules.

In the following, R denotes a given rule set, P is the set of rules discarded from R by pruning ($P \subseteq R$), and M is the set of selected rules which actually form the classifier (i.e., $M = R - P$).

Definition 5. (Idempotency). A pruning technique satisfies the idempotency property if applied once or multiple times to set R, it always provide the same rule set M.

Definition 6. (Transparency). A pruning technique satisfies the transparency property if the classifier built on set R has the same classification accuracy than the classifier built on set M.

The transparency property has a relevant application impact. The techniques that satisfy this property can be used to reduce the size of the classification model without affecting its accuracy.

Definition 7. (Commutativity). Let consider a rule set R and two pruning techniques, sequentially applied to it. The two techniques are said to be commutative if the same rule set M is obtained independently of their application order.

When two techniques are commutative, independently of their application order, the same rule set M is generated. Hence, independently of the algorithm used to build the classifier from set M, the same final classifier will be generated, in terms of number and type of selected rules, and classification accuracy.

We now define the concepts of specialization and general rule, and redundant and essential rule. These concepts will be used to characterize the set of pruned and unpruned rules in the set R.

Definition 8. (Rule specialization and general rule). Given two rules $r_i:X \rightarrow c$ and $r_j:Y \rightarrow c$, r_i is said to be a general rule of r_j (and r_j a specialization of r_i) if (i) r_i has fewer conditions in the rule antecedent than r_j, i.e., $X \subset Y$, and (ii) r_i and r_j have the same class label.

An alternative definition of general and specialistic rule has been proposed, similar to the one reported in this chapter, but a few less restrictive. With respect to Definition 8, in (Wang, Zhou, & He, 2000), a rule does not need to have the same class label of the rule whose it is specialization.

Based on the notion of specialization of rule, we introduce the concepts of essential and redundant classification rule. These rules characterize the more general (shorter) and more specific (longer) classification rules in a given classification rule set. Essential rules are referred also as not redundant rules.

Definition 9. (Redundant rule). Let R be a rule set, $>$ a total order relation on R, and r_i and r_j two rules in R. r_j is said to be redundant with respect to r_i if (i) r_i is a general rule of r_j, and (ii) r_i precedes r_j according to the order relation $>$, $r_i > r_j$.

Definition 10. (Essential rule). Let R be a rule set and $>$ a total order relation on R. A rule r_i is said to be essential if there is no rule r_j in R such as (i) r_i is a specialization of r_j, and (ii) $r_j > r_i$.

Let consider a rule set R, and an order relation $>$ defined on R. According to Definitions (9) and (10), the rules in R can be divided between the set of essential rules (denoted $S_>$) and the set of redundant rules (denoted $U_>$, $S_> = R - U_>$). When the order relation on set R is $>>$, the sets of essential and redundant rules are denoted as $S_{>>}$ and $U_{>>}$ ($S_{>>} = R - U_{>>}$). In this case, each rule in R precedes all the rules that are a specialization of it, and have either a lower confidence or equal confidence but a lower or equal support.

Nevertheless the formal analysis of the properties of the pruning techniques is performed in a general context, for the accuracy evaluation the present work relies on the most commonly used classification approach. Hence, rules are sorted based on $>>$ and they are selected for classification based on the MCF principle.

A REVIEW OF PRUNING METHODS

In this section, five of the main pruning techniques in the context of associative classification are reviewed and their properties are formally proven. Table 1 summarizes the mathematical properties satisfied by each pruning method and the characteristics of the selected rule sets in terms of essential and redundant rules.

Redundancy Removal

This pruning technique comes from the association rule cover approach introduced in (Toivonen, Klemettinen, Ronkainen, Hatonen, & Manilla, 1995). The approach relies on the idea that a general rule can replace, without information loss, the subset of rules that have lower rank and are a specialization of it. In fact, a general rule r_i matches a superset of the data covered by any its specialization rule r_j, since the antecedent of r_i has fewer conditions than r_j. Moreover, any data properly classified by r_j is also properly classified by r_i, since r_i and r_j assign the same class label.

Table 1. Summary of the properties of each pruning method

Pruning method	Idempotency	Commutativity with respect to	Transparency	Selected rules
Redundancy removal	Yes	Confidence-based pruning, database coverage, χ^2 test	Yes	The essential rule set
Confidence-based pruning	Yes	Redundancy removal	No	A subset of essential and redundant rules
Database coverage	Yes	Redundancy removal	No	A subset of essential rules
χ^2 test	Yes	Redundancy removal	No	A subset of essential and redundant rules
Pessimistic error rate based pruning	Yes	-	No	A subset of essential and redundant rules

Finally, r_i has to be preferred since it ranks higher than r_j. Hence, a general rule yields classification accuracy at least equal to the accuracy achieved by the whole set of rules redundant with respect to it. For this reason, the redundancy removal technique discards from a given set the rules that are redundant according to a certain order relation. Only rules that are essential are selected by the approach.

Definition 11. (Redundancy removal). Let R be a rule set, $>$ an order relation on R, and $U_>$ and $S_>$ the sets of redundant and essential rules in R according to $>$. The redundancy removal technique discards from R the rules in $U_>$. The selected rule set M is equal to $S_>$.

Starting from a given rule set R, the subset M selected by the pruning technique depends on the order relation adopted to rank the rules in R and thus identify redundant and essential rules.

The redundancy removal pruning technique satisfies the idempotency, transparency, and commutative properties.

Property 1. (Idempotency). Let R be a rule set and $>$ an order relation on R. The redundancy removal satisfies the idempotency property.

Proof. The idempotency property easily follows from the definition of redundant rules. □

The transparency property comes from the observation that when data are classified by means of the first sorted rule matching them (MCF principle), only the essential rules are used for classification. In a set R sorted by an order relation $>$, a rule r_i always precedes all the rules r_j that are redundant with respect to it. Due to the MCF principle, only r_i can be selected for classification but never r_j. Therefore, discarding redundant rules from R does not affect the classification accuracy yielded by R.

Property 2. (Transparency). Let R be a rule set, $>$ an order relation on R, and $S_>$ the subset of essential rules in R according to $>$. Let M be the subset selected by redundancy removal ($M=S_>$). R and M yield the same accuracy if in both the cases, for the classification task, rules are sorted by $>$ and rule selection is based on the MCF principle.

Proof. Under the conditions, for the set R only the rules in its subset $S_>$ are used for classification. The set M selected by redundancy removal is equal to $S_>$. Both sets M and $S_>$ are sorted by the same order relation $>$. Thus, the same rules in R

and in *M* are used for classifications, and the same accuracy is achieved by the two sets. □

From the transparency property it follows that the redundancy removal technique does not provide any accuracy improvement, but it can be exploited to reduce the size of the original rule set.

Property 3. (Commutativity). The redundancy removal satisfies the commutative property when combined with one of the following pruning techniques: (i) chi-square test, (ii) database coverage, (iii) confidence-based pruning.

The commutativity property will be proved in the following sections in which the mentioned techniques are detailed. Nevertheless the definition of redundant rules is valid for any order relation, usually the pruning technique is implemented sorting rules based on confidence and support according to >> (Liu, Hsu, & Ma, 1998).

Confidence-Based Pruning

The confidence-based pruning is the main approach traditionally used in the contexts of association rules and associative classification (Baralis, Chiusano, & Garza, 2008; Li, Han, & Pei, 2001; Liu, Hsu, & Ma, 1998; Liu, Ma, & Wong, 2000). The approach considers low confidence rules as less accurate than high confidence rules. Hence, it operates by selecting rules with confidence above a given threshold *minconf.* Differently from the support, the confidence does not satisfy the downward closure property. For this reason, pruning based on confidence is performed a-posteriori, after having extracted the rules.

In a rule set sorted based on the order relation >>, the pruning technique performs a "horizontally" cut of the original rule set. According to >>, rules are sorted by decreasing confidence and the approach discards the rules ranking below *minconf.* The accuracy achieved by the selected

rule set is always lower or equal than the accuracy by the initial set. Hence, similarly to redundancy removal, pruning based on confidence can reduce the size of the initial set, but it does not provide any accuracy improvement.

The confidence-based pruning satisfies the idempotency property and the commutative property when combined with the redundancy removal technique. In this case, the final rule set includes the essential rules with confidence above *minconf.* The confidence-based pruning does not satisfy the transparence property.

Property 4. (Idempotency). The confidence-based pruning satisfies the idempotency property.

Proof. The proof trivially follows from the definition of the confidence-based pruning technique. □

Property 5. (Commutativity). Let *R* be a rule set, >> the order relation on *R*, $S_{>>}$ the essential rule set in *R* according to >>, and *minconf* the confidence threshold. The redundancy removal and the confidence-based pruning are commutative. The rule set computed by joining the two techniques includes the rules in $S_{>>}$ with confidence above *minconf.*

Proof. Let r_i and r_j be two rules in *R*, with $r_i >> r_j$ and r_j redundant with respect to r_i. Since $conf(r_i) \geq conf(r_j)$, the confidence-based approach selects either both r_i and r_j, or only r_i, or none of the two, but never r_j and not r_i. By applying first the confidence-based approach, the rules below *minconf* are discarded from *R*; then the redundancy removal eliminates from the selected set the redundant rules. By inverting the application order, the redundancy removal selects the essential rules in *R*; then the confidence-based pruning discards rules below *minconf.* In both the cases, the final rule set includes the essential rules in the set *R* with confidence higher than *minconf.*

Database Coverage

The database coverage was introduced in (Liu, Hsu, & Ma, 1998) as a variation of the covering method proposed in (Michalski, 1980). The approach exploits the training set for both rule extraction and pruning. By means of a heuristic, it selects the minimal set of high-precedence rules needed to cover the training data. It discards from the original set the rules that either do not classify any training data or cause incorrect classifications only. First, a global order > is imposed on the rule set. Then, rules are considered one at a time according to the sort order. A rule is selected if it properly classifies at least one training data not covered yet by the rules previously analyzed. The database coverage consists of the following steps:

1. Sort the rules in R based on >.
2. Select from R the rule r with the highest precedence.
3. Compute the subset O of training data matched by r.
4. If at least one training data in O is correctly classified by r (i.e., the proper class label is assigned), include r in final rule set M and remove O from the training set. Otherwise, discard r.
5. Repeat from step 2 until all the rules in R have been considered or the training set became empty.

The characteristics of the selected rule set are summarized in the following proposition.

Proposition 1. (Database coverage). Let R be a rule set, > an order relation on R, and $S_>$ the set of essential rules in R according to >. The subset M of R selected by the database coverage is the minimal subset of essential rules of R ($M \subseteq S_>$) that have high-precedence and contribute to the correct classification of the training set.

Proof. Let first prove that none redundant rule in R belongs to M. Let r_i and r_j be two rule in R, r_j redundant with respect to r_i according to >. Let O_i and O_j be the subsets of training data that could be classified by r_i and r_j respectively, $O_j \subseteq O_i$ by construction. Since r_i precedes r_j according to >, the database coverage first classifies data with r_i, and it could update the training set. Later on, it classifies the remaining data with r_j. Two cases are possible. (a) At least one data in O_i is correctly classified. Thus, r_i is added to M and O_i is removed from the training set. Since $O_j \subseteq O_i$, O_j becomes an empty set and thus r_j will be pruned. (b) r_i does not match any training data or causes incorrect classifications only. Thus, r_i is pruned. Since $O_j \subseteq O_i$, r_j will be discarded for the same reason. The set M is a minimal set since each rule in M properly classifies at least one training data not covered the other rules in M. Finally, M includes high-precedence rules since the database coverage analyzes the rules in R for decreasing ranking values. □

The database coverage technique satisfies the idempotency property and the commutative property when combined with the redundancy removal technique.

Property 6. (Idempotency). Let R be a rule set and > an order relation on R. The database coverage satisfies the idempotency property.

Proof. The proof trivially follows from the definition of the database coverage pruning.

Property 7. (Commutativity). Let R be a rule set and > an order relation on R. The database coverage and the redundancy removal approach are commutative. The final rule set M is the rule set obtained by pruning R only by means of the database coverage.

Proof. The property easily follows from the fact that the redundancy removal selects the whole set $S_>$ of essential rules in R (see Definition 11) and the database coverage only a subset of $S_>$ (see Proposition 1).

From Property 7, it follows that the database coverage technique further compacts the rule set selected by redundancy removal.

The database coverage is described in this section according to its commonly adopted implementation (Baralis, Chiusano, & Garza, 2008; Liu, Hsu, & Ma, 1998; Liu, Ma, & Wong, 2000). Because of the implemented strategy, the selected rule set is strongly customized on the characteristics of the training set. As a main drawback, it may not be able to cover some discrepancies between the test and the training set. (Li, Han, & Pei, 2001) proposed a variation to limit the dependency of the selected rule set from the characteristics of the training set. Mainly, a data is discarded from the training set when it has been properly classified by at least δ rules, instead of by a single one.

Correlation Based Pruning: The Chi-Square Test

Many works discussed the limitation of the support-confidence framework for association rules selection (Brin, Motwani, & Silverstein, 1997; Liu, Hsu, & Ma, 1999; Meo, 2000). Mainly, this framework could not reflect the actual underline relationship among the data in the domain since negative implications are not taken into account. As main drawbacks, the evaluation of the rule relevance could be not enough accurate, and many rules are extracted but only a subset of them is actually significant (Brin, Motwani, & Silverstein, 1997; Liu, Hsu, & Ma, 1999; Meo, 2000). As an alternative, the chi-square test has been proposed in association rule mining (Brin, Motwani, & Silverstein, 1997; Liu, Hsu, & Ma, 1999) and in associative classification (Li, Han, & Pei, 2001) to identify the most significant rules.

Chi-square test (χ^2) is a widely used statistical method for testing independence or correlation of attributes (or variables) (Mills, 1965). It compares observed and expected frequencies, being the expected frequencies calculated under the assumption of independence. The closer the two frequencies are, greater is the evidence of independence. In the association rules context, the chi-square test has been initially proposed to study the correlation of a set of items (Brin, Motwani, & Silverstein, 1997). For classification rules (Baralis, Chiusano, & Garza, 2008; Li, Han, & Pei, 2001), the chi-square test has been used to check the correlation between the antecedent and consequent of a rule, to state whether a rule was statistically significant.

The correlation based pruning based on the chi-square test exclusively selects "correlated" rules. A rule is considered not relevant, and it is pruned, when its antecedent and its consequent are not correlated according to the chi-square test (i.e., the rule does not pass the chi-square test). Let consider a rule $r:X \rightarrow c$. To perform the chi-square test, the rule r is tested against the whole data set. The observed and expected frequencies of r are computed respectively as the actual support of the rule, indicated $O(r)$, and the support of the rule under the assumption of independence, indicated $E(r)$. By definition, $O(r)=sup(r)=sup(X \cup c)$, and $E(r)=sup(X)sup(c)/N$, being N the number of transactions in the data set. The chi-square test compares the observed and expected frequencies of $X \cup c$, with the observed and expected frequencies of X when labeled with classes different than c (denoted as $\neg c$), of c when appearing with itemsets different than X (denoted as $\neg X$), and of $\neg X \cup \neg c$. This corresponds to compare r with all the other rules in the data set, represented as $X \rightarrow \neg c$, $\neg X \rightarrow c$, and $\neg X \rightarrow \neg c$.

The information necessary to compute the chi-square value can be represented by means of a 2×2 contingency table where the four cells cover the cases mentioned before. In particular, Tables 2 and 3 are the observed and expected contingency tables and report the observed and expected frequencies for the four cases. Based on Table 2 and 3, the chi-square value for a rule $r:X \rightarrow c$ is defined as:

$$\chi^2(r) = \sum_{1 \leq i \leq 2, 1 \leq j \leq 2} \frac{(O(c_{ij}) - E(c_{ij}))^2}{E(c_{ij})} \quad (1)$$

being $O(c_{ij})$ and $E(c_{ij})$ the observed and expected frequencies in the cell c_{ij} in Table 2 and 3 respectively.

The χ^2 test relies on the concept of positive correlation, defined based on the chi-square value, to perform rule pruning. As a comparison, the support-confidence framework only exploits the content of the top-left cell in the contingency table. For this reason, in (Brin, Motwani, & Silverstein, 1997; Liu, Hsu, & Ma, 1999) the authors assert that the statistic significance expressed by means of the chi-square value is more reliable and the confidence measure in some cases can be misleading.

Definition 12. (Correlated and uncorrelated rule). Let s be a minimum support and l a significance level. Let r be a rule $r:X \rightarrow c$. X and c are said to be (s,l) correlated, or simply correlated, if (i) $sup(r)>s$ and (ii) $\chi^2(r)>l$. Instead, X and c are said

to be (s,l) uncorrelated, or simply uncorrelated, if (iii) $sup(r)>s$ and (iv) $\chi^2(r)<l$. Rule r is said to be correlated if X and c are correlated, uncorrelated otherwise.

The significance level usually adopted to check the correlation is equal to 3.84% (Baralis, Chiusano, & Garza, 2008; Li, Han, & Pei, 2001). A chi-square value of 0 implies the statistical independence of X and c.

Definition 13. (Positive and negative correlation). Let consider a rule $r:X \rightarrow c$. r is said to be a positive correlation if X and c are correlated and $(O(r)/E(r))>1$. r is said to be a negative correlation if X and c are correlated but $(O(r)/E(r))<1$. r is said to show independence if X and c are uncorrelated.

Definition 14. (Chi-square test based pruning). Let consider a rule set R. The chi-square based test prunes from R rules that are uncorrelated or negatively correlated. Only rules that are positively correlated are preserved by the approach.

Property 8. (Idempotency). The chi-square test satisfies the idempotency property.

Table 2. The 2x2 observed contingency table

	c	$\neg c$	Row total
X	$sup(X \cup c)$	$sup(X \cup \neg c)$	$sup(X)$
$\neg X$	$sup(\neg X \cup c)$	$sup(\neg X \cup \neg c)$	$sup(\neg X)$
Column total	$sup(c)$	$sup(\neg c)$	N transactions

Table 3. The 2x2 expected contingency table

	c	$\neg c$	Row total
X	$sup(X)sup(c)/N$	$sup(X)sup(\neg c)/N$	$sup(X)$
$\neg X$	$sup(\neg X)sup(c)/N$	$sup(\neg X)sup(\neg c)/N$	$sup(\neg X)$
Column total	$sup(c)$	$sup(\neg c)$	N transactions

Proof. The proof trivially follows from the definition of the chi-square based pruning. □

The chi-square test has been proved to satisfy the upward closure property when used to evaluate the correlation of sets of items (Brin, Motwani, & Silverstein, 1997). In other words, if a set of items is correlated at a certain significance level, then any its superset is also correlated at the same significance level. This property is no longer valid in the chi-square formalization for classification rules in equation (1). In fact, equation (1) evaluates the statistical correlation between the rule antecedent X and rule consequent c, but the correlation of the items in X is not directly taken into account. In the present work, it is shown that in the case of classification rules the chi-square test still satisfies a sort of downward closure property. Mainly, if a rule is positively correlated at a certain significance level l then any rule with higher or equal confidence and higher or equal support for the rule antecedent is also positively correlated at the same significance level. Before presenting the property let introduce an alternative formulation of equation (1) based on the concept of dependence value.

Definition 15. (Dependence value). The dependence value Δ of a rule $r:X{\to}c$ is the difference between the observed and expected occurrence of the rule: $\Delta = O(r) - E(r)$; $\Delta > 0$ when $(O(r)/E(r)) > 1$.

The dependence value has been presented in (Meo, 2000) as an alternative measure to represent the correlation of a set of items. It can be easily proved that the absolute value of the difference between the observed and expected occurrences in the four cases in the 2×2 contingency table is always equal to Δ. The chi-square in equation (1) can be expressed as a function of the dependence value in the following more compact form:

$$\chi^2(r) = \frac{N^3}{\sup(c)\sup(\neg c)} \times \frac{\Delta^2}{\sup(X)\sup(\neg X)}$$

(2)

where N is the number of transactions in the data set.

Let now present the downward closure property for the chi-square test in the case of classification rules.

Property 9. (Downward closure property). Let R be a rule set and $r_i:X{\to}c$ and $r_j:Y{\to}c$ two rules in R, with $conf(r_i) \geq conf(r_j)$ and $sup(X) \geq sup(Y)$. If $(O(r_j)/E(r_j)) > 1$ then it follows that (i) $(O(r_i)/E(r_i)) > 1$ and (ii) $\chi^2(r_i) \geq \chi^2(r_j)$.

Proof. Let first prove (i). The condition

$$\frac{O(r_j)}{E(r_j)} > 1$$

can be rewritten as

$$\frac{\sup(Y \cup c)N}{\sup(Y)\sup(c)} > 1$$

Being

$$\frac{\sup(X \cup c)}{\sup(X)} > \frac{\sup(Y \cup c)}{\sup(Y)}$$

because $conf(r_i) \geq conf(r_j)$, it follows that

$$\frac{\sup(X \cup c)N}{\sup(X)\sup(c)} > \frac{\sup(Y \cup c)N}{\sup(Y)\sup(c)} \qquad (3)$$

and therefore

$$\frac{O(r_i)}{E(r_i)} > \frac{O(r_j)}{E(r_j)} > 1$$

Let now prove (ii). In relation (3), $sup(X \cup c)$ can be replaced by

$$\frac{\sup(X)\sup(c)}{N} + \Delta_i,$$

and $sup(Y \cup c)$ by

$$\frac{\sup(Y)\sup(c)}{N} + \Delta_j$$

Being $sup(X) \geq sup(Y)$ the relation follows

$$\frac{\Delta_i}{\Delta_j} \geq \frac{sup(X)}{sup(Y)} \geq 1 \geq \frac{sup(\neg X)}{sup(\neg Y)} \qquad (4)$$

The chi-square of rule r_j can be expressed according to equation (2) as

$$\chi^2(r_j) = \frac{N^3}{sup(c)\,sup(\neg c)} \times \frac{\Delta_j^2}{sup(Y)\,sup(\neg Y)} \qquad (5)$$

From relation (4),

$$\frac{\Delta_j}{sup(Y)} \leq \frac{\Delta_i}{sup(X)}$$

and thus

$$\chi^2(r_j) \leq \frac{N^3}{sup(c)\,sup(\neg c)} \times \frac{\Delta_i}{sup(X)}\frac{\Delta_j}{sup(\neg Y)}$$

Again from relation (4),

$$\frac{\Delta_j}{sup(\neg Y)} \leq \frac{\Delta_i}{sup(\neg X)}$$

and thus

$$\chi^2(r_j) \leq \frac{N^3}{sup(c)\,sup(\neg c)} \times \frac{\Delta_i^2}{sup(X)\,sup(\neg X)}$$

Since

$$\frac{N^3}{sup(c)\,sup(\neg c)} \times \frac{\Delta_i^2}{sup(X)\,sup(\neg X)}$$

corresponds to $\chi^2(r_i)$ we proved that $\chi^2(r_i) \geq \chi^2(r_j)$.

Based on Property 9 the rules selected by the chi-square test can be characterized in terms of essential and redundant rules of R, based on the confidence and support values.

Proposition 2. (Correlation of essential and redundant rules). Let R be a rule set and $\gg$ the order relation on R. Let r_i be a rule in R. (i) Rule r_i is (s,l) positively correlated if at least one of the rules, redundant of r_i according to $\gg$, is (s,l)

positively correlated. (ii) $\chi^2(r_i)$ is higher or equal than the maximum chi-square values among the rules, redundant of r_i according to $\gg$ and (s,l) positively correlated.

Proof. Let consider $r_i:X \to c$ and $r_j:Y \to c$, r_j redundant of r_i according to $\gg$. By construction, $sup(r_i) \geq sup(r_j)$ and $sup(X) \geq sup(Y)$. If r_j is (s,l) positively correlated then also r_i is positively correlated, since $sup(r_i) \geq sup(r_j)$ and due to Property 9 $(O(r_i)/E(r_i)) > 1$ and $\chi^2(r_i) \geq \chi^2(r_j)$. Point (ii) is because the condition $\chi^2(r_i) \geq \chi^2(r_j)$ has to be satisfied for any rule r_j redundant of r_i and positively correlated.

However, a rule r_i may be (s,l) positively correlated also if none of its redundant rules is positively correlated, but the vice versa it is not true. From Proposition (2) it follows that when a rule r_j is selected by the chi-square based pruning, then all the rules r_i, with r_j redundant of r_i according to $\gg$, are also selected.

Proposition 3. (Selected rule set). Let R be a rule set, $\gg$ the order relation on R, and $S_{\gg}$ and $U_{\gg}$ the sets of essential and redundant rules in R according to $\gg$. Let M be the set of rules selected by the chi-square test. For any redundant rule r_j $(r_j \subset U_{\gg})$ included in M, M also includes all the essential rule r_i $(r_i \subset S_{\gg})$, such that r_j is a redundant rule of r_i.

Proposition (3) has two relevant implications. The redundant rules selected by the chi-square test are actually useless, when for the classification task rules are sorted by the order relation $\gg$ and data are covered by the first rule matching them (MCF principle). In fact, in the selected set each redundant rule is preceded by all the corresponding essential rules, and only these rules are used for classification according to the MCF principle. Moreover, from Proposition (3) the commutativity between the chi-square test and the redundancy removal technique follows.

Property 10. (Commutativity). Let R be a rule set, $\gg$ the order relation on R, and $S_{\gg}$ the set of essential rules in R according to $\gg$. The redundancy removal and chi-square test are commutative. By joining the two techniques, the rules in $S_{\gg}$ that are positively correlated at a given significance level are selected.

Proof. Let consider two rules $r_i:X \to c$ and $r_j:Y \to c$, with $r_i \gg r_j$ and r_j redundant of r_i. Since $r_i \gg r_j$ and r_j is redundant of r_i, it follows that $conf(r_i) \geq conf(r_j)$ and $sup(X) \geq conf(Y)$. By Property 9 it follows that the chi-square test selects either both r_i and r_j, or only r_i, or none of the two, but never r_j and not r_i. By applying first the chi-square test, the rules which are uncorrelated or negatively correlated are discarded from R; then the redundancy removal technique eliminates from the selected set the rules that are redundant. By inverting the application order, first the redundancy removal technique selects the essential rules in R; then the chi-square test discards those rules which are uncorrelated or negatively correlated. Therefore, in both the cases the final rule set includes the essential rules which are positively correlated.

Pessimistic Error Rate Based Pruning

The pessimistic error rate based pruning method relies on the concepts of pessimistic error rate (PER) and was initially proposed in C4.5 (Quinlan, 1993) for pruning decision trees. In this approach, the training set is used for both generating and pruning the rule set. C4.5 examines each decision node in the tree starting from the bottom, and replaces the subtree rooted by a node with either the leaf or the most frequently used branch which has fewer estimated errors. In associative classification pruning algorithms based on the pessimistic error rate have been proposed in (Liu, Hsu, & Ma, 1998). In the context of associative classification, the pessimistic error rate (PER) is used to evaluate the expected classification error of the rules. For a given rule, the approach compares the PER value of the rule with the PER values of its general rules. The rule is pruned if its PER value is higher than the PER value of at least one of its general rules. In this case the rule is expected to be less accurate than its general rules.

In the following the formal definitions are reported for the PER measure (Quinlan, 1993) and the pruning method based on PER as proposed in the context of associative classification (Liu, Hsu, & Ma, 1998).

Definition 16. (PER (I)) The pessimistic error rate $er(r)$ of a rule r is expressed as

$$er(r) = \frac{e(r)}{n(r)} + \frac{1}{2n(r)} \tag{6}$$

where, with respect to the training set, $e(r)$ is the number of data incorrectly classified by r and $n(r)$ the number of data matched by r. The term

$$\frac{1}{2n(r)}$$

is the continuity correction factor for binomial distribution introduced by Quinlan (1993).

Definition 17. (PER based pruning) Let R be a rule set. A rule r_j is discarded from R if there is a rule r_i in R such that (i) r_j is a specialization of r_i, (ii) $len(r_j) - len(r_i) = 1$, and (iii) $er(r_i) < er(r_j)$.

Differently from the database coverage, the PER based pruning does not eliminate either data from the training set or rules from the initial set until the end of the pruning process. Hence, each rule is always compared with any rule available in the initial set, and its pessimistic error rate is computed by considering the whole data set. The PER based pruning satisfies the idempotency property.

Property 11. (Idempotency). The PER based pruning satisfies the idempotency property.

Proof. The proof trivially follows from the definition of the PER based pruning. □

This chapter presents alternative formulations of the PER measure and pruning method which rely on the concepts of rule confidence and support. By means of these formulations, rules selected by the approach can be characterized in terms of essential and redundant rules of the original set. The following expression of the PER measure can be easily derived from equation (6) by considering that for a rule $r:X{\to}c$ is $n(r)=sup(X)$ and $e(r)=sup(X)-sup(X{\cup}c)$. By replacing these relations in equation (6), the alternative formulation of the PER measure in Proposition (4) follows.

Proposition 4. (PER (II)) The pessimistic error rate for a rule $r:X{\to}c$, can be expressed as

$$er(r) = 1 - conf(r) + \frac{1}{2\sup(X)} \qquad (7)$$

where the term

$$\frac{1}{2\sup(X)}$$

represents the continuity correction factor.

An alternative formalization of the PER based pruning method is obtained by replacing in the pruning condition $er(r_i)<er(r_j)$ the pessimistic error rates of the rules r_i and r_j, expressed in terms of confidence and support as in equation (7).

Proposition 5. (PER based pruning (II)) Let R be a rule set. A rule r_j is discarded from R if there is a rule r_i in R such that (i) r_j is a specialization of r_i, (ii) $len(r_j)-len(r_i)=1$, and (iii) $conf(r_i)>conf(r_j)-k$,

$$k = 0.5 \frac{\sup(X) - \sup(Y)}{\sup(X)\sup(Y)}, \; k{\geq}0.$$

The term k comes from the continuity correction factors in the PER expressions of the two rules; k is always positive since $sup(X){\geq}sup(Y)$ being r_j a specialization of r_i.

Proposition (5) states that the PER pruning method favors shorter rules with high values of confidence and support instead of longer rules. Longer rules with high confidence can be discarded if their high confidence is balanced by a

low support. A rule r_j is pruned if at least one rule among those having r_j as specialization (and length the r_j length minus one) has confidence higher than r_j. Otherwise, rule r_j is pruned if at least in one case the higher confidence of r_j is balanced by a lower support of the rule antecedent.

Proposition 6. (Selected rules) Let R be a rule set, $>>$ the order relation on R, and $S_{>>}$ and $U_{>>}$ the set of essential and redundant rules in R according to $>>$. The rule set M selected by PER based pruning includes (i) all the rules in $S_{>>}$ and a subset of $U_{>>}$, when the correction factor is null, and (ii) a subset of $U_{>>}$ and a subset of $S_{>>}$ otherwise.

Proof. Let first prove (i). When the correction factor is null (i.e., $k=0$), a rule r_j is pruned if there is a rule r_i where (a) r_j is a specialization of r_i with $len(r_j)-len(r_i)=1$ and (b) $conf(r_i)>conf(r_j)$. From (a) and (b), it follows that pruned rule r_j is a redundant rule of r_i according to the order relation $>>$. Let now prove (ii). When the correction factor is not null (i.e., $k{\neq}0$), a rule r_j can be pruned because of a rule r_i with (a) $len(r_j)-len(r_i)=1$, (b) $conf(r_i)>conf(r_j)-k$, but (c) $conf(r_i){\geq}conf(r_j)$. Due to (a), r_j is a specialization of r_i, but due to (c) rule r_j is not a redundant rule of r_i. Hence, either r_j is redundant with respect to a rule different from r_i or r_j is an essential rule.

From Proposition 6 it follows that for null correction factor the pessimistic error rate and the redundancy removal are commutative and the final rule set joining the two techniques includes all the essential rules in the initial set R.

EXPERIMENTAL RESULTS

This section reports the experimental results for the five pruning techniques considered in this chapter. The effects of pruning are investigated when the techniques are applied individually as well as when they are combined.

The five pruning techniques are evaluated by comparing the characteristics of the selected rule set M (i.e., unpruned rules) with respect to the characteristics of the initial rule set R. In particular, we analyzed the number of rules pruned by each technique and the quality of the rule sets M and R. In all the Tables, PER stands for pessimistic error rate based pruning, DBcov for database coverage, RR for redundancy removal pruning, and Conf for confidence-based pruning.

To run the experiments, the rule set R is extracted by setting as a unique constrain a minimum support of 1%, which is a standard value usually used to build associative classifiers (e.g., (Li, Han, & Pei, 2001; Liu, Hsu, & Ma, 1998)). For classification, a CBA-like approach is used (Liu, Hsu, & Ma, 1998). In particular, rules are sorted based on the order relation >> (see Definition 4) and are selected according to the MCF principle (see Definition 3). The 10 fold cross validation test (Liu, Hsu, & Ma, 1998) was applied to compute accuracy values. Since the 10 fold cross validation is based on multiple runs, it is less sensible to bias than the holdout method.

The experiments were run on 17 frequently used data sets downloaded from the UCI Machine Learning Repository (Asuncion & Newman, 2007). Continuous attributes were discretized by means of the same technique used by CBA (Liu, Hsu, & Ma, 1998). The experiments were performed on a 1GHz Pentium III PC with 1.0GB main memory, running Kubuntu 6.06.

Characteristics of Data Sets and Initial Rule Sets *R*

Table 4 summarizes the characteristics of the 17 UCI data sets and of the rule set R mined from each data set by setting a minimum support of 1%.

The average accuracy achieved by set R is 83.43%, the percentage of not classified data ($NC\%$) is always 0, and the average percentage of wrongly classified data ($WC\%$) is 16.57%. Therefore, the set R covers all the data in the data

sets, but on average in 16.57% of the cases the assigned class is not correct.

To analyze the information content for R, we also evaluated the maximum achievable accuracy of R. This value represents the maximum accuracy than can be achieved by using R if the right rules are selected during classification. Given a data set D and a rule set R extracted from D, the maximum achievable accuracy of R on D is the percentage of data in D for which there is at least one rule in R correctly covering it. Hence, it is the percentage of data in D that can be potentially correctly classified by at least one rule in R, if a proper rule is used during classification.

Results reported in Table 4 show that, except for Anneal, the maximum achievable accuracy for R is always equal to 100% (i.e., for each data in D there is at least one rule in R that can potentially correctly classify it). Thus, except for Anneal, R can potentially properly classify all the data if during classification a technique different from the MCF approach is used.

Experimental Comparison of Pruning Methods

This section compares the effects of the five pruning techniques when they are used individually. In particular, classification accuracy, percentage of pruned rules, model size, number of wrongly and not classified data, and the information content of the pruned and unpruned rule sets are analyzed.

Classification Accuracy Comparison

Table 5 reports the difference (Δacc) between the classification accuracy obtained by using M (the unpruned rule set) and the initial accuracy value obtained by using R. For each data set the Δacc of the pruning technique which achieves the highest accuracy value is in boldface.

The highest average accuracy improvement comes from the database coverage (1.57%), fol-

Table 4. Characteristics of data sets and initial rule sets R

Data set		R				
Name	Transactions	# of rules	Accuracy (acc%)	Not classified data (NC%)	Wrongly classified data (WC%)	Maximum achievable accuracy
Anneal	898	378122	93.32	0	6.68	99.10
Austral	690	312241	85.80	0	14.20	100
Breast	699	8005	95.57	0	4.43	100
Cleve	303	201522	79.87	0	20.13	100
Crx	690	577544	85.51	0	14.49	100
Diabetes	768	5034	78.13	0	21.88	100
Glass	214	9842	75.23	0	24.77	100
Heart	270	15115	82.22	0	17.78	100
Hepatic	155	55436	79.35	0	20.65	100
Iris	150	186	92.67	0	7.33	100
Labor	57	182489	91.23	0	8.77	100
Led7	3200	1788	71.81	0	28.19	100
Pima	768	5113	78.52	0	21.48	100
Sonar	208	125100	80.77	0	19.23	100
Tic-tac	958	9361	98.12	0	1.88	100
Vehicle	846	622294	58.63	0	41.37	100
Wine	178	181206	91.57	0	8.43	100
Average			83.43	0	16.57	99.95

lowed by the chi-square test (0.13%), and the pessimistic error rate based pruning (0.02%). The chi-square test has been implemented by considering the usual threshold of 3.84% (e.g., (Baralis, Chiusano, & Garza, 2008; Li, Han, & Pei, 2001)). Redundancy removal yields no accuracy improvement due to the transparency property as discussed in the previous section. Hence, this technique can be only used to reduce the size of the rule set R.

Results show that chi-square test or pessimistic error rate based pruning are quite conservative. These techniques reduce the size of the rule set but substantially preserve the initial accuracy. None improvement is yielded by the chi-square test except than in 4 data sets which slightly increase with respect to R. For the pessimistic error rate based pruning, the accuracy is slightly higher

than R in 4 cases, lower in 3 cases, and equal in the remaining cases. Instead, the database coverage yields higher accuracy in 11 cases and lower accuracy in 4 cases. Hence, it generates more accurate models, by selecting a subset of high quality rules and pruning harmful rules.

Confidence-based pruning yields no improvement or negative improvement. Since rules in R are sorted for decreasing confidence according to $\gg$, the approach cuts R "horizontally". In particular, the bottom rules are pruned. The experimental results show that when only low confidence rules are pruned (confidence threshold lower than 50%) the same accuracy of R is achieved. A lower accuracy is obtained when too many rules are pruned (confidence threshold higher than 50%), because not enough rules are available for classification. Thus, the 50% confidence threshold,

Table 5. Accuracy improvement given by each pruning technique

Data set	χ^2	RR	PER	DBcov	Conf 50%	Conf 70%	Conf 80%	Conf 90%
					Δacc%			
Anneal	0	0	0	**2.56**	0	0	0	-0.33
Austral	**0**	**0**	**0**	-0.72	**0**	**0**	**0**	**0**
Breast	0	0	**0.29**	0.14	0	0	0	0
Cleve	**0.66**	0	-0.99	1.65	0	0	0	0
Crx	**0**	**0**	**0**	-1.45	**0**	**0**	**0**	**0**
Diabetes	0	0	-0.13	0	0	0	-5.21	20.7
Glass	0	0	0.47	**1.87**	0	-8.88	-12.62	-35.51
Heart	0.37	0	0.37	**1.11**	0	0	0	0
Hepatic	0.65	0	0	**7.1**	0	0	0	0
Iris	0	0	0	**0.67**	0	0	0	0
Labor	**0**	**0**	**0**	-1.75	**0**	**0**	**0**	-1.75
Led7	0	0	0	**0.12**	0	-4.06	-17.56	-46.28
Pima	**0**	**0**	-0.13	**0**	**0**	**0**	-5.99	-20.31
Sonar	**0**	**0**	**0**	-2.40	**0**	**0**	**0**	**0**
Tic-tac	0	0	0	**0.73**	0	0	0	0
Vehicle	0.47	0	0.47	**10.87**	0	0	0	0
Wine	0	0	0	**6.18**	0	0	0	0
Average	0.13	0	0.02	**1.57**	0	-0.76	-2.43	-7.35

usually used in associative classification, seems to be appropriate to prune the rule set without affecting accuracy.

Percentage of Pruned Rules and Model Size

For each pruning technique, Table 6 reports the percentage of pruned rules, while Table 7 reports the model size (i.e., the number of unpruned rules).

The database coverage is the most aggressive pruning approach and discards the largest rule set (99.16%), followed by redundancy removal (90.99%), pessimistic error rate based pruning (77.16%), chi-square test (42.01%), and confidence-based pruning (17.95% with threshold 50%).

The database coverage prunes a large set of rules because it greedily selects the minimum number of rules needed to cover all the training data, by choosing at most one rule for each training data. It generates a compact and hence human-interpretable model (see Table 7). Also the redundancy removal approach prunes a high percentage of rules (about 91%). However, the majority of the generated models include thousands of rules and therefore they are less human-interpretable. The other approaches also prune on average a large set of rules, but they generate huge models that are not interpretable by a human being.

Table 6 shows that on average 90.99% of the rules in R are redundant rules. As discussed in the previous section, these rules are useless for the classification task when the MCF classification approach is used. Hence, most of the rules in R can be pruned without affecting the classification accuracy, but reducing the model size and therefore the classification time. While the

Table 6. Percentage of pruned rules

Data set	Percentage of pruned rules							
	χ^2	RR	PER	DBcov	Conf			
					50%	70%	80%	90%
Anneal	52.82	99.68	15.31	**99.99**	5.54	7.71	13.64	20.30
Austral	37.25	97.73	95.64	**99.95**	11.64	17.50	36.63	55.71
Breast	14.22	94.38	96.70	**99.21**	2.14	2.97	6.32	13.39
Cleve	64.61	99.26	96.09	**99.96**	14.24	20.90	41.73	56.58
Crx	33.78	98.39	61.96	**99.97**	9.93	15.02	32.07	53.21
Diabetes	54.87	96.50	85.76	**98.71**	28.97	41.27	65.00	81.99
Glass	41.64	95.32	62.51	**99.67**	41.99	50.89	64.46	74.17
Heart	75.27	96.17	95.43	**99.56**	25.74	35.40	56.66	68.14
Hepatic	20.42	99.09	98.52	**99.94**	0.19	0.34	2.21	6.81
Iris	41.40	71.51	72.58	**94.62**	29.57	31.18	38.17	45.16
Labor	98.19	99.78	59.38	**99.99**	1.23	2.93	3.89	4.10
Led7	20.30	35.46	35.91	95.92	72.47	77.22	90.73	**97.32**
Pima	54.55	96.60	86.29	**98.67**	29.87	42.85	66.69	82.26
Sonar	3.50	96.52	92.05	**99.96**	0.84	2.02	17.12	47.86
Tic-tac	63.50	73.21	76.22	**99.68**	18.57	32.32	61.34	75.56
Vehicle	7.81	98.10	84.95	**99.98**	9.88	17.83	38.84	51.69
Wine	30.98	99.06	96.48	**99.99**	2.41	3.06	6.06	8.28
Average	42.01	90.99	77.16	**99.16**	17.95	23.61	37.78	49.56

database coverage prunes all redundant rules in R, the other techniques discard only a subset of them. This behavior is showed by a percentage of pruned rules significantly lower than 90.99% for chi-square test, pessimistic error rate, and confidence-based pruning (with threshold 50%). Thus, many selected rules are useless for classification, and the model size could negatively affect the classification time.

Percentage of Not Classified and Wrongly Classified Data

This section analyzes the impact of each pruning technique on the percentage of not classified ($NC\%$) and wrongly classified data ($WC\%$). Table 8 reports the differences between the values of $NC\%$ ($\Delta NC\%$) and of $WC\%$ ($\Delta WC\%$) after and

before pruning, i.e., on set M with respect to R. The $NC\%$ value never decreases since $M \subseteq R$, while $WC\%$ decreases in correspondence of accuracy improvements.

For the redundancy removal technique, both $NC\%$ and $WC\%$ neither increase nor decrease due to the transparency property. Experiments show similar results for the confidence-based pruning with threshold 50%. For the chi-square test, $\Delta NC\%$ is always zero. Thus, the accuracy improvements in Table 5 are due to a reduction of $WC\%$. These results point out that the chi-square test selects a suitable and sufficient number of rules in R (i.e., it does not overprune the initial rule set). The pessimistic error rate based pruning, except in one case (Diabetes), shows a similar behavior, where $NC\%$ increases causing an accuracy value lower than of R.

Table 7. Model size

Data set	χ^2	RR	PER	DBcov	Conf			
					50%	70%	80%	90%
Anneal	178398	1210	320232	38	357174	348969	326546	301363
Austral	195931	7088	13614	156	275896	257599	197867	138292
Breast	6867	450	264	63	7834	7767	7499	6933
Cleve	71319	1491	7880	81	172825	159404	117427	87501
Crx	382450	9298	219698	173	520194	490797	388687	270233
Diabetes	2272	176	717	65	3576	2956	1762	907
Glass	5744	461	3690	32	5709	4833	3498	2542
Heart	3738	579	691	67	11224	9764	6551	4816
Hepatic	44116	504	820	33	55331	55248	54211	51661
Iris	109	53	51	10	131	128	115	102
Labor	3303	401	74127	18	180244	177142	175390	175007
Led7	1425	1154	1146	73	492	407	166	48
Pima	2324	174	701	68	3586	2922	1703	907
Sonar	120722	4353	9945	50	124049	122573	103683	65227
Tic-tac	3510	2508	2226	30	7623	6336	3619	2288
Vehicle	573693	11824	93655	124	560811	511339	380595	300630
Wine	125068	1703	6378	18	176839	175661	170225	166202

For the database coverage, the $NC\%$ value increases in almost all data sets. We experimentally verified that this increase does not affect the classification accuracy, since it is mainly due to data that were incorrectly classified by R. In addition, the approach appears to select suitable rules since in the majority of the cases $WC\%$ decreases (and thus the accuracy increases as shown in Table 5). Only in 4 cases (Austral, Crx, Labor, Sonar), lower accuracy values are obtained since the discarded rules were useless on the training set but they became useful on the test set.

Information Content of Unpruned and Pruned Rules

An interesting question we try to answer in this chapter is "Are pruned rules really useless?". To this aim, we have already analyzed the percent-age of not classified data. To give a more precise answer, we compared the maximum achievable accuracy of sets R and M. The difference between the two values represents the amount of information lost by applying the pruning techniques. It represents those data that can be potentially classified correctly by set R but not by M. Results are reported in Table 9.

Table 9 shows that the rule sets M selected by the confidence-based pruning (with threshold 50%) have the same maximum achievable accuracy of set R. Hence, M contains the same information of R, and the pruned rules are actually useless. For the redundancy removal technique, M and R always have the maximum achievable accuracy due to the transparency property.

The sets M obtained by chi-square, database coverage, and pessimistic error rate based pruning are characterized on average by a maximum

Table 8. Variation of not classified (NC) and wrongly classified (WC) data given by each pruning technique

Data set	ΔNC%					ΔWC%				
	χ^2	RR	PER	DBcov	Conf 50%	χ^2	RR	PER	DBcov	Conf 50%
Anneal	0	0	0	1.22	0	0	0	0	-3.79	0
Austral	0	0	0	1.45	0	0	0	0	-0.72	0
Breast	0	0	0	0.29	0	0	0	-0.29	-0.43	0
Cleve	0	0	0	1.32	0	-0.66	0	0.99	-2.97	0
Crx	0	0	0	0.87	0	0	0	0	0.58	0
Diabetes	0	0	13.02	0	0	0	0	-12.89	0	0
Glass	0	0	0	0.47	0	0	0	-0.47	-2.34	0
Heart	0	0	0	0.74	0	-0.37	0	-0.37	-1.85	0
Hepatic	0	0	0	0.65	0	-0.65	0	0	-7.74	0
Iris	0	0	0	0	0	0	0	0	-0.67	0
Labor	0	0	0	5.26	0	0	0	0	-3.51	0
Led7	0	0	0	0.13	0	0	0	0	-0.25	0
Pima	0	0	0	0	0	0	0	0.13	0	0
Sonar	0	0	0	1.44	0	0	0	0	0.96	0
Tic-tac	0	0	0	1.15	0	0	0	0	-1.88	0
Vehicle	0	0	0	0.12	0	-0.47	0	-0.47	-10.99	0
Wine	0	0	0	1.12	0	0	0	0	-7.3	0
Average	0	0	0.77	0.95	0	-0.13	0	-0.79	-2.52	0

achievable accuracy lower than set *R*. Therefore, these techniques discard some potentially useful rules. However, only the database coverage approach prunes a significant percentage of potentially useful rules (the maximum achievable accuracy lost is 9.73%). As discussed above, this technique performs a "greedy" pruning and selects a minimal subset of classification rules. Hence, even if it allows achieving on average the highest accuracy value, it potentially selects the least "rich" rule set. The database coverage pruning may be not the best choice if a classification approach different from the MCF principle is used.

Combining Pruning Techniques

This section analyses the accuracy values and the percentage of pruned rules when joining different pruning techniques. We performed experiments for all pairs of techniques analyzed in this chapter and for some combinations of more than two techniques. For the sake of clarity, detailed results are reported only for frequently used combinations (e.g., pessimistic error rate followed by database coverage (Liu, Hsu, & Ma, 1998) and chi-square followed by database coverage (Li, Han, & Pei, 2001)) and for combinations that yield significant accuracy values or prune high percentage of rules.

Table 9. Maximum achievable accuracy by the whole rule set R and the selected rule set M

Data set	Maximum Achievable Accuracy% by using *R*	by using *M*				
		χ^2	RR	PER	DBcov	Conf 50%
Anneal	99.10	99.10	99.10	99.10	96.90	99.10
Austral	100	99.90	100	100	89.10	100
Breast	100	99.90	100	100	98.00	100
Cleve	100	100	100	100	88.80	100
Crx	100	99.40	100	100	90.10	100
Diabetes	100	99.50	100	87.00	80.50	100
Glass	100	100	100	100	79.40	100
Heart	100	100	100	100	87.00	100
Hepatic	100	100	100	100	94.20	100
Iris	100	99.30	100	100	94.70	100
Labor	100	96.50	100	100	91.20	100
Led7	100	100	100	100	75.30	100
Pima	100	99.50	100	100	81.50	100
Sonar	100	100	100	100	89.40	100
Tic-tac	100	100	100	100	98.90	100
Vehicle	100	100	100	100	99.90	100
Wine	100	100	100	100	98.90	100
Average	99.95	99.59	99.95	99.18	90.22	99.95

Classification Accuracy Comparison

Table 10 shows the accuracy improvement with respect to set *R* when coupling two techniques. We omit the combinations where the redundancy removal technique follows another pruning technique. Due to the transparency property, these combinations yield the same accuracy values obtained when the techniques are applied separately (see Table 5).

The highest average accuracy improvement is given by the pessimistic error rate based pruning followed by the database coverage (+2.16%), but the most interesting combination is represented by the chi-square test followed by the database coverage (+1.86%). The first combination is more accurate than the database coverage alone only in 3 data sets, while the second combination in 9 data sets. The higher average accuracy by the first combination is mainly due to the accuracy on the Austral data set (about +11% with respect to the second combination).

When a pruning technique (the chi-square test or the pessimistic error rate based pruning) is applied after the database coverage, the final accuracy is almost always lower to or equal than by the database coverage alone. The database coverage selects a minimal rule set, where each rule classifies at least one training data uncovered by the rules with higher precedence in the set. Further pruning this set often decreases the accuracy. Hence, the database coverage should be preferably applied by last.

Combining in any order the chi-square test and the pessimistic error rate based pruning does not provide any interesting accuracy improvement.

These combinations achieve the same average accuracy values obtained when applying separately the two techniques.

The redundancy removal technique followed by the pessimistic error rate based pruning does not yield a positive effect on accuracy. In many data set it has no effect, while in some data sets the accuracy decreases significantly (-36.67% on Glass).

Percentage of Pruned Rules

Table 11 reports the percentage of pruned rules for the considered combinations of pruning techniques. Any combination including either the database coverage or the redundancy removal technique discards a large rule set, due to the tendency of the two approaches to prune many rules. As shown in Table 11, for each combination the final percentage of pruned rules is comparable to that obtained by applying the database coverage or the redundancy removal technique alone.

Since the redundancy removal technique satisfies the transparency property, it can be used as final pruning technique to compress a given rule set without affecting its accuracy. The selected rule set is more than halved for the chi-square test, and is about 15% smaller for the pessimistic error rate based pruning. It has no effect if applied after the database coverage, which selects only non-redundant rules.

Combination of More Than Two Pruning Techniques

This section briefly discusses the combinations of more that two pruning techniques. Experimental

Table 10. Accuracy combining different pruning techniques

Data set	χ^2+ DBcov	PER+DBcov	DBcov+ χ^2	DBcov+PER	PER+ χ^2	χ^2+ PER	RR+ PER
	Δacc%						
Anneal	-1.67	**2.56**	**2.56**	**2.56**	0	0	0
Austral	0	**11.01**	-0.72	-0.72	0	0	0
Breast	0.14	0	0.14	0.14	**0.29**	**0.29**	**0.29**
Cleve	**2.97**	1.65	1.32	1.98	0	0	-1.32
Crx	-0.58	-1.30	-1.45	-1.45	**0**	**0**	**0**
Diabetes	**0**	-0.13	-0.13	**0**	-0.13	-0.13	-0.13
Glass	1.41	0.93	0	**1.87**	0.47	0.47	0.47
Heart	**1.85**	1.11	-0.74	1.11	0.74	0.74	-36.67
Hepatic	5.81	6.45	3.87	**7.10**	0.65	0.65	0
Iris	0.66	**0.67**	**0.67**	**0.67**	0	0	0
Labor	**3.51**	-1.75	-1.75	-1.75	0	0	0
Led7	**0.25**	0.12	0.12	0.12	0	0	0
Pima	**-0.13**	**-0.13**	**-0.13**	**-0.13**	**-0.13**	**-0.13**	**-0.13**
Sonar	-0.96	-2.40	-2.40	-2.40	**0**	**0**	**0**
Tic-tac	**0.84**	0.73	0.73	0.73	0	0	0
Vehicle	10.76	**10.99**	10.87	10.87	0.47	0.47	0.47
Wine	**6.74**	6.18	6.18	6.18	0	-2.25	0
Average	1.86	**2.16**	1.13	1.58	0.14	0.01	-2.18

Table 11. Percentage of pruned rules combining different techniques

Data set	Percentage of pruned rules							
	χ^2+ DBcov	PER+DBcov	DBcov+ χ^2	DBcov+PER	RR+χ^2	RR+PER	χ^2+RR	PER+RR
Anneal	99.98	99.98	99.98	99.98	99.74	99.70	99.74	99.68
Austral	99.95	99.95	99.95	99.95	98.03	98.11	98.03	98.12
Breast	99.21	99.27	99.22	99.25	94.97	96.63	94.97	96.83
Cleve	99.96	99.96	99.96	99.96	99.46	99.41	99.46	99.41
Crx	99.96	99.96	99.97	99.96	98.58	98.67	98.56	98.64
Diabetes	98.70	98.78	98.78	98.74	97.13	96.90	97.13	96.96
Glass	99.67	99.68	99.70	99.67	96.48	95.69	96.48	95.69
Heart	99.55	99.56	99.61	99.56	96.89	96.95	96.89	96.91
Hepatic	99.94	99.94	99.94	99.94	99.20	99.17	99.20	99.16
Iris	94.62	95.16	94.62	95.16	82.79	77.95	82.79	78.40
Labor	99.99	99.99	99.90	99.99	99.90	99.84	99.90	99.79
Led7	95.92	95.92	95.92	95.92	37.30	35.90	37.30	35.90
Pima	98.67	98.76	98.74	98.76	97.16	97.04	97.16	97.02
Sonar	99.96	99.96	99.96	99.96	96.42	96.54	96.42	96.56
Tic-tac	99.67	99.67	99.67	99.67	82.46	76.88	82.46	77.04
Vehicle	99.97	99.97	99.97	99.97	98.15	98.10	98.15	98.10
Wine	99.99	99.99	99.99	99.99	99.13	99.21	99.13	99.19
Average	99.16	99.21	99.18	99.21	92.58	91.93	92.58	91.97

results show that these combinations on average do not achieve an accuracy improvement. For example, from results in Table 10, the chi-square test and pessimistic error rate based pruning provide higher accuracy values when followed by the database coverage. We evaluated the accuracy when the database coverage is preceded by both chi-square test and pessimistic error based pruning (in any order). The final accuracy is always lower to (on average about -1%) or equal than the accuracy obtained when only one of the two techniques precedes the database coverage.

We observe that the possible combinations of pruning techniques can be simplified based on the properties reported in Section "A review of pruning method". For the transparency property, the redundancy removal technique can follow any other combination without affecting the accuracy. Moreover, since the sequence redundancy re-

moval, database coverage is equivalent to database coverage alone, any combination containing this sequence can be simplified by applying only the database coverage. Hence, the number of applied pruning techniques can be reduced, by reducing on average the pruning time.

Comparison of the Pruning Techniques Using Various Metrics

Table 12 synthetically compares the five pruning techniques and some of their most interesting combinations. Both the techniques and their combinations are ranked by considering three criteria: average accuracy, average percentage of pruned rules, and average maximum achievable accuracy. For each pruning method (in row), Table 12 reports its rank with respect to the three ranking criteria (in columns). It also shows, in round brackets, the values of the ranking measures.

The pruning techniques usually achieve higher accuracy values and a smaller classification model when they are joined with another pruning technique. Only in few cases (e.g., redundancy removal followed by pessimistic error rate), the combination of two methods is less accurate than the single methods.

The highest accuracy values and percentage of pruned rules are obtained by means of the database coverage, either alone or combined with the other techniques. These combinations including the database coverage have a low rank when considering the maximum achievable accuracy. As already discussed, the database coverage performs a "greedy" rule selection, and the selected set is potentially the least "rich" set by an information content point of view. However, this aspect becomes relevant only when an approach different from the MCF principle is used.

The lowest average accuracy is obtained by joining the redundancy removal technique and the pessimistic error rate based approach. For the other combinations, the average accuracy values are quite close.

CONCLUSION

In this chapter, we analyzed five well-known pruning techniques that are frequently used to prune associative classification rules and select the rules for classification model generation. We formally described the pruning techniques and we proof which of them satisfy the mathematical properties of idempotency, commutativity, and transparency. Finally, by means of a large set of experiments, we empirically evaluated the

Table 12. Ranking of pruning methods using accuracy, percentage of pruned rules, and maximum achievable accuracy

Pruning method	Rank based on		
	accuracy	percentage of pruned rules	maximum achievable accuracy
PER+DBcov	1 (85.59%)	1 (99.21%)	11 (90.41%)
χ^2+DBcov	2 (85.29%)	4 (99.16%) .	12 (90.22%)
DBcov+PER	3 (85.01%)	1 (99.21%)	12 (90.22%)
DBcov	4 (85.00%)	4 (99.16%)	12 (90.22%)
DBcov+χ^2	5 (84.56%)	3 (99.18%)	15 (89.96%)
PER+χ^2	6 (83.57%)	6 (97.46%)	6 (99.18%)
RR+χ^2	7 (83.56%)	8 (92.58%)	3 (99.59%)
X^2+RR	7 (83.56%)	8 (92.58%)	3 (99.59%)
χ^2	7 (83.56%)	14 (42.01%)	3 (99.59%)
PER+RR	10 (83.45%)	10 (91.97%)	6 (99.18%)
PER	10 (83.45%)	13 (77.16%)	6 (99.18%)
χ^2+PER	12 (83.44%)	6 (97.46%)	6 (99.18%)
RR	13 (83.43%)	12 (90.99%)	1 (99.95%)
Conf (50%)	13 (83.43%)	15 (17.95%)	1 (99.95%)
RR+PER	15 (81.25%)	11 (91.93%)	6 (99.18%)

effects of each pruning technique, or a combination of techniques, on accuracy and percentage of pruned rules.

Experimental results show that the database coverage, either applied alone or together with other techniques, achieves on average the highest accuracy value and the most compact and human-interpretable classification model. However, the experimental results show that the database coverage prunes on average more potentially useful rules than other approaches. This aspect could be relevant if an approach different from the MCF principle is used for the classification task.

As an ongoing work, we are analyzing the effects of rule sorting and classification approaches different from those used in this chapter on the considered pruning methods and their combinations.

REFERENCES

Arunasalam, B., & Chawla, S. (2006). CCCS: a top-down associative classifier for imbalanced class distribution. In T. Eliassi-Rad & L. H. Ungar & M. Craven & D. Gunopulos (Eds.), *KDD'06: Proceedings of the 12th ACM SIGKDD international conference on Knowledge discovery and data mining* (pp. 517 - 522). Philadelphia, PA: ACM.

Asuncion, A., & Newman, D. J. (2007). *UCI Machine Learning Repository*. Retrieved May 31, 2007, from http://www.ics.uci.edu/~mlearn/MLRepository.html

Baralis, E., & Paolo, G. (2002). A Lazy Approach to Pruning Classification Rules. In V. Kumar & S. Tsumoto & N. Zhong & P. S. Yu & X. Wu (Eds.), *Proceedings of the 2002 IEEE International Conference on Data Mining* (pp. 35-42). Maebashi City, Japan: IEEE Computer Society.

Baralis, E., Chiusano, S., & Garza, P. (2008). A Lazy Approach to Associative Classification.

IEEE Transactions on Knowledge and Data Engineering, 20(2), 156-171.

Brin, S., Motwani, R., & Silverstein, C. (1997). Beyond Market Baskets: Generalizing Association Rules to Correlations. In J. Peckham (Ed.), *SIGMOD 1997, Proceedings ACM SIGMOD International Conference on Management of Data* (pp. 265-276). Tucson, AZ: ACM Press.

Dong, G., Zhang, X., Wong, L., & Li, J. (1999). CAEP: Classification by Aggregating Emerging Patterns. In S. Arikawa & K. Furukawa (Eds.), *Discovery Science, Second International Conference* (pp. 30-42). Tokyo, Japan: Springer.

Esposito, F., Malerba, D., & Semeraro, G. (1997). A Comparative Analysis of Methods for Pruning Decision Trees. *IEEE Transactions On Pattern Analysis and Machine Intelligence, 19*(5), 476-491.

Fayyad, U. M., & Irani, K. B. (1993). Multi-Interval Discretization of Continuous-Valued Attributes for Classification Learning. In R. Bajcsy (Ed.), *Proceedings of the 13th International Joint Conference on Artificial Intelligence* (pp. 1022-1029). Chambéry, France: Morgan Kaufmann.

Li, W., Han, J., & Pei, J. (2001). CMAR: Accurate and Efficient Classification Based on Multiple Class-Association Rules. In N. Cercone & T. Y. Lin & X. Wu (Eds.), *Proceedings of the 2001 IEEE International Conference on Data Mining* (pp. 369-376). San Jose, CA: IEEE Computer Society.

Liu, B., Hsu, W., & Ma, Y. (1998). Integrating Classification and Association Rule Mining. In R. Agrawal & P. E. Stolorz & G. Piatetsky-Shapiro (Eds.), *KDD'98: Proceedings of the Fourth International Conference on Knowledge Discovery and Data Mining* (pp. 80-86). New York City, NY: AAAI Press.

Liu, B., Hsu, W., & Ma, Y. (1999). Pruning and Summarizing the Discovered Associations. In

U. Fayyad & S. Chaudhuri & D. Madigan (Eds.), *KDD'99: Proceedings of the fifth ACM SIGKDD international conference on Knowledge discovery and data mining* (pp. 125-134). San Diego, CA: ACM.

Liu, B., Ma, Y., & Wong, C. K. (2000). Improving an Association Rule Based Classifier. In D. A. Zighed & H. J. Komorowski & J. M. Zytkow (Eds.), *Principles of Data Mining and Knowledge Discovery, 4th European Conference* (pp. 504-509). Lyon, France: Springer.

Meo, R. (2000). Theory of dependence values. *ACM Transactions on Database Systems, 25*(3), 380-406.

Michalski, R. S. (1980). Pattern recognition as rule-guided inductive inference. *IEEE Transactions on Pattern Analysis and Machine Intelligence, 2*(4), 349-361.

Mills, F. C. (1965). *Statistical Methods*. London: Sir Isaac Pitman and Sons.

Quinlan, J. R. (1993). *C4.5: Programs for Machine Learning*. San Francisco, CA: Morgan Kaufmann Publishers Inc.

Tan, P., Kumar, V., & Srivastava, J. (2002). Selecting the right interestingness measure for association patterns. In D. Hand & D. Keim & R. Ng (Eds.), *KDD'02: Proceedings of the Eighth ACM SIGKDD International Conference on Knowledge Discovery and Data Mining* (pp. 32-41). Edmonton, Alberta, Canada: ACM.

Thabtah, F. (2007). A review of associative classification mining. *The Knowledge Engineering Review, 22(1)*, 37-65.

Thabtah, F. A., Cowling, P. I., & Peng, Y. (2004). MMAC: A New Multi-Class, Multi-Label Associative Classification Approach. In R. Rastogi & K. Morik & M. Bramer ity & X. Wu (Eds.), *Proceedings of the 4th IEEE International Conference on Data Mining* (pp. 217-224). Brighton, UK: IEEE Computer Society.

Toivonen, H., Klemettinen, M., Ronkainen, P., Hatonen, K., & Manilla, H. (1995). Pruning and grouping discovered association rules. In Y. Kodratoff & G. Nakhaeizadeh & C. Taylor (Eds.), *Workshop Notes of the ECML-95 Workshop on Statistics, Machine Learning, and Knowledge Discovery in Databases* (pp. 47-52). Heraklion, Crete, Greece.

Wang, J., & Karypis, G. (2005). HARMONY: Efficiently Mining the Best Rules for Classification. In H. Kargupta & J. Srivastava & C. Kamath & A. Goodman (Eds.), *Proceedings of the Fifth SIAM International Conference on Data Mining* (pp. 205-216). Newport Beach, CA: SIAM.

Wang, K., Zhou, S., & He, Y. (2000). Growing decision trees on support-less association rules. In R. Ramakrishnan & S. Stolfo & R. Bayardo & I. Parsa (Eds.), *KDD'00: Proceedings of the sixth ACM SIGKDD international conference on Knowledge discovery and data mining* (pp. 265-269). Boston, MA: ACM.

Yin, X., & Han, J. (2003). CPAR: Classification based on Predictive Association Rules. In D. Barbarà & C. Kamath (Eds.), *Proceedings of the Third SIAM International Conference on Data Mining* (pp. 331-335). San Francisco, CA: SIAM.

Section V
Visualization and Representation of Association Rules

Chapter XI
Meta–Knowledge Based Approach for an Interactive Visualization of Large Amounts of Association Rules

Sadok Ben Yahia
Faculty of Sciences of Tunis, Tunisia

Olivier Couturier
Centre de Recherche en Informatique de Lens (CRIL), France

Tarek Hamrouni
Faculty of Sciences of Tunis, Tunisia

Engelbert Mephu Nguifo
Centre de Recherche en Informatique de Lens (CRIL), France

ABSTRACT

Providing efficient and easy-to-use graphical tools to users is a promising challenge of data mining, especially in the case of association rules. These tools must be able to generate explicit knowledge and, then, to present it in an elegant way. Visualization techniques have shown to be an efficient solution to achieve such a goal. Even though considered as a key step in the mining process, the visualization step of association rules received much less attention than that paid to the extraction step. Nevertheless, some graphical tools have been developed to extract and visualize association rules. In those tools, various approaches are proposed to filter the huge number of association rules before the visualization step. However both data mining steps (association rule extraction and visualization) are treated separately in a one way process. Recently different approaches have been proposed that use meta-knowledge to guide the user during the mining process. Standing at the crossroads of Data Mining and Human-Computer

Interaction, those approaches present an integrated framework covering both steps of the data mining process. This chapter describes and discusses such approaches. Two approaches are described in details: the first one builds a roadmap of compact representation of association rules from which the user can explore generic bases of association rules and derive, if desired, redundant ones without information loss. The second approach clusters the set of association rules or its generic bases, and uses a fisheye view technique to help the user during the mining of association rules. Generic bases with their links or the associated clusters constitute the meta-knowledge used to guide the interactive and cooperative visualization of association rules.

INTRODUCTION

Data mining techniques have been proposed and studied to help users better understand and scrutinize huge amounts of collected and stored data. In this respect, extracting association rules has grasped the interest of the data mining community. Thus, the last decade has been marked by a determined algorithmic effort to reduce the computation time of the interesting itemset extraction step. The obtained success is primarily due to an important programming effort combined with strategies for compacting data structures in main memory. However, it seems obvious that this frenzied activity loses sight of the essential objective of this step, *i.e.*, extracting a reliable knowledge, of exploitable size for users. Indeed, the unmanageably large association rule sets compounded with their low precision often make the perusal of knowledge ineffective, their exploitation time-consuming and frustrating for users. Moreover, unfortunately, this teenaged field seems to provide results in the opposite direction with the evolving "knowledge management" topic.

The commonly generated thousands and even millions of high-confidence rules – among which many are redundant (Bastide et al., 2000; Ben Yahia et al., 2006; Stumme et al., 2001; Zaki, 2004) – encouraged the development of more acute techniques to limit the number of reported rules, starting by basic pruning techniques based on thresholds for both the frequency of the represented pattern and the strength of the dependency between premise and conclusion. Moreover, this pruning can be based on patterns defined by the user (user-defined templates), on Boolean operators (Meo et al., 1996; Ng et al., 1998; Ohsaki et al., 2004; Srikant et al., 1997). The number of rules can be reduced through pruning based on additional information such as a taxonomy on items (Han, & Fu, 1995) or on a metric of specific interest (Brin et al., 1997) (*e.g.*, Pearson's correlation or $\chi 2$-test). More advanced techniques that produce only lossless information limited number of the entire set of rules, called generic bases (Bastide et al., 2000). The generation of such generic bases heavily draws on a battery of results provided by formal concept analysis (FCA) (Ganter & Wille, 1999). This association rule reduction can be seen as a "sine qua non" condition to avoid that the visualization step comes up short in dealing with large amounts of rules. In fact, the most used kind of visualization categories in data mining is the use of visualization techniques to present the information caught out from the mining process. Graphical visualization tools became more appealing when handling large data sets with complex relationships, since information presented in the form of images is more direct and easily understood by humans (Buono & Costabile, 2004; Buono et al., 2001). Visualization tools allow users to work in an interactive environment with ease in understanding rules.

Consequently, data mining techniques gain in presenting discovered knowledge in an interactive, graphical form that often fosters new insights.

Thus, the user is encouraged to form and validate new hypotheses to the end of better problem solving and gaining deeper domain knowledge (Bustos et al., 2003). Visual data analysis is a way to achieve such goal, especially when it is tightly coupled with the management of meta-knowledge used to handle the vast amounts of extracted knowledge.

It is important that this meta-knowledge has to be expressed in a convenient way, without bothering with the internal representation of knowledge (Pitrat, 1990). Constituting the basis of many optical illusions, Ralph Waldo Emerson said: "We see only what we are prepared to see"[1]. Thus, what can be seen or detected by the user is constrained in large part by the information structure. Avenues for future success of Data Mining techniques in stimulating and delighting the user include the presentation of meta-knowledge to analyze and infer small portions of knowledge.

We describe here research works that exploit generic bases (Bastide et al., 2000) in order to losslessly reduce the number of rules. Such bases contain the most informative association rules of minimal premises (*i.e.*, minimal generators (Bastide et al. 2000a)) and maximal conclusions (*i.e.*, closed itemsets (Pasquier et al., 2005)). In fact, visualization techniques are frequently employed to present the extracted knowledge in a form that is understandable to humans. This makes graphical visualization tools more appealing when handling large datasets with complex relationships.

In this chapter, we are interested in presenting different works that use meta-knowledge to guide the exploration of association rules. Two approaches are particularly presented in details. The first approach used a graphical-based visualization technique combined with the association rules technique to handle generic bases of association rules (Ben Yahia & Mephu Nguifo, 2008). The second approach used a fisheye view visualization technique combined with a clustering technique to handle generic bases of association rules (Couturier et al., 2007a).

The chapter is organized as follows. Section 2 overviews related work on association rules visualization techniques. Section 3 introduces basic notions for extraction of generic bases of association rules. Section 4 presents the meta-knowledge based approach for association rules visualization, focusing especially on the two different approaches mentioned above. It also discusses the scalability issue of both approaches when dealing with large number of association rules. Section 5 offers a detailed description of the prototypes we propose. Carried out experiments stressing on the ease of use and the scalability are sketched in Section 6. Finally, Section 7 ends with conclusion and points out avenues for future work.

RELATED WORKS

Compared to the stampede algorithmic effort for extracting frequent (condensed) patterns, only few works paid attention to visualizing association rules (Blanchard et al., 2003; Blanchard et al., 2007; Buono & Costabile, 2004; Chen et al., 2007; Couturier et al., 2005a; Ertek & Demiriz, 2006; Han & Cercone, 2000; Hofmann et al., 2000; Kuntz et al., 2000; Liu et al. 1999; Liu & Salvendy, 2005; Liu & Salvendy, 2006; Singh et al., 2007; Wong et al., 1999). In (Liu & Salvendy, 2005), the authors reported a survey of current state of art on the application of visualization techniques to facilitate association rules modelling process in terms of visualization of derived rules, visualization of rule evaluation and visual interactive rule derivation.

As pointed out earlier by Wong et *al.* (Wong et al., 1999), few of association rule visualization tools were able to handle more than dozens of rules, and none of them can effectively manage rules with multiple antecedents (see Figure 1a/1b). Thus, it was extremely difficult to visualize and understand the association information of a large data set even when all the rules were available.

In this situation, Wong et *al.* (Wong et al., 1999) introduced a visualization technique based on the application of the technology to a text mining study on large corpora. Thus, hundreds of multiple antecedent association rules in a three-dimensional display with minimum human interaction may be handled, with low occlusion percentage and no screen swapping. Besides, the approach presented by Buono and Costabile (2004) is noteworthy. In fact, the authors presented a visual strategy that exploits a graph-based technique and parallel coordinates to visualize the results of association rule mining algorithms. This helps data miners to get an overview of the rule set they are interacting with and enables them to deeply investigate inside a specific set of rules.

The work of Hofmann et *al.* (Hofmann et al., 2000) mainly focused on visual representation of association rules and presentation of the relationships between related rules using interactive mosaic plots (histograms) and double decker plots. In both of these approaches, there is no focus on rule reduction and the user interaction is limited, while, Liu et *al.* (Liu et al. 1999) presented an integrated system for finding interesting associations and visualizing them. Han and Cercone (2000) proposed an interactive model for visualizing the entire process of knowledge discovery and data mining. They focus mainly on the "parallel coordinates" technique to visualize rule induction algorithms.

Blanchard et *al.* (Blanchard et al., 2003; Blanchard et al., 2007) proposed an experimental prototype, called ArVis, which is intended to tackle the association rule validation problem by designing a human-centered visualization method for the rule rummaging task (see Figure 1e). This proposed approach, based on a specific rummaging model, relies on rule interestingness measures and on interactive rule subset focusing and mining.

In (Couturier et al., 2005a), Couturier et *al.* proposed an approach based on a hierarchical association rule mining, using a user-driven approach rather than on an automatic one. In this anthropocentric approach, the user is at the heart of the process by playing the role of an evolutionary heuristic. The work of Zaki et Phoophakdee (2003), introduced the MIRAGE tool which is the only one handling generic basis of association rules as defined by the authors in (Zaki, 2004) (see Figure 1c). Even though this basis is not informative, as outlined in (Gasmi et al., 2005), this system presents a new framework for mining and visually exploring the minimal rules. MIRAGE uses lattice-based interactive rule visualization approach, displaying the rules in a very compact form.

Recently different approaches were reported to treat semi-structured data (Chen et al., 2007; Singh et al., 2007). Chen et *al.* (Chen et al., 2007) proposed a visual data mining prototype framework to visualize and mine web usage data in order to understand web page access behaviours versus the connectivity structure. Singh et *al.* (Singh et al., 2007) introduced a new visual mining tool for social network data mining, by integrating a previous graph mining algorithm for interactive visualization.

Actually, all graphical representations present advantages and drawbacks which must be taken into account depending on users' preferences. For example, trees and graphs are easily interpretable thanks to their hierarchical structure. However, they are unreadable on dense data. Both 2D (see Figure 5) and 3D matrix (see Figure 1d) use colours in order to highlight metrics but they require cognitive efforts. Virtual reality allows introducing the user within the process in order to focus on a data subset but the metaphor choice requires a good data comprehension. As stated in the well known "No Free Lunch Theorems" (Wolpert & Macready, 1997), none of the graphical representations is the most efficient one for all types of data. Nevertheless, 3D matrix is a good compromise. We focused on 3D matrix "itemsets-itemsets". It is based on a 2D matrix but the third dimension is also projected on the screen plan.

Figure 1. Related works on association rules visualization

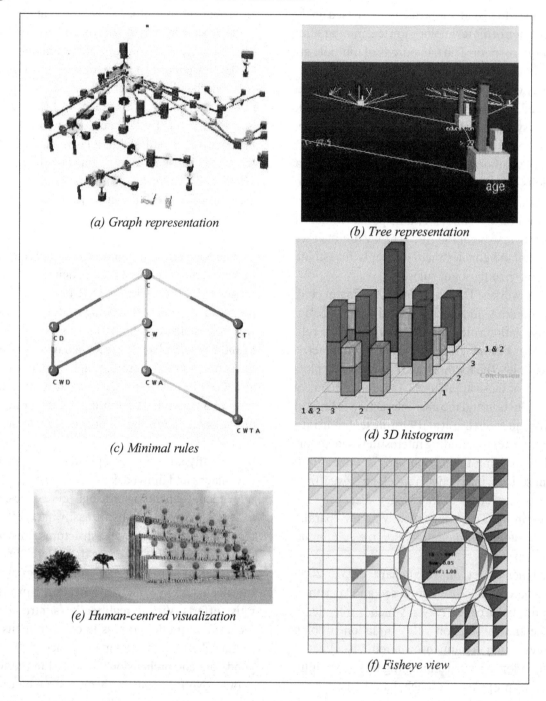

(a) Graph representation

(b) Tree representation

(c) Minimal rules

(d) 3D histogram

(e) Human-centred visualization

(f) Fisheye view

All these representations have a common limitation: they are not based on a global and detail view principle when displaying learned knowledge. Indeed, detail representations are quickly unreadable, whereas global representations do not present all information.

To sum up, the main moan that can be addressed to the existing representations is that they display all rules in a same screen space. Indeed, the user's visibility and understanding are proportionally reduced according to the number of rules. In addition, these representations are not adapted to clusters visualization, since they often treat only one set of rules that can be reduced with user's constraints.

In the area of information visualization, several kinds of known representations were proposed to study a large set of information as lenses and hyperbolic trees (Lamping et al., 1995), perspective walls (Mackinlay et al., 1991), fisheye views (FEV) (Furnas, 2006) or superposition of transparent views (Harrison & Vicente, 1996). In the literature, it is shown that FEV is adapted to this kind of problem (Couturier et al., 2007a). Indeed, at a glance Figure 1f highlights that FEV shows the point of interest in detail and the overview of the display in the same representation.

This is done by distorting the picture which, for this purpose, is not uniformly scaled. Objects far away from the focus point are shrunk while objects near the focus point are magnified. The degree of visual distortion depends on the distance from the focus point. Several tools implement FEV as AiSee[2], InfoVis (Fekete, 2004) and LARM (Couturier et al., 2005a). A first approach using a FEV in an association rule visualization method was proposed in (Couturier et al., 2007b) (see Figure 1f). In this work, authors exploited a merging representation in order to represent a set of association rules, in which the focus point is a detailed rule. One of the approaches that we describe further, CBVAR, also relies on the same idea and makes it of use to visualize the set of clusters (Couturier et al., 2007a).

In the following, we briefly recall basic notions on association rules and their underlying concepts, borrowed from the order theory. These notions are of need in the definition of the generic bases of association rules.

BACKGROUND KNOWLEDGE: NOTIONS ON ASSOCIATION RULES

Association rules, first introduced in 1993 (Agrawal et al., 1993), are used to identify relationships between a set of items in a database. These relationships are not based on inherent properties of the data itself (as with functional dependencies), but rather based on the co-occurrence of the data items. The discovered association rules can be used by management to increase the efficiency (and reduce the cost) of advertising, marketing, inventory, and stock shelving (Agrawal et al., 1993). Such contagious applicability was widespread to a number of various fields, *e.g.*, failure prediction in telecommunication networks, money laundering, etc.

The formal statement of the problem of mining association rules over basket data can be described as follows (Agrawal et al., 1993). Let $I = \{i_1, i_2, ..., i_m\}$ be a set of m distinct items. Each transaction t in a database D of transactions, has a unique identifier *TID*, and contains a set of items, such that $t \subseteq I$. An association rule is an expression $A \Rightarrow B$, where itemsets $A, B \subseteq I$, and $A \cap B = \varnothing$. Each itemset is said to have support s if $s\%$ of the transactions in D contain the itemset[3]. The association rule is said to have confidence c if $c\%$ of the transactions that contain A also contain B, *i.e.*,

$$c = \frac{\text{support}(A \cup B)}{\text{support}(A)} .[4]$$

Itemsets A and B are called, respectively, *premise* and *conclusion* of the rule R. *Valid association rules* are those with support (*resp.* confidence) value greater than or equal to the associated user-defined minimal threshold, called *minsup* (*resp. minconf*). If the confidence of a rule R is equal to 1 then it is called *exact association rule*, otherwise it is called *approximate association rule*.

In most real life databases, thousands or even millions of high-confidence rules are generated, among which many are redundant (Pasquier et al., 2005; Zaki, 2004). To this end, extracting "condensed" patterns is grasping the interest of the Data Mining community. In fact, avoiding the extraction of an overwhelming knowledge is of primary importance as it ensures extra value knowledge usefulness and reliability. In the association rule extraction domain, rule selection is mainly based on user-defined syntactic templates or on user-defined statistical interestingness metrics (Ohsaki et al., 2004). Lossless selection is mainly based on the determination of a generic subset of all association rules, called *generic basis*, from which the remaining (redundant) association rules are generated. In the following, we recall some key results from the Galois lattice-based paradigm in FCA and its connection with generic association rules mining.

Extraction context: An extraction context is a triplet $K = (O, I, R)$, where O represents a finite set of objects (or transactions), I is a finite set of items and R is a binary relation (*i.e.*, $R \subseteq O \times I$). Each couple $(o, i) \in R$ expresses that the transaction $o \in O$ contains the item $i \in I$. (see Figure 2 for an example).

We define two functions that map sets of objects to sets of items and *vice versa*. Thus, for a subset $O \subseteq O$, we define $\varphi(O) = \{i \mid \forall\, o \in O, (o, i) \in R\}$; and for $I \subseteq I$, $\psi(I) = \{o \mid \forall\, i \in I, (o, i) \in R\}$. Both functions φ and ψ form a Galois connection between the respective power sets $P(I)$ and $P(O)$ (Barbut & Monjardet, 1970). Consequently, both compound operators of φ and ψ are closure operators, in particular $\omega = \varphi \circ \psi$.

Closed itemset: An itemset $I \subseteq I$ is said to be *closed* if $I = \omega(I)$. For example, the itemset {a,e,k} is closed, while the itemset {c} is not closed since its closure is equal to {c,g}.

Frequent itemset: An itemset $I \subseteq I$ is said to be *frequent* with respect to the user-defined support threshold *minsup* if

$$support(I) = \frac{|\psi(I)|}{|O|} \geq minsup.$$

Frequent closed itemset: An itemset I is said to be *frequent closed* if it is frequent and closed.

Minimal generator: An itemset $g \subseteq I$ is *called minimal generator* of a closed itemset I, if and only if $\omega(g) = I$ and it does not exist $g_1 \subset g$ such that $\omega(g_1) = I$.

Iceberg lattice: When only frequent closed itemsets are considered with set inclusion, the resulting structure only preserves the joint operator. In the remaining of the paper, such structure is referred to as "*Iceberg lattice*" (Stumme et al., 2001).

With respect to (Guigues & Duquenne, 1986) and (Luxenburger, 1991), given an Iceberg lattice – representing closed itemsets ordered by means of a partial order relation (*i.e.*, $\subseteq$) – generic bases of association rules can be derived in a straightforward manner. We assume that, in such structure, each closed itemset is "decorated" with its associated list of minimal generators. Hence, generic approximate association rules represent "inter-node" implications, assorted with statistical information, *i.e.*, the confidence, from a sub-closed-itemset to a super-closed-itemset while starting from a given node in the Iceberg lattice. Conversely, generic exact association rules are "intra-node" implications extracted from each node in the partially ordered structure (Ben Yahia et al., 2006).

Example 1: Consider the extraction context K given by Figure 2 (Top left). By applying the PRINCE *algorithm (Hamrouni et al., 2005), the set of closed itemsets, with their associated minimal generators, is extracted. This set is shown by Figure 2 (Top right), in which the third column sketches the set of objects verified by the associated closed itemset. For*

$$minsup = \frac{1}{7} \text{ and } minconf = \frac{1}{5},$$

PRINCE also allows extracting the valid generic association rules presented in Figure 2 (Bottom).[5]

It is worth noting that the whole set of valid association rules for

$$minsup = \frac{1}{7} \text{ and } minconf = \frac{1}{5}$$

contains 60 rules.[6] From this set, only 16 rules are non-redundant (*cf.* Figure 2 (Bottom)). This clearly shows the benefit of relying on generic bases as an efficient step for drastically reducing the number of visualized rules without information loss. In this respect, as an example of redundant rules' derivation, the rule ckg⇒e is redundant *w.r.t.* the exact generic one ck⇒eg. Indeed, they have the same support

(equal to $\frac{1}{7}$)

and confidence (equal to 1). In addition, the premise (*resp.* conclusion) of the former is a superset (*resp.* subset) of that of the latter *w.r.t.* set inclusion. Indeed, ckg ⊇ ck and e ⊆ eg. By adopting the same reasoning, we have for example the approximate rule ek⇒a as redundant *w.r.t.* the approximate generic rule e⇒ak.

In our work, we intend to show that meta-knowledge can help to improve usability of visual data mining tools, when dealing with a huge set of association rules.

Figure 2. Example of generic association rules of a context. **Top left:** *Formal context K.* **Top right:** *List of closed itemsets associated to K and for each one, its minimal generators and the objects list where it appears.* **Bottom:** *The set of valid generic association rules for minsup* $= \frac{1}{7}$ *and minconf* $= \frac{1}{5}$ *.*

	a	c	e	g	k
1	×		×		×
2	×		×		×
3		×	×		
4		×	×	×	×
5				×	
6			×		×
7				×	×

Closed itemset	Minimal generators	Set of objects
g	g	$\{3,4,5,7\}$
k	k	$\{1,2,4,6,7\}$
cg	c	$\{3,4\}$
ek	e	$\{1,2,4,6\}$
gk	gk	$\{4,7\}$
aek	a	$\{1,2\}$
cegk	ce, ck, eg	$\{4\}$

\#	"⇒"
R_1	a⇒ ek
R_2	c⇒ g
R_3	e⇒ k
R_4	ce⇒ gk
R_5	ck⇒ eg
R_6	eg⇒ ck

Exact generic rules

Approximate generic rules		
\#	"⇒"	Confidence
R_7	gk⇒ec	0.5
R_8	g⇒c	0.5
R_9	g⇒cek	0.25
R_{10}	c⇒egk	0.5
R_{11}	k⇒e	0.8
R_{12}	k⇒ae	0.4
R_{13}	e⇒ak	0.5
R_{14}	k⇒ceg	0.2
R_{15}	e⇒cgk	0.25
R_{16}	g⇒k	0.5

META-KNOWLEDGE BASED INTERACTIVE VISUALIZATION OF (GENERIC) ASSOCIATION RULES

Visualization can be very beneficial to support the user in this task by improving the intelligibility of the large rule sets and enabling the user to navigate inside them. In order to find relevant knowledge for decision-making, the user needs to really rummage through the rules (Blanchard et al., 2007). During the last few years, different graphical approaches were proposed to present association rules in order to solve the major problem previously quoted. The common main drawback of previously reported works is that they do not offer a global and detailed view at the same time. None of those representations respects this global-detail view principle which is crucial in Human Computer Interaction (HCI) (Shneiderman, 1996).

Motivation and Proposal

The ultimate goal is to bring the power of visualization technology to every desktop to allow a better, faster, and more intuitive exploration of very large data resources (Bustos et al., 2003). However, faced with this deluge of association rules, a user may be asked to rely on a tedious and boring application of its perceptual abilities to explore such set of association rules. Even if we consider that we have to visualize a reduced number of generic association rules, their sufficiently high number[7] can dissuade users to perform a detailed exploration.

Thus, the scalability of the graphical visualization is shown to be of paramount importance. However, the use of the "scalability" term in this context may be misleading. Indeed, we mean by this term that a user has actually to explore both large and small amounts of knowledge with the same ease of use. Usually, the foggy and hazy interface that a user has to face when browsing a large amount of association rules is never showed when advertising graphical visualization systems (*e.g.*, the MineSet software[8], the ASSOCIATION RULE VIEWER[9] and the MIRAGE prototype (Zaki & Phoophakdee, 2003)).

Visual data exploration – also known as *the information seeking mantra* – usually follows the three steps as indicated by the *Schneiderman's* visual design guidelines (Shneiderman, 1996). The author recommended the following scheduling tasks "*Overview first, zoom and filter, then details on demand*". In fact, grasping a huge amount of rules can very often encourage the user to perform a superficial exploration instead of an in-depth one. That's why a visualization tool has to provide an overview of the association rules, which permits an overall knowledge direct access and interconnections within the knowledge space. Once the user focused on a portion of rules, a smooth user-zooming capability should be performed. When implementing the fisheye view technique to perform such task, it is very important to keep the context while zooming on the focused portion of knowledge. In addition to the complete description of the desired portion of rules (*i.e.*, premise, conclusion and confidence), the prototype has to display, *on user demand*, all the derivable rules that can be drawn from such generic association rule set.

The Scalability Issue: Clustering Generic Association Rules

Laying on "divide to conquer" idea, a clustering process makes it possible to portion an association rules set into smaller and, thus, manageable pieces of knowledge that can be easily handled. Thus, the "scalability" issue is tackled by performing a clustering on the generic association rule set. To do so, the K-MEANS algorithm (Steinhaus, 1956) is applied on a meta-context. In order to keep track of the confidence information, this meta-context should be a fuzzy binary relation. In this context, each $R(t^{\alpha}, j)$ couple means that the transaction *t* is covered by the rule R_j with a confidence value equal to $\alpha \in [0, 1]$. Thus we built a fuzzy meta-context where rows are transactions (or objects), columns are extracted generic association rules from the initial context, and a cell (t, j) contains the confidence α of the generic association rule j if it is verified by the transaction t; otherwise it contains zero. Figure 3 presents the fuzzy meta-context built from the generic association rule list given by Figure 2 (Bottom).

As output, a reduced cardinality set of clusters of generic association rules is obtained. Such a clustering makes possible to scalably handle large quantities of association rules. In addition, it provides a "guided" exploration based on a clustering of association rules.

The choice of K-MEANS algorithm is argued by the fact that it is one of the simplest unsupervised learning algorithms that solve the well known clustering problem. The procedure follows a simple and easy way to classify a given rule set through a certain number of clusters (say k) fixed beforehand. The main idea is to define k centroids, one for each cluster. These centroids should be placed in a cunning way because a different location may cause a different result. So, the better choice is to place them as much as possible far away from each other. The next step is to take each point belonging to a given rule set and to associate it to the nearest centroid (Steinhaus, 1956). When no point is pending, the first step is completed and an early gathering is done. At this point, we need to re-calculate k new centroids as barycenters of the clusters resulting from the previous step. After we have these k new centroids, a new binding has to be done between the same data set points and the nearest new centroid. As a result of this loop, we may notice that the k centroids change their location step by step until no more changes are done. As roughly described above, the K-MEANS algorithm can be viewed as a greedy algorithm for partitioning the n generic association rules into k clusters so as to minimize the sum of the squared distances to the cluster centers.

Nevertheless, the number of clusters k must be determined beforehand. Unfortunately, there is no general theoretical solution to find the optimal number of clusters for any given data set. To overcome such a drawback, the user currently has to introduce the number of clusters in the prototype and to compare the results of multiple runs with different k classes and choose the best partition matching its satisfactory criterion.

Providing Additional Knowledge on Demand

Let us keep in mind that given a generic association rule set, we aim to set up a graphical visualization prototype permitting to enhance the human-machine interaction by providing a contextual "knowledge exploration", minimizing a boring large amount of knowledge exploration. Here we come to a turning point: Why is it interesting to try to understand why a user and/or a knowledge expert may be interested in a particular rule, and to determine what interesting information

Figure 3. The associated fuzzy meta-context

	R_1	R_2	R_3	R_4	R_5	R_6	R_7	R_8	R_9	R_{10}	R_{11}	R_{12}	R_{13}	R_{14}	R_{15}	R_{16}
1	1		1								0.8	0.4	0.5			
2	1		1								0.8	0.4	0.5			
3		1						0.5								
4		1	1	1	1	1	0.5	0.5	0.25	0.5	0.8			0.2	0.25	0.5
5																
6			1								0.8					
7																0.5

or knowledge, not explicitly requested, we could provide him, in addition to the proper answer? Indeed, improving human-machine interaction by emulating a cooperative behavior has been proposed by some researchers through various techniques (Cuppens & Demolombe, 1989; Frantz, & Shapiro, 1991; Motro, 1987).

In (Motro, 1987), the author states: *"requests for data can be classified roughly into two kinds: specific requests and goals. A specific request establishes a rigid qualification, and is concerned only with data that matches it precisely. A goal, on the other hand, establishes a target qualification and is concerned with data which is close to the target".* For Cuppens and Demolombe (1989), *"the basic idea is that when a person asks a question, he is not interested to know the answer just to increase his knowledge, but he has the intention to realize some action, and the answer contains necessary or useful information to realize this action".*

In our context, when such additional knowledge is not supplied, this forces the user to retry a tedious rule exploration repeatedly, until obtaining a satisfactory "matching". In this respect, such additional knowledge is provided by a set of fuzzy meta-rules generated from the fuzzy meta-context. To do this, we use an approach of rules generation with constraints, where both premise and conclusion parts refer to classical generic association rules. The premise part is constraint to be a singleton with only one item which is a generic association rule.

The role of such fuzzy meta-rules is to highlight "connections" between association rules without losing rule's confidence information. In what follows, we describe our visualization prototypes.

DESCRIPTION OF THE PROPOSED VISUALIZATION TOOLS

We present here, respectively, GERVIS and CBVAR visualization prototypes as well as some screen snapshots implementing the driving above discussed issues.

GERVIS

The main aim of the GERVIS prototype is setting up a visualization tool that allows an effective exploration – of these generic association rules – guided by a back-end meta-knowledge (Ben Yahia & Mephu Nguifo, 2008). To retrieve such meta-knowledge, a meta-context is built. Once the fuzzy extraction meta-context is built, the associated set of fuzzy association rules (Sudkamp, 2005) is extracted. Interestingly enough, fuzzy association rules are very appealing from a knowledge representational point of view (Sudkamp, 2005).

Even though the user has the possibility to indicate which visualization technique he (she) prefers, the GERVIS tool can advise the user and automatically recommends a suitable visualization technique (Ben Yahia & Mephu Nguifo, 2008). The main recommendation claim is as follows: for generic rules extracted from sparse contexts, it is better to use 3D visualization technique, while, for those extracted from dense contexts, 2D visualization technique is advisable.

In the 3D histogram based visualization technique, matrix floor rows represent items and columns represent generic association rules (Figure 4). The red and blue blocks of each column (rule) in Figure 4 represent the premise and the conclusion, respectively[10]. Item identities are shown along the right side of the matrix. The associated confidence and support are represented by a scaled histogram. On a 2D matrix-based visualization technique, rule premise items are on one axis, and the rule conclusion items are on the other axis. The confidence value is indicated by different colors. The higher the confidence value is, the darker the color.

The GERVIS visualization prototype is implemented in JAVA. As input, it takes an XML (eXtensible Markup Language) file complying

Figure 4. Displaying clustered generic association rules

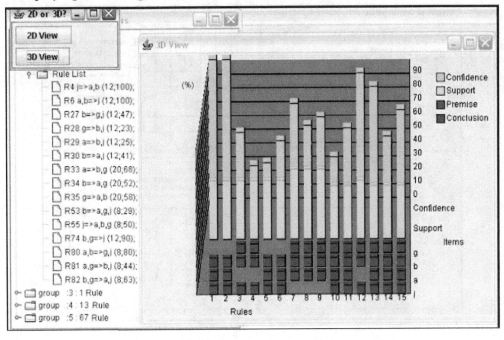

with the document type definition (DTD). This storing format is argued by the fact that XML has emerged as a new standard for data representation and exchange on the Internet. As output, the set of selected rules can be saved in a file with HTML or TXT format. At a glance, the associated DTD permits some interesting features:

- Represent generic rules in which the premise part is empty, by associating a dedicated symbol. Handling such kind of generic association rule, *e.g.*, the *IGB* basis (Gasmi et al., 2005), is of particular interest since it is informative and more compact than other generic basis requiring the non-emptiness of the premise part. The introduced categorization into "factual" and "implicative" also presents an appealing revisiting of generic association rule semantics.

- Represent "generalized" generic association rules, thanks to the "Deg" attribute. If

this degree value is set to belong to the unit interval, then we can handle fuzzy itemsets, while if it is equal to -1, then we can handle negative itemsets.

Once the displaying parameters have been set, the user can click on the "Cluster" tab. Next, the clusters are displayed in a new window as depicted in Figure 4. Once a cluster is of interest to the user, he (or she) can visualize only these intra-cluster generic rules graphically (2D or 3D) by activating the right option in the associated contextual menu. For example, Figure 4 depicts 98 generic association rules split into 5 clusters. If the user focuses on the second cluster, 15 generic association rules are displayed. By activating the right option, only these 15 generic association rules are graphically displayed. By zooming on these rules, their inter-cluster status seems to be meaningful. For example, Figure 4 presents only generic rules extracted from the itemset "a b j g" corresponding to the second cluster.

Figure 5. Displaying derived association rules

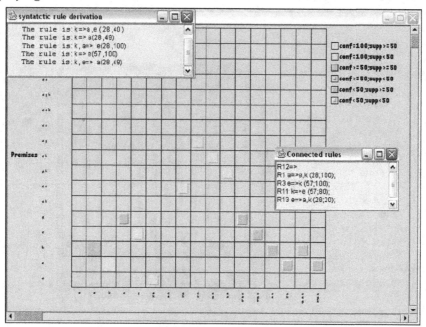

Figure 6. Displaying semantically connected association rules

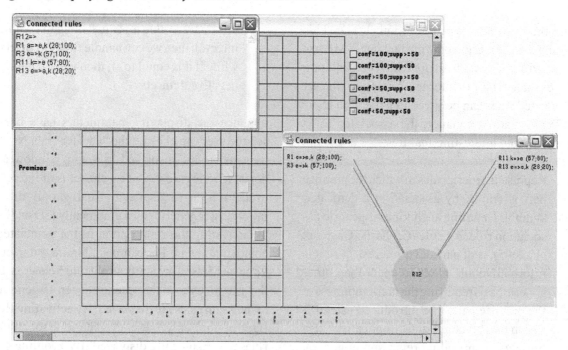

Aiming to fulfill the third recommendation *details on user demand*, the GERVIS prototype has to display not only all the derivable rules that can be drawn from such generic association rule set, but also all the semantically connected association rules. In what follows, these issues are discussed.

Displaying Derivable Rules

Once a user is interested in the graphical visualization window, then by activating the contextual menu, the first displayed two options "Syntactic Rule derivation" and "Rule derivation" are of interest. If the user selects the first option, then the system provides all syntactically derivable rules[11] in a new window, as shown in figure 5. Indeed, for these derivable rules the only available information is that their support and confidence values are at least equal, respectively, to those of the generic association rule used to derive them.

Displaying Semantically Connected Rules

Suppose that a user may be interested in a given rule. Then, by activating the contextual menu and selecting the "connected rules" option, all generic rules which are "semantically" connected to the chosen one are textually or graphically displayed in a new window. For example in Figure 6, four generic association rules are assessed as semantically connected if the user selects the generic association rule: k$\Rightarrow$ae.

CBVAR (Clustering-Based Visualizer of Association Rules)

Starting from the fact that the key to the success of a visualization prototype is to fully comply with the Visual Information-Seeking Mantra illustrated by Shneiderman (1996): *"Overview first, zoom and filter, then details on demand"*. First of all, graphical tools must provide a global

view of the system in order to deduce the main important points. The user must be able to determine the starting point of his analysis thanks to this global view. During his analysis, he must be able to explore in-depth particular areas if desired. Indeed, all details are not of need to be displayed at the same time. Unfortunately, all current representations do not respect this crucial point which is necessary in order to visualize large set of knowledge. The main thrust of CBVAR is to offer a global and detailed view at the same time, which is missing key feature in the approaches surveyed in the related works.

The CBVAR prototype (Couturier et al., 2007a) is implemented in JAVA and runs on Linux OS. The main feature of CBVAR is that it presents an integrated framework for extracting and shrewdly visualizing association rules. Thus, it avoids modifying the output format of the existing association rule mining algorithms to fit into the visualization module input requirements. The user has only to provide a data file and, at the end of the tunnel, association rules can be visualized.

CBVAR is composed of two independent parts: clustering and visualization of clustered association rules. Briefly, in order to obtain clusters, several existing tools are merged together and which are invocable from a shell-script. The well known K-MEANS algorithm (Steinhaus, 1956) is applied on data. As output, non-overlapping clusters are obtained, such that each one contains a reduced cardinality set of association rules.

Cluster Generation

The association rule extraction process takes a text file as input (such those of *dat* or *txt* extensions). The file type needs to be a textual one where each line contains the list of the distinct items composing a given object. Correspondent frequent closed itemsets and their associated minimal generators (Bastide et al., 2000a) as well as generic association rule bases are reported in a (.*txt*) file thanks to the PRINCE algorithm (Hamrouni et al., 2005). The latter also generates an XML file (*.xml*) containing information about the input file according to both user-specified minimum thresholds of support (*i.e.*, *minsup*) and confidence (*i.e.*, *minconf*). The *xml* file complies with the PMML standard (Predictive Model Markup Language[12]) to avoid limiting the scope of the prototype by using a specific DTD application. The choice of PMML can be argued by the fact that it is an XML-based language which provides a way for applications to define statistical and Data mining models and to share models between PMML compliant applications.

In addition, a meta-context file (*.gen*) can also be generated thanks to this algorithm. Even though this step is costly, it can be skipped if the meta-context has already been generated. Thus, the prototype keeps track of the generated meta-contexts and automatically uploads them in order to speed up the visualization process. During the latter step, a file (*.clu*) containing, for each rule, the attributed cluster identifier is generated. Note that the number of clusters *k* is specified by the user. The last step of the cluster set generation can begin according to the cluster

identifier file and the corresponding XML file. *k* files (*.xml*) corresponding to the *k* clusters are then generated with a meta-cluster file (*.cluxml*) and each one contains the associated part in the previously generated XML file. The package containing the (*.cluxml*) file and the *k* (*.xml*) files will constitute the starting point of the second part of CBVAR which is the visualization of all generated clusters. A complete toy example is described in Figure 7.

Each used tool is one parameter of the generation of the cluster set. It is possible to modify these intermediate tools by updating the shell-script. This script will be executed by CBVAR with several parameters specified by the user: support, confidence, meta-context file (if any) and the number of clusters.

Association Rule Visualization: Unravelling from Global to Detailed Views

Couturier et *al.* (Couturier et al., 2007a) have shown that the fisheye view (FEV) visualisation

Figure 7. Cluster generation: the case of the MUSHROOM dataset

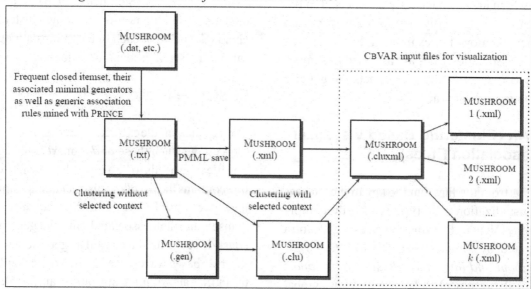

method is adapted for association rules visualization. Based on a merging representation, they represent a set of association rules, in which the focus point is a detailed rule. CʙVAR relies on the same idea to visualize the set of clusters (see Figure 8).

CʙVAR combines both 2D and 3D representations. The 2D representation allows having a global association rule view of one rule of each cluster. This rule is selected according to interestingness metric such as *support* or *confidence* (Agrawal et al., 1996) or *lift* (Brin et al., 1997). So, each area represents one rule of the corresponding cluster and we use the focus point of the FEV to detail the corresponding cluster, if the FEV parameter is active. To show it, the magnified focus point displays a 3D cabinet projection representation tackling occlusions appearance (Couturier et al., 2008) and 2D representation, respectively for sparse and dense contexts. It is worth noting that a dense context is characterized by the presence of at least one exact rule since minimal generators are different from their respective closures, which is not the case for sparse contexts. In the case of sparse or dense context, users can change the interestingness metric in real-time: *support* and *confidence*. Moreover, main information and rules of the cluster are given in dedicated text areas.

CʙVAR is dedicated to cluster visualization. Its purpose is not to detail in-depth information of the current cluster but to visualize all clusters in the

Figure 8. Displaying clustered association rules with CʙVAR

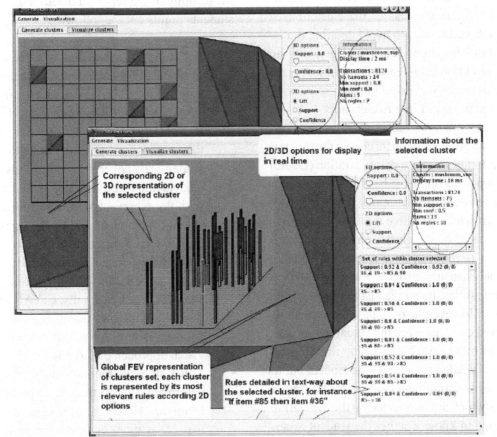

same time. Thanks to a double click on the chosen cluster, we propose to execute LARM (Couturier et al., 2008) which is able to obtain this detailed information. The main purpose of this hybrid representation is to combine advantages of both representations. The next section puts the focus on an evaluation of the CʙVAR prototype.

EXPERIMENTS

The evaluation of the CʙVAR prototype is composed of two parts. Firstly, the intuitiveness and the ease of use of the cluster-based representation are assessed. Secondly, the focus is put on the scalability issue.

Evaluation of the Cluster Representation

The aim of this preliminary evaluation was to assess the intuitiveness of the cluster-based representation. In order to avoid dodging the issue, a set of computer science students, with no preliminary knowledge on data mining visualization, was selected. The set of data used during the evaluation is split into five clusters.

Each test concerns one student and one observer. Each student is concerned by three parts: a free exploration (FE), a demonstration (Demo) and a second exploration (SE). The total evaluating time is equal to 15 minutes. Firstly, during the FE part which lasts five minutes, a person is placed in front of the cluster-based representation which is running on a computer. He (she) has neither instructions on the software nor on its functionalities. Its aim is just to explore as he (she) wish. However, he (she) has to comment its actions and explains what the visualization represents for him (her). Thus, during this step, an observer is needed not to help the student but to transcribe his actions and comments. The major questions which are mentioned on the evaluation form aimed to know whether the student estab-lished the links within the subsets of data (*i.e.*, the clusters) or not, and how the student reacts with the 2D and 3D notions. The second step (Demo) is a demonstration of the main functionalities by the observer during three minutes. Finally, the student can realize a last exploration (SE) during seven minutes. In this part, the aim was to interrogate the student, within an informal discussion, about the software (functionalities, easy-to-use points, etc.).

Even though the sample is reduced and may hamper to lead thorough statistics, the used evaluation methodology (*discount usability testing*) (Shneiderman & Plaisant, 2005) provides a correct evaluation of initial perceptions of the visualizing methodology of CʙVAR by real users. This kind of approach is efficient to highlight the main advantages and drawbacks of a user interface. Some major outlines (Shneiderman & Plaisant, 2005) appeared during this evaluation. A careful scrutiny of the reported discussions with the students points out the following:

- All students understood without explanations that the visualization represents several data subsets. They did not have an a priori knowledge on FEV notions but they used words as *groups* or *sets* in order to define their perception of the representation. Eight students discovered that options 2D/3D (sliders and radio buttons) were dependent with the representation. The comments of six students are related to the size of data (much, large, important). We can give two preliminary conclusions. Firstly, CʙVAR seems to be intuitive in order to represent subsets of data. Secondly, CʙVAR seems to be relevant for the students to analyze large datasets. These two points consolidate the visual approach of CʙVAR.

- Three students mentioned that the visual deformation allows to research particular information. However, seven students thought that 2D is more comprehensible than 3D.

Consequently, it is difficult for them to understand the information which is zoomed. However, eight students guessed that colors must have a signification, because they remarked that colors are variable. Several students criticized some functionalities of CBVAR as far as they interacted with the 3D representation in order to get out further detailed information. Six students understood that the cluster details are given in text-way but they thought this representation is not easy-to-understand. A global conclusion is that the visualization process using CBVAR is convivial as well as its global perception is clearly positive. Nevertheless, CBVAR still presents possibilities for improving its functionalities.

CBVAR Scalability Assessment

It was worth the effort to experiment in practice the potential benefits of the proposed prototype. Experiments were conducted on a Pentium IV 3 Ghz with 1 GB of main memory, running the Fedora UNIX distribution. Benchmark datasets used during these experiments are taken from the FIMI website[13]. In the remainder, the focus is put on both the MUSHROOM and the T10I4D100K datasets. The first dataset, composed of **8124** transactions for **119** items, is considered as typical dense dataset. The second dataset, composed of **100,000** transactions for **1,000** items, is considered

as typical sparse dataset. A large number of association rules is expected to be mined from both datasets, especially when lowering the *minsup* and *minconf* values. The number of extracted generic rules (denoted *# generic rules*) increases as far as we lower these two metrics: from **537** (when *minsup* = **0.4** and *minconf* = **0.4**) to **7,057** (when *minsup* = **0.2** and *minconf* = **0.2**) for the MUSHROOM dataset, and from **594** (when *minsup* = **0.006** and *minconf* = **0.006**) to **3,623** (when *minsup* = **0.004** and *minconf* = **0.004**) for the T10I4D100K dataset. The number of clusters is chosen according to the number x of association rules that will be contained in each cluster. The obtained results are depicted by Table 1. All XML files are already unreadable in the same screen space due to the relevant number of rules. Our approach allows visualizing these benchmark datasets in the same screen space in approximately the same time with a number of clusters equal to

$$\frac{\text{\# generic rules}}{100}$$

Tests with other numbers of clusters (*i.e.*, for x = **25** and x = **50**) require in general more time to be displayed. However, they make it possible to reduce the displaying time relative to each cluster, taken separately from the others, since each cluster contains less association rules (less than **100**).

Table 1 also compares the total number of association rules 1[14] (denoted *# rules*) with that of

Table 1. Displaying time for both MUSHROOM and T10I4D100K datasets

Dataset	*minsup*	*minconf*	*# rules*	*# generic rules*	Displaying time (ms)			
					Without clusters	With ($\frac{\text{\# generic rules}}{x}$) clusters		
						$x = 100$	$x = 50$	$x = 25$
MUSHROOM	0.4	0.4	7,020	537	828	375	375	594
MUSHROOM	0.3	0.3	94,894	2,184	2,250	1,782	3,250	5,750
MUSHROOM	0.2	0.2	19,197,504	7,057	-	17,953	-	-
T10I4D100K	0.006	0.006	928	594	1,453	516	813	1,594
T10I4D100K	0.005	0.005	2,216	1,231	2,475	1,375	2,329	4,125
T10I4D100K	0.004	0.004	8,090	3,623	-	6,078	11,750	27,000

generic ones. Statistics clearly show the benefits of generic bases towards presenting to users a set of interesting association rules that is as much compact as possible.

In order to interact in real-time, it is necessary to load all rules in main memory. However, we can observe that with a *minsup* (*resp. minconf*) value equal to **0.2** (*resp.* **0.2**) for the MUSHROOM dataset and with a *minsup* (*resp. minconf*) value equal to **0.004** (*resp.* **0.004**) for the T10I4D100K dataset, it is no more possible to load them in a classical visualization without clustering. CBVAR allows visualizing the first dataset in **17, 953** ms with

$$\frac{\text{\# generic rules}}{100}$$

clusters. The associated set contains **7, 057** rules which are represented in a same screen space (see Figure 9 (Left)).

The second dataset is displayed with our approach for the different values of x used in our tests. In this case, the association rule set contains **3, 623** rules (see Figure 9 (Right)).

CONCLUSION AND FUTURE WORK

In this chapter, we discussed the issue of efficient visualization of large amounts of association rules and presented two visualization prototypes. The driving idea of these prototypes is the use of a back-end meta-knowledge to guide association rule visualization through their clustering. Carried out experiments showed that thousands of rules can be displayed in few seconds and that the proposed clustering-based visualization can be an efficient tool to handle a large number of association rules, thanks to a merging representation which exploits both a 2D representation and a fisheye view (FEV).

Our goal is not to automatically select the best relevant rules as it might be done with other methods that use interestingness measures, but to propose an interactive and intuitive approach that allows the expert-user to be able to visualize the whole set of generated rules, and consequently to shed light on relevant ones. This approach is thus complementary to any kind of selective association rule methods, and can easily integrate any other visualization tool which is suitable for small set of rules.

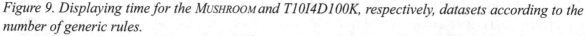

Figure 9. Displaying time for the MUSHROOM and T10I4D100K, respectively, datasets according to the number of generic rules.

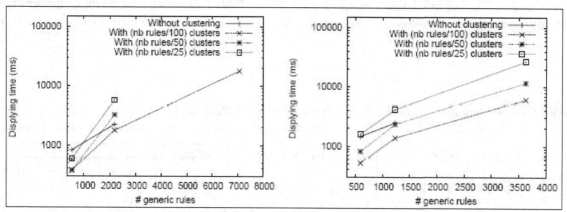

Other avenues for future work mainly address the following issues:

- The improvement of the clustering step in order to label clusters. In fact, these labels guide the user in the cluster selection in the current blind navigable hierarchy, which does not easily permit recovery from bad decisions. The MULTI-SOM approach (Ghouila et al., 2007), avoiding to users the setting-up of the number of clusters, may be a possible palliative issue.

- The cluster visualization by means of perspective wall-based approach (Lanzenberger et al., 2003; Mackinlay et al., 1991), which can be considered as an example of a general FEV approach, is a promising perspective. In fact, the perspective wall-based approach can be seen as an effective way of densely displaying large amounts of association rules by placing information on a flat plane which is tilted into the screen so that it shrinks back toward infinity. On focus, likely interesting association rules can be displayed at a closer location and thus appear larger than the less important association rules that are further away.

- The application of visualization within a user-driven approach for mining association rules is grasping the interest of the community (Couturier et al., 2007a; Couturier et al., 2008; Liu & Salvendy, 2006; Yamamoto et al., 2008). For example, in a level-wise exploration-based mining algorithm, getting out nuggets of clustered patterns of interest may be fruitful to withdraw not relevant patterns. Hence, two sighting facts may be outlined from which the mining process will benefit:

  ○ According to Hackman and Oldham (1975), the larger the user's skills involvement during the mining process, the stronger sense of independence and responsibility is.

  ○ The visualization tool is acting as a "background" pruning tool for shedding light on relevant association rules.

ACKNOWLEDGMENT

This work is partially supported by the French-Tunisian project PAI-CMCU 05G1412. We thank the anonymous reviewers as well as Mondher Maddouri for helpful remarks on previous drafts of this paper.

REFERENCES

Agrawal, R., Imielinski, T., & Swami, A. (1993). Mining association rules between sets of items in large databases. In *Proceedings of the ACM SIGMOD International Conference on Management of Data*, (pp. 207–216), Washington, USA.

Agrawal, R., Mannila, H., Srikant, R., Toivonen, H., & Verkamo, A. I. (1996). Fast discovery of association rules. In *Proceedings of Advances in Knowledge Discovery and Data Mining, AAAI Press*, (pp. 307–328), Menlo Park, California, USA.

Barbut, M. & Monjardet, B. (1970). *Ordre et classification. Algèbre et Combinatoire.* Hachette, Tome II.

Bastide, Y., Pasquier, N., Taouil, R., Lakhal, L., & Stumme, G. (2000). Mining minimal non-redundant association rules using frequent closed itemsets. In *Proceedings of the International Conference DOOD'2000, LNCS, Springer-Verlag*, (pp. 972–986), London, UK.

Bastide, Y., Taouil, R., Pasquier, N., Stumme, G., & Lakhal, L. (2000). Mining frequent patterns with counting inference. *SIGKDD Explorations*, *2*(2), 66–75.

Ben Yahia, S., Hamrouni, T., & Mephu Nguifo, E. (2006). Frequent closed itemset based algorithms: A thorough structural and analytical survey. In *ACM-SIGKDD Explorations*, *8*(1), 93–104.

Ben Yahia, S., & Mephu Nguifo, E. (2008). GERVIS: Scalable visualization of generic association rules. In *International Journal of Computational Intelligence Research (IJCIR)*, (to appear).

Blanchard, J., Guillet, F., & Briand, H. (2003). A user-driven and quality-oriented visualization for mining association rules. In *Proceedings of the Third IEEE International Conference on Data Mining*, (pp. 493–496), Melbourne, Florida.

Blanchard, J., Pinaud, B., Kuntz, P., & Guillet, F. (2007). A 2D–3D visualization support for human-centered rule mining. *Computers & Graphics*, *31*, 350–360.

Brin, S., Motawni, R., & Silverstein, C. (1997). Beyond market baskets: Generalizing association rules to correlations. In *Proceedings of ACM SIGMOD International Conference on Management of Data, ACM Press*, (pp. 265–276), Tucson, Arizona, USA.

Buono, P., & Costabile, M. F. (2004). Visualizing association rules in a framework for visual data mining. In *From Integrated Publication and Information Systems to Virtual Information and Knowledge Environments, Springer-Verlag*, *3379*(LNCS), 221–231.

Buono, P., Costabile, M. F., & Lisi, F. A. (2001). Supporting data analysis through visualizations. In *Proceedings of the International Workshop on Visual Data Mining co-located with ECML/PKDD 2001*, (pp. 67–78), Freiburg, Germany.

Bustos, B., D. Keim, A., Schneidewind, J., Schreck, T., & Sips, M. (2003). *Pattern visualization*. Technical report, University of Konstanz, Germany, Computer Science Department.

Chen, J., Zheng, T., Thorne, W., Zaiane, O. R., & Goebel, R. (2007). Visual data mining of web navigational data. In *Proceedings of the 11th International Conference on Information Visualization (IV'07), IEEE Computer Society Press*, (pp. 649–656), Zurich, Switzerland.

Couturier, O., Hamrouni, T., Ben Yahia S., & Mephu Nguifo, E. (2007). A scalable association rule visualization towards displaying large amounts of knowledge. In *Proceedings of the 11th International Conference on Information Visualization (IV'07), IEEE Computer Society Press,* (pp. 657-663), Zurich, Switzerland.

Couturier, O., Dubois, V., Hsu, T., & Mephu Nguifo, E. (2008). Optimizing occlusion appearances in 3D association rule visualization. In *4th IEEE International Conference on Intelligent Systems (IEEE-IS'08) (Vol. II, pp. 15:42-15:49)*, September, Varna, Bulgaria.

Couturier, O., Mephu Nguifo, E., & Noiret, B. (2005). A hierarchical user-driven method for association rules mining. In *Proceedings of the 11th International Conference on Human-Computer Interaction (HCI'05), Lawrence Erlbaum Associate Editions*, cdrom, Las Vegas, Nevada, USA.

Couturier, O., Rouillard, J., & Chevrin, V. (2007). An interactive approach to display large sets of association rules. In *Proceedings of the 12th International Conference on Human-Computer Interaction (HCI'07), Springer-Verlag, LNCS, 4557*, 258–267, Beijing, China.

Cuppens, F., & Demolombe, R. (1989). How to recognize interesting topics to provide cooperative answering. *Information Systems*, *14*(2), pp 163–173.

Ertek, G., & Demiriz, A. (2006). A Framework for Visualizing Association Mining Results. *In Proceedings of the 21st International Symposium ISCIS 2006*, (pp. 593-602), Istanbul, Turkey.

Fekete, J. D. (2004). The INFOVIS toolkit. In *Proceedings of the 10th IEEE Symposium on Information Visualization (INFOVIS'04)*, (pp. 167–174).

Frantz, V., & Shapiro, J. (1991). Algorithms for automatic construction of query formulations in Boolean form. *Journal of the American Society for Information Science, 1*(42), pp 16–26.

Furnas, G. W. (2006). A fisheyes follow-up: Further reflections on focus+context. In *Proceedings of the ACM Conference on Human Factors in Computing Systems (CHI'06), ACM Press,* (pp. 999–1008), Montréal, Canada.

Ganter, B., & Wille, R. (1999). *Formal Concept Analysis.* Springer-Verlag.

Gasmi, G., BenYahia, S., Mephu Nguifo, E., & Slimani, Y. (2005). *IGB*: A new informative generic base of association rules. In *Proceedings of the 9th International Pacific-Asia Conference on Knowledge Data Discovery (PAKDD'05), LNAI 3518,* (pp. 81–90)*,* Hanoi, Vietnam.

Ghouila, A., Ben Yahia S., Malouch, D., & Abdelhak, S. (2007). MULTI-SOM: A novel unsupervised classification approach. In *Proceedings of the 9th French Conference on Machine Learning (CAp'07),* (pp. 203–218), Grenoble, France.

Guigues, J. L., & Duquenne, V. (1986). Familles minimales d'implications informatives résultant d'un tableau de données binaires. *Mathématiques et Sciences Humaines, 95,* 5–18.

Hackman, J.R., & Oldham, G.R. (1975). Development of the job diagnostic survey. *Journal of Applied Psychology, 60,* 159–170.

Hamrouni, T., BenYahia, S., & Slimani, Y. (2005). PRINCE: An algorithm for generating rule bases without closure computations. In *Proceedings of the 7th International Conference on Data Warehousing and Knowledge Discovery (DaWaK'05), 3589,* 346–355, Copenhagen, Denmark.

Han, J., & Cercone, N. (2000). RULEVIZ: A model for visualizing knowledge discovery process. In *Proceedings of 6th ACM SIGKDD International Conference on Knowledge Discovery and Data Mining,* (pp. 244–253), Boston, MA, USA.

Han, J., & Fu, Y. (1995). Discovery of multiple-level association rules from large databases. In *Proceedings of the VLDB Conference,* (pp. 420–431).

Harrison, B. L., & Vicente, K. J. (1996). An experimental evaluation of transparent menu usage. In *Proceedings of the ACM Conference on Human factors in computing systems (CHI'96), ACM Press,* (pp. 391–398), New York, USA.

Hofmann, H., Siebes, A., & Wilhelm, A. F. X. (2000). Visualizing association rules with interactive mosaic plots. In *Proceedings of 6th ACM SIGKDD International Conference on Knowledge Discovery and Data Mining,* (pp. 227–235), Boston, MA, USA.

Kryszkiewicz, M. (2002). Concise representations of association rules. In D. J. Hand, N.M. Adams, and R.J. Bolton, editors, *Proceedings of Pattern Detection and Discovery, ESF Exploratory Workshop, 2447,* 92–109, London, UK.

Kuntz, P., Guillet, F., Lehn, R., & Briand, H. (2000). A user-driven process for mining association rules. In *Proceedings of the 4th European Symposium on Principles of Data Mining and Knowledge Discovery (PKDD'2000),* (pp. 483–489), Lyon, France.

Lamping, J., Rao, R., & Pirolli, P. (1995). A focus+context technique based on hyperbolic geometry for visualizing large hierarchies. In *Proceedings of the ACM Conference on Human Factors in Computing Systems (CHI'95), ACM Press,* (pp. 401–408), Denver, Colorado, USA.

Lanzenberger, M., Miksch, S., Ohmann, S., & Popow, C. (2003). Applying information visualization techniques to capture and explore the course of cognitive behavioral therapy. In *Proceedings of the ACM Symposium on Applied Computing 2003,* (pp. 268-274), Melbourne, Florida, USA.

Liu, B., Hsu, W., Wang, K., & Che, S. (1999). Visually aided exploration of interesting association rules. In *Proceedings of the 3rd International*

Conference on Research and Development in Knowledge Discovery and Data mining (PA-KDD'99), LNCS, volume 1574, Springer-Verlag, (pp. 380–389), Beijing, China.

Liu, Y., & Salvendy, G. (2005). Visualization support to facilitate association rules modeling: A survey. *International Journal of Ergonomics and Human Factors*, 27(1), 11–23.

Liu, Y., & Salvendy, G. (2006). Design and evaluation of visualization support to facilitate association rules modeling. *International Journal of HCI*, 21(1), 15–38.

Luxenburger, M. (1991). Implications partielles dans un contexte. *Mathématiques et Sciences Humaines*, 29(113), 35–55.

Mackinlay, J. D., Robertson, G. G., & Card, S. K. (1991). The perspective wall: detail and context smoothly integrated. In *Proceedings of the ACM Conference on Human Factors in Computing Systems (CHI'91), ACM Press*, (pp. 173–179), New Orleans, Louisiana, USA.

Meo, R., Psaila, G., & Ceri, S. (1996). A new SQL-like operator for mining association rules. In *Proceedings of the VLDB Conference*, (pp. 122–133), Bombay, India, 1996.

Motro, A. (1987). Extending the relational Databases Model to support Goal queries. In *Expert Database Systems*, (pp. 129–150).

Ng, R. T., Lakshmanan, V. S., Han, J., & Pang, A. (1998). Exploratory mining and pruning optimizations of constrained association rules. In *Proceedings ACM SIGMOD International Conference on Management of Data*, (pp. 13–24), Seattle, Washington, USA.

Ohsaki, M., Kitaguchi, S., Okamoto, K., Yokoi, H., & Yamaguchi, T. (2004). Evaluation of rule interestingness measures with a clinical dataset on hepatitis. In *Proceedings of the International Conference PKDD'04, Springer-Verlag*, 3202, 362–373, Pisa, Italy.

Pasquier, N., Bastide, Y., Taouil, R., Stumme, G., & Lakhal, L. (2005). Generating a condensed representation for association rules. *Journal of Intelligent Information Systems*, 24(1), 25–60.

Pitrat, J. (1990). *Métaconnaissance, Futur de l'Intelligence Artificielle (Metaknowledge, the future of artificial intelligence)*. Editions Hermès, Paris.

Shneiderman, B. (1996). The eyes have it: A task by data type taxonomy for information visualization. In *Proceedings of IEEE Symposium on Visual Languages (VL'96), IEEE Computer Society Press*, (pp. 336–343), Boulder, Colorado, USA.

Shneiderman, B., & Plaisant, C. (2005). *Designing the user interface*. Boston: Addison-Wesley.

Singh, L., Beard, M., Getoor, L., & Blake, M. B. (2007). Visual mining of multi-modal social networks at different abstraction levels. In *Proceedings of the 11th International Conference on Information Visualization (IV'07), IEEE Computer Society Press*, (pp. 672–679), Zurich, Switzerland.

Srikant, R., Vu, Q., & Agrawal, R. (1997). Mining association rules with item constraints. In *Proceedings of the 3rd International Conference on Knowledge Discovery in Databases and Data Mining*, (pp. 67–73), Newport Beach, California, USA.

Steinhaus, H. (1956). Sur la division des corps matériels en parties. In *Bull. Acad. Polon. Sci.*, Cl. III, volume IV, (pp. 801– 804).

Stumme, G., Taouil, R., Bastide, Y., Pasquier, N., & Lakhal, L. (2001). Intelligent structuring and reducing of association rules with formal concept analysis. In *Proceedings KI'2001 Conference, LNAI 2174, Springer-Verlag*, (pp. 335–350), Vienna, Austria.

Sudkamp, T. (2005). Examples, counterexamples, and measuring fuzzy associations. *Fuzzy Sets and Systems*, 149(1), 57–71.

Wolpert, D. H., & Macready, W.G. (1997). No free lunch theorems for optimization. *IEEE Transactions on Evolutionary Computation, 1*(1), 67–82.

Wong, P.C., Whitney, P., & Thomas, J. (1999). Visualizing association rules for text mining. In *Proceedings of the IEEE Symposium on Information Visualization*, (pp. 120–123), San Francisco, California, USA.

Yamamoto, C. H., Cristina, M., Oliveira, F., & Rezende, S. O. (2008). Including the user in the knowledge discovery loop: interactive itemset-driven rule extraction. In *Proceedings of the 23rd ACM Symposium on Applied Computing (SAC'08), ACM Press*, (pp. 1212–1217), Fortaleza, Ceara, Brazil.

Zaki, M. J. (2004). Mining Non-Redundant Association Rules. *Data Mining and Knowledge Discovery*, (9), 223– 248.

Zaki, M. J., & Phoophakdee, B. (2003). *Mirage: A framework for mining, exploring and visualizing minimal association rules*. Technical report, Computer Sciences Department, Rensselaer Polytechnic Institute, USA.

ENDNOTES

[1] Online Emerson's quotations. http://oaks.nvg.org/eg6ra16.html, date of access August 20, 2008.

[2] Available at http://www.aisee.com.

[3] The number of transactions containing A.

[4] The conditional probability that transactions contain the itemset B, given that they contain itemset A.

[5] We use a separator-free form for sets, *e.g.*, a e k stands for the set *{a, e, k}*.

[6] Due to size limitation, the reader can easily use an implementation of Apriori (Agrawal et al., 1996) to visualize the whole set of association rules.

[7] Specially those extracted from sparse contexts.

[8] Available at http://www.sgi.com/software/mineset/index.html.

[9] Available at http://www.lifl.fr/ jourdan/.

[10] In black and white displaying, red blocks are the dark ones while blue blocks are the clearer ones.

[11] The syntactic derivation is based on the *Cover* operator introduced in (Kryszkiewicz, 2002), *i.e.*, Cover(X$\Rightarrow$Y) = {X$\cup$Z $\Rightarrow$ V | Z, V $\subseteq$ Y $\wedge$ Z $\cap$ V = $\varnothing$ $\wedge$ V $\neq$ $\varnothing$}, with |Cover(X$\Rightarrow$Y)| = 3^m - 2^m where |Y|=m.

[12] http://www.dmg.org/.

[13] Available at http://fimi.cs.helsinki.fi/data.

[14] Provided by the implementation of B. Goethals available at: http://www.adrem.ua.ac.be/~goethals/software/.

Chapter XII
Visualization to Assist the Generation and Exploration of Association Rules

Claudio Haruo Yamamoto
Universidade de São Paulo, Brazil

Maria Cristina Ferreira de Oliveira
Universidade de São Paulo, Brazil

Solange Oliveira Rezende
Universidade de São Paulo, Brazil

ABSTRACT

Miners face many challenges when dealing with association rule mining tasks, such as defining proper parameters for the algorithm, handling sets of rules so large that exploration becomes difficult and uncomfortable, and understanding complex rules containing many items. In order to tackle these problems, many researchers have been investigating visual representations and information visualization techniques to assist association rule mining. In this chapter, an overview is presented of the many approaches found in literature. First, the authors introduce a classification of the different approaches that rely on visual representations, based on the role played by the visualization technique in the exploration of rule sets. Current approaches typically focus on model viewing, that is visualizing rule content, namely antecedent and consequent in a rule, and/or different interest measure values associated to it. Nonetheless, other approaches do not restrict themselves to aiding exploration of the final rule set, but propose representations to assist miners along the rule extraction process. One such approach is a methodology the authors have been developing that supports visually assisted selective generation of association rules based on identifying clusters of similar itemsets. They introduce this methodology and a quantitative evaluation of it. Then, they present a case study in which it was employed to extract rules from a real and complex dataset. Finally, they identify some trends and issues for further developments in this area.

INTRODUCTION

Huge volumes of data are now available, but we still face many difficulties in handling all such data to obtain actionable knowledge (Fayyad et al., 1996). Data visualization currently plays an important role in Knowledge Discovery processes, as it helps miners to create and validate hypotheses about the data and also to track and understand the behavior of mining algorithms (Oliveira & Levkowitz, 2003). Interactive visualization allows users to gain insight more easily by taking advantage of their vision system while performing complex investigation tasks. Combining the power of visual data exploration with analytical data mining, known as visual data mining (VDM), is now a trend.

Researchers (Ankerst, 2000, Oliveira & Levkowitz, 2003) identified three approaches for VDM: exploratory data visualization prior to mining, visualization of data mining models, and visualization of intermediate results or representations, during mining. The first approach concerns the use of visualization techniques during the data preprocessing stages of the knowledge discovery process. Visualization of data mining results focuses on visually representing the models extracted with data mining algorithms, to enhance comprehension. Finally, the third approach seeks to insert the miner into the knowledge discovery loop, not only to view intermediate patterns, but also to drive the process of exploring the solution space, for example, by providing feedback based on user previous knowledge about the domain or about the process itself.

Extracting association rules from a transaction database is a data mining task (association rule mining task) defined by Agrawal et al. (1993), in which the goal is to identify rules of the format A➜B satisfying minimum support and minimum confidence values. A and B denote one or multiple items occurring in the transactions. The rule extraction problem is split into two main stages:

(1) generating frequent itemsets; (2) extracting association rules from the frequent itemsets obtained. Several efficient algorithms have been designed for the first task, while the second one is actually trivial. A major problem, however, is that the process typically generates too many rules for analysis. Moreover, issues such as setting input parameters properly, understanding rules and identifying the interesting ones are also difficult. Visual representations have been proposed to tackle some of these problems. At first, visualization was employed mainly to assist miners in exploring the extracted rule set, based on visual representations of the rule space. There are also recent examples of employing visual representations to aid miners along the execution of the mining algorithm, e.g., to show intermediate results and to allow user feedback during the process.

This chapter is organized as follows. In the "Systematic survey" section we present a survey of approaches that employ visual representations in association rule mining. The survey is divided into two parts. In the first one, "Visualization of results of association rule mining", we discuss contributions that employ information visualization techniques at the end of the mining process to visually represent its final results. In the second part, "Visualization during association rule mining", we discuss contributions that employ visualization during the discovery process. In the third section, "An itemset-driven cluster-oriented approach", we introduce a rule extraction methodology which aims at inserting the miner into the knowledge discovery loop. It adopts an interactive rule extraction algorithm coupled with a projection-based graph visualization of frequent itemsets, an itemset-based rule extraction approach and a visually-assisted pairwise comparison of rules for exploration of results. We also introduce the I_2E System, that adopts the proposed methodology to enable an exploratory approach towards rule extraction, allowing miners to explore the rule space of a given transaction dataset. Furthermore, we present a quantitative evaluation of the methodology and a case study in which it is applied to a real and challenging dataset. Given the scenario, we then point out some challenges and trends for further developments in this area. Finally, we present some conclusions about this work.

SYSTEMATIC SURVEY

In this section we review the literature concerning the application of information visualization techniques in association rule mining. Further information on information visualization techniques in general can be found elsewhere (Keim & Kriegel, 1996, Keim, 2002).

Contributions are organized based on their publication date, following the timeline shown in **Figure 1**. The first identified contribution is the graph-based visualization by Klemettinen et al. (1994), which influenced several subsequent solutions, as indicated by the arrows. Visualization usage intensified after 1999, starting with the work by Wong et al. (1999), who proposed a grid-like visualization to discover association rules in text collections. We discuss approaches that focus on viewing mining results, namely the rule contents and/or their interest measure values, and also approaches that focus on displaying intermediate results, seeking to insert the miner into the process. To display association rules, the approaches typically list items appearing in the rules based on some ordering, e.g. alphabetical. To visualize intermediate results, the usual idea is to run the algorithm with an initial set of parameters and settings and present intermediate results, so a miner can decide whether execution follows a promising path or, otherwise, whether parameters should be changed.

Visualization of Results of Association Rule Mining

Typical visual representations to display results of association rule mining are grid-like structures and bar charts. The grid view consists of a 2D matrix of cells where each cell represents a rule, with one matrix dimension representing rule antecedents and the other one representing rule consequents. Each cell is filled with colored bars indicating rule support and confidence values. However, this representation often suffers from occlusion. Besides, it is difficult to represent antecedents (LHS) or consequents (RHS) with more than a single item. This restriction can be overcome by extending the matrix dimensions to represent combinations of items, but it becomes impracticable if there are too many different items.

Klemettinen et al. (1994) use bar charts to map interest measure values of association rules shown in a list, combined with templates to reduce the number of rules. Bar height maps the interest measure values – support, confidence and their product, named commonness – so that high values catch the miner's attention during rule exploration. The authors also present a graph-based visualization of rules where items are represented as nodes and associations as directed arcs. Arc thickness represents rule confidence or, alternatively, support, and colors can provide additional information mapping. Nonetheless, the graph suffers from a cluttering problem when displaying too many rules. A solution to avoid this problem is to use a template mechanism to reduce the number of rules based on user restrictions. An alternative solution is to limit rule size, e.g. in terms of the number of items at the LHS. Other ideas include merging multiple nodes from a cluster into a single node, or displaying nodes for the LHS and the RHS in separate regions of the screen.

Wong et al. (1999) introduced a representation based on two-dimensional matrices that maps rule-to-item rather than item-to-item relation-

Figure 1. Overview of approaches that employ visualization techniques for association rule mining tasks. The approaches shown in gray visualize mining results, while the ones in black employ visualization during the process. Approaches marked with an asterisk visualize only one rule at a time.

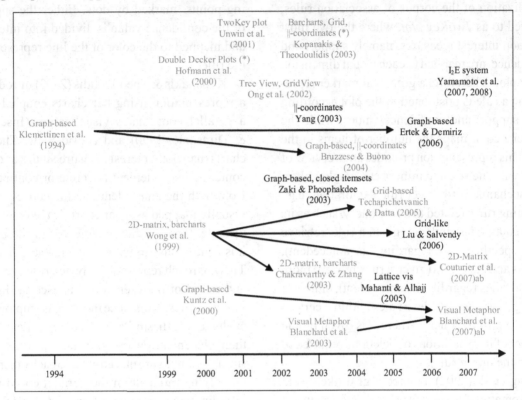

ships (or antecedent-to-consequent). Matrix rows represent items, whereas matrix columns represent rules. A block placed at the appropriate row-column intersection depicts a particular rule-to-item relationship, with blue blocks indicating rule antecedents and red ones indicating consequents. A three-dimensional view of the matrix is displayed, with support and confidence values represented as bar charts placed in the scene background.

Chakravarthy & Zhang (2003) proposed a two-step visualization of rules. First, rules are grouped according to the number of items at their antecedent, and bar charts represent their interest measures, namely, support and confidence. Each bar represents a quantity of items at the antecedent, and is sub-divided into interest measure range

values (for example, 80-90% confidence, 90-100% confidence and so on). This representation conveys a broader view of the rule set, and the miner may obtain a closer look by clicking on a bar, which causes a two-dimensional matrix view, similar to the previous one by Wong, to be shown – the major difference being that one of the matrix dimensions now represent rule consequents.

Hofmann et al. (2000) introduced a representation using Mosaic Plots and Double Decker Plots. They display a contingency table to represent an association rule. By mapping the support and confidence as areas proportional to their values, the representation provides deeper understanding of the correlation between the LHS and RHS of a rule. This approach considers only one rule at a time, and interpreting the visualization becomes difficult when three or more items appear either at the LHS or the RHS.

Unwin et al. (2001) proposed a scatter plot-like visualization of the corpus of association rules, referred to as *TwoKey plot*, where the two most common interest measures, namely support and confidence, are mapped to each visual dimension of the plot. Therefore, a graphical marker representing a rule is positioned in the plot according to its support and confidence values, while the marker's color maps the number of items in the rule. This representation provides an overview of the whole rule set, and miners can employ filtering mechanisms to direct rule exploration, e.g., obtaining rules related to a rule query, such as its children and descendants (given a rule, retrieve more specific rules regarding its antecedent), parents and ancestors (given a rule, retrieve more general rules regarding its antecedent), or neighbors (given a rule, retrieve rules within a certain distance *d* of the query, where *d* is given by the number of item additions or deletions required to obtain the query rule).

Ong et al. (2002) adopted a grid-like visual representation for association rules with columns ranked by confidence values and rows ranked by support. The rules are grouped in cells, according to their support and confidence, and represented as squares whose locations are determined by their support and confidence values. Filters based on support, confidence or item selection assist user navigation through the rule set. The authors pointed out that their method caters for rules of any size, with no limitations. However, only the interest measure values are visually represented. The same authors proposed a tree-like view of rules, which are grouped according to their antecedents and consequents. Antecedents are first shown as nodes, according to the number of items. Then, for each antecedent node, rules containing the consequents are shown as sub-nodes.

A grid-like rule visualization has been also employed later on by Techapichetvanich & Datta (2005), where two groups of lines represent items belonging to the antecedent and the consequent, respectively. Each rule is visually represented as a line that connects the item lines at intersecting points, marked by dots. Either the support or the confidence value is divided into intervals and mapped to the color of the line representing the rule.

Kopanakis & Theodoulidis (2003) introduced a representation using bar charts coupled with a parallel coordinates visualization (Inselberg & Dimsdale, 1990) and a grid view. The bar charts map both interest measure values and rule contents. Each element (discrete or continuous) from both the antecedent and the consequent is visually mapped as a bar chart. If the element is discrete, then a value is indicated in the bar; if it is continuous, an interval is indicated instead. This approach represents only one rule at a time, and a grid of representations is used to display multiple rules. A distance measure is employed to evaluate rule dissimilarity, in order to determine their placement on the grid, so that rules with similar contents are placed close to each other. The underlying rationale in the parallel coordinates visualization technique is to map data attributes (transaction items, in this case) to parallel axes, and map each data instance (rules, in this case) as a polyline intersecting each axis at a point corresponding to its particular value. However, this approach cannot represent continuous data. The grid representation offers a different perspective to visualize two or more rules simultaneously, by mapping attributes to each grid column and rules to each row.

In the graph-based representation of association rules by Bruzzese & Buono (2004) the color of a node represents the antecedent (red) or the consequent (green) of a rule, while edges connecting the nodes depict the associations. Confidence is mapped to the edge length, with color mapping the support, light and dark blue referring to low and high support, respectively. A miner may further explore subsets of rules using a parallel-coordinates representation. The technique was aimed at representing association rules in terms of the utility of each item in a rule antecedent – the authors state that the relevance of an item may be assessed by its utility. The polylines connecting the utility of each item for a given rule enable visual identification of items with the highest relevance for the whole rule set.

Kuntz et al. (2000) introduced a novel user-centered association rule extraction approach whose basic strategy is to depart from the frequent items, similarly to the *Apriori* algorithm. Then, users may select items of interest and obtain rules involving these and other items. This navigation-like operation is called forward chaining, and is graphically represented by a graph-based visualization (backward chaining is also supported). Besides being user-directed this strategy avoids generating unwanted rules.

Blanchard et al. (2003) proposed a user-centered rule exploration approach, which adopts a visual metaphor of two half-bowls to place rules of interest (e.g. user selected rules). The bowls hold the generalized and specialized rules separately. Each rule is represented by a sphere, whose radius maps its support, and by a cone, whose base width maps its confidence. Additionally, the colors of the sphere and cone redundantly represent a weighted average of the measures, with the position of the rule at the bowls representing the implication intensity. This work was later extended (Blanchard et al. 2007b) with two complementary visualizations: the first is the 3D visual metaphor and the other is a 2D visualization of rule sets and their neighborhood relations, some of them from the already mentioned work by Kuntz et al. (2000). Based on the neighborhood relations, the authors define rules that are closer to a selected rule according to predefined criteria. The relations are: *same antecedent*, *forward chaining*, *antecedent generalization* (which is opposite to forward chaining) and *same items*. In yet another extension, neighborhood relations were added to the ARVis interface (Blanchard et al., 2007a), inducing syntactic and interestingness measure

constraints. The former specifies items appearing at a rule antecedent or consequent, while the latter specifies valid interest measure ranges for the exploration. The initial list of relations was extended with the relations *agreement specialization*, *exception specialization*, *generalization* and *same consequent*.

Couturier et al. (2007b) combined several interactive visual representations of association rules with graphical fisheye views. Their goal is to give users details-on-demand while preserving an overview of the overall context. One of the visualizations shows rules in a 2D matrix, with antecedents and consequents mapped to each dimension and values for interest measures (support and confidence) displayed as colors within the corresponding cell, whose visual area is equally split among the measures. The same authors (Couturier et al., 2007a) proposed an approach for exploring association rules based on a visual representation of clusters of rules, obtained by applying the *k*-means algorithm over the rule characteristics. Each cluster is represented in a grid-cell, and colors map interest measure values.

A few approaches provide visual representations of individual rules (Hofmann et al., 2000, Kopanakis & Theodoulidis, 2003). They have the obvious advantage of using reduced screen space, but comparison of multiple rules is not supported. On the other hand, most visual representations of multiple rules cannot avoid a point of saturation, from where no rules can be further represented on the screen, a limitation faced by representations based on 2D matrices (Wong, 1999, Chakravarthy & Zhang, 2003, Couturier et al. 2007ab) and on grids (Techapichetvanich & Datta, 2005, Kopanakis & Theodoulidis 2003). Graph-based (Klemettinen et al., 1994, Kuntz et al. 2000, Bruzzese & Buono, 2004) and projection-based approaches (Unwin et al., 2001, Ong et al., 2002) are less sensitive to the saturation problem, but suffer from object occlusion, i.e., graphical markers overlap, and proper interaction mechanisms are required to handle the problem. The representation by Blanchard et al. (2007a,b) also suffers from visual clutter – though it may be reduced by changing the camera view, graphical objects may become very small, hampering perception. One possibility is to employ global approaches to get an overview of the rule set, then focus on subsets of rules and adopt visual representations capable of conveying more detailed information for further exploration.

The approaches discussed so far focus on exploring extracted rule sets. Those reviewed in the following section employ visualizations in order to allow miners to drive algorithm execution during rule extraction.

Visualization During Association Rule Mining

Although approaches aimed at visualizing the results of association rule mining help miners to find interesting rules within the typically huge corpora of rules inferred, they do not encourage active user participation in the process, e.g., by tracking execution and inputting feedback to the analytical algorithm. Active participation allows miners to input previous knowledge about the domain and/or knowledge acquired during the mining task into the process itself, which can be done both by driving the generation of frequent itemsets, and the extraction of association rules. Some approaches that favor user interference on the rule generation and discovery process are now discussed.

A visual interface to display the lattice of frequent itemsets obtained while extracting rules was suggested by Mahanti & Alhajj (2005), which displays the creation and deletion of lattice nodes for educational purposes. This representation is valuable for miners to monitor the construction of the lattice, as it provides an overview of the process of generating frequent itemsets that helps building a mental model of the algorithm's execution. The approach is targeted at learning the process, though, rather than at generating

rules, and it does not allow active user participation, e.g., to eliminate nodes, change parameters, etc. Moreover, the representation uses a lot of screen space and quickly becomes cluttered, as many objects are required to represent the lattice satisfactorily.

Zaki & Phoophakdee (2003), in their *Mirage* system, employ a graph-based visualization of closed itemsets to represent rules compactly. Their visualization is organized into layers according to the number of items in the closed itemset. Each closed itemset is mapped as a node and lines connect two closed itemsets if one of them is a subset of the other and there are no intermediate nodes between them (that can be connected).

Yang (2003) employed the parallel coordinates visualization to display frequent itemsets and association rules. Items are first arranged into groups so that items from the same group are laid out consecutively according to their frequencies. Then, n axes are drawn, such that n is the number of items in the largest itemset. Frequent itemsets are depicted as polylines connecting the axes at the positions corresponding to their items. Rules are represented similarly, by two polylines, one for the antecedent and another for the consequent. An arrow connects the polylines, and color may map interest measure values.

Ertek & Demiriz (2006), on the other hand, display frequent itemsets and rules using a graph-based technique. Items and itemsets are mapped as nodes and their inter-relationships are mapped as item-itemset connections. To visualize rules, items and rules are mapped as nodes, and item-rule connections map their relations, with directed lines to indicate the direction of the implication.

The approach by Zaki & Phoophakdee (2003) generates the closed frequent itemsets, and then visualizes them. The ones by Yang (2003) and Ertek & Demiriz (2006) generate the results and then visualize both intermediate results – frequent itemsets – and final results – association rules. However, they do not allow user interference during the analytical processing. A step in this direction is taken by Liu & Salvendy (2006), who allow exploring the frequent itemsets at each step of the *Apriori* algorithm. They employed a grid-like visual structure to represent frequent itemsets, where items and itemsets are mapped onto the rows and columns, respectively, so that each item-itemset relation can be mapped at a corresponding intersection cell. They also provide a visualization of rules, similar to the visualization of itemsets: items and rules are mapped in rows and columns, but an "A" or a "C" at the intersecting cell indicates whether the item belongs to the rule antecedent or to its consequent.

The later approach allows interactive generation of itemsets and generation of rules at each step of *Apriori*, but miners cannot fully drive the process, for two main reasons. First, rules are automatically generated for all the frequent itemsets obtained so far, it is not possible to focus on specific groups of itemsets at this moment. Moreover, miners do not have full control over algorithm execution, since the process can only proceed towards its end. In seeking an interactive approach for exploring the rule space, it is important for users to be able to undo some actions. For instance, if a user sets some parameters and realizes they are not suitable, the possibility of backtracking one step and restarting the process with different parameters would be desirable. This problem could be handled allowing miners to restart the process, to backtrack (or forward) one step, or to execute the process at user discretion, e.g. to its end.

Moreover, the visualizations adopted in most approaches reviewed so far demand considerable screen space, which is quite limited – typical screen resolutions in desktops and laptops are, e.g., 1,280x1,024 pixels or 1,024x768 pixels. Given the large amount of visual objects it is impossible to show all of the itemsets (or rules) simultaneously, so an overview of all the itemsets/rules is not feasible. Thus, compact visualizations in terms of space usage and number of objects are desirable. To reduce visual clutter on a limited screen

area, one either reduces the size of the objects or their number. Reducing object size introduces a limitation for interacting with the visual representations, anticipated by Fitt's law (Dix et al., 2003): the required time to move from one point to a target area is a function of the distance to the target and the size of the target.

Furthermore, none of the approaches reviewed considers employing a rule reduction policy, which is critical for association rule tasks, which may produce huge rule sets often with thousands or millions of rules. Exploring such large sets is not feasible, and analyzing them is time demanding and exhausting. Moreover, no approach supports a fully user-driven rule extraction process. Liu & Salvendy (2006) allow miners to interfere, e.g., to drop irrelevant frequent itemsets, but they have limited control, e.g. they are not allowed to backtrack and resume the process with different parameter settings. In the following section we introduce a visualization-supported methodology aimed at fully inserting miners into an association rule extraction process, seeking to tackle the limitations identified in the above discussion. It also employs a compact visual representation of rules that does not suffer from visual occlusion.

AN ITEMSET-DRIVEN CLUSTER-ORIENTED APPROACH

We believe some of the critical problems in association rule mining may be addressed by fostering a exploratory approach towards the task, assisted by visual representations. With this hypothesis in mind we introduced a novel user-driven rule extraction methodology (Yamamoto et al., 2007) and conducted an experimental validation on its effectiveness on extracting rules capable of representing the knowledge in a transaction data set. We presented elsewhere (Yamamoto et al., 2008) a case study describing how the methodology was applied to extract rules from a real dataset.

The proposed methodology relies on an interactive stepwise execution of *Apriori* aided by a visual representation of the space of itemsets, where each execution step identifies the frequent *k*-itemsets, according to the overall approach outlined in **Figure 2**. Miners can visualize and explore the frequent itemsets generated at the current step (*k*) before proceeding to the following one, that will generate the (*k+1*)-itemsets, interacting with a graph-based visualization of the itemsets extracted in the current step. They can also drive the rule extraction by changing the minimum support value and by filtering frequent itemsets based on their perceived relevance.

The itemset graph visualization groups together those itemsets that are more similar in content. It supports a user-driven selective rule extraction approach that produces fewer rules, but still includes rules representative of all different groups of similar itemsets identified. After rules are extracted a visual interface enables users to explore the complete rule space by queries based on pairwise rule comparisons. The user-driven

focus benefits miners for three main reasons. First, they can use previous knowledge, e.g. domain specific information to drive algorithm execution. Second, computational cost may decrease either because data complexity is reduced or the algorithm executes fewer operations. Finally, knowing intermediate results increases miners' awareness of the process, which favors knowledge acquisition. In this context, the methodology addresses four issues, discussed in the following.

The first issue relates to helping miners to determine proper parameter values, known to be a difficult task in association rule mining. A typical trial-and-error approach to establish a proper support value for a particular dataset and task may require five or more executions, which can be time-demanding and frustrating as it requires running the algorithm and inspecting the output several times before a decision can be made. Our method supports a flexible definition of the minimum support value, for though it may be pre-determined, as usual, it may also be modified on the fly between two consecutive steps. This considerably reduces the number of times the process needs to be completely redone.

The second issue is helping miners to learn about the data set and input what they learn into the rule extraction algorithm. This is supported by the graph-based visualization of the *k*-itemsets displayed after each itemset extraction step of *Apriori*. Each visualization represents one depth of the itemset lattice, and allows miners to navigate on the currently extracted frequent itemsets. Typically, users would perform this type of exploration by scrolling on a list of itemsets, which can be tiresome. Moreover, it is difficult to grasp an overview from a long list. The graph visualization displays frequent itemsets as circles (graph nodes, see **Figure 4**), with circles connected by lines (graph edges) when they have items in common. This representation permits identifying groupings of itemsets more easily. Node positioning on the screen is determined by projecting the itemsets in the two-dimensional space based on

Figure 2. Overall steps in the itemset-based cluster-oriented methodology to discover association rules. (Adapted from Yamamoto et al., 2007).

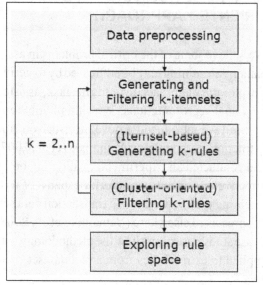

their content similarity, as discussed later. This visual representation of the itemsets is very compact, requiring less screen space than others found in the literature. Therefore, it helps miners to get an overview of the whole set of itemsets. The contents of a particular itemset can be shown by passing the mouse over its corresponding circle, and items may be also highlighted on a list by querying, or by a selection tool. Both the visualization of frequent itemsets and the list of items are coordinated, meaning that user actions affect both representations simultaneously. Also displayed to assist users in exploring the frequent itemsets is a histogram of their support distribution.

The third issue concerns a policy for reducing the size of the rule sets, in order to handle rule explosion and facilitate exploration. Conventional rule filtering approaches rely on defining thresholds for interest measure values, e.g. minimum confidence, minimum lift and so on, and preserving only those rules that satisfy those thresholds. However, filtering out rules based solely on interest metrics ignores their diversity. Some rules may be interesting because they contain many of the possible combination of items in the transactions, and we consider them to have a high 'semantic value'. Miners who know how rule generation takes place in an association rule mining scenario will likely know that, for each rule, other rules containing the same or similar sets of items are likely to be produced. However, we hypothesize that in an exploratory scenario not all these rules need to be explicitly shown. Thus, we introduced an itemset-based rule generation policy that considers also itemset diversity as a relevance factor, instead of only on rigid interest measure thresholds. The rationale was to select, for each itemset, some of the best rules relative to a set of user-defined interest measures, and name them as the representative rules for this itemset. Then, the rules extracted from the itemset are either placed in a visible set of representative rules, or are allocated to a separate, non visible, set. A complementary rule reduction policy may

be employed on groups of similar itemsets to remove the bottom ranked rules regarding the interest measures (further discussed in the following section).

Finally, miners may explore the rule space by comparing rules from the preselected representative set (visible) with those placed in the 'non-visible' set. This reduces the cognitive load on the miners, since the number of selected rules to be explored (the representative ones) is noticeably smaller. Moreover, semantic information is preserved because the previously non-selected less relevant rules can still be retrieved. A conventional approach towards exploring a rule set is typically based on inspecting minimum support and minimum confidence thresholds. However, rule sets may be huge and inspection may be tiresome even when applying semi-automated rule filtering policies. Our methodology allows miners to work on a much smaller, preselected representative rule set. The idea is to depart the exploration of the rule space from this representative set, comparing its rules to other somehow related ones allocated in the non-visible rule set, in order to find out which ones are actually relevant or interesting. A parallel coordinates' visualization of rule interestingness measures assists rule comparison.

In summary, the proposed methodology is a step forward towards including miners into the rule extraction process, and supports an exploratory approach towards the problem. In the following section we describe the I_2E System, which stands for *Interactive Itemset Extraction System*, designed to implement the features of the methodology just described and provide a platform for its validation.

The I_2E System

The I_2E System has been developed in Java, and comprises two modules: I_2E and *RulEx*. The former is the main module, supporting generation and visual exploration of itemsets and selective extraction of association rules. The latter supports exploration of association rule sets by visual pairwise comparison.

Playback Metaphor to Control Algorithm Execution

I_2E adopts a playback metaphor to control the stepwise execution of the *Apriori* algorithm, as shown in **Figure 3**. The playback controls are **rewind**, **backtrack one step**, **forward one step**, and **execute** (from this step to the end). The frame title informs the current status of the algorithm execution, i.e., the last step executed. In the figure, step 2 has just been executed, and therefore 2-itemsets have just been extracted.

The miner can visually observe the frequent itemsets obtained at each step and, before proceeding to the following step s/he can evaluate whether the minimum support threshold seems satisfactory. If not, support may be modified, affecting execution from now on. If the minimum support increases, the process just continues with the new support threshold, but it is restarted whenever the value is decreased. Itemsets considered not relevant by the miner can be discarded using filtering operations on the itemset graph visualization, described in the following.

Projection-Based Graph Visualization of Itemsets

The projection-based graph visualization of frequent itemsets is shown in **Figure 4**. This visualization is constructed by applying a multidimensional projection technique to feature vectors extracted from the itemsets, in order to obtain a two-dimensional layout. Multidimensional projections typically derive a two-dimensional layout for a set of high-dimensional objects (the feature vectors) while attempting to preserve, in the reduced (2D) space, the distance relationships observed amongst the objects in the original high-dimensional space. Thus, the output of a good projection is a 2D layout that emphasizes object similarity, as measured by the high-dimensional distance metric. I_2E employs a multidimensional projection technique called IDMAP, by Paulovich et al. (2006) with the Cityblock distance as the default dissimilarity metric (though other choices are possible). Thus, the resulting itemset visualization places similar itemsets (in terms of their constituent items) close to each other. A graph node (circle) represents a frequent itemset, while an edge connecting two nodes indicates they share common items. The size of the node maps how many items it contains, and edge thickness maps how many common items are shared between the two corresponding itemsets. Thus, regions concentrating lines indicate itemsets heavily connected, i.e., sharing many items. The groups of itemsets observed in the visualization actually reflect the items that appear more often in most itemsets in the group, especially in the initial steps, e.g. when generating 2 and 3-itemsets. In later steps, the projection tends to form well-defined

Figure 3. The main frame of the I_2E module. The playback metaphor controls lie at the second group of buttons in the toolbar, from left to right.

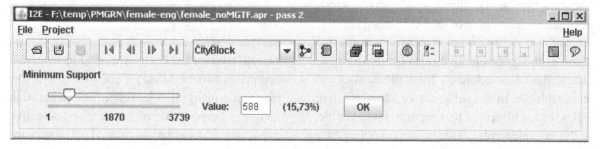

Figure 4. The frames of the frequent itemsets visualization at the center and the items list at the left. The histogram is shown at the lower left corner of the visualization frame. Controls for the search mechanism, color scale selection, springs threshold, cluster definition and selection are shown at the right side of the visualization frame.

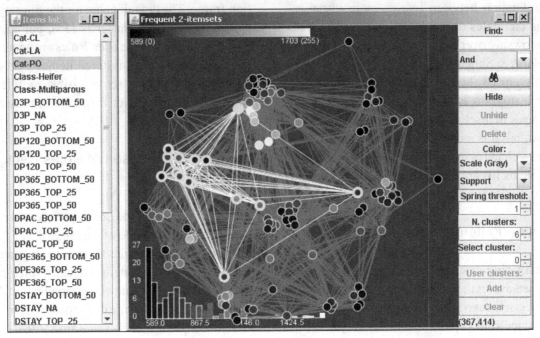

groups, which are possibly different variations of a very limited set of items. **Figure 4** shows a visualization of results from step 2 (2-itemsets just extracted). The white borders highlight the itemsets containing the item "Cat-PO", selected in the Items List.

In the visualization, the color of the nodes can map the support value of the itemset, or alternatively may indicate the cluster to which the itemset belongs – a functionality for clustering itemsets based on similarity is provided (discussed later on) to support selective filtering. Several color mapping scales are provided, obtained from (Levkowitz, 1997). The itemset visualization provides interaction tools to search and discard itemsets, to select the color scale, to select the color mapping attribute (support or the cluster identification), to un/hide the lines connecting nodes, to set clustering parameters, to select a

particular cluster (according to its identification number). It also includes controls for users to indicate the clusters manually on the projection-based visualization (clusters may be added to a cluster set, or cleared).

In the same window frame, the histogram shown in the bottom depicts either the distribution of the itemsets regarding their support values, or their cluster distribution (depending on which of these two, color or cluster pertinence is being mapped to color). Histogram ranges may be dynamically defined by the user.

A list of transaction items is also provided, which shows the items that appear in at least one frequent itemset shown at the visualization. Both the item list and the itemset visualization are coordinated, thus selecting an item in the list causes the itemsets in which it appears to be highlighted in the visualization. If multiple items are selected, those itemsets that include all the selected items are highlighted. Conversely, the items belonging to an itemset selected in the visualization are all highlighted in the items list. Coordination between two or more visualizations facilitates user interaction since it speeds up browsing over the set of itemsets – according to North & Shneiderman (2000ab) it can significantly enrich the visual exploration capability. The histogram is also coordinated both to the frequent itemset visualization and to the list of items, but it is a one-way coordination. In other words, changes in both visualization of itemsets and items list are reflected in the histogram, but the opposite is not true.

Clustering Itemsets for further Filtering

The filtering mechanism focused on clusters of itemsets avoids the locality problem when discarding itemsets based on interestingness metrics, e.g., to reduce rule explosion. The locality problem occurs when removing itemsets by filtering affects certain regions of the rule space more than others, thus reducing rule diversity – when it would be desirable to distribute the effect of the removal more uniformly over the whole set in order to preserve diversity.

To overcome this problem, a clustering algorithm is applied to identify clusters of similar itemsets. Itemset filtering is then performed on each cluster, rather than on the set as a whole, in order to make sure that rules representative of the different groups of similar itemsets will be extracted and displayed. Thus, the effect of filtering will be more uniformly distributed across the rule set. The clustering algorithm takes as input the feature vectors describing the frequent itemsets. Currently, the system implements the k-means clustering, which requires specifying the number of clusters to be identified. I_2E adopts an arbitrary default number, given by the square root of c, where c is the number of attributes in the feature vectors. This parameter may be modi-

fied by the miner, who can also define the itemset clusters manually by delimiting groups of similar itemsets in the graph visualization. Controls for both operations are provided in the visualization frame. The default value for the filtering cut percentage on each cluster is 15%, but again it may be modified by the user. Rules are generated from the remaining unfiltered itemsets on each cluster and kept in a set of visible preselected rules, which can be saved for exploration assisted by the *RulEx* module.

Pairwise Comparison of Rules Using Relations

Miners can explore the set of preselected rules with the *RulEx* module of I_2E, shown in **Figure 5**. They can identify rules that bear some relation a given rule of interest, and decide which rules are worth saving for knowledge acquisition. Five rule relation operators are defined to recover rules related to a query, namely ***same antecedent, same consequent, rules generated from a superset of the generating itemset, rules generated from a subset of the generating itemset*** and *rules generated from the same itemset*.

A parallel coordinates visualization of the rules interestingness measures assists comparison, where each axis maps one interest measure, on a scale given by the lower and upper ranges for the measure (so far, the ordering of the axes mapping measures is predefined and cannot be modified). Rules are displayed as polylines that intersect the axes on the points corresponding to its measure values. The visualization allows miners to rapidly compare the interest measure values for the selected rules and determine the most interesting ones.

In order to assess and validate the methodology we conducted a quantitative evaluation and a case study. The first one was conducted to measure the effectiveness of the rule reduction policy supported by the methodology. In the second one, we aimed at assessing the usefulness of

Figure 5. The RulEx module for pairwise comparison of association rules. The preselected rules are shown at the top left while the related rules are shown at the top right, and the final rules are shown at the bottom right. Filtering controls for the pre-selected rules are shown at the bottom left. The parallel coordinates visualization of interest measure values for the selected rules appears in a separate frame.

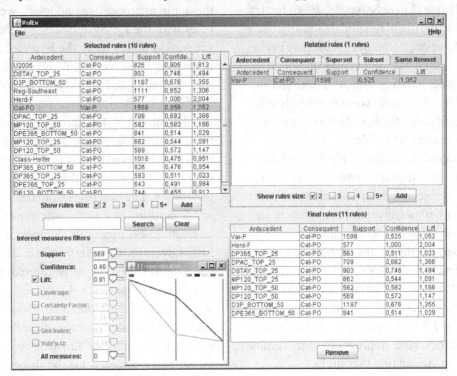

the methodology for a domain expert to explore a data set. Both evaluations are described in the following sections.

Evaluating the Methodology

Some works from the literature discuss how difficult it is to evaluate the effectiveness of information visualization techniques for data analysis (Chen & Yu, 2000, Plaisant, 2004). Similar difficulties apply to visual data mining. Evaluation is challenging for many reasons. First, a new approach may help identify patterns that no other existing approach has identified before, so direct comparison is not possible. Even when it is possible to compare different techniques one has

to consider that the user embedded in the process can contribute a bias that may distort results, i.e., different user proficiency levels on the analysis task can invalidate an experimental comparative study. Moreover, discovery is not an instantaneous event, and controlled experiments suffer from severe time constraints. Other difficulties include measuring user awareness in the process, using subjective metrics that are naturally fuzzy and error prone, and assessing the combined effect of visualizations. Even if all such issues have been correctly addressed, experimental studies must still be statistically valid in order to produce useful results. Moreover, there is always a discussion about the validity of controlled experimental studies to assess data analysis and exploration tasks that are far from controlled in real world situations.

From all the contributions that employ visualization to support rule mining discussed in this chapter, only one (Liu & Salvendy, 2006) relates a controlled experiment to validate the approach proposed. However, it employed subjective evaluation metrics, such as effectiveness of modeling, algorithm understanding and user satisfaction. This is actually an indication on how critical evaluation can be, and that further effort is required to address this particular problem.

We attempted to evaluate the methodology described in this chapter in two different ways. First, we used objective metrics to compare rules sets obtained with a conventional approach, i.e., rules automatically extracted with *Apriori* and filtering based on minimum support and minimum confidence, with rules sets obtained with the proposed methodology. Second, we conducted a subjective evaluation in which a domain specialist applied the I_2E tool on a real and challenging dataset, and describe impressions and results captured from conducting this study.

The goal of the quantitative evaluation was to assess the impact of the rule filtering policy introduced by the methodology. We thus defined itemset coverage as the evaluation metric. This is a measure of rule diversity, and is obtained as follows. Given the set of all itemsets I and a rule set R, the **Itemset Coverage** is given by the minimum number of itemsets from I necessary to generate the rules of the rule set R, divided by the total number of itemsets in I. It assesses the semantic information value of a rule set in terms of its diversity, i.e., the number of different itemsets covered by its rules. It is also useful to compare the semantic redundancy of two sets of rules.

In the first evaluation we compared the itemset coverage of the rule sets produced by our methodology and by the conventional approach. We used three datasets, two from the UCI Repository (Asuncion & Newman, 2007) – namely, Iris and Flags – and one made available by EMBRAPA

(*Empresa Brasileira de Pesquisas em Agropecuária*, in Portuguese) – namely, Coffee – containing 11,526 human expert evaluation records of coffee samples (12 attributes). In all datasets the same approach was adopted: we generated rules with the I_2E System using the default rule generation policy (only the best ranked rule per itemset is preserved) and then additional rule sets were obtained by varying the threshold for further rule filtering based on itemset clusters. We thus obtained 4 different rule sets, one with the basic filtering policy, 3 others with different levels of additional filtering. We then run *Apriori* with the same support threshold set for the I_2E generation. The best rules from the resulting rule set, according to a composite ranking of eight interestingness measures (Support, Confidence, Lift, Leverage, Certainty Factor, Jaccard, Gini index and Yule's Q), were filtered at different thresholds, to generate 4 rule sets of the same size of each of those obtained with I_2E. We then compared the rule coverage of the 8 rule sets, for each rule size and for all rules. Average results for all rules obtained for the three datasets are summarized in **Table 1**.

As expected, for all cut percentages used for rule filtering, the rule sets obtained with the I_2E System had better itemset coverage than those obtained with the conventional approach. Due to its selective filtering policy, our methodology produces rules that cover far more itemsets than a conventional approach with simple filtering based on composite ranking. One may also interpret this result as: the rule set obtained using our methodology has less redundant semantic information than the one obtained with a conventional filtering approach. Evaluating a semantically redundant rule set requires considerable more effort from a miner than analyzing a less redundant one. As the filtering cut percentage increases, itemset coverage decreases faster for I_2E System than for the conventional approach. However, itemset coverage remains superior for I_2E because it includes a set of facilities that give users direct control on itemset coverage.

Table 1. Average results for itemset coverage using the I_2E System with different configurations for the cut percentage, compared to rule sets of equivalent size obtained with Apriori and then filtered to keep the best rules according to a composite ranking of eight interest measures. Iris, Flags and Coffee data sets. (Adapted from Yamamoto et al., 2007).

Cut percentage (%)	Rule Coverage I_2E	Rule Coverage Conventional
0% (no cut)	100.00%	29.63%
15%	84.53%	25.20%
25%	74.07%	23.70%
50%	48.70%	17.90%

The second experiment is complementary to the first one, since it compares both the number of rules produced and the itemset coverage. It was conducted on a real dataset made available by PMGRN, which stands, in Portuguese, for *Program for Genetic Improvement of the Nellore Breeding* (Lôbo et al., 2008). This data set contains descriptive characteristics of bovines (females only – 3,739 records, 13 attributes) and information on cattle sales transactions conducted in Brazil. It was made available for specialists interested in discovering relevant information for marketing purposes – a comprehensive description of its attributes can be found elsewhere (Yamamoto et al., 2008). It is important to mention, however, that the values of different bovine quality attributes were binned into intervals named Bottom-50, Top-25 and Top-50 (between the previous ones), reflecting their quality rank.

This second study also compared results obtained with some configurations of the I_2E System with those obtained with a conventional rule extraction approach using *Apriori* and filtering, with different cuts keeping the best rules according to the same composite ranking of measures adopted in the previous experiment. The results, presented in **Table 2**, show that our methodology produces smaller rule sets than a conventional approach. Furthermore, considering rule sets with the same number of rules for both approaches,

the ones obtained with I_2E present better itemset coverage.

We further evaluated itemset coverage and associated rule coverage. On the same dataset, the domain specialist was asked to select only the relevant rules. At the end, with 54 rules selected, coverage of itemsets and rules were compared with that of rules obtained with the conventional approach, considering multiple executions of I_2E with different parameter settings. **Table 3** displays the results, featuring higher itemset coverages, but smaller rule coverages, for the rule sets obtained with the I_2E System. Nonetheless, rule coverage limitation can be easily overcome by exploring the visible representative rule set using *RulEx*, which allows miners to retrieve those rules missed by our methodology (the non-visible set) through their relations. Moreover, the methodology still has the advantage of producing more compact rule sets for exploration by the miner. We may intuitively infer that a reasonable value for the cut percentage lies between 75 and 85%, which shall be investigated in further experiments.

Case Study Using the I_2E System

We also conducted a case study on the PMGRN dataset with the aid of a domain specialist to evaluate the usefulness of the methodology. In this study, the domain specialist used the I_2E System

Table 2. Results for the number of rules obtained, the total itemsets covered and the itemset coverage using the I_2E System with various configurations for the filtering cut percentage, and using conventional Apriori with different filtering cuts of the best rules, according to a composite ranking of eight interest measures.

	Number of rules	Total itemsets	Itemset coverage
Conv-100	186	55	100.00%
Conv-85	158	46	83.64%
Conv-75	140	42	76.36%
Conv-50	93	30	54.55%
I_2E -100	**55**	**55**	**100.00%**
Conv-29.6	55	20	36.36%
I_2E -85	**47**	**47**	**85.45%**
Conv-25.3	47	18	32.73%
I_2E -75	**43**	**43**	**78.18%**
Conv-23.1	43	18	32.73%
I_2E -50	**31**	**31**	**56.36%**
Conv-16.7	31	13	23.64%

Table 3. Results for the itemset coverage and rule coverage of rule sets obtained using the I_2E System with different configurations for the filtering cut percentage, and using conventional Apriori with different filtering cuts to preserve only the best rules according to a composite ranking of eight interest measures.

Rule Set	Itemset coverage	Rule coverage
Conv-100	17 (100.00%)	54 (100.00%)
Conv-85	13 (76.47%)	42 (77.78%)
Conv-75	10 (58.82%)	35 (64.81%)
Conv-50	8 (47.06%)	16 (29.63%)
I_2E -100	**17 (100.00%)**	**17 (31.48%)**
Conv-29.6	3 (17.65%)	5 (9.26%)
I_2E -85	**14 (82.35%)**	**14 (25.96%)**
Conv-25.3	3 (17.65%)	5 (9.26%)
I_2E -75	**12 (70.59%)**	**12 (22.22%)**
Conv-23.1	3 (17.65%)	4 (7.41%)
I_2E -50	**9 (52.94%)**	**9 (16.67%)**
Conv-16.7	2 (11.76%)	3 (5.56%)

to discover relevant association rules from the PMGRN dataset. He wished to acquire general knowledge on the data executing four tasks: (1) to identify a profile of the commercialized female bovines by year; (2) by region; (3) identify specific characteristics of females of class heifer; and (4) identify specific characteristics of females of category PO (bovines with genealogy known).

At the beginning, the specialist set the minimum support to 1,131 and inspected the itemsets generated. After briefly inspecting the itemset visualization he redefined the support to 588. Satisfied with the current minimum support value, the specialist navigated on the space of itemsets displayed in the visualization. Then, he decided to focus on itemsets and rules of size 2, after removing itemsets with missing values, which reduced the number of objects shown in the visualization. For each task, the specialist selected the itemsets containing items relevant to the initial tasks, and generated rules that were then explored using the *RulEx* module. With the search mechanism, rules related to each task were compared with their corresponding related rules based on the relation operators defined. At the end of the process, the specialist selected the interesting rules and made some related inferences.

For the first task, he inferred that the quality of female bovines commercialized has increased due to an observed reduction on the number of rules having bottom-50 values from years 2004 to 2006. This is likely due to an increased awareness by owners of bovine herds on the need of improving the genetics of their animals. Regarding the second task, the specialist found out that the female bovines commercialized in the Southeast region of the country have bad genetic attributes, in contrast to the ones commercialized in the Central-West region. This reveals a segmentation of the heifers sales based on the region. Furthermore, heifers were mainly from the Central-West region and had good genetic attributes (task 3). Finally, female bovines from the Central-West region with category PO had mostly good genetic values (task 4). **Table 4** shows some of the rules chosen as interesting by the domain specialist. These inferences were actually used by the specialist on marketing material for prospective clients.

The specialist highlighted the comparison of rules as an important tool to aid rule analysis. It is important, for instance, when inspecting the strength of rules as compared to similar rules with the same antecedent or consequent. In some tasks, the specialist needed to compare the strength of a rule and of its inverse. This kind of task aims at determining the stronger direction of the rule, and it can be easily performed with the *same itemset* relation operator. The parallel coordinates

Table 4. Some of the rules from the dataset describing female bovines sales transactions selected by the specialist as the most interesting for the fourth task. (Adapted from Yamamoto et al., 2008).

Antecedent	Consequent	Support	Confidence	Lift
DP365-top-25	Cat-PO	583	0.511	1.023
DPAC-top-25	Cat-PO	709	0.682	1.366
DSTAY-top-25	Cat-PO	903	0.746	1.494
MP120-top-25	Cat-PO	662	0.544	1.091
MP120-top-50	Cat-PO	582	0.582	1.166
DP120-top-50	Cat-PO	569	0.572	1.147
D3P-bottom-50	Cat-PO	1,187	0.676	1.355
DPE365-bottom-50	Cat-PO	841	0.514	1.029

visualization was also very useful to compare interest measure values of related rules.

CONCLUSION AND FUTURE TRENDS

Since the definition of the association rule mining problem, practitioners have been facing the problems of establishing suitable input parameters and handling and interpreting huge rule sets. Approaches for handling rule exploration have been proposed based on filtering, templates and reduction techniques, to name a few, but no definitive solution has yet been found. Trying to address these problems researchers have been recently investigating the integration of information visualization techniques into rule extraction approaches. This chapter discussed relevant contributions in this area, considering both approaches that employ visualization to assist exploration of mining results, and approaches that seek to assist the rule extraction process and insert the user into the knowledge discovery loop. In this context, we also described a recent methodology that integrates several features in order to support user-driven rule extraction and exploration. The methodology contemplates flexible determination of the minimum support threshold during rule extraction, a projection-based visualization of frequent itemsets that is coordinated with a list of items, a cluster-oriented extraction of compact rule sets from similar itemsets, and a module to assist pairwise comparison of rules. Using the I_2E System, designed within the principles of this methodology, some experiments were conducted to compare the performance of the user-driven approach with a conventional rule extraction approach, and also to illustrate the possibilities of the user-driven solution. In a case study with a domain specialist, the usefulness of the methodology towards inserting the miner into the loop was confirmed. We believe that a closer contact with the discovery process allows miners to obtain better results faster than just running an algorithm as a black box. Of course, other approaches may be investigated regarding user participation, and further studies are desirable.

As for the trends, one observes that since the earlier uses of information visualization techniques there has been a shift from simply visualizing association rule mining results to inserting the user into the extraction process. We believe that this trend will remain and consolidate in the near future, though in a more elaborate manner due to possibilities open for exploration. One can mention, for example, the integration multiple coordinated visualizations to inspect the problem from several perspectives and the elaboration of better metaphors to facilitate user interaction with the systems. Other examples include using information visualization in the knowledge acquisition stage, for example, to retrieve sets of interesting rules through visual interfaces. Visualization of other existing solutions for rule extraction, such as maximal frequent itemsets and closed frequent itemsets may be useful to aid education, training and foster the practical use of these algorithms. Finally, an important issue in data mining is the incremental update of mining processes. Since these processes are computationally costly, it may be worthwhile to keep the mining results and add more results as more up-to-date data are mined. Visualization in this context is still incipient.

ACKNOWLEDGMENT

The authors acknowledge the financial support of CNPq (Grants 305861/2006-9 and 470272/2004-0) and CAPES.

REFERENCES

Agrawal, R., Imielinski, T., & Swami, A. (1993). Mining association rules between sets of items in large databases. In P. Buneman, S. Jajodia (Eds.), *1993 ACM SIGMOD International Conference on*

Management of Data (pp. 207-216). New York: Association for Computing Machinery.

Ankerst, M. (2000) *Visual Data Mining*. Ph.D. thesis. Fakultät für Mathematik und Informatik der Ludwig-Maximilians-Universität München.

Asuncion, A., & Newman, D. J. (2007). UCI Machine Learning Repository. *University of California, Irvine, School of Information and Computer Sciences*. Retrieved April 22, 2008, from http://www.ics.uci.edu/~mlearn/MLRepository.html.

Blanchard, J., Guillet, F., & Briand, H. (2003). A User-driven and Quality-oriented Visualization for Mining Association Rules. In J. Shavlik, X. Wu, A. Tuzhilin (Eds.), *Third IEEE International Conference on Data Mining* (pp. 493-496). Washington, DC: IEEE Computer Society.

Blanchard, J., Guillet, F., & Briand, H. (2007a). Interactive visual exploration of association rules with rule-focusing methodology. *Knowledge and Information Systems, 13*(1), 43-75.

Blanchard, J., Pinaud, B., Kuntz, P., & Guillet, F. (2007b). A 2D-3D visualization support for human-centered rule mining. *Computers & Graphics, 31*(3), 350-360.

Bruzzese, D., & Buono, P. (2004). Combining visual techniques for Association Rules exploration. In M. F. Costabile (Ed.), Working Conference on Advanced Visual Interfaces (pp. 381-384). New York: ACM Press.

Chakravarthy, S., & Zhang, H. (2003). Visualization of association rules over relational DBMSs. In G. B. Lamont, H. Haddad, G. A. Papadopoulos, B. Panda (Eds.), *ACM Symposium on Applied Computing* (pp. 922-926). New York: Association for Computing Machinery.

Chen, C. & Yu, Y. (2000). Empirical studies of information visualization: a meta-analysis. *International Journal of Human-Computer Studies, 53*(5), 851-866.

Couturier, O., Hamrouni, T., Yahia, S. B., & Mephu-Nguifo, E. (2007a). A scalable association rule visualization towards displaying large amounts of knowledge. In Proc. *11th International Conference on Information Visualization* (pp. 657-663). Washington: IEEE Computer Society.

Couturier, O., Rouillard, J., & Chevrin, V. (2007b). An interactive approach to display large sets of association rules. In M. J. Smith, G. Salvendy (Eds.), *International Conference on Human-Computer Interaction* (pp. 258-267). Heidelberg: Springer Berlin.

Dix, A., Finlay, J. E., Abowd, G. D., & Beale, R. (2003). *Human-Computer Interaction*. London: Prentice Hall.

Ertek, G., & Demiriz, A. (2006). A Framework for Visualizing Association Mining Results. In A. Levi, E. Savas, H. Yenigün, S. Balcisoy & Y. Saygin (Eds.), *21st International Symposium on Computer and Information Sciences* (pp. 593-602). Berlin: Lecture Notes in Computer Science.

Fayyad, U., Piatetsky-Shapiro, G., & Smyth, P. (1996). From data mining to knowledge discovery in databases. *AI Magazine, 17*(3), 37-54.

Hofmann, H., Siebes, A. P. J. & Wilhelm, A. F. X. (2000). Visualizing Association Rules with Interactive Mosaic Plots. In R. Ramakrishnan, R., S. Stolfo, R. Bayardo, I. Parsa (Eds.) *ACM International Conference on Knowledge Discovery and Data Mining* (pp. 227-235). New York: Association for Computing Machinery.

Inselberg, A., & Dimsdale, B. (1990). Parallel Coordinates: A Tool for Visualizing Multi-dimensional Geometry. In A. Kaufman (Ed.), *1st Conference on Visualization '90* (pp. 361-378). Prentice Hall.

Keim, D. A. (2002). Information Visualization and Visual Data Mining. *IEEE Transactions on Visualization and Computer Graphics, 8*(1), 1-8.

Keim, D. A., & Kriegel, H.-P. (1996). Visualization Techniques for Mining Large Databases: A Comparison. *IEEE Transactions on Knowledge and Data Engineering, 8*(6), 923-938.

Klemettinen, M., Mannila, H., Ronkainen, P., Toivonen, H., & Verkamo, A. I. (1994). Finding interesting rules from large sets of discovered association rules. In C. K. Nicholas, J. Mayfield (Eds.) *ACM International Conference on Information and Knowledge Management* (pp. 401-407). New York: Lecture Notes in Computer Science.

Kopanakis, I., & Theodoulidis, B. (2003). Visual data mining modeling techniques for the visualization of mining outcomes. *Journal of Visual Languages and Computing, 14*(6), 543–589.

Kuntz, P., Guillet, F., Lehn, R., Briand, H. (2000). A user-driven process for mining association rules. In D. A. Zighed, H. J. Komorowski, J. M. Zytkow (Eds.) *European Conference on Principles of Data Mining and Knowledge Discovery* (pp. 160-168). London: Springer-Verlag.

Levkowitz, H. (Ed.). (1997). *Color Theory and Modeling for Computer Graphics, Visualization and Multimedia Applications.* Kluwer Academic Publishers.

Liu, Y. & Salvendy, G. (2006). Design and Evaluation of Visualization Support to Facilitate Association Rules Modeling. *International Journal of Human Computer Interaction, 21*(1), 15-38.

Lôbo, R., Bezerra, L., Faria, C., Magnabosco, C., Albuquerque, L., Bergmann, J., Sainz, R., & Oliveira, H. (Eds.). (2008). *Avaliação Genética de Touros e Matrizes da Raça Nelore.* Ribeirão Preto: Associação Nacional de Criadores e Pesquisadores (in Portuguese).

Mahanti, A., & Alhajj, R. (2005). Visual Interface for Online Watching of Frequent Itemset Generation in Apriori and Eclat. In M. A. Wani, M. Milanova, L. Kurgan, M. Reformat, K. Hafeez (Eds.), *The Fourth International Conference on Machine Learning and Applications* (pp. 404-410). Washington, DC: IEEE Computer Society.

North, C., & Shneiderman, B. (2000)a. Snaptogether visualization: a user interface for coordinating visualizations via relational schemata. In V. D. Gesù, S. Levialdi, L. Tarantino (Eds.), *Advanced Visual Interfaces* (pp. 128-135). New York: ACM Press.

North, C. & Shneiderman, B. (2000b). Snaptogether visualization: can users construct and operate coordinated visualizations. *International Journal of Human-Computer Studies, 53*(5), 715-739.

Oliveira, M. C. F. de, & Levkowitz, H. (2003). From Visual Data Exploration to Visual Data Mining: A Survey. *IEEE Transactions on Visualization and Computer Graphics, 9*(3), 378-394.

Ong, H.-H., Ong, K.-L., Ng, W.-K., & Lim, E.-P. (2002, December). *CrystalClear: Active Visualization of Association Rules.* Paper presented at the IEEE International Workshop on Active Mining (AM-2002), Maebashi City, Japan.

Paulovich, F. V., Nonato, L. G., Minghim, R. (2006). Visual Mapping of Text Collections through a Fast High Precision Projection Technique. In A. Ursyn, E. Banissi (Eds.), *Tenth International Conference on Information Visualization* (pp. 282-290). London: IEEE Computer Society Press.

Plaisant, C. (2004). The challenge of information visualization evaluation. In M. F. Costabile (Ed.), *The working conference on Advanced Visual Interfaces* (pp. 109-116). New York: ACM Press.

Techapichetvanich, K., & Datta, A. (2005). VisAR: A New Technique for Visualizing Mined Association Rules. In X. Li, S. Wang, Z. Y. Dong (Eds.), *First International Conference on Advanced Data Mining and Applications* (pp. 88-95). New York: Lecture Notes in Computer Science.

Unwin, A., Hofmann, H., & Bernt, K. (2001). The TwoKey Plot for Multiple Association Rules Control. In L. D. Raedt, A. Siebes (Eds.), *Fifth European Conference on Principles of Data Mining and Knowledge Discovery* (pp. 472-483). London: Lecture Notes in Computer Science.

Wong, P. C., Whitney, P., & Thomas, J. (1999). Visualizing Association Rules for Text Mining. In S. Eick, G. Wills, & D. A. Keim (Eds.), *IEEE Symposium on Information Visualization* (pp. 120). Washington, DC: IEEE Computer Society.

Yamamoto, C. H., Oliveira, M. C. F. de, Fujimoto, M. L., & Rezende, S. O. (2007). An itemset-driven cluster-oriented approach to extract compact and meaningful sets of association rules. In M. A. Wani (Eds.), *The Sixth International Conference on Machine Learning and Applications* (pp. 87-92). Los Alamitos: Conference Publishing Services.

Yamamoto, C. H., Oliveira, M. C. F. de, Rezende, S. O., & Nomelini, J. (2008). Including the User in the Knowledge Discovery Loop: Interactive Itemset-Driven Rule Extraction. In R. L. Wainwright, H. M. Haddad, A. Brayner, R. Meneses, M. Viroli (Eds.), *ACM 2008 Symposium on Applied Computing* (pp. 1212-1217). New York: Association for Computing Machinery.

Yang, L. (2003). Visualizing frequent itemsets, association rules and sequential patterns in parallel coordinates. In V. Kumar, M. L. Gavrilova, C. J. K. Tan, & P. L'Ecuyer (Eds.), *Computational Science and Its Applications* (pp. 21-30). New York: Lecture Notes in Computer Science.

Zaki, M. J., & Phoophakdee, B. (2003). *MIRAGE: A framework for mining, exploring and visualizing minimal association rules* (Tech. Rep. No. 03-04). Troy, NY: Rensselaer Polytechnic Institute, Computer Sciences Department.

Chapter XIII
Frequent Closed Itemsets Based Condensed Representations for Association Rules

Nicolas Pasquier
University of Nice Sophia-Antipolis, France

ABSTRACT

After more than one decade of researches on association rule mining, efficient and scalable techniques for the discovery of relevant association rules from large high-dimensional datasets are now available. Most initial studies have focused on the development of theoretical frameworks and efficient algorithms and data structures for association rule mining. However, many applications of association rules to data from different domains have shown that techniques for filtering irrelevant and useless association rules are required to simplify their interpretation by the end-user. Solutions proposed to address this problem can be classified in four main trends: constraint-based mining, interestingness measures, association rule structure analysis, and condensed representations. This chapter focuses on condensed representations that are characterized in the frequent closed itemset framework to expose their advantages and drawbacks.

INTRODUCTION

Since the definition of association rules in the early 1990's by Agrawal *et al.* (1993), intensive studies have been conducted to produce efficient association rule mining algorithms from large datasets.

Association rules were defined as conditional rules depicting relationships between occurrences of attribute values, called *items*, in data lines[1]. An association rule $A \rightarrow C$ states that a significant proportion of data lines containing items in the *antecedent A* also contain items in the *conse-*

quent C. The *support* of a rule is the proportion, or number, of data lines containing all items in the rule to assess the scope, or frequency, of the rule. The confidence of a rule is the proportion of data lines containing the consequent among data lines containing the antecedent. The task of association rule mining consists in discovering all rules with support at least equal to the user defined minimum support threshold *minsup* and that have a confidence at least equal to the user defined minimum confidence threshold *minconf.* Such rules are called *valid* or *strong* association rules.

This approach to association rule mining suffers from several well-known drawbacks described in many researches and application reports (Brijs *et al.*, 2003). The first of these problems is the difficulty to define appropriate *minsup* and *minconf* thresholds. Choosing too high values may lead to the miss of important relations corresponding to association rules with support lower than *minsup.* Choosing too low values may lead to performance problems, as more itemsets are frequent, and to extract association rules that are irrelevant or useless because of their limited scope. The second problem is related to the confidence measure used to assess the precision of the rule. This measure does not consider the frequency, or support, of the consequent of the rule and thus, an association rule can exhibit a relation between two statistically uncorrelated itemsets (Brin *et al.*, 1997). The third problem is related to the huge number of association rules generated in most cases. This number can range from several thousands to several millions and the set of association rules can be difficult to manage and interpret (Toivonen *et al.*, 1995; Bayardo *et al.*, 2000). The fourth problems is related to the presence of many redundant association rules in the result. Redundant association rules are rules which information is contained in other rules and that can thus be deduced from them (Matheus *et al.*, 1993). These rules do not bring additional knowledge to the user and should be removed

from the result as they lower the result's accuracy and relevance and harden the management and interpretation of extracted rules.

The frequent closed itemsets framework was introduced to address the efficiency problem of association rule mining from dense and correlated data. Several posterior researches have shown that this framework is also well-fitted to address the problem of redundant association rules filtering. We first present association rule mining and frequent itemsets and frequent closed itemsets frameworks. Then, we briefly review several approaches proposed to address the four problems of association rule mining mentioned above. Then, we describe condensed representations and bases for association rules and characterize them in the frequent closed itemsets framework to show their advantages and drawbacks.

ASSOCIATION RULE MINING

In order to improve the extraction efficiency, most algorithms for mining association rules operate on binary data represented in a transactional or binary format. This also enables the treatment of mixed data types, resulting from the integration of multiple data sources for example, with the same algorithm. The transactional and binary representations of the example dataset *D*, used as a support in the rest of the chapter, are shown in Table 1. In the transactional or *enumeration* format represented in Table 1(a) each object, called *transaction* or *data line*, contains a list of items. In the binary format represented in Table 1(b) each object[2] is a *bit vector* and each bit indicates if the object contains the corresponding item or not.

An itemset is a lexicographically ordered set of items and the *support* of an itemset *A* is the proportion, or number, of objects containing it: *support*(A) = *count*(A) / *count*() where *count*(A) is the number of objects containing *A* and *count*() is the total number of objects. For example, the support of the itemset $\{b, c\}$, denoted *bc* for short,

Table 1. Dataset representations

Object	Items
1	a b c e
2	b c e
3	a b c e
4	a c d
5	b c e

Object	a	b	c	d	e
1	1	1	1	0	1
2	0	1	1	0	1
3	1	1	1	0	1
4	1	1	0	1	0
5	0	1	1	0	1

(a) Enumerations   (b) Bit vectors

is 2/5 in the example dataset D. The support of association rule $R: A \rightarrow C$ between two itemsets A and C is $support(R) = support(A \cup C)$ and it confidence is $confidence(R) = support(A \cup C) / support(C)$. For instance, in dataset D we have $support(a \rightarrow bc) = support(abc) = 2/5$ and $confidence(a \rightarrow bc) = support(abc) / support(a) = 2/3$. Association rule mining algorithms can be classified according to several criteria: The theoretical framework they are based on, the search space traversal they perform or the data structures they use. The two following sections present the main theoretical frameworks proposed for association rule mining: The *frequent itemsets* and the *frequent closed itemsets* frameworks.

Frequent Itemsets Framework

The frequent itemsets framework defined by Agrawal *et al.* (1993) is based on the following decomposition of the problem:

1. Extract frequent itemsets, i.e. itemsets that have a support at least equal to *minsup*.
2. Generate association rules between itemsets that have a confidence at least equal to *minconf*.

The second phase is straightforward once all frequent itemsets are discovered. However, the search space of the first phase is the itemset lattice,

or subset lattice, which size is exponential in the size of set of items and extracting all frequent itemsets was shown to be an NP-Complete problem (Angiulli *et al.*, 2001). The itemset lattice for the example dataset D is represented in Figure 1.

This lattice contains $2^{|I|}$ itemsets, where $I = \{a, b, c, d, e\}$ is the set of items and frequent itemsets for *minsup* = 2/5 are outlined. Frequent itemset identification requires lattice traversal and is thus computationally expensive. Optimized traversals of the search space and efficient data structures and implementation techniques are required to obtain acceptable response times. The frequent itemset approach was developed for extracting association rules from very large datasets containing weakly correlated data, such as market basket data. However, this approach faces important problems of efficiency with dense or highly correlated data as the number of frequent itemsets, and by the sequel of association rules, can be very large (Brin *et al.*, 1997). A recent review of association rule mining algorithms in these three trends can be found in Ceglar & Roddick (2006).

Frequent Closed Itemsets Framework

The frequent closed itemsets framework was introduced in Pasquier *et al.* (1998) with the Close algorithm to address the problem of association rule mining from dense datasets (Pasquier *et al.*,

Figure 1. Itemset lattice

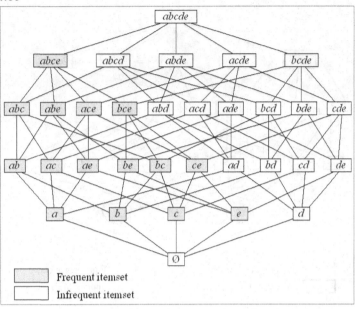

1999a). This framework is based on the closure operator of the Galois connexion used in Formal Concept Analysis (Ganter *et al.*, 2005). It defines frequent closed itemsets that constitute a minimal representation for frequent itemsets. The Galois closure $\gamma(A)$ of an itemset A is the intersection of all objects containing A and a closed itemset is an itemset that is equal to its closure. All frequent itemsets and their supports can be straightforwardly deduced from frequent closed itemsets. Algorithms based on the frequent closed itemset extraction use the following decomposition of the problem:

1. Extract frequent closed itemsets, i.e. closed itemsets that have a support at least equal to *minsup*.
2. Generate association rules that have a confidence at least equal to *minconf* from frequent closed itemsets.

The search space of the first phase is the closed itemset lattice and the potentially frequent closed itemsets for the example dataset *D* are outlined in Figure 3. A closed itemset is a maximal[3] set of items common to a set of objects. For instance, *ac* is a closed itemset since it is the maximal set of items common to objects 1, 3 and 4, that is their intersection. Frequent closed itemsets for the example dataset *D* and *minsup* = 2/5 are outlined in Figure 2. These frequent closed itemsets, with their respective supports, summarize all frequent itemsets and their supports (Pasquier *et al.*, 1998). See Ben Yahia *et al.* (2006), Pasquier (2005) and Valtchev *et al.* (2004) for reviews of frequent closed itemset based algorithms.

These algorithms use the closure property to exclude from the search space traversal many itemsets that are useless for association rule construction: The non closed frequent itemsets. Since the closure $\gamma(A)$ of an itemset A is the intersection of all objects containing A, the support of A is equal to the support of $\gamma(A)$. All itemsets are contained and have the same support as their closure, that is their first closed superset. For instance, in Figure 2, itemset *b*, *e*, *be*, *bc* and

Figure 2. Closed Itemsets and Equivalence Classes.

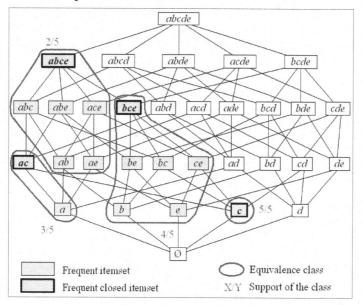

ce are deducible with support from the closed itemset *bce* and by consequence are useless for association rule mining. All itemsets with the same closure form an *equivalence class* (Bastide *et al.*, 2000b). Each equivalence class contains a unique maximal closed itemsets that is the closure of itemsets in the class.

Frequent closed itemset based algorithms eliminate from the search all subsets of identified frequent closed itemsets. However, improvements offered by this approach depend on data density and correlation. Experiments conducted on market basket data showed no efficiency improvement while experiments on census and biological data showed improvements both in execution times and memory usage. This is due to the sparse and weakly correlated nature of market basket data and the dense and correlated nature of census and biological data (Brin *et al.*, 1997; Pfaltz & Taylor, 2002). Despite these improvements, efficient search space traversals, data structures and implementation techniques are required to obtain acceptable response times when large

high-dimensional datasets are mined. Recent algorithms based on the frequent closed itemset approach have shown important improvements in response times and memory usage, increasing the capability to mine association rules from high-dimensional datasets with very low *minsup* and *minconf* values.

ASSOCIATION RULES FILTERING METHODS

Association rule mining has been applied in a wide variety of domains such as marketing, finance, telecommunications, bioinformatics, natural sciences and web usage. All these applications have highlighted important problems that often arise when extracted association rules are analyzed and interpreted: The problems of usability and relevance of extracted rules. This problem results mainly from both the number of rules generated and the presence of numerous redundancies among them. Indeed, in most applications several thousands, and sometimes millions, of association rules are generated. Moreover, the analyze of these rules shows that most often several rules were generated from the same objects and contain similar information. A small subset of these rules can summarize all information contained in this set of rules as other rules can be considered redundant and their suppression does not reduce information (Padmanabhan & Tuzhilin, 2000; Stumme *et al.*, 2001). This problem is crucial when data are dense or correlated since redundant rules may represent the majority of extracted rules in such data (Bastide *et al.*, 2000a; Zaki, 2000). Identifying and extracting only the most informative rules, from the user's viewpoint, among all rules has then become a crucial problem to improve usefulness of extracted association rules (Bayardo & Agrawal, 1999). Solutions proposed to address this problem can be classified in four main trends: The integration of constraints to select a subset of rules, the use of interestingness measures to evaluate the relevance of rules, the comparison of rules to filter similar ones and the extraction of condensed representations. The following subsections give a short overview of constraint-based mining, interestingness measures and association rule structure analysis approaches. Condensed representations for association rules are studied in more details in next the section.

Constraint-Based Mining

User specified constraints restrict combinations of items allowed to participate to association rules. They reduce the number of extracted association rules according to structural criteria corresponding to the user's preferences. These preferences are defined either as *templates* or as *item constraints*. Templates are rules containing boolean operators that define which items or combinations of items are allowed or forbidden in the antecedent and the consequent of extracted rules (Klemettinen *et al.*, 1994). In a post-processing phase, rules that do not match the user defined templates are discarded.

A template definition language, that is an extension of an SQL operator for extracting association rules from relational databases, was proposed in Baralis & Psaila (1997). A performance evaluation of the template approach is presented in Li *et al.* (2004). Item constraints are boolean expressions over the presence or absence of items in frequent itemsets and then association rules (Srikant *et al.*, 1997). These constraints are integrated during the frequent itemset discovery process to discard itemsets that do not match constraints and thus reduce the search space of frequent itemsets. An algorithm integrating item constraints in a depth-first frequent itemset mining approach was proposed in Lu *et al.* (2005).

Item constraints based approaches can naturally take advantage of structures describing hierarchical relations between items such as taxonomies or *is-a* hierarchies. In such hierarchies, items can be generalized in different ways and to different levels of abstraction according to hierarchical relations. Rules between items at different levels of abstraction, called *multi-level* (Srikant & Agrawal, 1995) or *generalized association rules* (Han & Fu, 1995), can then be generated. This approach can significantly reduce the number of extracted association rules as each higher-level rule may summarize several lower-level rules that can be derived given the corresponding item supports (Srikant & Agrawal, 1995). Moreover, with such hierarchies, item constraints can be defined at different levels of abstraction to simplify their definition when the items involved have common ancestors in the hierarchies.

Other general constraints can be integrated in the mining process. These constraints can be classified in *monotonic* and *anti-monotonic* constraints considering their impact on the mining process. Anti-monotonic constraints, such as the frequency constraint, reduce the search-space and can be pushed deep in the discovery process to optimize it (Bayardo *et al.*, 2000). Monotonic constraints, such as domain of values or class of items, can be checked once and no further checking is required for subsequent phases (Ng *et al.*,1998; Lakshmanan *et al.*, 1999). The problem of mining frequent itemsets satisfying a conjunction of anti-monotonic and monotonic constraints was studied in Pei *et al.* (2001), Boulicaut & Jeudy (2002) and Bonchi *et al.* (2005). Several studies concerned the integration of general constraints in frequent itemsets based algorithms (Pei & Han, 2002; Cheung & Fu, 2004; Leung *et al.*, 2002) and in frequent closed itemset based algorithms (Bonchi & Lucchese, 2004; Bonchi & Lucchese, 2006).

Interestingness Measures

The use of interestingness measures to assess statistical significance and operational value of rules was proposed in Piatetsky-Shapiro (1991). This approach was studied in a more general context, to select the most relevant association rules, in Toivonen *et al.* (1995). Interestingness measures are usually classified in *objective* and *subjective* measures. Objective measures assess the interestingness of rules according to a statistical significance criterion. Subjective measures compare rules with user's prior knowledge to assess the interestingness of rules according to *unexpectedness* and *actionability* criteria. Unexpected rules either contradict user's beliefs or represent previously unknown relations. Actionable rules are rules the user can act upon to his advantage. See McGarry (2005) for a review of objective and subjective interestingness measures for knowledge discovery. Recent studies showed that combining objective and subjective measures is required to select the most interesting rules: Objective measures first filter potentially interesting rules and then subjective measures select truly interesting rules (Carvalho *et al.*, 2005).

The support and confidence objective measures were introduced to evaluate the association rules interestingness from a statistical viewpoint (Brijs *et al.*, 2003). The use of statistical measures to assess rules' syntactic similarity and prune simi-lar rules was introduced in Piatetsky-Shapiro & Matheus (1994) and Toivonen *et al.* (1995). The use of other statistical measures to overcome support and confidence weakness, that is particularly important in dense correlated data, was suggested in Brin *et al.* (1997). This study was extended in (Silverstein *et al.*, 2000). Hilderman & Hamilton (1999) introduced and evaluated twelve heuristics for rule mining based on measures from information theory, statistics, ecology, and economics. This work was extended, considering four other measures, by Hilderman & Hamilton (2001). Hilderman & Hamilton (2003) also evaluated the combination of twelve objective measures with taxonomic hierarchies for mining generalized association rules. Tan *et al.* (2002) showed that no objective measure is more appropriate than others in all situations. They evaluated twenty objective measures, highlighting several of their key properties, to help the user choosing measures that are well-fitted to the application domain and his expectations. According to Freitas (1999), several factors, such as disjunct size, imbalance of class distributions, attribute interestingness, misclassification costs and asymmetry, should be considered additionally to the traditional coverage[4], completeness and confidence factors of objective measures. He also proposed a generic criterion taking into account all these factors. *Exception rules* are rules that contradict other rules with high support and confidence containing related items. Exception rules can be identified by using an induction algorithm and contingency tables to determine rules' deviation (Liu *et al.*, 1999) or objective measures based on relative entropy (Hussain *et al.*, 2000). See Geng & Hamilton (2006) and Lenca *et al.* (2008) for recent reviews on objective interestingness measures for association rules.

Many subjective measures to assess the interestingness of association rules by comparison with the user's prior knowledge were proposed. The use of background knowledge, such as user's beliefs, to identify *unexpected* association rules was introduced in Silberschatz & Tuzhilin (1996). In this approach, user's beliefs are defined in a knowledge base used during the mining process in combination with an unexpectedness heuristic to estimate rules' interestingness from the user's beliefs viewpoint. In Padmanabhan & Tuzhilin (1998), user's beliefs are represented in the same format as association rules and only rules that contradict existing beliefs are mined. In Liu *et al.* (1997), the user defines *general impressions* that express positive or negative relations between items. Association rules are then compared to this knowledge to rank *unexpected* or *confirming* rules. A confirming rule is a rule that matches user's beliefs. In Liu *et al.* (1999), the user's background knowledge is expressed in fuzzy rules and *unexpected, confirming* or *actionable* rules are extracted. In Wang *et al.* (2003), the user defines a preference model that characterizes how background knowledge should be used to evaluate rules' unexpectedness. Then, an algorithm extracts unexpected rules satisfying user defined thresholds of minimum *unexpectedness significance* and *unexpectedness strength*. In Jaroszewicz & Scheffer (2005), the interestingness of a rule is evaluated by comparing the difference between its support in the dataset and in a Bayesian network expressing user's prior knowledge. See Geng & Hamilton (2006) for a recent review of subjective measures of interestingness.

Association Rule Structure Analysis

Approaches in this category analyze the structure of association rules to suppress those containing information represented in other association rules. Each association rule is compared to all other rules and is suppressed if it is "similar" to another rule according to the items in its antecedent and its consequent.

Toivonen *et al.* (1995) proposed an algorithm to prune association rules by keeping only association rules with the minimal antecedent. In this approach, if the antecedent A of an association rule $R: A \rightarrow C$ is a superset of the antecedent A' of an association rule $R': A' \rightarrow C'$ with the same consequent, then R is suppressed. A similar approach was proposed in Liu *et al.* (1999) with the difference that the association rule R is suppressed if it does not show a positive correlation according to a χ^2 test with respect to R'. Padmanabhan & Tuzhilin (2000) combined an algorithm for mining association rules with minimal antecedent with an unexpectedness measure to mine a minimal set of unexpected association rules. However, the supports, precision measures and objects covered by R and R' are not taken into account by these methods. Thus, the precision measures of suppressed association rules cannot be deduced from the resulting set.

The extraction of A-maximal association rules to reduce the number of extracted association rules was proposed in Bayardo & Agrawal (1999). A-maximal association rules are association rules with maximal antecedent among all rules with the same support and the same consequent. Constraints defining which items are allowed, required or forbidden in the extracted A-maximal association rules can also be integrated to further reduce their number.

Succinct association rules defined in Deogun & Jiang (2005) are strong association rules filtered using a strategy based on a model called MaxPUF for maximal potentially useful association rules. As for other approaches in this category, the resulting set is not lossless since the capability to deduce all strong association rules with their statistical measures is not ensured.

CONDENSED REPRESENTATIONS

In this section, we characterize condensed representations for association rules using the frequent closed itemsets framework. To simplify this characterization, we distinguish two classes of association rules: *Approximate* or *partial association rules* that have a confidence less than 100

% and *exact association rules* that have a 100 % confidence. Approximate association rules have some counter-examples in the dataset whereas exact association rules have no counter-example in the dataset.

A condensed representation is a reduced set of association rules that summarizes a set of strong association rules. Strong association rules designate association rules extracted using a classical frequent itemset approach, that is all association rules with statistical measures, computed from itemset supports, at least equal to the user defined thresholds. A condensed representation is *lossless* if all strong association rules can be deduced from it. Information lossless condensed representations are called *generating sets*. Generating sets that are minimal with respect to the number of association rules are called *minimal covers* or *bases for association rules* (Pasquier *et al.*, 1999b; Zaki, 2000). A basis for association rules is thus a condensed representation with the two following properties:

1. **Non-redundancy:** A basis contains no redundant rule according to the inference rules[5] considered. That means each association rule in the basis cannot be deduced if suppressed from the basis. In other words, each association rule of the basis must contain information not deducible from other association rules of the basis.
2. **Generating set:** A basis enables the inference of all strong association rules according to the set of inference rules considered.

That means all strong association rules can be deduced from the basis.

Condensed representations and bases for association rules were defined to bring to the end-user a set of association rules as small as possible. Bases are condensed representations with more restrictive properties: They are minimal sets of association rules from which all strong association rules can be deduced by inference. This deduction, or inference, relies on a set of inference rules defining which association rules can be deduced from other association rules and are thus redundant. A set of inference rules is called an *inference system*.

Inference Systems

In the domains of databases and data analysis, such as Formal Concept Analysis, the closure of a set S of implication rules according to an inference system is the set $S+$ of all implication rules that can be inferred from S. Then, an implication rule is redundant if its suppression does not change this closure. Armstrong's axioms are inference rules proposed in the field of database conception for generating the closure of a set of functional dependencies between attribute values (Armstrong, 1974). Armstrong's inference system, recalled in Figure 3, is well-suited for association rules as implication rules are closely related to functional dependencies in the database domain (Maier, 1983; Valtchev *et al.*, 2004). Indeed, exact association rules are implication rules that are

Figure 3. Armstrong's axioms

Reflexivity	$: X \supseteq Y \vdash X \Rightarrow Y$
Augmentation	$: X \Rightarrow Y \vdash XZ \Rightarrow YZ$
Transitivity	$: X \Rightarrow Y \wedge Y \Rightarrow Z \vdash X \Rightarrow Z$
Union	$: X \Rightarrow Y \wedge X \Rightarrow Z \vdash X \Rightarrow YZ$
Decomposition	$: X \Rightarrow YZ \vdash X \Rightarrow Y \wedge X \Rightarrow Z$
Pseudo-transitivity	$: X \Rightarrow Y \wedge WY \Rightarrow Z \vdash XW \Rightarrow Y$

frequent enough in the dataset, according to the user defined frequency threshold *minsup*, and approximate association rules are partial implication rules that are frequent enough in the dataset to be considered useful (Valtchev *et al.*, 2004).

According to these definitions, several bases can be defined depending on the inference system considered. This inference system determines which association rules are considered redundant and are thus suppressed to constitute the basis.

Redundant Association Rules

To state the problem of redundant association rules, consider the three following rules that can be extracted from the example dataset D: $c \rightarrow b$, $c \rightarrow e$, $c \rightarrow be$. These approximate association rules have identical support (4/5) and confidence (4/5) as they are computed from the same objects (1, 2, 3 and 5). Obviously, the information in the two first rules is summarized by the third rule and thus, the two first are informatively useless. These two rules can be deduced using the union inference rule of Armstrong's axioms for instance.

Consider now objects 2 and 4 in Table 1 from which the following nine association rules can be extracted: $b \rightarrow c$, $b \rightarrow e$, $b \rightarrow ce$, $bc \rightarrow e$, $be \rightarrow c$, $e \rightarrow c$, $e \rightarrow b$, $e \rightarrow bc$, $ce \rightarrow b$. These exact association rules have a support of 4/5 and a confidence of 100 %. Using the deduction, augmentation and pseudo-transitivity inference rules of Armstrong's axioms, these nine rules can be inferred from the following two rules: $b \rightarrow ce$ and $e \rightarrow bc$. All information contained in the nine rules are contained in these two rules. Moreover, the presence of c in the antecedent of rules $bc \rightarrow e$ and $ce \rightarrow b$ is not significant since their statistical measures do not change if c is removed as *support*({b}) = *support*({bc}) and *support*({e}) = *support*({ce}). This reasoning also applies to the presence of e in the antecedent of rule $be \rightarrow c$.

In the database and Formal Concept Analysis domains, a functional dependency or an implication rule is redundant if its suppression does not modify the result of the closure of the set of dependencies or rules according to an inference system. This definition was adapted to association rules and a consensus among researchers is now established to consider that an association rule is redundant if its suppression does not modify the result of the closure of the set of association rules according to an inference system. In other words, a redundant association rule can be inferred from other strong association rules. Extracting only non-redundant association rules reduces as much as possible the number of rules without loosing the capability to retrieve other rules given the inference system. This greatly simplifies their post-processing, that is their management and exploration. In the literature, non-redundant association rules are sometimes called *non-derivable* or *non-deducible* association rules.

In the following, condensed representations for association rules are characterized using the frequent closed itemsets framework. These condensed representations are bases or minimal covers defined according to different sets of inference rules, corresponding to different goals, and thus have different properties with regard to their intelligibility for the end-user.

Duquenne-Guigues and Luxenburger Bases

The DG Basis (Duquenne & Guigues, 1986) and the Proper Basis (Luxenburger, 1991) for global and partial implications respectively were adapted to the association rule framework in Pasquier *et al.* (1999b). The mathematical, structural and informative properties of these bases was studied in several research papers (Cristofor & Simovici, 2002; Hamrouni *et al.*, 2006; Kryszkiewicz, 2002)

The DG Basis was defined in the context of implication rules and thus does not consider confidence in the inference system used to define redundant rules and deduce all strong rules from the bases. The DG Basis for exact association rules

Figure 4. DG inference rules

$$A \Rightarrow B \wedge C \Rightarrow D \vdash AC \Rightarrow BD$$
$$A \Rightarrow B \wedge B \Rightarrow C \vdash A \Rightarrow C$$

is defined by frequent pseudo-closed itemsets. A frequent pseudo-closed itemset A is a non-closed itemset that includes the closures of all frequent pseudo-closed itemsets included in A. This basis contains all association rules between a frequent pseudo-closed itemset and its closure. The DG Basis for the example dataset D and *minsup* = 2/5 and *minconf* = 2/5 is represented in Table 2.

The DG Basis for exact association rules is a minimal set, with respect to the number of extracted exact rules. All strong exact association rules can be deduced from the DG Basis using the inference rules given in Figure 4.

The DG Basis is the minimal generating set with respect to the number of rules for a set of implication rules (Ganter *et al.*, 2005). The same property was demonstrated for the DG Basis for association rules (Pasquier *et al.*, 1999b). However, statistical measures of all strong association rules inferred cannot be deduced from the DG Basis.

Association rules inferred using the first inference rule can have inferior support compared to the rules used for inferring them. Frequent closed itemset supports are then necessary to deduce statistical measures of all exact association rules from the DG Basis (Cristofor & Simovici, 2002; Kryszkiewicz, 2002).

The Proper Basis for association rules contains all association rules between two frequent closed itemsets related by inclusion. This basis contains exactly one association rule for each pair of equivalence classes which frequent closed itemsets are related by inclusion. The Proper Basis for the example dataset D and *minsup* = 2/5 and *minconf* = 2/5 is represented in Table 3.

The transitive reduction of the Proper Basis (Pasquier *et al.*, 1999b) is the reduction of the Proper Basis according to the transitivity inference rule such as defined in Armstrong's axioms. This inference rule states that given three frequent closed itemsets A, B and C such that $A \supset B \supset C$, the confidence of the association rule $A \rightarrow C$ can be computed from the confidences of association rules $A \rightarrow B$ and $B \rightarrow C$: *confidence*($A \rightarrow C$) = *confidence*($A \rightarrow B$) × *confidence*($B \rightarrow C$). Then, $A \rightarrow C$ is called a transitive associa-

Table 2. DG basis for exact association rules

Pseudo-closed itemset	Closure	Association rule	Support
{a}	{ac}	a → c	3/5
{b}	{bce}	b → ce	4/5
{e}	{bce}	e → bc	4/5

Table 3. Proper basis for approximate association rules

Subset	Superset	Association rule	Support	Confidence
⌊ac⌋	⌊abce⌋	ac → be	2/5	2/3
[bce]	[abce]	bce → a	2/5	2/4
[c]	[ac]	c → a	3/5	3/5
[c]	[bce]	c → be	4/5	4/5
[c]	[abce]	c → abe	2/5	2/5

tion rule. Considering rules in Table 3, the only transitive rule is c → *abe* and *confidence(c →* *abe)* = confidence(c → *be)* × *confidence(bce →* a) = 4/5 × 2/4 = 2/5. Another transitivity allows the inference of its confidence: *confidence(c →* *abe)* = confidence(c → *a)* × *confidence(ca → be)* = 3/5 × 2/3 = 2/5. This inference can be extended to all statistical measures of precision[6] computed using only supports of the itemsets included in the association rule.

These union of the DG Basis for exact association rules and the transitive reduction of the Proper Basis for approximate association rules is a minimal basis for association rules: No smaller set allows the deduction of the antecedent and consequent of all strong exact and approximate association rules (Pasquier *et al.*, 1999b).

Informative Bases

Bases defined in the database and data analysis domains, such as the DG Basis and the Proper Basis for implication rules, are minimal in their number of rules given an inference system. However, these bases do not consider the problem of exploration and interpretation of extracted rules by the end-user. They were defined for an automated treatment such as the computation of a database conceptual schema with normalization properties or to have a small set of rules that is easier to manage and treat, and from which all strong rules can be inferred on demand. They were not defined for human reasoning on the information they contain when the end-user explores them. However, in most data mining applications, the interpretation of extracted patterns by the end-user is a crucial step to maximize result's profitability. Consequently, the capability to get all information contained in the set of strong association rules should be considered as a criterion when defining which rules are presented to the end-user. To ensure this capability, the deduction of information contained in suppressed association rules must be natural (Goethals *et al.*, 2005). Thus,

to improve the relevance of the set of extracted association rules from the end-user interpretation viewpoint, a basis must possess the two additional properties:

1. **Itemset covering:** Association rules in the basis must cover all combinations of items covered by the set of all strong rules. That means all items contained in an association rule must be contained in an association rule of the basis, possibly containing other items.

2. **Objects covering:** Association rules in the basis must cover all sets of objects covered by the set of all strong rules. That means all association rule representing relationships between items contained in two given sets of objects must be deducible from an association rule of the basis concerning the same two sets of objects.

Bases with these two properties are called *informative bases* and their association rules are called *informative association rules* (Gasmi *et al.*, 2005; Hamrouni *et al.*, 2008; Pasquier *et al.*, 2005). Informative bases are condensed representations that are minimal generating sets of association rules bringing to the user all information about itemset co-occurrences as the set of all strong association rules. By information, we refer to both relationships between sets of items and statistical measure values that assess the frequency and the strength or precision of this relationship. The minimality of informative bases is ensured by eliminating redundant association rules containing information contained in other association rules. They are useless for the end-user interpretation and can be suppressed without reducing information. An inference system derived from Armstrong's axioms to define the informative bases was proposed by Cristofor & Simovici (2002). To characterize the properties of informative bases, the equivalence class framework is presented in the following section.

Kryszkiewicz (2002) demonstrated that the Proper Basis and the DG Basis, if supports of association rules are not considered, are lossless representations of strong exact and approximate association rules respectively. It was also demonstrated using Armstrong's axioms that both the DG Basis and the Proper Basis are not informative.

Equivalence Classes

Equivalence classes of itemsets are defined using the frequent closed itemsets framework (Bastide *et al.*, 2000b). An equivalence class is a set of itemsets that are contained in the same objects of the dataset, that is they cover the same objects. These itemsets have the same support that is the support of the equivalence class. A frequent equivalence class is an equivalence class which support is greater or equal to the *minsup* threshold. In the following, we refer to an equivalence class by its maximal itemset that is a closed itemset and is unique. For instance, [*bce*] refers to the equivalence class {*b*, *e*, *bc*, *be*, *ce*, *bce*}. Equivalence classes in the example dataset

D for *minsup* = 2/5 are represented in the lattice of frequent itemsets in Figure 5.

The confidence of an association rules $R: A \rightarrow C$ is *confidence(R) = support(AC) / support(A)*. We deduce that all association rules between two itemsets of the same equivalence class have the same support and a confidence of 100 %. We also deduce that all association rules between two equivalence classes, i.e. between itemsets of the same two equivalence classes, have the same support and the same confidence that is smaller than 100 %. This reasoning can be extended to all precision measures computed from supports of the antecedent and the consequent of the association rule. We show this for respectively exact and approximate association rules in the two following paragraphs.

Consider association rules between two itemsets of the equivalence class [*bce*] such as rule $b \rightarrow ce$, equivalent to $b \rightarrow bce$, between itemsets *b* and *bce*. Since these itemsets belong to the same class they have identical supports and

Figure 5. Frequent equivalence classes

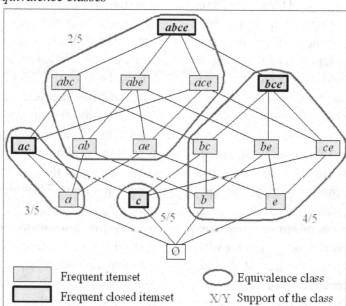

Figure 6. Exact association rules

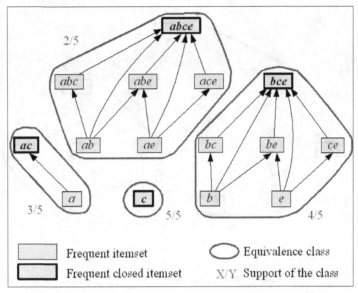

thus, all association rules between two of them have a confidence of 100 % (4/4). The support of these association rules is 4/5 that is the support of the equivalence class. These association rules constitute a *class of exact association rules*. Considering all equivalence classes, i.e. [*c*], [*ac*], [*bce*] and [*abce*], we obtain all strong exact association rules (Pasquier *et al.*, 2005). The nineteen strong exact association rules in the example dataset *D* for *minsup* = 2/5 are represented as directed links in Figure 6. They form three classes of exact association rules since no exact association rule is generated from the equivalence class [*c*] as it contains only the itemset *c*.

Consider now association rules between two itemsets of the equivalence classes [*ac*] and [*abce*] such as rule *a* → *bce* between *a* and *abce* and rule *ac* → *be* between *ac* and *abce*. These association rules are represented in Figure 7. Antecedents of these rules are itemsets in the class [*ac*] with *support* = 3/5 and consequents are determined by itemsets in the class [*abce*] with *support* = 2/5. These association rules thus all have a confidence of 2/3 and a support of 2/5. They constitute a *class*

of approximate association rules. Each pair of equivalence classes which frequent closed itemsets are related by inclusion, i.e. {[*ac*], [*abce*]}, {[*c*], [*ac*]}, {[*c*], [*bce*]}, {[*c*], [*abce*]} and {[*bce*], [*abce*]}, defines a class of approximate association rules (Pasquier *et al.*, 2005). These five classes of approximate association rules contain the thirty one strong approximate association rules in the

Figure 7. Approximate association rules

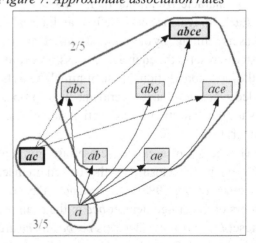

259

Figure 8. Frequent generators

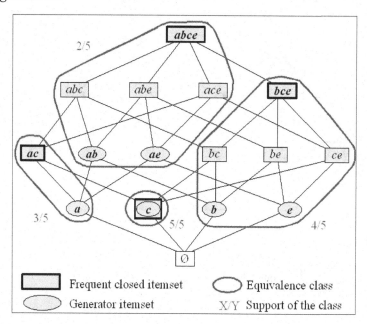

example dataset *D* for *minsup* = 2/5 and *minconf* = 2/5.

Each class of exact and approximate association rules regroups all association rules covering the same objects in the dataset. They are thus well-suited to characterize redundant exact and approximate association rules according to the definition of informative bases. Indeed, the space of strong association rules can be divided in classes of association rule and redundant association rules can be characterized inside their class.

Each equivalence class defines an interval of itemsets delimited by the minimal itemsets and the closed itemset of the equivalence class, according to the inclusion relation. These minimal itemsets, called *generators*, have several important properties for the definition of association rule bases.

Generators

Generators of a closed itemset are minimal itemsets which closure is the closed itemset (Pasquier *et al.*, 1998). For instance, the generators of the closed itemset *bce* in the example dataset *D* are *b* and *e*. Itemsets *bc*, *be* and *ce* are

not generators of *bce* since they are not minimal in the equivalence class {*b*, *e*, *bc*, *be*, *ce*, *bce*} of *bce* and *c* is a closed itemset and its own unique generator at the same time, since the closure of itemset *c* is *c*. Frequent generators are generators of frequent closed itemsets. Frequent generators in the example dataset *D* for *minsup* = 2/5 and *minconf* = 2/5 are shown in Figure 8.

Frequent generators constitute a relevant generating set for all frequent itemsets with supports and for all strong association rules or condensed representations (Hamrouni *et al.*, 2008; Liu *et al.*, 2007). Moreover, association rules can be computed more efficiently from frequent generators as they are shorter than frequent closed itemsets (Li *et al.*, 2006).

Minimal Antecedent and Consequent Association Rules

The extraction of the informative basis containing association rules with minimal antecedent and minimal consequent was proposed by Zaki

(2000). In this basis, redundant association rules are filtered inside each class of association rules: Rules with minimal antecedent and minimal consequent among all rules of the class are selected. This filtering is based on the observation that rules with fewer elements in the antecedent are easier to interpret and comprehend (Kryszkiewicz, 1998; Liu *et al.*, 1999; Mc Garry, 2005; Toivonen *et al.*, 1995).

Since generators are the minimal itemsets of an equivalence class, association rules with minimal antecedent in a class are association rules with a generator as antecedent. Considering all classes of association rules, we have a set of association rules covering all sets of items and objects covered by the set of all strong association rules. This basis is informative and lossless: All strong association rules can be deduced with support and precision measures from this set.

Considering classes of exact association rules, association rules with minimal antecedent and consequent are rules between the generators of the class and each of their first supersets in the equivalence class. Exact association rules with minimal antecedent and consequent for the example dataset *D* and *minsup* = 2/5 and *minconf* = 2/5 are presented in Table 4.

Approximate association rules with minimal antecedent and consequent are rules between a

generator *G* and each of their smallest supersets in another equivalence class which closure *C'* is a superset of the closure *C* of *G*. Strong approximate association rules with minimal antecedent and consequent in the example dataset *D* for *minsup* = 2/5 and *minconf* = 2/5 are presented in Table 5.

Zaki (2004) showed that the number of strong association rules with minimal antecedent and consequent is linear in the number of frequent closed itemsets and that the reduction in the number of association rules will thus be important in most cases. In the example dataset *D*, twenty one minimal antecedent and consequent association rules are strong whereas the set of all strong association rules contains fifty association rules.

Goethals *et al.* (2005) extended this approach to define another condensed representation containing only minimal antecedent and consequent association rules. However, the precision measures of some strong association rules cannot be deduced. It can only be approximated, given a user-specified error bound on the approximation used during the construction of the condensed representation. Thus, contrarily to the basis define by Zaki (2000), this condensed representation is not lossless.

Generic Bases for Association Rules

Generic bases for association rules were defined in Bastide *et al.* (2000a). They were conceived keeping two observations in mind: A basis for association rules presented to the end-user should be informative and rules with fewer elements in the antecedent are easier to interpret and comprehend (Kryszkiewicz, 1998; Liu *et al.*, 1999; Mc Garry, 2005; Toivonen *et al.*, 1995). The Generic bases for exact and approximate association rules contain association rules with minimal antecedent and maximal consequent. In these rules, the difference between the antecedent, that is the premise, and the consequent, that is the conclusion, is maximal and so is their scope as they cover more information. For instance, considering

Table 4. Min-Min exact association rules

Generator	Closure	Association rule	Support
{a}	{ac}	$a \rightarrow c$	3/5
{ab}	{abce}	$ab \rightarrow c$	2/5
{ab}	{abce}	$ab \rightarrow e$	2/5
{ae}	{abce}	$ae \rightarrow c$	2/5
{ae}	{abce}	$ae \rightarrow b$	2/5
{b}	{bce}	$b \rightarrow c$	4/5
{b}	{bce}	$b \rightarrow e$	4/5
{e}	{bce}	$e \rightarrow b$	4/5
{e}	{bce}	$e \rightarrow c$	4/5

Table 5. Min-Min approximate association rules

Generator	Equivalence class	Association rule	Support	Confidence
{a}	[abce]	$a \rightarrow bc$	2/5	2/3
{a}	[abce]	$a \rightarrow be$	2/5	2/3
{a}	[abce]	$a \rightarrow ce$	2/5	2/3
{b}	[abce]	$b \rightarrow ac$	2/5	2/4
{b}	[abce]	$b \rightarrow ae$	2/5	2/4
{c}	[ac]	$c \rightarrow a$	3/5	3/5
{c}	[bce]	$c \rightarrow b$	4/5	4/5
{c}	[bce]	$c \rightarrow e$	4/5	4/5
{c}	[abce]	$c \rightarrow ab$	2/5	2/5
{c}	[abce]	$c \rightarrow ae$	2/5	2/5
{e}	[abce]	$e \rightarrow ab$	2/5	2/4
{e}	[abce]	$e \rightarrow ac$	2/5	2/4

approximate association rules $c \rightarrow b$, $c \rightarrow e$ and $c \rightarrow be$ of the same class of association rules, $c \rightarrow be$ is the one with the highest scope as it contains the information contained in each other rule. Statistical measures of differential information use a similar criterion to evaluate rule interestingness (Mc Garry, 2005).

Generators and frequent closed itemsets are respectively the minimal and the maximal itemsets in a class of association rules. Consequently, association rules with minimal antecedent and maximal consequent are association rules between generators and frequent closed itemsets that are their supersets. If all classes of association rules are considered, we obtain a set of association rules covering all sets of items and objects covered by the set of all strong association rules. These rules are the informative association rules with minimal antecedent and maximal consequent. They are called *generic* or *min-max association rules*. They constitute the Generic Basis for association rules (Bastide *et al.*, 2000a).

From a structural viewpoint, an association rule R: $A \rightarrow C$ is a generic association rule if there is no association rule R': $A' \rightarrow C'$ with the same support and confidence, whose antecedent A' is a subset of the antecedent A of R and whose consequent C' is a superset of the consequent C of R. An inference system based on this definition of generic association rules was proposed in Cristofor & Simovici (2002). Kryszkiewicz (2002) demonstrated that the set of generic association rules is lossless and sound, and that both properties are important since condensed representations of strong association rules that are not sound are of no value even if lossless.

The Generic Basis for exact association rules contains all association rules between a frequent generator G and its closure C. Each of these association rules represents several rules within the same class of association rules and covering exactly the same objects and items. Then, the number of generic exact association rules is equal to the number of frequent generators in equivalence classes containing more than one itemset. The Generic Basis for exact association rules for the example dataset D and *minsup* = 2/5 and *minconf* = 2/5 is represented in Table 6.

The Generic Basis for approximate association rules contains all association rules between a frequent generator G and each of the frequent closed itemsets $C_1, ..., C_n$ that are supersets of the

Table 6. Generic basis for exact association rules

Generator	Closure	Association rule	Support
{a}	{ac}	a → c	3/5
{ab}	{abce}	ab → ce	2/5
{ae}	{abce}	ae → bc	2/5
{b}	{bce}	b → ce	4/5
{e}	{bce}	e → bc	4/5

closure of G. As for exact association rules, each generic approximate association rule represents several approximate association rules in the same class of association rules and covering exactly the same objects and items. The Generic Basis for approximate association rules for the example dataset D and *minsup* = 2/5 and *minconf* = 2/5 is represented in Table 7.

The transitive reduction of the Generic Basis for approximate association rules is the reduction according to the transitivity inference rule used to define the transitive reduction of the Proper Basis. Considering association rules in Table 7, the only transitive rule is $c \rightarrow abe$ and we have *confidence*($c \rightarrow abe$) = *confidence*($c \rightarrow be$) × *confidence*($b \rightarrow ace$) = 4/5 × 2/4 = 2/5. This rule can thus be deduced from rules $c \rightarrow be$ and $b \rightarrow ace$ or $e \rightarrow abc$, or from $c \rightarrow a$ and $a \rightarrow bce$. This rule has a lower confidence than the non-

transitive rules as its confidence is the product of their confidences that are lower than 100 %. This transitive reduction allows to further reduce the number of rules by suppressing the generic association rules that have the smallest confidences and are thus the least relevant for the end-user among generic association rules of the same class of association rules.

The union of the Generic bases for exact and approximate association rules is a basis for all strong association rules (Bastide *et al.*, 2000a). The Generic Basis for association rules was defined to provide the end-user with a set of association rules as small as possible, containing only the most relevant association rules and covering all strong co-occurrence relationships between two itemsets. This informative basis holds several properties:

- It contains informative association rules with minimal antecedent and maximal consequent. This property simplifies the interpretation by the end-user, as association rules with smaller antecedents are easier to interpret, and the information in each rule is maximized to minimize their number.
- It implicitly separates approximate association rules and exact association rules. This distinction can be made during the computation to extract a Generic Basis for exact, approximate or both association rules.

Table 7. Generic basis for approximate association rules

Generator	Closed superset	Association rule	Support	Confidence
{a}	{abce}	a → bce	2/5	2/3
{b}	{abce}	b → ace	2/5	2/4
{c}	{ac}	c → a	3/5	3/5
{c}	{bce}	c → be	4/5	4/5
{c}	{abce}	c → abe	2/5	2/5
{e}	{abce}	e → abc	2/5	2/4

- It is information lossless as all strong association rules can be deduced with their support and precision measures.

- Each generic association rule summarizes a set of association rules covering the same items and objects of the dataset. This property ensures that all information on itemset relationships are in the basis and can be presented to the end-user without having to perform a computation during the interpretation phase.

- Its generation does not require extra computation when a frequent closed itemset based algorithm is used as it can be integrated directly in the mining process.

- It can efficiently be generated from a set of strong association rules as a post-processing phase at little extra computation cost. This generation is straightforward and does not require accessing the dataset or the frequent itemsets. Algorithms for this generation are presented in Pasquier *et al.* (2005).

In the example dataset *D,* fifty association rules are strong for *minsup* = 2/5 and *minconf* = 2/5 whereas the Generic Basis contains eleven association rules. The number of association rules in this basis is linear in the number of frequent closed itemsets. It is not minimal with respect to the number of association rules, but it is a balanced solution for both reducing the number of rules and keeping an easy to interpret set of rules covering all existing relationships between itemsets. The Generic Basis constitutes an interesting starting point to reduce the size of the association rule set without information loss (Hamrouni *et al.,* 2006). Kryszkiewicz (2002) stated that the couple of the Generic bases for exact and approximate association rules combines the ideal properties of a condensed representation for association rules as it is lossless, sound and informative.

Extensions of the Generic Basis for Association Rules

The problem of defining a generating set that is minimal with respect to the number of association rules was the subject of several recent studies (Dong *et al.*, 2005; Gasmi *et al.*, 2005; Hamrouni *et al.*, 2006). These minimal generating sets are easier to manage and all strong association rules can be deduced from them, with support and precision measures, for interpretation by the end-user. From these generating sets, condensed representations such as the Generic Basis can be generated and presented to the end-user.

Dong *et al.* (2005) showed that some frequent generators can be deduced from other frequent generators by a subset substitution process. A condensed representation named SSMG for *Succinct System of Minimal Generators* from which all generators and all frequent closed itemsets can be inferred with their supports was proposed. In this condensed representation, only one generator, that is the first in the lexicographic order on itemsets, represents each class of association rules. However, Hamrouni *et al.* (2007) demonstrated that the SSMG set is not lossless and new definitions to ensure this lossless property were proposed in Hamrouni *et al.* (2008). A new lossless and sound basis for association rules relying on these definitions was also defined.

Gasmi *et al.* (2005) introduced the *IGB Basis* derived from the Generic bases for exact and approximate association rules. This basis introduces a novel characterization of generic association rules by discerning *factual* and *implicative* association rules instead of exact and approximate ones. Factual association rules have an empty antecedent and highlight unconditional correlations between items whereas implicative association rules have a non empty antecedent. They showed that the IGB basis is lossless and sound and an inference system with conditional reflexivity, augmentation and decomposition inference rules was defined to enable the inference all strong association rules.

The *Reliable Exact Basis* for exact association rules was defined by Xu & Li (2007) by relaxing the requirements for non-redundancy of the Generic bases and thus suppressing more association rules. This basis is constructed using the certainty factor measure or CF to evaluate generic association rules. The CF of an association rule $R: A \rightarrow C$ evaluates both the degree of the belief that the consequent C would be increased if the antecedent A was observed, and the degree of the disbelief that the consequent C would be increased by observing the same antecedent A. The Reliable Exact Basis is constructed using the CF to filter association rules in the Generic Basis with measures lower than some user defined thresholds. However, precision measures of all suppressed strong association rules cannot be deduced and this condensed representation is not lossless.

Cheng *et al.* (2008) defined δ-Tolerance Association Rules or δ-TARs using a new concept, called δ-tolerance, based on the approximation of frequent closed itemset supports. An inference system to infer all strong association rules from the δ-TARs, with approximated support and confidence, was also defined. The set of δ-TARs is a condensed representation for the set of strong association rules but is not lossless. The authors affirm that the set of association rules derived from the δ-TARs by this inference system is sound and complete and that approximations of supports and confidences are accurate.

FUTURE TRENDS

Extracting a set of association rules containing only the most interesting and useful association rules to the end-user is still an important research field. Several solutions addressing this problem have been proposed. These solutions can be classified in two main categories:

- Objective methods that are based on objective interestingness measures, association rule structural properties or hierarchical structures describing relations between items to filter, merge or generalize association rules in order to suppress redundant patterns.
- Subjective methods that integrate the user's beliefs and background knowledge in the domain to suppress uninteresting association rules and select the mot interesting association rules from the user's viewpoint.

An important research topic in this domain is: How can we integrate the different solutions from these two categories in order to select association rules that are the most interesting from both the statistical, the structural and the user's knowledge viewpoints?

Such a method, integrating both subjective and objective pruning criteria, was recently proposed by Chen *et al.* (2008). This method, based on semantic networks to represent user's knowledge, classifies association rules into five categories: Trivial, known and correct, unknown and correct, known and incorrect, unknown and incorrect. Preliminary experiments on a biomedical dataset showed that the reduction can be very important as more than 97 % strong association rules were identified as trivial or incorrect.

This preliminary work show that such methods could greatly improve the usefulness of association rule extraction. An interesting topic in this direction is the development of efficient methods to integrate user's knowledge in the discovery of condensed representations to select the most relevant association rules from the user's viewpoint. This integration could also be done during the visualization phase, by integrating quality measures and user defined constraints for instance.

CONCLUSION

The frequent closed itemsets theoretical framework was introduced in association rule mining to address the efficiency problem of mining large datasets containing dense or highly correlated data. Several posterior studies showed that this framework is also well-suited to address the problem of redundant association rules that is crucial in most applications. These association rules often constitute the majority of extracted association rules when mining large datasets. They are informatively useless and their suppression is highly desirable to improve the relevance of extracted association rules and simplify their interpretation by the end-user. This chapter focuses on condensed representations and bases for association rules. They are characterized in the frequent closed itemsets framework to show their properties from the theoretical, intelligibility, soundness and informativeness viewpoints.

Condensed representations are reduced sets of association rules summarizing a set of strong association rules. Several condensed representations such as the DG and Proper bases (Pasquier *et al.*, 1999b), the SSMG (Dong *et al.*; 2005), the Reliable Exact Basis (Xu & Li, 2007) and the δ-TARs set (Cheng *et al.*, 2008) were proposed in the literature. These condensed representations are not information lossless since some strong association rules cannot be deduced, with their supports and precision measures, from the rules in the basis. Even if they are not information lossless, they represent interesting alternatives for the presentation to the end-user of a very small set of association rules selected among the most relevant association rules according to objective criteria.

Condensed representations that are information lossless, i.e. from which all strong association rules can be deduced, are called generating sets. Generating sets are defined according to an inference system determining how this deduction is done. A generating set that is minimal with respect to the number of association rules is called a basis. Strong association rules that are deducible by inference are called redundant association rules and a basis contains only non-redundant association rules. A basis covering all itemsets and objects

covered by the set of strong association rules is called an informative basis. In other words, each strong association rule must be represented by an association rule of the informative basis. This property is important for the intelligibility of the basis as it ensures that all information are present in the basis and that no computation is required during the interpretation phase.

The minimal antecedent and consequent basis (Zaki, 2000), the Generic Basis (Bastide *et al.*, 2000a) and the IGB Basis (Gasmi *et al.*, 2005) are informative bases defined according to different criteria that correspond to different inference systems. Several studies have shown that these bases are lossless, sound and contain a small number of association rules, that is the minimal number of rules with respect to their inference system. The minimal antecedent and consequent basis was defined outside the scope of the frequent closed itemsets framework. It was defined according to the property that rules with the smallest antecedents are the easiest to interpret for the end-user. By construction, they also have a minimal consequent. The Generic Basis, defined according to the frequent closed itemsets framework, contains rules with the smallest antecedent and the maximal consequent, in order to ease their interpretation and maximize the information in each rule (Mc Garry, 2005). The Generic Basis brings to the end-user all knowledge contained in the strong association rules in a minimal number of association rules without information loss. This basis maximizes the information contained in each association rule and several rules of the minimal antecedent and consequent basis can be summarized by one rule of the Generic Basis. The IGB Basis is an extension of the Generic Basis. It introduces a new kind of rules with an empty antecedent that represent unconditional co-occurrences of items in the dataset. Then, the association rules of the Generic Basis that can be deduced using these item co-occurrence rules are suppressed to form the IGB Basis. These three informative bases define a compact set of relevant association rules that is easier to interpret for the end-user. Since their size is reduced and as they are generating sets, they also constitute efficient solutions for the long-term storage on secondary memories and the computer-aided management of a set of strong association rules.

REFERENCES

Agrawal, R., Imielinski, T., & Swami, A.N. (1993). Mining association rules between sets of items in large databases. *Proceedings of the SIGMOD Conference* (pp. 207-216).

Angiulli, F., Ianni, G., & Palopoli, L. (2001). On the complexity of mining association rules. *Proceedings of the SEBD conference* (pp. 177-184).

Armstrong, W. W. (1974). Dependency structures of data base relationships. *Proceedings of the IFIP congress* (pp. 580-583).

Baralis, E., & Psaila, G. (1997). Designing templates for mining association rules. *Journal of Intelligent Information Systems, 9*, 7-32.

Bastide, Y., Pasquier, N., Taouil, R., Lakhal, L., & Stumme, G. (2000a). Mining minimal non-redundant association rules using frequent closed itemsets. *Proceedings of the CL conference* (pp. 972-986).

Bastide, Y., Pasquier, N., Taouil, R., Stumme, G., & Lakhal, L. (2000b). Mining frequent patterns with counting inference. *SIGKDD Explorations, 2*(2), 66-75.

Bayardo, R. J., & Agrawal, R. (1999). Mining the most interesting rules. *Proceedings of the KDD conference* (pp. 145-154).

Bayardo, R. J., Agrawal, R., & Gunopulos, D. (2000). Constraint-based rule mining in large, dense databases. Knowledge Discovery and Data Mining, *4*(2), 217-240.

Ben Yahia, S., Hamrouni, T., & Nguifo, E.M. (2006). Frequent closed itemset based algorithms: A thorough structural and analytical survey. *SIGKDD Explorations, 8*(1), 93-104.

Bonchi, F., Giannotti, F., Mazzanti, A., & Pedreschi, D. (2005). Efficient breadth-first mining of frequent pattern with monotone constraints. *Knowledge and Information Systems, 8*(2), 131-153.

Bonchi, F., & Lucchese, C. (2004). On closed constrained frequent pattern mining. *Proceeding of the IEEE ICDM conference* (pp. 35-42).

Bonchi, F., & Lucchese, C. (2006). On condensed representations of constrained frequent patterns. *Knowledge and Information Systems, 9*(2), 180-201.

Boulicaut, J. F., Bykowski, A., & Rigotti, C. (2003). Free-sets: A condensed representation of boolean data for the approximation of frequency queries. *Data Mining and Knowledge Discovery, 7*, 5-22.

Boulicaut, J. F., Jeudy, B. (2002). Optimization of association rule mining queries. *Intelligent Data Analysis Journal, 6*, 341–357.

Brin, S., Motwani, R., Ullman, J. D., & Tsur., S. (1997). Dynamic itemset counting and implication rules for market basket data. *Proceedings ACM SIGMOD conference* (pp. 255-264).

Brijs, T., Vanhoof, K., & Wets, G. (2003). Defining interestingness for association rules. *International Journal of Information Theories and Applications, 10*(4), 370–376.

Ceglar, A., & Roddick, J.F. (2006). Association mining. *ACM Computing Surveys, 38*(2).

Cheng, J., Ke, Y., & Ng, W. (2008). Effective elimination of redundant association rules. *Data Mining and Knowledge Discovery, 16*(2), 221-249.

Chen, P., Verma, R., Meininger, J. C., & Chan, W. (2008). Semantic analysis of association rules.

Proceedings of the FLAIRS Conference, Miami, Florida.

Cheung, Y.-L., & Fu, A. (2004). Mining frequent itemsets without support threshold: With and without item constraints. *IEEE Transactions on Knowledge and Data Engineering, 16*(9), 1052-1069.

Cristofor, L., & Simovici, D.A. (2002). Generating an informative cover for association rules. *Proceedings of the ICDM conference.*

Deogun, J.S., & Jiang, L. (2005). SARM - succinct association rule mining: An approach to enhance association mining. *Proceedings ISMIS conference* (pp. 121-130), *LNCS 3488.*

Dong, G., Jiang, C., Pei, J., Li, J., & Wong, L. (2005). Mining succinct systems of minimal generators of formal concepts. *Proceeding of the DASFAA conference* (pp. 175-187). *LNCS 3453.*

Duquenne, V., & Guigues, J.-L. (1986). Famille minimale d'implications informatives résultant d'un tableau de données binaires. *Mathématiques et Sciences Humaines, 24*(95), 5-18.

Freitas, A. (1999). On rule interestingness measures. *Knowledge-Based Systems, 12*(5), 309-315.

Carvalho, D. R., Freitas, A. A., & Ebecken, N. F. (2005). Evaluating the correlation between objective rule interestingness measures and real human interest. *Proceedings of the PKDD conference* (pp. 453-461).

Ganter, B., Stumme, G., & Wille, R. (2005). Formal Concept Analysis: Foundations and applications. *Lecture Notes in Computer Science, 3626.*

Gasmi, G., Ben Yahia, S., Nguifo, E. M., & Slimani, Y. (2005). IGB: A new informative generic base of association rules. *Proceedings of the PAKDD conference* (pp. 81-90).

Geng, L., & Hamilton, H. J. (2006). Interestingness measures for data mining: A survey. *ACM Computing Surveys, 38*(3).

Goethals, B., Muhonen, J., & Toivonen, H. (2005). Mining non-derivable association rules. *Proceedings of the SIAM conference.*

Hamrouni, T., Ben Yahia, S., & Mephu Nguifo, E. (2006). Generic association rule bases: Are they so succinct? *Proceedings of the CLA conference* (pp. 198-213).

Hamrouni, T., Ben Yahia, S., Mephu Nguifo, E., & Valtchev, P. (2007). About the Lossless Reduction of the Minimal Generator Family of a Context. *Proceedings of the ICFCA conference* (pp. 130-150).

Hamrouni, T., Ben Yahia, S., & Mephu Nguifo, E. (2008). Succinct system of minimal generators: A thorough study, limitations and new definitions. *Lecture Notes in Computer Science, 4923,* 80-95.

Han, J., & Fu, Y. (1995). Discovery of multiple-level association rules from large databases. *Proceedings of the VLDB conference* (pp. 420-431).

Hilderman, R., & Hamilton, H. (1999). Heuristic measures of interestingness. *Proceedings of the PKDD conference* (pp. 232-241).

Hilderman, R., & Hamilton, H. (2001). Knowledge Discovery and Measures of Interest. Kluwer Academic Publishers.

Hussain, F., Liu, H., Suzuki, E., & Lu, H. (2000). Exception rule mining with a relative interestingness measure. *Proceedings of the PAKDD conference* (pp. 86–97).

Jaroszewicz, S., & Scheffer, T. (2005). Fast discovery of unexpected patterns in data relative to a bayesian network. *Proceeding of the ACM SIGKDD conference* (pp. 118-127).

Klemettinen, M., Mannila, H., Ronkainen, P., Toivonen, H., & Verkamo, A.I. (1994). Finding interesting rules from large sets of discovered association rules. *Proceedings of the CIKM conference* (pp. 401-407).

Kryszkiewicz, M. (1998). Representative association rules and minimum condition maximum consequence association rules. *Proceedings of the PKDD conference* (pp. 361-369), *LNCS 1510*.

Kryszkiewicz, M. (2002). Concise representations of association rules. *Lecture Notes in Computer Science, 2447*, 187-203.

Lakshmanan, L., Ng, R., Han, J., & Pang, A. (1999). Optimization of constrained frequent set queries with 2-variable constraints. *Proceeding of the ACM SIGMOD international conference* (pp. 157-168).

Lenca, P., Meyer, P., Vaillant, B., & Lallich, S. (2008). On selecting interestingness measures for association rules: User oriented description and multiple criteria decision aid. *European Journal of Operational Research, 184*(2), 610-626.

Leung, C., Lakshmanan, L., & Ng, R. (2002). Exploiting succinct constraints using FP-Trees. *ACM SIGKDD Explorations, 4*(1), 40-49.

Li, J., Li, H., Wong, L., Pei, J., & Dong, G. (2006). Minimum description length (MDL) principle: Generators are preferable to closed patterns. *Proceedings of the AAAI conference* (pp. 409-414).

Li, J., Tang, B., & Cercone, N. (2004). Applying association rules for interesting recommendations using rule templates. *Proceedings of the PAKDD conference* (pp. 166-170).

Liu, B., Hsu, W., Mun, L.-F. & Lee, H.-Y. (1999). Finding interesting patterns using user expectations. *Knowledge and Data Engineering, 11*(6), 817-832.

Liu, B., Hsu, W., & Chen, S. (1997). Using general impressions to analyze discovered classification rules. *Proceedings of the KDD conference* (pp. 31-36).

Liu, B., Hsu, W., & Ma, Y. (1999). Pruning and summarizing the discovered associations. *Proceedings of the ACM SIGKDD conference* (pp. 125-134).

Liu, H., Lu, H., Feng, L., & Hussain, F. (1999). Efficient search of reliable exceptions. *Proceedings of the PAKDD conference* (pp. 194-204).

Liu, G., Li, J., & Limsoon, W. (2007). A new concise representation of frequent itemsets using generators and a positive border. *Knowledge and Information Systems, 13*.

Lu, N., Wang-Zhe, C.-G. Zhou; J.-Z. Zhou. (2005). Research on association rule mining algorithms with item constraints. *Proceedings of the CW conference*.

Luxenburger, M. (1991). Implications partielles dans un contexte. *Mathématiques, Informatique et Sciences Humaines, 29*(113), 35-55.

McGarry, K. (2005). A survey of interestingness measures for knowledge discovery. *The Knowledge Engineering Review.* Cambridge University Press.

Maier, D. (1983). *The theory of Relational Databases*. Computer Science Press.

Matheus, C. J., Chan, P. K., & Piatetsky-Shapiro, G. (1993). Systems for knowledge discovery in databases, *IEEE Transactions on Knowledge and Data Engineering, 5*(6), 903-913.

Ng, R., Lakshmanan, L., Han, J., & Pang, A (1998). Exploratory mining and pruning optimizations of constrained associations rules. *Proceeding of the ACM SIGMOD conference* (pp. 13–24).

Padmanabhan, B., & Tuzhilin, A. (1998). A belief driven method for discovering unexpected patterns. *Proceedings of the KDD conference* (pp. 94-100).

Padmanabhan, B., & Tuzhilin, A. (2000). Small is beautiful: Discovering the minimal set of unexpected patterns. *Proceedings of the KDD conference* (pp. 54-63).

Pasquier, N., Bastide, Y., Taouil, R., & Lakhal, L. (1998). Pruning closed itemset lattices for association rules. *Proceedings of the BDA conference* (pp. 177-196).

Pasquier, N., Bastide, Y., Taouil, R., & Lakhal, L. (1999a). Efficient mining of association rules using closed itemset lattices. *Information Systems*, 24(1), 25-46.

Pasquier, N., Bastide, Y., Taouil, R., & Lakhal, L. (1999b). Discovering frequent closed itemsets for association rules. *Proceedings of the ICDT conference* (pp. 398-416).

Pasquier, N., Taouil, R., Bastide, Y., Stumme, G., & Lakhal, L. (2005). Generating a condensed representation for association rules. *Journal of Intelligent Information Systems*, 24(1), 29-60.

Pasquier, N. (2005). Mining association rules using frequent closed itemsets. In J. Wang (Ed.), *Encyclopedia of Data Warehousing and Mining* (pp. 752-757). Idea Group Publishing.

Pei, J., Han, J., & Lakshmanan, L. V. (2001). Mining frequent itemsets with convertible constraints. *Proceedings of the ICDE conference* (pp. 433–442).

Pei, .J, & Han, J. (2002). Constrained frequent pattern mining: A pattern-growth view. *ACM SIGKDD Explorations*, 4(1), 31-39.

Pfaltz, J., & Taylor, C. (2002). Closed set mining of biological data. *Proceedings of the BioKDD conference* (pp. 43-48).

Piatetsky-Shapiro, G. (1991). Discovery, analysis, and presentation of strong rules. *Knowledge Discovery in Databases* (pp. 229-248), AAAI/MIT Press.

Piatetsky-Shapiro, G., & Matheus, C. (1994). The interestingness of deviations. *Proceedings of the KDD conference* (pp. 25-36).

Silberschatz, A., & Tuzhilin, A. (1996). What makes patterns interesting in knowledge discovery systems. *IEEE Transaction on Knowledge and Data Engineering*, 8(6), 970-974.

Silverstein, C., Brin, S., Motwani, R., & Ullman, J. D. (2000). Scalable techniques for mining causal structures. *Data Mining and Knowledge Discovery*, 4(2), 163-192.

Srikant, R., & Agrawal, A. (1995). Mining Generalized Association Rules. *Proceedings of the VLDB conference* (pp. 407-419).

Srikant, R., Vu, Q., & Agrawal, R. (1997). Mining association rules with item constraints. *Proceedings of the KDD conference* (pp. 67-73).

Stumme, G., Pasquier, N., Bastide, Y., Taouil, R., & Lakhal, L. (2001). Intelligent structuring and reducing of association rules with formal concept analysis. *Proceeding of the KI conference* (pp. 335-350). *LNCS 2174*.

Tan, P., Kumar, V., & Srivastava, J. (2002). Selecting the right interestingness measure for association patterns. *Proceedings of the ACM SIGKDD conference* (pp. 32-41).

Toivonen H., Klemettinen, M., Ronkainen, P., Hätönen, K., & Mannila, H. (1995). Pruning and grouping discovered association rules. *Proceedings of the ECML workshop* (pp. 47-52).

Valtchev, P., Missaoui, R., & Godin, R. (2004). Formal concept analysis for knowledge discovery and data mining: The new challenges. *Lecture Notes in Computer Science*, 2961, 352-371.

Wang, K., Jiang, Y., & Lakshmanan, L. (2003). Mining unexpected rules by pushing user dynamics. *Proceeding of the ACM SIGKDD conference* (pp. 246–255).

Xu, Y., & Li, Y. (2007). Generating concise association rules. *Proceedings of the ACM CIKM conference* (pp. 781-790).

Zaki, M.J. (2000). Generating non-redundant association rules. *Proceedings of the KDD conference*.

Zaki, M.J. (2004). Mining non-redundant association rules. *Data Mining and Knowledge Discovery*, 9(3), 223-248.

ENDNOTES

[1]   Data lines correspond to data rows when the dataset is represented as a data matrix and to transactions when the dataset is represented as a transactional database. Each data line contains a set of items and the set of data lines constitute the dataset.

[2]   The generic term *object* refers to a data line represented either as a data row or as a transaction.

[3]   Maximal and minimal itemsets are defined according to the inclusion relation.

[4]   The set of objects *covered* by an association rule is defined as the set of objects containing the items in the antecedent and the consequent of the rule.

[5]   A set of inference rules define a procedure which combines association rules in the basis to deduce, or infer, other strong association rules.

[6]   In the rest of the chapter, statistical measures of precision computed from supports of the antecedent and consequent itemsets of association rule only are noted "precision measures" for simplicity.

Section VI
Maintenance of Association Rules and New Forms of Association Rules

Chapter XIV
Maintenance of
Frequent Patterns:
A Survey

Mengling Feng
Nanyang Technological University, Singapore
National University of Singapore, Singapore

Jinyan Li
Nanyang Technological University, Singapore

Guozhu Dong
Wright State University, USA

Limsoon Wong
National University of Singapore, Singapore

ABSTRACT

This chapter surveys the maintenance of frequent patterns in transaction datasets. It is written to be accessible to researchers familiar with the field of frequent pattern mining. The frequent pattern maintenance problem is summarized with a study on how the space of frequent patterns evolves in response to data updates. This chapter focuses on incremental and decremental maintenance. Four major types of maintenance algorithms are studied: Apriori-based, partition-based, prefix-tree-based, and concise-representation-based algorithms. The authors study the advantages and limitations of these algorithms from both the theoretical and experimental perspectives. Possible solutions to certain limitations are also proposed. In addition, some potential research opportunities and emerging trends in frequent pattern maintenance are also discussed[1].

INTRODUCTION

A frequent pattern, also named as a frequent itemset, refers to a pattern that appears frequently in a particular dataset. The concept of frequent pattern is first introduced in Agrawal et al. (1993). Frequent patterns play an essential role in various knowledge discovery and data mining (KDD) tasks, such as the discovery of association rules (Agrawal et al. 1993), correlations (Brin et al.1997), causality (Silverstein et al. 1998), sequential patterns (Agrawal et al. 1995), partial periodicity (Han et al. 1999), emerging patterns (Dong & Li 1999), etc.

Updates are a fundamental aspect of data management in frequent pattern mining applications. Other than real-life updates, they are also used in interactive data mining to gauge the impact caused by hypothetical changes to the data. When a database is updated frequently, repeating the knowledge discovery process from scratch during each update causes significant computational and I/O overheads. Therefore, it is important to analyse how the discovered knowledge may change in response to updates, so as to formulate more effective algorithms to maintain the discovered knowledge on the updated database.

This chapter studies the problem of frequent pattern maintenance and surveys some of the current work. We give an overview of the challenges in frequent pattern maintenance and introduce some specific approaches that address these challenges. This should not be taken as an exhaustive account as there are too many existing approaches to be included.

The current frequent pattern maintenance approaches can be classified into four main categories: 1) *Apriori*-based approaches, 2) *Partition*-based approaches, 3) *Prefix-tree*-based approaches and 4) *Concise-representation*-based approaches. In the following section, the basic definitions and concepts of frequent pattern maintenance are introduced. Next, we study some representative frequent pattern maintenance approaches from

both theoretical and experimental perspectives. Some potential research opportunities and emerging trends in frequent pattern maintenance are also discussed.

PRELIMINARIES AND PROBLEM DESCRIPTION

Discovery of Frequent Patterns

Let $I = \{i_1, i_2, ..., i_m\}$ be a set of distinct literals called 'items'. A 'pattern', or an 'itemset', is a set of items. A 'transaction' is a non-empty set of items. A 'dataset' is a non-empty set of transactions. A pattern P is said to be contained or included in a transaction T if $P \subseteq T$. A pattern P is said to be contained in a dataset D, denoted as $P \in D$, if there is $T \in D$ such that $P \subseteq T$. The 'support count' of a pattern P in a dataset D, denoted $count(P,D)$, is the number of transactions in D that contain P. The 'support' of a pattern P in a dataset D, denoted $sup(P,D)$, is calculated as $sup(P,D) = count(P,D)/|D|$. Figure 1(a) shows a sample dataset, and all the patterns contained in the sample dataset are enumerated in Figure 1(b) with their support counts.

A pattern P is said to be *frequent* in a dataset D if $sup(P,D)$ is greater than or equal to a pre-specified threshold $ms_\%$. Given a dataset D and a support threshold $ms_\%$, the collection of all frequent itemsets in D is called the 'space of frequent patterns', and is denoted by $F(ms_\%,D)$. The task of frequent pattern mining is to discover all the patterns in the space of frequent patterns. In real-life applications, the size of the frequent pattern space is often tremendous. According to the definition, suppose the dataset has l distinct items, the size of the frequent pattern space can go up to 2^l. To increase computational efficiency and reduce memory usage, concise representations are developed to summarize the frequent pattern space.

Concise Representations of Frequent Patterns

The concise representations of frequent patterns are developed based on the *a priori* (or anti-monotone) property (Agrawal et al. 1993) of frequent patterns.

FACT 1 (A priori Property). Given a dataset D and a support threshold $ms_\%$, if pattern $P \in F(D, ms_\%)$, then for every pattern $Q \subseteq P$, $Q \in F(D, ms_\%)$; on the other hand, if pattern $P \notin F(D, ms_\%)$, then for every pattern $Q \supseteq P$, $Q \notin F(D, ms_\%)$.

The *a priori* property basically says that all subsets of frequent patterns are frequent and all supersets of infrequent patterns are infrequent.

The commonly used concise representations of frequent patterns include maximal patterns (Bayardo 1998), closed patterns (Pasquier et al.1999), key patterns (a.k.a. generators) (Pasquier et al. 1999) and equivalence classes (Li et al. 2005). Figure 1(b) graphically demonstrates how the frequent pattern space of the sample dataset can

be concisely summarized with maximal patterns, closed patterns and key patterns, and Figure 1(c) illustrates how the pattern space can be compactly represented with equivalence classes.

Maximal Pattern Representation

Maximal patterns are first introduced in Bayardo (1998). Frequent maximal patterns refer to the longest patterns that are frequent, and they are formally defined as follows.

Definition 1 (Maximal Pattern). Given a dataset D and a support threshold $ms_\%$, a pattern P is a frequent 'maximal pattern', iff $sup(P,D) \geq ms_\%$ and, for every $Q \supset P$, it is the case that $sup(Q,D) < ms_\%$.

The maximal pattern representation is composed of a set of frequent maximal patterns annotated with their support values. The maximal pattern representation is the most compact representation of the frequent pattern space. As shown in Figure 1(b), one maximal pattern is already sufficient to represent the entire pattern

Figure 1. (a) An example of transaction dataset. (b) The space of frequent patterns for the sample dataset in (a) when $ms_\% = 25\%$ and the concise representations of the space. (c) Decomposition of frequent pattern space into equivalence classes.

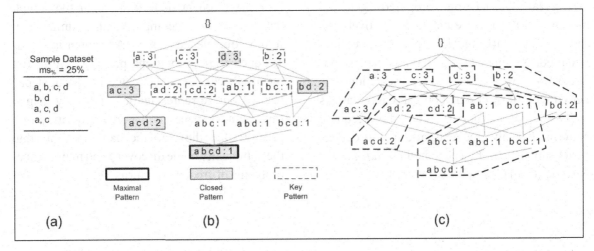

space that consists of 15 patterns. Based on the *a priori* property (Agrawal et al. 1993) of frequent patterns, one can enumerate all frequent patterns from the frequent maximal patterns. However, the representation lacks the information to derive the exact support of frequent patterns. Therefore, the maximal pattern representation is a lossy representation.

Closed Pattern and Key Pattern Representations

Unlike the maximal pattern representation, both the closed pattern and key pattern representations are lossless concise representations of frequent patterns. We say a representation is lossless if it is sufficient to derive and determine the support of all frequent patterns without accessing the datasets. The concepts of closed patterns and key patterns are introduced together in Pasquier (1999).

Definition 2 (Closed Pattern). Given a dataset D, a pattern P is a 'closed pattern', iff for every $Q \supset P$, it is the case that $sup(Q,D) < sup(P,D)$.

For a dataset D and support threshold $ms_\%$, the closed pattern representation is constructed with the set of frequent closed patterns, denoted as $FC(D,ms_\%)$, and their corresponding support information. Algorithms, such as *FPclose* (Grahne et al. 2003), *CLOSET* (Pei et al 2000) & *CLOSET+* (Wang et al 2003), have been proposed to generate the closed pattern representation effectively. As shown in Figure 1(b), the closed pattern representation is not as compact as the maximal representation. However, it is a lossless representation. The closed pattern representation can enumerate as well as derive the support values of all frequent patterns. For any frequent pattern P in dataset D, its support can be calculated as: $sup(P,D) = max\{sup(C,D)|C \supseteq P, C \in FC(D,ms_\%)\}$.

Definition 3 (Key Pattern). Given a dataset D, a pattern P is a 'key pattern', iff for every $Q \subset P$, it is the case that $sup(Q,D) > sup(P,D)$.

For a dataset D and support threshold $ms_\%$, the key pattern representation is constructed with the set of frequent key patterns, denoted as $FG(D,ms_\%)$, and their corresponding support information. The key pattern representation is also lossless. For any frequent pattern P in dataset D, its support can be calculated as: $sup(P,D) = min\{sup(G,D)|G \subseteq P, G \in FG(D,ms_\%)\}$.

Equivalence Class Representation

Li et al. (2005) have discovered that the frequent pattern space can be structurally decomposed into sub-spaces --- equivalence classes.

Definition 4 (Equivalence Class). Let the 'filter', $f(P,D)$, of a pattern P in a dataset D be defined as $f(P,D) = \{T \in D \mid P \subseteq T\}$. Then the 'equivalence class' $[P]_D$ of P in a dataset D is the collection of patterns defined as $[P]_D = \{Q \mid f(P,D) = f(Q,D),$ Q *is a pattern in* $D\}$.

In other words, two patterns are 'equivalent' in the context of a dataset D iff they are included in exactly the same transactions in D. Thus the patterns in a given equivalence class have the same support. Figure 1(c) graphically illustrates how the frequent pattern space of the sample dataset can be decomposed and summarized into 5 equivalence classes. As shown in Figure 1, concise representations provide us effective means to compress the space of frequent patterns. Concise representations not only help to save memory spaces, but, more importantly, they greatly reduce the size of the search space and thus the complexity of the discovery and maintenance problems of frequent patterns.

MAINTENANCE OF FREQUENT PATTERNS

Data is dynamic in nature. Datasets are often updated in the applications of frequent pattern mining. Data update operations include addition/ removal of items, insertion/deletion of transactions, modifications of existing transactions, etc. In this chapter, we focus on the two most common update scenarios, where new transactions are inserted into the original dataset and obsolete transactions are removed.

When new transactions are added to the original dataset, the new transactions are called the 'incremental dataset', and the update operation is called the 'incremental update'. The associated maintenance process is called the 'incremental maintenance'. When obsolete transactions are removed from the original dataset, the removed transactions are called the 'decremental dataset', and the update operation is called the 'decremental update'. The associated maintenance process is called the 'decremental maintenance'. For the rest of the chapter, we use notations D_{org} to denote the original dataset, D_{upd} to denote the updated dataset, d^+ to denote the incremental dataset and d^- to denote the decremental dataset. In incremental updates, where new transactions d^+ are added, we have $D_{upd} = D_{org} \cup d^+$ and thus $|D_{upd}| = |D_{org}| + |d^+|$. On the other hand, in decremental updates, where existing transactions are removed, we have $D_{upd} = D_{org} - d^-$ and thus $|D_{upd}| = |D_{org}| - |d^-|$.

To effectively maintain the space of frequent patterns, we first need to understand how the space evolves in the response to data updates. Suppose we have a dataset D_{org} and the corresponding frequent pattern space $F(ms_\%, D_{org})$ under support threshold $ms_\%$. We can characterize the evolution of the frequent pattern space by studying the behaviour of individual patterns. In incremental updates, we observe that, for every pattern P, exact one of the following 4 scenarios holds:

1. $P \notin F(ms_\%, D_{org})$ and P is not in d^+. This corresponds to the scenario where pattern P is infrequent in D_{org} and it is not contained in d^+. In this case, pattern P remains infrequent and no update action is required.

2. $P \in F(ms_\%, D_{org})$ and P is not in d^+. This corresponds to the scenario where pattern P is frequent in D_{org} but it is not contained in d^+. In this case, $count(P, D_{upd}) = count(P, D_{org})$, and since $|D_{upd}| = |D_{org}| + |d^+| > |D_{org}|$, $sup(P, D_{upd}) < sup(P, D_{org})$. The support count of P remains unchanged but its support decrease. Then we have two cases: first, if $count(P, D_{upd}) \geq |D_{upd}| \times ms_\%$, pattern P remains to be frequent, and only its support value needs to be updated; second, if $count(P, D_{upd}) < |D_{upd}| \times ms_\%$, pattern P becomes infrequent in D_{upd} and it needs to be discarded.

3. $P \notin F(ms_\%, D_{org})$ and P is in d^+. This corresponds to the scenario where pattern P is infrequent in D_{org} but it is contained in d^+. In this case, $count(P, D_{upd}) = count(P, D_{org}) + count(P, d^+)$. Then we have two cases: first, if $count(P, D_{upd}) \geq |D_{upd}| \times ms_\%$, pattern P emerges to be frequent in D_{upd}, and it needs to be included in $F(ms_\%, D_{upd})$; second, if $count(P, D_{upd}) < |D_{upd}| \times ms_\%$, pattern P remains to be infrequent, and no update action is required.

4. $P \in F(ms_\%, D_{org})$ and P is in d^+. This corresponds to the scenario where pattern P is frequent in D_{org} and it is contained in d^+. Similar to scenario 3, $count(P, D_{upd}) = count(P, D_{org}) + count(P, d^+)$. Again we have two cases: first, if $count(P, D_{upd}) \geq |D_{upd}| \times ms_\%$, pattern P remains to be frequent, and only its support value needs to be updated; second, if $count(P, D_{upd}) < |D_{upd}| \times ms_\%$, pattern P becomes infrequent in D_{upd}, and it needs to be discarded.

For decremental updates, similar scenarios can be derived to describe the evolution of the frequent pattern space. (Detailed scenarios can be derived easily based on the duality between incremental updates and decremental updates. Thus, details are not included.) The key observation is that both incremental and decremental updates may cause existing frequent patterns to become infrequent and may induce new frequent patterns to emerge. Therefore, the major tasks and challenges in frequent pattern maintenance are to:

1. Find out and discard the existing frequent patterns that are no longer frequent after the update.
2. Generate the newly emerged frequent patterns.

Since the size of the frequent pattern space is usually large, effective techniques and algorithms are required to address these two tasks.

MAINTENANCE ALGORITHMS

The maintenance of frequent patterns has attracted considerable research attention in the last decade. The proposed maintenance algorithms fall into four main categories: (1) *Apriori*-based, (2) *Partition*-based, (3) *Prefix-tree*-based and (4) *Concise-representation*-based. In this section, we will study these four types of approaches first from the theoretical perspective and then proceed on to the experimental investigation of their computational effectiveness.

Apriori-Based Algorithms

Apriori (Agrawal et al. 1993) is the first frequent pattern mining algorithm. *Apriori* discovers frequent patterns iteratively. In each iteration, it generates a set of candidate frequent patterns and then verifies them by scanning the dataset. *Apriori* defines a 'candidate-generation-verification' framework for the discovery of frequent patterns. Therefore, in *Apriori* and *Apriori-based* algorithms, the major challenge is to generate

the minimum number of unnecessary candidate patterns.

FUP (Cheung et al. 1996) is the representative *Apriori*-based maintenance algorithm. It is proposed to address the incremental maintenance of frequent patterns. Inspired by *Apriori*, *FUP* updates the space of frequent patterns based on the candidate-generation-verification framework. Using a different approach from *Apriori*, *FUP* makes use of the support information of the previously discovered frequent patterns to reduce the number of candidate patterns. *FUP* effectively prunes unnecessary candidate patterns based on the following two observations.

FACT 2. Given a dataset D_{org}, the incremental dataset d^+, the updated dataset $D_{upd} = D_{org} \cup d^+$ and the support threshold $ms_\%$, for every pattern $P \in F(ms_\%, D_{org})$, if $P \notin F(ms_\%, D_{upd})$, then for every pattern $Q \supseteq P$, $Q \notin F(ms_\%, D_{upd})$.

FACT 2 is an extension of the *a priori* property of frequent patterns. It is to say that, if a previously frequent pattern becomes infrequent in the updated dataset, then all its supersets are definitely infrequent in the updated dataset and thus should not be included as candidate patterns. FACT 2 facilitates us to discard existing frequent patterns that are no longer frequent. FACT 3 then provides us a guideline to eliminate unnecessary candidates for newly emerged frequent patterns.

FACT 3. Given a dataset D_{org}, the incremental dataset d^+, the updated dataset $D_{upd} = D_{org} \cup d^+$ and the support threshold $ms_\%$, for every pattern $P \notin F(ms_\%, D_{org})$, if $sup(P, d^+) < ms_\%$, $P \notin F(ms_\%, D_{upd})$.

FACT 3 states that, if a pattern is infrequent in both the original dataset and the incremental dataset, it is definitely infrequent in the updated dataset. This allows us to eliminate disqualified candidates of the newly emerged frequent patterns based on their support values in the incremental dataset. The support values of candidates can be obtained by scanning only the incremental dataset. This greatly reduces the number of scans of the original dataset and thus improves the effectiveness of the algorithm. (In general, the size of the incremental dataset is much smaller than the one of the original dataset.)

In Cheung et al. (1997), *FUP* is generalized to address the decremental maintenance of frequent patterns as well. The generalized version of *FUP* is called *FUP2H*. Both *FUP* and *FUP2H* generate a much smaller set of candidate patterns compared to *Apriori*, and thus they are more effective. But both *FUP* and *FUP2H* still suffer from two major drawbacks:

1. they require multiple scans of the original and incremental/decremental datasets to obtain the support values of candidate patterns, which leads to high I/O overheads, and
2. they repeat the enumeration of previously discovered frequent patterns.

To address Point 2, Aumann et al (1999) proposed a new algorithm---*Borders*.

Borders is inspired by the concept of the 'border pattern', introduced in Mannila & Toivonen (1997). In the context of frequent patterns, the 'border pattern' is formally defined as follows.

Definition 5 (Border Pattern). Given a dataset D and minimum support threshold $ms_\%$, a pattern P is a 'border pattern', iff for every $Q \subset P$, $Q \in F(ms_\%, D)$ but $P \notin F(ms_\%, D)$.

The border patterns are basically the shortest infrequent patterns. The collection of border patterns defines a borderline between the frequent patterns and the infrequent ones. Different from *FUP*, *Borders* makes use of not only the support information of previously discovered patterns but also the support information of the border patterns.

We illustrate the idea of *Borders* using an incremental update example. When the incremental dataset d^+ is added, *Borders* first scans through d^+ to update the support values of the existing frequent patterns and the border patterns. If no border patterns emerge to be frequent after the update, the maintenance process is finished. Otherwise, if some border patterns become frequent after the update, new frequent patterns and border patterns need to be enumerated. Those border patterns that emerge to be frequent after the update are called the 'promoted border patterns'. The pattern enumeration process follows the *Apriori* candidate-generation-verification method. But, distinct from *Apriori* and *FUP*, *Borders* resumes the pattern enumeration from the 'promoted border patterns' onwards and thus avoids the enumeration of previously discovered frequent patterns.

Since *Borders* successfully avoids unnecessary enumeration of previously discovered patters, it is more effective than *FUP*. However, similar to *FUP*, *Borders* requires multiple scans of original and incremental/decremental datasets to obtain the support values of newly emerged frequent pattern and border patterns. *Borders* also suffers from heavy I/O overheads. One possible way to solve this limitation of *FUP* and *Borders* is to compress the datasets into a prefix-tree (Han et al. 2000). The prefix-tree is a data structure that compactly records datasets and thus enables us to obtain support information of patterns without scanning of the datasets. Details will be discussed in the section of Prefix-tree-based algorithms.

Partition-Based Algorithms

Partition-based maintenance algorithms, similar to *Apriori*, enumerate frequent patterns based on the candidate-generation-verification framework, but they generate candidate patterns in a different manner. Candidate patterns are generated based on the 'partition-based heuristic' (Lee et al. 2005):

given a dataset D that is divided into n partitions $p_1, p_2, ..., p_n$, if a pattern P is a frequent pattern in D, then P must be frequent in at least one of the n partitions of D.

Sliding Window Filtering (*SWF*) (Lee et al. 2005) is a recently proposed partition-based algorithm for frequent pattern maintenance. *SWF* focuses on the pattern maintenance of time-variant datasets. In time-variant datasets, data updates involve both the insertion of the most recent transactions (incremental update) and the deletion of the most obsolete transactions (decremental update).

Given a time-variant dataset D, *SWF* first divides D into n partitions and processes one partition at a time. The processing of each partition is called a *phase*. In each *phase*, the local frequent patterns are discovered, and they are carried over to the next *phase* as candidate patterns. In this manner, candidate patterns are cumulated progressively over the entire dataset D. The set of cumulated candidate patterns is called the 'cumulative filter', denoted by *CF*. According to the 'partition-based heuristic', *CF* is the superset of the set of frequent patterns. Finally, *SWF* scans through the entire dataset to calculate the actual support of the candidate patterns and to decide whether they are globally frequent. To facilitate the maintenance of frequent patterns,

SWF records not only the support information but also the 'start partition' of each candidate pattern. The 'start partition' attribute of candidate patterns refers to the first partition that the candidate pattern is first introduced. When the most obsolete transactions are removed, the 'start partition' attribute allows us to easily locate and thus update the candidate patterns that are involved in the obsolete transactions. When new transactions are added, the incremental dataset d^+ will be treated as a partition of the dataset and will be involved in the progressively generation of candidate patterns.

The major advantage of *SWF* is that, based on the 'partition-based heuristic', *SWF* prunes most of the false candidate patterns in the early stage of the maintenance process. This greatly reduces the computational and memory overhead. Moreover, *SWF* requires only one scan of the entire time-variant dataset to verify the set of candidate patterns. We will demonstrate in our experimental studies later that it is this very advantage of *SWF* that allows it to significantly outperform *Apriori* and *FUP*.

PREFIX-TREE-BASED ALGORITHMS

The prefix-tree is an effective data structure that compactly represents the transactions and thus

Figure 2. (a) The original dataset. (b) The projected dataset from the original dataset. (c) The construction process of FP-tree.

Original Dataset $ms_\% = 50\%$		Projected Dataset		Root	Root	Root	Root
Tid	Item_list	Tid	Item_list				
1	a, d, c, e, b, g	1	a, b, d, e	a : 1	a : 2	a : 3	a : 4
2	a, f, d, c, b	2	a, b, d, e	b : 1	b : 2	b : 2	b : 3
3	a	3	a				
4	b, d, a	4	a, b, d	d : 1	d : 2	d : 2	d : 3
				e : 1	e : 2	e : 2	e : 2
(a)		(b)		(c)			

Figure 3. (a) The construction of CATS tree. (b) The construction of CanTree.

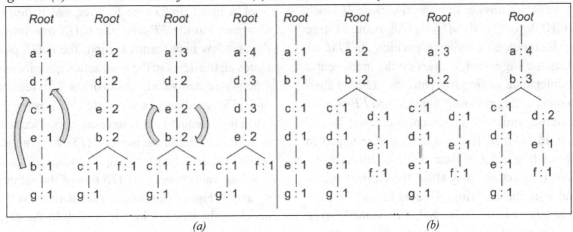

(a)   *(b)*

the frequent patterns in datasets. The usage of the prefix-tree is a tremendous breakthrough in frequent pattern discovery. With the prefix-tree, we can compress the transactional dataset and store it in the main memory. This enables fast access of the support information of all the frequent patterns. More importantly, we can now generate frequent patterns by traversing the prefix-tree without multiple scanning of the dataset and generation of any candidate patterns (Han et al. 2000). To better appreciate the idea of prefix-tree, let us study the *FP-tree*, the most commonly used prefix-tree, as an example.

The *FP-tree*, in full 'frequent pattern tree', is first proposed in Han et al. (2000). The *FP-tree* is a compact representation of all relevant frequency information in a database. Every branch of the *FP-tree* represents a 'projected transaction' and also a candidate pattern. The nodes along the branches are stored in decreasing order of support values of the corresponding items, so leaves are representing the least frequent items. Compression is achieved by building the tree in such a way that overlapping transactions share prefixes of the corresponding branches. Figure 2 demonstrates how the *FP-tree* is constructed

for the sample dataset given a support threshold $ms_\%$. First, the dataset is transformed into the 'projected dataset'. In the 'projected dataset', all the infrequent items are removed, and items in each transaction are sorted in descending order of their support values. Transactions in the 'projected dataset' are named the 'projected transactions'. The 'projected transactions' are then inserted into the prefix-tree structure one by one, as shown in Figure 2(c). It can be seen that the *FP-tree* effectively represents the sample dataset in Figure 2(a) with only four nodes.

Based on the idea of *FP-tree*, a novel frequent pattern discovery algorithm, known as *FP-growth*, is proposed. *FP-growth* generates frequent pattern by traversing the *FP-tree* in a depth-first manner. *FP-growth* only requires two scans of the dataset to construct the *FP-tree* and no candidate generations. (The detailed frequent pattern generation process can be referred to Han et al. (2000)). *FP-growth* is a very effective algorithm. It is experimentally shown that *FP-growth* can outperform *Apriori* by orders of magnitudes.

Now the question is, when the dataset is updated, how to effectively update the prefix-tree and thus to achieve efficient maintenance of frequent patterns? To answer this question, Koh & Shieh (2004) developed the *AFPIM* (Adjusting FP-tree for Incremental Mining) algorithm *AFPIM*, as the name suggested, focuses on the incremental maintenance of frequent patterns. *AFPIM* aims to update the previously constructed *FP-tree* by scanning only the incremental dataset. Recall that, in *FP-tree*, frequent items are arranged in descending order of their support values. Insertions transactions may affect the support values and thus the ordering of items in the *FP-tree*. When the ordering is changed, items in the *FP-tree* need to be adjusted. In *AFPIM*, this adjustment is accomplished by re-sorting the items through bubble sort. Bubble sort sorts items by recursively exchanging adjacent items. This sorting process is computational expensive, especially when the ordering of items are dramatically affected by the data updates. In addition, incremental update may induce new frequent items to emerge. In this case, the *FP-tree* can no longer be adjusted using *AFPIM*. Instead, *AFPIM* has to scan the updated dataset to construct a new *FP-tree*.

To address the limitations of *AFPIM*, Cheung & Zaïane (2003) proposed the *CATS tree* (Com-pressed and Arranged Transaction Sequences tree), a novel prefix-tree for frequent patterns. Compared to the *FP-tree*, the *CATS tree* introduces a few new features. First, the *CATS tree* stores all the items in the transactions, regardless whether the items are frequent or not. This feature of *CATS tree* allows us to update *CATS tree* even when new frequent items have emerged. Second, to achieve high compactness, *CATS tree* arranges nodes based on their local support values. Figure 3(a) illustrates how the *CATS tree* of the sample dataset in Figure 2(a) is constructed and how the nodes in the tree are locally sorted. In the case of incremental updates, the *CATS tree* is updated by merging the newly inserted transactions with the existing tree branches. According to the construction method of *CATS tree*, transactions in incremental datasets can only be merged into the *CATS tree* one by one. Moreover, for each new transaction, searching though the *CATS tree* is required to find the right path for the new transaction to merge in. In addition, since nodes in *CATS tree* are locally sorted, swapping and merging of nodes are required during the update of the *CATS tree* (as shown in Figure 3(a)).

Figure 4. (a) Sample dataset. (b) The backtracking tree of the sample dataset when ms%=40%. Bolded nodes are the frequent maximal patterns, nodes that are crossed out are enumeration termination points, and nodes that are linked with a dotted arrow are skipped candidates.

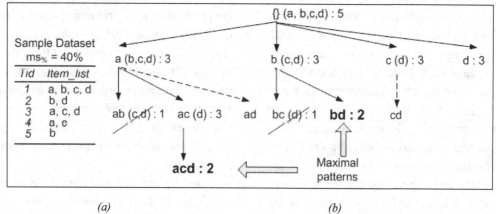

(a)   *(b)*

CanTree (Leung et al. 2007), Canonical-order Tree, is another prefix-tree designed for the maintenance of frequent patterns. The *CanTree* is constructed in a similar manner as the *CATS tree*, as shown in Figure 3(b). But in the *CanTree*, items are arranged according to some canonical order, which can be determined by the user prior to the mining process. For example, items in the *CanTree* can be arranged in lexicographic order, or, alternatively, items can be arranged based on certain property values of items (e.g. their prices, their priority values, etc.). Note that, in *CanTree*, once the ordering of items is fixed, items will follow this ordering for all the subsequent updates. To handle data updates, the *CanTree* allows new transactions to be inserted easily. Unlike the *CATS tree*, transaction insertions in the *CanTree* require no extensive searching for merge-able paths. Also since the canonical order is fixed, any changes in the support values of items caused by data updates have no effect on the ordering of items in the *CanTree*. As a result, swapping/merging nodes are not required in the update of *CanTree*. The simplicity of the *CanTree* makes it a very powerful

prefix-tree structure for frequent pattern maintenance. Therefore, in our experimental studies, we choose *CanTree* to represent the prefix-tree-based maintenance algorithms.

Concise-Representation-Based Algorithms

It is well known that the size of the frequent pattern space is usually large. The tremendous size of frequent patterns greatly limits the effectiveness of the maintenance process. To break this bottleneck, algorithms are proposed to maintain the concise representations of frequent patterns, instead of the entire pattern space. We name this type of maintenance algorithms as the concise-representation-based algorithms.

ZIGZAG (Veloso et al. 2002) and *TRUM* (Feng et al. 2007) are two representative examples of this type of algorithms. *ZIGZAG* (Veloso et al. 2002) maintains only the maximal frequent patterns. *ZIGZAG* updates the maximal frequent patterns with a backtracking search, which is guided by the outcomes of the previous mining iterations.

Figure 5. The evolution of frequent equivalence classes under decremental updates

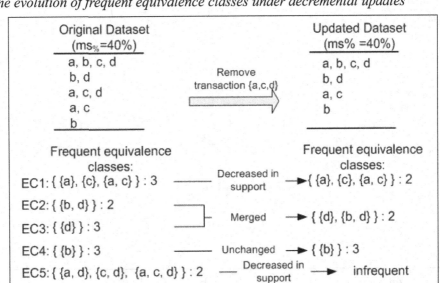

The backtracking search method in *ZIGZAG* is inspired by its related work *GenMax* (Guoda 2001). *ZIGZAG* conceptually enumerates the candidates of maximal frequent patterns with a 'backtracking tree'. Figure 4(b) shows an example of backtracking tree. In the backtracking tree, each node is associated with a frequent pattern and its 'combination set'. For a particular frequent pattern *P*, the 'combination set' refers to the set of items that form potential candidates by combining with *P*. Take the backtracking tree in Figure 4(b) as an example. Node {*a*} is associated with combination set {*b, c, d*}. This implies that the union of {*a*} and the items in the combination set, which are {*a, b*}, {*a, c*} and {*a, d*}, are potential candidates for maximal frequent patterns.

ZIGZAG also employs certain pruning techniques to reduce the number of generated false candidates. First, *ZIGZAG* prunes false candidates based on the *a priori* property of frequent pat-terns. If a node in the backtracking tree is not frequent, then all the children of the node are not frequent, and thus candidate enumeration of the current branch can be terminated. In Figure 4(b), crossed out nodes are the enumeration termination points that fall in this scenario. Second, *ZIGZAG* further eliminates false candidates based on the following fact.

FACT 4. Given a dataset *D* and a support threshold $ms_\%$, if a pattern *P* is a maximal frequent pattern, then for every pattern $Q \supset P$, *Q* is not a maximal frequent pattern.

FACT 4 follows the definition of the maximal frequent pattern. In Figure 4(b), nodes, which are pointed with a dotted line, are those pruned based on this criterion.

On the other hand, *TRUM* (Transaction Removal Update Maintainer) maintains the equivalence classes of frequent patterns. *TRUM* focuses on the decremental maintenance. In Feng et al. (2007),

Figure 6. (a) The original dataset and the frequent equivalence classes in the original dataset when $ms_\%=40\%$. (b) The Tid-tree for the original dataset. (c) The update of the Tid-tree under decremental update.

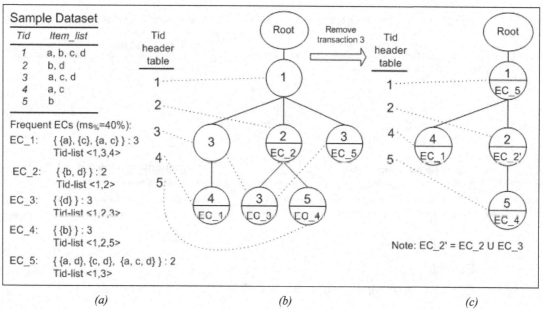

Table 1. Summary of various maintenance algorithms

	Algorithm	Strengths		Weaknesses
Apriori-based	**FUP**	•	Makes use of the support information of the previously discovered frequent patterns to reduce the number of candidate patterns	• Generates large amount of unnecessary candidates • Requires multiple scans of datasets
	Borders	•	Avoids enumeration of previous discovered patterns • Effective enumeration of new frequent patterns from the border patterns	• Generates large amount of unnecessary candidates • Requires multiple scans of datasets
Partition-based	**SWF**	•	Prunes most of the false candidates in the early stage based on the 'partition-based heuristic' • Requires only one full scan of dataset	• Still generates unnecessary candidates
Prefix-tree-based	**AFPIM**	•	Dataset is summarized into a prefix-tree and requires only two scans of the dataset • No false candidate is enumerated	• Inefficient update of the prefix-tree: the whole tree needs to be re-organized for each update • The prefix-tree needs to be rebuild if new frequent items emerge
	CATS tree	•	Dataset is summarized into a prefix-tree and requires only two scans of the dataset • No false candidate is enumerated • Items are locally sorted, which allows the tree to be locally updated • The tree update mechanism allows new frequent items to emerge	• Node swapping and merging, which are computational expensive, are required for the local update of prefix-tree
	CanTree	•	Dataset is summarized into a prefix-tree and requires only two scans of the dataset • No false candidate is enumerated • Items are arranged in a canonical-order that will not be affected by the data update, so that no re-sorting, node swapping and node merging are needed while updating the prefix tree	• CanTree is less compact compared to CATS tree
Concise-representation-based	**ZIGZAG**	•	Updates the maximal frequent patterns with a backtracking search • Prunes infrequent and non-maximal patterns in the early stage	• Maximal patterns are lossy representations of frequent patterns
	TRUM	•	Maintains frequent patterns based on the concept of equivalence class --- a lossless representation of frequent patterns • Employs an efficient data structure *Tid-tree* to facilitate the maintenance process	• Handles only the decremental maintenance

it is discovered that, in response to decremental updates, an existing frequent equivalence class can evolve in exactly three ways as shown in Figure 5. The first way is to remain unchanged without any change in support. The second way is to remain unchanged but with a decreased support. If the support of an existing frequent equivalence class drops below the minimum support threshold, the equivalence class will be removed. The third way is to grow by merging with other classes. As a result, the decremental maintenance of frequent equivalence classes can be summarized into two tasks. The first task is to update the support values of existing frequent equivalence classes. The second task is to merge equivalence classes that are to be joined together.

TRUM accomplishes the two maintenance tasks effectively with a novel data structure called the *Tid-tree*. The *Tid-tree* is developed based on the concept of Transaction Identifier List, in short *Tid-list*. Tid-lists, serve as the vertical projections of items, greatly facilitate the discovery of frequent itemsets and the calculation of their support. Moreover, *Tid-lists* can be utilized as the identifiers of equivalence classes. According to the definition of the equivalence class, each frequent equivalence class is associated with a unique *Tid-list*. The *Tid-tree* is a prefix tree of the *Tid-lists* of the frequent equivalence classes. Figure 6(b) shows how the *Tid-lists* of frequent equivalence classes in Figure 6(a) can be stored in a *Tid-tree*. The *Tid-tree* has two major features: (1) Each node in the *Tid-tree* stores a *Tid*. If the *Tid* of the node is the last *Tid* in some equivalence class's *Tid-list*, the node points to the corresponding equivalence class. Moreover, the depth of the node reflects the support of the corresponding equivalence class. (2) The *Tid-tree* has a header table, where each slot stores a linked list that connects all the nodes with the same *Tid*.

When transactions are removed from the original dataset, the *Tid-tree* can be updated by removing all the nodes corresponding to the *Tids*

of the deleted transactions. This can be accomplished effectively with the help of the *Tid* header table. As demonstrated in Figure 6(c), after a node is removed, its children re-link to its parent to maintain the tree structure. If the node points to an equivalence class, the pointer is passed to its parent. When two or more equivalence class pointers collide into one node, they should be merged together. E.g. in Figure 4, equivalence classes EC 2 and EC 3 of the original dataset merge into EC 2' after the update. With the *Tid-tree*, two decremental maintenance tasks are accomplished in only one step.

We have reviewed the representative maintenance algorithms for frequent patterns. The strengths and weaknesses of these algorithms are summarized in Table 1.

Experimental Studies

We have discussed the different types of maintenance algorithms from theoretical and algorithmic perspectives. In this section, we justify our theoretical observations with experimental results. The performance of the discussed algorithms is tested using several benchmark datasets from the *FIMI* Repository, http://fimi.cs.helsinki.fi. In this chapter, the results of *T10I4D100K, mushroom, pumsb_star* and *gazelle* (a.k.a *BMS-WebView-1*) are presented. These datasets form a good representative of both synthetic and real datasets. The detailed characteristics of the datasets are presented in Table 1. The experiments were run on a PC with 2.8GHz processor and 2GB main memory.

Table 2. Characteristics of datasets

Datasets	Size	#Trans	#Items	MaxTL	AvgTL
T10I4D100K	3.93MB	100,000	870	30	10.10
mushroom	0.56MB	8,124	119	23	23
pumsb_star	11.03MB	49,046	2,088	63	50.48
gazelle	0.99MB	59,602	497	268	2.51

The performance of the maintenance algorithms is investigated in two ways. First, we study their computational effectiveness over various update intervals for a fixed support threshold $ms_\%$. For incremental updates, the update interval, denoted as Δ^+, is defined as $\Delta^+=|d^+|/|D_{org}|$. For decremental updates, the update interval, denoted as Δ^-, is defined as $\Delta^-=|d^-|/|D_{org}|$. Second, we study the computational effectiveness of the maintenance algorithms over various support thresholds $ms_\%$ for a fixed update interval. To better evaluate the maintenance algorithms, their performance is compared against two representative frequent pattern mining algorithms: *Apriori* (Agrawal et al. 1993) and *FP-growth* (Han et al. 2000).

First, let us look at the *Apriori*-based algorithms: the *FUP* and the *Borders*. The experimental results of *FUP* and *Borders* are summarized in Figure 7(a) and 8(a). It is discovered that both *FUP* and *Borders* outperform *Apriori* over various datasets and update intervals. *FUP* is on average around twice faster than *Apriori*, and, especially for the *mushroom* dataset, *FUP* outperforms *Apriori* up to 5 times when the update interval gets larger. Compared with *FUP*, *Borders* is much more effective. *Borders* outperforms *Apriori* on average an order of magnitude. This shows that the 'border pattern' is a useful concept that helps to avoid redundant enumeration of existing frequent patterns. However, both *FUP* and *Borders* are much slower compared to *FP-growth*, the prefix-tree based frequent pattern mining algorithm. This is mainly because both *FUP* and *Borders* require multiple scans of datasets and thus cause high I/O overhead. To solve this limitation, we employ a prefix-tree structure with the *Borders* algorithm, and we name the improved algorithm *Borders(prefixTree)*. It is experimentally demonstrate that the employment of a prefix-tree greatly improve the efficiency of *Borders*. *Borders(prefixTree)* is faster then the original *Borders* by at least an order of magnitude, and it even beats *FP-growth* in some cases.

Second, the performance results of *SWF*, the partition-based algorithm, are presented in Figure 7(b) and 8(b). *SWF* is found to be more effective than *Apriori*. *SWF* outperforms *Apriori* on average about 6 times. However, since *SWF* still follows the candidate-generation-verification framework, its performance is not as efficient as *FP-growth*, which discovers frequent patterns without generation of any candidates.

Third, we have *CanTree*[2], a prefix-tree-based algorithm. Its performance is also summarized in Figure 7(b) and 8(b). It is observed that *CanTree* is a very effective maintenance algorithm. *CanTree* is faster than both *Apriori* and *FP-growth*. It outperforms *Apriori* at least an order or magnitude. *CanTree* performs the best on the *mushroom* dataset, where it is almost 1000 times faster than *Apriori* and about 10 times faster than *FP-growth*.

Lastly, we study *ZIGZAG* and *TRUM*, which maintain the concise representations of frequent patterns. The effectiveness of *ZIGZAG* and *TRUM* is evaluated under decremental updates. They are also compared with *FUP2H*, the generalized version of *FUP*. Experimental results are summarized in Figure 7(c) and 8(c). *ZIGZAG* and *TRUM* maintains only the concise representations of frequent patterns, where the number of involved patterns is much smaller compared to the size of frequent pattern space. Therefore, they are more effective, especially for small update intervals, than the algorithms that discover or maintain frequent patterns. However, it is also observed that the advantage of *ZIGZAG* and *TRUM* diminish as the update interval increases. For some cases, *ZIGZAG* and *TRUM* are even slower than *FP-growth*. Among the comparing maintenance algorithms --- *FUP2H*, *ZIGZAG* and *TRUM*, *TRUM* is the most effective decremental maintenance algorithm.

In summary, for incremental maintenance, we found that *CanTree* is the most effective algorithm; on the other hand, for decremental maintenance, *TRUM* is the most effective one. In general, it is observed that the advantage of maintenance algorithms diminishes as the update interval increases. This is because, when more transactions are inserted/deleted, a larger number of frequent patterns are affected, and thus a high computational cost is required to maintain the pattern space. It is inevitable that, when the update interval reaches a certain level, the frequent pattern space will be affected so dramatically that it will be better to re-discover the frequent patterns than maintaining them. In addition, it is also observed that the advantage of maintenance algorithms becomes more obvious when the support threshold $ms_\%$ is small. It is well known that the number of frequent patterns and thus the size of the frequent pattern space grow exponentially as the support threshold drops. Therefore, when the support threshold is small, the space of frequent patterns becomes relatively large, and the discovery process becomes more 'expensive'. In this case, updating the frequent pattern space with maintenance algorithms becomes a better option.

FUTURE OPPORTUNITIES

We have reviewed the frequent pattern maintenance algorithms for conventional transaction datasets. Due to the advance in information technologies, a lot of data now is recorded continuously like a stream. This type of data is called 'data streams'.

A 'data stream' is an ordered sequence of transactions that arrives in timely order. Data streams are involved in many applications, e.g. sensor network monitoring (Halatchev & Gruenwald 2005), internet packet frequency estimation (Demaine et al. 2004), web failure analysis (Cai et al. 2004), etc. Data steams are updated constantly. Thus effective algorithms are needed for the maintenance of frequent patterns in data streams. Compared with the conventional trans-

action dataset, the frequent pattern maintenance in data streams is more challenging due to the following factors: first, data streams are continuous and unbounded (Leung & Khan 2006). While handling data streams, we no longer have the luxury of performing multiple data scans. Once the streams flow through, we lose them. Second, data in streams are not necessarily uniformly distributed (Leung & Khan 2006). That is to say currently infrequent patterns may emerge to be frequent in the future, and vice versa. Therefore, we can no longer simply prune out infrequent patterns. Third, updates in data streams happen more frequently and are more complicated. Data streams are usually updated in the 'sliding windows' manner, where, at each update, one obsolete transaction is removed from the window and one new transaction is added. Data streams are also updated in the 'damped' manner, in which every transaction is associated with a weight and the weight decrease with age.

The maintenance of frequent patterns in data streams faces more challenges compared to the conventional one. Some new algorithms (Manku et al 2002 & Metwally et al 2005) have been proposed to address the problem. However, certain existing ideas in the maintenance algorithms of transaction datasets could be useful to the maintenance in data streams, e.g. the prefix-tree (Leung & Khan 2006). In our opinion, to explore how the existing maintenance techniques can be used to benefit the frequent pattern maintenance in data streams is a potential and promising research direction.

CONCLUSION

This chapter has reviewed the maintenance of frequent patterns in transaction datasets. We focused on both incremental and decremental updates. We have investigated how the space of frequent patterns evolves in the response to the

Figure 7. Computational performance over various update intervals. (a) The Apriori-based algorithms --- FUP, Borders and Borders(prefixTree). (b) Partition-based algorithm SWF and prefix-tree-based algorithm CanTree. (c) Concise-representation-based algorithms --- ZIGZAG and TRUM.

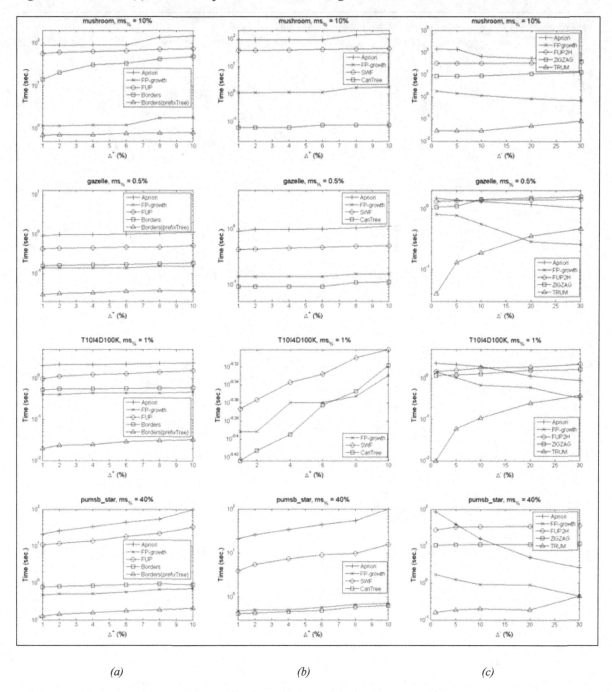

(a)   (b)   (c)

Figure 8. Computational performance over various support thresholds. (a) The Apriori-based algorithms --- FUP, Borders and Borders(prefixTree). (b) Partition-based algorithm SWF and prefix-tree-based algorithm CanTree. (c) Concise-representation-based algorithms --- ZIGZAG and TRUM.

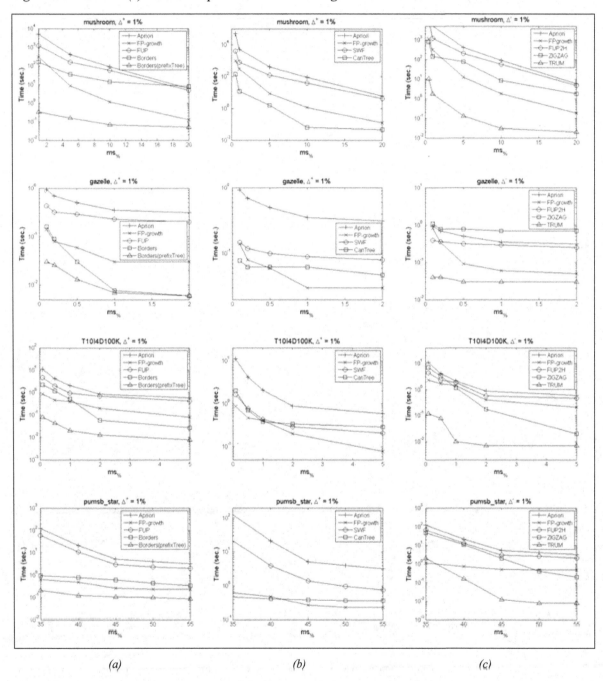

(a)   (b)   (c)

data updates. It is observed that both incremental and decremental updates may cause existing frequent patterns to become infrequent and may induce new frequent patterns to emerge. We then summarized the major tasks in frequent pattern maintenance is to 1) locate and discard previously frequent patterns that are no longer qualified and to 2) generate new frequent patterns.

We have surveyed four major types of maintenance algorithms, namely the *Apriori*-based algorithms, the partition-based algorithms, the prefix-tree-based algorithms and the concise-representation-based algorithms. The characteristics of these algorithms have been studied from both theoretical and experimental perspectives. It is observed that algorithms that involve multiple data scans suffer from high I/O overhead and thus low efficiency. We have demonstrated that this limitation can be solved by employing a prefix-tree, e.g. *FP-tree*, to summarize and store the dataset. According to the experimental studies, for incremental maintenance, the prefix-tree-based algorithm, *CanTree*, is the most effective algorithm. On the other hand, *TRUM*, which maintains the equivalence classes of frequent patterns, is the most effective method for decremental maintenance.

In addition, it is a challenging and potential research direction to explore how the existing maintenance techniques for transaction data can be applied to effectively maintain frequent patterns in data streams.

REFERENCES

Agrawal, R., Imielinski, T., & Swami, A. (1993). Mining association rules between sets of items in large databases. *Proceedings of the 1993 ACM SIGMOD International Conference on Management of Data* (pp. 207-216).

Agrawal, R., & Srikant, R. (1995). Mining sequential patterns. *Proceedings of the Eleventh International Conference on Data Engineering* (pp. 3-14).

Aumann, Y., Feldman, R., Lipshtat, O. & Manilla, H. (1999). Borders: An efficient algorithm for association generation in dynamic databases. *Intelligent Information Systems, 12*(1), 61-73.

Bayardo, R. J. (1998). Efficiently mining long patterns from databases. *Proceedings of the 1998 ACM SIGMOD International Conference on Management of Data* (pp. 85-93).

Brin, S., Motwani, R., & Silverstein, C. (1997). Beyond market basket: Generalizing association rules to dependence rules. *Data Mining and Knowledge Discovery, 2*(1), 39-68.

Cai, Y. D., Clutter, D., Pape, G., Han, J., Welge, M., & Auvil L. (2004). MAIDS: mining alarming incidents from data streams. *Proceedings of the 2004 ACM SIGMOD international conference on Management of data* (pp. 919-920).

Cheung, D., Han, J., Ng, V. T., & Wong, C. Y. (1996). Maintenance of discovered association rules in large databases: an incremental update technique. *Proceedings of the 1996 International Conference on Data Engineering* (pp. 106-114).

Cheung, D., Lee, S. D., & Kao, B. (1997). A general incremental technique for maintaining discovered association rules. *Database Systems for Advanced Applications* (pp. 185-194).

Cheung, W., & Zaïane, O. R. (2003). Incremental mining of frequent patterns without candidate generation or support constraint. *Proceedings of the 2003 International Database Engineering and Applications Symposium* (pp. 111-116).

Demaine, E. D., López-Ortiz, A., & Munro, J. I. (2002). Frequency estimation of internet packet streams with limited space. *Proceedings of the 10th Annual European Symposium on Algorithms* (pp. 348-360).

Dong, G., & Li, J. (1999). Efficient Mining of Emerging Patterns: Discovering Trends and Differences. *Proceedings of the Fifth ACM SIG-KDD International Conference on Knowledge Discovery and Data Mining* (pp. 15-18).

Feng, M., Dong, G., Li, J., Tan, Y-P., & Wong, L. (2007). Evolution and maintenance of frequent pattern space when transactions are removed. *Proceedings of the 2007 Pacific-Asia Conference on Knowledge Discovery and Data Mining* (pp. 489-497).

Grahne, G., & Zhu, J. (2003). Efficiently using prefix-trees in mining frequent itemsets. *Proceedings 1st IEEE ICDM Workshop on Frequent Itemset Mining Implementations, 2003.*

Guoda, K., & Zaki, M. J. (2001). Efficiently mining maximal frequent itemsets. *Proceedings of the 2001 IEEE International Conference on Data Mining* (pp. 163-170).

Han, J., Dong, G., & Yin, Y. (1999). Efficient mining of partial periodic patterns in time series database. *International Conference on Data Engineering,* (pp. 106-115).

Han, J., Pei, J., & Yin, Y. (2000). Mining frequent patterns without candidate generation. *2000 ACM SIGMOD International. Conference on Management of Data* (pp. 1-12).

Halatchev, M., & Gruenwald, L. (2005). Estimating missing values in related sensor data streams. *International Conference on Management of Data* (pp. 83-94).

Jiang, N., & Gruenwald, L. (2006). Research issues in data stream association rule mining. *ACM SIGMOD Record, 35*(1), 14-19.

Koh, J-L., & Shieh, S-F. (2004) An efficient approach for maintaining association rules based on adjusting FP-tree structures. *Proceedings of the 2004 Database Systems for Advanced Applications* (pp. 417-424).

Lee, C-H., Lin, C-R., & Chen, M-S. (2005). Sliding window filtering: an efficient method for incremental mining on a time-variant database. *Information Systems, 30*(3), 227-244.

Leung, C. K-S., & Khan, Q. I. (2006). DSTree: A Tree Structure for the Mining of Frequent Sets from Data Streams. *Proceedings of the Sixth International Conference on Data Mining* (pp. 928 - 932).

Leung, C. K-S., Khan, Q. I., Li Z., & Hoque, T. (2007). CanTree: a canonical-order tree for incremental frequent-pattern mining. *Knowledge and Information Systems, 11*(3), 287-311.

Li, H., Li, J., Wong, L., Feng, M., & Tan, Y-P. (2005). Relative risk and odds ratio: A data mining perspective. *Symposium on Principles of Database Systems* (pp. 368-377).

Manku, G. S., & Motwani, Q. (2002). Approximate frequency counts over data streams. *VLDB* (pp. 346-357).

Mannila. H.. & Toivonen, H. (1997). Levelwise search and borders of theories in knowledge discovery. *Data Mining and Knowledge Discovery, 1*(2), 241-258.

Metwally, A., Agrawal, D., & Abbadi, A. E. (2005) Efficient computation of frequent and top-k elements in data streams. *International Conference on Data Theory* (pp. 398-412).

Pasquier N., Bastide Y., Taouil R., & Lakhal, L. (1999). Efficient mining of association rules using closed itemset lattices. *Information Systems, 24*(1), 25-46.

Pei ,J., Han, J. & Mao R. (2000). CLOSET: An efficient algorithm for mining frequent closed itemsets. *SIGMOD Workshop on Research Issues in Data Mining and Knowledge Discovery 2000* (pp 21-30).

Silverstein, C., Brin, S., & Motwani, R. (1998). Scalable techniques for mining causal structures. *Data Mining and Knowledge Discovery, 4*(2), 163-192.

Veloso, A. A., Meira ,W. Jr.,Carvalho, M. B., Possas, B., Parthasarathy, S., & Zaki, M. J. (2002). Mining frequent itemsets in evolving databases. *SIAM International Conference on Data Mining, 2002.*

Wang, J., Han, J., & Pei, J. (2003). CLOSET+: Searching for the best strategies for mining frequent closed itemsets. *Proceedings of the Ninth ACM SIGKDD International Conference on Knowledge Discovery and Data Mining* (pp. 236-245).

ENDNOTES

[1] This work is partially supported by an A*STAR SERC PSF grant, a MOE AcRF Tier 1 grant, and an A*STAR AGS scholarship.

[2] The *CanTree* algorithm in our experimental studies is implemented by us based on Leung et al. 2007.

Chapter XV
Mining Conditional Contrast Patterns

Guozhu Dong
Wright State University, USA

Jinyan Li
Nanyang Technological University, Singapore

Guimei Liu
National University of Singapore, Singapore

Limsoon Wong
National University of Singapore, Singapore

ABSTRACT

This chapter considers the problem of "conditional contrast pattern mining." It is related to contrast mining, where one considers the mining of patterns/models that contrast two or more datasets, classes, conditions, time periods, and so forth. Roughly speaking, conditional contrasts capture situations where a small change in patterns is associated with a big change in the matching data of the patterns. More precisely, a conditional contrast is a triple (B, F_1, F_2) of three patterns; B is the condition/context pattern of the conditional contrast, and F_1 and F_2 are the contrasting factors of the conditional contrast. Such a conditional contrast is of interest if the difference between F_1 and F_2 as itemsets is relatively small, and the difference between the corresponding matching dataset of $B \cup F_1$ and that of $B \cup F_2$ is relatively large. It offers insights on "discriminating" patterns for a given condition B. Conditional contrast mining is related to frequent pattern mining and analysis in general, and to the mining and analysis of closed pattern and minimal generators in particular. It can also be viewed as a new direction for the analysis (and mining) of frequent patterns. After formalizing the concepts of conditional contrast, the chapter will provide some theoretical results on conditional contrast mining. These results (i) relate conditional *contrasts with closed patterns and their minimal generators, (ii) provide a concise representation for conditional contrasts, and (iii) establish a so-called dominance-beam property. An efficient algorithm will be proposed based on these results, and experiment results will be reported. Related works will also be discussed.*

INTRODUCTION

This chapter formalizes the notions of conditional contrast patterns (C2Ps) and conditional contrast factors (C2Fs), and studies the associated data mining problem. These concepts are formulated in the abstract space of patterns and their matching datasets.

Roughly speaking, C2Ps are aimed at capturing situations or contexts (the conditional contrast bases or C2Bs) where small changes in patterns to the base make big differences in matching datasets. The small changes are the C2Fs and their cost is measured by the average number of items in the C2Fs. The big differences are the differences among the matching datasets of the C2Fs; we use the average size of the differences to measure the impact (of the C2Fs). Combining cost and impact allows us to find those C2Fs

which are very effective difference makers. In formula, a C2P is a pair $\langle B, \{F_1, ..., F_k\}\rangle$, where k >1, and B and F_i are itemsets; B is the C2B and the F_i's are the C2Fs.

For $k=2$, Figure 1 (a) shows that F_1 and F_2 are small itemset changes to B. Panel (b) shows that the matching datasets of $B \cup F_1$ and $B \cup F_2$ are significantly different from each other. The $k>2$ case is similar.[1]

We use the impact-to-cost ratio, defined as the impact divided by the cost, as well as other measures, to evaluate the goodness of C2Ps and C2Fs. Observe that one can also consider other factors involving class, financial benefit or utility in defining this ratio.

Example 1.1. *C2Ps can give new insights to many, especially medical/business, applications. We illustrate the concepts using a medical dataset.*

Figure 1. Conditional contrast patterns/factors: (a) F_1 and F_2 are small itemset changes to B, and (b) the matching dataset of $B \cup F_1$ is very different from that of $B \cup F_2$.

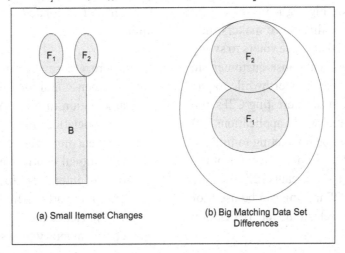

(a) Small Itemset Changes

(b) Big Matching Data Set Differences

From a microarray gene expression dataset used in acute lymphoblastic leukemia subtype study [Yeoh et al, 2002], we got a number of C2Ps, including the following[2].

P_L=⟨{gene-38319-at≥15975.6}, {{gene-33355-at < 10966}, {gene-33355-at ≥ 10966}}⟩

Here {gene-38319-at ≥15975.6} is the C2B, {gene-33355-at < 10966} is F_1, and {gene-33355-at ≥ 10966} is F_2. This C2P says that the samples that satisfy gene-38319-at ≥ 15975.6 (which are the samples of B-lineage type) are split into two disjoint parts: the first part are the E2A-PBX1 subtype (18 samples), and the other part are the other B-lineage subtypes (169 samples). Expressed as a rule, P_L says: Among the samples satisfying gene-38319-at ≥ 15975.6, if the expression of gene-33355-at is less than 10966, then the sample is E2A-PBX1; otherwise, it belongs to the other types of B-lineage.

This C2P nicely illustrates how the regulation of gene-38319-at and gene-33355-at splits patients into different acute lymphoblastic leukemia subtypes.

Typically, an individual C2F of a C2P does not make the big differences between matching datasets; the differences are made by two or more C2Fs of the C2P. For example, in a C2P with two C2Fs F_1 and F_2, the set of items in $F_1 \cup F_2$ makes the differences.

The mining of C2Ps/C2Fs has several interesting applications. We highlight a few here. (a) The C2Fs of a C2P are difference makers, in a sense similar to issues that cause voters to swing in elections, or factors that cause customers to switch companies. It may be worthwhile to pay more attention to the most interesting C2Fs and the items in them in real world applications. (b) Given a dataset, it may be interesting to find the most significant C2Ps as important states of the dataset, and the most significant C2Fs as state transitions. (c) C2P/C2F mining can be used for unsupervised feature selection, for association

mining, clustering, and other forms of knowledge pattern mining. (d) We note that one can also define some indices which can be used to identify important "distinguishing items," based on how frequently the items occur in C2Bs or C2Fs.

Besides formulating the concepts of C2Ps and C2Fs, we make the following contributions: (a) We present theoretical results on properties of C2Ps and C2Fs, concerning a so-called dominance beam property (DBP), relationship to closed and key (generator) patterns, and concise representation of C2Ps and C2Fs. The results are useful for expansion-based search for situations where anti-monotonicity does not hold. (b) We present an algorithm for mining C2Ps, called C2Pminer. It utilizes the theoretical results on the relationship of C2Ps/C2Fs with closed itemsets and keys, and the dominance beam property, for efficient mining. It produces all C2Ps under a special C2P representation. (c) We report experiment results performed on some data sets for cancer research and some datasets from the UCI repository.

Section 1.1 discusses related works. Section 2 formulates the main concepts. Section 3 presents the dominance beam property. Section 4 considers representation issues. Section 5 presents the C2P-miner algorithm. Section 6 gives an experimental evaluation. Section 7 concludes.

Related Work

This chapter is related six groups of previous studies.

1. There are several interesting differences between conditional contrast mining and association mining [Agrawal et al., 1993]. In association mining one is interested in frequent itemsets or association rules. In conditional contrast pattern (C2P) mining one is interested in interactions among groups of patterns (namely the C2B and the C2Fs). Hence the C2P pattern type is quite complementary to association mining.

2. This work leads to new insights to the field of Formal Concept Analysis (FCA) [Ganter & Wille, 1999] and to the direction of closed pattern mining [Mineau & Ganter, 2000, Pasquier et al., 1999, Zaki & Hsiao, 2002, Wang et al., 2003]. It relates C2P/C2F mining with closed pattern and key mining. Moreover, a C2P can be considered as identifying important groups of concepts, and C2Fs can be viewed as small patterns that cause big data changes to the formal concepts.

3. This work is related to the direction on mining of contrast patterns (including patterns on changes and differences) [Dong & Li, 1999, Bay & Pazzani, 2001, Ganti et al., 1999, Liu et al., 2000, Webb et al., 2003, Ji et al, 2005], in a non-temporal, non-spatial, and unsupervised setting. The mining of emerging patterns and contrast (classification) patterns have been limited to situations where a number of classes are given. In this work, there is no need to have classes; the data cohorts corresponding to the C2B-C2F combinations can be viewed as dynamically discovered "classes," and the C2Fs can be viewed as the emerging/contrast patterns between those dynamically discovered "classes."

4. The notion of conditional contrast pattern is somehow related to the (generalized) disjunction free representation [Bykowski & Rigotti, 2001] for itemsets. Our study on representation issues of conditional contrast patterns is also related to other studies on concise representation of frequent itemsets and association rules [Kryszkiewicz, 2001, Calders & Goethals, 2002]. It is also related to the rough set approach [Pawlak, 1991].

5. This work is also related to interestingness [Tan et al., 2002] of association rules, especially the so-called "neighborhood based" interestingness [Dong & Li, 1998], and related to actionable rules [Jiang et al., 2005].

6. The mining of C2Ps/C2Fs can be used for unsupervised feature selection [Liu & Motoda, 1998]. Indeed, C2Fs and the items in them can be viewed as important features, since they participate in making big differences between data cohorts. Moreover, C2P/C2F mining does not depend on the existence of classes.

BACKGROUND: CONCEPTS OF CONDITIONAL CONTRAST PATTERNS

We formulate here the concepts of conditional contrast patterns (C2Ps) and conditional contrast factors (C2Fs), together with cost, impact, and (relative) impact-to-cost ratio.

Let I be a set of *items*. An *itemset*, or a *pattern*, is a set of items. A *transaction* is a non-empty set of items, which is also associated with a unique *transaction identity* (TID). A *dataset* is a non-empty multi-set of transactions. Following a popular convention, we write an itemset such as $\{a, b, c\}$ as *abc,* and an TID set such as *{1,2,3,5}* as *1235*. A transaction T is said to *contain* a pattern X if $X \subseteq T$. The *matching dataset* of an itemset X, denoted mat(X), is the set of transactions containing X. The *support* of a pattern X in a dataset D, denoted supp(X), is the number |mat(X)|. A pattern X is *frequent* w.r.t. *ms* in a dataset D if supp(X) $\geq$ *ms*, where *ms* is a given support threshold.

We now turn to the main concepts. We first define potential conditional contrast patterns, and then add restrictions to define the true conditional contrast patterns and conditional contrast factors. Intuitively, a conditional contrast pattern consists of a base and a set of conditional contrast factors, where small changes—the conditional contrast factors—make big differences.

Definition 2.1. *A potential conditional contrast pattern[3] (or PC2P for short) is an ordered pair P = $\langle B, \{F_1, ..., F_k\} \rangle$ where:*

- $k>1$, *an integer, is the* arity *of the PC2P,*
- B, *an itemset, is the* conditional contrast base *(C2B) of the PC2P,*
- $F_1,..., F_k$, *k distinct itemsets, are the* conditional contrast factors *(C2Fs) of the PC2P, and* $\{F_1,...,F_k\}$ *is the* conditional contrast factor set *(C2FS) of the PC2P.*

Example 2.2. The pair $P = \langle abc, \{d, ef\}\rangle$ is a PC2P; abc is the C2B, d and ef are the C2Fs, and $\{d, ef\}$ is the C2FS consisting of two C2Fs.

We are interested in the C2Fs' ability to effectively make big differences among their matching datasets, at a low cost. A C2B is like an efficient "watershed", where the C2Fs are "small" and they separate and direct the data into different valleys. The C2Fs can be considered as "tipping patterns/factors", since these small patterns are associated with big differences. Figure 1 illustrates these points.

To capture the intuition of "small changes making big differences," we need two functions on PC2Ps: cost measures how expensive the first change is, and impact measures how significant the second (induced) change is. They measure different properties: the former is focused on syntax (items) and the latter on the behavior (matching datasets, etc).

Definition 2.3. Given a PC2P $P = \langle B, \{F_1,...,F_k\}\rangle$, we define cost($P$) to be the average number of items used in the C2Fs, and impact(P) to be the average size of the matching dataset differences among the C2Fs; in formula[4].

$$\text{cost}(P) = \frac{\sum_{i=1}^{k}|F_i|}{k}$$

$$\text{impact}(P) = \frac{\sum_{1\le i<j\le k}\left|\text{mat}(B\cup F_i)\Delta\text{mat}(B\cup F_j)\right|}{k(k-1)/2}$$

Combining the two, we define a ratio to measure "per-item ability of conditional contrast factors to make dataset changes".

Definition 2.4. The impact-to-cost ratio and *relative impact-to-cost ratio* of a PC2P P are respectively defined by:

$$\text{icr}(P) = \frac{\text{impact}(P)}{\text{cost}(P)}$$

$$\text{ricr}(P) = \frac{\text{icr}(P)}{\text{supp}(B)}$$

The ricr can be more useful than icr, since it is relative to (the size of) mat(B).

Example 2.5 Let D be a dataset which contains 8 transactions and which satisfies the following (for brevity, the data set itself is omitted): mat(abc) = 12345678, mat($abcd$) = 12345, mat($abcef$) = 13468, and mat($abcg$) = 12678. For $P = \langle abc, \{d, g\}\rangle$, we have:

$$\text{cost}(P) = (|d| + |g|)/2 = 1$$

$$\text{impact}(P) = |\text{mat}(abcd)\Delta\text{mat}(abcg)| = 6$$

$$\text{ricr}(P) = \frac{\text{impact}(P)/\text{cost}(P)}{|\text{mat}(B)|} = \frac{6/1}{8} = 0.75.$$

By letting $B' = B \cup \cap_{i=1}^{k} F_i$ and $F_i' = F_i - B'$, a PC2P $P = \langle B, \{F_1, ..., F_k\}\rangle$ can be simplified into a PC2P $P' = \langle B', \{F_1', ..., F_k'\}\rangle$ where the following hold: icr(P')$\ge$icr(P), $\cap_{i=1}^{k} F_i' = \varnothing$, $B' \supseteq B$, and for each i, $B'\cap F_i' = \varnothing$, $F_i' \subseteq F_i$ and mat($B\cup F_i$) = mat($B'\cup F_i'$) (C2Fs of P' describe the same datasets as C2Fs of P). Below we assume PC2Ps satisfy these conditions unless specified otherwise.

Definition 2.6. Given a threshold $\eta > 0$, an η-conditional contrast pattern is a PC2P $P = \langle B, \{F_1, ..., F_k\}\rangle$ such that ricr(P) $\ge \eta$.

Example 2.7. Continuing with Example 2.5, we have: $P = \langle abc, \{d, g\}\rangle$ is a 0.75-C2P, but it is not a 0.8-C2P.

The conditional contrast factors (C2Fs) can be viewed as "actionable" patterns for the situation described by the C2B: By "making" certain C2Fs false or true through "item-changing actions" (such as financial incentives or medical treatments), certain objects in one C2F's matching dataset may be switched into another C2F's matching dataset. As noted earlier, one can also use C2Fs to identify globally important individual items, which participate in many small C2Fs that make big differences.

We can also modify the icr/ricr definition to encourage the C2Fs to contain different classes or conditions on some (financial) utility attributes, and to consider the varying degree of difficulty in changing items over general attributes.[5]

One may use additional measures to help select interesting C2Ps, especially when there are globally rare items. Consider a dataset D containing a very rare item a. There can be many C2Ps P = <B, {a, {}}> where supp(B) and ricr(P) are high, due to the global rarity of a, not by a's interesting interaction with B; we are not interested in such C2Fs. We can use the minC2Fsupp threshold to fix the problem. We also use the minC2Bsupp threshold to help find C2Ps which cover relatively large number of tuples/transactions.

DOMINANCE BEAM RESULTS

We now consider properties of C2Ps, especially the "dominance beam" property (DBP), for efficient C2P mining. We motivate and define this property, and then establish the results concerning this property which are used in our algorithm.

The Dominance Beam Property

One might be tempted to try to adapt the frequently used anti-monotone property for efficient C2P mining. One may define a measure function f (e.g. ricr) to be *anti-monotone* over the C2Ps w.r.t. a partial order $\leq$ if $f(X) \geq f(Y)$ for all C2Ps X and Y such that $X \leq Y$. (We need to replace the usual $\subseteq$ for itemsets by $\leq$ for C2Ps, since C2Ps are no longer sets.) Unfortunately, it is not clear if there exist such partial orders $\leq$ over C2Ps for which ricr has the anti-monotone property.

Note: The f function discussed in the above paragraph has the C2Ps as its domain. Its range can be any type that has a partial order on it. For example, the range can be the real numbers when f is ricr.

Let us see what anti-monotonicity gives us. It is well known that it allows efficient search by join-based expansion, where one needs to examine a candidate Y only if every immediate subset X of Y is a valid result.

The "dominance beam property" introduced below can also be used for efficient search, and it is a dual of anti-monotonicity in some sense: we need to examine a candidate Y if at least one of its immediate predecessors X is a valid result; in other words, we only need to search along the branches of the search tree whose nodes are all valid results.

Definition 3.1. A function f has the dominance beam property (DBP) w.r.t. a partial order $\leq$ over C2Ps if, for each C2P P, there exists some C2P P' such that P' is an immediate predecessor of P under $\leq$ and $f(P') \geq f(P)$.

The DBP can be used for efficient mining when anti-monotonicity does not hold. This applies to C2P mining. Suppose f has the DBP, σ is a threshold, and we want to mine all C2Ps P such that $f(P) \geq \sigma$. The mining can proceed as follows: We start by constructing an initial set of C2Ps, to consist of all minimal C2Ps P (under

$\leq$) such that $f(P)\geq\sigma$. Then we expand the search by recursively generating all immediate successors of the computed C2Ps P which satisfy $f(P) \geq\sigma$; the DBP ensures that this search will find all desired C2Ps.

One can define several natural partial orders over the C2Ps, including those based on C2B containment, C2FS containment, or C2F containment. Among them, the most useful for us is the one based on C2FS containment. Luckily, we can establish the dominance property for this partial order.

Dominance Beam w.r.t. Conditional Contrast Factor Set

We now present our most useful dominance beam results, for beams which link C2Ps that differ by exactly one C2F. Such results are especially useful because they imply that we only need to search by adding/replacing one C2F at a time when mining C2Ps.

The partial order for such dominance beams is $\leq_{C2FS}$ defined by: Given C2Ps $P1 = \langle B, FS_1 \rangle$ and $P2 = \langle B, FS_2 \rangle$, we say $P_1 \leq_{C2FS} P_2$ if $FS_1 \subseteq FS_2$. In this partial order, P_1 is an immediate predecessor of P_2, and P_2 is an immediate successor of P_1, if $FS_2 - FS_1$ contains exactly one itemset (viewed as a C2F). Moreover, only C2Ps with identical C2Bs are comparable.

Proposition 3.2. (ricr Dominance Beam w.r.t. C2FS) Let $P = \langle B, FS \rangle$ and $FS = \{F_1, .., F_k\}$ where $k>2$. Then for each $1<k'<k$, there is a $P'= \langle B,FS' \rangle$, where $FS' \subset FS$ and $|FS'| = k'$, such that icr$(P') \geq$ icr(P) and ricr$(P') \geq$ ricr(P). In particular, the above is true for $k' = k - 1$.

Proof. By induction, it suffices to consider $k' = k - 1$. For each $J \subset \{1, ..., k\}$ with $|J| = k - 1$, define $ssd(J)= \Sigma_{i,j \in J, i<j}|mat(B \cup F_i)\Delta$mat$(B \cup F_j)|$, and $sz(J)= \Sigma_{i \in J}|F_i|$.

Let us suppose, for a contradiction, that for all $J \subset \{1, ..., k\}$ where $|J| = k - 1$, we have:

$$\frac{ssd(J)}{sz(J)} < \text{icr}(P)*(k-2)/2.$$ So $ssd(J) < sz(J) * \text{icr}(P) * (k-2)/2.$

Summing over all possible J, we get $\Sigma_J ssd(J) < \Sigma_J sz(J)*\text{icr}(P)*(k-2)/2$.

For each pair of distinct $i, j \in \{1, ..., k\}$, there are:

$$\binom{k-2}{k-3} = k - 2$$

subsets J of $\{1,...,k\}$, where $|J| = k - 1$ and $\{i, j\} \subseteq J$. Hence $\Sigma_J ssd(J)=(k-2) *\Sigma_{1\leq i<j\leq k}|mat(B\cup F_i)$ Δmat$(B\cup F_j)| = (k-2)*impact(P)*k *(k-1)/2$. For each $i \in \{1,...,k\}$, there are:

$$\binom{k-1}{k-2} = k - 1$$

subsets J of $\{1,...,k\}$, where $|J|=k-1$ and $i \in J$. Hence $\Sigma_J sz(J)=(k-1)*\Sigma_{1\leq i\leq k}|F_i| = k *(k-1)*$cost$(P)$. Plugging these equalities into $\Sigma_J ssd(J)<\Sigma_J sz(J)*\text{icr}(P) *(k-2)/2$, we get $(k-2)*impact(P)*k *(k-1)/2 < \text{icr}(P)* $cost$(P)*k *(k-1) *(k-2)/2$. It follows that icr$(P) >$ icr(P), a contradiction.

So there is a $J \subset \{1,...,k\}$ where $|J| = k - 1$ and

$$\frac{ssd(J)}{sz(J)} \geq \text{icr}(P)*(k-2)/2,$$

proving the icr case. Since the conditional contrast bases for P and P' are identical, the statement for ricr follows.

Proposition 3.2 says that the impact-to-cost ratio can be increased by deleting C2Fs. Such increase can be achieved until the C2P is reduced to just two C2Fs. No more deletion is possible, since a C2P must have $\geq$ 2 C2Fs by definition.

One may wonder what happens when we further simplify a C2P with just two C2Fs. Here we note that the impact-to-cost ratio still can increase after we replace one of the C2Fs by {}.

Proposition 3.3 Let $P = \langle B, \{F_1, F_2\}\rangle$. Then there exists i such that $\text{icr}(P_i) \geq \text{icr}(P)$ and $\text{ricr}(P_i) \geq \text{ricr}(P)$, where $P_i = \langle B, \{F_i, \{\}\}\rangle$.

Proof. Suppose to the contrary that $\text{icr}(P_i) < \text{icr}(P)$ for each i. Then $|\text{mat}(B \cup F_i) \Delta \text{mat}(B)| < \text{icr}(P) * |F_i|/2$. So $|\text{mat}(B \cup F_1) \Delta \text{mat}(B \cup F_2)| < |\text{mat}(B \cup F_i) \Delta \text{mat}(B)| < \text{icr}(P) * (|F_1| + |F_2|)/2$. This leads to $\text{icr}(P) < \text{icr}(P)$, a contradiction. Hence $\text{icr}(P_i) \geq \text{icr}(P)$ for some i. Since the conditional contrast base has remained the same, we have also $\text{ricr}(P_i) > \text{ricr}(P)$ for some i.

REPRESENTATION ISSUES AND RELATIONSHIP WITH CLOSED PATTERNS AND MINIMAL GENERATORS

A conditional contrast pattern is intended to capture changes in the underlying dataset under some given condition. It is possible for two distinct C2Ps to correspond to exactly the same changes. We consider here the issue of representing such changes and the corresponding C2Ps of such changes. We also discuss C2P/C2F's relationship with closed patterns and minimal generators.

We first define denotational equivalence on PC2Ps, then we take icr into consideration. Let D be a fixed data set.

Definition 4.1. The denotation $[|P|]$ of a PC2P $P = \langle B, FS\rangle$ is defined to be the collection $\{\text{mat}(B \cup F) \mid F \in FS\}$ of sets. The equivalence class $[P]$ of P is defined to be the set $\{P' \mid [|P'|] = [|P|]\}$ of PC2Ps that have the same denotations as P. Moreover, we say that $P = \langle B, FS\rangle$ is redundant if $\|[|P|]\| < |FS|$—i.e., there are distinct $F, F' \in FS$ such that $\text{mat}(B \cup F) = \text{mat}(B \cup F')$.

Before discussing Definition 4.1, we give some background definitions. The *equivalence class* $[X]$ of an itemset X is defined as the set of patterns Y that occur in exactly the same transactions as

X in the given dataset D—viz., $[X] = \{Y \mid \text{mat}(X) = \text{mat}(Y)\}$. The closed patterns are defined as the most specific patterns in these equivalence classes—viz., X is a closed pattern if $X \supseteq Y$ for all $Y \in [X]$. The key patterns are defined as the most general patterns (or equivalently, minimal patterns) in these equivalence classes—viz., X is a key pattern, if there is no pattern $Y \in [X]$ such that $Y \subseteq X$ and $Y \neq X$. It is well known that (i) $[X]$ is convex ($\forall Y_1, Y_2$, and Z, $Z \in [X]$ holds if $Y_1, Y_2 \in [X]$ and $Y_1 \subseteq Z \subseteq Y_2$); (ii) $[X]$ has exactly one closed pattern and it has one or more key patterns.

The definition of $[|P|]$ is set theoretic and ignores the icr. There can be multiple PC2Ps in an equivalence class. The definition of redundancy is aimed at avoiding uninformative C2Fs. Consider $P_1 = \langle B, \{F_1, \{\}\}\rangle$, $P_2 = \langle B, \{F_2, \{\}\}\rangle$, and $P_{12} = \langle B, \{F_1, F_2, \{\}\}\rangle$, where $B \cup F_1$ and $B \cup F_2$ are distinct key patterns of $[B \cup F_1]$. Then P_1, P_2 and P_{12} are in the same equivalence class. The C2Fs F_1 and F_2 in P_{12} are referring to the same underlying matching dataset, which is why P_{12} is redundant. The definition ensures that every C2F in a non-redundant PC2P refers to a distinct matching dataset. We focus on non-redundant PC2Ps from now on.

Equivalence classes have some nice structural properties.

Proposition 4.2. Let $P = \langle B, \{F_1, ..., F_k\}\rangle$ be a PC2P. For each i, let cF_i be the closed itemset of $[B \cup F_i]$.

1. Let $\text{BS}([P]) = \{B' \mid$ there is a FS' where $\langle B', FS'\rangle \in [P]\}$ be the set of all C2Bs that occur in $[P]$. Then $\text{BS}([P])$ is convex, $\{\}$ is its most general (minimum) itemset, and $\hat{B} = \cap_{i=1}^{k} cF_i$ is its most specific (maximum) itemset.

2. Given itemset $B' \in \text{BS}([P])$ and $i \in [1..k]$, let $\text{FBS}([P], B', i) = \{F' \mid$ there is a FS' such that $\langle B', FS'\rangle \in [P]$, $F' \in FS'$, and $\text{mat}(B' \cup F') = \text{mat}(B \cup F_i)\}$. That is, $\text{FBS}([P], B', i)$ is the set of all C2Fs that can substitute for F_i for a fixed C2B B'. Then $\text{FBS}([P], B', i)$ is convex and cF_i is its most specific itemset.

Proof. To prove Part (1), note that $\langle\{\},$ $\{cF_1,...,cF_k\}\rangle$ and $\langle\hat{B}, \{cF_1,...,cF_k\}\rangle$ are clearly in $[P]$. Thus $\{\}$ and $\hat{B}$ are in $BS[P]$. It is obvious that $\{\}$ is minimum in $BS[P]$.

To show that $\hat{B}$ is maximum in $BS([P])$, let $P' = \langle B', FS'\rangle$ be an arbitrary PC2P in $[P]$. Then $[|P'|] = \{mat(B' \cup F) \mid F \in FS'\} = [|P|] = \{mat(B \cup F_1),...,mat(B \cup F_k)\}$. Since B' occurs in all transactions in the denotations of P', we know that B' occurs in all transactions in $mat(B \cup F_i)$, for $1 \le i \le k$. Then $B' \subseteq cF_i$ for $1 \le i \le k$, since cF_i is the closed pattern of $[B \cup F_i]$. Hence $B' \subseteq \hat{B} = \cap_{i=1}^{k} cF_i$. Therefore $\hat{B}$ is the maximum among all the C2Bs of $[P]$.

To show that $BS([P])$ is convex, suppose $X \subseteq Y \subseteq Z$ and $X, Z \in BS([P])$. Then $Y \subseteq Z \subseteq \hat{B} = \cap_{i=1}^{k} cF_i$. Then $mat(Y \cup cF_i) = mat(cF_i) = mat(B \cup F_i)$ for $1 \le i \le k$. Thus $\langle Y, \{cF_1, ..., cF_k\}\rangle \in [P]$. So $Y \in BS([P])$, proving Part (1).

To prove Part (2), note that for any $B' \in BS([P])$, it is the case that $\langle B', \{cF_1, ..., cF_k\}\rangle \in [P]$. Thus $cF_i \in FBS([P], B', i)$, for $B' \in BS([P])$ and $1 \le i \le k$. Suppose $F' \in FBS([P], B', i)$. Then $mat(B' \cup F') = mat(B \cup F_i) = mat(cF_i)$ by construction. Since cF_i is the closed pattern of $mat(B \cup F_i)$, we have $B' \cup F' \subseteq cF_i$. Thus $F' \subseteq cF_i$. So cF_i is the most specific itemset in $FBS([P], B', i)$.

To show that $FBS([P], B', i)$ is convex, suppose $X \subseteq Y \subseteq Z$ and $X, Z \in FBS([P], B', i)$. Then $mat(B' \cup X) = mat(B' \cup Z) = mat(B \cup F_i)$ by construction. Thus $B' \cup X \in [B \cup F_i]$ and $B' \cup Z \in [B \cup F_i]$. Then $B' \cup Y \in [B \cup F_i]$ by convexity of $[B \cup F_i]$. So $mat(B' \cup Y) = mat(B \cup F_i)$. It follows that $\langle B', \{cF_1, ..., cF_{i-1}, Y, cF_{i+1}, ..., cF_k\}\rangle \in [P]$. Thus $Y \in FBS([P], B', i)$. So $FBS([P], B', i)$ is convex as required.

We note that a C2B can influence the choice of patterns that can be used as C2Fs. Specifically, a C2B $B' \in BS([P])$ cannot be too specific, since it must leave some items in cF_i for use in the C2Fs to uniquely identify $mat(B \cup F_1), ..., mat(B \cup F_k)$; but it can be very general.

We now show that the equivalence classes of C2Ps can be represented by key and closed patterns.

Proposition 4.3. Let $P = \langle B, FS\rangle$ be a PC2P, where $FS = \{F_1, ..., F_k\}$. Let cF_i be the closed pattern of $[B \cup F_i]$ for $1 \le i \le k$. Let $\hat{B} = \cap_{i=1}^{k} cF_i$. Then:

1. $\langle\hat{B}, \{cF_i - \hat{B} \mid 1 \le i \le k\}\rangle \in [P]$.
2. $\langle\cap_{1 \le i \le k} kF_i, \{kF_j - \cap_{1 \le i \le k} kF_i \mid 1 \le j \le k\}\rangle \in [P]$, where kF_i is a key pattern of $[B \cup F_i]$ for $1 \le i \le k$.
3. $\langle\hat{B}, \{kF_i - \hat{B} \mid 1 \le i \le k\}\rangle \in [P]$, where kF_i is a key pattern of $[B \cup F_i]$.
4. $\langle B', FS'\rangle \in [P]$ iff (a) for each $F' \in FS'$, there is $F \in FS$ satisfying $kF \subseteq B' \cup F' \subseteq cF$; and (b) for each $F \in FS$, there is $F' \in FS'$ satisfying $kF \subseteq B' \cup F' \subseteq cF$, where kF is a key, and cF is the closed, pattern of $[B \cup F]$.

Proof. Parts (1), (2), and (3) follow from the fact that $[B \cup F_i] = [cF_i] = [kF_i]$ for $1 \le i \le k$. Part (4) follows from the fact that, for any pattern X and Y, it is the case that $Y \in [X]$ iff $kX \subseteq Y \subseteq cX$, where kX is a key pattern of $[X]$ and cX is the closed pattern of $[X]$.

Consequently, for any PC2P $P = \langle B, \{F_1, ..., F_k\}\rangle$, the following are possible choices for a "canonical" representative of its equivalence class $[P]$ (where cF_i is the closed pattern of $[B \cup F_i]$ for $1 \le i \le k$):

- minCP is the (singleton) set of non-redundant PC2Ps in CP $= \{\langle \cap_{1 \le i \le k} cF_i, \{cF_j - \cap_{1 \le i \le k} cF_i \mid 1 \le j \le k\}\rangle\}$;
- minKP is the set of non-redundant PC2Ps in KP $= \{\langle\cap_{1 \le i \le k} kF_i, \{kF_j - \cap_{1 \le i \le k} cF_i \mid 1 \le j \le k\}\rangle \mid kF_i$ is a key pattern of $[B \cup F_i]\}$; and
- minCKP is the set of non-redundant PC2Ps in KCP $= \{\langle\cap_{1 \le i \le k} cF_i, \{kF_j - \cap_{1 \le i \le k} cF_i \mid 1 \le j \le k\}\rangle \mid kF_i$ is a key pattern of $[B \cup F_i]$ for $1 \le i \le k\}$.

The choice of minCP as a canonical representative of the equivalence class is nice in the sense that it is guaranteed to be a unique representative. But it has one weakness because it often has low—though not always the lowest[6]—impact-to-cost ratio in PC2Ps of its equivalence class.

On the other hand, PC2Ps in the set minKP generally have high—though not always the highest[7]—impact-to-cost ratios among the PC2Ps in [P]. Similar to minCKP, they do not guarantee a unique canonical representative. They are worse than minCKP is this aspect. All the PC2Ps in minCKP have exactly the same conditional contrast base, because of the uniqueness of closed patterns. In contrast, the PC2Ps in minKP may not have the same conditional contrast base.

As mentioned above, the PC2Ps in the set minCKP do not guarantee a unique canonical representative, even though they have the same conditional contrast base. Nevertheless, they are nice in a different way. Specifically, they have the highest impact-to-cost ratios among the non-redundant PC2Ps in [P]. For this reason, we recommend the PC2Ps in minCKP as canonical representatives, and think that the mining of conditional contrast patterns should be restricted to these canonical PC2Ps.

Proposition 4.4. (Optimality of minCKP) For each non-redundant PC2P $P'' \in [P]$, there is a $P' \in$ minCKP$\subseteq[P]$, such that icr(P') $\geq$ icr(P'') and ricr(P') $\geq$ ricr(P''). Consequently, the PC2Ps in minCKP are among the non-redundant PC2Ps having the highest icr and ricr in [P].

Proof. Let $P = \langle B, \{F_1, ..., F_k\}\rangle$. Let $P'' = \langle B'', \{F_1'', ..., F_k''\}\rangle$ be a non-redundant PC2P in [P]. By rearrangement if necessary, by Part (4) of Proposition 4.3, we can assume that $kF_i \subseteq B'' \cup F_i'' \subseteq cF_i$, where cF_i is the closed pattern of $[B \cup F_i]$ and kF_i is some key pattern of $[B \cup F_i]$, for $1 \leq i \leq k$.

Now, let $B' = \cap_{1 \leq i \leq k} cF_i$, $F_i' = kF_i' - B'$, and $P' = \langle B', \{F_1', ..., F_k'\}\rangle$. By Proposition 4.2, we have $B' \subseteq B$. For each $1 \leq i \leq k$, from $kF_i \subseteq B'' \cup F_i''$, we get $F_i' = kF_i' - B' \subseteq (B' \cup F_i'') - B' \subseteq F_i''$. So (i) cost($P'$) $\leq$ cost(P'').

We know by construction that $[B' \cup F_i'] = [kF_i'] = [B'' \cup F_i'']$. So mat($B' \cup F_i'$) = mat($B'' \cup F_i''$), for $1 \leq i \leq k$. This implies (ii) impact(P')$\geq$impact(P''). Combining (i) and (ii), we obtain (iii) icr(P')$\geq$icr(P'').

By Proposition 4.2, we have $B'' \subseteq B'$. So supp(B'')$\geq$supp(B'). Combined with (iii), we get ricr(P')$\geq$ricr(P).

Another nice property enjoyed by minCKP is that the unique C2B in these PC2Ps is a closed pattern. This special property is useful for the mining of conditional contrast patterns, as it allows us to anchor the mining process on closed patterns.

Proposition 4.5 Given an equivalence class [P], the C2B of the PC2Ps in minCKP is unique and is a closed pattern.

In practice, one may want to be able to easily test whether an arbitrary PC2P P' is in the equivalence class of another PC2P P. Representing an equivalence class by a single canonical PC2P does not facilitate such tests. We suggest that the equivalence class [P] of a (non-redundant) PC2P $P = \langle B, \{F_1, ..., F_k\}\rangle$ be represented by a set of borders $\langle B', \{\langle K_1', C_1'\rangle, ..., \langle K_k', C_k'\rangle\}\rangle$, where C_i is the closed pattern of $[B \cup F_i]$, K_i is the set of key patterns of $[B \cup F_i]$, $B' = \cap_{1 \leq i \leq k} C_i$, $C_i' = C_i - B'$, and $K_i' = \{K - B' | K \in K_i\}$, for $1 \leq i \leq k$. This representation allows us to readily test if a PC2P is in a particular equivalence class as per Part (4) of Proposition 4.3. It also let us quickly enumerate all minCKP, which are the PC2Ps having the highest impact-to-cost ratios in [P].

THE C2PMINER ALGORITHM

In this section, we present our C2PMiner algorithm for mining conditional contrast patterns. The algorithm uses four thresholds: minC2Pricr, maxC2Fcost, minC2Bsupp and minC2Fsupp. The first two thresholds ensure that only interesting conditional contrast patterns with low cost and high ricr are discovered. The last two parameters ensure that the mined conditional contrast patterns have big absolute changes, and the big changes are not caused by conditional contrast

Box 1. Algorithm 1 C2PMiner

Input: A dataset D and four thresholds: minC2Bsupp, minC2Fsupp, maxC2Fcost, minC2Pricr.

Output:

All desired C2Ps satisfying the thresholds, under the minCKP representation.

Description:

1: Use a modified GcGrowth to mine a) the set of frequent closed itemsets CS_b wrt minC2Bsupp and all of their keys, and b) the set of closed itemsets CS_f and their keys such that for each closed itemset $X \in CS_f$, there exists a closed itemset $Y \in CS_b$ such that $X \supset Y$, $|kX - Y| \leq maxC2Fcost$ and $supp(kX - Y) \geq minC2Fsupp$. Build inverted files on $CS_b \cup CS_f$ to facilitate subsequent superset search.

2: For each closed itemset $B \in CS_b$ do:

2.a) Use the inverted files to find all the supersets of B. For each superset X, test and generate C2Ps of the form $P = \langle B, \{kX - B, \{\}\}\rangle$, where kX is a key of X satisfying $|kX - B| \leq maxC2Fcost$ and $supp(kX - B) \geq minC2Fsupp$. Maintain all the generated C2Fs $kX - B$ in a list CandC2Fs. Output P if $ricr(P) \geq minC2Pricr$.

2.b) Call DFSMineC2P(B, CandC2Fs, |CandC2Fs|) to generate all the C2Ps with B as conditional contrast base and containing more than one non-empty C2Fs. This procedure uses the dominance beam properties to search for C2Ps meeting the thresholds.

---

factors alone but caused by adding conditional contrast factors to conditional contrast bases. A conditional contrast pattern $P = \langle B, \{F_1, F_2, .., F_k\}\rangle$ is called desired if P satisfies $supp(B) \geq minC2Bsupp$, $ricr(P) \geq minC2Pricr$, $|F_i| \leq maxC2Fcost$ and $supp(F_i) \geq minC2Fsupp$ for all $i \in [1, k]$.

The C2PMiner algorithm first mines frequent closed itemsets and keys with respect to minC2Bsupp simultaneously using the GcGrowth algorithm [Li et al., 2005]. The frequent closed itemsets are used as candidate conditional contrast bases. We modified the GcGrowth algorithm to mine those closed itemsets X and their keys kX such that $|kX - B| \leq maxC2Fcost$, $supp(kX - B) \geq minC2Fsupp$ and $B \subset X$, where B is some frequent closed itemset. We build inverted files on closed itemsets to facilitate subsequent superset search. Next C2PMiner generates all C2Ps containing only one non-empty conditional contrast factor, and then uses these C2Ps as starting patterns to generate all the C2Ps containing more than one non-empty C2Fs based on the dominance-beam properties given in Section 3. The pseudo-code of the C2PMiner algorithm is given in Algorithm 1. It calls a procedure DFSMineC2P(B, CandC2Fs,

L) to generate all the C2Ps containing more than one non-empty C2Fs. This procedure uses the dominance beam properties to search for C2Ps meeting the thresholds.

Now we describe how DFSMineC2P(B, CandC2Fs, L) works. Besides using the dominance-beam properties, C2PMiner uses the relative impact of conditional contrast factors with respect to conditional contrast bases to prune the search space. The relative impact of a conditional contrast factor F with respect to a conditional contrast base B is defined as $rimp(F,B) = (supp(B) - supp(B \cup F))/supp(B)$.

Lemma 5.1. Let $P = \langle B, \{F_1, ..., F_k\}\rangle$. If $ricr(P) \geq minC2Pricr$, then we have $\sum_{i-1}^{k} rimp(F_i, B) \geq k'* minC2Pricr/2$, where k' is the number of non-empty conditional contrast factors in P. (see Box 2)

When generating the C2Ps containing only one non-empty conditional contrast factor, C2PMiner also maintains the list of candidate conditional contrast factors for each conditional contrast base B, denoted as CandC2Fs(B), and calculates

Box 2. Lemma 5.1 proof

$$minC2Pricr \leq ricr(P) = \frac{\sum_{1 \leq i < j \leq k} supp(B \cup F_i) + supp(B \cup F_j) - 2supp(B \cup F_i \cup F_j)}{supp(B) * (k-1)/2 * \sum_{i=1}^{k} |F_i|}$$

$$\leq \frac{\sum_{1 \leq i < j \leq k}(supp(B) - supp(B \cup F_i) + supp(B) - supp(B \cup F_j))}{supp(B) * (k-1)/2 * \sum_{i=1}^{k} |F_i|}$$

$$\leq \frac{(k-1)\sum_{i=1}^{k}(supp(B) - supp(B \cup F_i))}{supp(B) * (k-1)/2 * k'}$$

$$= \frac{2\sum_{i=1}^{k} rimp(F_i, B)}{k'}$$

Proof:

Hence we have $\sum_{i-1}^{k} rimp(Fi, B) \geq k'* minC2Pricr/2$.

Box 3. Algorithm 2 DFSMineC2P(B, CandC2Fs, L)

Input:

B is a conditional contrast base, *CandC2Fs* is the set of candidate C2Fs of B and L is the size of *CandC2Fs*

Output:

All desired C2Ps containing more than one non-empty C2Fs with B as base.

Description:

1: **for** i=1 to L **do**

2:   $FS = FS \cup CandC2Fs[i]$;

3:   $rimp\_sum = rimp\_sum + rimp(CandC2Fs[i], B)$;

4:   **if** $CandC2Fs[i] \neq \emptyset$ **then**

5:     $k' = k'+1$;

6:   **if** $k' \geq 2$ AND $ricr(P=\langle B, FS \rangle) \geq minC2Pricr$ **then**

7:     Output $P = \langle B, FS \rangle$;

8:     **if** $k_{max} < |FS|$ **then**

9:       $k_{max} = |FS|$;

10:   **if** $i>0$ AND $|FS| \leq k_{max}$ AND ($rimp\_sum \geq k'* minC2Pricr/2$ OR $rimp(CandC2Fs[i-1], B) \geq minC2Pricr/2$) **then**

11:       DFSMineC2P(B, CandC2Fs, i–1));

12:   $FS = FS - CandC2Fs[i]$;

13:   $rimp\_sum = rimp\_sum - rimp(CandC2Fs[i], B)$;

14:   **if** $CandC2Fs[i] \neq \emptyset$ **then**

15:     $k' = k' - 1$;

the relative impact of the candidate conditional contrast factors. Here we say a conditional contrast factor F is a candidate conditional contrast factor of B if $|F| \leq maxC2Fcost$ and $supp(F) \geq minC2Fsupp$. Any combination of the candidate conditional contrast factors can form a conditional contrast factor set of B, so the search space of conditional contrast factor set wrt B is the power set of $CandC2Fs(B)$. The C2PMiner algorithm explores the search space in the depth-first order. It sorts the candidate conditional contrast factors of B in ascending order of relative impact. The candidate extensions of a conditional contrast factor include all the conditional contrast factors that are before it in the ascending order. During the mining process, C2PMiner maintains the accumulated relative impact of the C2Fs on the current path, denoted as *rimp_sum*. Let F be the current candidate C2F to be appended. If *rimp_sum* $< k'^*$ *minC2Pricr/2* and *rimp(F)* $<$ *minC2Pricr/2*, where k' is the number of non-empty C2Fs on the current path, then there is no need to explore the current branch further based on Lemma 5.1.

The C2PMiner algorithm uses the dominance beam property with respect to C2FS as follows. It explores the search space in ascending order of relative impact of the conditional contrast factors, and the candidate extensions of a condi-

tional contrast factor includes all the conditional contrast factors that are before it in the ascending order of relative impact. Therefore, the subsets of a conditional contrast factor set *FS* are always discovered before *FS*. C2PMiner maintains the maximal number of conditional contrast factors contained in the desired conditional contrast patterns that have been generated, denoted as k_{max}. If the current exploration depth is greater than k_{max}, it means that none of the immediate subsets of the current conditional contrast factor set *FS* satisfies the minC2Pricr threshold, so there is no need to explore further based on Proposition 3.2.

Algorithm 2 shows the pseudo-codes of the DFSMineC2P(B, *CandC2Fs*, L) procedure. During the depth first exploration, C2PMiner maintains the set of C2Fs on the current path, denoted as *FS*, the accumulated relative impact of the C2Fs in *FS*, denoted as *rimp_sum*, the number of non-empty C2Fs in *FS*, denoted as k' and the maximal number of conditional contrast factors contained in the conditional contrast factor sets that have been generated, denoted as k_{max}. Initially, *rimp_sum* and k' are set to 0, k_{max} is set to 2 and *FS* is set to {}.

The correctness and completeness of the C2P-Miner algorithm is guaranteed by Proposition 3.2, Proposition 3.3 and Lemma 5.1.

Figure 2. Runtime vs. ricr

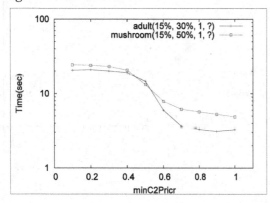

Figure 3. Runtime vs. minC2Bsupp

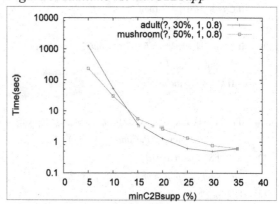

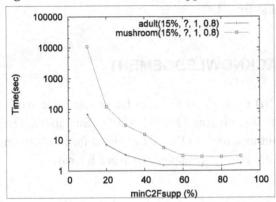

Figure 4. Runtime vs. minC2Fsupp

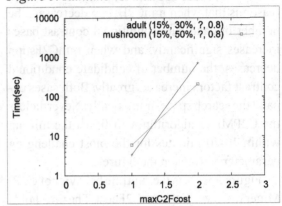

Figure 5. Runtime vs. maxC2Fcost

EXPERIMENTAL EVALUATION

This section describes an experimental evaluation of the performance of the C2Pminer algorithm. We will show that the algorithm is effective in C2P mining; there is of course still room for further improvement. Since this is the first paper on C2P mining, there are no previous algorithms to compare against. The program was written in C++. The experiments were performed on a machine running Microsoft Windows XP professional, with a 3.00GHz CPU and 2GB memory.

Datasets used: In this paper (here and Section 1) we consider four datasets: two microarray gene expression datasets (one for acute lymphoblastic leukemia sub-type study [Yeoh et al, 2002] and another for prostate cancer [Singh et al., 2002]), and two datasets from the UCI repository. All are dense datasets and frequently used in data mining evaluations. An entropy-based method [Fayyad & Irani, 1993] was used to discretize continuous attributes into ≥2 bins. (-23, 24] represents an interval; <11 represents the interval of $(-\infty, 11)$. Each gene has an ID of the form 36533_at. The other two datasets are available at the UCI repository. The adult dataset was extracted from the 1994 U.S. Census. It was originally collected to predict whether an individual's income exceeds $50K

per year based on census data. The attributes are concerned with personal economical, educational, and family conditions etc. Each sample contains 15 features. The mushroom dataset consists of 8124 hypothetical mushroom samples. Each sample has 23 features.

Runtime performance: The first experiment evaluates C2PMiner's efficiency w.r.t. the four thresholds. We conducted this experiment on datasets adult and mushroom. Figures 2–5 show the results. In the figures, a question mark "?" indicates that the threshold is the varying one.

Figure 2 reports the runtime behavior of C2P-miner when varying minC2Pricr. The thresholds are fixed at (10%, 30%, 1,?) for adult, and at (10%, 50%, 1,?) for mushroom. The figure shows that execution time grows at roughly a linear speed when ricr decreases.

Figure 3 reports the runtime behavior of C2P-Miner when varying minC2Bsupp. The thresholds are fixed at (?, 30%, 1, 0.8) for adult, and at (?, 50%, 1, 0.8) for mushroom.

Figure 4 reports the runtime behavior when varying minC2Fsupp. The thresholds are fixed at (10%, ?, 1, 0.8) for both datasets.

Figures 3 and 4 show that the running time of C2PMiner grows much faster than linear when minC2Bsupp or minC2Fsupp decreases. The reason is that when minC2Bsupp decreases, the number of candidate conditional contrast bases increases significantly, and when minC2Fsupp decreases, the number of candidate conditional contrast factors increases greatly. Both cases expand the search space dramatically. Nevertheless the C2PMiner algorithm can finish the mining within 10-20 minutes for the most challenging parameter settings in the figures.

Figure 5 reports the runtime behavior of C2P-Miner when varying maxC2Fcost. The thresholds are fixed at (10%, 50%, ?, 0.8) for adult, and at (10%, 60%, ?, 0.8) for mushroom. When individual C2F size of 2 is allowed, the execution time becomes much longer than when it is limited to 1. The reason is: The most expensive step in the C2PMiner algorithm generates all the C2Ps containing more than one non-empty conditional contrast factors, and the search space of conditional contrast factor sets is exponential to the number of candidate conditional contrast factors; moreover, when maxC2Fcost increases from 1 to 2, the number of potential candidate conditional contrast factors increases sharply.

CONCLUDING REMARKS

This chapter introduced the concepts of conditional contrast patterns and conditional contrast factors, as pattern types for data mining. These concepts capture small patterns that make big matching dataset differences. The paper presented theoretical results on the dominance beam property (which allows expansion-based search), on representation issues of conditional contrast patterns, and on relationship of conditional contrast patterns/conditional contrast factors with closed itemsets and keys/generators. It also designed an algorithm called C2PMiner based on those results. Experimental results demonstrated the performance of the algorithm, and produced inter-esting patterns from datasets on cancer research and from UCI.

ACKNOWLEDGEMENT

Part of work by Guozhu Dong was done while he was visiting I2R and NUS of Singapore. The authors wish to thank Lei Duan for his help on converting the paper into Word format.

REFERENCES

Agrawal, R., Imielinski, T., & Swami, A. (1993). Mining Association Rules between Sets of Items in Large Databases. *In Proc. ACM-SIGMOD Int. Conf. Management of Dat*a (pp. 207–216).

Bay, S. D., & Pazzani, M. J. (2001). Detecting Group Differences: Mining Contrast Sets. *Data Mining and Knowledge Discovery*.

Bykowski, A., & Rigotti, C. (2001). A condensed representation to find frequent patterns. *In Proc. of PODS*.

Calders, T., & Goethals, B. (2002). Mining all non-derivable frequent itemsets. *In Proc. of PKDD*. (pp. 74–85).

Dong, G., & Li, J. (1998). Interestingness of Discovered Association Rules in terms of Neighborhood-Based Unexpectedness. *In Proc. Pacific Asia Conf. on Knowledge Discovery and Data Mining*.

Dong, G., & Duan, L. (2008). *Mining Class Converters for Converting Undesirable Objects into Desirable Ones*. Submitted for publication.

Dong, G., & Li, J. (1999). Efficient mining of emerging pat-terns: Discovering trends and differences. *In Proc. of the 5th ACM SIGKDD Int'l Conf. on Knowledge Discovery and Data Mining*.

Fayyad, U., & Irani, K. (1993). Multi-interval discretization of continuous-valued attributes for classification learning. *In Proceedings of the 13th International Joint Conference on Artificial Intelligence.*

Ganter, B., & Wille, R. (1999). *Formal Concept Analysis: Mathematical Foundations.* Springer, Heidelberg.

Ganti, V., Gehrke, J., Ramakrishnan, R., & Loh, W. Y. (1999). A Framework for Measuring Changes in Data Characteristics. *In Proc. of ACM PODS* (pp. 126–137).

Ji, X., Bailey, J., & Dong, G. (2005). Mining Minimal Distinguish-ing Subsequence Patterns with Gap Constraints. *In Proc. of ICDM.*

Jiang, Y., Wang, K., Tuzhilin, A., & Fu, A. (2005). Mining Patterns That Respond to Actions. *In Proc. of IEEE International Conference on Data Mining.*

Kryszkiewicz, M. (2001). Concise Representation of Frequent Patterns Based on Disjunction-Free Generators. *In Proc. of ICDM* (pp. 305–312).

Li, H., Li, J., Wong, L., Feng, M., & Tan, Y.-P. (2005). Relative Risk and Odds Ratio: A Data Mining Perspective. In Proceedings of 23rd ACM Symposium on Principles of Database Systems (pp. 368–377).

Liu, B., Hsu, W., Han, H.-S., & Xia, Y. (2000). Mining Changes for Real-Life Applications. *In Proc. of DaWaK* (pp. 337–346).

Liu, H., & Motoda, H. (1998). *Feature Selection for Knowl-edge Discovery and Data Mining.* Kluwer Academic Publishers.

Mineau, G., & Ganter, B. (Eds.) (2000). Proceedings of International Conference on Conceptual Structures, 2000. *LNCS 1867*, Springer.

Tan, P. N., Kumar, V., & Srivastava, J. (2002). Selecting the right interestingness measure for association patterns. *In Proceedings of KDD.*

Pasquier, N., Bastide, Y., Taouil, R., & Lakhal, L. (1999). Discovering Frequent Closed Itemsets for Association Rules. *In Proc. of ICDT 1999* (pp. 398–416).

Pawlak, Z. (1991). *Rough Sets: Theoretical Aspects of Reasoning About Data.* Kluwer Academic Publishers.

Pei, J., Han, J., & Lakshmanan, L. V. S. (2001). Mining Frequent Item Sets with Convertible Constraints. *In Proceedings of the 17th International Conference on Data Engineering* (pp. 433–442).

Singh, D., et al (2002). Gene expression correlates of clinical prostate cancer behavior. *Cancer Cell, 1*, 203–209.

Wang, J., Han, J., & Pei, J. (2003). CLOSET+: Searching for the Best Strategies for Mining Frequent Closed Itemsets. *In Proceedings of KDD.*

Webb, G. I., Buttler, S., & Newlands, D. (2003). On Detecting Differences Between Groups. *In Proceedings of KDD.*

Yeoh, E. J., et al (2002). Classification, subtype discovery, and prediction of outcome in pediatric acute lymphoblastic leukemia by gene ex-pression profiling. *Cancer Cell, 1*, 133–143.

Zaki, M., & Hsiao, C. (2002). CHARM: An efficient algorithm for closed itemset mining. *In Proceedings of SDM.*

ENDNOTES

[1] There is no $k = 1$ case. To contrast the matching dataset of $B \cup F_1$ against that of B, one can use the C2P of $\langle B, \{F_1, \{\}\} \rangle$.

[2] We also found similar C2Ps from other datasets, including a prostate cancer microarray gene expression dataset [Singh et al., 2002] and some datasets from the UCI repository.

3   One may also define a PC2P as a set $\{X_1, ..., X_k\}$ of itemsets, and define the C2B and C2Fs as

$$B = \cap_{i=1}^{k} X_i \text{ and } F_i = X_i - B.$$

4   We denote the symmetric set difference as Δ. Given two sets X and Y, the set X Δ Y is defined to be *(X-Y)* $\cup$ *(Y-X)*.

5   Reference [Jiang et al., 2005] considers changing utility attributes for actionable rules. Reference [Dong & Duan, 2008] considers the mining of converter sets (each of which is a set of attribute changes) to convert undesirable objects into desirable ones.

6   To see that the unique PC2P in minCP does not have the lowest icr among PC2Ps in [P], consider D = {*abcdk, abek, abfgjk, bg, ah*} and P = $\langle b, \{ak, fg\}\rangle$. Then minCP = {$P'$} = {$\langle abk, \{\{\}, fgj\}\rangle$} and icr(P)=1<4/3=icr($P'$).

7   To see that PC2Ps in minKP do not have the highest icr among PC2Ps in [P], consider D = {*abcdk, abek, abfk, bg, ah*}. Let P = $\langle b, \{a, f\}\rangle$. Then one of PC2Ps in minKP is P'= $\langle\{\}, \{ab, f\}\rangle$. Clearly, icr($P'$)<icr(P).

Chapter XVI
Multidimensional Model–Based Decision Rules Mining

Qinrong Feng
Tongji University, China

Duoqian Miao
Tongji University, China

Ruizhi Wang
Tongji University, China

ABSTRACT

Decision rules mining is an important technique in machine learning and data mining, it has been studied intensively during the past few years. However, most existing algorithms are based on flat data tables, from which sets of decision rules mined may be very large for massive data sets. Such sets of rules are not easily understandable and really useful for users. Moreover, too many rules may lead to over-fitting. Thus, a method of decision rules mining from different abstract levels was provided in this chapter, which aims to improve the efficiency of decision rules mining by combining the hierarchical structure of multidimensional model and the techniques of rough set theory. Our algorithm for decision rules mining follows the so called separate-and-conquer strategy. Namely, certain rules were mined beginning from the most abstract level, and supporting sets of those certain rules were removed from the universe, then drill down to the next level to recursively mine other certain rules which supporting sets are included in the remaining objects until no objects remain in the universe or getting to the primitive level. So this algorithm can output some generalized rules with different degree of generalization.

INTRODUCTION

Decision rules mining is an important technique in data mining and machine learning. It has been widely used in business, medicine and finance, etc. A multitude of promising algorithms of decision rules mining (Xiaohua Hu & Nick Cercone, 1997, 2001; Michiyuki Hirokane, et al. 2007; María C. Fernández, et al. 2001) have been developed during the past few years.

The aim of decision rules mining is to find a good rule set, which has a minimum number of rules and each rule should be as short as possible. We all know, each row of a decision table specifies a decision rule that determine decisions in terms of conditions. Thus, a set of decision rules mined from a decision table may be very large for a massive data set. Such a set of rules are not easily understandable and really useful for users. Moreover, too many rules may lead to over-fitting. Most existing methods to this problem follow the strategy of post-processing for those mined decision rules.

Marek Sikora and Marcin Michalak (2006) summed up that post-processing of decision rules mining can be implemented in two ways: rules generalization (rules shortening and rules joining) and rules filtering (rules that are not needed in view of certain criterion are removed from the final rules set). The technique of rules generalization is to obtain rules from detailed level first, and then use the techniques of generalization for these rules, combination or joining to reduce the number of decision rules. The technique of rules filtering is accomplished by template, interestingness or constraint to further process those rules mined from detailed level.

Most existing algorithms of decision rules mining only manipulate data at individual level, namely, they have not consider the case of multiple abstract levels for the given data set. However, in many applications, data contain structured information which is multidimensional and multilevel in nature, such as e-commerce, stocks, scientific data, etc. That is, there exists partial order relation among some attribute values in the given dataset, such as *day, month, quarter* and *year* for *Time* attribute. The partial order relation among attribute values for each attribute can be represented by a tree or a lattice, which constitutes a concept hierarchy. Obviously, there exists the relation of generalization or specification among concepts at different levels.

In this chapter, an approach to mine decision rules from various abstract levels is provided, which aims to improve the efficiency of decision rules mining by combining the multidimensional model (Antoaneta Ivanova & Boris Rachev, 2004) and rough set theory (Z. Pawlak, 1991; Wang Guoyin, 2001; Zhang Wenxiu et al. 2003).

Multidimensional model is a variation of the relational model that uses multidimensional structures to organize data and express the relationships among data, in which the data is presented as a data cube. A multidimensional model includes a number of dimensions that each includes multiple levels of abstraction defined by concept hierarchies, where hierarchy is a way to organize data at different levels of granularity. This organization provides users with the flexibility to view data from different perspectives. The most advantage of multidimensional model is that data can be visualized and manipulated by a compact and easy-to-understand way.

By using the hierarchical structure of a multidimensional model it is possible to "scan" the given data set at the different levels of abstraction to find some interesting patterns or rules. At each level, the techniques of rough sets can then be used to discover and analyze significant patterns or rules.

The advantage of our multidimensional model is that the contents of cells in data cube is a set of objects (an equivalence class induced by those dimension members located at the edges of the cell in data cube) not a numerical data as usual.

Consequently, the operation of aggregate in this multidimensional model is the union of the contents of cells. That is, the contents of those cells at the higher abstract level are those of unions of those cells at the lower abstract level correspondingly. In the multidimensional model, we can not only reduce the data scale by the operation of roll-up along the multiple dimensions simultaneously, but also improve the quality of data with incompleteness, uncertainty or inconsistent. To our knowledge, this kind of multidimensional model has not been reported in the existing literature.

In this chapter, we notice that attribute values are hierarchical in many applications, so a method of decision rules mining from multiple abstract levels is provided. Our algorithm follows the so-called separate-and-conquer strategy. Namely, certain rules are mined beginning from the most abstract level, and remove supporting sets of those certain rules from the universe, then drill down to the next level to recursively mine other certain rules which supporting sets is included in the remaining objects until no objects remain in universe or getting to the primitive level. Firstly, data are generalized along members of dimensions by the characteristic of dimension hierarchies and then we will obtain data at the different abstract level. This can decreases the number of tuples in the given dataset greatly. Secondly, data are processed by the top-down strategy. Decision rules are mined from every abstract level by rough set theory (attribute reduction and attribute value reduction), and the relation of these rules at the different level are analyzed. Those certain rules mined from higher abstract level remain certain at the lower level. Those possible rules mined from higher abstract level may be decomposed to a part of certain rules and a part of possible rules. Thus, we only need to further process those possible rules at the lower level.

BACKGROUND

Ivan Bruha and A. Famili (2000) pointed out that post-processing as an important component of KDD consists of many various procedures and methods that can be categorized into the following groups: (a) Knowledge filtering, (b) Interpretation and explanation, (c) Evaluation, and (d) Knowledge integration. As an important technique in machine learning and data mining, the post-processing of decision rules mining is also subject to the methods as mentioned above.

Marek Sikora and Marcin Michalak (2006) summed up that post-processing of decision rules mining can be implemented in two ways: rules generalization (rules shortening and rules joining) and rules filtering (rules that are not needed in view of certain criterion are removed from the final rules set).

Michal Mikolajczyk(2002) presented a solution for reducing the number of rules by joining rules from some clusters, which leads to a smaller number of more general rules. A. An, S. Khan & X. Huang (2006) propose two algorithms for grouping and summarizing association rules. The first algorithm recursively groups rules according to the structure of the rules and generates a tree of clusters as a result. The second algorithm groups the rules according to the semantic distance between the rules by making use of a semantic tree-structured network of items. Rafal Latkowski & Michal Mikolajczyk (2004) provided an algorithm for decision rule joining to obtain the final rule set from partial rule sets, and a smaller set of rules will be obtained, it has better classification accuracy than classic decision rule induction methods. Keith Shwayder (1975) briefly showed that the techniques for minimizing logic circuits can be applied to the combination of decision rules to provide a more powerful solution for simplifying decision table. Hanhong Xue & Qingsheng Cai (1998) introduced an approach of condition combination to generate rules in a decision table.

All of these algorithms reduce the scale of rules set by rules generalization.

Ken Mcgarry(2005) presented a review of the available literature on the various interesting-ness measures, which are generally divided into two categories: objective (data-driven) measures (Hussain et al., 2000), and subjective (user-driven) measures (Ning Zhong, Y.Y.Yao et al., 2003) . Rules interestingness measures can also used to reduce the scale of rules set.

All of the above algorithms are all process data at single level. That is, they process data only at flat table.

Xiaohua Hu et al. (2001) proposed a method to learn maximal generalized decision rules from databases by integrating discretization, generalization, and rough set feature selection. This method reduces the data horizontally and vertically. But, data are still processed at single level although the hierarchical structure of data is considered in advance.

R. Srikant and R. Agrawal (1997) introduce the problem of generalized Association Rules using taxonomy. They also present a new interest-measure for rules which uses information of the taxonomy.Tzung-Pei Hong et al. (2008) noticed that hierarchical attribute values are usually predefined in real-world applications and can be represented by hierarchical trees, and then pro-vided a method to deriving rules on cross-level. W. Ziarko (2003) proposed a technique to create a linearly structured hierarchy of decision tables through hierarchical methods of boundary area reduction. All of these works have not offer an effective representation for hierarchical structure of the given data set. While multidimensional data models can provide a way to organize data at different levels of granularity, which may be an effective data structure for processing hier-archical data.

Multidimensional model (Antoaneta Ivanova & Boris Rachev, 2004) is a variation of the rela-tional model that uses multidimensional structures to organize data and express the relationships among data, in which data are presented as a data cube. A multidimensional model includes a number of dimensions that each includes multiple levels of abstraction defined by concept hierarchies (Yijun Lu, 1997), where hierarchy is a way to or-ganize data at different levels of granularity. This organization provides users with the flexibility to view data from different perspectives.

To the best of our knowledge, Kamber et al. (1997) were the first who introduced mining in multidimensional environment. But, the proposed algorithm in (Kamber et al., 1997) misses the hierarchies which are relevant to the multidi-mensionality.

The rest of the paper is organized as follows. Some preliminaries about rough set theory and multidimensional model will be introduced in section 3. In section 4, we analyze the necessity of data transformation and illustrate the proce-dure of transform a relational data table to a data cube. An algorithm of decision rules mining from multiple levels is proposed in section 5, which aims to improve the efficiency of decision rules mining by combining the hierarchical structure of multidimensional model and the techniques of rough set theory, and an example is given to illus-trate the algorithm of decision rules mining from multiple levels. Finally, we conclude the chapter and point out the future research direction.

PRELIMINARIES

In this section, we will introduce some preliminar-ies of Rough set theory (RST) and multidimen-sional model for the purpose of decision rules mining.

Rough Set Theory

Rough Set Theory was introduced by Z. Pawlak as a mathematical tool to deal with inexact, uncer-tain or vague knowledge in artificial intelligence applications. It was used for the discovery of data dependencies, data reduction, data mining, and rule extraction from databases, etc. **Rough set theory** is based on the ability to classify the observed and measured data, and some method based on rough set theory are applied to deal with decision. In this chapter, we will use the rough sets theory to decision rule mining at different abstract levels.

In this section, we will first review some basic notions related to information systems and rough sets which can make reference to (*Z. Pawlak, 1991; Z. Pawlak,2005; Z. Pawlak & Andrzej Skowron, 2007*), and then define a concept of supporting set for a rule.

Indiscernibility Relation

The starting point of rough set theory is the indiscernibility relation, which is generated by information about objects of interest. The indiscernibility relation expresses the fact that due to a lack of information (or knowledge) we are unable to discern some objects employing available information. This means that, in general, we are unable to deal with each particular object but we have to consider granules (clusters) of indiscernible objects as a fundamental basis for RST.

An information system is a quadruple IS=(U,A,V,f), where U is a non-empty, finite set of objects, called the universe, and A is a non-empty, finite set of attributes,

$$V = \bigcup_{a \in A} V_a$$

where V_a is the value set of a, called the domain of a. f is an information function from U to V, which assigns particular values from domains of attributes to objects such that $f_a(x_i) \in V_a$ for all $x_i \in U$ and $a \in A$.

Let IS=(U,A,V,f) be an information system. For every set of attributes $B \subseteq A$ and $B \neq \varnothing$, then $\cap B$ (intersection of all equivalence relations belong to B) is also an equivalence relation, and will be denoted by IND(B). It will be called an indiscernibility relation over A, defined by

x IND(B) y if and only if a(x)=a(y) , for every a∈B,

where a(x) denotes the value of attribute a for object x.

The family of all equivalence classes of IND(B), i.e., the partition determined by B, will be denoted by U/IND(B), or simply U/B, $[x]_B$ denotes the block of the partition U/B containing x, moreover, $[x]_{IND(B)} = \bigcap_{r \in B} [x]_r$.

Lower and Upper Approximations

The indiscernibility relation will be further used to define basic concepts of rough set theory. Suppose we are given an information system IS=(U,A,V,f). With each subset X⊆U and an equivalence relation R∈A we associate two subsets:

$$\underline{R}X = \cup \{x \in U : [x]_R \subseteq X\}, \ \bar{R}X = \cup \{x \in U : [x]_R \cap X \neq \varnothing\}$$

called the R-lower and R-upper approximate of X, respectively.

Assuming P and Q are equivalence relations over U, then P-positive region of Q is the set of all objects of the universe U which can be properly classified to classes of U/Q employing knowledge expressed by the classification U/P. it is defined as:

$$POS_P(Q) = \bigcup_{X \in Q} \underline{P}X$$

A positive region contains all patterns in U that can be classified in attribute set Q using the information in attribute set P.

Attribute Reduction

A special case of information system called decision table. A decision table is an information system of the form DT=(U,C∪D,V,f), where D is a distinguished attribute called the decision. The elements of C are called conditions.

A decision table DT=(U,C∪D,V,f), if for any x,y∈U, a∈C, a(x)=a(y), then d(x)=d(y), we will call this decision table consistent, otherwise, decision table is inconsistent.

In a decision table DT=(U,C∪D,V,f), there often exist some condition attributes that do not provide any additional information about the objects in U. So, we should remove those attributes since the complexity and cost of decision process can be reduced if those condition attributes are eliminated

Definition 1. Given a decision table DT=(U,C∪D,V,f), $r \in C$, if POS $_{C-\{r\}}$ (D)=POS $_C$ (D), then r is a dispensable attribute of C with respect to D, otherwise, r is a indispensable attribute of C with respect to D.

Definition 2. Given a decision table DT=(U,C∪D,V,f) and an attribute set $P \subseteq C$, if for $\forall r \in P$, POS $_{P-\{r\}}$ (D)≠POS $_P$ (D), then P is independent with respect to D.

Definition 3. Given a decision table DT=(U,C∪D,V,f), an attribute set $P \subseteq C$ is a D-reduct of C if:

1. POS $_{C-\{r\}}$ (D)=POS $_C$ (D)
2. For $\forall r \in P$, POS $_{P-\{r\}}$ (D)≠POS $_P$ (D).

The intersection of all D-reducts is called a D-core (core with respect to D). Because the core is the intersection of all reducts, it is included in every reduct, i.e., each element of the core belongs to some reduct. Thus, in a sense, the core is the most important subset of attributes, since none of its elements can be removed without affecting the classification power of attributes.

Decision Rules

Each object of a decision table determines a decision rule. A decision rule $\varphi \rightarrow \psi$ read "if φ then ψ", where φ is called the antecedent of the rule, and ψ is called the consequent of the rule.

Decision rules corresponding to some objects can have the same condition part but different decision part. Such rules are called **possible rules** (inconsistent, nondeterministic, conflicting); otherwise the rules are called **certain rules** (consistent, sure, deterministic) rules.

Several numerical quantities of interest can be associated with a decision rule. In a decision table DT=(U,C∪D, V,f), we often call attribute-value pairs (a,v) or in short a$_v$ are atomic formulas for any a∈C∪D and v∈V$_a$, combined by means of sentential connectives (and, or, not etc.) in a standard way, forming compound formulas.

Definition 4. Given a decision table DT=(U,C∪D,V,f), $\varphi \rightarrow \psi$ is a rule in DT, the number of objects satisfying formula $\varphi \rightarrow \psi$ is called its support and is denoted by supp(φ,ψ), and the number supp$_x$(φ,ψ)=| $\varphi(x) \cap \psi(x)$|.

In some cases, it isn't enough to know only the support of a rule. What we want to know most is the supporting elements of a rule. So a supporting set was defined for a rule as follows.

Definition 5. Given a decision table DT=(U,C∪D,V,f), $\varphi \rightarrow \psi$ is a rule in DT, we will say that an object x∈U supports rule $\varphi \rightarrow \psi$ iff x satisfies both φ and ψ, we call the set consist of x satisfies both φ and ψ the supporting set of $\varphi \rightarrow \psi$, and denoted by SS($\varphi \rightarrow \psi$).

A decision rule $\varphi \rightarrow \psi$ may only reveal a part of the overall picture of the decision system from which it was derived. It may happen that the decision system contains objects that match the rule's antecedent φ, but that have a different value for the decision attribute than the one indicated by the rule's consequent ψ. Hence, we are interested in the probability of the consequent ψ being correct, given φ.

Definition 6. The certainty factor of a decision rule $\varphi \rightarrow \psi$ is defined as cer($\varphi \rightarrow \psi$)= | $\varphi(x) \cap \psi(x)$|/ | $\varphi(x)$|.

Apparently, if cer($\varphi \rightarrow \psi$)=1, then the decision rule is certain, otherwise, the decision rule is uncertain or possible.

Multidimensional Model

Multidimensional model (Manpreet Singh et al., 2007) is a variation of the relational model that uses multidimensional structures to organize data and express the relationships among data, in which the data is presented as a data cube. A multidimensional model includes a number of dimensions that each includes multiple levels of abstraction defined by **concept hierarchies**, where hierarchy is a way to organize data at different levels of granularity. This organization provides users with the flexibility to view data from different perspectives. The most advantage of **multidimensional model** is that data can be visualized and manipulated by a compact and easy-to-understand way.

A number of OLAP (on-line analytical processing) data cube operators exist to materialize these different views, such as the operation of roll-up and drill-down can make us handling data conveniently at various levels of abstraction. The structure of data cubes provide us to generalize or specialize attributes along several dimensions simultaneously.

Dimensions are hierarchical by nature. For example, dimension Time can be described by the members Year, Quarter, Month, and Day. Alternatively, the members of a dimension may be organized into a lattice, which indicates a partial order for the dimension. That is, the same Time dimension can have Year, Quarter, Month, Week, and Day instead. With this scheme, the Time dimension is no longer a hierarchy because some weeks in the year may belong to different months.

Therefore, if each dimension contains multiple levels of abstraction, the data can be viewed from different perspectives flexibly. A number of typical **data cube** operations and their functions are listed as follows (Manpreet Singh et al., 2007):

a. **Roll-up** (increasing the level of abstraction)
b. **Drill-down** (decreasing the level of abstraction or increasing detail)
c. Slice and dice (selection and projection)
d. Pivot (re-orienting the multidimensional view of data).

These operations are known as On-Line Analytic Processing (OLAP).

There are many features of multidimensional data model (Manpreet Singh, et al., 2007) which offer us a great help in designing our algorithm, such as (1) Explicit hierarchies in dimensions, (2) Symmetric treatment of dimension and measures, (3) Multiple hierarchies in each dimension, (4) Handling different levels of granularity, etc.

INFORMATION GENERALIZATION

We usually face a flat data table in data analysis applications, from which the hierarchical characteristic of data itself is difficult to be reflected. While multidimensional data cube can not only reflect the inherent hierarchical characteristic easily, but also provide a more compact representation for data. Moreover, we can obtain a compressed, high-level, generalized data by the hierarchical structure of a multidimensional model. So it is necessary to generalize the given flat data table, that is, to transform a flat data table to a multidimensional **data cube**.

Concept Hierarchy

In a multidimensional model, data are organized into multiple dimensions, and each dimension contains multiple members which form multiple abstract levels defined by concept hierarchies

(Yijun Lu, 1997). A concept hierarchy (or lattice) defines certain generalization relationships for the concepts in one or a set of attributes. When the flat data table was generalized along multiple dimensions level-by-level, and as a result, we will transform a large, low-level, detailed data into a compressed, high-level, generalized data.

Concept hierarchies, which is used for expressing knowledge in concise and high-level terms, and facilitating mining knowledge at multiple levels of abstraction, is to organize data or concepts into a hierarchical structure since a large quantity of information is hierarchically structured, for instance, manuals, directory structures, internet addressing, library cataloging, computer programs and so on.

Concept hierarchies, is usually in the form of tree. It is an important tool for capturing the generalization relations among objects. It has been used in many data mining applications, such as multi-level association rules mining, data warehouse, etc. As far as multiple level decision rules mining is concerned, there is usually more than one possible way to building concept hierarchies for every dimension, different users may prefer different hierarchies. So concept hierarchies are usually built by combining the given data set with some relevant domain knowledge, or it can be given by domain experts directly.

Concept hierarchies may also be defined by discretizing or grouping values for a given dimension, that is, discretizing numerical data into interval, and grouping categorical attribute values into a generalized abstract concept. A total or partial order can be defined among groups of values.

There have some other methods to built concept hierarchies. Huang-Cheng Kuo et al. (2005) provided a method of building concept hierarchies from a distance matrix, which is modifying the traditional hierarchical clustering algorithms. Huang-Cheng Kuo et al. (2006) provided another method of building concept hierarchies by modifying the traditional agglomerative hierarchical clustering.

Next we will illustrate concept hierarchies through an example.

Example 1 Building a concept hierarchy for every attributes in Table 1.

Table 1 is a decision table, where attributes "Education-level" and "Vocation" is condition attributes, "Salary" is decision attribute. We can see that the attributes "Education-level" and "Vocation" are categorical attributes, while attribute "Salary" is a numerical attribute. To building concept hierarchies for these attributes, we should use the technique of discretizing attribute "Salary" and grouping for attributes "Education-level"

Table 1. Training data set

	Education-level	Vocation	Salary(unit:yuan)
1	Doctoral student	Private enterprise	Above 10000
2	Postgraduate student	State-owned enterprise	6000-10000
3	Others	Education	Under 2000
4	Undergraduate	Private enterprise	2000-6000
5	Undergraduate	State-owned enterprise	2000-6000
6	Postgraduate student	State-owned enterprise	2000-6000
7	Undergraduate	State-owned enterprise	6000-10000
8	Undergraduate	Civil servant	2000-6000
9	Doctoral student	Education	2000-6000
10	Others	State-owned enterprise	2000-6000

and "Vocation" respectively according to some relevant domain knowledge.

We can build a concept hierarchy which is structured as a tree for every attribute in Table 1, in which, every node in concept hierarchy represent a concept. Every concept includes its intent and extent. The intent of a concept is attribute value that the concept possessed, while the extent of a concept is a subset of object which has attribute value specified by the intent of the concept.

Those leaves nodes on a concept hierarchy are actual attribute values appearing in the given data set which determine an equivalence class. Those internal nodes represent generalized attribute values of their child-nodes. As we all know, every attribute value determine an equivalence class in a decision table, so we can attach a subset of objects to every leaf node, which is an equivalence class determined by the attribute value, and the subset of objects attached to internal nodes are unions of those equivalence classes attached to their child-nodes, which is also an equivalence class.

In essence, every node of a concept hierarchy is a concept, the attribute value also a node's label is its intent, and the subset of objects attached is its extent.

Next, we will build concept hierarchies for every attributes in Table 1. In a concept hierarchy, each level can be assigned with a level number k. The level number of the leaf nodes will be assigned with the number of 0, and the level number for each of the other concepts is one plus its child's level number. In this case, the concepts at each level could be called a concept at level k (see Figure 1).

According to relevant domain knowledge, we will build a two-level concept hierarchical structure for attributes "Education-level" and "Vocation" in Table 1 as shown in Figure 1. Of course, not all of attributes have the same number of levels in general. For simplicity of notation, we denote attribute "Education-level" as A, "Vocation" as B and "Salary" as C respectively. Every node in concept trees is denoted by the symbol in bracket near it.

Figure 1. Concept hierarchies of attributes in Table 1

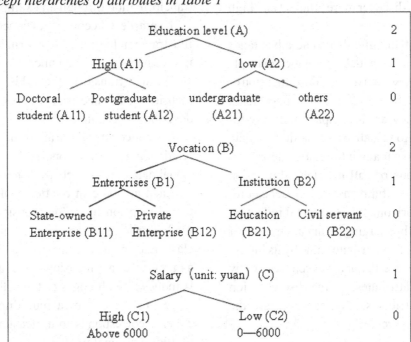

Data Transformation

Data transformation, also known as data consolidation, it is a phase in which the selected data is transformed into forms appropriate for the mining procedure.

In reality, dataset often has characters of multi-dimension and multi-level. However, the data set we usually obtained is represented as a flat data table. It is difficult to reflect some hierarchical characteristics of data from it. The quantity of knowledge mined from different level is usually different, and the preference for different users may also different. Thus, to mine more useful information from the given dataset, we will transform a flat data table to a multidimensional data cube.

Multidimensional model provides a tool to enhance data with generalization along one or more dimensions. Generalizing or enhancing data (Shichao Zhang, Chengqi Zhang & Qiang Yang, 2004) is critical in generating a data set that is cleaner, clearer and smaller than the original, which can improve data mining's efficiency significantly. So we should enhance information from raw data to discover more efficient and high quality knowledge.

In addition, there are also some advantages of multidimensional model. It provides multiple perspectives to view data from multi-dimension or multi-level. A major benefit of multidimensional model is that they are a compact and easy-to-understand way to visualize and manipulate data elements that have many interrelationships.

The operations of **roll-up** along dimension hierarchies in a multidimensional model can reduce the data horizontally. Horizontal reduction is accomplished by merging identical tuples after the substitution of an attribute value by its higher level value in a pre-defined concept hierarchy for categorical attributes, or the discretization of numerical attributes. This can decrease the number of tuples greatly.

In a multidimensional model, data are organized as a **data cube**, which is composed of multiple dimensions and measures. Every dimension is consists of multiple dimension members, which can be organized as a tree or lattice. There are many cells in a data cube, where the edges of a cell are dimension members, and the content of a cell is measure.

Multidimensional model has been used widely in OLAP during the past few years, which mainly tend to the trend analysis. Thus, measures in multidimensional model are usually numerical. However, we mainly focus on the task of decision rules mining in this chapter, the advantage of our multidimensional model is that the content of every cell in data cube is a set of objects, which is an equivalence class induced by all edges of the cell of a multidimensional data cube. The operation of aggregate becomes unions of subsets during the course of roll-up. With the implementation of rolling-up along dimensions level by level, the contents of cells will be merged step by step until getting to the most abstract level. That is, the highest level in the multidimensional model.

Next, we will illustrate the procedure of data transformation through an example as follows.

Example 2 According to concept hierarchies illustrated in Figure 1, transform the Table 1 to a multidimensional data cube.

We will transform the Table 1 to a multidimensional data cube using the concept hierarchies described as example 1.

We noticed that there are some corresponding relations between relational table and multidimensional data cube, which are listed as follows.

Each attribute in relation table corresponds to a dimension in multidimensional data cube. Each attribute value induces an equivalence class. Each edge of a cell in data cube represents a member for a dimension. An equivalence class is induced by all edges of the cell and then it is placed in the cell of a multidimensional data cube. It corresponds to a measure of the usual multidimensional model.

We will transform Table 1 to a data cube after we understand the corresponding relation between a relational table and a multidimensional data cube. The result of transformation according to level 0 for every condition attributes is illustrated as Figure 2.

We will further roll-up data cube illustrated as Figure 2 along every dimension, and we will obtain a multidimensional data cube as Figure 3 according to level 1 for every attributes in Table 1.

The relational table corresponds to the multidimensional data cube illustrated as Figure 3 is Table 2.

Because every dimensions have rolled-up to its most abstract level, and thus the data cube illustrated in Figure 3 can't be rolled up further. So we obtain a two-level multidimensional model. How do we mine decision rules based on this multidimensional model, the solution will be given following.

MULTI-LEVEL DECISION RULES MINING

Decision rules mining has been used widely in business, medicine and finance, etc. The aim of it is to find a concise rule set, which has a minimum number of rules and each rule should be as short as possible.

Figure 2. Data cube transformed from Table 1

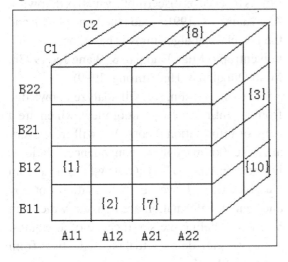

Figure 3. Data cube corresponding concept hierarchy 1

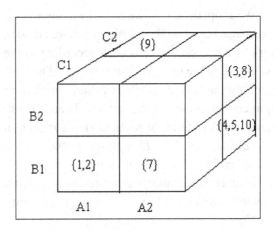

Table 2. Data table corresponding to Figure 3

	Education level	Vocation	Salary
{1,2}	High	Enterprise	High
{3,8}	Low	Institution	Low
{4,5,10}	Low	Enterprise	Low
{6}	High	Enterprise	Low
{7}	Low	Enterprise	High
{9}	High	Institution	Low

To this end, we should first simplify a given decision table, i.e. eliminate the irrelevant or superfluous attributes and attribute values without losing essential information about the original decision table. As a result, a set of concise and meaningful rules will be produced. Then, we will mine decision rules at the different abstract levels using the hierarchical structure of multidimensional model.

After the phase of information generalization mentioned above, for every levels of abstraction k, the procedure of decision rules mining consists of the following three steps:

1. Find a reduct of a given decision table, which is equivalent to elimination of some column from the decision table and elimination of duplicate rows.
2. Eliminate superfluous values of attributes.
3. Generate decision rules.

We adopt the top-down strategy to mine decision rules based on the multidimensional model. Firstly, a decision table is built according to the data cube at the highest abstract level. Then, attribute reduction and attribute value reduction are implemented on this decision table. There already have fruitful literature about attribute reduction (Z. Pawlak,1991; Miao Duoqian et al. 1997b; Miao Duoqian & Hu Guirong1999). In this chapter, we will reduce the number of attributes by a heuristic method based on information entropy (Thomas M. Cover & Joy A. Thomas, 1991).

Attribute Reduction

Attribute reduction is one of the important concepts in rough set theory. It has been intensively studied during the past few years. As we all known that a decision table usually has more than one reduct. This means that the set of rules derived from reduction of knowledge is not unique. In practice, it is always hoped to obtain the set of the most concise rules. Therefore, people have been attempting to find a minimal reduct of decision tables, which means that the number of attributes contained in the reduct is minimal. Unfortunately, it has been proved that finding a minimal reduct of a decision table is an NP-hard problem (Wong S K M & W. Ziarko, 1985).Thus, we have to seek a near-optimal solution for attribute reduction. Heuristic reduction algorithms are a good choice if time cost is considered.

To design an effective heuristic algorithm, the most important is to effectively measure and then rank the relative significance of different attributes in a decision system. The attribute significance can be defined from different aspects. To the best of our knowledge, existing heuristic reduction algorithms can be classified into three classes: Among the first class of algorithms, the attribute significance is defined based on positive region (Z. Pawlak,1991), the second class of algorithms is based on discernibility matrix (Skowron A & Rauszer C,1991; Miao Duoqian, 1997a); and the last class of algorithms is based on information entropy (Miao Duoqian & Wang Jue,1997b; Miao Duoqian & Hu Guirong, 1999).

In this section, we will analyze knowledge from an entirely new point of view, which are a view of information theory. We will treat every attribute (knowledge or equivalence relations) in decision table DT=(U,C∪D,V,f) as a random variable defined over U. Information entropy and mutual information are defined, which can be used to define the significance of attributes. Then we can define attribute reduction from the view of information theory. Based on these definitions, a bottom-up strategy for constructing a reduct was proposed by using the core as the starting point.

Next, we will list some definitions about attribute reduction from the view of information theory, and which is equivalent to those definitions given by Z. Pawlak.

Definition 7. (Miao Duoqian & Wang Jue,1999; Miao Duoqian et al.2007) Given a decision table DT=(U, C∪D, V, f,), $P, Q \subseteq C \cup D$, which can be considered as random variables defined over U, Let $X = U/P = \{X_1, X_2, \cdots, X_n\}$, $Y = U/Q = \{Y_1, Y_2, \cdots, Y_m\}$, then their probability distribution are defined as follows respectively:

$$[X;p] = \begin{pmatrix} X_1 & X_2 & \cdots & X_n \\ p(X_1) & p(X_2) & \cdots & p(X_n) \end{pmatrix}$$

$$[Y;p] = \begin{pmatrix} Y_1 & Y_2 & \cdots & Y_m \\ p(Y_1) & p(Y_2) & \cdots & p(Y_m) \end{pmatrix}$$

and their joint probability distribution is

$$[XY;p] =$$
$$\begin{pmatrix} X_1 \cap Y_1 & \cdots & X_i \cap Y_j & \cdots & X_n \cap Y_m \\ p(X_1 Y_1) & \cdots & p(X_i Y_j) & \cdots & p(X_n Y_m) \end{pmatrix}$$

Where:

$$p(X_i) = \frac{card(X_i)}{card(U)}, \text{ i=1,2,...,n,}$$

$$p(Y_j) = \frac{card(Y_j)}{card(U)}, \text{ j=1,2,...,m}$$

$$p(X_i Y_j) = \frac{card(X_i \cap Y_j)}{card(U)}, \text{ i=1,2,...,n,j=1,2,...,m,}$$

U/P means the family of all equivalence classes of P over U, and card denotes the cardinality of a set.

According to information theory (Thomas M. Cover & Joy A. Thomas,1991), the entropy of P and the conditional entropy of Q given P are defined as follows:

Definition 8. (Miao Duoqian et al., 2007) Given a decision table DT=(U, C∪D, V, f), $P, Q \subseteq C \cup D$, the entropy of knowledge P and the conditional entropy of Q given P are defined as follows respectively,

$$H(P) = -\sum_{i=1}^{n} p(X_i) \log p(X_i),$$

$$H(Q|P) = -\sum_{i=1}^{n} p(X_i) \sum_{j=1}^{m} p(Y_j | X_i) \log p(Y_j | X_i).$$

Definition 9. (Thomas M. Cover & Joy A. Thomas, 1991) Given a decision table DT=(U, C∪D, V, f), $P, Q \subseteq C \cup D$, the mutual information of P and Q is defined as I(P;Q)=H(Q)-H(Q|P).

We can define some basic concepts relative to attribute reduction for information system or decision table based on the concept of information entropy. In this chapter, we will mainly focus on decision table. Those related concepts based on information entropy for information system can reference to (Miao Duoqian,1997a; Miao Duoqian & Wang Jue1999; Miao Duoqian, Feng Qinrong, Wang Ruizhi. 2007).

Definition 10. Given a decision table DT=(U, C∪D, V,f) , $r \in C$, if I(C-{r};D)=I(C;D), then r is a dispensable attribute of C with respect to D, otherwise, r is a indispensable attribute of C with respect to D.

Definition 11. Given a decision table DT=(U, C∪D, V,f) and an attribute set $P \subseteq C$, if for $\forall r \in P$, I(P-{r};D)<I(P;D), then P is independent with respect to D.

Definition 12. Given a decision table DT=(U, C∪D, V,f), an attribute set $P \subseteq C$ is a reduction of C with respect to D if:

1.   I(C;D)=I(P;D);
2.   For $\forall r \in P$, I(P-{r};D)<I(P;D).

For brevity and readability, the concept of conditional mutual information and the relationship between conditional mutual information and conditional entropy are introduced.

Definition 13. Let P,Q,R are equivalence relations over set U, and partitions induced by P,Q,R are U/P={X_1,X_2,...,X_n}, U/Q={Y_1,Y_2,...,Y_m }, and U/R={Z_1,Z_2,...,Z_l} respectively, then the conditional mutual information between P and Q given R is defined by

$$I(P;Q|R) =$$

$$\sum_r \sum_s \sum_t p(X_i, Y_j, Z_k) \log \frac{p(X_i, Y_j | Z_k)}{p(X_i | Z_k) p(Y_j | Z_k)}$$

The amount of conditional mutual information is equal to the amount of information about P which is obtained from Q given R.

Proposition 1. Given a decision table DT=(U,C∪D, V, f), $R \subseteq C$, denote I(D;{a}|R) the conditional mutual information between decision attribute D and any $a \in C - R$ given R, then the relation between conditional information entropy and the conditional mutual information is as follows: I(D;{a}|R)=H(D|R)-H(D|R∪{a}).

Definition 14. Given a decision table DT=(U,C∪D, V, f), $R \subseteq C$, then for any $a \in C - R$, its significance is defined as Sig(a,R,D)=I(D;{a}|R).

This is equal to the amount of information about decision attribute D obtained from attribute a given R.

The definition of attribute significance indicates that the greater the value sig(a,R,D), the more important the attribute a with respect to decision attribute D. So we can reduce the search space by using sig(a,R,D) as a heuristic message.

Lemma 1. Given a consistent decision table DT=(U,C∪D,V,f), where U is the universe, C is a set of conditional attributes, D is the decision attribute, $P,Q \subseteq C$, if $POS_P(D)=POS_Q(D)$, then I(P;D)=I(Q;D).

The proof is reference to Miao Duoqian's Ph D dissertation (1997).

Lemma 2. Given a consistent decision table DT=(U,C∪D,V,f), where U is the universe, C is

a set of conditional attributes, D is the decision attribute, $P,Q \subseteq C$, if I(P;D)=I(Q;D) and $P \subseteq Q$ (or $Q \subseteq P$), then $POS_P(D)=POS_Q(D)$.

The proof is reference to Miao Duoqian(1997a).

Theorem 1. Given a consistent decision table DT=(U,C∪D,V,f), where U is the universe, C is a set of conditional attributes, D is the decision attribute. $P \subseteq C$, and for any r∈P, we will say that r is D-dispensable in P, if and only if I(P;D)=I(P-{r};D).

Corollary 1. Given a consistent decision table DT=(U,C∪D,V,f), where U is the universe, C is a set of conditional attributes, D is the decision attribute. $P \subseteq C$, and for any r∈P, we will say that r is D-indispensable in P, if and only if I(P;D)≠I(P-{r};D).

Theorem 2. Given a consistent decision table DT=(U,C∪D,V,f), where U is the universe, C is a set of conditional attributes, D is the decision attribute. $P \subseteq C$, then P is D-independent, if and only if for any r∈P , I(P;D)>I(P-{r};D).

Theorem 3. Given a consistent decision table DT=(U,C∪D,V,f), where U is the universe, C is a set of conditional attributes, D is the decision attribute. $P \subseteq C$, then P will be called a D-reduct in C, if and only if:

1. I(P;D)=I(Q;D)
2. For any r∈P , I(P;D)>I(P-{r};D).

These results indicate that we can represent some basic concepts relate to consistent decision table based on the concept of mutual information, and we call this information representation for rough sets. In the information representation, those classical operations of set in rough sets can be transformed to those efficient operations of information entropy and some effective and efficient algorithms can be designed for rough sets.

The following is an efficient algorithm for knowledge reduction based on mutual information.

Algorithm 1
(Miao Duoqian & Hu Guirong, 1999)
(Mutual Information-Based Algorithm for Reduction of Knowledge, MIBARK)

- **Input:** A decision table DT=(U, C∪D, V,f)
- **Output:** A near-optimal relative reduct of the given decision table.
  - Step 1: Compute the mutual information $I(C;D)$.
  - Step 2: Compute the relative core $C_0=CORE_D(C)$ and $I(C_0;D)$. In general, $I(C_0;D)<I(C;D)$, especially, if $C_0=\varnothing$, then $I(C_0;D)=0$.
  - Step 3: Set C_0 to B, repeat while C-B $\neq\varnothing$
    1. Compute $I(p;D|B)$ for any $p\in C-B$;
    2. Select the attribute p which satisfies the following equation: $$I(p;D|B)=\max_{p\in C-B}\{I(p;D|B)\},$$ and set $B\cup\{p\}$ to B.
    3. If $I(B;D)=I(C;D)$, then turn to step 4, otherwise, turn to substep 3(1).
  - Step 4: Output the result B, which is a near-optimal relative reduct of C with respect to D.

Attribute Value Reduction

The process which the maximum number of condition attribute values are removed without loosing essential information is called **attribute value reduction**, and the resulting rule is called minimal length. Computing minimal length rules is of particular importance in knowledge discovery since they represent general patterns existing in the data.

For the sake of simplicity, we assume that the set of condition attributes is already reduced, i.e. there have no superfluous condition attributes in the decision table.

Attribute reduction can only discard some redundant attributes in decision table to some extent, but it can't discard all of the redundant information sufficiently. To this end, we can obtain a more simplified decision table by further processing it. That is, we should discard those redundant attribute values by performing value reduction.

When data are rolled up to the most abstract level in a multidimensional model, the number of objects will decreased considerably, in that many objects have same attribute values can be merged as one. This can reduce the complexity of attribute value reduction greatly because of its mainly related to the number of objects.

There are some algorithms for attribute value reduction in (Z.Pawlak,1991; Miao Duoqian & Li daoguo. 2008; Wang Guoyin, 2001). So we will not describe those at here.

Decision Rules Mining

Each row of a decision table specifies a decision rule that determines decisions in terms of conditions. So it is difficult to process data in flat data table directly when we face massive data sets in real world applications. Multidimensional model provide an effective tool to reduce the amount of data. In a multidimensional model, the amount of data can be reduced greatly by the operation of roll-up, which can generalize all dimensions simultaneously. In other words, more and more non-empty cells in data cube will be merged during the roll-up process, which will reduce the number of non-empty cells to a great extent.

During the roll-up process, a new data cube will be produced once the roll-up operation is performed. The produced data cube can be transformed to a decision table. That is, a data cube corresponds to a decision table at every abstract level.

For the decision table which corresponds to the data cube at the kth abstract level, we will call it the kth level decision table. The term "the kth level decision table" and "data cube at the kth abstract level" will be used exchangeably hereinafter. Denote the finest level decision table, namely the decision table at the primitive level by DT_0. With the implementation of roll-up each time, the index i of the decision table DT_i will add one, e.g., when we implement roll-up one time from DT_0, we will get decision table DT_1.

In order to analyze the relation among decision tables at the different level, we will give a definition as follows.

Definition 15. Denote the kth level decision table by $DT_k=(U_k,C\cup D,V_k,f_k)$, and (k-1)th level decision table by $DT_{k-1}=(U_{k-1}, C\cup D,V_{k-1},f_{k-1})$, if for every $X_i\in U_{k-1}$, there always exists $Y_j\in U_k$, such that $X_i\subseteq Y_j$, then we will say that the decision table DT_k is coarser than DT_{k-1}, or DT_{k-1} is finer than DT_k, denoted by $DT_{k-1}\preceq DT_k$. If $DT_{k-1}\preceq DT_k$ and $DT_{k-1}\neq DT_k$, then we will say that DT_k is strictly coarser than DT_{k-1}, denoted by $DT_{k-1}\prec DT_k$.

Obviously, the coarser/ finer relation among decision tables at different levels is a partial order relation. These decision tables can be organized as a lattice. We only discuss the simplest case in this chapter, that is, a total order case. If we assume that there are m levels in a given multidimensional data cube, we will have $DT_0\preceq DT_1\preceq ... \preceq DT_m$. Of course, the coarser/finer relation of different decision tables is determined by the object granularity in the corresponding set of object.

Proposition 2. Let $DT_k=(U_k,C\cup D,V_k,f_k)$ be the kth level decision table, and denote $POS_k(C,D)$ the positive region for the kth level decision table, assume that there are m level in the given multidimensional data cube, then we have $POS_0(C,D)\supseteq POS_1(C,D)\supseteq\cdots\supseteq POS_m(C,D)$.

Obviously, the result can be derived from the definition 15.

Proposition 3. Given the kth level decision table $DT_k=(U_k, C\cup D,V_k,f_k)$, a rule induced from this decision table is certain iff the supporting set of this rule is included in the positive region of the decision table.

This result can be obtained easily by combining the definition of certain rule and positive region of a decision table.

Proposition 4. Given two decision tables $DT_i=(U_i, C\cup D,V_i,f_i)$ and $DT_j=(U_j, C\cup D,V_j,f_j)$, where $DT_i\preceq DT_j$, then those certain decision rules mined from DT_j remain certain in DT_i.

Proof. A rule is certain iff it is induced from the lower approximate of a concept. Obviously, if a rule is induced from the positive region of a decision table, it must be a certain rule. In other words, if the supporting set of a rule is included in the positive region of the decision table, it is certain.

Since $DT_i\preceq DT_j$, namely, decision table DT_i is finer than DT_j, we have $POS_i(C,D)\supseteq POS_j(C,D)$ by proposition 2. A rule is certain in DT_j that means the supporting set of this rule being included in $POS_j(C,D)$. So it is included in $POS_i(C,D)$. Thus, the proposition holds.

We can construct a decision table based on the data cube at the coarsest level. Now, the number of objects will decrease largely because many duplicative objects are merged which have same attribute values. Thus, the number of decision rules is also decreased greatly than that at the primitive level. We will say that the decision table at the coarsest level is the coarsest decision table.

In the coarsest decision table, each row of it determines a decision rule, of course, redundant information maybe exist in this decision table. So we should further simplify it. **Attribute reduction** will eliminate those redundant columns in decision table without losing the classification ability. This can simplify the decision table vertically and horizontally since some duplicative tuples will be merged. **Attribute value reduction** will discard those redundant attribute values on the premise of keeping the classification ability unchanged. This can make those rules mined from the simplified decision table much fewer and shorter than the original decision table.

As it has been discussed in the previous section, **rough set theory** is particularly well suited to deal with inconsistency in a decision table. If a decision table is inconsistent then lower and upper approximations of the decision classes are computed. For each decision class, certain decision rules are generated from objects belonging to its lower approximation. Possible decision rules are generated either from the upper approximation or from the boundaries of this decision class. We notice that **certain rules** indicate unique decision value while **possible rules** lead to a few possible decisions.

Our algorithm for **decision rules mining** follows the so-called **separate-and-conquer strategy** (Johannes Fürnkranz,1999), which has been coined by Pagallo and Haussler(1990), because of the way of developing a theory that characterizes this learning strategy: learn a rule that covers a part of the given training examples, remove the covered examples from the training set (the separate part) and recursively learn another rule that covers some of the remaining examples(the conquer part) until no examples remain.

In our algorithm, we first load data into a pre-assigned multidimensional data cube, roll up along the specified members of dimensions to the most abstract level, and build the coarsest decision table from it; then mine certain rules from this coarsest decision table, and remove the supporting sets from the set of objects; at last, drill down to the next level and recursively mine other rules that support the remaining examples until no examples remain or getting to the primitive level. Thus, the

output result of our algorithm will include rules mined from different abstract levels. This can obtain not only generalized rules, but also rules mined from various levels of abstraction.

In a multidimensional model, we can choose one dimension as a decision dimension according to the application requirement, and the others as conditional dimensions. Every dimension is composed of multiple levels, so we can classify the task of decision rules mining in data cube to three cases. (1) Keeping the decision dimension level unchanged and perform level-wise **drill-down** for every conditional dimension. (2) Keeping all conditional dimension level unchanged and performing levelwise **drill-down** for every decision dimension. (3) Conditional dimensions and decision dimension are all **drill-down** level by level. In this chapter, we only focus on the first case, and other cases will be studied in the future.

With respect to a fixed decision level, we adopt the top-down strategy starting from the coarsest level of conditional dimensions to the finest level. We have proved that **certain rules** mined from this level remain certain at the lower level. So we can save these certain rules into a rule set and remove their supporting set from the current universe; then drill down to the next level, and further process those **possible rules**. The algorithm will terminate until no objects remain or getting to the primitive level.

The aim of this algorithm is to find a set of decision rules which are concise to the greatest extent, that is, the number of rules is as fewer as possible and the length of every rule is as shorter as possible. Furthermore, this algorithm provides us to mine all certain rules with different degree of generalization from different abstract levels.

To summarize, the procedure of **decision rules mining** from a data cube is described in the following algorithm.

Algorithm 2
(Multi-Level Decision Rules Mining)

- **Input:** a given decision table $DT=(U,C\cup D,V,f)$.
- **Output:** a set of decision rules RS.
  - Step 1: Build concept hierarchies for every conditional attributes in DT.
  - Step 2: Transform the given decision table to a multidimensional data cube according to concept hierarchies obtained from step 1.
  - Step 3: Roll up the data cube at the primitive level along all conditional dimension simultaneously, until get to the most abstract level, set the label of the most abstract level to k, set $RS=\varnothing$, U is the universe of the given decision table.
  - Step 4: Building the decision table DTk based on the data cube at the kth level, set $RSk=\varnothing$.
  - Step 5: Simplify the decision table DTk (Implement attribute reduction and attribute value reduction for DTk), and generate decision rules, combine those duplicative decision rules as one, and merge their supporting set of the duplicative decision rules.
  - Step 6: For every decision rules, if the certainty factor of the rule is equal to 1, then it is certain. Otherwise, it is uncertain.
    Save those certain decision rules to RSk, and set $RS\cup RSk$ to RS, That is, $RS=RS\cup RSk$.
    Compute the supporting set SS(RSk) of RSk, set U- SS(RSk) to U.
  - Step 7: If $U=\varnothing$ or k=0, then turn to step 8, otherwise, k=k-1, turn to step 4.
  - Step 8: Merging those rules induced from the remaining examples to RS, and the algorithm is terminated.

The algorithm performs the following three main tasks:

1. Information generalization. This task consists of step 1 to step 3, which mainly complete the procedure of data transforming, that is, transform the given flat decision table to a multidimensional data cube.
2. Simplify the decision table for each level k. This task consists of step 4 to step 5, which can shorten those mined rules.
3. Mine those certain rules for each level k.

Table 3. Training data set

	Education-level	Vocation	Salary
1	Doctoral student	Private enterprise	High
2	Postgraduate student	State-owned enterprise	High
3	Others	Education	Low
4	Undergraduate	Private enterprise	Low
5	Undergraduate	State-owned enterprise	Low
6	Postgraduate student	State-owned enterprise	Low
7	Undergraduate	State-owned enterprise	High
8	Undergraduate	Civil servant	Low
9	Doctoral student	Education	Low
10	Others	State-owned enterprise	Low

Eventually, the algorithm returns the final certain rule set with various levels of abstraction.

An example will be illustrated to demonstrate how algorithm 2 works. The decision table is shown in Table 3, which contain 10 objects, and 2 conditional attributes. There are exist inconsistencies tuples in this data set.

Example 3 Suppose a two-layer decision system is considered as Figure 1. The training data used in this example is in Table 3. Illustrate the procedure of algorithm 2 by data Table 3.

(1) Building concept hierarchies for every attribute in Table 3 as illustrated in Figure 1, and then transforming the Table 3 to a data cube as Figure 2.

Roll-up the data cube as illustrated in Figure 2 along dimensional "Educational-level" and "Work", we will obtain a data cube as in Figure 3.

For the data cube in Figure 3, its corresponding decision table is as Table 4.

After merged the duplicative objects of Table 4, we will obtain a simplified table as Table 2.

(2) Compute the reduct of Table 2 or Table 4 using algorithm MIBARK, a minimal reduct of Table 2 or Table 4 is {Vocation}. Of course the core of it is also {Vocation}.

Now, we have climbed to the highest abstract level due to its two-level structure for this decision table, and we will mine decision rules begin from this highest abstract level.

(3) Rules mined from Table 2 are presented in Table 5.

Rules mined from the highest abstract level are presented in Table 5. We can see that there are only three items of decision rules, which are fewer than the number of objects in the original data set. These generalized rules will provide us more concise and easy-to-understand information than the original data set. Of course, if you are unsatisfied with this mining result, you can proceed to this procedure by drilling down to the next level.

Table 4. Data set roll-up to concept level 1

	Education-level	Vocation	Salary
1	High	Enterprise	High
2	High	Enterprise	High
3	Low	Institution	Low
4	Low	Enterprise	Low
5	Low	Enterprise	Low
6	High	Enterprise	Low
7	Low	Enterprise	High
8	Low	Institution	Low
9	High	Institution	Low
10	Low	Enterprise	Low

Table 5. Rules mined from Table 2 or Table 4

	Decision rules	Supporting set	Certainty factor
1	If Vocation="Enterprise" then Salary="High"	{1,2,7}	0.5
2	If Vocation ="Enterprise" then Salary ="Low"	{4,5,6,10}	0.5
3	If Vocation ="Institution" then Salary ="Low"	{3,8,9}	1

From Table 5, we know that the rule "IF Vocation= 'Institution' THEN Salary= 'Low'" is a certain one, so the subset {3,8,9} can be removed from the universe according to the algorithm 2, and those possible rules were processed further by drilling-down along all conditional dimensions to the next level, which is the primitive level in this example.

(4) In this situation, data Table 3 decreased as Table 6, the minimal reduct of Table 6 is {Education-level, Vocation} and the core is also {Education-level, Vocation}.

(5) The rules mined from Table 6 is as follows:

Certain Rules

1. IF Educational-level= "Doctoral student" THEN Salary= "High"
2. IF Educational-level= "Undergraduate" AND Vocation= "Private enterprise" THEN Salary= "Low"
3. IF Educational-level= "Others" THEN Salary= "Low"

Possible Rules

4. IF Educational-level= "Postgraduate student" AND Vocation= "State-owned enterprise" THEN Salary= "High"
5. IF Educational-level= "Postgraduate student" AND Vocation= "State-owned enterprise" THEN Salary= "LOW"

6. IF Educational-level= "Undergraduate" AND Vocation= "State-owned enterprise" THEN Salary= "LOW"
7. IF Educational-level= "Undergraduate" AND Vocation= "State-owned enterprise" THEN Salary= "High"

(6) So the final output is as follows.

Certain Rules

1. IF Vocation= "Institution" THEN Salary= "Low"
2. IF Educational-level= "Doctoral student" THEN Salary= "High"
3. IF Educational-level= "Undergraduate" AND Vocation= "Private enterprise" THEN Salary= "Low"
4. IF Educational-level= "Others" THEN Salary= "Low"

Possible Rules

5. IF Educational-level= "Postgraduate student" AND Vocation= "State-owned enterprise" THEN Salary= "High"
6. IF Educational-level= "Postgraduate student" AND Vocation= "State-owned enterprise" THEN Salary= "LOW"
7. IF Educational-level= "Undergraduate" AND Vocation= "State-owned enterprise" THEN Salary= "LOW"
8. IF Educational-level= "Undergraduate" AND Vocation= "State-owned enterprise" THEN Salary= "High"

Table 6. Remaining data set

	Education-level	Vocation	Salary
1	Doctoral student	Private enterprise	High
2	Postgraduate student	State-owned enterprise	High
4	Undergraduate	Private enterprise	Low
5	Undergraduate	State-owned enterprise	Low
6	Postgraduate student	State-owned enterprise	Low
7	Undergraduate	State-owned enterprise	High
10	Others	State-owned enterprise	Low

We can see that the number of decision rules mined from higher abstract level is much fewer than those mined from the lower level. In this example, there are only three items of decision rules mined from higher level, while there are ten items of decision rules mined from primitive level. Furthermore, we can mine all certain rules with different degree of generalization from different abstract levels.

CONCLUSION AND DISCUSSION

Decision rules mining is an important technique in machine learning and data mining. It has been studied intensively during the past few years. However, most existing algorithms are based on flat data tables. Sets of decision rules mined from flat data table can be very large for massive data sets. Such sets of rules are not easy to understand. Moreover, too many rules may lead to over-fitting.

In real world applications, we notice that data are hierarchical in nature. So a method of multi-level decision rules mining is provided in this chapter, which aims to improve the efficiency of decision rules mining by combining the hierarchical structure of multidimensional model and the techniques of rough set theory. This algorithm can output some generalized rules with different degree of generalization.

We also notice that our algorithm will obtain different results for different type of decision tables, i.e. consistent decision table and inconsistent tables. For a consistent decision table, the universe will be reduced to an empty set when the algorithm terminates. That is, we can mine all certain rules with different degree of generalization at different levels. While for an inconsistent decision table, the universe can't be an empty set even though the algorithm is terminated. That is, there still exist some unprocessed objects in the universe.

FUTURE TRENDS

Hierarchical structure of data has received much attention in recent years. It has been used in many areas, such as hierarchical reduction, multi-level association rules mining, hierarchical text classification, etc. However, there is not an effective representation and operations for hierarchical data at present.

Multidimensional model is a variation of the relational model that uses multidimensional structures to organize data, in which the data is presented as a data cube. The main advantage of multidimensional model is that they offer a powerful way to represent hierarchical structured data. Moreover, there are a number of typical data cube operations, which are very fit to hierarchical data.

Thus, based on hierarchical structure of multidimensional model, there are some works need to study further in the forthcoming future, such as rules property preserving at multiple levels, attribute value reduction at multiple levels, etc. These will be paid close attention by more and more researchers.

ACKNOWLEDGMENT

We would like to express my sincere gratitude to those anonymous reviewers. This work was supported by National Natural Science Foundation of China (Serial No. 60475019, 60775036) and The Research Fund for the Doctoral Program of Higher Education (Serial No. 20060247039).

REFERENCES

An, A., Khan, S., & Huang, X. (2006). Hierarchical grouping of association rules and its application to a real-world domain. International Journal of Systems Science, 37(13). 867-878.

Bruha, I., & Famili, A. F. (2000). Postprocessing in machine learning and data mining. In R. Ng (Ed.), Proceedings of the sixth ACM SIGKDD international conference on Knowledge discovery and data mining, (pp.20-23). Boston, MA, USA.

Cover, T. M., & Thomas, J. A. (1991). Elements of Information Theory. 1st edition. New York: Wiley-Interscience.

Duoqian, M., & Daoguo, L. (2008). Rough sets theory, Algorithms and Applications. Beijing, China: Tsinghua University Press.

Duoqian, M. (1997a). Rough set theory and its application in machine learning. Ph D dissertation (in Chinese). Institute of automation, Chinese academy of sciences.

Duoqian, M., & Guirong, H. (1999). A heuristic algorithm for reduction of knowledge.

Duoqian, M., & Jue, W. (1997b). Information-based algorithm for reduction of knowledge. IEEE International conference on intelligent processing systems (pp.1155-1158). Beijing, China. International AcademicPublishers.

Duoqian, M., & Jue, W. (1999). An information representation of concepts and operations in rough set theory. Journal of Software (in Chinese), 10(2). 113-116.

Duoqian, M., Qinrong, F., & Ruizhi, W. (2007). Information Entropy and Granular Computing. In D. Miao, et al. (Eds.), Granular Computing: Past, Present, and the Future Perspectives, (pp.142-180). Beijing: China Academic Press.

Fernández, M. C., Menasalvas, F., et al. (2001). Minimal decision rules based on the APRIORI algorithm. International Journal of Applied Mathematics and Computer Science. 11(3), 691-704.

Furnkranz, J. (1999). Separate-and-Conquer Rule Learning, Artificial intelligence Review, 13, 3-54.

Guoyin, W. (2001). Rough set theory and knowledge acquisition. Xi'an, China: Xi'an Jiaotong University Press.

Hirokane, M., Konishi, H., et al.(2007). Extraction of minimal decision algorithm using rough sets and genetic algorithm. Systems and Computers in Japan, 38(4), 39-51.

Hong, T-P., Lin, C-E., & Lin, J-H. (2008). Learning cross-level certain and possible rules by rough sets. Expert Systems with Applications, 34(3), 1698-1706.

Hu, X., & Cercone, N. (1997). Learning maximal generalized decision rules via discretization, generalization and rough set feature selection. In Proceedings of the 9th IEEE International Conference of Tools on Artificial Intelligence (pp. 548-556). Newport Beach, California, USA.

Hu, X., & Cercone, N. (2001). Discovering maximal generalized decision rules through horizontal and vertical data reduction, Computational Intelligence, 17(4), 685-702.

Hussain, F., Liu, H., Suzuki, E., & Lu, H. (2000). Exception rule mining with a relative interestingness measure. In T. Terano, et al. (Eds.), 4th Pacific-Asia Conference on Knowledge Discovery and Data Mining, Current Issues and New Applications (pp. 86–97). Springer-Verlag.

Ivanova, A., & Rachev, B. (2004). Multidimensional models—Constructing DATA CUBE. *In Proceedings of international conference on computer systems and technologies —ComSysTech'2004.* (pp. V.5-1—V.5-7). 17-18 June 2004, Rousse, Bulgaria.

Kamber, M., Han, J., & Chiang, J. Y (1997). Metarule-Guided Mining of Multi-Dimensional Association Rules Using Data Cubes. In D. Heckerman et al. (Eds.), Proceeding of the 3rd International Conference on Knowledge Discovery and Data Mining. (pp. 207-210) Newport Beach, California, USA.

Kuo, H-C., & Huang, J-P. (2005). Building a Concept Hierarchy from a Distance Matrix. In M. A. Klopotek, et al. (Eds.), Intelligent Information Processing and Web Mining (pp. 87-95). Springer.

Kuo, H-C., Tsai, T-h., & Huang, J-P. (2006). Building a Concept Hierarchy by Hierarchical Clustering with Join/Merge Decision. In H. D. Cheng, et al. (Eds.), Proceedings of the 9th Joint Conference on Information Sciences (JCIS 2006), (pp.142-145). Kaohsiung, Taiwan, ROC, October 8-11, 2006. Atlantis Press.

Latkowski, R., & Michal Mikolajczyk (2004). Data Decomposition and Decision Rule Joining for Classification of Data with Missing Values. In S. Tsumoto et al. (Eds.), RSCTC 2004, Lecture Notes in Artificial Intelligence 3066. (pp. 254–263). Springer-Verlag Berlin Heidelberg .

Lu, Y. (1997). Concept hierarchy in data mining: specification, generation and implementation. Master thesis. Simon Fraser University, Canada.

Mcgarry, K. (2005). A survey of interestingness measures for knowledge discovery. The Knowledge Engineering Review, 20(1), 39-61.

Mikolajczyk, M. (2002). Reducing Number of Decision Rules by Joining. In J. J. Alpigini, J. F. Peters, et al. (Eds.), RSCTC 2002. Lecture Notes in Artificial Intelligence 2475. (pp. 425-432). Springer-verlag Berlin Heidelberg.

or from http://csdl2.computer.org/comp/mags/ex/2004/02/x2012.pdf.

Pagallo, G., & Haussler, D. (1990). Boolean feature discovery in empirical learning. Machine learning, 5, 71-99.

Pawlak, Z. (1991). Rough Sets: Theoretical Aspects of Reasoning About Data. Dordrecht: Kluwer Academic Publishing.

Pawlak, Z. (2005). Rough sets and decision algorithms. In W. Ziarko & Y. Yao (Eds.), RSCTC 2000, Lecture Notes of Artificial Intelligence 2005 (pp. 30-45). Springer-Verlag Berlin Heidelberg.

Pawlak, Z., & Andrzej Skowron (2007). Rudiments of rough sets. Information Sciences, 177. 3-27.

Shwayder, K. (1975). Combining decision rules in a decision table. Communications of the ACM, 18(8), 476-480.

Sikora, M., & Michalak, M. (2006). NetTRS Induction and Postprocessing of Decision Rules. In S. Greco et al.. (Eds.), RSCTC 2006. Lecture Notes in Artificial Intelligence 4259. (pp. 378-387). Springer-verlag, Berlin.

Singh, M., Singh, P., & Suman (2007). Conceptual multidimensional model, In: Proceedings of world academy of science, engineering and technology, 26, 709-714.

Skowron, A., & Rauszer, C. (1991). The Discernibility Matrices and Functions in Information Systems. In R. Slowinski (Eds.), Intelligent Decision Support—Handbook of application and advances of the rough sets theory (pp. 331-362).

Srikant, R., & Agrawal, R. (1997). Mining generalized association rules. Future Generation Computer Systems, 13, 161-180.

Wong, S. K. M., & Ziarko, W. (1985). On optimal decision rules in decision tables. Bulletin of Polish Academy of Sciences, 33, 693-696.

Xue, H., & Cai, Q. (1998). Rule Generalization by Condition Combination. In X. Wu, et al. (Eds.), Research and Development in Knowledge Discovery and Data Mining, Second Pacific-Asia Conference, PAKDD-98, (pp. 420-421). Melbourne, Australia. Springer, ISBN 3-540-64383-4.

Zhang, S., Zhang, C., & Yang, Q. (2004), Information Enhancement for Data Mining. IEEE Intelligent System (pp. 12-13).

Zhang, W. X., Wu, W. Z., & Liang, J. (2003). Rough set Theory and Methods. Beijing, China: Science Press.

Zhong, N., Yao, Y. Y., & Ohishima, M. (2003). Peculiarity oriented multidatabase mining. IEEE Transactions on Knowledge and Data Enginering, 15(4), 952–960.

Ziarko, W. (2003). Acquisition of hierarchy-structured probabilistic decision tables and rules from data. Expert Systems, 20(5), 305-310.

Compilation of References

Adamo, J.-M. (2001). *Data Mining for Association Rules and Sequential Patterns*. Springer-Verlag.

Aggarwal, C. C., & Yu, P. S. (1998). Mining Large Itemsets for Association Rules. *In Bulletin of the Technical Committee, IEEE Computer Society, 21(1)* 23-31.

Aggarwal, C. C., & Yu, P. S. (2001). Mining associations with the collective strength approach. *IEEE Transactions on Knowledge and Data Engineering, 13*(6), 863–873.

Aggarwal, C. C., & Yu, P. S. (1998). Online generation of association rules. In *ICDE* (pp. 402-411).

Agrawal, R., & Psaila, G. (1995). Active data mining. In U. M. Fayyad, & R. Uthurusamy, (Eds.), *Proceedings of the 1st ACM SIGKDD International Conference on Knowledge Discovery and Data Mining*, (pp. 3–8), Montreal, Quebec, Canada. AAAI Press, Menlo Park, CA, USA.

Agrawal, R., & Shafer, J. (1996). Parallel Mining of Association Rules: Design, Implementation, and Experience. *Technical Report RJ10004, IBM Almaden Research Center*, San Jose, California, USA.

Agrawal, R., & Srikant R. (1994). Fast Algorithms for Mining Association Rules in Large Databases. *In Proceedings of the 20th International Conference on Very Large Data Bases,* Santiago, Chile (pp. 478-499).

Agrawal, R., & Srikant, R. (1995). Mining sequential patterns. *Proceedings of the Eleventh International Conference on Data Engineering* (pp. 3-14).

Agrawal, R., Imielinski, T., & Swami, A. (1993). Mining association rules between sets of items in large databases. In *Proceedings of the ACM SIGMOD International Conference on Management of Data,* (pp. 207–216), Washington, USA.

Agrawal, R., Mannila, H., Srikant, R., Toivonen, H., & Verkamo, A. I. (1996). Fast Discovery of Association Rules. In U. Fayyad, G. Piatetsky-Shapiro, P. Smyth, & R. Uthurusamy (Ed.), *Advances in Knowledge Discovery and Data Mining* (pp. 307–328). Menlo Park, CA: AAAI Press / MIT Press.

An, A., Khan, S., & Huang, X. (2006). Hierarchical grouping of association rules and its application to a real-world domain. International Journal of Systems Science, 37(13). 867-878.

Angiulli, F., Ianni, G., & Palopoli, L. (2001). On the complexity of mining association rules. *Proceedings of the SEBD conference* (pp. 177-184).

Anick, P., & Pustejovsky, J. (1990). An Application of lexical Semantics to Knowledge Acquisition from Corpora. *30th International Conf. on Computational Linguistics (COLING'90), 3,* 7–12. Helsinki, Finland.

Ankerst, M. (2000) *Visual Data Mining*. Ph.D. thesis. Fakultät für Mathematik und Informatik der Ludwig-Maximilians-Universität München.

Antonie, M.-L., & Zaïane, O. R. (2002). Text document categorization by term association. In *Proceedings of ICDM,* (pp. 19–26).

Antonie, M.-L., & Zaïane, O. R. (2004). An associative classifier based on positive and negative rules. In *9th ACM SIGMOD Workshop on Research Issues in Data*

Mining and Knowledge Discovery (DMKD-04), (pp. 64–69), Paris, France.

Antonie, M.-L., & Zaïane, O. R. (2004). Mining positive and negative association rules: An approach for confined rules. In *8th European Conference on Principles and Practice of Knowledge Discovery in Databases (PKDD 04)*, (pp. 27–38), Pisa, Italy.

Antonie, M.-L., & Zaïane, O.R. (2002). Text document categorization by term association. In *IEEE Data Mining (ICDM)*, (pp. 19–26).

Antonie, M.-L., & Zaïane, O.R. (2004). An associative classifier based on positive and negative rules. In *DMKD '04: Proceedings of the ACM SIGMOD workshop on Research issues in data mining and knowledge discovery*, (pp. 64–69), New York, NY, USA.

Antonie, M.-L., Zaïane, O. R., & Holte, R. (2006). Learning to use a learned model: A two-stage approach to classification. *In Proceedings of ICDM*, (pp. 33–42).

Armstrong, W. W. (1974). Dependency structures of data base relationships. *Proceedings of the IFIP congress* (pp. 580-583).

Arunasalam, B., & Chawla, S. (2006). CCCS: a top-down associative classifier for imbalanced class distribution. In T. Eliassi-Rad & L. H. Ungar & M. Craven & D. Gunopulos (Eds.), *KDD'06: Proceedings of the 12th ACM SIGKDD international conference on Knowledge discovery and data mining* (pp. 517 - 522). Philadelphia, PA: ACM.

Arunaslam, B., & Chawla, S. (2006). *CCCS: A top-down associative classifier for imbalanced class distribution* (Technical report). University of Sydney, School of IT.

Ashrafi, M. Z., Taniar, D., & Smith, K. (2007). Redundant association rules reduction techniques. *International Journal of Business Intelligence and Data Mining, 2*(1), 29-63.

Asuncion, A., & Newman, D. J. (2007). UCI Machine Learning Repository. *University of California, Irvine,*

School of Information and Computer Sciences. Retrieved April 22, 2008, from http://www.ics.uci.edu/~mlearn/MLRepository.html.

Au, W.-H., & Chan, K. (2005). Mining changes in association rules: A fuzzy approach. *Fuzzy Sets and Systems, 149*(1), 87–104.

Aumann, Y., Feldman, R., Lipshtat, O. & Manilla, H. (1999). Borders: An efficient algorithm for association generation in dynamic databases. *Intelligent Information Systems, 12*(1), 61-73.

Aze, J., & Kodratoff, Y. (2002). A study of the effect of noisy data in rule extraction systems. In Rappl, R. (Ed.), *Proceedings of the Sixteenth European Meeting on Cybernetics and Systems Research (EMCSR'02), 2,* 781–786.

Baesens, B., Viaene, S., & Vanthienen, J. (2000). Postprocessing of association rules. *In Proceedings of the Sixth ACM SIGKDD International Conference on Knowledge Discovery and Data Mining (KDD'2000),* Boston, Massachusetts, 20-23 Aug 2000 (pp. 2-8).

Baeza-Yates, R. A., & Ribeiro-Neto, B. A. (1999). *Modern Information Retrieval.* ACM Press / Addison-Wesley.

Bai, Y., Thakkar, H., Wang, H., Luo, C., & Zaniolo, C. (2000). A data stream language and system designed for power and extensibility. In *CIKM* (pp.337-346).

Baralis, E., & Chiusano, S. (2004). Essential Classification Rule Sets. *ACM Transactions on Database Systems, 29*(4), 635-674.

Baralis, E., & Paolo, G. (2002). A Lazy Approach to Pruning Classification Rules. In V. Kumar & S. Tsumoto & N. Zhong & P. S. Yu & X. Wu (Eds.), *Proceedings of the 2002 IEEE International Conference on Data Mining* (pp. 35-42). Maebashi City, Japan: IEEE Computer Society.

Baralis, E., & Psaila, G. (1997). Designing templates for mining association rules, *Journal of Intelligent Information Systems, 9*(1), 7-32.

Baralis, E., Chiusano, S., & Garza, P. (2008). A Lazy Approach to Associative Classification. *IEEE Transactions on Knowledge and Data Engineering, 20*(2), 156-171.

Barbut, M. & Monjardet, B. (1970). *Ordre et classification. Algèbre et Combinatoire.* Hachette, Tome II.

Baron, S., Spiliopoulou, M., & Günther, O. (2003). Efficient monitoring of patterns in data mining environments. In *Proc. of 7th East-European Conf. on Advances in Databases and Inf. Sys. (ADBIS'03)*, LNCS, (pp. 253–265). Springer.

Bastide, Y., Pasquier, N., Taouil, R., Lakhal, L., & Stumme, G. (2000). Mining minimal non-redundant association rules using frequent closed itemsets. In *Proceedings of the International Conference DOOD'2000, LNCS, Springer-Verlag*, (pp. 972–986), London, UK.

Bastide, Y., Pasquier, N., Taouil, R., Lakhal, L., & Stumme, G. (2000). Mining minimal non-redundant association rules using frequent closed itemsets. *Proceedings of the CL conference* (pp. 972-986).

Bastide, Y., Pasquier, N., Taouil, R., Stumme, G., & Lakhal, L. (2000). Mining minimal non-redundant association rules using frequent closed itemsets. In *First International Conference on Computational Logic* (pp. 972-986).

Bastide, Y., Taouil, R., Pasquier, N., Stumme, G., & Lakhal, L. (2000). Mining frequent patterns with counting inference. *ACM SIGKDD Exploration Journal, 2*(2), 66–75.

Basu, S., Mooney, R. J., Pasupuleti, K. V., & Ghosh J. (2001). Evaluating the Novelty of Text-Mined Rules using Lexical Knowledge. *7th ACM SIGKDD International Conference on Knowledge Discovery in Databases* (pp. 233–238). San Francisco, CA: ACM Press.

Bathoorn, R., Koopman, A., & Siebes, A. (2006). *Frequent Patterns that Compress.* Institute of Information and Computing Sciences, Technical reports, UU-CS-2006-048, Utrecht University.

Bay, S. D., & Pazzani, M. J. (2001). Detecting Group Differences: Mining Contrast Sets. *Data Mining and Knowledge Discovery.*

Bayardo, Jr., R. J., & Agrawal, R. (1999). Mining the most interesting rules. *In Proceedings of the 5th ACM SIGKDD International Conference on Knowledge Discovery and Data Mining*, (pp. 145–154).

Bayardo, R. (1997). Brute-force mining of high-confidence classification rules. In *SIGKDD 1997*, (pp. 123–126).

Bayardo, R. J. (1998). Efficiently Mining Long Patterns from Databases. *In Proceedings of the ACM SIGMOD International Conference on Management of Data* (pp. 85-93).

Bayardo, R. J., & Agrawal, R. (1999). Mining the most interesting rules. In *Proceedings of ACM KDD'1999*, (pp. 145–154). ACM Press.

Bayardo, R. J., Agrawal, R., & Gunopulos, D. (2000). Constraint-based rule mining in large, dense databases. Knowledge Discovery and Data Mining, *4*(2), 217-240.

Ben Yahia, S., & Mephu Nguifo, E. (2008). GERVIS: Scalable visualization of generic association rules. In *International Journal of Computational Intelligence Research (IJCIR)*, (to appear).

Ben Yahia, S., Hamrouni, T., & Mephu Nguifo, E. (2006). Frequent closed itemset based algorithms: A thorough structural and analytical survey. In *ACM-SIGKDD Explorations, 8*(1), 93–104.

Berrado, A., & Runger, G. C. (2007). Using metarules to organize and group discovered association rules. *Data Mining and Knowledge Discovery, 14*(3), 409-431.

Berzal, F., & Cubero, J.C. (2007). Guest editors' introduction, *Data & Knowledge Engineering, Special section on Intelligent Data Mining, 60*, 1-4.

Blake, L. C., & Merz, J. C. (1998). *UCI Repository of Machine Learning Databases.* Department of Information and Computer Science, University of California, Irvine, http://www.ics.uci.edu/~mlearn/MLRepository.html.

Blanchard, J. (2005). *Un système de visualisation pour l'extraction, l'évaluation, et l'exploration interactives des règles d'association*. PhD thesis, University of Nantes.

Blanchard, J., Guillet, F., & Briand, H. (2003). A user-driven and quality-oriented visualization for mining association rules. In *Proceedings of the Third IEEE International Conference on Data Mining*, (pp. 493–496), Melbourne, Florida.

Blanchard, J., Guillet, F., & Briand, H. (2007). Interactive visual exploration of association rules with rule-focusing methodology. *Knowledge and Information Systems*, *13*(1), 43-75.

Blanchard, J., Guillet, F., & Briand, H. (2007). Interactive visual exploration of association rules with rule-focusing methodology. *Knowledge and Information Systems*, *13*(1), 43-75.

Blanchard, J., Guillet, F., Briand, H., & Gras, R. (2005). Assessing rule interestingness with a probabilistic measure of deviation from equilibrium. In *Proceedings of the 11th international symposium on Applied Stochastic Models and Data Analysis ASMDA-2005*, (pp. 191–200).

Blanchard, J., Guillet, F., Gras, R., & Briand, H. (2005). Using information-theoretic measures to assess association rule interestingness. In *Proceedings of the fifth IEEE international conference on data mining ICDM'05*, (pp. 66–73). IEEE Computer Society.

Blanchard, J., Kuntz, P., Guillet, F., & Gras, R. (2003). Implication intensity: from the basic statistical definition to the entropic version. In *Statistical Data Mining and Knowledge Discovery*, (pp. 473–485). Chapman & Hall.

Blanchard, J., Pinaud, B., Kuntz, P., & Guillet, F. (2007). A 2D-3D visualization support for human-centered rule mining. *Computers & Graphics*, *31*(3), 350-360.

Boettcher, M., Nauck, D., & Spott, M. (2005). Detecting Temporally Redundant Association Rules. In *Proceedings of the 4th International Conference on Machine Learning and Applications*, (pp. 397-403). IEEE Computer Science Press.

Boettcher, M., Nauck, D., Ruta, D., & Spott, M. (2006). Towards a framework for change detection in datasets. In *Proceedings of the 26th SGAI International Conference on Innovative Techniques and Applications of Artificial Intelligence*, (pp. 115–128). Springer.

Boettcher, M., Spott, M., & Nauck, D. (2007). A framework for discovering and analyzing changing customer segments. In *Proceedings of the 7th Industrial Conference on Data Mining (ICDM'2007)*, LNAI 4597, (pp. 255–268). Springer.

Bonchi, F., & Lucchese, C. (2004). On closed constrained frequent pattern mining. *Proceeding of the IEEE ICDM conference* (pp. 35-42).

Bonchi, F., & Lucchese, C. (2006). On condensed representations of constrained frequent patterns. *Knowledge and Information Systems*, *9*(2), 180-201.

Bonchi, F., Giannotti, F., Mazzanti, A., & Pedreschi, D. (2005). Efficient breadth-first mining of frequent pattern with monotone constraints. *Knowledge and Information Systems*, *8*(2), 131-153.

Boole, G. (1847). *The Mathematical Analysis of Logic*. Cambridge: Macmillan, Barclay and Macmillan.

Boole, G. (1854). *An Investigation of the Laws of Thought*. Cambridge: Macmillan and Co.

Borgelt, C. (2000). *Apriori software*. Available from http://www.borgelt.net/software.html.

Borgelt, C. (2003). Efficient implementations of apriori and éclat. *In Workshop on Frequent Itemset Mining Implementations*. Melbourne, FL.

Borgelt, C., & Kruse, R. (2002). Induction of association rules: Apriori implementation. *Proceedings of the 15th Conference on Computational Statistics*, (pp. 395-400). Berlin, Germany.

Boulicaut, J. F., Bykowski, A., & Rigotti, C. (2003). Free-sets: a condensed representation of boolean data for the approximation of frequency queries. *Data Mining and Knowledge Discovery, 7*(1), 5-22.

Boulicaut, J. F., Jeudy, B. (2002). Optimization of association rule mining queries. *Intelligent Data Analysis Journal, 6*, 341–357.

Bradley, A. P. (1996). ROC curves and the x^2 test. *Pattern Recognition Letters, 17*(3), 287-294.

Bradley, A. P. (1997). The use of the area under the ROC curve in the evaluation of machine learning algorithms. *Pattern Recognition, 30*(7), 1145-1159.

Brijs, T., Swinnen, G., Vanhoof, K., & Wets, G. (1999). Using association rules for product assortment decisions: a case study. *Proceedings of the fifth ACM SIGKDD international conference on Knowledge discovery and data mining,* (pp. 254-260).

Brijs, T., Vanhoof, K., & Wets, G. (2000). Reducing Redundancy in Characteristic Rule Discovery By Using Integer Programming Techniques. *Intelligent Data Analysis Journal, 4*(3), 229-240.

Brijs, T., Vanhoof, K., & Wets, G. (2003). Defining interestingness for association rules. *International Journal of Information Theories and Applications, 10*(4), 370–376.

Brin, S., Motawni, R., & Silverstein, C. (1997). Beyond market baskets: Generalizing association rules to correlations. In *Proceedings of ACM SIGMOD International Conference on Management of Data, ACM Press,* (pp. 265–276), Tucson, Arizona, USA.

Brin, S., Motwani, R., & Silverstein, C. (1997). Beyond market basket: Generalizing association rules to dependence rules. *Data Mining and Knowledge Discovery, 2*(1), 39-68.

Brin, S., Motwani, R., & Silverstein, C. (1997). Beyond market baskets: Generalizing association rules to correlations. *SIGMOD Record, 26*(2), 265–276.

Brin, S., Motwani, R., Ullman, J. D., & Tsur, S. (1997). Dynamic itemset counting and implication rules for market basket data. *In SIGMOD '97: Proceedings of the 1997 ACM SIGMOD international conference on Management of data,* Tucson, Arizona, USA (pp 255-264).

Bruha, I. (2000). From machine learning to knowledge discovery: Survey of preprocessing and postprocessing. *Intelligent Data Analysis, 4*(3-4), 363-374.

Bruha, I., & Famili, A. F. (2000). Postprocessing in machine learning and data mining. In R. Ng (Ed.), Proceedings of the sixth ACM SIGKDD international conference on Knowledge discovery and data mining, (pp.20-23). Boston, MA, USA.

Bruzzese, D., & Buono, P. (2004). Combining visual techniques for Association Rules exploration. In M. F. Costabile (Ed.), Working Conference on Advanced Visual Interfaces (pp. 381-384). New York: ACM Press.

Bruzzese, D., & Davino, C. (2001). Statistical pruning of discovered association rules. *Computational Statistics, 16(3),* 387-398.

Buono, P., & Costabile, M. F. (2004). Visualizing association rules in a framework for visual data mining. In *From Integrated Publication and Information Systems to Virtual Information and Knowledge Environments, Springer-Verlag, 3379*(LNCS), 221–231.

Buono, P., Costabile, M. F., & Lisi, F. A. (2001). Supporting data analysis through visualizations. In *Proceedings of the International Workshop on Visual Data Mining co-located with ECML/PKDD 2001,* (pp. 67–78), Freiburg, Germany.

Burdick, D., Calimlim, M., & Calimlim, M. (2001). MAFIA: A Maximal Frequent Itemset Algorithm for Transactional Databases. *Proceedings of the 17th International Conference on Data Engineering,* IEEE Computer Society (pp. 443-452).

Bustos, B., D. Keim, A., Schneidewind, J., Schreck, T., & Sips, M. (2003). *Pattern visualization.* Technical report, University of Konstanz, Germany, Computer Science Department.

Bykowski, A., & Rigotti, C. (2001). A condensed representation to find frequent patterns. *In Proc. of PODS.*

Cai, Y. D., Clutter, D., Pape, G., Han, J., Welge, M., & Auvil L. (2004). MAIDS: mining alarming incidents from data streams. *Proceedings of the 2004 ACM SIGMOD international conference on Management of data* (pp. 919-920).

Calders, T., & Goethals, B. (2002). Mining all non-derivable frequent itemsets. *In Proc. of PKDD.* (pp. 74–85).

Calders, T., & Goethals, B. (2007). Non-derivable itemset mining. *Data Mining and Knowledge Discovery, 14,* 171-206.

Calders, T., Goethals, B., & Prado, A. (2006) Integrating pattern mining in relational databases. In *PKDD,* volume 4213 of *Lecture Notes in Computer Science* (pp. 454-461). Springer.

Calders, T., Rigotti, C., & Boulicaut, J. F. (2006). A Survey on Condensed Representations for Frequent Sets, In: J.F. Boulicaut, L.D. Raedt, & H. Mannila (Ed.), *Constraint-based mining and Inductive Databases* (pp. 64-80), Springer.

Carmona-Saez, P., Chagoyen, M., Rodriguez, A., Trelles, O., Carazo, J. M., & Pascual-Montano, A. (2006). Integrated analysis of gene expression by association rules discovery. *BMC Bioinformatics, 7(54).*

Carvalho, D. R., Freitas, A. A., & Ebecken, N. (2005). Evaluating the correlation between objective rule interestingness measures and real human interest. *Knowledge Discovery in Databases. Lecture Notes in Artificial Intelligence 3731* (pp. 453–461). Springer-Verlag Press.

Carvalho, V. O., Rezende, S. O., & Castro, M. (2007). Obtaining and evaluating generalized association rules. In *Proceedings of the 9th International Conference on Enterprise Information Systems (ICEIS),* Volume 2 Artificial Intelligence and Decision Support Systems, (pp. 310–315).

Carvalho, V. O., Rezende, S. O., & Castro, M. (2007) An analytical evaluation of objective measures behavior for generalized association rules. In *Proceedings of the IEEE Symposium on Computational Intelligence and Data Mining (CIDM-2007),* (pp. 43–50).

Castelo, R., Feelders, A., & Siebes, A. (2001). MAMBO: Discovering association rules based on conditional independencies. *In Proceedings of 4th International Symposium on Intelligent Data Analysis,* Cascais, Portugal.

Ceglar, A., & Roddick, J. F. (2006). Association mining. *ACM Computing Surveys, 38*(2), 5.

Chakrabarti, S., Sarawagi, S., & Dom, B. (1998). Mining surprising patterns using temporal description length. In *Proceedings of the 24th International Conference on Very Large Databases,* (pp. 606–617). Morgan Kaufmann Publishers Inc.

Chakravarthy, S., & Zhang, H. (2003). Visualization of association rules over relational DBMSs. In G. B. Lamont, H. Haddad, G. A. Papadopoulos, B. Panda (Eds.), *ACM Symposium on Applied Computing* (pp. 922-926). New York: Association for Computing Machinery.

Chan, R., Yang, Q., & Shen, Y.-D. (2003). Mining high utility itemsets Data Mining, *In ICDM 2003: Third IEEE International Conference on Data Mining,* Melbourne, Florida, USA (pp. 19-26).

Chatfield, C. (2003). *The Analysis of Time Series: An Introduction, Sixth Edition (Texts in Statistical Science).* Chapman & Hall/CRC.

Chawla, S., Davis, J., & Pandey G. (2004). **On local pruning of association rules using directed hypergraphs. In** Proceedings of the 20th International Conference on Data Engineering (pp. 832-841).

Chen, C. & Yu, Y. (2000). Empirical studies of information visualization: a meta-analysis. *International Journal of Human-Computer Studies, 53*(5), 851-866.

Chen, J., Zheng, T., Thorne, W., Zaiane, O. R., & Goebel, R. (2007). Visual data mining of web navigational data. In *Proceedings of the 11th International Conference on Information Visualization (IV'07), IEEE Computer Society Press,* (pp. 649 656), Zurich, Switzerland.

Chen, M.-C., Chiu, A.-L., & Chang, H.-H. (2005). Mining changes in customer behavior in retail marketing. *Expert Systems with Applications, 28*(4), 773–781.

Chen, P., Verma, R., Meininger, J. C., & Chan, W. (2008). Semantic analysis of association rules. *Proceedings of the FLAIRS Conference*, Miami, Florida.

Cheng, J., Ke, Y., & Ng, W. (2008). Effective elimination of redundant association rules. *Data Mining and Knowledge Discovery, 16*(2), 221-249.

Cherfi, H., Napoli, A., & Toussaint, Y. (2006). Towards a text mining methodology using frequent itemsets and association rules. *Soft Computing Journal - A Fusion of Foundations, Methodologies and Applications, 10*(5), 431–441. Special Issue on Recent Advances in Knowledge and Discovery. Springer-Verlag.

Cheung, D., Han, J., Ng, V. T., & Wong, C. Y. (1996). Maintenance of discovered association rules in large databases: an incremental update technique. *Proceedings of the 1996 International Conference on Data Engineering* (pp. 106-114).

Cheung, D., Lee, S. D., & Kao, B. (1997). A general incremental technique for maintaining discovered association rules. *Database Systems for Advanced Applications* (pp. 185-194).

Cheung, W., & Zaïane, O. R. (2003). Incremental mining of frequent patterns without candidate generation or support constraint. *Proceedings of the 2003 International Database Engineering and Applications Symposium* (pp. 111-116).

Cheung, Y.-L., & Fu, A. (2004). Mining frequent itemsets without support threshold: With and without item constraints. *IEEE Transactions on Knowledge and Data Engineering, 16*(9), 1052-1069.

Chi, Y., Wang, H., Yu, P. S., & Muntz, R. R. (2004). Moment: Maintaining closed frequent itemsets over a stream sliding window. In *ICDM* (pp 59-66).

Clark, P., & Boswell, R. (1991). Rule induction with CN2: Some recent improvements. In *EWSL'91: Proceedings of the European Working Session on Machine Learning*, (pp. 151–163). Springer.

Coenen, F., & Leng, P. (2004). An evaluation of approaches to classification rule selection. In *ICDM 2004*, (pp. 359–362).

Coenen, F., & Leng, P. (2007). The effect of threshold values on association rule based classification accuracy. In *Journal of Data and Knowledge Engineering, 60*(2), 345–360.

Cohen, J. (1960). A coefficient of agreement for nominal scales. *Educational and Psychological Measurement*, (20), 37–46.

Collins A., & Loftus E. (1975). A spreading-activation of semantic processing. *Psychological Review, 82*(6), 407–428.

Couturier, O., Dubois, V., Hsu, T., & Mephu Nguifo, E. (2008). Optimizing occlusion appearances in 3D association rule visualization. In *4th IEEE International Conference on Intelligent Systems (IEEE-IS'08)*, September, Varna, Bulgaria.

Couturier, O., Hamrouni, T., Ben Yahia S., & Mephu Nguifo, E. (2007). A scalable association rule visualization towards displaying large amounts of knowledge. In *Proceedings of the 11th International Conference on Information Visualization (IV'07), IEEE Computer Society Press*, (pp. 657-663), Zurich, Switzerland.

Couturier, O., Mephu Nguifo, E., & Noiret, B. (2005). A hierarchical user-driven method for association rules mining. In *Proceedings of the 11th International Conference on Human-Computer Interaction (HCI'05), Lawrence Erlbaum Associate Editions*, cdrom, Las Vegas, Nevada, USA.

Couturier, O., Rouillard, J., & Chevrin, V. (2007). An interactive approach to display large sets of association rules. In *Proceedings of the 12th International Conference on Human-Computer Interaction (HCI'07), Springer-Verlag, LNCS, 4557*, 258–267, Beijing, China.

Cover, T. M., & Thomas, J. A. (1991). Elements of Information Theory. 1st edition. New York: Wiley-Interscience.

Cox, D., & Stuart, A. (1955). Some quick sign tests for trend in location and dispersion. *Biometrika, 42,* 80–95.

Cristofor, L., & Simovici, D.A. (2002). Generating an informative cover for association rules. *Proceedings of the ICDM conference.*

Cuppens, F., & Demolombe, R. (1989). How to recognize interesting topics to provide cooperative answering. *Information Systems, 14*(2), pp 163–173.

De Morgan, A. (1847). *Formal Logic or, The Calculus of Inference, Necessary and Probable.* London: Taylor and Walton.

Demaine, E. D., López-Ortiz, A., & Munro, J. I. (2002). Frequency estimation of internet packet streams with limited space. *Proceedings of the 10th Annual European Symposium on Algorithms* (pp. 348-360).

Deogun, J.S., & Jiang, L. (2005). SARM - succinct association rule mining: An approach to enhance association mining. *Proceedings ISMIS conference* (pp. 121-130), *LNCS 3488.*

Dice, L. (1945). Measures of the amount of ecologic association between species. *Ecology,* (26), 297–302.

Dix, A., Finlay, J. E., Abowd, G. D., & Beale, R. (2003). *Human-Computer Interaction.* London: Prentice Hall.

Domingues, M. A., & Rezende, S. O. (2005). Post-processing of Association Rules using Taxonomies. *In Proceedings of Portuguese Conference on Artificial Intelligence* (pp. 192-197).

Domingues, M. A., & Rezende, S. O. (2005). Using taxonomies to facilitate the analysis of the association rules. In *Proceedings of ECML/PKDD'05 – The Second International Workshop on Knowledge Discovery and Ontologies (KDO-2005),* (pp. 59–66).

Dong, G., & Duan, L. (2008). *Mining Class Converters for Converting Undesirable Objects into Desirable Ones.* Submitted for publication.

Dong, G., & Li, J. (1998), Interestingness of discovered association rules in terms of neighborhood-based unex-pectedness. *In Pacific-Asia Conference on Knowledge Discovery and Data Mining.* Melbourne, Australia (pp. 72-86).

Dong, G., & Li, J. (1999). Efficient mining of emerging patterns: Discovering trends and differences. *In Proceedings of the 5th ACM SIGKDD International Conference on Knowledge Discovery and Data Mining,* (pp. 43–52).

Dong, G., Jiang, C., Pei, J., Li, J., & Wong, L. (2005). Mining succinct systems of minimal generators of formal concepts. *Proceeding of the DASFAA conference* (pp. 175-187). *LNCS 3453.*

Dong, G., Zhang, X., Wong, L., & Li, J. (1999). CAEP: Classification by Aggregating Emerging Patterns. In S. Arikawa & K. Furukawa (Eds.), *Discovery Science, Second International Conference* (pp. 30-42). Tokyo, Japan: Springer.

Drummond, C., & Holte, R. (2006). Cost curves: An improved method for visualizing classification performance. *Machine Learning, 65*(1), 95--130.

Dunn, J. M. (1986). Relevance logic and entailment. In D. Gabbay, & F. Guenthner (Ed.), *Handbook of Philosophical Logic, 3,* 117–224. Kluwer Academic Publishers.

Duoqian, M. (1997). Rough set theory and its application in machine learning. Ph D dissertation (in Chinese). Institute of automation, Chinese academy of sciences.

Duoqian, M., & Daoguo, L. (2008). Rough sets theory, Algorithms and Applications. Beijing, China: Tsinghua University Press.

Duoqian, M., & Guirong, H. (1999). A heuristic algorithm for reduction of knowledge.

Duoqian, M., & Jue, W. (1997). Information-based algorithm for reduction of knowledge. IEEE International conference on intelligent processing systems (pp.1155-1158). Beijing, China. International Academic Publishers.

Duoqian, M., & Jue, W. (1999). An information representation of concepts and operations in rough set theory. Journal of Software (in Chinese), 10(2). 113-116.

Duoqian, M., Qinrong, F., & Ruizhi, W. (2007). Information Entropy and Granular Computing. In D. Miao, et al. (Eds.), Granular Computing: Past, Present, and the Future Perspectives, (pp.142-180). Beijing: China Academic Press.

Duquenne, V., & Guigues, J.-L. (1986). Famille minimale d'implications informatives résultant d'un tableau de données binaires. *Mathématiques et Sciences Humaines, 24*(95), 5-18.

Egan, J. P. (1975). *Signal detection theory and ROC analysis*. New York: Academic Press.

Elder, J. F., & Pregibon, D. (1996). A statistical perspective on knowledge discovery in databases. In U. M. Fayyad, G. Piatetsky-Shapiro, P. Smyth, & R. Uthurusamy, (Eds.), *Advances in knowledge discovery and data mining*, (pp. 83–113). AAAI/MIT Press.

Ertek, G., & Demiriz, A. (2006). A Framework for Visualizing Association Mining Results. In A. Levi, E. Savas, H. Yenigün, S. Balcisoy & Y. Saygin (Eds.), *21st International Symposium on Computer and Information Sciences* (pp. 593-602). Berlin: Lecture Notes in Computer Science.

Esposito, F., Malerba, D., & Semeraro, G. (1997). A Comparative Analysis of Methods for Pruning Decision Trees. *IEEE Transactions On Pattern Analysis and Machine Intelligence, 19*(5), 476-491.

Ester, M., Kriegel, H.-P., Sander, J., Wimmer, M., & Xu, X. (1998). Incremental clustering for mining in a data warehousing environment. In *VLDB* (pp. 323-333).

Faure, C., Delprat, D., Boulicaut, J. F., & Mille, A. (2006). Iterative Bayesian Network Implementation by using Annotated Association Rules. *15th Int'l Conf. on Knowledge Engineering and Knowledge Management – Managing Knowledge in a World of Networks, Vol. 4248 of Lecture Notes in Artificial Intelligence – LNAI* (pp. 326–333). Prague, Czech Republic: Springer-Verlag.

Fawcett, T. (2006). An introduction to ROC analysis. *Pattern Recognition Letters, 27*(8), 861-874.

Fawcett, T. (2008). PRIE: A system to generate rulelists to maximize ROC performance. *Data Mining and Knowledge Discovery Journal, 17*(2), 207-224.

Fawcett, T., & Flach, P. A. (2005). A Response to Webb and Ting's On the Application of ROC Analysis to Predict Classification Performance Under Varying Class Distributions. *Machine Learning, 58*(1), 33-38.

Fayyad, U. M., & Irani, K. B. (1993). Multi-Interval Discretization of Continuous-Valued Attributes for Classification Learning. In R. Bajcsy (Ed.), *Proceedings of the 13th International Joint Conference on Artificial Intelligence* (pp. 1022-1029). Chambéry, France: Morgan Kaufmann.

Fayyad, U. M., Piatetsky-Shapiro, G., & Uthurusamy, R. (2003). Summary from the KDD-03 panel: Data mining–the next 10 years. *SIGKDD Explorations Newsletter, 5*(2), 191–196.

Fayyad, U. M., Piatetsky-Shapiro, G., Smyth, P., & Uthurusamy, R. (1996). *Advances in Knowledge Discovery and Data Mining*. AAAI Press and MIT Press, Menlo Park and Cambridge, MA, USA.

Fayyad, U., & Irani, K. (1993). Multi-interval discretization of continuous-valued attributes for classification learning. *In Proceedings of the 13th International Joint Conference on Artificial Intelligence.*

Fayyad, U., Piatetsky-Shapiro, G., & Smyth, P. (1996). From data mining to knowledge discovery in databases. *AI Magazine, 17*(3), 37-54.

Fayyad, U., Piatetsky-Shapiro, G., Smyth, P., & Uthurusamy, R. (1996). *Advances in Knowledge Discovery and Data Mining*. Menlo Park, CA: AAAI Press / MIT Press.

Fekete, J. D. (2004). The INFOVIS toolkit. In *Proceedings of the 10th IEEE Symposium on Information Visualization (INFOVIS'04)*, (pp. 167–174).

Feng, M., Dong, G., Li, J., Tan, Y-P., & Wong, L. (2007). Evolution and maintenance of frequent pattern space when transactions are removed. *Proceedings of the 2007*

Pacific-Asia Conference on Knowledge Discovery and Data Mining (pp. 489-497).

Fernádez, M. Z., Menasalvas, E., Marbán, O., Peña, J. M., & Millán S. (2001). Minimal Decision Rules Based on the Apriori Algorithm, *Internal Journal of Applied Mathematics and Computer Science, 11*(3), 691-704.

Fienberg, S. E., & Shmueli, G. (2005). Statistical issues and challenges associated with rapid detection of bio-terrorist attacks. *Statistics in Medicine, 24(4),* 513-529.

FIMI Dataset Repository. (2003). Available from http://fimi.cs.helsinki.fi/data/.

Flach, P. A. (2003). The geometry of ROC space: Understanding machine learning metrics through ROC isometrics. *Proceedings of the Twentieth International Conference on Machine Learning,* (pp. 194–201).

Fogel, D. B. (1997). The advantages of evolutionary computation. In D. Lundh, B. Olsson, & A. Narayanan, (Eds.), *Bio-Computing and Emergent Computation.* World Scientific Press, Singapore.

Frantz, V., & Shapiro, J. (1991). Algorithms for automatic construction of query formulations in Boolean form. *Journal of the American Society for Information Science, 1*(42), pp 16–26.

Freitas, A. (1999). On rule interestingness measures. *Knowledge-Based Systems Journal, 12*(5-6), 309–315.

Freitas, A. (1999). On rule interestingness measures. *Knowledge-Based Systems, 12*(5), 309-315.

Freitas, A. A. (1998). On Objective Measures of Rule Surprisingness. *PKDD '98: Proceedings of the Second European Symposium on Principles of Data Mining and Knowledge Discovery,* Springer-Verlag, Nantes, France (pp. 1-9).

Furnas, G. W. (2006). A fisheyes follow-up: Further reflections on focus+context. In *Proceedings of the ACM Conference on Human Factors in Computing Systems (CHI'06), ACM Press,* (pp. 999–1008), Montréal, Canada.

Furnkranz, J. (1999). Separate-and-Conquer Rule Learning, Artificial intelligence Review, 13, 3-54.

Ganascia, J. G. (1991). Deriving the learning bias from rule properties. In *Machine intelligence 12: towards an automated logic of human thought,* (pp. 151–167). Clarendon Press.

Ganter, B., & Wille, R. (1999). *Formal Concept Analysis: Mathematical Foundations.* Springer, Heidelberg.

Ganter, B., Stumme, G., & Wille, R. (2005). Formal Concept Analysis: Foundations and applications. *Lecture Notes in Computer Science, 3626.*

Ganti, V., Gehrke, J., Ramakrishnan, R., & Loh, W. Y. (1999). A Framework for Measuring Changes in Data Characteristics. *In Proc. of ACM PODS* (pp. 126–137).

Gasmi, G., BenYahia, S., Mephu Nguifo, E., & Slimani, Y. (2005). *IGB*: A new informative generic base of association rules. In *Proceedings of the 9th International Pacific-Asia Conference on Knowledge Data Discovery (PAKDD'05), LNAI 3518,* (pp. 81–90), Hanoi, Vietnam.

Geng, L., & Hamilton, H. J. (2006). Interestingness measures for data mining: A survey. *ACM Computing Surveys, 38*(3), 9.

Geng, L., & Hamilton, H. J. (2007). Choosing the right lens: Finding what is interesting in data mining. In F. Guillet & H. J. Hamilton (Ed.), *Quality Measures in Data Mining,* volume 43 of *Studies in Computational Intelligence,* (pp. 3–24). Springer.

Ghouila, A., Ben Yahia S., Malouch, D., & Abdelhak, S. (2007). MULTI-SOM: A novel unsupervised classification approach. In *Proceedings of the 9th French Conference on Machine Learning (CAp'07),* (pp. 203–218), Grenoble, France.

Goethals, B., Muhonen, J., & Toivonen, H. (2005). Mining non-derivable association rules. *Proceedings of the SIAM conference.*

Gouda, K., & Zaki, M. J. (2001). Efficiently Mining Maximal Frequent Itemsets. *ICDM '01: Proceedings of the 2001 IEEE International Conference on Data Mining,* San Jose, California, USA (pp. 163-170).

Grahne, G., & Zhu, J. (2003). Efficiently using prefix-trees in mining frequent itemsets. *Proceedings 1st IEEE ICDM Workshop on Frequent Itemset Mining Implementations*, 2003.

Gras, R. (1996). *L'implication statistique : nouvelle méthode exploratoire de données.* La Pensée Sauvage Editions.

Gras, R., & Kuntz, P. (2008). An overview of the statistical implicative analysis development. In Gras, R., Suzuki, E., Guillet, F., & Spagnolo, F. (Ed.), *Statistical Implicative Analysis: Theory and Applications*, volume 127 of *Studies in Computational Intelligence*, (pp. 21–52). Springer.

Gray, B., & Orlowska, M. (1998). CCAIIA: Clustering categorical attributes into interesting association rules. *In Pacific-Asia Conference on Knowledge Discovery and Data Mining*, Melbourne, Australia (pp. 132-143).

Guigues, J. L., & Duquenne, V. (1986). Familles minimales d'implications informatives résultant d'un tableau de données binaires. *Mathématiques et Sciences Humaines, 95*, 5–18.

Guillet, E., & Hamilton, H. J. (Ed.). (2007). *Quality Measures in Data Mining.* Studies in Computational Intelligence. Springer.

Guillet, P. F., & Hamilton, H. J. (2007). *Quality Measures in Data Mining.* Springer.

Guoda, K., & Zaki, M. J. (2001). Efficiently mining maximal frequent itemsets. *Proceedings of the 2001 IEEE International Conference on Data Mining* (pp. 163-170).

Guoyin, W. (2001). Rough set theory and knowledge acquisition. Xi'an, China: Xi'an Jiaotong University Press.

Hackman, J.R., & Oldham, G.R. (1975). Development of the job diagnostic survey. *Journal of Applied Psychology, 60*, 159–170.

Halatchev, M., & Gruenwald, L. (2005). Estimating missing values in related sensor data streams. *International Conference on Management of Data* (pp. 83-94).

Hamrouni, T., Ben Yahia, S., & Mephu Nguifo, E. (2006). Generic association rule bases: Are they so succinct? *Proceedings of the CLA conference* (pp. 198-213).

Hamrouni, T., Ben Yahia, S., & Mephu Nguifo, E. (2008). Succinct system of minimal generators: A thorough study, limitations and new definitions. *Lecture Notes in Computer Science, 4923*, 80-95.

Hamrouni, T., Ben Yahia, S., Mephu Nguifo, E., & Valtchev, P. (2007). About the Lossless Reduction of the Minimal Generator Family of a Context. *Proceedings of the ICFCA conference* (pp. 130-150).

Hamrouni, T., BenYahia, S., & Slimani, Y. (2005). PRINCE: An algorithm for generating rule bases without closure computations. In *Proceedings of the 7th International Conference on Data Warehousing and Knowledge Discovery (DaWaK'05), 3589*, 346–355, Copenhagen, Denmark.

Han, J., & Cercone, N. (2000). RULEVIZ: A model for visualizing knowledge discovery process. In *Proceedings of 6th ACM SIGKDD International Conference on Knowledge Discovery and Data Mining*, (pp. 244–253), Boston, MA, USA.

Han, J., & Fu, Y. (1995). Discovery of multiple-level association rules from large databases. *Proceedings of the VLDB conference* (pp. 420-431).

Han, J., Dong, G., & Yin, Y. (1999). Efficient mining of partial periodic patterns in time series database. *International Conference on Data Engineering*, (pp. 106-115).

Han, J., Pei, J., & Yin, Y. (2000). Mining frequent patterns without candidate generation. *2000 ACM SIGMOD International. Conference on Management of Data* (pp. 1-12).

Han, J., Pei, J., Yin, Y., & Mao, R. (2004). Mining frequent patterns without candidate generation. *Data Mining and Knowledge Discovery, 8*, 53-87.

Harrison, B. L., & Vicente, K. J. (1996). An experimental evaluation of transparent menu usage. In *Proceedings of the ACM Conference on Human factors in computing systems (CHI'96), ACM Press*, (pp. 391–398), New York, USA.

Hartigan, J. A., & Kleiner, B. (1981). Mosaics for contingency tables. In W. F. Eddy (Ed.), *13th Symposium on the Interface Between Computer Science and Statistics*, New York: Springer-Verlag.

Hébert, C., & Crémilleux, B. (2007). A unified view of objective interestingness measures. In Petra Perner (Eds.)*, Machine Learning and Data Mining in Pattern Recognition* (pp. 533-547). Springer-Verlag Press.

Hilderman, R. J., & Hamilton, H. J. (2001). Evaluation of interestingness measures for ranking discovered knowledge. In D. W. Cheung, G. J. Williams, Q. Li (Eds.), *Proceedings of the 5th Pacific-Asia Conference on Knowledge Discovery and Data Mining* (pp. 247–259). Springer-Verlag Press.

Hilderman, R., & Hamilton, H. (1999). Heuristic measures of interestingness. *Proceedings of the PKDD conference* (pp. 232-241).

Hilderman, R., & Hamilton, H. (2001). Knowledge Discovery and Measures of Interest. Kluwer Academic Publishers.

Hirokane, M., Konishi , H., et al.(2007). Extraction of minimal decision algorithm using rough sets and genetic algorithm. Systems and Computers in Japan, 38(4), 39-51.

Hofmann, H., & Wilhelm, A. (2001). Visual comparison of association rules. *Computational Statistics, 16(3)*, 399-415.

Hofmann, H., Siebes, A. P. J. & Wilhelm, A. F. X. (2000). Visualizing Association Rules with Interactive Mosaic Plots. In R. Ramakrishnan, R., S. Stolfo, R. Bayardo, I. Parsa (Eds.) *ACM International Conference on Knowledge Discovery and Data Mining* (pp. 227-235). New York: Association for Computing Machinery.

Holt, J. D., & Chung, S. M. (2007). Parallel mining of association rules from text databases. *The Journal of Supercomputing, 39(3),* 273-299.

Hong, T-P., Lin, C-E., & Lin, J-H. (2008). Learning cross-level certain and possible rules by rough sets. Expert Systems with Applications, 34(3), 1698-1706.

Hu, X., & Cercone, N. (1997). Learning maximal generalized decision rules via discretization, generalization and rough set feature selection. In Proceedings of the 9th IEEE International Conference of Tools on Artificial Intelligence (pp. 548-556). Newport Beach, California, USA.

Hu, X., & Cercone, N. (2001). Discovering maximal generalized decision rules through horizontal and vertical data reduction, Computational Intelligence, 17(4), 685-702.

Hussain, F., Liu, H., & Lu, H. (2000). Relative measure for mining interesting rules. In *4th European Conference on Principles and Practice of Knowledge Discovery in Databases - Workshop in Knowledge Management: Theory and Applications* (pp. 117-132). Springer-Verlag Press.

Hussain, F., Liu, H., Suzuki, E., & Lu, H. (2000). Exception rule mining with a relative interestingness measure. In T. Terano, et al. (Eds.), 4th Pacific-Asia Conference on Knowledge Discovery and Data Mining, Current Issues and New Applications (pp. 86–97). Springer-Verlag.

Huynh, X.-H., Guillet, F., & Briand, H. (2006). Evaluating interestingness measures with linear correlation graph. In *Proceedings of the 19th International Conference on Industrial, Engineering and Other Applications of Applied Intelligent Systems (IEA/AIE)*, volume 4031 of *Lecture Notes in Computer Science*, (pp. 312–321). Springer.

Inselberg, A., & Dimsdale, B. (1990). Parallel Coordinates: A Tool for Visualizing Multi-dimensional Geometry. In A. Kaufman (Ed.), *1st Conference on Visualization '90* (pp. 361-378). Prentice Hall.

Ivanova, A., & Rachev, B. (2004). Multidimensional models—Constructing DATA CUBE. *In Proceedings of international conference on computer systems and technologies —ComSysTech'2004* (pp. V.5-1—V.5 7). 17-18 June 2004, Rousse, Bulgaria.

Jaakkola, T., & Siegelmann, H. (2001). Active information retrieval. In *Advances in Neural Information Processing Systems, 14*, 777–784. MIT Press.

Jaccard, P. (1901). Etude comparative de la distribution florale dans une portion des Alpes et du Jura. *Bulletin de la Société Vaudoise des Sciences Naturelles*, (37), 547–579.

Jacquemin, C. (1994). FASTR: A unification-based front-end to automatic indexing. *Information multimedia, information retrieval systems and management* (pp. 34–47). New-York, NY: Rockfeller University.

Jacquenet, F., Largeron, C., & Udrea, C. (2006). Efficient Management of Non Redundant Rules in Large Pattern Bases: A Bitmap Approach. *In Proceedings of the International Conference on Enterprise Information Systems*, 2006 (pp. 208-215).

Jaroszewicz, S., & Scheffer, T. (2005). Fast Discovery of Unexpected Patterns in Data, Relative to a Bayesian Network. *ACM SIGKDD Conference on Knowledge Discovery in Databases* (pp. 118–127). Chicago, IL: ACM Press.

Jaroszewicz, S., & Simovici, D. A. (2001). A general measure of rule interestingness. In *Proceedings of PKDD'2001*, (pp. 253–265). Springer.

Jaroszewicz, S., & Simovici, D. A. (2004) Interestingness of Frequent Itemsets using Bayesian networks as Background Knowledge. *ACM SIGKDD Conference on Knowledge Discovery in Databases* (pp. 178–186). Seattle, WA: ACM Press.

Jaroszewicz, S., & Simovici, D.A. (2002). Pruning Redundant Association Rules Using Maximum Entropy Principle. *In Proceedings of the 6th Pacific-Asia Conference on Knowledge Discovery and Data Mining*, 2002 (pp. 135-147).

Jeffreys, H. (1935). Some tests of significance treated by the theory of probability. In *Proceedings of the Cambridge Philosophical Society*, (pp. 203–222).

Jevons, W. S. (1890). *Pure Logic and Other Minor Works*. London: Macmillan.

Ji, X., Bailey, J., & Dong, G. (2005). Mining Minimal Distinguish-ing Subsequence Patterns with Gap Constraints. *In Proc. of ICDM*.

Jiang, N., & Gruenwald, D. L. (2006). Cfi-stream: mining closed frequent itemsets in data streams. In *SIGKDD* (pp. 592-597).

Jiang, N., & Gruenwald, L. (2006). Research issues in data stream association rule mining. *ACM SIGMOD Record, 35*(1), 14-19.

Jiang, Y., Wang, K., Tuzhilin, A., & Fu, A. (2005). Mining Patterns That Respond to Actions. *In Proc. of IEEE International Conference on Data Mining*.

Jorge, A., Poças, J., & Azevedo, P. (2002). A post-processing environment for browsing large sets of association rules. In *Proceedings of Second International Workshop on Integration and Collaboration Aspects of Data Mining, Decision Support and Meta-Learning* (pp. 53-64). Springer-Verlag Press.

Kamber, M., Han, J., & Chiang, J. Y (1997). Metarule-Guided Mining of Multi-Dimensional Association Rules Using Data Cubes. In D. Heckerman et al. (Eds.), Proceeding of the 3rd International Conference on Knowledge Discovery and Data Mining. (pp. 207-210) Newport Beach, California, USA.

Kawano, H., & Kawahara, M. (2002). Extended Association Algorithm Based on ROC Analysis for Visual Information Navigator. *Lecture Notes In Computer Science, 2281*, 640-649.

Keim, D. A. (2002). Information Visualization and Visual Data Mining. *IEEE Transactions on Visualization and Computer Graphics, 8*(1), 1-8.

Keim, D. A., & Kriegel, H.-P. (1996). Visualization Techniques for Mining Large Databases: A Comparison. *IEEE Transactions on Knowledge and Data Engineering, 8*(6), 923-938.

Keller, R., & Schlögl, A. (2002). *PISSARRO: Picturing interactively statistically sensible association rules reporting overviews*. Department of Computer Oriented Statistics and Data Analysis, Augsburg University, Germany.

Kimball, R. (1996). *Data Warehouse Toolkit: Practical Techniques for Building High Dimensional Data Warehouses*. John Wiley & Sons.

Klemettinen, M., Mannila, H., & Verkamo, A. I. (1999). Association rule selection in a data mining environment. *Principles of Data Mining and Knowledge Discovery (Proc. 4th European Conf.-PKDD-99), LNAI, 1704*, 372-377.

Klemettinen, M., Mannila, H., Ronkainen, P., Toivonen, H., & Verkamo, A.I. (1994). Finding interesting rules from large sets of discovered association rules. *In Proceedings of the Third International Conference on Information and Knowledge Management (CIKM'94),* Gaithersburg, Maryland, USA (pp. 401-408).

Kodratoff, Y. (2000). Extraction de connaissances à partir des données et des textes. In *Actes des journées sur la fouille dans les données par la méthode d'analyse statistique implicative,* (pp. 151–165). Presses de l'Université de Rennes 1.

Kodratoff, Y. (2001). Comparing machine learning and knowledge discovery in databases: an application to knowledge discovery in texts. In Paliouras, G., Karkaletsis, V., and Spyropoulos, C. (Ed.), *Machine Learning and Its Applications,* volume 2049 of *Lecture Notes in Artificial Intelligence,* (pp. 1–21). Springer.

Koh, J-L., & Shieh, S-F. (2004). An efficient approach for maintaining association rules based on adjusting FP-tree structures. *Proceedings of the 2004 Database Systems for Advanced Applications* (pp. 417-424).

Kopanakis, I., & Theodoulidis, B. (2003). Visual data mining modeling techniques for the visualization of mining outcomes. *Journal of Visual Languages and Computing, 14*(6), 543–589.

Kraemer, H. (1988). Assessment of 2 × 2 associations: generalization of signal-detection methodology. *The American statistician, 42*(1), 37-49.

Kraemer, H. (1992). *Evaluating medical tests*. Newbury Park, CA: Sage Publications.

Kryszkiewicz, M. (1998). Representative Association Rules and Minimum Condition Maximum Consequence Association Rules. *In Proceedings of the Principles of Data Mining and Knowledge Discovery Conference* (pp. 361-369).

Kryszkiewicz, M. (2001). Concise Representation of Frequent Patterns Based on Disjunction-Free Generators. *In Proc. of ICDM* (pp. 305–312).

Kryszkiewicz, M. (2002). Concise representations of association rules. In D. J. Hand, N.M. Adams, and R.J. Bolton, editors, *Proceedings of Pattern Detection and Discovery, ESF Exploratory Workshop, 2447*, 92–109, London, UK.

Kryszkiewicz, M. (2005). Generalized disjunction-free representation of frequent patterns with negation. *Journal of Experimental and Theoretical Artificial Intelligence, 17*(1-2), 63-82.

Kulczynski, S. (1927). Die pflanzenassoziationen der pieninen. *Bulletin International de l'Académie Polonaise des Sciences et des Lettres. Classe des Sciences Mathématiques et Naturelles,* (suppl. II), 57–203. série B.

Kumar, K. B., & Jotwani, N. (2006). Efficient algorithm for hierarchical online mining of association rules. In *COMAD*.

Kuntz, P., Guillet, F., Lehn, R., & Briand, H. (2000). A User-Driven Process for Mining Association Rules. In D. Zighed, H. Komorowski, & J. Zytkow (Eds.), *4th Eur. Conf. on Principles of Data Mining and Knowledge Discovery (PKDD'00), Vol. 1910 of Lecture Notes in Computer Science – LNCS* (pp. 483–489), Lyon, France: Springer-Verlag.

Kuo, H-C., & Huang, J-P. (2005). Building a Concept Hierarchy from a Distance Matrix. In M. A. Klopotek, et al. (Eds.), Intelligent Information Processing and Web Mining (pp. 87-95). Springer.

Kuo, H-C., Tsai, T-h., & Huang, J-P. (2006). Building a Concept Hierarchy by Hierarchical Clustering with Join/Merge Decision. In H. D. Cheng, et al. (Eds.),

Proceedings of the 9th Joint Conference on Information Sciences (JCIS 2006), (pp.142-145). Kaohsiung, Taiwan, ROC, October 8-11, 2006. Atlantis Press.

Lakshmanan, L., Ng, R., Han, J., & Pang, A. (1999). Optimization of constrained frequent set queries with 2-variable constraints. *Proceeding of the ACM SIGMOD international conference* (pp. 157-168).

Lamping, J., Rao, R., & Pirolli, P. (1995). A focus+context technique based on hyperbolic geometry for visualizing large hierarchies. In *Proceedings of the ACM Conference on Human Factors in Computing Systems (CHI'95), ACM Press*, (pp. 401–408), Denver, Colorado, USA.

Lanzenberger, M., Miksch, S., Ohmann, S., & Popow, C. (2003). Applying information visualization techniques to capture and explore the course of cognitive behavioral therapy. In *Proceedings of the ACM Symposium on Applied Computing 2003*, (pp. 268-274), Melbourne, Florida, USA.

Latkowski, R., & Michal Mikolajczyk (2004). Data Decomposition and Decision Rule Joining for Classification of Data with Missing Values. In S. Tsumoto et al. (Eds.), RSCTC 2004, Lecture Notes in Artificial Intelligence 3066. (pp. 254–263).Springer-Verlag Berlin Heidelberg .

Lavrač, N., Flach, P., & Zupan, R. (1999). Rule evaluation measures: A unifying view. In S. Dzeroski, P. Flach (Eds.), *Proceedings of the 9th International Workshop on Inductive Logic Programming*, ILP 1999, Volume 1634 of Lecture Notes in Artificial Intelligence, (pp. 174–185). Springer-Verlag.

Lee, C-H., Lin, C-R., & Chen, M-S. (2005). Sliding window filtering: an efficient method for incremental mining on a time-variant database. *Information Systems, 30*(3), 227-244.

Lehmann, E. (1959). *Testing Statistical Hypotheses*. Wiley, New York.

Lenca, P., Meyer, P., Vaillant, B., & Lallich, S. (2008). On selecting interestingness measures for association rules: User oriented description and multiple criteria decision aid. *European Journal of Operational Research, 184*(2), 610-626.

Lenca, P., Vaillant, B., Meyer, P., & Lallich, S. (2007). Association rule interestingness measures: Experimental and theoretical studies. In Guillet, F. and Hamilton, H. J. (Ed.), *Quality Measures in Data Mining*, volume 43 of *Studies in Computational Intelligence*, (pp. 51–76). Springer.

Lent, B., Swami, A. N., & Widom, J. (1997). Clustering Association Rules. *Proceedings of the Thirteenth International Conference on Data Engineering*. Birmingham U.K., IEEE Computer Society (pp. 220-231).

Lerman, I. C. (1981). *Classification et analyse ordinale des données*. Dunod.

Lerman, I. C. (1993). Likelihood linkage analysis (LLA) classification method: An example treated by hand. *Biochimie, 75*(5), 379–397.

Leung, C. K., & Carmichael, C. (2007). *Frequent itemset visualization* (Technical report). University of Manitoba.

Leung, C. K-S., & Khan, Q. I. (2006). DSTree: A Tree Structure for the Mining of Frequent Sets from Data Streams. *Proceedings of the Sixth International Conference on Data Mining* (pp. 928 - 932).

Leung, C. K-S., Khan, Q. I., Li Z., & Hoque, T. (2007). CanTree: a canonical-order tree for incremental frequent-pattern mining. *Knowledge and Information Systems, 11*(3), 287-311.

Leung, C., Lakshmanan, L., & Ng, R. (2002). Exploiting succinct constraints using FP-Trees. *ACM SIGKDD Explorations, 4*(1), 40-49.

Leung, C.-S., Khan, Q., & Hoque, T. (2005). Cantree: A tree structure for efficient incremental mining of frequent patterns. In *ICDM* (pp. 274-281).

Levkowitz, H. (Ed.). (1997). *Color Theory and Modeling for Computer Graphics, Visualization and Multimedia Applications*. Kluwer Academic Publishers.

Li, H., Li, J., Wong, L., Feng, M., & Tan, Y.-P. (2005). Relative Risk and Odds Ratio: A Data Mining Perspective. In Proceedings of 23rd ACM Symposium on Principles of Database Systems (pp. 368–377).

Li, H., Li, J., Wong, L., Feng, M., & Tan, Y.-P. (2005). Relative risk and odds ratio: A data mining perspective. *Symposium on Principles of Database Systems* (pp. 368-377).

Li, J. (2006). On Optimal Rule Discovery. *IEEE Transactions on Knowledge and Data Engineer, 18*(4), 460-471.

Li, J., Li, H., Wong, L., Pei, J., & Dong, G. (2006). Minimum description length (MDL) principle: Generators are preferable to closed patterns. *Proceedings of the AAAI conference* (pp. 409-414).

Li, J., Tang, B., & Cercone, N. (2004). Applying association rules for interesting recommendations using rule templates. *Proceedings of the PAKDD conference* (pp. 166-170).

Li, W., Han, J., & Pei, J. (2001). CMAR: Accurate and Efficient Classification Based on Multiple Class-Association Rules, *In Proceedings of the 2001 IEEE International Conference on Data Mining*, 2001 (pp. 369-376).

Li, W., Han, J., & Pei, J. (2001). CMAR: Accurate and Efficient Classification Based on Multiple Class-Association Rules. In N. Cercone & T. Y. Lin & X. Wu (Eds.), *Proceedings of the 2001 IEEE International Conference on Data Mining* (pp. 369-376). San Jose, CA: IEEE Computer Society.

Lim, W.-K., Ong E.-P., & Ng, K.-L (2001). Multi-level rules with recurrent items using fp'-tree. In *Proceedings of ICICS*.

Liu, B., & Hsu, W. (1996). Post-Analysis of Learned Rules. *AAAI/IAAI, 1*(1996), 828-834.

Liu, D., Hsu, W., & Chen, S. (1997). Using general impressions to analyze discovered classification rules. In *Proceedings of the 3rd ACM SIGKDD International Conference on Knowledge Discovery and Data Mining*, (pp. 31–36).

Liu, B., Hsu, W., & Ma, Y. (1998). Integrating Classification and Association Rule Mining. In R. Agrawal & P. E. Stolorz & G. Piatetsky-Shapiro (Eds.), *KDD'98: Proceedings of the Fourth International Conference on Knowledge Discovery and Data Mining* (pp. 80-86). New York City, NY: AAAI Press.

Liu, B., Hsu, W., & Ma, Y. (1999). Pruning and summarizing the discovered associations. *Proceedings of the fifth ACM SIGKDD international conference on Knowledge discovery and data mining (KDD-99)*, ACM Press (pp. 125-134).

Liu, B., Hsu, W., & Ma, Y. (1999). Pruning and Summarizing the Discovered Associations. In U. Fayyad & S. Chaudhuri & D. Madigan (Eds.), *KDD'99: Proceedings of the fifth ACM SIGKDD international conference on Knowledge discovery and data mining* (pp. 125-134). San Diego, CA: ACM.

Liu, B., Hsu, W., & Ma, Y. (2001a). Discovering the set of fundamental rule changes. In *Proceedings of the 7th ACM SIGKDD International Conference on Knowledge Discovery and Data Mining*, (pp. 335–340).

Liu, B., Hsu, W., Chen, S., & Ma, Y. (2000). Analyzing the subjective interestingness of association rules. *IEEE Intelligent Systems, 15*(5), 47–55.

Liu, B., Hsu, W., Han, H.-S., & Xia, Y. (2000). Mining Changes for Real-Life Applications. *In Proc. of DaWaK* (pp. 337–346).

Liu, B., Hsu, W., Mun, L., & Lee, H. (1999). Finding interesting patterns using user expectations. *IEEE Transactions on Knowledge and Data Engineering, 11*(6), 817-832.

Liu, B., Hsu, W., Wang, K., & Che, S. (1999). Visually aided exploration of interesting association rules. In *Proceedings of the 3rd International Conference on Research and Development in Knowledge Discovery and Data mining (PAKDD'99), LNCS, volume 1574, Springer-Verlag*, (pp. 380–389), Beijing, China.

Liu, B., Hu, M., & Hsu, W. (2000). Multi-level organization and summarization of the discovered rules. In *Knowledge Discovery and Data Mining* (pp. 208-217).

Liu, B., Ma, Y., & Lee, R. (2001). Analyzing the interestingness of association rules from the temporal dimension. In *Proceedings of the IEEE International Conference on Data Mining*, (pp. 377–384). IEEE Computer Society.

Liu, B., Ma, Y., & Wong, C. K. (2000). Improving an Association Rule Based Classifier. In D. A. Zighed & H. J. Komorowski & J. M. Zytkow (Eds.), *Principles of Data Mining and Knowledge Discovery, 4th European Conference* (pp. 504-509). Lyon, France: Springer.

Liu, B., Ma, Y., Wong, C., & Yu, P. (2003). Scoring the Data Using Association Rules. *Applied Intelligence, 18*(2), 119–135.

Liu, G., Li, J., & Limsoon, W. (2007). A new concise representation of frequent itemsets using generators and a positive border. *Knowledge and Information Systems, 13*.

Liu, H., & Motoda, H. (1998). *Feature Selection for Knowl-edge Discovery and Data Mining*. Kluwer Academic Publishers.

Liu, H., Lu, H., Feng, L., & Hussain, F. (1999). Efficient search of reliable exceptions. *Proceedings of the PAKDD conference* (pp. 194-204).

Liu, Y. & Salvendy, G. (2006). Design and Evaluation of Visualization Support to Facilitate Association Rules Modeling. *International Journal of Human Computer Interaction, 21*(1), 15-38.

Liu, Y., & Salvendy, G. (2005). Visualization support to facilitate association rules modeling: A survey. *International Journal of Ergonomics and Human Factors, 27*(1), 11–23.

Lôbo, R., Bezerra, L., Faria, C., Magnabosco, C., Albuquerque, L., Bergmann, J., Sainz, R., & Oliveira, H. (Eds.). (2008). *Avaliação Genética de Touros e Matrizes da Raça Nelore*. Ribeirão Preto: Associação Nacional de Criadores e Pesquisadores (in Portuguese).

Loevinger, J. (1947). A systematic approach to the construction and evaluation of tests of ability. *Psychological Monographs, 61*(4).

Lu, N., Wang-Zhe, C.-G. Zhou; J.-Z. Zhou. (2005). Research on association rule mining algorithms with item constraints. *Proceedings of the CW conference.*

Lu, Y. (1997). Concept hierachy in data mining: specification, generation and implementation. Master thesis. Simon Fraser University, Canada.

Luxenburger, M. (1991). Implications partielles dans un contexte. *Mathématiques, Informatique et Sciences Humaines, 29*(113), 35-55.

Mackinlay, J. D., Robertson, G. G., & Card, S. K. (1991). The perspective wall: detail and context smoothly integrated. In *Proceedings of the ACM Conference on Human Factors in Computing Systems (CHI'91), ACM Press*, (pp. 173–179), New Orleans, Louisiana, USA.

Mahanti, A., & Alhajj, R. (2005). Visual Interface for Online Watching of Frequent Itemset Generation in Apriori and Eclat. In M. A. Wani, M. Milanova, L. Kurgan, M. Reformat, K. Hafeez (Eds.), *The Fourth International Conference on Machine Learning and Applications* (pp. 404-410). Washington, DC: IEEE Computer Society.

Maier, D. (1983). *The theory of Relational Databases.* Computer Science Press.

Manku, G. S., & Motwani, Q. (2002). Approximate frequency counts over data streams. *VLDB* (pp. 346-357).

Mann, H. (1945). Nonparametric tests against trend. *Econometrica, 13,* 245–259.

Mannila. H.. & Toivonen, H. (1997). Levelwise search and borders of theories in knowledge discovery. *Data Mining and Knowledge Discovery, 1*(2), 241-258.

Mao, G., Wu, X., Zhu, X., Chen, G., & Liu, C. (2007). Mining maximal frequent itemsets from data streams. *Information Science* (pp. 251-262).

Martins, C. D., & Rezende, S. O. (2006) Construção semi-automática de taxonomias para generalização de regras de associação. In *Proceedings of International Joint Conference IBERAMIA/SBIA/SBRN 2006 – 3rd Workshop on MSc dissertations and PhD thesis in Artificial Intelligence (WTDIA)*. São Carlos: ICMC/USP. v. 1. 10 p. (In Portuguese).

Matheus, C. J., Chan, P. K., & Piatetsky-Shapiro, G. (1993). Systems for knowledge discovery in databases, *IEEE Transactions on Knowledge and Data Engineering, 5*(6), 903-913.

McGarry, K. (2005). A survey of interestingness measures for knowledge discovery. *The Knowledge Engineering Review, 20*(1), 39–61.

McNicholas, P. D. (2007). Association rule analysis of CAO data. *Journal of the Statistical and Social Inquiry Society of Ireland, 36.*

McNicholas, P. D., Murphy, T. B., & O'Regan, M. (2008). Standardising the Lift of an Association Rule, *Computational Statistics and Data Analysis, 52(10)*, 4712-4721.

Melanda, E. A. (2004) *Post-processing of Association Rules.* PhD thesis, Instituto de Ciências Matemáticas e de Computação – USP – São Carlos. (In Portuguese).

Melanda, E. A., & Rezende, S. O. (2004). Combining quality measures to identify interesting association rules. In C. Lemaître, C. A. Reyes, J. A. González (Eds.), *Advances in Artificial Intelligence* (pp. 441-453). Springer-Verlag Press.

Meo, R. (2000). Theory of dependence values. *ACM Transactions on Database Systems, 25*(3), 380-406.

Meo, R., Psaila, G., & Ceri, S. (1996). A new SQL-like operator for mining association rules. In *Proceedings of the VLDB Conference*, (pp. 122–133), Bombay, India, 1996.

Metwally, A., Agrawal, D., & Abbadi, A. E. (2005) Efficient computation of frequent and top-k elements in data streams. *International Conference on Data Theory* (pp. 398-412).

Michalski, R. S. (1980). Pattern recognition as rule-guided inductive inference. *IEEE Transactions on Pattern Analysis and Machine Intelligence, 2*(4), 349-361.

Mikolajczyk, M. (2002). Reducing Number of Decision Rules by Joining. In J. J. Alpigini, J. F. Peters, et al. (Eds.), RSCTC 2002. Lecture Notes in Artificial Intelligence 2475. (pp. 425-432). Springer-verlag Berlin Heidelberg.

Mills, F. C. (1965). *Statistical Methods.* London: Sir Isaac Pitman and Sons.

Mineau, G., & Ganter, B. (Eds.) (2000). Proceedings of International Conference on Conceptual Structures, 2000. *LNCS 1867*, Springer.

Mosteller, F. (1968). Association and estimation in contingency tables. *Journal of the American Statistical Association, 63*(321), 1–28.

Motro, A. (1987). Extending the relational Databases Model to support Goal queries. In *Expert Database Systems*, (pp. 129–150).

Mozafari, B., Thakkar, H., & Zaniolo, C. (2008). Verifying and mining frequent patterns from large windows over data streams. *ICDE* (pp. 179-188).

Mueller A. (1995). Fast sequential and parallel methods for association rule mining: A comparison. *Technical Report CS-TR-3515, Department of Computer Science, University of Maryland*, College Park, MD.

Natarajan, R., & Shekar, B. (2005). A relatedness-based data-driven approach to determination of interestingness of association rules. In H. Haddad, L. M. Liebrock, A. Omicini, R. L. Wainwright (Eds.), *Proceedings of the 2005 ACM Symposium on Applied Computing* (pp. 551–552). ACM Press.

Ng, R. T., Lakshmanan, V. S., Han, J., & Pang, A. (1998). Exploratory mining and pruning optimizations of constrained association rules. In *Proceedings ACM SIGMOD International Conference on Management of Data*, (pp. 13–24), Seattle, Washington, USA.

Ng, R., Lakshmanan, L. V. S., Han, J., & Mah, T. (1999). Exploratory mining via constrained frequent set queries. *Proceedings of the 1999 ACM SIGMOD international conference on Management of data*, (pp. 556-558).

North, C. & Shneiderman, B. (2000). Snap-together visualization: can users construct and operate coordinated visualizations. *International Journal of Human-Computer Studies, 53*(5), 715-739.

North, C., & Shneiderman, B. (2000). Snap-together visualization: a user interface for coordinating visualizations via relational schemata. In V. D. Gesù, S. Levialdi, L. Tarantino (Eds.), *Advanced Visual Interfaces* (pp. 128-135). New York: ACM Press.

Ochiai, A. (1957). Zoogeographic studies on the soleoid fishes found in japan and its neighbouring regions. *Bulletin of the Japanese Society of Scientific Fisheries*, (22), 526–530.

Ohsaki, M., Kitaguchi, S., Okamoto, K., Yokoi, H., & Yamaguchi, T. (2004). Evaluation of rule interestingness measures with a clinical dataset on hepatitis. In J.-F. Boulicaut, F. Esposito, F. Giannotti, D. Pedreschi (Eds.), *Proceedings of the 8th European Conference on Principles and Practice of Knowledge Discovery in Databases*, PKDD 2004, Volume 3202 of Lecture Notes in Artificial Intelligence, (pp. 362–373). Springer-Verlag New York, Inc.

Oliveira, M. C. F. de, & Levkowitz, H. (2003). From Visual Data Exploration to Visual Data Mining: A Survey. *IEEE Transactions on Visualization and Computer Graphics*, *9*(3), 378-394.

Omiecinski, E. R. (2003). Alternative Interest Measures for Mining Associations in Databases. *IEEE Transactions on Knowledge and Data Engineering*, *15*, 57-69.

Ong, H.-H., Ong, K.-L., Ng, W.-K., & Lim, E.-P. (2002, December). *CrystalClear: Active Visualization of Association Rules*. Paper presented at the IEEE International Workshop on Active Mining (AM-2002), Maebashi City, Japan.

Padmanabhan, B., & Tuzhilin, A. (1998). A belief driven method for discovering unexpected patterns. *Proceedings of the KDD conference* (pp. 94-100).

Padmanabhan, B., & Tuzhilin, A. (1999). Unexpectedness as a measure of interestingness in knowledge discovery. *Decision Support Systems*, *27*(3), 303–318.

Padmanabhan, B., & Tuzhilin, A. (2000). Small is beautiful: discovering the minimal set of unexpected patterns. In *Proceedings of the 6th ACM SIGKDD International Conference on Knowledge Discovery and Data Mining*, (pp. 54–63).

Padmanabhan, B., & Tuzhilin, A. (2002). Knowledge refinement based on the discovery of unexpected patterns in data mining. *Decision Support Systems*, *33*(3), 309–321.

Pagallo, G., & Haussler, D. (1990). Boolean feature discovery in empirical learning. Machine learning, 5, 71-99.

Palshikar, G. K., Kale, M. S., & Apte, M. M. (2007). Association rules mining using heavy itemsets. *Data & Knowledge Engineering*, *61*(1), 93-113.

Park, J. S., Chen, M. S., & Yu, P. S. (1995). Efficient Parallel Data Mining of Association Rules. *In Fourth International Conference on Information and Knowledge Management*, Baltimore, Maryland. (pp. 31-36).

Park, J. S., Chen, M.-S., & Yu, P. S. (1995). An effective hash-based algorithm for mining association rules. In *SIGMOD* (pp. 175-186).

Paroubek, P. (2007). Evaluating Part-Of-Speech Tagging and Parsing – On the Evaluation of Automatic Parsing of Natural Language (Chapter 4). In L. Dybkaer, H. Hemsen, & W. Minker (Eds.), *Chapter 4 of Evaluation of Text and Speech Systems* (pp. 99–124). Springer.

Pasquier N., Bastide Y., Taouil R., & Lakhal, L. (1999). Efficient mining of association rules using closed itemset lattices. *Information Systems*, *24*(1), 25-46.

Pasquier, N. (2005). Mining association rules using frequent closed itemsets. In J. Wang (Ed.), *Encyclopedia of Data Warehousing and Mining* (pp. 752-757). Idea Group Publishing.

Pasquier, N., Bastide, Y., Taouil, R., & Lakhal, L. (1998). Pruning closed itemset lattices for association rules. *Proceedings of the BDA conference* (pp. 177-196).

Pasquier, N., Bastide, Y., Taouil, R., & Lakhal, L. (1999). Discovering Frequent Closed Itemsets for Association Rules. *Proceeding of the 7th International Conference on Database Theory*, Lecture Notes in Computer Science (LNCS 1540), Springer, 1999, 398-416.

Pasquier, N., Taouil, R., Bastide, Y., Stumme, G., & Lakhal, L. (2005). Generating a Condensed Representation for Association Rules. *Journal of Intelligent Information Systems*, *24*(1), 29-60.

Paulovich, F. V., Nonato, L. G., Minghim, R. (2006). Visual Mapping of Text Collections through a Fast High Precision Projection Technique. In A. Ursyn, E. Banissi (Eds.), *Tenth International Conference on Information Visualization* (pp. 282-290). London: IEEE Computer Society Press.

Pawlak, Z. (1991). *Rough Sets: Theoretical Aspects of Reasoning About Data*. Kluwer Academic Publishers.

Pawlak, Z. (2005). Rough sets and decision algorithms. In W. Ziarko & Y. Yao (Eds.), RSCTC 2000, Lecture Notes of Artificial Intelligence 2005 (pp. 30-45). Springer-Verlag Berlin Heidelberg.

Pawlak, Z., & Andrzej Skowron (2007). Rudiments of rough sets. Information Sciences, 177. 3-27.

Pearl, J. (1988). *Probabilistic Reasoning in Intelligent Systems: Networks of Plausible Inference*. San Fransisco, CA: Morgan Kaufmann.

Pearson, K. (1896). Mathematical contributions to the theory of evolution: regression, heredity and panmixia. *Philosophical Transactions of the Royal Society Of London*, series A(187), 253–318.

Pei ,J., Han, J. & Mao R. (2000). CLOSET: An efficient algorithm for mining frequent closed itemsets. *SIGMOD Workshop on Research Issues in Data Mining and Knowledge Discovery 2000* (pp 21-30).

Pei, .J, & Han, J. (2002). Constrained frequent pattern mining: A pattern-growth view. *ACM SIGKDD Explorations*, *4*(1), 31-39.

Pei, J., Han, J., & Lakshmanan, L. V. S. (2001). Mining Frequent Item Sets with Convertible Constraints. *In Proceedings of the 17th International Conference on Data Engineering* (pp. 433–442).

Pei, J., Han, J., & Mao, R. (2000). CLOSET: An efficient algorithm for mining frequent closed itemsets. *Proceedings of ACM SIGMOD Workshop on Research Issues in Data Mining and Knowledge Discovery*, 2000.

Pei, J., Han, J., Mortazavi-Asl, B., Wang, J., Pinto, H., Chen, Q., Dayal, U., & Hsu, M. (2004). Mining sequential patterns by pattern-growth: The PrefixSpan approach. *IEEE TKDE*, *16*(11), 1424-1440.

Pfaltz, J., & Taylor, C. (2002). Closed set mining of biological data. *Proceedings of the BioKDD conference* (pp. 43-48).

Piatetsky-Shapiro, G. (1991). Discovery, analysis, and presentation of strong rules. In G. Piatetsky-Shapiro, W. Frawley (Eds.), *Knowledge Discovery in Databases* (pp. 229-248). AAAI/MIT Press.

Piatetsky-Shapiro, G. (2000). Knowledge discovery in databases: 10 years after. *SIGKDD Explorations Newsletter*, *1*(2), 59–61.

Piatetsky-Shapiro, G., & Matheus, C. J. (1994). The interestingness of deviations. In *Proceedings of the AAAI Workshop on Knowledge Discovery in Databases*, (pp. 25–36).

Piatetsky-Shapiro, G., Piatetsky-Shapiro, G., Frawley, W. J., Brin, S., Motwani, R., Ullman, J. D., et al. (2005). Discovery, Analysis, and Presentation of Strong Rules. *Proceedings of the 11th international symposium on Applied Stochastic Models and Data Analysis ASMDA*, *16*, 191-200.

Pitrat, J. (1990). *Métaconnaissance, Futur de l'Intelligence Artificielle (Metaknowledge, the future of artificial intelligence)*. Editions Hermès, Paris.

Plaisant, C. (2004). The challenge of information visualization evaluation. In M. F. Costabile (Ed.), *The working conference on Advanced Visual Interfaces* (pp. 109-116). New York: ACM Press.

Poulin, B., Eisner, R., Szafron, D., Lu, P., Greiner, R., Wishart, D.S., Fyshe, A., Pearcy, B., MacDonnell, C., & Anvik, J.. Visual explanation of evidence in additive classifiers. *In Proceedings of the Conference on Innovative Applications of Artificial Intelligence*, (pp. 1–8).

Prati, R., & Flach, P. (2005). ROCCER: an algorithm for rule learning based on ROC analysis. *Proceeding of the 19th International Joint Conference on Artificial Intelligence. Edinburgh, Scotland.*

Provost, F., & Fawcett, T. (2001). Robust Classification for Imprecise Environments. *Machine Learning, 42*(3), 203-231.

Provost, F., Fawcett, T., & Kohavi, R. (1998). The case against accuracy estimation for comparing induction algorithms. Proceedings of the Fifteenth International Conference on Machine Learning, (pp. 445–453).

Quinlan, J. R. (1993). *C4.5: Programs for Machine Learning.* San Francisco, CA: Morgan Kaufmann Publishers Inc.

Rak, R., Stach, W., Zaïane, O.R., & Antonie, M. (2005). Considering re-occurring features in associative classifiers. In *PAKDD'05: Pacific-Asia Conf. on Knowledge Discovery and Data Mining,* (pp. 240–248).

Rogers, D., & Tanimoto, T. (1960). A computer program for classifying plants. *Science,* (132), 1115–1118.

Ruß, G., Boettcher, M., & Kruse, R. (2007). Relevance feedback for association rules using fuzzy score aggregation. In *Proc. Conf. North American Fuzzy Information Processing Society (NAFIPS 2007),* (pp. 54–59).

Ruß, G., Kruse, R., Nauck, D., & Boettcher, M. (2008). Relevance feedback for association rules by leveraging concepts from information retrieval. In M. Bramer, (Ed,), *Research and Development in Intelligent Systems, 24* of *Proceedings of AI-2007,* (pp. 253–266). BCS SGAI, Springer.

Russel, P., & Rao, T. (1940). On habitat and association of species of anopheline larvae in south-eastern madras. *Journal of the Malaria Institute of India,* (3):153–178.

Sadri, R., Zaniolo, C., Zarkesh, A., & Adibi, J. (2001). Optimization of sequence queries in database systems. In *PODS* (pp. 71-81).

Sahar, S. (1999). Interestingness via What is Not Interesting. In S. Chaudhuri, & D. Madigan, (Eds.), *5th ACM SIGKDD International Conference on Knowledge Discovery and Data Mining (KDD'99).* (pp. 332–336). San Diego, CA: ACM Press.

Salton, G. (1971). *The SMART Information Retrieval System.* Englewood Cliffs, NJ: Prentice Hall.

Salton, G., & Buckley, C. (1987). Term weighting approaches in automatic text retrieval. *Information Processing and Management, 5*(24), 513– 523.

Savasere, A., Omiecinski, E., & Navathe, S. B. (1998). Mining for strong negative associations in a large database of customer transactions. *Proceedings of the 14th International Conference on Data Engineering,* Washington DC, USA, 1998, (pp. 494–502).

Sebag, M., & Schoenauer, M. (1988). Generation of rules with certainty and confidence factors from incomplete and incoherent learning bases. In *Proceedings of EKAW88,* (pp. 28.1–28.20).

Sheikh, L., Tanveer, B., & Hamdani, M. (2004). Interesting measures for mining association rules. *Multitopic Conference INMIC, 8th International* (pp. 641-644).

Shekar, B., & Natarajan, R. (2004). A framework for evaluating knowledge-based interestingness of association rules. *Fuzzy Optimization and Decision Making, 3*(2), 157-185.

Shneiderman, B. (1996). The eyes have it: A task by data type taxonomy for information visualization. In *Proceedings of IEEE Symposium on Visual Languages (VL'96), IEEE Computer Society Press,* (pp. 336–343), Boulder, Colorado, USA.

Shneiderman, B., & Plaisant, C. (2005). *Designing the user interface.* Boston: Addison-Wesley.

Shwayder, K. (1975). Combining decision rules in a decision table. Communications of the ACM, 18(8), 476-480.

Sikora, M., & Michalak, M. (2006). NetTRS Induction and Postprocessing of Decision Rules. In S. Greco et al.. (Eds.), RSCTC 2006. Lecture Notes in Artificial Intelligence 4259. (pp. 378-387). Springer-verlag, Berlin.

Silberschatz, A., & Tuzhilin, A. (1996). User-assisted knowledge discovery: how much should the user be involved. In *Proceedings of the 1996 SIGMOD work-*

shop on research issues on data mining and knowledge discovery (DMKD).

Silberschatz, A., & Tuzhilin, A. (1996). What Makes Patterns Interesting in Knowledge Discovery Systems. *IEEE Transactions on Knowledge and Data Engineering, IEEE Educational Activities Department, 8,* 970-974.

Silverstein, C., Brin, S., Motwani, R., & Ullman, J. D. (2000). Scalable techniques for mining causal structures. *Data Mining and Knowledge Discovery, 4*(2), 163-192.

Silverstien, C., Brin, S., & Motwani, R. (1998). Beyond Market Baskets: Generalizing Association Rules to Dependence Rules. *Data Mining and Knowledge Discovery, 2(1),* 39-68.

Singh, D., et al (2002). Gene expression correlates of clinical prostate cancer behavior. *Cancer Cell, 1,* 203–209.

Singh, L., Beard, M., Getoor, L., & Blake, M. B. (2007). Visual mining of multi-modal social networks at different abstraction levels. In *Proceedings of the 11th International Conference on Information Visualization (IV'07), IEEE Computer Society Press,* (pp. 672–679), Zurich, Switzerland.

Singh, M., Singh, P., & Suman (2007). Conceptual multidimensional model, In: Proceedings of world academy of science, engineering and technology, 26, 709-714.

Skowron, A., & Rauszer, C. (1991). The Discernibility Matrices and Functions in Information Systems. In R. Slowinski (Eds.), Intelligent Decision Support—Handbook of application and advances of the rough sets theory (pp. 331-362).

Smyth, P., & Goodman, R. M. (1992). An information theoretic approach to rule induction from databases. *IEEE Transactions on Knowledge and Data Engineering, 4*(4), 301–316.

Sokal, R., & Michener, C. (1958). A statistical method for evaluating systematic relationships. *University of Kansas Science Bulletin,* (38), 1409–1438.

Spiliopoulou, M., Baron, S., & Günther, O. (2003). Efficient monitoring of patterns in data mining environments. In *Proceedings of the 7th East-European Conference*

on Advances in Databases and Information Systems (ADBIS'03), (pp. 253–265). Springer.

Srikant, R., & Agrawal, R. (1995). Mining Generalized Association Rules. *In Proceedings of the 1995 Int. Conf. Very Large Data Bases, Zurich, Switzerland,* 1995 (pp. 407-419).

Srikant, R., & Agrawal, R. (1996). Mining sequential patterns: Generalizations and performance improvements. In *EDBT* (pp. 3-17).

Srikant, R., & Agrawal, R. (1997). Mining generalized association rules. Future Generation Computer Systems, 13, 161-180.

Srikant, R., Vu, Q., & Agrawal, R. (1997). Mining association rules with item constraints. In *Proceedings of the 3rd International Conference on Knowledge Discovery in Databases and Data Mining,* (pp. 67–73), Newport Beach, California, USA.

Steinhaus, H. (1956). Sur la division des corps matériels en parties. In *Bull. Acad. Polon. Sci.,* Cl. III, volume IV, (pp. 801– 804).

Stumme, G., Taouil, R., Bastide, Y., Pasquier, N., & Lakhal, L. (2001). Intelligent structuring and reducing of association rules with formal concept analysis. In *Proceedings KI'2001 Conference, LNAI 2174, Springer-Verlag,* (pp. 335–350), Vienna, Austria.

Sudkamp, T. (2005). Examples, counterexamples, and measuring fuzzy associations. *Fuzzy Sets and Systems, 149*(1), 57–71.

Tamir, R., & Singer, Y. (2006). On a confidence gain measure for association rule discovery and scoring. *The VLDB Journal The International Journal on Very Large Databases, 15*(1), 40–52.

Tan, P. N., Kumar, V., & Srivastava, J. (2002). Selecting the right interestingness measure for association patterns. Proceedings of the eighth ACM SIGKDD international conference on Knowledge discovery and data mining, (pp. 32-41).

Tan, P. N., Kumar, V., & Srivastava, J. (2004). Selecting the right objective measure for association analysis.

In *Knowledge Discovery and Data Mining, 29*(4), 293–313.

Tan, P., & Kumar, V. (2000). *Interestingness measures for association patterns: A perspective.* Technical Report 00-036, Department of Computer Science, University of Minnesota.

Tan, P., Kumar, V., & Srivastava, J. (2002). Selecting the right interestingness measure for association patterns. In D. Hand & D. Keim & R. Ng (Eds.), *KDD'02: Proceedings of the Eighth ACM SIGKDD International Conference on Knowledge Discovery and Data Mining* (pp. 32-41). Edmonton, Alberta, Canada: ACM.

Tan, P.-N., & Kumar, V. (2000). Interestingness measures for association patterns: a perspective. In *Proceedings of the KDD-2000 workshop on postprocessing in machine learning and data mining.*

Tan, P.-N., Kumar, V., & Srivastava, J. (2004). Selecting the right objective measure for association analysis. *Information Systems, 29*(4), 293–313.

Tang, Z., Maclennan, J., & Kim, P. (2005). Building data mining solutions with OLE DB for DM and XML analysis. *SIGMOD Record, 34*(2), 80-85.

Techapichetvanich, K., & Datta, A. (2005). VisAR: A New Technique for Visualizing Mined Association Rules. In X. Li, S. Wang, Z. Y. Dong (Eds.), *First International Conference on Advanced Data Mining and Applications* (pp. 88-95). New York: Lecture Notes in Computer Science.

Teng, W. G., Hsieh, M. J., & Chen, M. S. (2002). On the mining of substitution rules for statistically dependent items. In *Proceedings of ICDM,* (pp. 442–449).

Thabtah, F. (2007). A review of associative classification mining. *The Knowledge Engineering Review, 22(1),* 37-65.

Thabtah, F. A., Cowling, P. I., & Peng, Y. (2004). MMAC: A New Multi-Class, Multi-Label Associative Classification Approach. In R. Rastogi & K. Morik & M. Bramer ity & X. Wu (Eds.), *Proceedings of the 4th IEEE*

International Conference on Data Mining (pp. 217-224). Brighton, UK: IEEE Computer Society.

Thakkar, H., Mozafari, B., & Zaniolo, C. (2008). Designing an inductive data stream management system: the stream mill experience. In *SSPS* (pp. 79-88).

Toivonen, H., Klemettinen, M., Ronkainen, P., Hatonen, K., & Manilla, H. (1995). Pruning and grouping discovered association rules. In Y. Kodratoff & G. Nakhaeizadeh & C. Taylor (Eds.), *Workshop Notes of the ECML-95 Workshop on Statistics, Machine Learning, and Knowledge Discovery in Databases* (pp. 47-52). Heraklion, Crete, Greece.

UMLS (2000). *The Unified Medical Language System.* (11th edition). National Library of Medicine.

Uno, T., Asai, T., Arimura, H. & Uchida, Y. (2003). LCM: An Efficient Algorithm for Enumerating Frequent Closed Item Sets. *In Proceedings of ICDM'03 Workshop on Frequent Itemset Mining Implementations* (pp. 1-10).

Unwin, A., Hofmann, H., & Bernt, K. (2001). The TwoKey Plot for Multiple Association Rules Control. In L. D. Raedt, A. Siebes (Eds.), *Fifth European Conference on Principles of Data Mining and Knowledge Discovery* (pp. 472-483). London: Lecture Notes in Computer Science.

Valtchev, P., Missaoui, R., & Godin, R. (2004). Formal concept analysis for knowledge discovery and data mining: The new challenges. *Lecture Notes in Computer Science, 2961,* 352-371.

Veloso, A. A., Meira, W. Jr., Carvalho, M. B., Possas, B., Parthasarathy, S., & Zaki, M. J. (2002). Mining frequent itemsets in evolving databases. *SIAM International Conference on Data Mining,* 2002.

Waitman, L. R., Fisher, D. H., & King P. H. (2006). Bootstrapping rule induction to achieve rule stability and reduction. *Journal of Intelligent Information System, 27,* 49–77.

Wang, H., & Zaniolo, C. (2003). Atlas: a native extension of sql for data minining. In *Proceedings of Third SIAM Int. Conference on Data Mining* (pp.130-141).

Wang, H., Fan, W., Yu, P. S., & Han, J. (2003). Mining concept-drifting data streams using ensemble classifiers. *In SIGKDD (pp. 226-235).*

Wang, J., & Karypis, G. (2005). HARMONY: Efficiently Mining the Best Rules for Classification. In H. Kargupta & J. Srivastava & C. Kamath & A. Goodman (Eds.), *Proceedings of the Fifth SIAM International Conference on Data Mining* (pp. 205-216). Newport Beach, CA: SIAM.

Wang, J., Han, J., & Pei, J. (2003). CLOSET+: Searching for the best strategies for mining frequent closed itemsets. *Proceedings of the Ninth ACM SIGKDD International Conference on Knowledge Discovery and Data Mining* (pp. 236-245).

Wang, K., Jiang, Y., & Lakshmanan, L. V. S. (2003). Mining unexpected rules by pushing user dynamics. In L. Getoor, T. E. Senator, P. Domingos, C. Faloutsos (Eds.), *Proceedings of the Ninth International Conference on Knowledge Discovery and Data Mining* (pp. 246-255). ACM Press.

Wang, K., Zhou, S., & He, Y. (2000). Growing decision trees on support-less association rules. In R. Ramakrishnan & S. Stolfo & R. Bayardo & I. Parsa (Eds.), *KDD'00: Proceedings of the sixth ACM SIGKDD international conference on Knowledge discovery and data mining* (pp. 265-269). Boston, MA: ACM.

Wang, W., Bich Do, D., & Lin, X. (2005). Term graph model for text classification. In *Advanced Data Mining and Applications*, pages 19–30.

Wang, W., Yang, J., & Yu, P. (2004). War: Weighted association rules for item intensities. *Knowledge and Information Systems, 6,* 203–229.

Webb, G. I., & Zhang, S. (2005). *K* Optimal Rule Discovery. *Data Mining and Knowledge Discovery, 10*(1), 39-79.

Webb, G. I., Buttler, S., & Newlands, D. (2003). On Detecting Differences Between Groups. *In Proceedings of KDD.*

Webb, G. I. (2000). Efficient search for association rules. In *Proceedings of the 6th ACM SIGKDD International Conference on Knowledge Discovery and Data Mining,* (pp. 99–107).

Weiß, C. H. (2008). Statistical mining of interesting association rules. *Statistics and Computing, 18*(2), 185-194.

Wilhelm, A. (2002). Statistical tests for pruning association rules. *In Computational Statistics: 15th Symposium,* Berlin, Germany.

Witten, I. H., & Frank, E. (2000). *Data Mining: practical machine learning tools and techniques with Java implementations.* Morgan Kaufmann.

Witten, I. H., & Frank, E. (2005). Data Mining: Practical machine learning tools and techniques. Morgan Kaufman, 2nd edition.

Wolpert, D. H., & Macready, W.G. (1997). No free lunch theorems for optimization. *IEEE Transactions on Evolutionary Computation, 1*(1), 67–82.

Won, D., & McLeod, D. (2007). Ontology-driven rule generalization and categorization for market data. *Data Engineering Workshop, 2007 IEEE 23rd International Conference on* (pp. 917-923).

Wong, P. C., Whitney, P., & Thomas, J. (1999). Visualizing Association Rules for Text Mining. In S. Eick, G. Wills, & D. A. Keim (Eds.), *IEEE Symposium on Information Visualization* (pp. 120). Washington, DC: IEEE Computer Society.

Wong, S. K. M., & Ziarko, W. (1985). On optimal decision rules in decision tables. Bulletin of Polish Academy of Sciences, 33, 693-696.

Wu, X., Zhang, C., & Zhang, S. (2002). Mining both positive and negative association rules. In *Proceedings of ICML,* (pp. 658–665).

Xiao, Y., Yao, J., Li, Z., & Dunham, M. H. (2003). Efficient Data Mining for Maximal Frequent Subtrees. *ICDM '03: Proceedings of the Third IEEE International Conference on Data Mining,* IEEE Computer Society, *379.*

Xu, Y., & Li, Y. (2007). Generating concise association rules. *Proceedings of the ACM CIKM conference* (pp. 781-790).

Xue, H., & Cai, Q. (1998). Rule Generalization by Condition Combination. In X. Wu, et al. (Eds.), Research and Development in Knowledge Discovery and Data Mining, Second Pacific-Asia Conference, PAKDD-98, (pp. 420-421). Melbourne, Australia. Springer, ISBN 3-540-64383-4.

Yager, R. R. (1988). On ordered weighted averaging aggregation operators in multicriteria decisionmaking. *IEEE Trans. Syst. Man Cybern., 18*(1), 183–190.

Yager, R. R. (1997). On the inclusion of importances in owa aggregations. In *The ordered weighted averaging operators: theory and applications,* (pp. 41–59), Norwell, MA, USA. Kluwer Academic Publishers.

Yamamoto, C. H., Oliveira, M. C. F. de, Fujimoto, M. L., & Rezende, S. O. (2007). An itemset-driven cluster-oriented approach to extract compact and meaningful sets of association rules. In M. A. Wani (Eds.), *The Sixth International Conference on Machine Learning and Applications* (pp. 87-92). Los Alamitos: Conference Publishing Services.

Yamamoto, C. H., Oliveira, M. C. F. de, Rezende, S. O., & Nomelini, J. (2008). Including the User in the Knowledge Discovery Loop: Interactive Itemset-Driven Rule Extraction. In R. L. Wainwright, H. M. Haddad, A. Brayner, R. Meneses, M. Viroli (Eds.), *ACM 2008 Symposium on Applied Computing* (pp. 1212-1217). New York: Association for Computing Machinery.

Yang, L. (2003). Visualizing frequent itemsets, association rules and sequential patterns in parallel coordinates. In V. Kumar, M. L. Gavrilova, C. J. K. Tan, & P. L'Ecuyer (Eds.), *Computational Science and Its Applications* (pp. 21-30). New York: Lecture Notes in Computer Science.

Yao, Y. Y., & Zhong, N. (1999). An analysis of quantitative measures associated with rules. In *PAKDD'99: Proceedings of the Third Pacific-Asia Conference on*

Methodologies for Knowledge Discovery and Data Mining, pages 479–488. Springer.

Yeoh, E. J., et al (2002). Classification, subtype discovery, and prediction of outcome in pediatric acute lymphoblastic leukemia by gene ex-pression profiling. *Cancer Cell, 1*, 133–143.

Yin, X., & Han, J. (2003). CPAR: Classification based on predictive association rules. In *Proceedings of SDM.*

Yin, X., & Han, J. (2003). CPAR: Classification based on Predictive Association Rules. In D. Barbarà & C. Kamath (Eds.), *Proceedings of the Third SIAM International Conference on Data Mining* (pp. 331-335). San Francisco, CA: SIAM.

Yu, J., Chong, Z., Lu, H., Zhang, Z., & Zhou, A.. A false negative approach to mining frequent itemsets from high speed transactional data streams. *Inf. Sci.* 176(14).

Yule, G. (1900). On the association of attributes in statistics. *Philosophical Transactions of the Royal Society of London,* series A(194), 257–319.

Yule, G. U. (1903). Notes on the theory of association of attributes in statistics. *Biometrika, 2*(2), 121–134.

Zaïane, O. R., & Antonie, M.-L. (2005) On pruning and tuning rules for associative classifiers. In *KES'05: Knowledge-Based Intelligence Information & Engineering Systems,* (pp. 966–973).

Zäiane, O. R., El-Hajj, M., & Lu, P. (2001). Fast Parallel Association Rule Mining without Candidacy Generation. *In First IEEE International Conference on Data Mining* (pp. 665-668).

Zaïane, O. R., Han, J., & Zhu, H. (2000). Mining recurrent items in multimedia with progressive resolution refinement. In *Proceedings of ICDE,* (pp. 461–470).

Zaki, M. J. (2004). Mining Non-Redundant Association Rules. *Data Mining and Knowledge Discovery, 9,* 223-248.

Zaki, M. J., & Hsiao, C. (2002). CHARM: An efficient algorithm for closed itemset mining. In *SIAM.*

Zaki, M. J., & Hsiao, C. (2005). Efficient Algorithms for Mining Closed Itemsets and Their Lattice Structure. *IEEE Transactions on Knowledge and Data Engineering, 17*, 462-478.

Zaki, M. J., & Phoophakdee, B. (2003). *MIRAGE: A framework for mining, exploring and visualizing minimal association rules* (Tech. Rep. No. 03-04). Troy, NY: Rensselaer Polytechnic Institute, Computer Sciences Department.

Zaki, M. J., Parthasarathy, S., Ogihara, M., & Li, W. (1997). New algorithms for fast discovery of association rules. *Technical Report 651, Computer Science Department, University of Rochester*, Rochester, NY 14627.

Zaki, M., & Hsiao, C. (2002). CHARM: An efficient algorithm for closed itemset mining. *In Proceedings of SDM.*

Zaki, M.J. (2000). Generating non-redundant association rules. *Proceedings of the KDD conference.*

Zaki, M.J. (2004). Mining non-redundant association rules. *Data Mining and Knowledge Discovery, 9*(3), 223-248.

Zembowicz, R., & Zytkow, J. M. (1996). From contingency tables to various forms of knowledge in databases.

In *Advances in knowledge discovery and data mining,* (pp. 328–349). American Association for Artificial Intelligence.

Zhang, S., Zhang, C., & Yang, Q. (2004), Information Enhancement for Data Mining. IEEE Intelligent System (pp. 12-13).

Zhang, W. X., Wu, W. Z., & Liang, J. (2003). Rough set Theory and Methods. Beijing, China: Science Press.

Zhang, X., Dong, G., & Kotagiri, R. (2000). Exploring constraints to efficiently mine emerging patterns from large high-dimensional datasets. In *Proceedings of the 6th ACM SIGKDD International Conference on Knowledge Discovery and Data Mining,* (pp. 310–314).

Zheng, C., & Zhao, Y. (2003). A distance-based approach to find interesting patterns. In Y. Kambayashi, K. Mohania, W. Wöß (Eds.), *Data Warehousing and Knowledge Discovery* (pp. 299-308). Springer-Verlag Press.

Zhong, N., Yao, Y. Y., & Ohishima, M. (2003). Peculiarity oriented multidatabase mining. IEEE Transactions on Knowledge and Data Enginering, 15(4), 952–960.

Ziarko, W. (2003). Acquisition of hierarchy-structured probabilistic decision tables and rules from data. Expert Systems, 20(5), 305-310.

About the Contributors

Yanchang Zhao is a Postdoctoral Research Fellow in Data Sciences & Knowledge Discovery Research Lab, Centre for Quantum Computation and Intelligent Systems, Faculty of Engineering & IT, University of Technology, Sydney, Australia. His research interests focus on association rules, sequential patterns, clustering and post-mining. He has published more than 30 papers on the above topics, including six journal articles and two book chapters. He served as a chair of two international workshops, and a program committee member for 11 international conferences and a reviewer for 8 international journals and over a dozen of international conferences.

Chengqi Zhang is a Research Professor in Faculty of Engineering & IT, University of Technology, Sydney, Australia. He is the director of the Director of UTS Research Centre for Quantum Computation and Intelligent Systems and a Chief Investigator in Data Mining Program for Australian Capital Markets on Cooperative Research Centre. He has been a chief investigator of eight research projects. His research interests include Data Mining and Multi-Agent Systems. He is a co-author of three monographs, a co-editor of nine books, and an author or co-author of more than 150 research papers. He is the chair of the ACS (Australian Computer Society) National Committee for Artificial Intelligence and Expert Systems, a chair/member of the Steering Committee for three international conference.

Longbing Cao is an Associate Professor in the Faculty of Engineering and IT, University of Technology, Sydney (UTS), Australia. He is the Director of the Data Sciences & Knowledge Discovery Research Lab at the Centre for Quantum Computation and Intelligent Systems at UTS. He also holds the position of Research Leader of the Data Mining Program at the Australian Capital Markets Cooperative Research Centre. His research interests focus on data mining, multi-agent systems, and the integration of agents and data mining. He is a Senior Member of the IEEE Computer Society and SMC Society. He has over 100 publications, including monographs and edited books. He has led the investigation of around 20 research and industry projects in data mining and intelligent systems. He has served as an organiser and program committee member on over 30 international conferences and workshops in data mining and multi-agent systems.

* * *

Maria-Luiza Antonie received her MSc degree in Computing Science from University of Alberta. Her main research interests focus on building and improving Associative Classifiers. She is interested in data mining and machine learning and their application in healthcare. She has published more than 10 articles in international venues and has reviewed scientific articles for multiple prestigious conferences. She is currently a PhD candidate in the Department of Computing Science, University of Alberta.

Julien Blanchard earned his PhD in 2005 from Nantes University (France) and is currently an assistant professor at Polytechnic School of Nantes University. He is the author of 3 book chapters and 8 journal and international conference papers in the areas of visualization and interestingness measures for data mining.

Mirko Boettcher studied computer science and psychology at the University of Magdeburg, Germany. After graduating in 2005 with distinction with a MSc in computer science he joined the Intelligent Systems Research Centre of BT Group plc, United Kingdom, as a Research Scientist where he conducted research into industrial applications of temporal and change mining. Currently he is undertaking a PhD with the University of Magdeburg. In parallel, he is working as a software architect specialized in data mining systems. His research interests +include association rules, decision trees, approaches of change mining, and dynamic aspects of data mining in general.

Veronica Oliveira de Carvalho received her BS degree in Computer Science from UNIP (Brazil), in 2000, the MS degree in Computer Science from UFSCar (Brazil), in 2003, and the PhD degree in Computer Science from USP (Brazil), in 2007. Currently she is a professor at Faculty of Informatics, University of Oeste Paulista at Presidente Prudente, Brazil. Her research interests include machine learning and data mining.

Hacène Cherfi is presently a PhD – Research Engineer in Semantic Wed and Text Mining at INRIA - Sophia Antipolis, France. His research interests are Knowledge Engineering for texts using Natural Language Processing, and Knowledge representation with semantic Web technologies. He is involved in European research project on Semantic Virtual Engineering Environment for Product Design. Hacène CHERFI got his PhD degree in 2004 from the Henri Poincare University in Nancy, France. His PhD dissertation is about Text Mining techniques using association rules to represent textual corpora. He got in 2005 a Post-doctoral position at UQO: University of Quebec in Ottawa (Canada) dealing with automatic illustration of a text with images using their labels. Hacène CHERFI has an active publication record among which a journal (Soft Computing) and major international conferences (ECAI, ICCS on conceptual structures, Web intelligence).

Silvia Chiusano received the master's and PhD degrees in computer engineering from the Politecnico di Torino. She has been an assistant professor in the Dipartimento di Automatica e Informatica, Politecnico di Torino, since January 2004. Her current research interests are in the areas of data mining and database systems, in particular, integration of data mining techniques into relational DBMSs and classification of structured and sequential data.

David Chodos received an MMath in Computer Science from the University of Waterloo in 2007, and is currently pursuing a PhD in Computing Science at the University of Alberta. His research interests include data mining, web-based software, and virtual environments, with a focus on the use of virtual environments in educational settings. His research is funded by an NSERC scholarship, and involves collaboration with people from various fields including healthcare, educational psychology and business.

Olivier Couturier received the PhD degree in computer science from University of Artois, Lens, France, in 2005. He focuses on data mining user driven approach and post mining (visualization of large amount of data). He was ATER between 2005 and 2007. He has been technical reviewer of different national and international workshops. He is currently engineer in Jouve group.

Guozhu Dong is a professor at Wright State University. He received his PhD from the University of Southern California in 1988. His main research interests are databases, data mining, and bioinformatics. He has published over 110 research papers, published a book entitled "Sequence Data Mining," holds 3 US patents, and won the Best Paper Award from IEEE ICDM 2005. He was a program committee co-chair of the 2003 International Conference on Web-Age Information Management (WAIM) and the 2007 Joint International APWeb/WAIM Conferences. He serves on the steering committee of the WAIM conference series and the editorial board of International Journal of Information Technology. He served on over 60 conference program committees. His research has been funded by government agencies (NSF, ARC, AFRL) and private corporations. He is a senior member of IEEE and a member of ACM.

Mengling Feng is a research assistant at School of Computing, National University of Singapore. He is currently pursuing his PhD degree from Nanyang Technological University. He received his Bachelor degree in 2003 from Nanyang Technological University. His main research interests are in data mining, especially pattern mining and pattern maintenance.

Qinrong Feng was born in Shanxi, China, in 1972. She received her BS in Computational Mathematics in 1994 from Shanxi University, MS in Computer Algebra in 2000 from Shanxi Normal University. She is now a PhD candidate of Computer Sciences at Tongji University of China. Her research interests include Data Mining, Rough Sets, and Granular Computing.

Magaly Lika Fujimoto Fujimoto received her BS degree in Informatics from USP (Brazil), in 2006, and the MS degree in Computer Science from USP (Brazil), in 2008. Currently she works as analyst of development in a company called ITG at São Paulo, Brazil. Her research interests include machine learning and data mining.

Paolo Garza received the master's and PhD degrees in computer engineering from the Politecnico di Torino. He has been a postdoctoral fellow in the Dipartimento di Automatica e Informatica, Politecnico di Torino, since January 2005. His current research interests include data mining and database systems. In particular, he has worked on the classification of structured and unstructured data, clustering, and itemset mining algorithms.

Fabrice Guillet is currently a member of the LINA laboratory (CNRS 2729) at Polytechnic School of Nantes University (France). He holds a PhD in Computer Science in 1995 from the Ecole Nationale Supérieure des Télécommunications de Bretagne. He is author of 35 international publications in data mining and knowledge management. He is a foundator and a permanent member of the Steering Committee of the annual EGC French-speaking conference.

Tarek Hamrouni is a PhD student at the Faculty of Sciences of Tunis (Tunisia) since 2006. He obtained his master thesis in July 2005 from the Faculty of Sciences of Tunis. Since, he is an Assistant at the Computer Sciences Department at the Faculty of Sciences of Tunis. His research interests include efficient extraction of informative and compact covers of interesting patterns, visualization of association rules, etc. He has been technical reviewer of different international conference, like ICFCA, CLA, FUZZ-IEEE. He published papers in international conferences, like DaWaK, ICFCA, CLA, IVVDM, and international journals, like IJFCS, SIGKDD.

Rudolf Kruse received his PhD in mathematics in 1980 and his Venia legendi in mathematics in 1984. From 1986 to 1996 he was Professor for Computer Science at the University of Braunschweig. Since 1996 he is Professor for Computer Science at the Otto-von-Guericke University of Magdeburg, Germany. His research interests are in neuro-fuzzy systems and computational intelligence. Among others, he is associate editor of Transactions on Fuzzy Systems and area editor of Fuzzy Sets and Systems.Research achievements include, among others, an IEEE fellowship in 2005.

Pascale Kuntz received the MS degree in Applied Mathematics from Paris-Dauphine University and the PhD degree in Applied Mathematics from the Ecole des Hautes Etudes en Sciences Sociales, Paris in 1992. From 1992 to 1998 she was assistant professor in the Artificial Intelligence and Cognitive Science Department at the Ecole Nationale Supérieure des Télécommunications de Bretagne. In 1998, she joined the Polytechnic School of Nantes University (France), where she is currently professor of Computer Science in the LINA laboratory (CNRS 2729). She is the head of the team "KOD - KnOwledge and Decision". She is member of the board of the French Speaking Classification Society. Her research interests include classification, graph mining and graph visualization, and post-mining.

Jinyan Li received the PhD degree in computer science from the University of Melbourne in 2001. He is an associate professor in the School of Computer Engineering, Nanyang Technological University. He has published over 90 articles in the fields of bioinformatics, data mining, and machine learning. His research focus is currently on protein structural bioinformatics, mining of statistically important discriminative patterns, mining of interaction subgraphs, and classification methods.

Guimei Liu is a research fellow at School of Computing, National University of Singapore. She received her BSc in 2000 from Peking University and her PhD in 2005 from Hong Kong University of Science & Technology. Her main research interests are in data mining and bioinformatics, especially frequent pattern mining, graph mining, protein interaction network analysis and medical data analysis.

Huawen Liu received his BSc degree in computer science from Jiangxi Normal University in 1999, and MSc degree in computer science from Jilin University, P.R. China, in 2007. At present, he is a PhD candidate in Jilin University. His research interests involve data mining, machine learning, pattern recognition and rough set, and several papers have been accepted by international journals and conferences during past two years.

Paul D. McNicholas was educated at Trinity College Dublin, Ireland, where he read an MA in mathematics, an MSc in high performance computing and a PhD in statistics. He was awarded the Barrington Medal by the Statistical and Social Inquiry Society of Ireland during the 2006/07 session for an application of association rules to the university application system in Ireland and, as such, he was the 120th Barrington Lecturer. His work in association rules has since focused on interestingness measures, while his other research focuses on model-based clustering. Following completion of his PhD, he accepted the position of Assistant Professor at the Department of Mathematics and Statistics at the University of Guelph in Guelph, Ontario, Canada.

Edson Augusto Melanda received his MS degree in Civil Engineering from UFSCar (Brazil), in 1998, and the PhD degree in Computer Science from USP (Brazil), in 2004. Currently he is a professor of the Federal University of São Carlos, São Carlos, Brazil, and has been engaged in teaching and researching in Urban Planning area, with emphasis in Geoprocessing. His main research topics are spatial data mining and data mining on geographic information systems.

Duoqian Miao was born in Shanxi, China, in 1964. He received his Bachelor of Science degree in Mathematics in 1985, Master of Science degree in Probability and Statistics in 1991 both from Shanxi University, and Doctor of Philosophy in Pattern Recognition and Intelligent System at Institute of Automation, Chinese Academy of Sciences in 1997. He is a Professor and Vice dean of the school of Electronics and Information Engineering of Tongji University, P.R.China. His present research interests include Rough Sets, Granular Computing, Principal Curve, Web Intelligence, and Data Mining etc. He has published more than 100 scientific articles in refereed international journals, books, and conferences. In addition, he has published 3 academics books. He is committee member of International Rough Sets Society, a senior member of the China Computer Federation (CCF).

Barzan Mozafari is currently a PhD candidate in computer science at UCLA. He has been conducting research on several topics under the supervision of Professor Carlo Zaniolo, since 2006. He is mainly interested in data stream mining, online recommendation systems and privacy preserving data mining. He has spent the summer of 2007 at Yahoo headquarters, enhancing their real-time targeting system as a research intern. He has also experienced from another internship at Microsoft Research Center (Redmond, summer 2008) working on distributed systems, extending their query language, and optimizing dynamic aggregations in a Map-Reduce model. Barzan received his MSc degree from UCLA in computer science and his BSc from SBU in computer engineering.

Amedeo Napoli is a computer scientist (directeur de recherche CNRS) with a doctoral degree in Mathematics (thèse de doctorat) and an habilitation degree in computer science (thèse d'état). He is currently the head of the Orpailleur research team at LORIA Laboratory in Nancy, whose main research theme is knowledge discovery guided by domain knowledge. The scientific interests of Amedeo Napoli are firstly knowledge discovery with formal and relational concept analysis, itemset and association rule extraction, text mining, and secondly, knowledge representation and reasoning, with description logics, classification-based reasoning and case-based reasoning. Amedeo Napoli has been involved in many research projects in these research domains and has authored or co-authored more than a hundred publications.

Detlef Nauck joined the Intelligent Systems Research Centre at BT in 1999. He leads the Intelligent Data Analysis Team in the Computational Intelligence Group (CIG). Detlef holds a Masters degree in Computer Science (1990) and a PhD in Computer Science (1994) both from the University of Braunschweig. He also holds a Venia Legendi (Habilitation) in Computer Science from the Otto-von-Guericke University of Magdeburg (2000), where he is a Visiting Senior Lecturer. He is a regular member of program committees for conferences on computational intelligence. Detlef's current research interests include the application of Computational Intelligence, Intelligent Data Analysis and Machine Learning in different areas of Business Intelligence. His current projects include research in pro-active intelligent data exploration and platforms for real-time business intelligence and predictive analytics in customer relationship management.

Engelbert Mephu Nguifo is currently full professor at University Blaise Pascal (UBP, Clermont-Ferrand) and is member of the computer science, system design and optimization laboratory (LIMOS, CNRS 6158). He received the PhD degree in computer science from University of Montpellier 2, France, in 1993. He was assistant (1994-2001) and associate (2001-2008) professor at University of Artois (Institute of Technology of Lens), France, where he has served as head of computer science department from 1998 to 2004, and head of the technology transfer service from 2005 to 2008. He has authored and co-authored more than eighty technical papers and book chapters. He has served in the program committees of over 10 international conferences and has been technical reviewer of different international journals. He has also served as guest editors of six international journals. He is currently member of the steering committee of the international conference on Concept Lattices and their Applications (CLA). He is member of the ACM SIGKDD, and different French scientific societies (Artificial Intelligence - AFIA, Data Mining -EGC, Bioinformatics - SFBI, Classification - SFC). His main research interests are: data mining, machine learning, artificial intelligence, neural networks, bioinformatics, formal concept analysis, ontology.

Maria Cristina Ferreira de Oliveira received the BSc in Computer Science from the Universidade de São Paulo, Brazil, in 1985, and the PhD degree in Electronic Engineering from the University of Wales, Bangor, UK, in 1990. She is currently a Full Professor at the Computer Science Department of the Instituto de Ciências Matemáticas de São Carlos, at the Universidade de São Paulo, Brazil, and has been a visiting scholar at the Institute for Visualization and Perception Research at University of Massachusetts, Lowell, in 2000/2001. Her research interests are on development, implementation and validation of techniques, tools and technologies for data visualization, scientific visualization, information visualization, visual data mining and visual analytics. She has published ca. 19 papers in refereed journals and ca. 45 full papers in conference proceedings (Brazilian and International). She has also supervised 13 MSc and 6 PhD dissertations successfully completed from 1993-2007. She is a member of the Association for Computing Machinery (ACM) and of the Brazilian Computer Society (SBC).

Nicolas Pasquier received his PhD in computer science from the University Blaise Pascal of Clermont-Ferrand, France, in January 2000. He received the Junior Researcher Award from the INFORSID association on information systems, databases and decision systems in 2000 for his contribution to the design of efficient association rule extraction methods. He is now a faculty member as senior lecturer at the University of Nice Sophia-Antipolis and member of the GLC research group of the I3S Laboratory of Computer Science, Signals and Systems of Sophia Antipolis (CNRS UMR-6070) in France. His current research interests include bioinformatics, data mining, knowledge discovery in databases and ontologies.

Ronaldo Cristiano Prati was awarded both the MSc and PhD in computer science from the University of São Paulo, Brazil (2003 and 2006, respectively). His research interests include machine learning, data and text mining. Currently he holds a postdoctoral research position at the Laboratory of Computational Intelligence at the Institute of Mathematics and Computer Science of the University of São Paulo, Campus São Carlos.

Solange Oliveira Rezende received her MS degree in Computer Science from USP (Brazil), in 1990, the PhD degree from the Faculty of Mechanical Engineering at USP (Brazil), in 1993, and the post-doctorate degree from the University of Minnesota (USA), in 1995. Currently she is an associate professor of the University of São Paulo, São Carlos, Brazil, and has been engaged in teaching and re-searching in Computer Science area, with emphasis in Artificial Intelligence. Her main research topics are data and text mining and machine learning.

Georg Ruß received his master's degree in computer science in 2006. Since October 2006 he is research assistant at the computational intelligence group at the Otto-von-Guericke-University of Magdeburg. His interests are focused on data mining and computational intelligence, especially on the application side. Currently, he is involved in data mining and prediction technologies in the area of precision agriculture and in optimization in regard to wind energy grid interfaces.

Roberta Akemi Sinoara received her BS degree in Informatics from USP (Brazil), in 2002, and the MS degree in Computer Science from USP (Brazil), in 2006. Currently she is working as a system analyst in a company called Ícaro at Campinas, Brazil. She is interested in the data mining research.

Jigui Sun received his MSc degree in mathematics and PhD degree in computer science from Jilin University in 1988 and 1993, respectively. He became a lecturer in the College of Computer Science and Technology of Jilin University in 1993. Currently, he is a professor with Jilin University, P.R. China, and dean of Key Laboratory of Symbolic Computation and Knowledge Engineering of Ministry of Education. He has wide research interests, mainly including artificial intelligence, machine learning, data mining, automation reasoning, intelligent planning and intelligent decision support system, and more than 200 papers have been accepted or published by journals and conferences.

Hetal Thakkar is currently a PhD candidate in the UCLA Computer Science Department. Since 2003, he has been working with Professor Zaniolo on data stream management systems and their languages. He has also worked as a research intern at Google (summer 2007) and IBM Almaden Research Center (summer 2005 and summer 2006), investigating click streams, data stream languages, RFID data, Web 2.0 applications, etc. His current research interests include data stream mining systems and data stream languages. Hetal received an MS in Computer Science in winter 2005 and expects to complete his PhD in fall 2008.

Yannick Toussaint is a senior researcher at INRIA in Nancy, France. His research activity combines Natural Language processing (information extraction from texts) with Data Mining techniques (knowledge model building in a given domain). The applications concern text mining in the context of semantic web: building ontologies from texts and semantic annotation. He was involved in the KW: Knowledge Web Network of Excellence - project funded by the European Commission 6th Framework Programme (2004–2007). Yannick TOUSSAINT is also involved in several French national projects of various domains such as mining texts in astronomy, detecting signals in pharma-vigilance. He is presently developing semantic annotation tools guided by the domain knowledge.

Ruizhi Wang received her BS in Computer Science in 1992 from China National University of Defense Technology, MS in Computer Science in 2003 from Anshan University of Science and Technology, China. She is now a PhD candidate of Computer Sciences at Tongji University of China. Her research interests include data mining, statistical pattern recognition, and bioinformatics. She is currently working on biclustering algorithms and their applications to various tasks in gene expression data analysis.

Limsoon Wong is a professor of computer science and a professor of pathology at the National University of Singapore. He currently works mostly on knowledge discovery technologies and is especially interested in their application to biomedicine. Prior to that, he has done significant research in database query language theory and finite model theory, as well as significant development work in broad-scale data integration systems. Limsoon has written about 150 research papers, a few of which are among the best cited of their respective fields. He was conferred (along with a co-author of this chapter, Jinyan Li, and two other colleagues) the 2003 FEER Asian Innovation Gold Award for their work on treatment optimization of childhood leukemias. He serves on the editorial boards of Journal of Bioinformatics and Computational Biology (ICP), Bioinformatics (OUP), Drug Discovery Today (Elsevier), Information Systems (Elsevier), as well as International Journal of Information Technology (SCS). He received his BSc(Eng) in 1988 from Imperial College London and his PhD in 1994 from University of Pennsylvania.

Sadok Ben Yahia he is an associate professor at the Computer Sciences department at the Faculty of Sciences of Tunis since October 2002. He obtained his PhD in Computer Sciences from the Faculty of Sciences of Tunis in September 2001. Currently, He is leading a small group of researchers in Tunis, whose research interests include efficient extraction of informative and compact covers of association rules, visualization of association rules and soft computing. He has served in the program committees of over 8 international conferences and has been technical reviewer of different international journals. He has also served is co-guest editor of three international journals special issues. He is currently member of the steering committee of the international conference on Concept Lattices and their Applications (CLA).

Claudio Haruo Yamamoto received his BSc degree in Computer Science from the Universidade Federal de Goiás, Brazil, in 2001, and the MSc degree in Computer Science from Universidade Federal de São Carlos, Brazil, in 2003. He is currently a DSc student at Universidade de São Paulo, Brazil. He worked as a professor at Universidade Federal de Goiás and Universidade Católica de Goiás from 2003-2004. His research interests are visual data mining, information visualization, database indexing and their applications.

Osmar Zaïane received an MSc in electronics from the University of Paris XI, France, in 1989 and an MSc in Computing Science from Laval University, Canada, in 1992. He received his PhD in Computing Science from Simon Fraser University in 1999 specializing in data mining. He is an Associate Professor at the University of Alberta with research interest in novel data mining techniques and currently focuses on e-learning as well as Health Informatics applications. He regularly serves on the program committees of international conferences in the field of knowledge discovery and data mining and was the program co-chair for the IEEE international conference on data mining ICDM'2007. He is the editor-in-chief of ACM SIGKDD Explorations and Associate Editor of Knowledge and Information Systems.

Carlo Zaniolo is a professor of computer science at UCLA, which he joined in 1991 as the N. Friedmann Chair in Knowledge Science. Before that, Zaniolo was a researcher at AT&T Bell Laboratories and the associate director of the Advanced Computer Technology Program of MCC, a U.S. research consortium in Austin, Texas. He received a degree in electrical engineering from Padua University, Italy, in 1969 and a PhD in computer science from UCLA in 1976. A prolific authors and program chair or co-chair of major IS conferences, his recent research focuses on data stream management systems, data mining and archival IS.

Huijie Zhang received her BSc and MSc degrees in computer science from Jilin University, P.R. China, in 1998 and 2004, respectively. Then she jointed the department of computer science, Northeast Normal University, P.R. China. Currently, she works as a lecturer. She mainly focuses her research interests on Geographical Information System (GIS), data mining and pattern recognition.

Index